# Real World Research

*To Mark and Catherine*

# Real World Research

*A Resource for Social Scientists and Practitioner–Researchers*

## SECOND EDITION

## COLIN ROBSON

Blackwell
Publishing

350 Main Street, Malden, MA 02148-5018, USA
108 Cowley Road, Oxford OX4 1JF, UK
550 Swanston Street, Carlton South, Melbourne, Victoria 3053, Australia
Kurfürstendamm 57, 10707 Berlin, Germany

First published 1993 by Blackwell Publishing Ltd
Second edition published 2002
Reprinted 2002, 2003

*Library of Congress Cataloging-in-Publication Data*

Robson, Colin.
    Real world research : a resource for social scientists and
practitioner – researchers / Colin Robson. – 2nd ed.
        p.    cm.
    Includes bibliographical references and index.
    ISBN 0–631–21304–X (hardcover : alk. paper) – ISBN 0–631–21305–8
(pbk. : alk. paper)
    1. Social sciences—Research—Methodology.
    2. Psychology—Research—Methodology. I. Title.
    H62.R627   2002
    300'.7'2—dc21

                                                        2001001503

A catalogue record for this title is available from the British Library.

Set in 10.5 on 13 pt Galliard
by Best-set Typesetter Ltd, Hong Kong
Printed and bound in the United Kingdom
by T. J. International Ltd, Padstow, Cornwall

For further information on
Blackwell Publishing, visit our website:
http://www.blackwellpublishing.com

# Contents

# Preface to the Second Edition

I have been heartened and emboldened by the positive response to the first edition of *Real World Research*. It was with some trepidation that I sent off the original manuscript to the publishers. I was conscious of being likely to offend some of my erstwhile colleagues within experimental psychology by displaying a less than totally enthusiastic espousal of the experiment as representing the 'gold standard' for all research, and by my advocacy of qualitative approaches as having an important place in the pantheon of research involving people. The intervening years have seen a substantially increased acceptance of the value of qualitative approaches within psychology, and the appearance of a positive plethora of methods texts, from a variety of disciplinary perspectives, exploring how they might be used in an appropriately systematic manner. This was an aspiration of mine in the first edition and, climbing on others' shoulders, I have attempted to address the question more adequately in the second.

I was also very conscious of straying into the perceived purviews of other disciplines and of perhaps revealing a naïveté of the 'fools rush in' variety. My co-existence over a number of years with sociologists and other social scientists undoubtedly influenced my mind-set (and reading) to the extent that at the time I was preparing the first edition, it came to me, with an almost 'road to Damascus' suddenness, that I had made the transition from being a biological to a social scientist (unfortunately, more or less at the time when psychologists in the United Kingdom were just appreciating the financial benefits from funding formulae in portraying their subject as a firmly biological, laboratory-based enterprise!). However, colleagues, reviewers and others have been very gentle with some undoubtedly simplistic assertions and presentations in the first edition. I have always been fully in agreement with the old adage that teaching a topic is one of the best ways of learning about it. I would now add that writing a methods text similarly gives point and direction to one's reading and thinking about doing research.

In approaching the task of revising the text, I was influenced initially by the remark made more than once that I was a 'closet realist'. If this were so, it was essentially from ignorance rather than from a wish to keep quiet about an affiliation which might be viewed negatively in some quarters. However, it did spur me on to a reading binge about something variously described as 'scientific realism', 'critical realism' and 'fallibilistic realism', among other labels. The publication of Ray Pawson and Nick Tilley's *Realistic Evaluation* in 1997 provided a particularly clear exemplar of 'cometh the hour – cometh the book': surprisingly often, when one is wrestling with a particular intellectual problem, the right book comes along at the right time. I tend to ascribe this to the Zeitgeist; but it could be a beneficent providence. Pawson and Tilley provide a stimulating and provocative manifesto for realism as the paradigm of choice when carrying out evaluations. As Elliot Stern puts it in a refreshingly non-saccharine quotation on the back cover, 'It is the kind of book that clarifies your thoughts, even when you disagree with everything they say.' It certainly fulfilled the first of these functions as far as I was concerned, and a reading of this edition of *Real World Research*, particularly chapter 2, will reveal a significant influence from their exposition, which may make it obvious that I found much that was persuasive. I was further encouraged to discover that several of the methodologists whose work I admired, including in particular Matthew Miles and Michael Huberman, had adopted a realist stance.

So, just in case anyone is at all interested, I am out of the closet and am now a self-confessed realist (specifically a critical realist). However, as one temperamentally inclined toward broad-church, inclusive formulations, I have attempted to provide an account which should not alienate relatively flexible readers comfortable with very different views of the nature of the social science research enterprise. Clearly this stance will be anathema to some of those espousing positivistic and social constructivist methodologies. I can live with losing the first group. To be (I hope) uncharacteristically rude, if you have not yet appreciated that positivism as a basis for social research is a god that failed, then either you haven't done sufficient reading and thinking, or you are impervious to evidence. I would be sad, however, to lose all social constructivists, partly because some of those I respect and have worked with take this position, and partly because it is a clearly healthy and thriving perspective. My view is that rapprochement is feasible between the realist framework proposed here and the more forgiving versions of social constructivism. And I remain sufficient of a pragmatist to retain pragmatism as a suggested fall-back position for those not grabbed by realism. However, these arguments are to be developed in the text rather than here.

At a superficial level, there is a degree of consonance between a 'real world' approach and realism as an underlying philosophy for the approach. The metaphor of 'real world research' is retained virtually unchanged from the first edition. As emphasized in the original preface (reproduced below), it has its problems, but I think it still helps denote a stance in which I wholeheartedly believe. What realism does is to try to fill what I now see as a rather glaring inconsistency in the first edition. While stressing the value of theories in designing and carrying out research, the book actually said very little about them. In fact, as is not uncommonly the case with methods texts, it was essentially atheoretical. This approach has the advantage of not upsetting those with particular theoretical perspectives, but I have come to see it as something of a cop-out. So in this edition I have attempted to use the language of, and to some extent the conceptual framework provided by, realist philosophy to fill this gap. I hope and intend that this will help the reader both to gain a firmer grasp on the role of theory in social research and, more particularly, actually to develop theories which help in understanding the situations being researched and why interventions have the effects, or lack of effects, that they do.

The text should still provide support for those who take a more practical view about the doing of research, interested above all in delivering a competent piece of work relevant to some clear issue or problem. Such readers may consider that theory is low on their list of priorities. While the ordering of priorities remains your prerogative, I hope to persuade that theory can help.

In addition to this development, the book is somewhat differently organized, though it retains the overall structure of the first edition. A basic distinction has been made between *fixed designs* and *flexible designs*. I prefer the fixed/flexible labels for the designs commonly referred to as 'quantitative' and 'qualitative', since designs that make use primarily of qualitative data can also include some element of quantitative data collection; the shift in usage also signals a move on from the often rancorous quantitative vs qualitative debates. Within each of these broad approaches to design, the book covers a range of research traditions. For fixed designs (where most if not all of the design work is carried out 'up-front' before the main effort of data collection proper starts) there is coverage of both experimental and non-experimental traditions. The latter, which were not covered explicitly in the first edition (apart from in relation to surveys – here repositioned as a 'method' rather than a strategy), focus on answering research questions using quantitative methods in contexts where it is not feasible or ethical to carry out the kind of deliberate manipulation of variables called for in doing experiments.

The 1990s saw an explosion of interest in qualitative research and its design, and it now appears feasible to isolate a number of traditions of such enquiry. All these are flexible in that many aspects of the design are decided during the process of the study. For the purposes of this text three main types have been highlighted. These are the case study, ethnographic and grounded theory traditions. Each is widely used and has a strong foothold in many applied settings.

Two major changes are that the analysis of quantitative data is now covered in the context of the use of SPSS (the Statistical Program for the Social Sciences), and the analysis of qualitative data in that of NUD*IST (Non-numerical Data Indexing Searching and Theory-building). SPSS has now to a considerable extent cornered the market for a statistical software package and its more recent manifestations are substantially easier to use than those available at the time of writing the first edition. The field for qualitative software packages is rather more open but NUD*IST, as well as being probably the most widely used currently, can be used in support of a wide range of different approaches to qualitative data analysis. Overall, the position is still taken that, for all but the most trivial of quantitative data analysis tasks, it makes sense to use a software package such as SPSS. When analysing qualitative data, there are clear advantages to using specialist software packages such as NUD*IST, but it is argued that you shouldn't dismiss out of hand the use of a general word-processing package in tandem with traditional paper-based approaches.

Greater attention has been given at various points in the text to the contribution made by feminist researchers and methodologists. The coverage of individual data collection techniques has been expanded and, it is hoped, improved. The construction and use of tests and scales is given a separate chapter. There is also coverage – not uncritical – of focus groups, in part reflecting their increasing use in the land of New Labour (and elsewhere). In response to other pleas, protocol analysis has also been added, together with a nod in the direction of some less widely used techniques which may be worth considering in particular situations. Material in the last two chapters of the first edition on 'Intervention and Change' and 'Researchers and Practitioners' has been repositioned. The opportunity has been taken to update and revise all sections of the book, including the 'Further Reading' sections – the last seven years having seen a deluge of methods and methods-related texts. The 'Further Reading' sections, as the term suggests, are brief lists of works, at the end of each chapter, particularly relevant to that chapter's subject. The author and date references in the text relate to the 'References' section at the end of the book. This section also functions as an author index by including (in bold) the numbers of the pages in the text where that work is referred to. Another additional tool is provided in this edition in the form of a glossary at the end of the book providing short explanations of the meaning, in the context of this book, of a number of important terms.

It has been extremely encouraging to note that readers from a very wide range of disciplines and areas appear to have found the first edition of value to them. These include students and staff in several fields, such as design and architecture, development studies, politics, criminology and legal studies, of which I have essentially no direct experience. I have attempted to extend the range of examples covered. In particular, partly because of my own present concerns in supervising research students and advising on research design matters, there are additional references in the fields of social policy and social work, and several health-related fields including nursing. However, I have tried not to leave behind my old field of educational research and the concerns of educational, clinical and other professional psychology groups.

Overall my message remains unchanged, and I have tried to ensure that it shines through the text. At the heart of it is the research question: i.e. developing appropriate questions answerable within your constraints of time and other resources. You don't just dream up these research questions. They are derived from theory. And to know what I mean by that – read the book.

# Preface to the First Edition

This book is about doing your own research, and about assisting others to do research. (I have found that 'research' tends to put some people off. They see it as some esoteric enterprise necessarily done by outside experts. In fact it is simply another word for 'enquiry', and the two terms are used interchangeably here.) It is for those who want to carry out 'real world enquiry': research on and with people, outside the safe confines of the laboratory. The focus is on the relatively small-scale study carried out by an individual or by a group of colleagues, rather than on the big project. It is about 'human' research not only in the sense of covering studies about people, but also in trying to take account of the advantages accruing from the enquirers themselves being people. The experience and understanding that we bring to the research, and which we develop during it, are an important ingredient of the research.

I have tried to walk the tightrope between stressing how easy the enquiry task is – because much of what you have to do is common sense – and how difficult it is for exactly the same reason. The core skills are watching people and talking to them. These are based on very common human activities and any reader will have had extensive experience of them. The trick is to avoid 'de-skilling' yourself by devaluing this experience, while appreciating the need to do these things with an uncommon degree of both system and sensitivity.

As an experimental psychologist I started with a virtually unquestioned assumption that rigorous and worthwhile enquiry entailed a laboratory, and the statistical analysis of quantitative data obtained from carefully controlled experiments. More recently I have developed doubts – in part planted by working in a department alongside social psychologists and sociologists who seemed to go about things in very different ways; and not without their own very different dogmatisms. Also, my developing interests in more 'applied' fields, in particular working with practitioners in schools and hospitals, precipitated a fundamental reconsideration of the style and approach to enquiry which are appropriate if one wants to say something sensible about such complex, messy, poorly controlled 'field' settings.

The book is for the person wanting to say something sensible and helpful about such settings. There are many methods of enquiry which can be used in this task, and I have attempted to give a fair run to several of them, with a nod in the direction of others that might be considered. All methods have their strengths and weaknesses. Recognizing this leads to a preference for multi-method approaches. A theme of the book is that several methods of enquiry are likely to be better than any single one in shedding light on an issue. Another theme is that very often the real-world enquirer has a direct research interest in and concern for the particular setting or situation under investigation (rather than seeing it simply as a sample from which generalizations about a wider population are made). These two themes are brought together in an advocacy of multi-method case studies as a serious and respectable research strategy for real world investigations.

'Wanting to say something helpful' raises the issue that we are often seeking not simply to understand something, but also to try to change it. Effectively, many real world studies are evaluations. They try to provide information about how some intervention, procedure, system, or whatever, is functioning; and how it might be improved. This kind of involved, 'action', agenda brings to the fore many difficult practical and ethical issues, which form a third theme.

The book tries to meet the needs of that large proportion of those trained in psychology and the social sciences who do not go on to profess their discipline directly, but who are called upon to carry out some empirical enquiries as part of their job. It is highly unlikely that this will involve laboratory experimentation. The book also addresses the needs of the specialist acting in a consultancy role for 'real world' studies. Practitioners and professionals in 'people' jobs in industry and commerce as well as education and the helping and caring professions, are increasingly being called upon to carry out evaluative and other enquiry projects. My experience has been that with advice and support, which can at least in part be provided by the type of material here, they are often in a position to do very effective studies.

As a course text it is targetted at those higher education courses which seek to prepare students to carry out empirical investigations. While initially developed for undergraduate use, I have found that it provides a useful framework for the formal research training increasingly called for in preparation for research degrees and postgraduate courses. It links with the growing number of more 'applied' courses in psychology and the social sciences, and at professional courses for teachers, health and social services related fields, and in business and management. Although it is written from the perspective of a psychologist, I have made particular efforts to incorporate approaches and methods traditionally seen as falling within other disciplines (e.g. in the coverage of participant observation and other approaches which generate qualitative data). This is a deliberate attempt to break down a form of apartheid which in my view serves little useful purpose.

Other features include an attempt to come to terms with the microcomputer revolution as far as the analysis of data (both qualitative and quantitative) is concerned. The treatment of quantitative analysis is influenced by 'exploratory data analysis' approaches, which appear to be particularly apposite for 'real world' studies; that of qualitative analysis by a wish to see it achieve a corresponding degree of rigour to that conventionally expected of quantitative analysis. The hegemony of the journal article as *the* preferred style of reporting is also put into question by giving serious attention to the notion of 'audience'; i.e. by considering who the report is for, and what one is seeking to achieve by writing it. Both the language of the book, and the general approach to enquiry which is advocated within it, are intended to be non-sexist and take note of recent feminist critiques of social science methodology. Wherever possible, results of research on research (on the presentation of graphical information, the effects of experimenters on experimental results, etc.) have been incorporated and referenced.

Finally, I do appreciate that the 'real world' is something of a questionable concept. Attempts have been made to wean me off it, but it is the best metaphor I can come up with to express my intentions. As the text suggests, it is more of a state of mind than a real 'real world'.

# Acknowledgements

I am grateful to many colleagues and students who, over the years, have contributed much to my education. I have been fortunate in working at Huddersfield with several groups of extraordinarily committed colleagues, initially in education, then in behavioural sciences, and more latterly in social work and health-related areas. It would, in these connections, be invidious to name names – as it would in the case of the group of enriching and invigorating research students which it has been my privilege to supervise. I am ever grateful for the stylistic advice generously provided by my wife, Pat. I am sure that readers will be too.

In the preparation of this edition, I am particularly indebted to Darren Langdridge for SPSS help in the writing of chapter 13, and to Graham Gibbs for casting his NUD*IST eye over the following chapter; also to Margaret Weaver and colleagues at Huddersfield University library for helping to open my eyes to the wonders of the internet as a bibliographic tool. I also wish to give sincere thanks to Tony Gale and Joe Maxwell who, in reviewing the text, provided extremely helpful, detailed and constructive comments. I have found working with colleagues from Blackwell a totally positive experience in both of the editions of this book. For this edition Sarah Bird gave invaluable editorial support and Gillian Bromley provided a model of the mixture of sensitivity and punctiliousness called for by the copy-editing task.

I would also wish to give formal acknowledgement of permissions given to reprint the following material. To Sage Publications Inc. (figure 5.6, from Thyer and Geller, 1987, *Environment and Behavior*, 19, figure 2, p. 490, © Sage Publications Inc.; figure 3.1, from Miles and Huberman, 1994, *Qualitative Data Analysis*, pp. 114, box 5.2, 158, figure 6.4, 159, figure 6.5; figure 14.2, from Miles and Huberman, 1994, *Qualitative Data Analysis*, p. 109 table 5.6. © Sage Publications Inc.; figure 8.1, from Czaja and Blair, 1996, *Designing Surveys: A Guide to Decisions and Procedures*, p. 53 exhibit 4.1, Pine Forge Press © Sage Publications Inc.). To Routledge/ITPS (figure 5.1 from

Marsh, 1982, *The Survey Method: The Contribution of Surveys to Sociological Explanation*, p. 74, model 4.1). To Professor Ned Flanders (box 8.6, from Flanders, 1970, *Analysing Teaching Behavior*, p. 34). To the *Journal of Applied Behavior Analysis* (figure 5.8, from Engelman et al., 1999, *Journal of Applied Behavior Analysis*, 32, figure 1, p. 109, © *Journal of Applied Behavior Analysis*). To the American Psychological Association (box 9.8, from Fibel and Hale, 1978, *Journal of Consulting and Clinical Psychology*, 46, p. 931, © 1978 American Psychological Association). To Dallas Cliff (box 9.3, interview schedule, *Looking for Work in Kirklees*). To Graham Gibbs (figure 8.2, questionnaire on 'Consumer behaviour and green attitudes'). Thanks are extended to SPSS UK Ltd for permission to use copies of SPSS for Windows screens. SPSS is a registered trademark of SPSS Inc.

# Ways of Using the Book

## Recommendations

- If you are following a course of some kind, then the needs of the course will shape your use. Broadly speaking, however, it is likely that the course will be about methods and methodology of investigation. To get an appreciation of the issues involved, my view is that it is best to start at the beginning and work through to the end. My own preference is to go through initially at some speed so that your momentum keeps you going through any bits that you don't take in fully. From this you get a feeling for the general lie of the land, and can then return at more leisure to sections which are important for your needs or which you found difficult.

- If you want to use the book to help you carry out an enquiry, then you have two main choices. You could do the same as suggested above and effectively use the book as a self-study course guide – then home in on the bits you need. Alternatively, you could jump straight in and use it more as a 'how to' cook book. To do this, use the marked (tinted) pages, which are intended to provide an overview of the main stages of the enquiry process and appear at intervals throughout the book. They can be picked out from the contents list where their headings are given in italic type.

- If you want to use this book to help others to carry out enquiries, you are likely to be familiar with much of the material in the text and a quick glance should locate aspects to recommend to those working with you. Some of the material differs from the traditional, however (particularly in the first two parts), and you are recommended to review these sections to key you in to the line taken.

## Disclaimers

- No single text could hope to cover all you need to carry out 'real world enquiry'. This text is wide-ranging and tries to give the reader a feeling for the issues involved in designing, carrying out, analysing and reporting on different kinds of study, so that you will appreciate some of the many possibilities open to you. The intention has been to try to provide a clear overall structure, while seeking to address some of the complexities and controversies in current social research. Each chapter contains annotated suggestions for further reading. This is particularly important in the case of specific methods and techniques of investigation and analysis, where it is highly likely that you will have to go beyond what is provided here.
- All the reading in the world won't make you into a skilled enquirer. There is the danger of the centipede problem (it never moved again after trying to work out which leg it moved first) and much to be said for jumping in, carrying out enquiries and developing skills through experience – using this text as a reference along the way. This is, in fact, an important feature of flexible research design. It is flexible in the sense that the design changes and develops as a result of your data-gathering experiences. Fixed designs (such as experiments and surveys) do call for considerable pre-planning before the main data collection, but you can, and should, gain experience through pilot work.

## A Note on Gender and Language

In order to avoid both the suggestion that all real world researchers and others involved are males (or females) and the clumsy 'she/he', I use the plural 'they' whenever feasible. If the singular is difficult to avoid, I use 'she' and 'he' in fairly random sequence.

### Carrying out an enquiry

To carry out an enquiry you need to give attention to a wide range of things. These are some of the main ones:

- deciding on the focus;
- developing the research questions;
- choosing a research strategy;

- selecting the method(s);
- arranging the practicalities;
- collecting the data;
- preparing for analysis; and
- reporting what you have found.

The book is concerned with giving advice and suggestions on these activities. Some of them are relatively straightforward and can be dealt with in a page or so. Others need more detailed consideration. For example, before deciding on a research strategy, you need to know something about the possibilities open to you, the reasons why you might go for a flexible rather than a fixed design, and the implications of this choice. Part II covers what might be, at first sight, a dauntingly wide range of possibilities. Similarly, there is a wide variety of different methods or techniques (interviews of various types; structured or participant observation; documentary analysis, etc.) for collecting and analysing data, which take up further chapters.

   You will find *general* discussion on these issues at various points in the book, as indicated below. These general discussion pages are marked in the same way that this section is.

# Part I
## Before You Start

Before leaping into an enquiry or project, you need to have an idea about what you are letting yourself in for. Many real world studies take place on someone else's territory. False moves can inoculate a firm, school or other institution against future involvements, not only with you, but with other potential researchers – and, possibly, against the whole idea of systematic enquiry as an approach to dealing with problems or understanding situations. Other commonly occurring real world studies may involve you researching some aspect of the situation in which you work or are already involved in some way. Here you will have to live with any mess you make.

This is not to argue that everything has to be cut and dried before you start. Any proposals you make for carrying out the enquiry will benefit from some real world exposure by discussing your suggestions with 'stakeholders' – those likely to have an interest in the research, either because it might involve them in some additional efforts or trouble, or because they might be affected by the findings. Indeed, there is much to be said in favour of collaborative ventures, where such persons have a substantial say in the enterprise.

## Keeping a Research Diary

It is good practice to keep a full and complete record of all the various activities with which you are involved in connection with the project. Sometimes this is limited to the stages when you are collecting data. Then it is certainly invaluable as it helps to keep in one place details of appointments and meetings, what data were actually collected, where, when, etc. However, there is much to be said for starting the diary on day one of planning the project. It can take a variety of formats, but an obvious one is an actual diary, with at least a page for each day. Keeping it on your computer is attractive, providing you have good computer housekeeping habits.

The kinds of things which might be entered include:

- notes of things you have read; references (get into good habits of taking full references, the effort now will save you pain later when you are trying to chase up missing details);
- any thoughts relevant to the project; particularly when you decide to modify earlier intentions; reminders to yourself of things to be done; people to be chased up, etc.;
- appointments made, and kept, together with an aide-memoire of where you have put anything arising from the meeting (one strategy is to include everything here in the diary);
- stocktaking of where you are in relation to each phase of the project; short interim reports of progress, problems and worries; suggestions for what might be done.

The diary can be very valuable when you get to the stage of putting together the findings of the research and writing any reports. In particular, with some styles of flexible design research where it is expected that you produce a *reflexive report* (an account reflecting on the process of the research), the research diary is indispensable.

# 1
# Real World Enquiry

This chapter:

- explains what is meant by focusing on the real world;
- introduces possible approaches to real world enquiry and makes the case for your knowing something about methodology (the fundamental principles on which the methods of social research are based) as well as the methods themselves;
- stresses that much real world research is concerned with evaluating some intervention, innovation, service or program, and that
- there is often a concern for action or change;
- reveals the author's assumptions about what you are looking for in using this book; and
- concludes by attempting to give something of the flavour of real world enquiry.

## Focusing on the Real World

The purpose of this book is to give assistance, ideas and confidence to those who, for good and honourable reasons, wish to carry out some kind of investigation involving people in 'real life' situations; to draw attention to some of the issues and complexities involved; and to generate a degree of informed enthusiasm for a particularly challenging and important area of work.

The 'real life' situation refers in part to the actual context where whatever we are interested in occurs, whether it be an office, school, hospital, home, street or sports stadium. This book is not primarily about studies carried out in purpose-built laboratories. Not that there is anything particularly unreal about a laboratory. Indeed, a study of the 'real life' in a laboratory makes a fascinating topic almost worthy of a soap opera – see for example Lynch (1985), a study of 'shop work and shop talk in a research laboratory'. Roll-Hansen (1998) discusses a range of such 'laboratory studies' carried out by sociologists and other social scientists. The point about the laboratory is that it permits a large degree of control over conditions; what is done to people can be very carefully determined and standardized. The slightly sinister under-tone which the term 'experiment' tends to have, particularly when one hears about 'experiments with human beings', is a reflection of the fact that deliberate and active control over what is done to people is central to the experimental approach.

In the 'real world' – or 'the field', as the part of the world focused on is often referred to by social researchers (conjuring up visions of intrepid inves-tigators in pith helmets) – that kind of control is often not feasible, even if it were ethically justifiable. Hence, one of the challenges inherent in carrying out investigations in the 'real world' lies in seeking to say something sensible about a complex, relatively poorly controlled and generally 'messy' situation. Another way of saying this, developed later in the book, is that the laboratory approx-imates to a 'closed' system shut off from external influences, while studies outside the laboratory operate in 'open' systems.

## Fixed and Flexible Designs

Experiments, particularly those involving randomized controlled trials (RCTs), are viewed by many as the 'gold standard' for social research (e.g. MacDonald, 1996; Oakley, 1996). Surveys continue to be widely used. Czaja and Blair (1996, p. xv) claim with some justification that 'Few areas of the social sciences are more widely used and valued by our society than survey research.' Experiments and surveys are examples of what Anastas and Mac-Donald (1994) refer to as *fixed* research designs. Their hallmark is that a very substantial amount of pre-specification about what you are going to do, and how you are going to do it, should take place before you get into the main part of the research study. Carried out in real world settings, they require a developed conceptual framework or theory so that you know in advance what to look for, and extensive pilot work to establish what is going to be feasible. Even when this has been achieved, they call for a degree of control by the researcher which may not be possible. They also have clear specifications about what is needed in order to carry them out to a professional standard. To a large extent, this involves following tried and tested steps and procedures.

However, there is an increasing recognition of the value of some very dif-ferent approaches to social research. Virtually all fields (including educational research, health-related research, social work research and market research) and disciplines (including psychology, sociology, anthropology and geography) now have strong advocates for what are commonly called *qualitative designs*. (Hammersley, 2000, provides a well-argued defence of qualitative designs against recent attacks on their relevance to policy-making and practice.) These designs come in many forms and arise from a variety of theoretical positions. Anastas and MacDonald (1994) refer to such designs as *flexible*. The two labels, 'qualitative' and 'flexible', capture important features of such designs. They typically make substantial use of methods which result in qualitative data (in many cases in the form of words). They are also flexible in the sense that much less pre-specification takes place and the design evolves, develops and (to use a term popular with their advocates) 'unfolds' as the research proceeds. I prefer the 'flexible' label because such designs may well make some use of methods which result in data in the form of numbers (quantitative) as well as in the form of words; hence, labelling them as qualitative can be misleading. Indeed, one of the arguments in this text is that there can be considerable advantage in using *mixed-method* designs, that is, designs which make use of two or more methods, and which may yield both quantitative and qualitative data.

Flexible research designs are much more difficult to pin down than fixed designs. This is in part because it is only in recent years that researchers have given consideration to the design issues which they raise. Previously, there had been a tradition in the disciplines of social anthropology and sociology, from which these approaches largely derive, of an 'apprenticeship' model, whereby skill in their use was developed by working alongside someone already skilled. However, since the early 1990s the design of flexible studies using qualitative methods has excited much interest and generated many publications, and an attempt is made in this book to suggest ways in which this task might be approached.

Fixed designs, with their reliance on quantitative data and statistical generalization, are considered by their proponents to be 'scientific'. The scientific status of flexible designs is more in dispute. There are those, mainly from qualitative traditions, who have no wish to have their research viewed as 'science'. My own view, elaborated in the next chapter, is that there are strong arguments for characterizing both fixed and flexible designs as scientific – provided that they are carried out in a systematic, principled, fashion.

## Can All This Be Safely Skipped?

I sense that those approaching this text in an instrumental vein – perhaps attracted by the notion that they are in fact going to get the advice, support and assistance in carrying out investigations in the real world which was promised – may be somewhat dismayed to find that they are letting themselves in for a brief detour into methodology and the nature of science. Obviously, one of the beauties and enduring strengths of books is that they are 'random access devices'. It is up to readers what they select or skip. The marked pages, chapter headings and index are all ways of giving rapid and direct access to the more 'nuts and bolts' aspects of the subject, such as the choice and use of different methods of gathering evidence, analysing different kinds of data, writing a report appropriate to a particular audience, and so on.

Far be it from me to seek to constrain your freedom of access. However, entering into any kind of investigation involving other people is necessarily a complex and sensitive undertaking. To do this effectively and ethically, you need to know what you are doing. If you opt for a fixed design, there are well-established principles and procedures for carrying out a study of high quality which you ignore at your peril. By contrast, it is not possible to specify in advance many of the details of flexible designs. Such designs are necessarily interactive, enabling the sensitive enquirer to capitalize on unexpected even-tualities. It is my belief that this process is facilitated by your acquiring some knowledge and understanding of these more general matters covered in the early chapters.

There is a secondary reason for their inclusion which I should make explicit. Advocating flexible designs as a serious possibility for enquiry in the real world is still likely to be viewed as a radical and risky departure in some disciplines, especially those steeped in the statistical sampling paradigm. Justification is called for.

Taking a stance that there are some circumstances where fixed designs are to be preferred, and others where flexible ones are more appropriate, and claiming that the whole can be regarded as a scientific enterprise, is also likely to antagonize those of both scientific and humanistic persuasions. There is a strongly held view that there is an ideological divide between qualitative and quantitative approaches, and that these particular twain should never meet. Following Bryman (1988a) and later commentators such as Tashakkori and Teddlie (1998), my view is that many of these differences are more apparent than real and that there can be advantages in combining qualitative and quantitative approaches.

## Evaluation, Action Research and Change

Much enquiry in the real world is essentially some form of *evaluation*. Is the organization of educational provision for children with special needs such as learning difficulties, or problems with sight or hearing, working effectively in a particular local authority area? Does a service catering for abused children actually serve the interests of the children concerned? Can a business improve its interviewing procedures for new sales staff? Evaluation brings to the fore a very different agenda of issues from those usually associated with 'pure' research. For example, issues to do with change (How can it be implemented? What are the barriers to implementation? How might they be overcome?) often loom large. There are influential approaches within applied social research, such as *action research*, which regard supporting and engineering change as an integral part of the research process. Evaluation and action research form the main focus of chapter 7.

Should you, as a researcher, get involved in these processes? One possible stance is that the researcher's responsibility stops with achieving some understanding of what is going on, and communicating that information to those directly concerned. An alternative view is that it is part of the researcher's job to use this understanding to suggest ways in which desirable change might take place, and perhaps to monitor the effectiveness of these attempts. There are no general solutions to these questions. The answers in each case depend to a considerable extent on the situation in which you find yourself. Certainly, someone attempting to carry out a form of enquiry into the situation in which they themselves are working or living may find that the change aspects become virtually impossible to separate out from the enquiry itself.

This mention of what amounts to 'self-evaluation' opens up a further Pandora's Box. At one extreme, some would doubt the feasibility of insiders carrying out any worthwhile, credible or objective enquiry into a situation in which they are centrally involved. At the other extreme, those associated with movements such as 'collaborative research' (e.g. Schensul and Schensul, 1992), 'participatory action research' (Kemmis and Wilkinson, 1998) or 'participatory evaluation' (e.g. Cousins and Earl, 1995) maintain that outsider research is ineffective research, at least as far as change and development are concerned. My sympathies tend to lie in the latter camp, though I recognize both the problems and stresses of doing 'insider' research, and the need for specialists in research and methodology. The role that such specialists should take on then becomes an important issue. One thing they need to be able to do is to 'give away' skills – an important skill in its own right.

All of this carries with it the implication that the 'real world enquirer' needs to have knowledge, skills and expertise in areas outside the likely competence of most laboratory-oriented researchers. How change comes about in individuals and groups is itself an immense research area, some knowledge of which is likely to be helpful if you are involved in its implementation. At a more down-to-earth level, a very strong sense of audience is needed to guide the style, content and length of any report or other communication arising from the enquiry. If an important objective is concerned with change, then a report which does not get its findings across to the decision-makers in that situation is a waste of time.

## The Audience for this Book

*The main focus is on those wanting to carry out, or advise on the carrying out of, small-scale projects about individuals and groups and their problems and concerns, and/or about the services, systems and organizations in which they find themselves.*

In part, this is an attempt to arm potential social researchers with tools and expertise that they can both use for themselves and 'give away' to others to use. I also have the hope, based on experience, that it will help to equip practitioners in the helping and caring professions, and others working with people, to undertake useful enquiry into their own and others' practice, with a view to understanding, developing and changing it.

### A word to those with a social science background

It is my strong impression that, for carrying out real world enquiry, the exact social science disciplinary background of the potential researcher is not all that important. A psychology graduate is likely to have been well steeped in experimental design and to know little about qualitative approaches (although such approaches are now being taken seriously by an increasing proportion of departments), whereas a sociology graduate will be likely to have had the reverse experience.

The approach taken in this book is deliberately promiscuous. Strategies and techniques which have tended to be linked to different disciplines have been brought together in the attempt to give enquirers a range of options appropriate to the research questions they are asking. Hence it is hoped that those from a range of social science disciplines will find material which is both useful and accessible.

### A word to practitioners and those without a social science background

My experience is that the approaches advocated here can be accessible to those without a background or training in the social sciences. The things that social researchers do are not all that different from those done in a variety of other trades and professions. Northmore (1996), for example, writing for investigative journalists, reveals many similarities. The research task has also been compared with that of the detective: information is gathered; a 'case' is made on the basis of evidence; the 'modus operandi' of a suspect is studied; decisions are made about the best explanation, etc. (Scriven, 1976). There are obvious linkages, too, with the approaches taken by therapists and counsellors, and others in the helping professions; and in humanities disciplines such as history. It remains a matter of controversy how far the practice of social research is 'common sense' (see e.g. the debate between Lamal, 1991, and Locke and Latham, 1991). A problem is that you 'know not what it is that you know not' and may rush in blindly or blithely without realizing the complexity of the situation. My advice is that you seek to appreciate the implications of carrying out a *scientific* study. If you are not from a scientific background, or are 'anti-science', please try to keep your prejudices in check. The next chapter aims, among other things, to clear away some common misconceptions about the scientific approach. You won't be expected to wear a white coat or, necessarily, to crunch numbers.

Associated with the scientific approach is the need for rigour and for rules or principles of procedure. However, as has already been stressed, many real world studies both permit and require a flexibility in design and execution which may well appeal to those with a background in the arts or humanities. Well-written-up research designed on a flexible model can provide a compelling account. A major theme of this book is how to introduce rigour into all aspects of enquiry so that we achieve a justified credibility and trustworthiness in what we find and write up.

If you do not have a social science background, you will be at a disadvantage compared to those who do in two main ways. First, the carrying out of a systematic enquiry calls for a set of particular skills – for example, in observing and interviewing, designing, analysing, interpreting and reporting. The development of these skills requires practice, which takes time. This can and should have taken place during a training in most social science subjects; but in the absence of such a training, you will have to learn 'on the job', or to sub-contract some or all of these tasks out to others who do have the necessary skills.

Second – and this is more difficult to remedy – the social sciences have a substantive content of theories, models and findings which in general you will not know about. I am genuinely unsure as to how much of a disadvantage this constitutes. One obvious solution is to work in partnership, or on some kind of consultancy basis, with a professional social researcher. If you are a practitioner or professional, trained and experienced in the field forming the subject of the research, then you will have at your disposal a corresponding, and possibly more useful, set of theories, models etc. to those deriving from the 'pure' social science disciplines. This is not to minimize the importance of theory. It simply makes the point that a theoretical framework can be acquired by a variety of means (including interaction with, and analysis of, the data you have collected).

When, as will often be the case, the intention is to assist individuals, groups or organizations to understand, and possibly develop or change, some aspect of themselves and the situation in which they find themselves, there is virtue in staying close to the concepts and language they themselves use. Certainly, unassimilated jargon often accentuates the commonly acknowledged theory/practice divide.

The basic claim being made here is that principled enquiry can be of help in gaining an understanding of the human situation and its manifestations in an office, factory, school, hospital or any other environment, and in initiating sensible change and development. It is important not to claim too much, however. Common sense, management fiat, hunches, committee meetings and the like are going to continue to form the main precursors to action. But getting enquiry on the agenda, as something likely to be of assistance if there is an important decision to be made or problem to be dealt with, would be a step forward. And if you can consult a sympathetic expert for advice and support, you may well find that your efforts are more effective.

## Returning to the Real World

The proposal for a real world emphasis is as much about an attitude of mind as an invitation to come out of the laboratory closet. It is reflected in several dichotomies – suggesting, for example, applied research rather than pure or basic research; policy research, not theoretical research. These dichotomies are probably not very helpful as they suggest absolute distinctions. Hakim (1987) sees the differences more in terms of emphasis. For her, the main features that distinguish policy research from theoretical research are:

> an emphasis on the substantive or practical importance of research results rather than on merely 'statistically significant' findings, and second, a multi-disciplinary approach which in turn leads to the eclectic and catholic use of any and all research designs which might prove helpful in answering the questions posed. (p. 172)

As Rossi (1980) has pointed out, well-designed policy research can not only be of value to those concerned with determining policy, but may also be of interest to one or more academic disciplines. Trist (1976) goes further and claims that while the natural sciences first generate pure research findings and then apply them, social sciences make theoretical progress only through application. The argument is that the only way to get the proper access needed to study people in real life settings is through proving your 'competence in supplying some kind of service' (p. 46). Hence practice helps to improve theory, which in turn helps to improve practice. This is the 'action research' perspective, discussed in chapter 7. It is an overstatement to claim that all real world research must follow this pattern, but an active symbiotic link between researcher and researched is a very common feature.

Hall and Hall (1996) view this link as a partnership:

> The research relationship is between equals and is not exploitative: the client organization is not being 'used' merely to develop academic theory or careers nor is the academic community being 'used' (brains being picked). There is a genuine *exchange*. The research is negotiated. (p. 12; emphasis in original)

The emphases associated with adopting the metaphor of the real world are very different from those of laboratory-based experimentalists. Box 1.1 suggests some of the dimensions involved. Weick (1985) provides contrasting examples of 'artificial' and 'real world' approaches. In crude terms, you might be better able to vary anticipatory stress experimentally and control other factors in a laboratory study, but there is much to be gained by transferring the enquiry to the dentist's chair (Anderson et al., 1991).

Bickman (1980) presents an extended analysis of these differing emphases in the context of approaches to social psychology research. Not all of the aspects shown in box 1.1 will occur in any particular enquiry, but together they go some way to capturing the kind of enterprise that this book is seeking to foster. Academic researchers may not feel that the suggestions about open-ended availability of time and money chime in too well with their experience but, to take a strict line, there is little point in their carrying out studies intended to advance their discipline if the resources available are inadequate. In the real world context, the game is different – in its crudest form, you tell the sponsors what they will get for their money, and either they buy it or they don't!

Entering into this kind of real world enquiry could, with some justice, be viewed as capitulation to the values of an enterprise culture. There are obvious dangers in being a 'hired hand'. You may, overtly or covertly, be serving the agendas of those in positions of power (Scheurich, 1997): perhaps being hired to seek sticking-plaster solutions to complex and intractable problems. However, there is the advantage that letting society, in the guise of the client or sponsor, have some role in determining the focus of an enquiry makes it more likely that the findings will be both usable and likely to be used. Some support for this assertion comes from a study by Weiss and Bucuvalas (1980). They analysed fifty studies in the field of mental health. Thirteen were commissioned to answer specific questions; the rest were initiated by researchers. At least six decision-makers rated each study. Although differences were small, the commissioned research studies tended to get higher ratings on usefulness than the others. It is important to note, though, that the quality of the research

# Box 1.1

## Characterizing real world enquiry

In real world enquiry the emphasis tends to be on:

| | | |
|---|---|---|
| *solving problems* | rather than | *just gaining knowledge* |
| *getting large effects* (looking for robust results) and *concern for actionable factors* (where changes are feasible) | rather than | *relationships between variables* (and assessing statistical significance) |
| *field* | rather than | *laboratory* |
| *outside organization* (industry, business, school, etc.) | rather than | *research institution* |
| *strict time constraints* | rather than | *as long as the problem needs* |
| *strict cost constraints* | rather than | *as much finance as the problem needs* (or the work isn't attempted) |
| *little consistency of topic from one study to the next* | rather than | *high consistency of topic from one study to the next* |
| *topic initiated by sponsor* | rather than | *topic initiated by researcher* |
| *often generalist researchers* (need for familiarity with range of methods) | rather than | *typically highly specialist researchers* (need to be at forefront of their discipline) |
| *multiple methods* | rather than | *single methods* |
| *oriented to the client* (generally, and particularly in reporting) | rather than | *oriented to academic peers* |
| *currently viewed as dubious by many academics* | rather than | *high academic prestige* |
| *need for well developed social skills* | rather than | *some need of social skills* |

was seen as a more important factor than whether the research was commissioned or researcher-initiated. Studies rated higher on methodological quality were judged significantly more useful. The need, then, is for high-quality, methodologically sophisticated research – both where researchers follow their own noses, and also where they work on others' questions.

Enquiry may be thought of as a way of solving problems, which may range from the purely theoretical to the totally practical. Box 1.2 presents a list of

---

# Box 1.2

## Approaches to problem-solving

*A    The traditional approach: 'science only'*

**1**    Basic research. Application to problem-solving in the real world not usually seen as an objective.

**2**    Less basic, but still 'pure' or 'theoretical'. Application not a high priority and is usually left to others.

**3**    Research on practical problems. Application seen as a possible but not a necessary outcome, and is often left to others.

*B    Building bridges between researcher and user*

**4**    Researcher believes work has practical implications and should be used. Seeks to disseminate results widely and in accessible language.

**5**    Researcher obtains client collaboration on researcher-designed project. Researcher would like client to be influenced by research outcome.

**6**    As (5), but in addition researcher takes steps to give client regular feedback on progress, problems and outcomes. During feedback, client has an opportunity to check on interim findings and contribute own analysis and interpretation. Researcher attempts to help in implementation.

*C    Researcher–client equality*

**7**    Researcher and client together discuss problem area(s) and jointly formulate research design. Research involves active collaboration and some measure of control on part of client. Implementation is part of the collaborative design. May be termed 'research action' as fact-finding takes precedence over implementation.

*continued*

**8**   As (7), but initiative taken by client who identifies the problem. This is taken by researcher as the 'presenting problem'. Early stages of the research consider whether there are other issues which should receive primary attention. 'Research action' or 'action research' depending on relative attention to research and implementation.

**9**   As (8), but the problem identified by the client is not questioned and research proceeds on that basis. Likely to be 'action research' with the researcher paying most attention to implementation.

### D   Client–professional exploration

**10**   A client with a problem requests help from a researcher/academic. Collection of new data (if any) is minimal. Advice or recommendation is based on researcher's past experience and knowledge of the field. If this takes place in an organization, then training or organization development is a frequent outcome.

### E   Client-dominated quest

**11**   Client requests help from a specialist or colleague with social science background. Specialist examines problem, interprets 'best current knowledge', makes a diagnosis and suggests a line of action.

**12**   As (11), but help is requested from non-specialist without social science background (may be familiar with more popular literature). 'Best current knowledge' will be interpreted at second or third hand, heavily influenced by personal experience and 'common sense'.

(Adapted and abridged from Heller, 1986, pp. 4–6.)

different possible approaches to problem-solving. It describes a dimension from pure to applied, and of increasing contribution from the client. The main thrust of this book is towards the mid-range of these approaches, say from type 3 through to type 9. Where a particular study will lie on this continuum depends crucially on your individual circumstances. The more client-dominated approaches (from type 10 to type 12) do not concern us here, irrespective of any views one might have about them, as they involve little or no empirical data collection. There is no intention to make a value judgement suggesting that any one of the mid-range methods is intrinsically superior or inferior to any other. Heller (1986) claims that, in terms of utilization of research outcomes, there is evidence in favour of the approaches within section B ('Building bridges between researcher and user') and section C ('Researcher–client equality'). He goes on to point out, however, that the limitation of depending on these approaches is their emphasis on current issues:

> Research on the effect of the media on imitative behaviour should not wait for an increase in violence or political misgivings. Research on trade-union decision-making practices should not wait until there is a political demand for change: social cost research should precede redundancy crises. (p. 10)

This argues for a broad spread of approaches, with researchers choosing the one most suitable to the research questions that interest them. However, before getting down to design specifics, the next chapter tries to provide a more general context.

## Further Reading

Burton, D., ed. (2000) *Research Training for Social Scientists*. London: Sage. Comprehensive and wide-ranging set of short contributions. Aimed at postgraduate student researchers but more widely relevant.

Hall, D. and Hall, I. (1996) *Practical Social Research: Project Work in the Community*. London: Macmillan. Accessible introduction to applied social research. Emphasis on collaborative research in partnership with local organizations.

Kaplan, A. (1964) *The Conduct of Inquiry: Methodology for Behavioral Science*. San Francisco: Chandler. Classic book on methodology by friendly but critical philosopher. Emphasizes the common concerns of the different disciplines and the community of scholarship between the humanities and the social sciences. Wise, readable and challenging.

Mertens, D. M. (1998) *Research Methods in Education and Psychology: Integrating Diversity with Quantitative and Qualitative Approaches*. Thousand Oaks, Calif., and London: Sage. Big text with full treatment of both quantitative and qualitative approaches. Focus on issues of race, gender and disability.

Oskamp, S. and Schultz, P. W. (1998) *Applied Social Psychology*, 2nd edn. Upper Saddle River, NJ: Prentice-Hall. Emphasizes real world problems and social issues including health care, environmental problems, legal issues, educational questions, the mass media and life in organizations. Multidisciplinary; covers work by sociologists, communication researchers and economists as well as social psychologists. Discusses applicability and the applied vs theoretical conflict (ch. 1).

Scheurich, J. J. (1997) *Research Method in the Postmodern*. London: Falmer. Postmodern theory challenges preconceptions about research method. This text shows its implications for research practice.

# 2
# Approaches to Social Research

This chapter:

- explores what it means to be 'scientific' and argues for its advantages;
- considers the standard positivist view of science and, following a discussion of critiques of this view, rejects it as a basis for real world research;
- discusses relativist views of social science and, in their more extreme versions, similarly rejects them;
- reviews two main current approaches to social research: post-positivism and constructivism;
- gives a voice to emancipatory approaches; and, after
- considering the attractions of a realist approach in providing a possible synthesis of attractive features of post-positivism and constructionism,
- plumps for 'critical realism' as the version which (incorporating emancipatory ideals) is particularly appropriate for real world research, but also
- offers a pragmatic approach for any unpersuaded readers.

## Introduction

When carrying out real world research involving people, can we, or should we, be scientific? This question raises a wide set of issues. What does 'being scientific' mean? And why might we either want, or not want, to be scientific?

In seeking to disentangle some of these issues, the route taken will be as follows. First, there is a discussion of the nature of scientific activity and of the general scientific attitude to carrying out research which underpins it. This is followed by consideration of a common but seriously misleading view of science which is held not only by laypeople but by many scientists themselves.

After clarification of what is meant by the so-called 'scientific method', there is consideration of the differences between natural and social sciences, including whether it is feasible or desirable for the methods of the natural sciences to be used in applied research involving people. A hearing is then given to those who do not accept the term 'science' for the research that they do, either because of a dislike of what they consider this to involve or because they do not believe such a social science to be possible.

A resolution is then sought which seeks to retain a scientific approach when carrying out real world research, spelling out the advantages of doing this. However, it is seen as necessary to get rid of the standard, positivistic, view of science because of its inadequacies as a description or explanation of science (whether natural or social). A case is made for the adoption of critical realism. This stance, currently influential within the philosophy of science, rejects both traditional positivistic science and purely relativistic approaches which consider science to give but one of a number of equally valid accounts. The further claim is made that critical realism can encompass a range of post-positivistic approaches to social science which are currently influential.

Critical realism is seen as providing a particularly appropriate framework for designing real world studies. At the very least it provides a language and way of thinking about these studies which facilitate their design and analysis, and which help in seeking an explanation of what is going on. However, rather than alienate those who find realism unconvincing or misguided, a pragmatic approach is also developed which, at the expense of some theoretical coherence, provides a way forward.

## Being Scientific

At the time of writing this edition, science is getting a bad press. There is a lack of public confidence in scientists and their pronouncements. This has been fuelled in the United Kingdom by the scandal of BSE (so-called 'mad cow disease') and throughout Europe by the development of genetically modified organisms (GMOs) by large multinational corporations. Scientists are seen as providing information potentially biased to suit their sponsors. Health scares about potential side-effects of science-based initiatives such as the contraceptive pill or vaccination programmes crop up on a regular basis, suggesting dangers lurking behind even the best efforts of scientists.

Admittedly, social science hits the headlines more rarely. Some social researchers, indeed, have strong reservations about being labelled as 'scientific' – a term which is commonly associated by them, and to some extent by the public at large as well, with doing particular types of study: specifically, those that involve collecting 'hard' data, usually in the form of numbers which are subsequently analysed using statistical methods. Their preference may be for 'softer' styles of enquiry involving methods such as relatively unstructured interviews or participant observation, which result in data typically in the form of words, to which they would be unlikely to apply any form of statistical analysis.

A major message of this text is that those following what some call 'qualitative' approaches (here referred to as 'flexible' designs) *need* not shun being 'scientific'. They may *wish* to do, of course, and that is their privilege. I hope that they will still find information and advice in this text which helps them to carry out research. My own view, as is no doubt obvious, is that aspiring to be scientific in the ways developed in this chapter has much to commend it.

## A scientific attitude

A great deal of effort has been expended in seeking to establish what is meant by the 'scientific method'. Is there a particular set of procedures which, if followed, give the seal of approval that the result is 'science'? This question is discussed in some detail below. For the moment I simply propose to assert that, for much real world research, it is valuable to have what I will call a 'scientific attitude'.

By this I mean that the research is carried out *systematically*, *sceptically* and *ethically*:

- *systematically* means giving serious thought to what you are doing, and how and why you are doing it; in particular, being explicit about the nature of the observations that are made, the circumstances in which they are made and the role you take in making them;
- *sceptically* means subjecting your ideas to possible disconfirmation, and also subjecting your observations and conclusions to scrutiny (by yourself initially, then by others);
- *ethically* means that you follow a code of conduct for the research which ensures that the interests and concerns of those taking part in, or possibly affected by, the research are safeguarded.

The intention behind working in this way is to seek the 'truth' about whatever is the subject of the research. 'Truth' is a term to be approached with considerable caution and the intention can, perhaps, be best expressed in negative terms. You should not be seeking to promote or 'sell' some particular line, or to act simply and solely as an advocate. Some of these issues can become very problematic when carrying out real world research. For example, a *part* of your role may well be to act as an advocate for the sponsor of the research or for a disadvantaged group whose cause you are seeking to assist.

A commitment to carrying out the research in an ethically responsible manner, while it might not be viewed by some as a defining characteristic of a scientific attitude, appears to me to be central. You are working with people and may do them harm. Such empirically based, systematic, sceptical and ethical research should, in the real world, also be in some sense influential or effective if it is to be worthwhile.

Why is it valuable to have this attitude? The main reason is that working in this way – systematically, being explicit about all aspects of your study, and opening up what you have done to scrutiny by others – is likely to lead to better-quality, more useful research. While some might object to the 'science' tag, I am sure that no responsible researchers would wish to dissociate themselves from these aspirations.

*For some small, straightforward, enquiries, where the questions to be answered are clearly specified initially, and the method of data collection self-evident, this attitude will in itself take you a substantial way. Obviously, craft skills in the use of the method chosen and in analysis of the resulting data are needed; but if you are working systematically, sceptically and ethically, you should be able to do something worthwhile.*

However, in practice, very few actual real world studies turn out to be as straightforward as this. This book tries to provide a framework for designing and carrying out studies where things are not cut and dried, and where you need to take difficult decisions about how to proceed. To do this, we need to delve rather more deeply into what is implied by 'being scientific'.

## The standard view of science

Contrary to common preconceptions, including those held by many who regard themselves as scientists, and not a few who would be disturbed to be so labelled, it is not obvious what is meant by 'science' or the 'scientific method'. Chalmers (1982), for example, spends nearly 200 pages trying to answer his own question: 'What is this thing called science?'

The so-called 'standard view' of science derives directly from a philosophical approach known as *positivism* which is still embraced by many scientists. As is the case for many philosophical positions which have been worked on over the years, positivism can be defined in different ways. Outhwaite (1987, pp. 5–8) distinguishes three generations: nineteenth-century positivists, such as Auguste Comte (from whom the term derives, arising from 'positive' in the sense of progressive) and Herbert Spencer; logical positivism, associated particularly with the work of A. J. Ayer in the early twentieth century; and a post-Second World War account developed by Carl Hempel, emphasizing the importance of value-free evidence, hard facts and prediction in policy development by government and other organisations. Positivism is sometimes labelled empiricism, but the latter is a broader term and there are important differences (see Smith, 1998, ch. 3).

Box 2.1 gathers together some features of the positivist approach. (For a more extensive account of the main ideas of positivism and the critiques of these ideas, see Bentz and Shapiro, 1998, appx C, pp. 177–85). In this standard view, science, including social science, has explanation as a central aim. But explanation is thought of in a particular, very restricted, manner: namely, if you can relate an event, observation or other phenomenon to a general law (sometimes called a 'covering' law), then you have explained it. Outhwaite (1987, p. 7) presents as an example the freezing of a car radiator. This is explained by the operation of general laws covering the behaviour of water in conjunction with particular conditions (low temperature).

---

## Box 2.1

### Assumptions of positivism: the 'standard view' of science

1   Objective knowledge (facts) can be gained from direct experience or observation, and is the only knowledge available to science. Invisible or theoretical entities are rejected.

2   Science separates facts from values; it is 'value-free'.

3   Science is largely based on quantitative data, derived from the use of strict rules and procedures, fundamentally different from common sense.

4   All scientific propositions are founded on facts. Hypotheses are tested against these facts.

5   The purpose of science is to develop universal causal laws. The search for scientific laws involves finding empirical regularities where two or more things appear together or in some kind of sequence (sometimes called a 'constant conjunction' of events).

6   Cause is established through demonstrating such empirical regularities or constant conjunctions – in fact, this is all that causal relations are.

7   Explaining an event is simply relating it to a general law.

8   It is possible to transfer the assumptions and methods of natural science from natural to social science.

The theory of causation invoked here comes from the eighteenth-century philosopher David Hume (1888 [1738]). According to this view, all that it is possible to observe is the 'constant conjunction' of events. In other words, if there are freezing temperatures, then this causes water-filled radiators to burst. What we observe is the co-occurrence of these events, and this is all that we can observe. In the standard view of science, this is all we need to know.

Essentially, positivists look for the existence of a constant relationship between events, or, in the language of experimentation, between two variables. This can be relatively straightforward when dealing with the natural world, although calling for considerable ingenuity and the ability to control the conditions of the experiment – which is why laboratories exist. However, when people are the focus of the study, particularly when it is taking place in a social real world context, 'constant conjunction' in a strict sense is so rare as to be virtually non-existent. In other words, as has often been lamented (e.g. Koch 1959, vol. 3, ch. 1), psychology and the social sciences do not appear to have produced any 'scientific' laws yet, even though they have been at it for at least a century. This 'failure' has led some to consider that the whole scientific approach is inappropriate for social science.

*The argument advanced here is that it is the 'standard' positivistic scientific view which is wrong: both as providing an account of how natural science takes place, and as a model for the social sciences.*

Somewhat paradoxically, adherence to positivist views appears to linger more tenaciously in social science than in natural science (Klee, 1997), and the position still has its defenders (e.g. Turner, 1992). Many of the individual tenets of positivism have been subjected to severe criticism from a range of philosophical standpoints, as summarized in box 2.2. Bhaskar (1986) and Stockman (1983) provide more detailed analysis. For example, the positivist notion is that science becomes credible and possible because every scientist looking at the same bit of reality sees the same thing. However, it has been amply demonstrated that what observers 'see' is not determined simply by the characteristics of the thing observed; the characteristics and perspective of the observer also have an effect.

Positivistic approaches and their quantitative practices have also come in for severe criticism from within social research, notably by feminist researchers and others who take a qualitative stance. Box 2.3 presents several of their criticisms. Such criticisms of positivism and the quantitative practices associated with it in social research have considerable force. However, rather than throw out the scientific baby with the positivist bath-water, perhaps one can nurture this frail infant by reconceptualizing the view of science so that it provides both a more adequate representation of what scientists do and a more

---

## Box 2.2

### Philosophical critiques of the 'standard view'

**1**   The claim that direct experience can provide a sound basis for scientific knowledge is open to question.

**2**   The view that science should deal only with observable phenomena is rejected.

**3**   It is impossible to distinguish between the language of observation and of theory.

**4**   Theoretical concepts do not have a $1:1$ correspondence with 'reality' as it is observed.

**5**   Scientific laws are not based on constant conjunctions between events in the world.

**6**   'Facts' and 'values' cannot be separated.

(After Blaikie, 1993, p. 101.)

---

promising basis for social science. This task is returned to after discussion below of a very different view of how research involving people could and should be carried out.

## Relativist Approaches

Relativism crops up in several guises and contexts. In its extreme form, philosophical relativism maintains that there is no external reality independent of human consciousness; there are only different sets of meanings and classifications which people attach to the world. The philosopher of science Feyerabend (1978) views science as just one cultural tradition among many. It does not have a privileged position by comparison with other traditions such as religion or astrology. 'Reality' can be constructed only by means of a conceptual system, and hence there can be no objective reality because different cultures and societies have different conceptual systems.

   Such a position appears to be at odds with the world as we know it – or perhaps I should say, the world as I know it. The standard counter-example is the fall of a tree in a forest where there is no person to hear it. Do you believe it makes a sound while falling? Or does the event require a hearer? Many would

# Box 2.3

## Critiques of the 'standard view' in relation to social research

1   Social phenomena exist not 'out there' but in the minds of people and their interpretations.

2   Reality cannot be defined objectively but only subjectively: reality is interpreted social action.

3   The overemphasis positivists place on quantitative measurement is wrong and unjustifiable, for it cannot capture the real meaning of social behaviour.

4   Quantitative research restricts experience in two ways: first by directing research to what is perceived by the senses; and second by employing only standardized tools, based on quantifiable data, to test hypotheses.

5   Quantitative research attempts to neutralize the researchers, or to reduce or eliminate as far as possible their influence on the researched.

6   Quantitative research takes natural sciences as a model. However, the methods of natural sciences are not suitable for social research. People are not just natural elements but social persons, acting individuals with their own wishes, perceptions and interests.

7   Because quantitative research works on the principles of natural sciences (objectivity, neutrality), research objects are seen as scientific objects and are treated as such. Respondents are therefore treated as *objects* and as informants or producers of data. But social sciences are not natural sciences, and respondents are not objects but partners and 'experts' whose views are sought.

8   Quantitative researchers endeavour to achieve objectivity in their research; they consider this to be one of the most important properties of social research, and employ several methods to achieve it, such as standardization.

9   Standardization and distance from the research object do not guarantee objectivity because the perceptions and meanings of the researcher penetrate the research process in many ways. Standardization results in converting the social world under study into an artificial world which has nothing in common with the real world. Objectivity is not necessary. The personal involvement of the researcher is required in order to help to take the position of the respondent and see human life as seen by people themselves.

(Abridged from Sarantakos, 1998, pp. 43–5.)

agree with Trigg (1989) that the idea that there is no reality separate from the conceptual systems employed by people accords quite ludicrous powers to human thought. Or, as Hughes and Sharrock (1997, p. 163) put it, 'The notion of the world as "mind independent", regardless of whatever way we believe it to be, is one of the keys to our whole way of thinking and can only be denied at the risk of absurdity. Believing that one has won the lottery is – alas! – obviously not the same as winning the lottery.' If we are to recognize the role of common sense as an adjunct to our thinking about research, full relativity seems an engaging idea which we rapidly put aside. As Davidson and Layder (1994) point out:

> It is possible to accept that neither natural nor social scientists ever rely purely on observation and that their observations are never completely detached from their pre-conceived beliefs and theories about the world without having to argue that empirical observations are therefore useless, or that they are invariably disregarded by scientists, or the science is merely the subjective process by which they go about confirming their own prejudices. It is essential to recognise that empirical observations are not the be all and end all of scientific research, and that a commitment to natural science methods and procedures does not offer the final, ultimate, reliable and objective way to obtain knowledge, without abandoning all belief in reality or all hope of advancing human knowledge. (p. 26)

Within social science there are influential relativistic approaches. They are variants of what is commonly referred to as 'qualitative' research, as distinguished from the 'quantitative' research typical of the positivistic tradition; and these views helped shape the criticisms of positivistic approaches listed in box 2.3 above. Other labels include 'constructivist', 'naturalistic' or 'interpretive'. Within this tradition there is almost invariably a rejection of the view that 'truths' about the social world can be established by using natural science methods. This is essentially because of the nature of the subject matter of the social sciences – people. People, unlike the objects of the natural world, are conscious, purposive actors who have ideas about their world and attach meaning to what is going on around them. In particular, their behaviour depends crucially on these ideas and meanings.

This central characteristic of humans has implications for doing research involving them. Their behaviour, what they actually do, has to be interpreted in the light of these underlying ideas, meanings and motivations. Davidson and Layder (1994), for example, cite the pattern whereby females typically do more housework than their male partners, fathers and sons:

> But since women are not drawn to the kitchen sink by some irresistible, physical force (they are not *compelled* to conform to this social convention in the same way that they would be compelled to obey the law of gravity if they jumped from a cliff), social scientists cannot hope to formulate general laws on the basis of

observing this pattern. Instead, they have to ask questions about the beliefs people hold and the meanings they attach to action. They have to concern themselves with the inner world of their subjects in order to understand why they act as they do. (p. 31, emphasis in original)

Box 2.4 lists some of the features characteristic of relativistic qualitative approaches to social research. As with other attempts to provide a simple summary of complex matters which researchers and philosophers have fought over for decades, the exact features accepted as typifying these approaches will vary from one advocate to another. However, the first point made in box 2.4 is central to a strict or thoroughgoing relativist position, and it is this which

---

## Box 2.4

## Features of relativistic approaches

1   Scientific accounts and theories are not accorded a privileged position; they are equivalent to other accounts (including lay ones). Different approaches are alternative ways of looking at the world and should be simply described, rather than evaluated in terms of their predictive power, explanatory value or truth value.

2   It is not accepted that there are rational criteria for choosing among different theoretical frameworks or explanations; moral, aesthetic or instrumental values or conventions always play an essential part in such choices.

3   Reality is represented through the eyes of participants. The existence (or accessibility, which has the same consequences) of an external reality independent of our theoretical beliefs and concepts is denied.

4   The role of language is emphasized, both as an object of study and as the central instrument by which the world is represented and constructed.

5   The importance of viewing the meaning of experience and behaviour in context, and in its full complexity, is stressed.

6   The research process is viewed as generating working hypotheses rather than immutable empirical facts.

7   The attitude towards theorizing emphasizes the emergence of concepts from data rather than their imposition in terms of a priori theory.

8   Qualitative methodologies are used.

(After Fletcher, 1996, p. 414; additional material from Steinmetz, 1998.)

---

effectively destroys any claim that such relativists might have to be 'doing science' (not that they would necessarily worry too much about this). As Fletcher (1996, p. 415) puts it, 'by discarding the criteria or aims concerned with truth or objectivity and adopting a full-blown constructionism, such theories become entangled in a web of internal contradictions.' This criticism is not new, having been initially developed by Socrates (see Siegel, 1987 for a detailed analysis).

It might be argued that these accounts are not presented as being 'true'. They are simply an invitation to view things from a particular perspective. In Gergen's (1985) view, 'the success of theoretical accounts depends primarily on the analyst's capacity to invite, compel, stimulate, or delight the audience, and not on criteria of veracity' (p. 272). To which a rejoinder might be that these aims need not be in opposition; those who regard striving for veracity as fundamental must also strive to fully engage their audience. However, as discussed below, many relativists do not deny the possibility of some kind of underlying reality, and there are other aspects of the relativist critique of positivistic approaches which have undoubtedly contributed to the methodology of social science research. These include the notion of science as a socially constituted construction; the recognition that science is not value free; and that there is a much looser connection between data and theory confirmation (or disconfirmation) than assumed in positivist doctrine.

## Current Views of Social Research

'Positivism is dead. By now it has gone off and is beginning to smell' (Byrne, 1998, p. 37). Given this widely accepted, though not usually as trenchantly expressed, view of the demise of positivism as a viable philosophical underpinning for research, including social research, what is the current state of play? This section seeks to provide an overview of approaches to social research which appear to be alive and well at the beginning of the millennium.

Different commentators nominate different candidates. Bentz and Shapiro (1998) list ten 'cultures' of enquiry; ethnography, quantitative behavioural science, phenomenology, action research, hermeneutics, evaluation research, feminist research, critical social science, historical–comparative research, and theoretical research. More typically, there is an attempt to isolate two broader strands, commonly labelled 'post-positivist' and 'constructivist', as the heirs respectively of the quantitative and qualitative traditions within social research. It is perhaps helpful to separate out a third approach, which may be labelled 'emancipatory' and which, while closer to the qualitative tradition, criticizes both the post-positivist and the constructivist approaches.

## Post-positivism

Post-positivism recognizes the force of the criticisms made of positivism and attempts to come to terms with them. For example, while positivists hold that the researcher and the researched person are independent of each other, there is an acceptance by post-positivists that the theories, hypotheses, background knowledge and values of the researcher can influence what is observed (Reichardt and Rallis, 1994). However, there is still a commitment to objectivity, which is approached by recognizing the possible effects of these likely biases.

Similarly, positivists maintain that one reality exists and that it is the researcher's job to discover what it is. Post-positivists also believe that a reality does exist, but consider that it can be known only imperfectly and probabilistically because of the researcher's limitations. Post-positivist researchers can be viewed as recognizing, sometimes reluctantly, that the battle for positivism has been lost, but as still hankering after the mantle of respectability and authority that it conferred. It is argued below that they can find their salvation in critical realist approaches.

## Constructivism

This is but one of many labels used to denote the current state of qualitative research (see Tesch, 1990, for what is probably the most exhaustive list, with a total of twenty-six different labels). 'Constructivism' is helpful because it flags a basic tenet of the approach, namely, that reality is socially constructed. However, it is also commonly called 'interpretive' (see Schwandt, 1994) or 'naturalistic' (Lincoln and Guba, 1985; Guba and Lincoln, 1994).

Constructivist researchers, as heirs to the relativist tradition, have grave difficulties with the notion of an objective reality which can be known. They consider that the task of the researcher is to understand the multiple social constructions of meaning and knowledge. Hence they tend to use research methods such as interviews and observation which allow them to acquire multiple perspectives. The research participants are viewed as helping to construct the 'reality' with the researchers. And, because there are multiple realities, the research questions cannot be fully established in advance of this process.

Some constructionists accept that there are valid criticisms of full-blown relativism that debar it from any aspirations to scientific credibility. Parker (1999) is 'Against relativism in psychology, on balance.' Parker (1998) and his contributors (see especially Burr, 1998; Collier, 1998; Davies, 1998; Merttens, 1998) provide a comprehensive exploration of the many and different claims made within constructionist research for what can be known about reality.

While this appears to have the characteristics of the start of a long-running debate, it provides encouragement for the view developed below that a sophisticated realist approach can provide a framework not only for post-positivists but also for constructionists.


## Feminist and other emancipatory approaches

This heading covers a varied range of approaches also commonly referred to as *critical approaches* (e.g. Everitt and Hardiker, 1996). Marxists, action researchers and many feminist researchers share similar concerns. Guba and Lincoln (1994) provide a detailed account. Their central criticism of both post-positivist and constructivist researchers is that they are relatively powerful experts researching relatively powerless people. They try to find ways of overcoming this imbalance in power. Box 2.5 summarizes some of the features of this general approach.

Feminist researchers have focused on gender imbalances. They share the well-established belief that, historically, women have not enjoyed the same power and privileges as men, and that they still live in an oppressive society; and a concern for 'understanding and improving the lives and relations between women and men' (Martusewicz and Reynolds, 1994, p. 13). The claim is made that feminist research is significantly different from traditional male-dominated research because it raises problems and concerns important to women rather than to men. The purpose of feminist enquiry is to facilitate female emancipation and the understanding of women's views of the world.

---

## Box 2.5

### Features of the emancipatory paradigm

1  It focuses on the lives and experiences of diverse groups (e.g. women, minorities, and persons with disabilities) that traditionally have been marginalized.

2  It analyses how and why resulting inequities are reflected in asymmetric power relationships.

3  It examines how results of social enquiry into inequities are linked to political and social action.

4  It uses an emancipatory theory to develop the research approach.

(After Mertens et al., 1994.)

---

It is also commonly asserted that feminist research is built on a different, more equal relationship between the researcher and the researched.

Some feminists have been happy to follow post-positivist approaches (e.g. Harding, 1986). Other feminists criticize this stance as merely replicating male norms of scientific research. Feminist relativists, particularly those influenced by postmodernism, reject the idea of any type of science as just another way in which the experiences of women are used and taken over by 'experts'. May (1997, pp. 21–5) provides a detailed account of this view. Feminists in their turn have been criticized for ignoring other imbalances. Thus Gordon (1995) highlights racist domination, and Oliver (1992) that experienced by persons with disabilities.

## Realism and Real World Research

Realism has a long tradition in the philosophy of science, including social science (Manicas, 1987). While early forms of the approach, sometimes referred to as 'naïve realism', attracted severe criticism, more recent formulations have a strong current position in the philosophy of both natural and social science. The writings of Roy Bhaskar and Rom Harré have been particularly influential (e.g. Bhaskar, 1978, 1982, 1990; Harré, 1981, 1986), while the text by Ray Pawson and Nick Tilley (Pawson and Tilley, 1997) provides a stirring, though controversial (because of its polemical style) manifesto for the use of realism in evaluation research. The 'new' realism is variously labelled (among other terms) as 'scientific realism', 'critical realism', 'fallibilistic realism', 'subtle realism' and 'transcendental realism', each variant stressing particular features. For example, fallibilistic realism focuses on

> the evident *fallibility* of our knowledge – the experience of getting things wrong, of having our expectations confounded, and of crashing into things – that justifies us in believing that the world exists regardless of what we happen to think about it. If by contrast, the world itself was a product or construction of our knowledge, then our knowledge would surely be infallible, for how could we ever be mistaken about anything? (Sayer, 2000, p. 2)

In the interests of simplicity, I will simply use 'realism' here, before opting eventually for 'critical realism'.

*Realism can provide a model of scientific explanation which avoids both positivism and relativism.*

Realism is an attractive choice for those doing social research who wish to characterize what they are doing as scientific. Its advocates claim that it is scientific, in a sense which is fully in accord with currently influential approaches to the philosophy of science. It also has the potential of incorporating features highlighted by the emancipatory approach, such as taking note of the perspectives of participants, and even of promoting social justice (House, 1991). Bhaskar's (1986) text is entitled *Scientific Realism and Human Emancipation*, elaborating his concern for 'emancipatory social practice' (Corson, 1991). Realism has been seen as particularly appropriate for research in practice- and value-based professions such as social work (Anastas, 1998).

The potential utility of realism for social research has been appreciated widely. Examples of work discussing or advocating its use occur in many fields, including applied linguistics (Corson, 1997); criminology (Young and Matthews, 1992); economics (Mäki, 1988); education (House, 1991; Nash, 1999; Scott, 2000); geography (Pratt, 1995; Yeung, 1997); health (Kaneko, 1999; Williams, 1999); international studies (Patomäki and Wight, 2000); learning disabilities (Warner, 1993); medical education (Colliver, 1996); management (Mutch, 1999); nursing (Porter and Ryan, 1996; Wainwright, 1997); organisational analysis (Reed, 1997); political science (Lane, 1996); psychology (Fletcher, 1996; Manicas and Secord, 1983; Shames, 1990); social work (Anastas, 1998; Kazi, 2000; Kazi and Ward, 2001); sociology (Nash, 1999; Steinmetz, 1998); and urban and regional studies (Banai, 1995)

## Realist explanation

The example of gunpowder is commonly used to illustrate the principles of realist explanation. Does gunpowder blow up when a flame is applied? Yes, if the conditions are right. It doesn't ignite if it is damp, or if the mixture is wrong, or if no oxygen is present, or if heat is applied only for a short time. In realist terms, the *outcome* (the explosion) of an *action* (applying the flame) follows from *mechanisms* (the chemical composition of the gunpowder) acting in particular *contexts* (the particular conditions which allow the reaction to take place). This is illustrated in figure 2.1.

## A realist view of doing experiments

Experimenters need to have a very substantial knowledge of the phenomenon they are interested in before it is worth their while to set up a formal experiment. Through theory and observation, and as a result of previous experiments, they develop knowledge and understanding about the mechanism through which an action causes an outcome, and about the context which provides the ideal conditions to trigger the mechanism. There may well be several

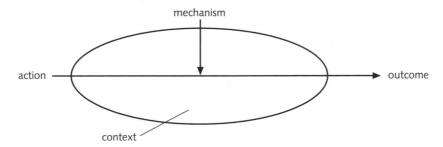

**Figure 2.1**   Representation of realist explanation.

such mechanisms, as well as other mechanisms which could have the effect of blocking the effect of the action. Disabling the latter mechanisms is known as *experimental* (or *laboratory*) *control*. The laboratory in the physical sciences is essentially a special space devoted to this kind of control where temperature, vibration, air quality, etc. are all carefully monitored to ensure that their variation cannot influence the outcome. Note that this has nothing to do with control groups.

The whole enterprise differs radically from the logic of experimental design as traditionally expounded in research methods texts. There, the experimenter simply manipulates one variable and looks for resultant change in a second one. In positivist science, the experimenter looks for this 'constant conjunction' (change in one variable reliably leading to a change in the second variable). If this is found, it constitutes a 'law'.

The realist experimenter is engaged in a very different kind of exercise. In Bhaskar's (1979, p. 53) terminology, you 'first . . . must trigger the mechanism under study to ensure that it is active; and secondly must prevent any interference with the operation of the mechanism.' This is a more active task; it is to 'manipulate the entire experimental system, so as to *manufacture* the desired interrelationship between independent and dependent variable. The experimentalist is indeed a *system builder* and the crucial evidence is produced not by controlled observation but by *work*' (Pawson and Tilley, 1997, p. 60, emphasis in original). Some realists are heavily critical of experimental designs. Pawson and Tilley (1997, ch. 2), for example, consider the standard control group design to be fatally flawed. Byrne (1998) contends that 'by its own criteria experimentalism only works when the world is linear and when causes are simple and single' (p. 65); non-linearity and complex causation are not too difficult to demonstrate.

Studies of the history of how physical scientists actually go about their trade (e.g. Koyré, 1968) reveal that it fits in well with this type of realist explanation. Theory is gradually and hesitantly developed so that eventually experiments can be done which make clear the mechanisms in operation. The studies also reveal that the process bears little resemblance to the kind of logical positivist analysis derived from Hume and John Stuart Mill which underpins traditional views of how experiments should be done. Box 2.6 lists some of the main features of the realist view of science; Blaikie (1993, esp. pp. 58–62, 94–5, and 114–18) provides a more detailed account. Note that, as with the discussions earlier in this chapter of positivist and relativist views, the summary presented here is an amalgam of features common in realist writing but to which it would be difficult to get different realist theorists to sign up *in toto*. In particular, the chief protagonists Roy Bhaskar and Rom Harré differ considerably in their stance and terminology (Lewis, 2000). Harré argues for an interpretive social psychology, whereas Bhaskar has been substantially

---

## Box 2.6

### A realist view of science

1   There is no unquestionable foundation for science, no 'facts' that are beyond dispute. Knowledge is a social and historical product. 'Facts' are theory-laden.

2   The task of science is to invent theories to explain the real world, and to test these theories by rational criteria.

3   Explanation is concerned with how mechanisms produce events. The guiding metaphors are of structures and mechanisms in reality rather than phenomena and events.

4   A law is the characteristic pattern of activity or tendency of a mechanism. Laws are statements about the things that are 'really' happening, the ongoing ways of acting of independently existing things, which may not be expressed at the level of events.

5   The real world is not only very complex but also stratified into different layers. Social reality incorporates individual, group and institutional, and societal levels.

6   The conception of causation is one in which entities act as a function of their basic structure.

7   Explanation is showing how some event has occurred in a particular case. Events are to be explained even when they cannot be predicted.

(Partly after House, 1991.)

concerned initially with the natural sciences and is much closer to materialist views. While they both agree that social science is a search for the fundamental structures and mechanisms of social life, Harré prefers to talk about 'reason explanations' in the social sciences as analogous to 'mechanism explanations' in the natural sciences.

This terminology may well be preferable to many social scientists uncomfortable with the obvious machine-like connotations of 'mechanisms'. However, I will stick to the term 'mechanism' in this account. The secondary dictionary definition as 'arrangement and action by which a result is produced' is to my ears helpful and exact. Readers who require further softening up are recommended to browse an engaging short text by Jon Elster (1989) entitled *Nuts and Bolts for the Social Sciences* which 'offers a tool-box of mechanisms – nuts and bolts, cogs and wheels – that can be used to explain quite complex social phenomena' (p. 3).

There is much more to the realist view than simply asserting that an external reality exists. As indicated in box 2.6, it provides a coherent model for science which is very different from that of positivism. Nevertheless, at the heart of realism is the assumption that there is a reality which exists independently of our awareness of it. This is taken for granted by all but a few recalcitrant (though logically impregnable) philosophers when considering the everyday world of the physical objects around us. It becomes more debatable when considering very small things such as electrons, viruses and genes, which we cannot 'see' or otherwise sense directly. However, realism claims that the various 'things' described by theories actually exist. As Hacking (1983, p. 21) puts it, 'Protons, photons, fields of force and black holes are as real as toenails, turbines, eddies in the stream, and volcanoes.' Note, however, that this does not commit one to the position that everything is real. Maxwell and Delaney (1999) make the point that

> Within psychology a realistic interpretation might be given to a brain mechanism that you hypothesize is damaged on the basis of the poor memory performance of a brain-injured patient. However, the states in a mathematical model of memory such as working memory may be viewed instrumentally, as simply convenient fictions or metaphors that allow estimation of the probability of recall of a particular item. (p. 23)

One of the advantages of realism is that it allows one to take on board some of the attractive features of relativist positions as discussed above (p. 25). They have, for example, made explicit the value-laden and political nature of research. However, in thoroughgoing relativist accounts, it is difficult to see how competing values and political interests can be reconciled. Realism can acknowledge values in a way not open to positivists, who claim their activities are value-free. And because there is a reality to which reference can be made, there is a basis for choice among different theories. Similarly, realists do not aspire to the universalist claims of positivism, but see knowledge as a social and historical product that can be specific to a particular time, culture or situation. It is the task of science to invent theories that aim to represent the world. Manicas and Secord stress the diametrically opposed positions of realism and positivism on the status of theoretical entities and observation. For positivists, observations are the unquestioned foundation and theoretical entities merely hypothetical; but

> *for realists, 'theoretical entities are not hypothetical, but real; observations are not the rock bottom of science, but are tenuous and always subject to reinterpretation.' (Manicas and Secord, 1983, p. 406)*

This inversion of the traditional view is central to an appreciation of a realist approach.

The practices of the sciences generate their own rational criteria in terms of which theory is accepted or rejected. These criteria can be rational because there is a world independent of our experience of it. The theories may be wrong because they are based on what is currently known about the world, which is necessarily incomplete.

The world and science are stratified; the things of the world are complex composites. Manicas and Secord (1983, p. 401) give table salt as an example: it is not simply sodium chloride but will also contain other chemicals, even if only in very small amounts. At another level, sodium chloride is a compound of the elements sodium and chlorine, both of which have different properties which are also different from the properties of the compound. At a further level, both the elements are themselves complexes of electrons, neutrons, etc. In a similar way, the activities of people in society constitute a set of interacting things and structures at different levels. The task of the social scientist is to establish their existence and properties through both theoretical and experimental work.

## Realism and social research

Moving from carrying out natural or physical science in laboratories to studies on or about people in real world settings calls for two giant leaps. Studying people, in whatever setting, is very different from studying physical objects or non-human organisms. Also, outside the laboratory, the kind of experimental control discussed above becomes difficult, often bordering on the impossible. It effectively means a move from a closed, controlled situation to an open, more fluid one. These features in no way invalidate the realist analysis but do complicate the carrying out of research.

What about social reality? Are there social 'objects'? Realism accepts that there are fundamental differences between natural and social phenomena. This means that different methods have to be used for different subject matters. However, although their procedures will differ, natural and social sciences share common principles. For realists there are social objects which can be studied scientifically, but the methods chosen must fit the subject matter. As Bhaskar (1979, p. 30, n. 40) puts it, 'it is obvious that one can no more set out to experimentally identify . . . the causes of the French revolution than one can contemplate interviewing a gene.'

Realism permits a new integration of what are usually referred to as subjectivist and objectivist approaches in social theory. The former approaches (e.g. action theory, phenomenology, ethnomethodology, interpretive sociologies) emphasize that action is meaningful and intentional, that it is social behaviour, that meanings are social meanings, and that intentionality involves reflexive monitoring of conduct in a social milieu. However, they have tended to deny an objective character for society. Objectivist approaches (e.g. the structural functionalism of Durkheim and Parsons), while emphasizing the reality of society, tend to deny the causal role of agency.

The new integration argues that social structure is at the same time the relatively enduring product, and also the medium, of motivated human action. This allows both subjectivist and objectivist approaches to co-exist. Social structures such as language are both reproduced and transformed by action, but they also pre-exist for individuals. They permit persons to act meaningfully and intentionally while at the same time limit the ways in which they can act. People may marry for personal, psychological reasons, but an unintended consequence of their actions is to reproduce the family structure.

## Mechanisms and contexts

It has already been stressed that, for realists, explanation is constructed in terms of *mechanisms*. We understand why gunpowder explodes when we know that the properties of the mixture of chemicals are such that when heat is applied under appropriate known conditions, a violent reaction takes place. It is claimed that, for many sufferers, drinking a large strong black coffee immediately the first signs of a migraine attack appears stops it developing. A dyed-in-the-wool sceptic, such as myself, finds this more persuasive now that a pharmacological mechanism for its analgesic properties has been demonstrated (Sawynok, 1995; Barnard, 1999).

Byrne (1998, pp. 38–40) provides a clear example from a study by Bradbury (1933) of the incidence and causes of tuberculosis on Tyneside in the north of England (further details are given in Byrne et al., 1986). He concluded that three main factors (mechanisms) were involved in its development:

- 'poor housing conditions', leading to overcrowding and facilitating transmission of the TB bacillus;
- 'poor feeding', in particular insufficient consumption of milk, making it easier for the infection to take hold;
- 'being Irish', which meant less generational exposure to the disease.

'In other words the causal mechanisms for clinical TB were complex and contingent. Good housing and good food blocked the disease' (p. 39). Byrne cites strong epidemiological support for this account.

Realists also look for explanations of social phenomena. For example, Pawson and Tilley (1997, pp. 78–82) use a realist approach to analyse attempts to reduce car park crime through the introduction of closed-circuit television (CCTV). Clearly the cameras do not in themselves make cars more difficult to break into. If they do work, it must be through processes in the minds of potential thieves, parkers of cars, car park attendants, police and others. From a knowledge of the situation, combined with observation in car parks, it is possible to suggest a range of mechanisms that may be at work. Pawson and Tilley suggest eight possibilities, including:

a    'caught in the act': offenders are more likely to be observed, arrested, punished and deterred;
b    'increased usage': drivers feel that the car park is safer, leading to increased usage; with more people around, potential offenders are deterred;
c    'appeal to the cautious': cautious drivers who lock their cars and use alarms and immobilizers are attracted to parks with CCTV, displacing more vulnerable cars.

More than one mechanism may be involved in a particular situation, and whether or not a particular mechanism operates will depend on the *context*. If, for example, much of the crime in a particular car park is committed by a single offender, then increasing the probability of apprehension, as in mechanism (a), will be likely to have a much more dramatic effect on car crime than if many thieves were involved. Mechanisms (b) and (c) will be largely inoperative in commuter car parks which already fill up early in the morning and remain virtually full until workers return in the evening. However, parks which are currently little used, and where each parked car has a relatively high chance of being broken into, may provide an appropriate context for firing the 'increased usage' mechanism.

Pawson and Tilley point out that their list of mechanisms and contexts is speculative, there being – as in much real world research – little social science background from which they might have been derived; or, as they put it, 'there being no existing sociology of the car park' (1997, p. 80). However, it may be worthwhile to search for existing studies in similar situations such as shopping malls, football stadiums and town centres where CCTV cameras are employed, and where the same mechanisms may occur (Brown, 1995). And, as in much real world research, it is not a difficult task for practitioners and others with a well-developed and intimate knowledge of the situation (and for researchers with whom they have shared this knowledge) to come up with a set of proposals for the mechanisms and contexts likely to be relevant. Box 2.7 gives an example of this process.

These proposals help to focus the research effort. They may suggest avenues which were not initially obvious. In the car park example, while data relating to break-ins would almost certainly be routinely collected, assessing the operation of an 'appeal to the cautious' mechanism suggests an examination

---

## Box 2.7

### Practitioner proposals for mechanisms

A client organization wished to know why some residents from a nearby centre for adults with learning difficulties attended their evening club but others did not. Some explanations were suggested by the key worker of the client organization and others by the students undertaking the project.

1    Perhaps some residents did not want to make the journey to the club or did not have adequate transport.
2    Perhaps the residents wanted to be accompanied on the journey.
3    Perhaps they did not have enough information (or any information) about the club.
4    Perhaps the club did not provide the kinds of activities which the residents liked.
5    Perhaps the club was not friendly enough.

Consideration of these suggestions indicates the possibility of the following mechanisms affecting club attendance:

*    an *accessibility mechanism* (1 and 2);
*    an *information mechanism* (3);
*    a *needs and expectations mechanism* (4 and 5).

Evidence about the operation of these mechanisms could be sought in a project.

(Example taken from Hall and Hall, 1996, p. 31; NB The original is not described in terms of mechanisms.)

of unmolested cars. Are there changes in the numbers and proportions of cars left unlocked; or with visible stealable goods; or without an armed alarm? Other mechanisms may suggest some attention to what is stolen, or to the locations of the crimes, or to their timing, etc. You will also have to concern yourself with what is technically feasible; for example, it is only recently that CCTV pictures have been of sufficiently high definition to provide unequivocal identification of offenders, and hence potentially operate the 'caught in the act' mechanism.

Following up these leads fits in most appropriately with the initial exploratory phase which is common to a large proportion of real world research. In some situations, this may have to be 'virtual' exploratory work where, without further observation or other direct data gathering, you explore with those who are knowledgeable about the setting which mechanisms and contexts appear to be the 'bankers', i.e. those agreed to be the ones to concentrate on. Or you may be in the fortunate position where you are building on previous work (your own or others'), or even have a developed theoretical framework, either of which may provide strong pointers to the mechanisms and contexts to work on in detail.

'Working on in detail' constitutes the main phase of your research. It can, in principle, follow any of the fixed or flexible designs covered in the following chapters. The desirable end-state of this process for realists is that you come up with one or more postulated mechanisms which are capable of explaining the phenomena; that, from the research, you have good reason to believe in their existence; and that you can specify the contexts in which these mechanisms operate. This discussion has been couched in terms of mechanisms which operate to produce an outcome or effect, but there may also be mechanisms operating which block the outcome or effect. In particular, your research will be set in some social system or situation where existing mechanisms may be blocking the change or outcome you are seeking.

## Embeddedness

Human actions can only be understood in terms of their place within different strata or layers of social reality. The usual realist example is the act of signing a cheque. This is accepted for payment because of its place within the social organization known as the banking system. The action of presenting a signed cheque leads causally to the outcome of receipt of goods because of accepted social relations within a wider system.

In order to explain what is going on in social systems, it seems inevitable that we will have to call on mechanisms at various levels: micro and macro, group and organizational, etc. Consider, for example, the effectiveness of a new approach to curriculum in schools, say the introduction of a 'literacy hour'. Realists would argue that it is too simplistic to limit our assessment of its efficacy to changes made by individual pupils following the new curriculum. At one level the curriculum does consist of content, ideas and skills introduced into children's minds. However, the curriculum is delivered via interaction in the classroom where there are expectations and rules about the behaviour of both teachers and pupils which may or may not vary from class to class, teacher to teacher, school to school, etc. The teacher will have aims which may be shared by some pupils but be very different from those of other pupils. Both teachers and pupils bring their own backgrounds and experiences to the classroom. Teachers' loyalties may be to the school and the new curriculum; or they may be primarily to colleagues, or their union (particularly in times of strife). Children may be motivated by their own or parents' aspirations to success, or by the need to appear 'cool' to their peers.

The innovation necessarily has a history, perhaps a centrally perceived general inadequacy in literacy providing the spur for its introduction. It will be likely to 'play' differently in a school under stress, or in transition, and in one with acclaimed success and clear leadership. Similarly, the future as represented by the opportunities and constraints in later education and life prospects is likely to influence the value put on literacy.

A realist researcher into the effects that such an innovation has in schools would look for possible mechanisms and contexts at the different levels within this complex social system. Given different contexts, there is no expectation that the same set of releasing or blocking mechanisms would be operating universally. As discussed in chapter 7, the typical result for large-scale social interventions of this type is to show, at best, a disappointingly small overall change. However, following the realist path effectively rephrases the question from 'What will produce the greatest overall change?' to *'What works best, for whom, and under what circumstances?'* In other words, the focus shifts to seeking an understanding not only of the combination of circumstances where substantial gains have been achieved, but also where the innovation has been totally ineffective or possibly negative in outcome. Understanding the mechanisms at work and the contexts in which they operate provides a theoretical understanding of what is going on which can then be used to optimize the effects of the innovation by appropriate contextual changes, or by finding alternative ways of countering blocking mechanisms, or even by changing the innovation itself so that it is more in tune with some of the contexts where positive change has not been achieved.

## Open and closed systems

Scientific laws in a realist analysis are about the causal properties of structures that exist and operate in the world. Salt will usually dissolve in water. In the real world, there may be some conditions where this does not happen. Studies carried out under strict laboratory conditions would be able to specify in detail the situations where it does or does not dissolve. To do this, we have to set up a *closed system* where all aspects are under the researcher's control. Realism recognizes that in social science it is essentially impossible to approach that degree of closure. Because we are dealing with *open systems*, we have to accept that we are dealing with tendencies and probabilities. Causal processes may sometimes, even usually, lead to particular outcomes. But on some occasions, and in some circumstances, they may not. Our hypothesis is that there are one or more mechanisms at work which will trigger these outcomes; and that there are other mechanisms which will interfere so that the outcome does not occur.

The research task is to obtain evidence about the actual existence of these hypothesized mechanisms. Positivistic science, with its Humean view of causation, is concerned with establishing predictable regularities, taking the view that, without them, laws do not apply. As Outhwaite (1987) makes clear:

> Unlike a constant conjunction analysis, which logically presupposes that the system within which 'causal' relations are observed is isolated from extraneous influences, a realist analysis of causality can account for the interaction of various causal tendencies within the complex and open systems among which we live, and which we ourselves are. (p. 22)

Realists believe that even in the absence of the degree of closure needed to establish predictable regularities, the laws still apply. They seek to show how it is that, in the particular situation in which the research took place, there was a particular causal configuration involving a set of mechanisms that had the particular pattern of results achieved. In other words, we are seeking causal explanations. The task is to carry out an analysis of the possible causes which were in operation while eliminating alternatives which might have been involved.

In the open systems of real world research, the hospital ward, housing estate, business, or whatever forms the focus of our research cannot be hermetically sealed from external influences. People, information and all other aspects of the situation are likely to change in ways that may or may not have anything to do with the focus of our investigation. These are systems which are open in the sense that they can be entered and exited, both literally and figuratively, at any time. There is an arbitrariness about what we consider to be the context of our study and what its actual content.

Manicas and Secord (1983) make the more general claim that social and psychological reality exists in inherently open systems. They stress the complexity of the task.

> The acts of persons in life settings are open-systemic events that involve an enormous range of codetermining structures and systems. One needs knowledge only of physics to account for the fall of a person from a precipice; one needs knowledge of biological structures and processes to comprehend birth or death; one needs psychology to have an understanding of the structures and processes that underlie performances – and of course this is made more difficult by the fact that the relevant intrinsic structures of persons are complexly related and causally codetermining. (p. 407)

In open systems, we can well be in a position to explain some event after it has occurred even though we were not able to predict it. In closed systems, explanation and prediction are symmetrical; if we can explain, we can predict, and vice versa. But in open systems, the actual configurations of structures and processes are constantly changing, making definite prediction impossible. This means that while the future cannot be predicted, the past can be explained by establishing the particular configuration which was in existence.

## Critical realism

Of the various adjectives used to indicate variants of realism, *critical* appears preferable for the purposes of this text. It is the term used by Roy Bhaskar in developing his influential realist philosophy of the social sciences (Bhaskar, 1989). Note that this is not an easy read; Sayer (2000, pp. 10–28) provides an excellent short introduction (see also Collier, 1994).

This version of realism is critical in the sense that it provides a rationale for a critical social science; one that criticizes the social practices that it studies. For example:

> Gender relations are usually informed and reproduced through beliefs that gender is natural rather than a product of socialization, so that the disadvantages suffered by women are seen implicitly as natural too. Social scientists who merely reproduce this explanation uncritically in their accounts so that they merely reported that gender was a product of biological difference would fail to understand gender. To explain such phenomena one has to acknowledge this dependence of actions on shared meanings while showing in what respects they are false, if they are. (Sayer, 2000, pp. 18–19)

If false understandings, and actions based on them, can be identified, this provides an impetus for change (Bhaskar, 1986). Hence adopting a critical realist stance not only provides a third way between positivism and relativism, but might also help fulfil the emancipatory potential of social research.

Realism and replication

Replication in research – the attempt to repeat a study – is a major corner-stone of natural science. A finding is not regarded as secure unless it has been independently replicated on several occasions, and 'failure to replicate' has dealt a death blow to many promising lines of research. In real world research, and social science more generally, attempts to replicate are rare. Some quali-tative researchers consider it an impossibility; to them, each study is essentially unique. Certainly it is just not feasible to repeat a study exactly with the same people in the same situation.

The realist views any of these approaches to replication as an attempt to confirm the structures and mechanisms identified in the original study under similar contingent conditions. However, replication does not produce con-clusive verification of their existence (or, put in other terms, of the theory). Similarly, a failure to replicate previous findings does not conclusively falsify the theory. As Tsang and Kwan (1999) put it:

> One explanation of this failure is that the structures and mechanisms as postu-lated in the theory are inaccurate: in this case we have a true falsification. However, another possible explanation is that, in the replicated study, there is a different set of contingencies that either modifies the postulated mechanisms or invokes previously inactive countervailing mechanisms. This results in a differ-ent set of events being observed. (p. 769)

Given the relatively primitive stage of our understanding of what is hap-pening in many real world situations, a sensible strategy, with some hope of progress in that understanding, would appear to be to capitalize on any studies where there are relatively strong findings giving support to a particular theory suggesting the operation of certain mechanisms in the contexts of the study. This would be done most effectively by trying to set up as exact a replication as feasible in the first instance. After that, and given some success in that repli-cation, effort could be put into generalizing the findings.

## A Pragmatic Approach

Critical realism has been proposed in this chapter as a way forward, ac-knowledging that positivism has been discredited but avoiding the divorce from science implied by a thoroughgoing relativist approach. It seeks to achieve a detente between the different paradigms of a post-positivist approach within the empirical tradition on the one hand, and less thoroughgoing versions of relativism found in some constructionist approaches on the other.

This solution to the so-called 'paradigm wars' endemic in the social sciences for the past three decades between positivists (empiricists, quantitative researchers) and constructionists (phenomenologists, qualitative researchers; e.g. Reichardt and Rallis, 1994; Guba, 1990) calls for a radical reappraisal by warriors on both sides of this divide. It may well be a step too far for both qualitative and quantitative adherents; nevertheless, I hope that you will at least go along with it as far as seeing how a critical realist approach actually 'cashes out' in design and analysis terms in the following chapters.

As noted by Tashakkori and Teddlie (1998, pp. 3–11) it does appear that the qualitative/quantitative debate, while it might have been necessary in the 1980s and early 1990s, has now become increasingly unproductive (see also Datta, 1994). Some argue that this is because it is now clear that there is a basic incompatibility between the two approaches, hence it is time to stop the talking and get on with one's own thing (e.g. Smith and Heshusios, 1986). An alternative approach is to follow the lead of Bryman (1988a), who points out that in practice there is a greater rapprochement between workers in the two traditions than would appear to be the case from studying their philosophical underpinnings, and hence a greater compatibility of approach in practice. This is probably particularly true of those working in applied fields. Others have advocated a pragmatic approach: use whatever philosophical or methodological approach works best for a particular research problem at issue. This leads to mixed-method studies where both quantitative and qualitative approaches are adopted (e.g. Brewer and Hunter, 1989); these are discussed in chapter 12 below.

Pragmatism is itself a philosophical position with a respectable, mainly American, history going back to the work of Peirce, William James and Dewey (Cherryholmes, 1992; Howe, 1988). For these pragmatists, truth is 'what works'. Hence the test is whether or not it is feasible to carry out worthwhile studies using qualitative and quantitative approaches side by side (Tashakkori and Teddlie, 1998, pp. 137–70, provide an extensive set of examples).

Reichardt and Rallis (1994, p. 85) contend that this pragmatic approach is feasible because the fundamental values of current quantitative and qualitative researchers are actually highly compatible and include the following beliefs:

- the value-ladenness of enquiry;
- the theory-ladenness of facts;
- that reality is multiple, complex, constructed and stratified; and
- the underdetermination of theory by fact (i.e. that any particular set of data is explicable by more than a single theory).

This is a list which is remarkably similar to that put forward above in box 2.6 as underlying the realist position, suggesting a helpful compatibility between the realist and the pragmatic.

## Further Reading

Archer, M., Bhaskar, R., Collier, A., Lawson, T. and Norrie, A. (1998) *Critical Realism: Essential Readings*. London and New York: Routledge. Definitive set of readings on critical realism.

Blaikie, N. (1993) *Approaches to Social Enquiry*. Cambridge: Polity. A comprehensive, balanced and up-to-date text covering both the philosophy and the methodology of the social sciences.

Byrne, D. (1998) *Complexity Theory and the Social Sciences: An Introduction*. London: Routledge. Fascinating introduction to chaos/complexity theories and their implications for social research. Written from a realist perspective.

Delanty, G. (1997) *Social Science: Beyond Constructivism and Realism*. Buckingham: Open University Press. Concise challenging text arguing for a synthesis of constructivism and realism.

Elster, J. (1989) *Nuts and Bolts for the Social Sciences*. Cambridge: Cambridge University Press. Short, engaging and idiosyncratic introduction to the philosophy of the social sciences. After reading this your world will be full of mechanisms.

Pettigrew, T. F. (1996) *How to Think Like a Social Scientist*. New York: HarperCollins. Concise, personal style. Fosters critical thinking on important issues such as theory, comparison, causation, sampling, levels, etc. Big on healthy scepticism.

Sayer, A. (2000) *Realism and Social Science*. London: Sage. Authoritative guide to critical realism including its implications for social science research.

Smith, M. J. (1998) *Social Science in Question*. London: Sage/Milton Keynes: Open University Press. Comprehensive and well-structured account of current dilemmas and debates in the philosophy of the social sciences and their implications for research practice.

# 3
# Developing Your Ideas

This chapter:

- reviews differences in developing fixed and flexible design research;
- helps you decide on the focus of your enquiry, emphasizing the advantages of 'starting where you are';
- considers tactics for researching the background, including database searches;
- discusses how this focus can be refined into research questions, and
- the role of theory in this process;
- emphasizes the importance of ethical issues;
- highlights questionable practices that you should avoid;
- stresses the political arena within which real world research is carried out; and
- concludes with some warnings about sexism in research.

## Introduction

The task of carrying out an enquiry is complicated by the fact that there is no overall consensus about how to conceptualize the doing of research. This shows in various ways. There are, for example, different views about the place and role of theory; also about the sequence and relationship of the activities involved. One model says that you need to know exactly what you are doing before collecting the data that you are going to analyse; and that you collect all this data before starting to analyse it. A different approach expects you to develop your design through interaction with whatever you are studying, and has data collection and analysis intertwined. These approaches were referred to in chapter 1 as *fixed designs* and *flexible* designs respectively. The former have their antecedents in the traditions variously labelled as positivistic, natural-science based, hypothetico-deductive, quantitative or even simply 'scientific'; the latter in ones known as interpretive, ethnographic or qualitative – among several other labels.

Spradley (1980) compares these two research approaches to petroleum engineers and explorers respectively:

> The [petroleum] engineer has a specific goal in mind; to find oil or gas buried far below the surface. Before the engineer even begins an investigation, a careful study will be made of the maps which show geological features of the area. Then, knowing ahead of the time the kinds of features that suggest oil or gas beneath the surface, the engineer will go out to 'find' something quite specific. (p. 26)

To follow the fixed design route, you have to be in the position of knowing what you are looking for. However, those following flexible designs begin much more generally. They explore,

> gathering information, going first in one direction then perhaps retracing that route, then starting out in a new direction. On discovering a lake in the middle of a large wooded area, the explorer would take frequent compass readings, check the angle of the sun, take notes about prominent landmarks, and use feedback from each observation to modify earlier information. (p. 26)

For those interested in carrying out relatively small-scale real world investigations, each of these traditional models presents difficulties. A problem in following fixed designs is that one is often forced to work with maps that are sketchy at best. In other words, the firm theoretical base that is called for is difficult to get hold of. Similarly, free-range exploring is rarely on the cards. For one thing, there isn't the time; and the real world enquirer often has some idea of the 'lie of the land', and is looking for something quite specific while still being open to unexpected discoveries.

This suggests that real world researchers may need to be somewhat innovative in their approach, not automatically following research traditions when they do not quite fit the purposes and context of the research task. Fortunately, researchers do already seem to be more eclectic in their actual research practice than methodologists urge them to be. Bryman (1988a) makes out a strong case that many of the differences between the two traditions exist in the minds of philosophers and theorists, rather than in the practices of researchers. For example, he concludes that

> the suggestion that quantitative research is associated with the testing of theories, whilst qualitative research is associated with the generation of theories, can be viewed as a convention that has little to do with either the practices of many

researchers within the two traditions or the potential of the methods of data collection themselves. (p. 172)

Undoubtedly there are situations and topics where a fixed design following a quantitative approach is called for, and others where a flexible qualitative study is appropriate. But there are 'still others [which] will be even better served by a marriage of the two traditions' (p. 173). This view that the differences between the two traditions can be best viewed as technical rather than epistemological, enabling the enquirer to 'mix and match' both methodologies and methods according to what best fits a particular study, is developed in chapter 12 below.

## Deciding on the focus

### A   The need for a focus

Before you can start, you obviously need to have some idea of what area you are going to deal with. This amounts to deciding on your focus. My experience is that this tends either to be quite straightforward, almost self-evident (especially when you are told what to do!); or pretty problematic (when you have an open field).

Finding the focus involves identifying what it is that you want to gather information about. Until you have done this, further planning is impossible. If you are deciding for yourself, with few or no external constraints, the decision will be driven by what you are interested in and concerned about. Any research or enquiry experience that you already have can be a legitimate influence on this decision, but you should beware of this having a straitjacket effect (e.g. simply looking for topics where you might use your survey experience). Conversely, it is also legitimate to select a focus which leads you to branch out and gain experience of a strategy or technique not already within your 'toolbag'.

Sometimes the idea comes from your own direct experience or observation (see 'Starting where you are' below). Or it may arise from discussion with others about what would be timely and useful. Much real world research is sparked off by wanting to solve a problem, or a concern for change and improvement in something to do with practice. Neuman (1994, p. 110) suggests, in addition, curiosity based on something in the media, personal values, everyday life, and topics of current interest and concern where funding is more likely.

*It is helpful to try to write down the research focus at this stage, even if you can only do this in a vague and tentative form.* Later stages in the process will help to refine it and get it more clearly focused. Box 3.1 gives a varied set of examples.

*continued*

---

# Box 3.1

## Examples of initial proposals for research foci

- The 'quality of life' in the community for ex-patients of a closed-down psychiatric hospital
- A successful 'job club'
- The effectiveness of 'Work-Link' in providing jobs for the young disabled
- Helping carers of geriatric relatives
- Evaluating a short course in Rogerian counselling
- Dramatherapy with sexually abused children
- Approaches to curriculum in 16–19-year-old pupils with severe learning difficulties
- Facilitating change in small organizations through a computer version of the Delphi Nominal Group approach
- The 'Young Terriers': youth section of a football supporters club
- Failing the first year of an engineering degree: how not to do it
- The social function of a hairdressing salon
- Introducing a student-led assessment into a course
- Woman-centred maternity care

---

## B   Making a group decision

If you are proposing to carry out a group project with colleagues or friends, it is valuable for each member independently to think about, and write down, their proposals for the research focus. The group then comes together to decide on an agreed focus. In this way, all members of the group have some input into the process, and ideas of combining individual input with group collaboration and negotiation get built in at an early stage. Hall and Hall (1996, pp. 22–7) provide useful practical advice on working in groups, covering areas such as group development, unwritten contracts, team roles and leadership.

## C   Having the decision made for you

In many cases, the focus of a real world enquiry is given to the investigator(s) as a part of the job, or as a commission or tender. That is not to say that the people giving the task to the investigators necessarily know what they want, or that the investigators agree that this is what they should be wanting. The main task in this situation is clarificatory: translating the problem presented into something researchable and, moreover, 'do-able' within the limits of the time, resources and finance that can be made available.

*continued*

## D Starting where you are

If you do have some say in the choice of topic, there are several factors which might be taken into account. *Interest* is probably the most important. *All enquiry involves drudgery and frustration, and you need to have a strong interest in the topic to keep you going through the bad times.* Such interest in the focus of the research is not the same thing as having a closed and pre-judged view of the nature of the phenomenon to be researched or the kind of outcomes that will be found, which is likely to affect the objectivity and trustworthiness of the research. All of these aspects, however, are a part of what Lofland and Lofland (1995) call 'starting where you are'. Box 3.2 gives examples. As Kirby and McKenna (1989) put it: 'Remember that who you are has a central place in the research process because you bring your own thoughts, aspirations and feelings, and your own ethnicity, race, class, gender, sexual orientation, occupation, family background, schooling, etc. to your research' (p. 46).

This open acknowledgement of what the enquirer brings to the enquiry is more common in some research traditions than others. However, even in traditional laboratory experimentation, the work of Robert Rosenthal and colleagues (e.g. Rosnow and Rosenthal, 1997) has led to a recognition of 'experimenter effects' of various kinds, although they tend to be viewed solely in terms of the difficulties they produce.

---

## Box 3.2

### Examples of 'starting where you are'

| *Where they were:* | *What they did:* |
| --- | --- |
| An expectant parent exploring birthing options | DeVries, G. (1985) Regulating birth: midwives, medicine and the law |
| Serving as escorts at an abortion clinic | Dilorio, J. A. and Nusbaumer, M. R. (1993) Securing our sanity: anger management among abortion escorts |
| Working at a small iron foundry when a wildcat strike occurred | Fantasia, R. (1988) Cultures of solidarity: consciousness, action, and contemporary American workers |
| Leaving a nunnery | Ebaugh, H. R. F. (1988) Becoming an EX: the process of role exit |
| In prison | Irwin, J. (1985) *The Jail: Managing the Underclass in American Society* |

(Abridged from Lofland and Lofland, 1995, pp. 12–13, who provide additional examples.)

*continued*

Enquirers selecting their own foci make the choice for a variety of reasons. It may be, for example, to address a problem of 'practice'. That is, as professionals (psychologists, social workers, health service workers, teachers, managers, personnel officers, etc.) they wish to look at, perhaps evaluate or change, some aspect of practice that interests or concerns them. It may be their own, or colleagues', practice or professional situations, or those of others whom they have a responsibility to advise or support. Frequently encountered problems are obviously a sensible choice for a research focus as anything useful that you find out has a direct spin-off; and, importantly, there will be no shortage of instances to study.

In such situations you are also likely to know a lot about the topic even before starting the research, which can assist in planning the research. Maxwell (1996) comments: 'Traditionally, what you bring to the research from your background and identity has been treated as *bias*, something whose influence needs to be eliminated from the design, rather than a valuable component of it' (p. 27; emphasis in original).

Because of this there is a tendency, particularly in proposals from students, to ignore what the proposer can bring to the study from their own experience about the settings and issues to be studied. Maxwell's view is that such *experiential knowledge* can be profitably capitalized on. The potential for bias still exists, of course, and it will be necessary to seek to counter this by examining the assumptions and values you bring to the situation. One approach to this is to use an *experience memo* which articulates the expectations, beliefs and understandings you have from previous experience. Maxwell (1996, pp. 30–1) and Grady and Wallston (1988, p. 41) provide examples.

## E   Researching the background

The approach to deciding on the research focus suggested here differs from traditional views of the origins of research tasks. These see them as rooted in the academic discipline, revealed through the research literature and theoretical or methodological concerns. This places a considerable onus on researchers. They must have a thorough and up-to-date understanding of the 'literature'; detailed background knowledge of the relevant discipline; technical proficiency; and substantial time and resources. Bentz and Shapiro (1998, pp. 72–4) provide useful suggestions for getting started in more traditional research.

In many 'real world' studies, it can be argued that the research literature, and the discipline, provide a *background resource* rather than the essential starting point for research designs (Walker, 1985, p. 13). This change of view is important because of the change in power relationship between investigator and practitioner that it suggests. The researcher does not set the agenda in isolation, but acts in partnership with a variety of client groups. One way in which this can be implemented is for those who have been, in the past, the *subjects* of research now to play a role in carrying out the research. This applies with particular force to the part of the enquiry that is concerned with conceptualizing the task and deciding on the research questions. (*Note:* There is a recent change in terminology in experimental research. It is advocated that those taking part, formerly referred to as 'subjects', should now be 'participants'. This very rarely indicates that they do anything other than what the experimenter has pre-ordained; nevertheless, it is a recognition of the negative connotations of the previous term. This change is adopted in chapter 5, p. 110.)

A good understanding about what is already known, or established, does not then have the absolutely central role in applied real world enquiry that it does in fundamental, discipline-developing research. However, it can still be of considerable value. It may be possible to get background information from persons who have done related work, either directly or through the 'literature'. Unfortunately, for many real world topics, that literature tends to be somewhat inaccessible and fragmentary.

A general strategy would start with the various databases which contain bibliographic information relating to your area of interest. Box 3.3 gives a selection of widely used sources. Mertens (1998, p. 40) and Thomas (1996, p. 135) list other sources. While several of these sources are available in print form, they can be more efficiently and effectively searched using CD-ROM versions or on-line via World Wide Web (WWW) sites. Such databases typically include journal articles, books and book chapters. Often abstracts are provided which help in judging whether something is likely to be of interest. Watson and Richardson (1999) provide an interesting comparative analysis of Medline and PsychINFO showing substantial problems in the necessary search strategies and suggesting that while such searches

## Box 3.3

### Sources for an initial database search

| | |
|---|---|
| *ASSIA* | Applied Social Sciences Index and Abstracts |
| *ERIC* | Educational Resources; includes journals, research reports, conference proceedings, etc.; American based. |
| *BEI* | British Education Index; UK equivalent of ERIC |
| *Medline* | Covers medicine, nursing, pharmacology, pharmacy and other health-related areas |
| *CINAHL* | Cumulative Index to Nursing and Allied Health Literature |
| *PsychINFO* | Electronic version of *Psychological Abstracts* (American Psychological Association) |
| *Sociofile* | Covers wide range of journals in sociology, anthropology and social work. Also covers 'social' areas of education, health and psychology |
| *SSCI* | Social Sciences Citation Index. Lists works which cite a particular article. |

*continued*

will find relevant material, they are likely to fail to identify substantial amounts of other relevant studies.

Citation indices (of which the Social Sciences Citation Index – SSCI – is likely to be of particular interest) are invaluable as they enable you to travel forward in time from a particular reference via later authors who have cited the initial work. My experience has been that with real world research, there are likely to be very few really central references that you can get hold of, and citation indices help you to see how others have taken them forward.

Most of these databases work on very similar lines, and it is worth investing time and effort in becoming familiar with them. *Key word searches* (i.e. for words occurring in the title, abstract and/or descriptors of the article) and *subject searches* (for the descriptors used by the compilers of the database to categorize the article, which are listed in the thesaurus of the database) can be an efficient way of pin-pointing relevant material. In doing this, one usually starts by getting an unmanageably large number of 'hits'; or, less frequently, very few of them.

A more focused search is obtained by combining the words or terms you use. Thus, asking for 'A and B' restricts the search to articles having both of whatever words or terms A and B represent. The search can be broadened by asking for 'A or B', and also by using truncated versions of key terms (e.g. when searching for material in the field of 'disability' , 'disab*' will pick up 'disabilities', 'disabled' and anything else starting with 'disab' as well – but note that the truncation symbol, here shown as '*', varies from one database to another). You will often also get ideas for broadening the search by noting other descriptors of articles you have picked out, which did not occur to you originally.

You should use on-line 'help' facilities to find out exactly how to refine your search for specific databases. Also seek help and advice from librarians. Cooper (1998) gives details on the use of these technological aids to reviewing existing literature. Burton (2000) and Hart (1998) provide more general advice on the task.

From the information and abstracts in the databases, you then move on to primary material in books and journals. Increasingly, full-text journal articles are available for downloading through the internet, although these may have to be paid for unless you have links to libraries which take out subscriptions to these journals. Some journals are available only in electronic format (e-journals). Some are of high quality and can contain very up-to-date material. However, it may be difficult, as with much WWW material, to assess its quality. Looking through contents pages of journals (whether in paper or electronic format ) containing the references located from the database can be helpful. My experience has been that quite often when key words have indicated a specific journal article, adjacent articles in the same journal have been of greater interest or relevance (perhaps a variant of the dictionary phenomenon, where words next to the one you are looking up are often more interesting!).

*Note:* Copyright conditions for the use of electronic databases usually permit their use for academic and non-profit-making research purposes, but exclude use for research, consultancy or services for commercial purposes. This may be an issue for some real world research.

*Documenting your search*   It is not too difficult to use these suggestions for the starting point of a hunt through what is currently in print which is relevant to your study. As this proceeds, it is important to ensure that you keep a record of what you have found. Bibliographic information needs to be full and accurate. If you just jot down a name and a date, you may have to spend hours later trying to find the full details. There are several styles. A common one (followed broadly but not slavishly in this text) is based upon the American Psychological Association's (1994) 'Publication Manual'. The APA also provides recommendations for electronic reference formats. Thus their document on this topic should be cited as:

*Electronic reference formats recommended by the American Psychological Association (2000, September 5). Washington, DC: American Psychological Association. Retrieved October 31, 2000 from the World Wide Web: http://www.apa.org/journals/webref.html*

Note the need to give the date of retrieval for documents on the Web which can change, move or disappear; website addresses themselves, however, are typically presented undated.

When building up a database of the books and articles to which you have referred, a major decision is whether to follow the traditional route of paper index cards or to use bibliographic software such as Endnote and ProCite (both published by ISI ResearchSoft) or Idealist (Blackwell, 1995). The latter option is worthwhile if you are going to build up big lists of references. However, you need to be careful to keep up good housekeeping practices, ensuring that you have up-to-date copies at all times. Losing a large list of references two days before you have to complete a report is no joke!

You will usually want to supplement the reference itself with notes of what you have got from it. How you do this is very much up to you, but there is little to be said for laboriously transcribing great chunks of material. Orna with Stevens (1995, pp. 43–58) provide an excellent set of suggestions.

*Networking*   Searching through databases can be supplemented by networking in various ways. It is highly likely that people are already doing work linked to the topic you are interested in. If your research is being supervised, perhaps for some award or qualification, then your supervisor or supervisors should be key resources. (If they are not, perhaps you should do something about it!) Networking through conferences and meetings of professional associations can give good leads. Internet discussion groups ('Listservs') now form a virtual equivalent. I have found it very heartening to see how, in a list such as EVALTALK (devoted to discussions on evaluation research topics), senior figures in the field often take the time to respond to pleas for help and advice from beginning researchers. Whatever means you use, communicating with people who have done some work in the area often turns up new sources, perhaps giving you access to unpublished material or to accounts of work in progress.

In personal contacts, you should aim for a symbiotic relationship where you give as well as get. It is discourteous, as well as likely to be counter-productive, to seek to pick other's brains on topics where you have nothing to contribute. If you are new to a field, or indeed to research in general, only network in this way after you have spent time researching the background and have at least some idea of what you might do. You are then less likely to waste others' time, and can throw your own ideas into the discussion. You may even get direct advice.

Some researchers are very cautious about revealing what they are proposing, thinking that others are just waiting to steal their ideas. A colleague seeking permission to carry out a study with the co-operation of hospital consultants was refused permission by one of them who then carried out a very similar study using the same test instruments. Such behaviour is clearly unethical and raises issues about 'whistle-blowing', i.e. whether and how it should be reported (Wenger et al., 1999). Obviously there are situations where you have to be careful, perhaps for reasons of organizational sensitivity, but openness usually pays dividends.

From researching the background in these ways, you go some way towards finding out what is known about the topic, what is seen as problematic, the approaches that have been taken, etc. It helps to get a good feel for this. However, it is all too easy to be imprisoned by what others have done into a particular way of looking at, and of investigating, the topic. Beware.

## F   Acknowledging the constraints

Any real world study must obviously take serious note of real world constraints. Your choice of research focus must be realistic in terms of the time and resources that you have available. If you have a maximum of three weeks to devote to the project, you choose something where there is a good chance of 'getting it out' in that time. Access and co-operation are similarly important, as well as having a nose for situations where any enquiry is likely to be counter-productive (getting into a sensitive situation involving, say, the siting of a hostel for mentally handicapped adults when your prime aim is to develop community provision is not very sensible if a likely outcome is the stirring up of a hornet's nest). These are themes which will recur throughout our discussions and are particularly important when deciding on the kind of research strategy to be used and the practicalities of actually carrying out the study; but they need to be present, at least in the background, when considering the research focus.

## Deciding on the Research Questions

There is no foolproof, automatic way of generating research questions. While the sequence envisaged here, of first deciding on a general research focus or area, and then refining that down into a small number of relatively specific research questions, has an intuitive reasonableness, things may not work out like this. A question, or questions, may come first – perhaps stimulated by theoretical concerns. You then seek an appropriate context, a research focus, in which to ask the question. More commonly, as indicated above, the general focus comes first.

There is evidence, however, that some ways of approaching the generation of research questions are more likely to result in successful and productive enquiries than others. J. T. Campbell et al. (1982) have looked at these issues by using a range of empirical techniques, including contrasts between studies judged by their originators as being either successful or unsuccessful. Their remit was limited to research in industrial and organizational psychology, but many of their conclusions seem to have general relevance to studies in the social sciences.

An idea that emerges strongly from their work is that the selection of innovative research questions is not a single act or decision. Significant research is a process, an attitude, a way of thinking. Significant research is accomplished by people who are motivated to do significant research, who are willing to pay the cost in terms of time or effort (p. 109).

Box 3.4 lists features considered by researchers to be associated with their successful and unsuccessful projects. Campbell et al. view the choice process for selecting the research questions as being often non-linear and involving considerable uncertainty and intuition. Research starting with mechanistic linear thinking, closely tied to the known and understood, may be clean and tidy but is unlikely to be of any significance. However, something that starts out as poorly understood, given considerable theoretical effort to convert it into something which is clearly defined, logical and rational, could well be of value.

Campbell et al. also conducted a relatively informal interview study with investigators responsible for what are considered important 'milestone' studies in the study of organizations, and reached conclusions which supported their previous ones. Specifically, it did not appear that these milestone studies had arisen simply from seeking to test, or extend, an existing theory previously used in that field of research. In fact, in virtually all cases, the relevant theory or knowledge was imported from some other field. What was clear was that these important studies were driven by some specific problem to be solved; that they were characterized by a problem in search of a technique, rather than the reverse. Each of the researchers was deeply involved in the substantive area of study, and it was interesting to note that many of them reported an element of luck in either the creation or the development of the research problem. However, it is well known in scientific creativity that Lady Luck is more willing to bestow her favours on the keenly involved and well prepared (see e.g. Medawar, 1979, p. 89).

## Box 3.4

### Features considered by researchers to characterize the antecedents of their successful and unsuccessful research

*Successful research develops from:*

1  *Activity and involvement*   Good and frequent contacts both out in the field and with colleagues.

2  *Convergence*   Coming together of two or more activities or interests (e.g. of an idea and a method; interest of colleague with a problem or technique).

3  *Intuition*   Feeling that the work is important, timely, 'right' (rather than logical analysis).

4  *Theory*   Concern for theoretical understanding.

5  *Real world value*   Problem arising from the field and leading to tangible and useful ideas.

*Unsuccessful research starts with:*

1  *Expedience*   Undertaken because it is easy, cheap, quick or convenient.

2  *Method or technique*   Using it as a vehicle to carry out a specific method of investigation or statistical technique.

3  *Motivation by publication, money or funding*   Research done primarily for publication purposes rather than interest in the issue.

4  *Lack of theory*   Without theory the research may be easier and quicker, but the outcome will often be of little value.

(Adapted from Campbell et al., 1982, pp. 97–103.)

## Developing the research questions

### A   Know the area

It obviously helps to be really familiar with the area on which your research focuses. A good strategy to force yourself into this position is to 'go public' in some way – produce a review paper, do a seminar or other presentation with colleagues whose comments you respect (or fear!).

## B   Widen the base of your experience

You should not be limited by the research (and research questions) current in the specific field you are researching. Researchers in other fields and from other disciplines may well be wrestling with problems similar to yours, or from which useful parallels can be drawn. An afternoon's trawling through journals in cognate disciplines is one way. Contact and discussion with practitioners may give a different perspective on what the questions are.

## C   Consider using techniques for enhancing creativity

There is a substantial literature on creativity and on methods of promoting innovation which is relevant to the process of generating research questions. Lumsdaine and Lumsdaine (1995) provide comprehensive coverage. While their text is primarily addressed to engineers, there is much of relevance here to real world researchers. The methods include *brainstorming* (e.g. Tudor, 1992; Rawlinson, 1981); the *nominal group* and *Delphi techniques* (e.g. Delbecq, 1986); and *focus groups*. (see chapter 9 below, p. 284).

*Note:* The techniques for enhancing creativity are primarily concerned with groups. Even if you are going to carry out the project on an individual basis, there is much to be said for regarding this initial stage of research as a group process and enlisting the help of others.

Consider, for example, the Delphi technique. In this context it might mean getting together a group of persons, either those who are involved directly in the project or a range of colleagues with interests in the focus of the research. (Bear in mind the point made in section B, that there is advantage in including in the group colleagues from other disciplines and practitioners.) Each individual is then asked to generate *independently*, i.e. not in a group situation, say, up to three specific research questions in the chosen area. They may be asked also to provide additional information, perhaps giving a justification for the questions chosen. The responses from each individual are collected, and all responses are passed on in an unedited and unattributed form to all members of the group. A second cycle then takes place. This might involve individuals commenting on other responses, and/or revising their own contribution in the light of what others have produced. Third and fourth cycles might take place, either of similar form or seeking resolution or consensus through voting, or ranking, or categorizing responses. Endacott et al. (1999) and Gibson (1998) provide examples of different uses of the technique.

## D   Avoid the pitfalls of

- *Allowing a pre-decision on method or technique to decide the questions to be asked.* A variant of this concerning the use of computerized packages for statistical analysis is also worth flagging. Developing research questions *simply* on the basis that they allow the use of a particular package that you have available is almost as big a research sin as designing and carrying out a fixed research design study that you don't know how to analyse.

- *Posing research questions that can't be answered* (either in general or by the methods that it is feasible for you to use).
- *Asking questions that have already been answered satisfactorily* (deliberate replication resulting from a concern about the status of a finding is different from ignorance of the literature).

## E   Cut it down to size

Thinking about the focus almost always leads to a set of research questions that is too large and diffuse. Grouping questions together and constructing a hierarchy of sub-questions nested within more general ones helps to bring some order. It is important not to arrive at premature closure, even on a list of questions threatening to get out of hand. What commonly happens is that something like a research programme emerges, which has within it several relatively separate research projects.

However, the time will come when you have to make hard decisions about where your priorities are – and in particular about what is feasible, given the time and other resources that you have available. In fixed designs you need to have done this to a very large extent even before you pilot; the role of the pilot is, among other things, to fine-tune the questions. In flexible design, you keep things much more open when starting data collection. Even here, though, it is wise to have a concern for feasibility at an early stage. The flexibility comes in modifying and developing the questions as data collection and analysis proceeds. An important criterion for such development is getting a better understanding of what is likely to be feasible as the research process continues.

Guidelines for the number of research questions you might be able to address in a single study vary from three to over ten. Obviously this depends on the nature of the specific research questions and the resources at your disposal, but my experience is that very few small-scale real world studies can cope adequately with more than six questions, and that four to six such questions is a fair rule of thumb. Box 3.5 suggests characteristics of good research questions.

## F   Think in terms of the purposes of your research

Clarifying the purpose or purposes of your research can go a long way towards sorting out the research questions. A tripartite classification is commonly used, distinguishing between *exploratory*, *descriptive* and *explanatory* purposes. Following Marshall and Rossman (1999, p. 33) it seems appropriate to add a fourth *emancipatory* category signalling the 'action' perspective present in many real world studies (see also the discussion in chapter 2 above, p. 28). These are summarized in box 3.6. *A particular study may be concerned with more than one purpose*, possibly all four, but often one will predominate. *The purpose may also change as the study proceeds*. Box 3.7 gives an example of links between research questions and purpose.

## Box 3.5

## Good research questions

*Good questions are:*

- *Clear*   They are unambiguous and easily understood.
- *Specific*   They are sufficiently specific for it to be clear what constitutes an answer.
- *Answerable*   We can see what data are needed to answer them and how those data will be collected.
- *Interconnected*   The questions are related in some meaningful way, forming a coherent whole.
- *Substantively relevant*   They are worthwhile, non-trivial questions worthy of the research effort to be expended.

(Based on Punch, 1998, p. 49.)

## Box 3.6

## Classification of the purposes of enquiry

1   *Exploratory*

- To find out what is happening, particularly in little-understood situations.
- To seek new insights.
- To ask questions.
- To assess phenomena in a new light.
- To generate ideas and hypotheses for future research.
- Almost exclusively of flexible design.

2   *Descriptive*

- To portray an accurate profile of persons, events or situations.
- Requires extensive previous knowledge of the situation etc. to be researched or described, so that you know appropriate aspects on which to gather information.
- May be of flexible and/or fixed design.

3   *Explanatory*

- Seeks an explanation of a situation or problem, traditionally but not necessarily in the form of causal relationships.

- • To explain patterns relating to the phenomenon being researched.
- • To identify relationships between aspects of the phenomenon.
- • May be of flexible and/or fixed design.

4    *Emancipatory*

- • To create opportunities and the will to engage in social action.
- • Almost exclusively of flexible design.

---

## Box 3.7

### Linking research questions to purpose

In an evaluation of an innovatory reading programme for children with special needs, an *explanatory study* might focus on:

1    Do the children read better as a result of this programme?

*or*

2    Do the children read better in this programme compared with the standard programme?

*or*

3    For what type of special need, ability level, class organization or school is the programme effective?

*Note*: The 'as a result of' in (1) indicates that the concern is whether the programme caused the improvement. Questions (2) and (3) also imply a concern for causation, although this is not explicit. Question (3) is couched in terms of the realist concern for 'what works for whom in what context'.

An *exploratory study* might focus on:

4    What is the experience of children following the programme?

*Note*: With an established, rather than an innovatory, programme it may be that sufficient is known about this question for it to be approached as a *descriptive* task.

A *descriptive study* might focus on:

5    What are teachers' views about the programme?

*and/or*

**6** To what extent are parents involved in and supportive of the programme?

*Note*:   This is a descriptive task if it is felt that sufficient is known about the dimensions of teachers' likely views, or of parents' involvement, etc. If not, it would be an *exploratory* task. Given the focus of the study, it could also have an *emancipatory* role if the programme helps to extend the abilities of children with special needs; or is shown to enrich their experience; or helps empower their parents or teachers.

A study, with adequate resources, might cover each of these questions, though it is likely that the focus would be primarily on one of these purposes.

(Box 4.4 returns to this example when considering the links between research questions and strategy)

It is taken as given that all enquiry is concerned with *contributing to knowledge*. Real world enquiry also commonly seeks a potential usefulness in relation to policy and practice. The information from J. T. Campbell et al. (1982) and related studies discussed in the previous section provides some practical suggestions for the strategies one might adopt in generating research questions.

## The Place of Theory

The findings of J. T. Campbell et al. (1982), summarized in box 3.4, emphasize the value of theory in carrying out quality applied research. Or, as Kurt Lewin put it many years ago, when advising applied social psychologists, 'there is nothing so practical as a good theory' (1951, p. 169). This view is contested. Scriven (1991, p. 360) regards theories as a luxury in evaluation research, while Thomas (1997), writing in the context of education, advocates the abandonment of all theory because of its stifling effect on practice. The view that 'what works' is enough is closely linked to influential 'evidence-based' approaches in many areas (e.g. Hargreaves, 1997; but see Atkinson, 2000 for a spirited defence of the value of theories).

'Theory' can mean very different things to different people. In very general terms it is an explanation of what is going on in the situation, phenomenon or whatever that we are investigating. Theories can range from formal large-scale systems developed in academic disciplines to informal hunches or speculations from laypersons, practitioners or participants in the research.

Obviously, there are advantages if links can be made to current formal theories. This provides some assurances that what you are doing is in tune with other researchers' attempts to understand what is happening. As a result, as well as carrying out a higher-quality study, you may well be able to make some small contribution to the development of theory itself. For example, Johnson (1997; see also Johnson and Robson, 1999) was able to gain a greater understanding of the transition of mature female students into professionally oriented courses of higher education through viewing this process in terms of Breakwell's (1986) theory of 'threatened identities'.

Admittedly, it may well not be feasible to make this kind of symbiotic connection between the research topic and existing theory in many real world studies. The topic may be novel and appropriate theories elusive. Time pressures may be such that there is not the opportunity to do the necessary delving into what is often quite difficult literature. Don't despair. In thinking about the focus of the research, you will develop what amounts to a personal theory about what might be going on and how it might be understood (what Argyris and Schön, 1974, describe as a 'theory-in-use' or 'tacit theory'). There are highly likely to be others around who can help: perhaps staff members, professionals, practitioners, clients who may have had a much longer experience with the situation than you and who, if asked, may have highly pertinent observations about how and why 'it' will or won't 'work'. Again, it will be advantageous if you can move beyond this to more formal theory and concepts, but this is by no means an essential feature of many real world studies.

A distinction is sometimes made between 'theory verification' and 'theory generation' research. Positivist methodology, which has traditionally formed the basis for fixed design experimental studies, starts with a theory, deduces formal hypotheses from it, and designs the study to test these hypotheses. The tradition in much flexible design research, quintessentially in grounded theory studies (see chapter 6), is theory generation. Here researchers do not start with a theory but aim to end up with one, developed systematically from the data collected. However, these connections are by no means universal. Quantitative, fixed design research can be used for theory generation; qualitative, flexible designs for theory verification (Hammersley, 1992). The position taken here is that there is a place for both theory generating and theory verification approaches. Which is most appropriate will depend on the particular circumstances and context of your research. Obviously, if an apparently serviceable theory relevant to your proposed study already exists, the sensible task is to test its utility. If you are casting around for a plausible theory, then theory generation is indicated. What is important is that you have a theory on completion of the study; i.e. you have achieved some understanding about what is going on.

The view that you will have some personal theories, and indeed should seek to make them explicit, is to some extent at odds with the grounded theory approach which specifies that you start with a clean sheet and that theory should be developed only as and when data are collected. This seems to me unrealistic (although the grounded theory veto on extensive prior literature searching does have its attractions!). Also, in most real world studies time is at a premium and there is advantage in not delaying theory development.

## Conceptual frameworks and realist mechanisms

The theory about what is going on, what is happening and why, particularly when expressed in diagrammatic form, is sometimes referred to as a *conceptual framework*. This term is sometimes defined rather more widely, for example as 'the system of concepts, assumptions, expectations, beliefs, and theories that supports and informs your research' (Maxwell, 1996, p. 25). In my experience, most (though by no means all) researchers new to the game find it very helpful to try to produce such a diagram – and to refine it through discussion and, in flexible designs, as data collection and analysis continue. Figure 3.1 gives examples of different types proposed by Miles and Huberman (1994). Similar approaches have been suggested by other writers under the headings of *concept maps* (Novak and Gowin, 1984), *integrative diagrams* (Strauss, 1987, p. 170), *systems* (or *Venn*) *diagrams* (Blackmore and Ison, 1998, p. 52), and *conceptual modelling* (Blackmore and Ison, 1998, p. 55).

The realist approach, as discussed and exemplified in chapter 2 above, can be used to generate a particular kind of conceptual framework. The task is to specify the various enabling and disabling mechanisms operating in a particular situation, and the contexts relevant to their operation.

*A note on replication studies, critical realism, and theory development*   It may be worthwhile to reiterate the plea made in chapter 2 (p. 42) that you give serious consideration to carrying out some form of replication study. This may be of an earlier study you have carried out, or (assuming you can find one) a relevant study by another researcher. Or, as discussed in chapter 4, you can build replication into your design by having, say, a set of linked case studies which share important characteristics. Attempts to replicate are all too rare in the applied social sciences. This may, in part, be linked to the desire on the part of researchers to do something new and innovatory. It could also come from a view that replication, while occupying a central role in the progress of natural science, is not feasible in social science. However, as argued in chapter 2 (p. 41), adoption of a critical realist perspective can provide a sound basis for the use of replication in the development and refinement of theories.

*A note on hypotheses*   Some readers, particularly those with a quantitative background, may be familiar with discussions of research couched in terms of

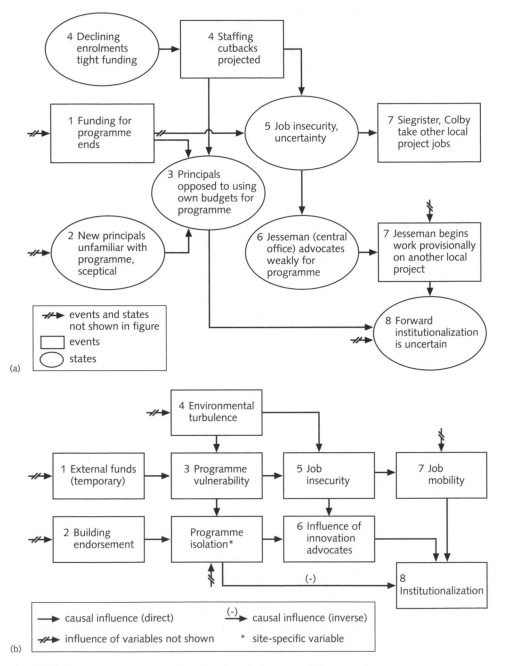

**Figure 3.1** Examples of different types of conceptual framework.
(a) Excerpt from an event–state network: Perry-Parkdale School.
(b) Excerpt from a causal network: Perry-Parkdale School.
*Source*: Miles and Huberman (1994).

hypothesis testing, with detailed definitions of null and alternative hypotheses. As discussed above, this text favours (largely because of its wider applicability) the approach of seeking answers to research questions. Following Punch (1998, pp. 39–41) *a simple definition of the hypothesis as the predicted answer to a research question is proposed.* A theory (whether expressed in terms of mechanisms or otherwise) explains why a particular answer is predicted. Talking in terms of hypotheses best fits fixed design research, where we should be in a position to make predictions before the data are gathered. In flexible design research, we are likely to be in this position only after, and as a result of, the data gathering. The outcomes can be used to support the existence of particular mechanisms in the context studied, even if they could not be predicted.

## Ethical Considerations

Participants in real world studies may sometimes be involved without their knowledge. They may be misled about the true nature of the study. Or they may be faced with situations that cause stress or anxiety. Should they be? In other words, is the investigator acting ethically? Put baldly like this, the answer seems to be clearly: no. However, there is another way of looking at the question. These considerations might be put alongside your time and effort as 'costs' of carrying out the enquiry, to be set against 'benefits' including the knowledge gained from the study, and possible changes and improvements to situations or services.

These questionable practices arise from the kind of research questions we are asking, and the methods used to seek answers, particularly the procedures used to avoid misleading results. It may be that we can go about things differently and avoid deception, stress and the like. If this is not possible, then there is a conflict. How is our 'right to know' balanced against the participants' right to privacy, dignity and self-determination? And should the investigator act as both judge and jury?

It is vital that, at a very early stage of your preparations to carry out an enquiry, you give serious thought to these ethical aspects of what you are proposing. Ethics refers to rules of conduct; typically, to conformity to a code or set of principles (Reynolds, 1979). Many professions working with people have adopted such codes. Examples include those of the British Psychological Society (2000), British Sociological Association (n.d.), British Association of Social Workers (1996), American Psychological Association (1992), American Sociological Association (1997) and American Educational Research Association (1992). The American Psychological Association has also published (Bersoff, 1999) a useful and stimulating text on ethical conflicts. You should familiarize yourself with the code or codes most relevant to your work, and ensure that you follow it/them scrupulously. Note that web addresses, where available, have been included in the references to the various codes mentioned above. You should follow these up and ensure that you have the current version.

A distinction is sometimes made between *ethics* and *morals*. While both are concerned with what is good or bad, right or wrong, ethics are usually taken as referring to general principles of what one ought to do, while morals are usually taken as concerned with whether or not a *specific* act is consistent with accepted notions of right or wrong. For example, a psychologist might punctiliously follow the profession's ethical guidelines but still be accused of behaving immorally. Controversial research on perception in kittens, involving the sewing together of their eyelids, is a case which illustrates this divide sharply. Views about the morality or otherwise of this work depend crucially, of course, on what constitute 'accepted' notions of right and wrong. One position would be that it is simply and absolutely wrong to do this to an animal. An opposing view would seek to balance the costs (to the animal, and possibly to the researcher through adverse publicity) and the benefits (to science, with possible medical or other 'spin-offs').

The terms 'ethical' and 'moral' are subsequently used interchangeably in this text to refer to 'proper' conduct, except where the context makes codified principles relevant. Ethical and moral concerns in scientific studies have come to the fore alongside the changing views of the nature of science discussed in chapter 2. The traditional view was that science was 'value-free' or 'value-neutral', and the task of the scientist simply to describe what *is* in an objective manner. This is a different task from determining what *ought* to be done to behave ethically. If, however, objectivity cannot be guaranteed when doing science, and the values of the researcher are inevitably involved in the research, the worlds of 'is' and 'ought' become much more difficult to disentangle.

Experimental research with people poses ethical problems in sharp forms. Control over what people do obviously has a moral dimension. While this is self-evident in experimental situations, ethical dilemmas lurk in *any* research involving people. In real world research we may not be able to, or wish to, control the situation, but there is almost always the intention or possibility of change associated with the study. This forces the researcher, wittingly or not, into value judgements and moral dilemmas. Suppose we are looking at a new approach to the teaching of reading. It is highly likely that we start with the premise that this looks like being a 'good thing', probably an improvement on what is currently on offer. Life – your own and the participants' – is too short to waste it on something which does not appear to have this 'prima facie' value. A possible exception would be where the latest educational fad was sweeping the schools and a demonstration of its drawbacks might be a useful inoculation for the system – although even in this case, my experience has been that the conclusion ends up something like: 'If you want to take on this new approach, these are the conditions under which it seems to be most effective.'

Reverting to consideration of the likely 'good' intervention, an immediate issue becomes 'Which schools are to be involved?' Do you choose the fertile soil of a friendly, innovative school? Or the stony ground of a setting where there is probably a greater, though unacknowledged, need for something new? These are partly research issues, but they have a clear ethical dimension.

Ethical problems start at the very beginning of a study. It may appear unethical to select certain foci for research because of the likely exacerbation of an explosive situation simply by carrying out research in that area. Problems continue through into the choice of a venue, and indeed can permeate the whole of a study. For example:

- Is the giving of necessary additional resources of staff, equipment or whatever to the places where the research takes place, simply part of the deal, the investigator showing good faith by giving as well as taking? Or is it unfair coercion to take part, reminiscent of prisoners gaining food or early release for taking part in trials of potentially dangerous drugs?
- Do individuals have the right not to take part? And even if they do, are there any overt or covert penalties for non-participation ('It will look good on your reference if you have taken part in this study')?
- Do they know what they are letting themselves in for? Is their consent 'fully informed'? (Herrera, 1999, and Clarke, 1999, present critiques of the defences sometimes put forward for omitting informed consent.)
- Will individuals participating be protected, not only from any direct effects of the intervention, but also by the investigator ensuring that the reporting of the study maintains confidentiality?
- Is confidentiality, on the other hand, always appropriate? If people have done something good and worthwhile, and probably put in extra effort and time, why shouldn't they get credit for it? Conversely, if inefficiency or malpractice is uncovered in the study, should the investigator let the guilty ones hide?
- What responsibility do investigators have for the knowledge that they have acquired? Are they simply the 'hired hands' doing the bidding of the paymaster? Or – changing the metaphor to one used by Carl Rogers – are they simply ammunition wagons, loaded with powerful knowledge just waiting to be used, whether the users are the 'good guys' or the 'bad guys'? Incidentally, Rogers' (1961) view is: 'Don't be a damn ammunition wagon, be a rifle.' That is, those doing applied studies have to target their knowledge and take responsibility for what they 'hit'.

Each of these issues is complex. Although general guidelines can be given, as in the various codes discussed above, the issues must be carefully thought through in each specific situation.

Consider, for example, whether or not people should always be asked in advance whether they are prepared to take part. It may not be possible or practicable to do this. You may have good grounds for believing that telling them would alter the behaviour you are interested in. But not telling them means that you have taken away their right not to participate.

There are several questions you can ask to help you decide. Will the study involve them doing things they would not otherwise do? If not, it is less of an infringement. So, an observational study of naturally occurring behaviour is less questionable than a field experiment where you contrive something which would not otherwise happen. Not that all experiments are equivalent. One which involved you stalling a car when the traffic lights turn green to study the effects on driver behaviour, while questionable in its own right, is probably less so than a simulated mugging on a tube train to study bystander behaviour. Reasonable things to take into account are the degree of inconvenience, and of likely emotional involvement, to participants. In studies where the judgement is made that prior permission must be sought, it is increasingly the practice to present all potential participants with an 'informed consent' form (see p. 380 below).

However, even this apparently highly ethical procedure can have its pitfalls. In research on socially sensitive topics such as drug abuse or AIDS, it is possible that the investigator would be under legal pressure to disclose all research information, including such signed forms. American investigators have been served with subpoenas requiring their attendance in court, and in a similar situation, journalists have faced prison rather than reveal their sources. Hence, in such situations, it might be preferable to proceed informally, and not use a form as such. More generally, while discussion of ethical principles rightly stresses the potential risks to the participants in the research, researchers themselves, in common with professionals such as hospital staff and teachers, can be at risk. Craig et al. (2000), in a useful discussion of safety in social research, list the following types of potential risk:

- risk of physical threat or abuse;
- risk of psychological trauma or consequences, as a result of actual or threatened violence, or the nature of what is disclosed during the interaction;
- risk of being in a compromising situation, in which there might be accusations of improper behaviour;
- increased exposure to general risks of everyday life and social interaction: travel, infectious disease, accident.

They provide draft suggestions for a 'code of practice' for the safety of social researchers which are well worth considering, particularly if you are likely to be involved in risky fieldwork situations.

Box 3.8 presents a list of questionable practices in which you might be tempted to indulge. The presumption is that you do not do so, unless in a particular study you can convince yourself, and an appropriate 'ethical committee', that the benefits accruing outweigh the costs. Note that, in particular, the use of deception was formerly widespread in social psychological experimentation. Adair et al. (1985) reported that 'upwards of 81% of studies published in the top social psychological journals use deception in their procedures.' This practice is now called into question, in part because participants appear increasingly to appreciate that they are likely to be deceived, resulting in their non-cooperation (Taylor and Shepperd, 1996). Recent commentators call for the complete outlawing of all forms of deception (Ortmann and Hertwig, 1997).

Ethical committees are now commonplace in many settings. Gregg and Jones (1990) provide suggestions for arrangements and procedures for such

---

## Box 3.8

### Ten questionable practices in social research

1   Involving people without their knowledge or consent.

2   Coercing them to participate.

3   Withholding information about the true nature of the research.

4   Otherwise deceiving the participant.

5   Inducing participants to commit acts diminishing their self-esteem.

6   Violating rights of self-determination (e.g. in studies seeking to promote individual change).

7   Exposing participants to physical or mental stress.

8   Invading privacy.

9   Withholding benefits from some participants (e.g. in comparison groups).

10   Not treating participants fairly, or with consideration, or with respect.

(Kimmel, 1988 provides further discussion on these issues, together with useful exercises on ethical issues.)

committees. They are not necessarily separate committees; for example ethical considerations may be one of the responsibilities for a more general approving committee whose agreement must be sought before a study is started.

## Working with vulnerable groups

There are particular ethical problems associated with working with some groups, such as children, persons with mental handicap or mental disturbance, prisoners and other 'captive' populations (e.g. persons in homes for the aged). The issues are whether such participants can rationally, knowingly and freely give informed consent. In the case of legally under-age children, and others who may not be in a position to appreciate what is involved, the parents or guardians should be asked for their consent (Esbensen et al., 1996, discuss the issues involved in detail). In many cases, the child will be able to appreciate at least something of what is involved and should be asked directly in addition to the parent. Ethical committees or review boards, including laypersons and legal experts as well as experienced researchers, can play a key role in such situations. They are particularly important in studies of relatively powerless groups such as the elderly or homeless.

The use of students on a course (common in many psychological experiments) raises similar issues (Banyard and Hunt, 2000). Indeed, whenever anyone takes part in a study for a 'consideration' of some kind, whether financial or as an explicit or implicit part of their duties or position, there are ethical implications. The situation can lead to researchers and participants taking on employer and employee roles respectively. The 'employer' has to guard against the notion that payment justifies placing the participant at risk. On the 'employee's' side, there is the likely tendency to 'give them whatever I think that I am being paid for'.

Certain styles of real world research carry with them additional ethical implications. For example, 'action research' (discussed in chapter 7) goes beyond the usual concerns for consent, confidentiality and respect for the participants' interests covered in the preceding discussion. There is a commitment to genuine participation in the research to the extent that this is seen as a collaborative effort between researcher and 'researched'. Ethical guidelines for this type of research, as presented for example by Kemmis and McTaggart (1981, pp. 43–4) bring the need for negotiation with participants to the fore.

## General ethical responsibilities

Real world research can lead to the researcher finding out about practices or conduct which present ethical dilemmas. In the most serious cases you discover something illegal, such as sexual or physical abuse of children. This must be reported to the police or other appropriate authority. The requirement to report over-rides any confidentiality agreements you have made (in situations where it is known that laws may be broken, it may be sensible to make it clear at the outset that you will have to report illegal acts).

Other situations, while not revealing illegal or unlawful activities, may cause concern. Suppose that in an office, school or hospital setting, you observe serious and persistent bullying by someone in a position of power; or that people are being put at physical or other risk by someone's dereliction of duty. There are no general rules applying to all such situations. In the first instance, they should be discussed with research supervisors or colleagues. If they concur with your assessment of the seriousness of what you have found, and with the need for action, then this will have to be taken up formally with your contacts in the organization or an appropriate senior figure. This may mean that you will have to withdraw from any involvement with the people involved.

An alternative scenario might be that after further thought and discussion you come to the view that what initially disturbed you may be accepted and commonplace in the setting, and perhaps that you are seeking to impose your own values and expectations, whereas the ethical course is to try to seek an understanding of what is going on by 'telling it as it is'. Remember that while you have particular ethical responsibilities as a researcher, this does not mean that you have a privileged voice on what constitutes ethical behaviour in others.

## Ethical reporting of research

A further agenda of ethical issues arises in connection with the research report. This is discussed in chapter 15 below (p. 501).

## Values in research

The above discussion of ethics has touched on values at several points. This is inevitable because values and value judgements are closely linked to morals and moral judgements. In the traditional positivist view, science and scientists are 'value free', facts and values are fundamentally different, and scientific research which is based on facts arising from empirical data has no role in making value judgements.

As discussed in chapter 2 (p. 21) the positivist position has been largely discredited. This is in part because of successful critiques of the notion of value-free science by philosophers of science as well as feminist and critical theorists. Where this leaves the position of values in social research is disputed.

Even traditional positivist researchers would accept that the actual choice of a research project and the kind of research questions asked involves value judgements. A topic is chosen because it is viewed as more worthwhile than another. Defining, say, the use of soft drugs as a social problem with high priority for research resources indicates a particular set of values. The recommendations for action or practice arising from evaluation research similarly contain value judgements.

The argument is more about the position of values in the actual conduct, analysis and interpretation of social research. Some regard the attempt to differentiate facts and values as misconceived. Others, while accepting the value-laden nature of what are taken to be facts, seek to establish and state explicitly when value judgements are being made. Viewing sweeping judgements (on the part of the researcher) about something being 'good' or 'bad', 'effective' or 'ineffective' as suspect is itself a value judgement. However, it is a position not difficult to defend as part of the 'scientific attitude' discussed in chapter 2 (p. 18).

## Politics and social research

Acknowledging that values and value judgements are involved in various ways in the process of social research provides a basis for the argument that such research is political. Hammersley (1995, ch. 6) provides a clear and detailed analysis of the question 'Is social research political?' He discusses four ways in which values are implicated in research:

- The research commitment to producing knowledge – i.e. the presupposition that knowledge is to be preferred to ignorance – shows that, in a fundamental sense, research cannot be value free or politically neutral.
- Research requires resources. Given that they could be used for other purposes, allocating them to research represents a political and value choice.
- Research is founded upon presuppositions reflecting the values of the researcher which may derive, for example, from their gender and ethnicity.
- Research has effects on people's lives through their being involved in the research and/or being in a context affected by the research findings. Ethical concerns about such possible consequences provide another route whereby the researcher's values influence the research.

Such features are not specific to research. They are characteristic of many human activities which therefore have a similar political dimension. The point is worth stressing, however, when views of science as value free or value neutral still linger.

A second way in which social research may be considered as political arises from the view of politics as to do with the exercise of power. Whether or not researchers were ever autonomous, simply following their own noses uninfluenced by any external forces, is questionable. In the current climate in many countries, those with power influence virtually all aspects of the research process from the choice of research topic (controlled by which projects get funding or other resources) to the publication of findings. This is typically viewed as a malign corrupting influence. The line taken in this text (see chapter 1, p. 11) is that, while there are undoubtedly dangers in this situation, if it is unavoidable you should not waste time and effort trying to avoid it; and that there are advantages to a more inclusive, participatory style of research where working to an agreed shared agenda with sponsors and others in positions of power increases the possibility of research being more useful and more widely used. Some specific influences to be watched out for are covered in box 3.9.

Do researchers themselves have power? Yes – but not a lot. The claim is that because they have specialist expertise, their voice and their findings should command attention. This privileged position is disputed by constructionists and others taking a relativist stance (see chapter 2, p. 25). As discussed in that chapter, the realist position is that researchers can claim only limited and fallible authority in relation to the production of knowledge (see also Hammersley, 1995, p. 107; also Hammersley and Scarth, 1993, which discusses instances of researchers exceeding the boundaries of their authority). Their power is also limited by the fact that research findings are not a major contributor to the development of public policy and that, in general, the impact of research is weak (this issue is discussed in more detail in chapter 7, p. 219).

Political issues come into sharpest focus in evaluation research, and are discussed in greater detail in this context (see chapter 7, p. 210).

## Sexism and social research

Feminist commentators and researchers have made a convincing case for the existence of sexist bias in research. This is seen in all areas of science, including the natural sciences (e.g. Harding and Hintikha, 1983), but is obviously of great concern in the social sciences where the human, in one or both genders, is the enquirer and the enquired-upon. There is now a substantial literature on this area (e.g. Harding, 1987; Roberts, 1981; Stanley and Wise, 1983; Smith, 1987; Hollway, 1989; Eichler, 1980; Maynard and Purvis, 1994; Neilsen, 1990; Reinharz, 1992).

## Box 3.9

### Political influences on research

The person(s) or agencies sponsoring, funding or otherwise providing resources, access or facilities for the research may influence some or all of the following:

**1** *Selection of research focus*   Not a problem providing that you consider the project feasible and ethical. Decisions about the topics which will receive funding is strongly influenced by policy and ideological considerations.

**2** *Selection of research design (research questions, strategy, methods etc.)* Again, not a problem providing that you consider the design feasible and ethical. It may be important to fall in with their preferences (e.g. for a fixed or flexible design) as this could influence the utilization of findings.

**3** *Granting of access*   A problem only when access is refused, which may be due to fear of exposure, general dislike or distrust of research and researchers, and/or previous unfortunate experiences with projects. Rare when funded by the organization involved.

**4** *Publication of findings*   Can cause severe problems. It is important that this is clarified in the contract or agreement made when starting the project. This should cover both their and your rights of publication (including who has final control over the content and whether they can prohibit your separate publication). You must decide at the outset whether the conditions are acceptable. Jenkins (1984) provides a graphic example of how things can go wrong. Journal publication is strongly influenced by dominant ideologies and powerful interest groups.

**5** *Use made by sponsor of findings*   This is likely to be outside your control. Findings may be misrepresented, used partially or suppressed totally. Provided this falls within the terms of the contract or agreement, you just put this down to experience. Or you may even get a publication discussing what happened!

*Note*: Knowledge that a research project has been sponsored by a particular agency may affect the *credibility* of its findings (e.g. a study funded by a pharmaceutical company on the environmental effects of genetically modified organisms will have low credibility with some audiences). There is undoubtedly the possibility that funded researchers will, wittingly or unwittingly, produce 'favourable' results. If you consider the project worthwhile and can live with criticism, your responsibility if you proceed is to guard against bias and generally observe all ethical considerations.

Eichler (1988), in a clear and readable analysis applicable to all social science disciplines, suggests that sexism in research arises from four 'primary problems': androcentricity, overgeneralization, gender insensitivity and double standards. She also argues that there are three further problems, which, while logically derived from and falling within the primary problems, occur so frequently as to merit separate identification: sex appropriateness, familism and sexual dichotomism. Box 3.10 gives an indication of the meaning of these terms.

---

# Box 3.10

## Sexism in research: sources of bias

1  *Androcentricity*   Viewing the world from a male perspective: e.g. when a test or other research instrument is developed and tested on males, and then assumed to be suitable for use with females. Note that *gynocentricity* (viewing the world from a female perspective) is, of course, also possible, though relatively rare.

2  *Overgeneralization*   When a study deals with only one sex but presents itself as generally applicable: e.g. a study dealing solely with mothers which makes statements about parents. *Overspecificity* can also occur when single-sex terms are used when both sexes are involved; e.g. many uses of 'man', either by itself or as in 'chairman'.

3  *Gender insensitivity*   Ignoring sex as a possible variable: e.g. when a study omits to report the sex of those involved.

4  *Double standards*   Evaluating, treating or measuring identical behaviours, traits or situations by different means for males and females: e.g. using female-derived categories of social status for males (or vice versa). This may well be not inappropriate in a particular study, but nevertheless could lead to bias which should be acknowledged.

5  *Sex appropriateness*   A common form of 'double standards': e.g. that child rearing is necessarily a female activity.

6  *Familism*   A particular instance of 'gender insensitivity'. Consists of treating the family as the smallest unit of analysis when it would be possible and appropriate to treat an individual as the unit.

7  *Sexual dichotomism*   Another instance of 'double standards': treating the sexes as two entirely distinct social groups rather than as groups with overlapping characteristics.

(Adapted from Eichler, 1988.)

This analysis covers a much wider range of issues than the use of sexist language. It is now generally accepted that such language should be avoided when reporting research, as discussed in chapter 15 (p. 503).

Problems arising from sexism can affect all aspects and stages of the research process, and both female and male readers and researchers are urged to be on their guard. Eichler (1988, pp. 170–5) provides a comprehensive 'Nonsexist Research Checklist' giving examples of how the various problems arise in the concepts employed in the research, its design, methods, data interpretation, etc.

## Further Reading

Ballenger, B. (1998) *The Curious Researcher*, 2nd edn. Boston: Allyn & Bacon. The early sections ('The First Week' and 'The Second Week') provide many practical tips for getting started with a 'research paper' but equally relevant to a project. Very down-to-earth.

Becker, H. S. (1998) *Tricks of the Trade: How to Think about Your Research While You're Doing It*. Chicago: University of Chicago Press. Howard Becker shows once again that it is possible to be a sociologist and write clearly and accessibly. Presents a set of techniques for helping you to think about research projects.

Hall, D. and Hall, I. (1996) *Practical Social Research: Project Work in the Community*. London: Macmillan. First chapter gives helpful advice on undertaking small applied projects based on participation with local groups and emphasizing an ethical basis.

Homan, R. (1991) *The Ethics of Social Research*. London: Longman. Readable and thorough analysis of ethical issues. Seeks to keep open the debate between covert and overt methods of social research.

Newman, D. L. and Brown, R. D. (1996) *Applied Ethics for Program Evaluation*. Thousand Oaks, Calif.: Sage. Provides a practical framework for ethical decision-making by practitioners. Gives a range of practical dilemmas.

Prilleltensky, I. (1994) *The Morals and Politics of Psychology: Psychological Discourse and the Status Quo*. New York: State University of New York Press. Deals with the social ethics of psychology. Argues that applied psychology strengthens the societal status quo, hence contributing to the perpetuation of social injustice. Raises important issues that many choose to ignore.

Thomas, A. et al., eds (1998) *Finding Out Fast: Investigative Skills for Policy and Development*. London: Sage. Highly practical guide to carrying out policy-oriented research when time is short and resources are limited.

# Part II
## Designing the Enquiry

It is useful to distinguish between the *strategy* and the *tactics* you adopt when carrying out an enquiry. Strategy refers to the general broad orientation taken in addressing research questions – the style, if you like. These strategic considerations are the major concern of this second part of the book. Tactics, the specific methods of investigation, are dealt with in Part III.

# 4

# General Design Issues

This chapter:

- develops a framework for designing a real world study linking purpose, theory, research questions, methods and sampling strategy;
- provides a range of examples of fixed, flexible and multiple research strategies from different disciplines and areas;
- sensitizes the reader to the issues involved in selecting a research strategy;
- introduces experimental and non-experimental fixed design strategies, and
- three flexible design strategies seen as particularly appropriate for real world research: case studies, ethnographic studies and grounded theory studies;
- emphasizes that it is advisable to read the other chapters in part II before making decisions about strategy;
- concludes by considering the trustworthiness of research findings, and its relationship to research design.

## Introduction

*Design is concerned with turning research questions into projects.*

This is a crucial part of any enquiry, but it is often slid over quickly without any real consideration of the issues and possibilities. There is a strong tendency for both those carrying out projects, and those who want them carried out, to assume that there is no alternative to their favoured approach. Comments have already been made on the assumption by many psychologists that an experimental design is inevitably called for. For other social scientists, and for quite a few clients when commissioning studies, designs involving the statistical analysis of sample survey data are seen as the only possible approach.

Manstead and Semin (1988) make the obvious but often neglected point that the strategies and tactics you select in carrying out a piece of research depend very much on the type of research question you are trying to answer. They adopt a river-crossing analogy. The task of crossing the river corresponds to the general *research focus*. Specific *research questions* are analogous to asking how many people want to cross the river; the frequency with which they want to cross; the current of the river; and so on. The choice of *research strategy* is akin to a choice among swimming, walking, flying or sailing across. The *research tactics* (or methods of investigation) concern the particular type of boat, bridge, aircraft, etc. to be used in the crossing.

> *The general principle is that the research strategy or strategies, and the methods or techniques employed, must be appropriate for the questions you want to answer.*

Hakim (1987), in one of the few books which focuses on design issues across a range of social science disciplines, makes a comparison between designers of research projects and architects, and then goes on to extend this to suggest that those who actually carry out projects are like builders. For her:

> design deals primarily with aims, purposes, intentions and plans within the practical constraints of location, time, money and availability of staff. It is also very much about *style*, the architect's own preferences and ideas (whether innovative or solidly traditional) and the stylistic preferences of those who pay for the work and have to live with the finished result. (p. 1)

In small-scale research the architect–designer and builder–enquirer are typically one and the same person. Hence the need for sensitivity to design issues, to avoid the research equivalent of the many awful houses put up by speculative builders without benefit of architectural expertise.

Such muddling through should be distinguished from the opportunity to develop and revise the original plan, which is easier in a small-scale project than in one requiring the co-ordination of many persons' efforts. Design modification is more feasible with some research strategies than with others – indeed, it is an integral part of flexible designs. However, this kind of flexibility calls for a concern for design *throughout* the project, rather than providing an excuse for not considering design at all.

## A Framework for Research Design

Design, in the sense discussed above, concerns the various things which should be thought about and kept in mind when carrying out a research project. Many models have been put forward, and figure 4.1 is my attempt. The components are:

- *Purpose(s)* What is this study trying to achieve? Why is it being done? Are you seeking to describe something, or to explain or understand something? Are you trying to assess the effectiveness of something? Is it in response to some problem or issue for which solutions are sought? Is it hoped to change something as a result of the study?
- *Theory* What theory will guide or inform your study? How will you understand the findings? What conceptual framework links the phenomena you are studying?
- *Research questions* To what questions is the research geared to providing answers? What do you need to know to achieve the purpose(s) of the study? What is it feasible to ask given the time and resources that you have available?
- *Methods* What specific techniques (e.g. semi-structured interviews, participant observation) will you use to collect data? How will the data be analysed? How do you show that the data are trustworthy?
- *Sampling strategy* From whom will you seek data? Where and when? How do you balance the need to be selective with the need to collect all the data required?

All these aspects need to be inter-related and to be kept in balance. Figure 4.1 suggests that there is some directionality about the whole process. Both your purposes and theory feed into, and help you specify, the research questions. When you know something about the research questions you want to be answered, then you are able to make decisions about the methods to be used and the strategy to be used in sampling. However, unless you are dealing with a fixed design which is tightly pre-specified, this should not be taken to imply a once-and-for-all consideration of the different aspects.

In flexible designs, there should be a repeated revisiting of *all* of the aspects as the research takes place. In other words, the detailed framework of the design *emerges* during the study. The various activities – collecting and analysing data; refining and modifying the set of research questions; developing theory; changing the intended sample to follow up interesting lines, or to seek answers to rather different questions; and perhaps even reviewing the purposes of the study in the light of a changed context arising from the way in which the other aspects are developing – are all likely to be going on together.

This might suggest that a better representation of the relationship among these aspects in flexible designs would show two-way arrows between the components in the figure. Maxwell (1996, p. 5) approximates to this in a very similar diagram which he refers to as an 'interactive' model of qualitative research design. Or one might even revert to what Martin (1981) has called

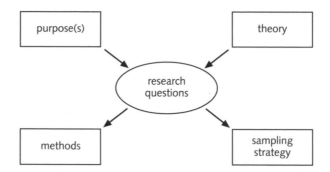

**Figure 4.1**    Framework for research design.

the 'garbage can' model of research design, where the components are swirling 'around in the garbage can or decision space of the particular research project' (Grady and Wallston, 1988, p. 12). However, providing the interactive nature of what goes on in this kind of project is understood, figure 4.1 has the advantage of presenting a simple and logical structure.

A good design framework will have high compatibility among purposes, theory, research questions, methods and sampling strategy.

- If the only research questions to which you can get answers are not directly relevant to the purposes of the study, then something has to change – probably the research question.
- If your research questions do not link to theory it is unlikely that you will produce answers of value (see chapter 3, p. 61 for a discussion of the value of theory in producing work of high quality). In this case, theory needs developing or the research questions need changing.
- If the methods and/or the sampling strategy are not providing answers to the research questions, something should change. Collect additional data, extend the sampling or cut down on or modify the research questions.

In fixed research designs you should get all of this right before embarking on the major phase of data collection. Hence the importance of pilot work, where you have the opportunity of testing out the feasibility of what you propose.

In flexible research designs you have to get all of this sorted out by the *end* of the study. As Brewer and Hunter (1989, p. 63) put it, 'Once a study is published, it is in many ways irrelevant whether the research problem prompted the study or instead emerged from it.' This is not a licence to rewrite history. In many qualitative research traditions, there is an expectation that you provide an account of your journey, documenting the various changes made along the way. However, you are definitely not bound to some form of 'honour code' where, say, you declare your initial set of research questions and then stick to them through thick and thin. Your aim is to come up with a final set of research questions, which are relevant to the purposes of the study (which may, or may not, have been renegotiated along the way), which show clear linkage to theory (from whatever source it has obtained) and for which the sampling has been such that the data you have collected and analysed provide answers to those questions.

In the real world, of course, it won't be as neat and tidy as this. Some research questions may remain stubbornly unanswerable, given the amount of sampling and data collection your resources permit. This is not a capital offence. Provided you have answers to some of the questions which remain on your agenda, then you have made worthwhile progress. And the experience will no doubt be salutary in helping you to carry out more realistically designed projects in the future. You could even claim this for a study where you ended up with no answers to relevant research questions, but this is not going to further your career as a researcher.

It may also be that you come up with unexpected findings which appear interesting and illuminative. You may be able to incorporate these findings into your framework by appropriate extension or modification of the research questions. There is nothing wrong with adding a further question providing it is relevant to your purposes and it can be incorporated within a (possibly modified) theoretical framework. If your ingenuity fails, and you can't link it in, then simply regard this as a bonus to be reported under the heading of 'an interesting avenue for further research'.

## Getting a Feel for Design Issues

The marked pages which follow give an overview of what is involved in choosing a research strategy, including a short description of the strategies you might consider. Chapters 5 and 6 give more detailed discussion of fixed and flexible designs respectively, concentrating on design issues specific to each strategy. Chapter 7 discusses two approaches, evaluation research and action research, which are of particular importance in applied real world studies; they are viewed here as approaches which have distinctive purposes but which make use of the general strategies for doing research discussed in the preceding chapters.

This might be a good time for you to get hold of the reports of a range of published studies and to read them through to get a feel for different designs. Try not to get bogged down in the detail, and don't be put off by complex analyses. When you get on to the detailed design of your own study and its analysis, you can seek assistance on such matters. The obvious sources are academic and professional journals close to your own concerns, but there is a lot to be said for what anthropologists call 'spending some time in the next village'. If your field is, say, social work, browse through a few health-related, educational or management journals. The purpose here is not so much to build up knowledge of directly relevant literature, or to find something you can repli-cate, although both of these are reputable aims in their own right. It's the overall design that you are after. Box 4.1 gives brief details of a mixed bag of fixed and flexible design studies worth chasing up and looking through. Note that they won't necessarily use the terminology adopted here of research ques-tions, purposes, etc. (it is instructive to try to work these out as an exercise).

If you follow up these examples, you will notice that many of them involve evaluating some practice, intervention or programme, or have an action per-spective where they are concerned with change of some kind taking place. Chapter 7 covers the additional features to be considered in studies which have these purposes.

---

## Box 4.1

### Examples of a range of fixed, flexible and multiple design strategy studies

*A   Fixed designs*

*Carlsson et al. (1997)* Randomized controlled trial with one-year follow-up to determine the effectiveness of a nurse-monitored prevention programme in improving the lifestyle of adults following an acute heart attack. (See also commentary by Brand, 1998.)

*Clifford et al. (1999)* Non-experimental study focusing on the development and initial validation of a Punjabi version of the Edinburgh Post-natal Depression Scale for use in health visiting practice.

*Diaper (1990)* Experiment comparing the relative effectiveness of three variants of 'paired reading' (a technique involving the use of parents as teachers) in the teaching of reading in a primary school. Pre-post admini-stration of a standardized reading test.

*Engelman et al. (1999)* Single case experimental design analysing the efforts of nursing assistants to increase the engagement of older adults with dementia in daily living activities.

*Harrison et al. (1999)* Quasi-experimental design seeking to determine the effectiveness of a twelve-week family-based intervention for troubled children. Weak pre-test post-test single group design. Two instruments used: a questionnaire developed by the research team and a pre-existing 'child behaviour checklist'. Problems with low response rates.

*King and Kennedy (1999)* Quasi-experimental design comparing patients with spinal cord injury receiving a theory-based 'coping effectiveness training' programme with matched controls. Pre and post measures.

*Monnickendam and Markus (1996)* Quasi-experimental post-test only comparison group design to determine the effects of a practice-centred cognitive-oriented computer course on the attitudes to computers of social work students.

*Newcomb et al. (1991)* Non-experimental survey of student views on drinking and driving, focusing on respondents who had been in the situation where they had seen someone they thought was too drunk to drive during the last year. Used to compare with laboratory studies of 'helping' behaviour.

*Norwich (1999)* Non-experimental study of pupils' reasons for learning and behaving or for not learning and not behaving at secondary school level. Development of a 'why I learn' inventory through semi-structured interviews which was then administered in a second stage. Results discussed in terms of self-determination theory.

## B  Flexible designs

*Backman and Hentinen (1999)* Grounded theory study aiming to develop a model to understand self-care of elderly persons living at home. Interview based.

*Barrett and Cooperrider (1990)* Case study by consultants brought in to assist a hotel linked to a hospital to move it up-market to become a 'four star' facility. History of interpersonal and interdepartmental conflicts impeding change. Multiple methods including initial survey, use of visiting managers as field researchers conducting interviews and observing. (See also commentary by Krantz, 1990.)

*Brez and Taylor (1997)* Multiple case study design used to develop a conceptual model of how adults with low literacy levels respond to assessments of their literacy. Use of semi-structured interviews and participant observation. (See also commentary by Carlisle, 1998.)

*Fortier (1998)* Ethnographic study of two London Italian social clubs, each run by a religious congregation. Focuses on their role in constructing an

Italian group identity for an immigrant, multigenerational population which is a religious and linguistic minority in Britain.

*Foster (1995)* Ethnographic study of informal social control and community crime prevention on a housing estate with high crime rates and many of the 'design failures' of public housing.

*Morrow and Smith (1995)* Grounded theory study of surviving and coping with childhood sexual abuse. Use of in-depth interviews, focus group documentary evidence, participant checks and collaborative analysis, leading to the development of a theoretical model.

*Onyskiw et al. (1999)* Case study design to evaluate a collaborative community-based child abuse prevention project. Use of semi-structured interviews and client records.

*Pervin and Turner (1998)* Case study of bullying of teachers by pupils in an inner London school. Questionnaire-based study seeking to document the extent of bullying experienced by teachers.

## C    Multiple designs (i.e. incorporating both fixed and flexible elements)

*Kopinak (1999)* Study of refugee well-being through a combination of ethnographic interviews and observation, health questionnaires and collection of demographic information. Discusses the advantages and pitfalls of this triangulation approach.

*Tolson et al. (1999)* An investigation of the components of best nursing practice in the care of acutely ill hospitalized older patients with coincidental dementia. Multimethod design incorporating survey methodology, documentary analysis and critical incident interviews yielding qualitative data.

*Winchester (1999)* Study of the experiences of lone fathers. Use of individual interviews to provide information in depth on the causes of marital breakdown and post-marital conflict, and to pilot the use of a structured questionnaire which generated quantitative data.

## Choosing a research strategy

This section seeks to sensitize you to the issues involved in choosing a research strategy.

*continued*

## A   Is a FIXED or a FLEXIBLE design strategy appropriate?

- A *fixed design strategy* calls for a tight pre-specification before you reach the main data collection stage. If you can't pre-specify the design, don't use the fixed approach. Data are almost always in the form of numbers; hence this type is commonly referred to as a *quantitative* strategy.
- A *flexible design* evolves during data collection. Data are typically non-numerical (usually in the form of words); hence this type is often referred to as a *qualitative* strategy.

  *While a design cannot be fixed and flexible at the same time, it could have a flexible phase followed by a fixed phase (or, more rarely, the reverse sequence). Or there could be a separate flexible element within an otherwise fixed design, as discussed in the note following E below.*

*Note:* Flexible designs can include the collection of quantitative data. Fixed designs rarely include qualitative data (but could do).

## B   Is your proposed study an EVALUATION?

Are you trying to establish the worth or value of something such as an intervention, innovation or service? This could be approached using either a fixed or a flexible strategy, depending on the specific purpose of the evaluation. If the focus is on *outcomes*, a *fixed design* is probably indicated: if it is on *processes*, a *flexible design* is probably indicated. See chapter 7, p. 202 for further details.

## C   Do you wish to carry out ACTION RESEARCH?

Is an action agenda central to your concerns? This typically involves direct participation in the research by others likely to be involved, coupled with an intention to initiate change. A *flexible design* is probably indicated. See chapter 7, p. 215 for further details.

## D   If you opt for a FIXED design strategy, which type is most appropriate?

Two broad traditions are widely recognized: *experimental* and *non-experimental* designs. Box 4.2 summarizes their characteristics.

## E   If you opt for a FLEXIBLE design strategy, which type is most appropriate?

Flexible designs have developed from a wide range of very different traditions. However, three of these appear particularly relevant to real world studies. These

*continued*

## Box 4.2

### Traditional fixed design research strategies

*Experimental strategy*

> *The central feature is that the researcher actively and deliberately intro-*
> *duces some form of change in the situation, circumstances or experience*
> *of participants with a view to producing a resultant change in their*
> *behaviour.*

In 'experiment-speak' this is referred to as measuring the effects of manipulating one variable on another variable. The details of the design are
fully pre-specified before the main data collection begins (there is typically a 'pilot' phase before this when the feasibility of the design is
checked and changes made if needed).

*Typical features:*

- selection of samples of individuals from known populations;
- allocation of samples to different experimental conditions;
- introduction of planned change on one or more variables;
- measurement on small number of variables;
- control of other variables;
- usually involves hypothesis testing.

*Non-experimental strategy*

> *The overall approach is the same as in the experimental strategy but the*
> *researcher does not attempt to change the situation, circumstances or ex-*
> *perience of the participants.*

The details of the design are fully pre-specified before the main data
collection begins (there is typically a 'pilot' phase before this when the
feasibility of the design is checked and changes made if needed).

*Typical features:*

- selection of samples of individuals from known populations;
- allocation of samples to different experimental conditions;
- measurement on small number of variables;
- control of other variables;
- may or may not involve hypothesis testing.

are *case studies*, *ethnographic studies* and *grounded theory* studies. Box 4.3 summarizes their characteristics.

*Note:* The research strategies discussed above by no means cover all possible forms of enquiry. They are more of a recognition of the camps into which researchers have tended to put themselves, signalling their preferences for certain ways of working. Such camps have the virtue of providing secure bases within which fledgling researchers can be inculcated in the ways of the tribe; more generally, they enable the maintenance of high professional standards. They carry the danger of

---

## Box 4.3

## Three traditional flexible design research strategies

*Case study*

> *Development of detailed, intensive knowledge about a single 'case', or of a small number of related 'cases'.*

The details of the design typically 'emerge' during data collection and analysis.

*Typical features:*

- selection of a single case (or a small number of related cases) of a situation, individual or group of interest or concern;
- study of the case in its context;
- collection of information via a range of data collection techniques including observation, interview and documentary analysis.

*Ethnographic study*

> *Seeks to capture, interpret and explain how a group, organization or community live, experience and make sense of their lives and their world.*

It typically tries to answer questions about specific groups of people, or about specific aspects of the life of a particular group (Bentz and Shapiro, 1998, p. 117).

*Typical features:*

- selection of a group, organization or community of interest or concern;
- immersion of the researcher in that setting;
- use of participant observation.

*Grounded theory study*

> *The central aim is to generate theory from data collected during the study.*

Particularly useful in new, applied areas where there is a lack of theory and concepts to describe and explain what is going on. Data collection, analysis and theory development and testing are interspersed throughout the study.

*Typical features:*

- applicable to a wide variety of phenomena;
- commonly interview-based;
- a systematic but flexible research strategy which provides detailed prescriptions for data analysis and theory generation.

*Notes:* There are other genres of flexible design, some of which are summarized in chapter 6. Many studies involving flexible designs focus on a particular 'case' in its context and can be conceptualized as case studies. Case studies can follow an ethnographic or grounded theory approach, but don't have to.

enquiry being 'strategy driven' in the sense that someone skilled in, say, the ways of experiments assumes automatically that every problem has to be attacked through that strategy.

It may well be that some *hybrid strategy* falling somewhere between these 'ideal types' is appropriate for the study with which you are involved. For example, there is nothing to stop you collecting a substantial amount of largely standardized survey-type data from a relatively small number of cases. As mentioned in A above, it can also make a lot of sense to *combine strategies* in an investigation. One or more case studies might be linked to an experiment. Alternatively, a small experiment might be incorporated actually within a case study.

## F    The purpose(s) help in selecting the strategy

The strategies discussed above represent different ways of collecting and analysing empirical evidence. Each has its particular strengths and weaknesses. It is also commonly suggested that there is a hierarchical relationship between the different strategies, related to the purpose of the research: namely, that

- flexible (qualitative) strategies are appropriate for exploratory work;
- non-experimental fixed strategies are appropriate for descriptive studies; and
- experiments are appropriate for explanatory studies.

There is some truth in these assertions. However these are not necessary linkages. For example, there have been exploratory, descriptive and explanatory case studies (Yin, 1993, 1994).

Real world studies are very commonly evaluations; i.e. their purpose is to assess the worth or value of something. A fixed or flexible design may be appropriate depending on the specific focus of the evaluation (see B above).

If a purpose is to initiate change and/or to involve others, then an action research strategy is called for. A flexible design is probably called for (see C above).

## G  The research questions influence the choice of strategy

The research questions to which you seek answers also help in determining the strategy. For example, 'what?' questions (asking 'how many?' or 'how much?', 'who?' and 'where?'), suggest the use of a non-experimental fixed strategy such as a survey. 'What' questions concerned with 'what is going on here?' lend themselves to some form of flexible design study. 'How?' and 'why?' questions are more difficult to pin down. They often indicate a flexible design. However, if the investigator has control over events, quantitative data are preferred and there is substantial knowledge about the likely mechanisms involved, an experiment would be the strategy of choice.

Box 4.4 considers the research questions set out in box 3.7, p. 60, and discusses the research strategies that might be appropriate.

---

### Box 4.4

### Linking research questions to research strategy

Consider the research questions discussed in box 3.7 (p. 60):

**1**  Do the children read better as a result of this programme?

*or*

**2**  Do the children read better in this programme compared with the standard programme?

*or*

**3**  For what type of special need, ability level, class organization or school is the programme effective?

If the interest is in quantitative outcome measures, and it is feasible to exert some degree of control over the situation (e.g. setting up different groups of children for the innovatory and standard programmes), these questions could be approached using an *experimental* strategy. If random allocation is used this becomes a true *experiment*; if not a *quasi-experiment*.

---

If this control were not feasible, or not desired, but quantitative data were still sought, a *non-experimental fixed* design is possible.

If there is a broader notion of what is meant by 'reading better' or of an 'effective' programme than that captured by a small number of quantitative variables, some type of *flexible* strategy is called for. This is likely to be a multimethod *case study*, and could also be *ethnographic* or *grounded theory* in style.

A *hybrid* approach where the *case study* could incorporate, say, an *experimental* component, could be considered.

**4**   What is the experience of children following the programme?

**5**   What are teachers' views about the programme?

*and/or*

**6**   To what extent are parents involved in and supportive of the programme?

These questions could be approached using any of the *flexible* strategies; though (4) might particularly indicate an *ethnographic* approach.

Questions (5) and (6) could, alternatively or additionally, follow a *non-experimental fixed* design if quantitative data are sought

*The overall message is that, while the research questions help in deciding research strategy, much is still dependent on your own preferences and on the type of design and data which are going to speak most strongly to the stakeholders.*

## H   Specific methods of investigation need not be tied to particular research strategies

The methods or techniques used to collect information, what might be called the *tactics of enquiry*, such as questionnaires or various kinds of observation, are sometimes regarded as necessarily linked to particular research strategies. Thus, in fixed non-experimental designs, surveys may be seen as being carried out by structured questionnaire; and experiments through specialized forms of observation, often requiring the use of measuring instruments of some sophistication. In flexible designs, grounded theory studies were often viewed as interview-based, and ethnographic studies seen as entirely based on participant observation.

However, this is not a tight or necessary linkage. For example, while participant observation is a central feature of the ethnographic approach, it can be augmented by interviews and documentary analysis. Similarly, there is no reason in principle for particular fixed design studies to be linked to specific data collection techniques. Non-experimental surveys could well be carried out using observation, the effect of an experiment assessed through questionnaire responses.

You should now have some appreciation of what is involved in selecting an appropriate research strategy. Before plunging in and making a decision, you need to know more about the issues involved in working within each of the traditional strategies to help you get a feel for what might be involved. The following two chapters cover fixed and flexible strategies respectively.

## Establishing Trustworthiness

How do you persuade your audiences, including most importantly yourself, that the findings of your enquiry are worth taking account of? What is it that makes the study believable and trustworthy? What are the kinds of argument that you can use? What questions should you ask? What criteria are involved?

In this connection *validity* and *generalizability* are central concepts. Validity is concerned with whether the findings are 'really' about what they appear to be about. Generalizability refers to the extent to which the findings of the enquiry are more generally applicable outside the specifics of the situation studied. These issues, together with the related one of *reliability* (the consistency or stability of a measure; for example, if it were to be repeated, would the same result be obtained?), were initially developed in the context of traditional fixed designs collecting quantitative data, and there is considerable debate about their applicability for flexible designs with qualitative data. Hence trustworthiness is considered separately in the two following chapters, covering fixed and flexible designs respectively.

## Further Reading

Bentz, V. M. and Shapiro, J. J. (1998) *Mindful Inquiry in Social Research*. Thousand Oaks, Calif.: Sage. A helpful guide to those confused by the complexities of post-modernism and the maze of research traditions now on offer. Seeks to empower researchers by putting them at the centre of the research process.

Davidson, J. O'C. and Layder, D. (1994) *Methods, Sex and Madness*. London: Routledge. A refreshingly different text which grounds a discussion of research methodology in the areas of madness and sex.

Hakim, C. (1987) *Research Design: Strategies and Choices in the Design of Social Research*. London: Allen & Unwin. Systematic coverage of all aspects of design; applicable to a wide range of disciplines. Includes both pure and applied (policy) research.

Marshall, C. and Rossman, G. B. (1999) *Designing Qualitative Research*, 3rd edn. Thousand Oaks, Calif.: Sage. Very accessible text on a wide range of issues involved in research design. Focus on qualitative, but much of general relevance. Extensive use of illustrative vignettes.

Maxwell, J. A. (1996) *Qualitative Research Design: An Interactive Approach*. Thousand Oaks, Calif.: Sage. Detailed discussion on purposes, conceptual context and research questions, following a similar approach to that taken here.

Mertens, D. M. (1998) *Research Methods in Education and Psychology: Integrating Diversity with Quantitative and Qualitative Approaches*. Thousand Oaks, Calif.: Sage. Encyclopedic text with balanced, even-handed treatment of quantitative and qualitative approaches. Strong on the emancipatory paradigm, including the perspectives of feminists, ethnic/racial minorities and persons with disabilities.

# 5
# Fixed Designs

This chapter:

- covers general features of fixed design research, typically involving the collection of quantitative data;
- discusses how the trustworthiness (including reliability, validity and generalizability) of findings from this style of research can be established;
- explores the attractions and problems of doing experiments in real world research;
- gives particular attention to the randomized controlled trial (RCT) and whether it can legitimately be viewed as the 'gold standard' of research designs;
- differentiates between true experimental, quasi-experimental and single case experimental designs;
- provides a range of examples of each of these types of experimental design;
- concludes by considering a range of non-experimental fixed designs, distinguishing between relational and comparative types.

## Introduction

This chapter deals with approaches to social research where the design of the study is fixed before the main stage of data collection takes place. In these approaches, the phenomena of interest are typically quantified. This is not a necessary feature. As pointed out by Oakley (2000, p. 306), there is nothing intrinsic to such designs which rules out qualitative methods or data (see Murphy et al., 1998 for examples of purely qualitative studies, and of others using both qualitative and quantitative methods, in the field of health promotion evaluation).

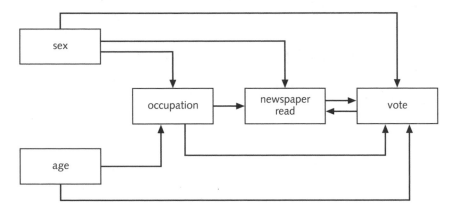

**Figure 5.1**   Causal model for voting.
*Source*: Marsh (1982).

It has already been argued in chapter 3 that there can be considerable advantage in linking research to theory. With fixed designs, that link is straightforward; *fixed designs are theory-driven*. The only way in which we can, as a fixed design requires, specify in advance the variables to be included in our study, and the exact procedures to be followed, is by having a reasonably well articulated theory of the phenomenon we are researching. To put this in other terms, we must already have a substantial amount of conceptual understanding about a phenomenon before it is worthwhile following the risky strategy of investing precious time and resources in such designs. This understanding may be in the form of a model, perhaps represented pictorially as a conceptual framework as discussed in chapter 3, where several examples were presented in figure 3.1, p. 64). Figure 5.1 presents a further example.

Such models help to make clear the multiple causality of most things studied in social research. They also emphasize that while some variables may have a direct effect on others (e.g. that of sex on occupation), others have an indirect effect (that of sex on vote through newspaper readership). Hard thinking to establish this kind of model before data collection is invaluable. It suggests the variables we should target; those to be manipulated or controlled in an experiment; and those to be included in non-experimental studies.

In critical realist terms, this means that you have a pretty clear idea about the mechanisms likely to be in operation and the specific contexts in which they will, or will not, operate. If the study does deliver the expected relationships, it provides support for the existence of these mechanisms, and their actual operation in this study. This does not preclude your following up interesting or unexpected patterns in the data. They may suggest the existence of other mechanisms which you had not thought of.

Large-scale studies can afford to cast the net relatively wide. Large numbers of participants can be involved; several sub-groups established; perhaps a range of different contexts covered; more possible mechanisms tested out. For the small-scale studies on which this text focuses, and in real world settings where relevant previous work may be sparse or non-existent, there is much to be said for a *combined strategy design*, with an initial flexible design stage of primarily exploratory purpose. This seeks to establish, both from discussions with professionals, participants and others involved in the initial phase, and from the empirical data gathered, likely 'bankers' for mechanisms operating in the situation, contexts where they are likely to operate, and the characteristics of participants best targeted. The second fixed design phase then incorporates a highly focused experiment or other fixed design study.

Even with a preceding exploratory phase, *fixed designs should always be piloted*. A pilot is a mini-version of the study carried out before committing yourself to the big one. This is done in part so you can sort out technical matters to do with methods of data collection to ensure that, say, the questions in a questionnaire are understandable and unambiguous. Just as importantly, it gives you a chance to ensure you are on the right lines conceptually. Have you 'captured' the phenomenon sufficiently well for meaningful data to be collected? Do you really have a good grasp of the relevant mechanisms and contexts? This is an opportunity to revise the design, to sharpen up the theoretical framework, develop the research questions, rethink the sampling strategy – and perhaps to do a further pilot.

Also, while the central part of what you are going to do with your data should be thought through in advance – in other words, in implementing a fixed design you are primarily engaged in a *confirmatory* task – there is nothing to stop you also carrying out *exploratory data analysis*. It may be that there are unexpected patterns or relationships which reveal inadequacies in your initial understanding of the phenomenon. You cannot expect to confirm these revised understandings in the same study, but they may well provide an important breakthrough suggesting a basis for further research.

This chapter seeks to provide a critical realist view of fixed design research. There is coverage of *true experimental, single case experimental, quasi-experimental* and *non-experimental fixed designs*. The differences between these types of design are brought out and some examples given. In the 'true' experiment, two or more groups are set up. The defining feature of the true experiment is that there is random allocation of people to the groups. The experimenter then actively manipulates the situation so that different groups get different treatments. Single case design, as the name suggests, focuses on individuals rather than groups and effectively seeks to use a person as their own control, subjecting them to different experimentally manipulated conditions at different times. Quasi-experiments lack the random allocation to different conditions found in true experiments. Non-experimental fixed designs lack an active manipulation of the situation by the researcher However, the different fixed designs are similar in many respects, as discussed in the following section.

## General Features of Fixed Designs

Fixed designs are usually concerned with aggregates, with group properties and with general tendencies. In traditional experiments, results are reported in terms of group averages rather than what individuals have done. Single case designs are an interesting exception to this rule. Most non-experimental fixed research also deals with averages and proportions. The relative weakness of fixed designs is that they cannot capture the subtleties and complexities of individual human behaviour. Even single case designs are limited to quantitative measures of a single simple behaviour, or at most a small number of such behaviours. The advantage of fixed designs lies in their ability to transcend individual differences and identify patterns and processes which can be linked to social structures and group or organizational features.

Fixed designs traditionally assume a 'detached' researcher, to guard against the researcher's having an effect on the findings of the research. In experimental research the *experimenter effect* is well known. It is now widely acknowledged that the beliefs, values and expectations of the researcher can influence the research process at virtually all of its stages (Rosnow and Rosenthal, 1997). Hence the stance now taken is that all potential biases should be brought out into the open by the researcher and every effort made to counter them.

Generally, researchers using fixed methods remain at a greater physical and emotional distance from the study than those using flexible, qualitative methods. There are often long periods of preparation and design preliminaries before data collection, and a substantial period of analysis (almost certainly involving computer software packages) after data collection. This does not, of course, in any way absolve the researcher from familiarity with the topic of the research, which is typically acquired vicariously from others, or from a familiarity with the literature, or from an earlier qualitative study. There will be involvement during the data collection phase, but with some studies, such as postal surveys, this may be minimal. Your personal preference for a relatively detached, or a more involved, style of carrying out research is an important factor in deciding the focus of your research project and the selection of a fixed or flexible design.

It is fashionable in some academic and professional circles to denigrate the contribution of quantitative social research. As Bentz and Shapiro (1998) comment, in a text primarily covering qualitative approaches:

There is currently an anti-quantitative vogue in some quarters, asserting or implying that quantitative research is necessarily alienating, positivistic, dehumanizing, and not 'spiritual'. In fact, it is clear that using quantitative methods to identify causes of human and social problems and suffering can be of immense practical, human, and emancipatory significance, and they are not necessarily positivistic in orientation. For example, quantitative methods are currently being used in the analysis of statistics to help identify the principal causes of rape. Baron and Straus have analyzed police records on rape quantitatively to look at the relative roles of gender inequality, pornography, gender cultural norms about violence, and social disorganization in causing rape (1989). Clearly knowing the relative contribution of these factors in causing rape would be of great significance for social policy, economic policy, the law, socialization, and the criminal justice system, and it is difficult to see how one would arrive at compelling conclusions about this without quantitative analysis. (p. 124)

They also point out that quantitative and experimental methods have been used for the purposes of critical social science (i.e. in relation to the emancipatory purposes discussed in chapter 2): that is, to understand social problems and criticize prevailing ideologies in a way which contributes to social change and the alleviation of human suffering (e.g. Adorno et al., 1950; Lerner, 1980).

Oakley (2000) suggests that this antipathy to quantitative, and in particular experimental, research derives in part from the influence of feminist methodologists who have viewed quantitative research as a masculine enterprise, contrasting it with qualitative research which is seen as embodying feminine values. She rejects this stereotyping, and in her own work has made the transition from being a qualitative researcher to a staunch advocate of true randomized experiments.

## Variables in fixed design research

The concept of 'variable' is part of the quantitative worldview central to fixed design research; indeed, it is such a fundamental part of this worldview that most statistics and research methods books never really explain what a 'variable' is, giving a brief definition and then taking the concept for granted (a deficiency shared by the draft version of this text, tactfully pointed out by a reviewer, Joe Maxwell; this section owes much to material kindly provided by him.)

In this worldview, reality is conceptualized as consisting of properties of things, properties that can vary and thus be measured and compared. These properties may be seen as categorical – gender, nationality, teaching style (authoritarian or democratic), etc. – or as continuous – age, SAT score, knowledge of some topic, etc.

*The term 'variable' refers to some defined property or characteristic of a person, thing, group or situation that can be measured in some way, and for which these measurements vary, so that they can be compared to one another.*

IQ is a variable; so are class size, household income, ethnicity, number of students (in a class or school), personality type, and so on. While there's nothing inherently quantitative about the idea of a variable, quantitative fixed design research can deal with reality only by translating it into variables, measuring these, and comparing and mathematically manipulating their values. Quantitative data all consist of values – measurements – of variables for particular individuals or other units. In contrast, most flexible design qualitative researchers do not see the world in terms of variables Your ability to understand quantitative research articles, and to design your own quantitative fixed design research, depends on your ability to 'see' the research in terms of variables, to identify what variables are being studied, and to distinguish different types of variables (such as independent and dependent variables).

## Establishing Trustworthiness in Fixed Design Research

This is to a considerable extent a matter of common sense. Have you done a good, thorough and honest job? Have you tried to explore, describe or explain in an open and unbiased way? Or are you more concerned with delivering the required answer or selecting the evidence to support a case? If you can't answer these questions with yes, yes and no respectively, then your findings are essentially worthless in enquiry terms. However, pure intentions do not guarantee trustworthy findings. You persuade others by clear, well-written and presented, logically argued accounts which address the questions that concern them. These are all issues to which we will return in chapter 15 on reporting.

This is not simply a presentational matter, however. Fundamental issues about the enquiry itself are involved. Two key ones are *validity* and *generalizability*. Validity, from a realist perspective, refers to the accuracy of a result. Does it 'really' correspond to, or adequately capture, the actual state of affairs? Are any relationships established in the findings 'true', or due to the effect of something else? (The scare quotes around 'really' and 'true' are intended to sensitize you to the problematic nature of these concepts.) Generalizability refers to the extent to which the findings of the enquiry are more generally applicable, for example in other contexts, situations or times, or to persons other than those directly involved.

## Validity

Suppose that we have been asked to carry out some form of enquiry to address the research question:

*Is educational achievement in primary schools improved by the introduction of standard assessment tests at the age of seven?*

Let us leave on one side issues about whether or not this is a sensible question and about the most appropriate way to approach it. Suppose that the findings of our enquiry indicated a 'yes' answer – possibly qualified in various ways. In other words, we measure educational achievement, and it appears to increase following the introduction of the tests. Is this relationship what it appears to be – is there a 'real', direct, link between the introduction of the tests and improved educational achievement?

Central to the scientific approach is a degree of scepticism about our findings and their meaning (and even greater scepticism about other people's). Can we have been fooled so that we are mistaken about them? Unfortunately, yes – there is a wide range of possibilities for confusion and error.

*Reliability*    Some problems come under the heading of reliability. This is the stability or consistency with which we measure something. For example, consider how we are going to assess educational achievement. This is no easy task. Possible contenders, each with its own problems, might include:

*   a formal 'achievement test' administered at the end of the primary stage of schooling;
*   teachers' ratings, also at the end of the primary stage;
*   the number, level and standard of qualifications gained throughout life.

Let's say we go for the first. It will not be difficult to devise something which will generate a score for each pupil. However, this might be unreliable in the sense that if a pupil had, say, taken it on Thursday rather than Wednesday, she would have got a quite different score. There are logical problems in assessing this, which can be attacked in various ways (e.g. by having parallel forms of the test which can be taken at different times, and their results compared). These are important considerations in test construction – see chapter 10, p. 292 for further details.

Unless a measure is reliable, it cannot be valid. However, while reliability is necessary, it is not sufficient to ensure validity. A test for which all pupils always got full marks would be totally consistent but would be useless as a way of discriminating between the achievements of different pupils (there could, of course, be good educational reasons for such a test if what was important was mastery of some material).

Unreliability may have various causes. One is *participant error*. In our example, the pupil's performance might fluctuate widely from occasion to occasion on a more or less random basis. Tiredness due to late nights could produce changes for different times of the day, pre-menstrual tension monthly effects, or hay fever seasonal ones. There are tactics which can be used to ensure that these kinds of fluctuations do not bias the findings, particularly when specific sources of error can be anticipated: for example, keeping testing away from the hay fever season. More problematic from a validity point of view are sources of *participant bias*. It could be that pupils might seek to please or help their teacher, knowing the importance of 'good results', by making a particularly strong effort at the test. Here it would be very difficult to dis-entangle whether this was simply a short-term effect which had artificially boosted the test scores, or a desirable more long-lasting side-effect of a more testing-oriented primary school educational system. Consideration of poten-tial errors of these kinds is part of the standard approach to experimental design (see p. 104).

*Observer error* is another possible source of unreliability. This would be most obvious if the second approach, making use of teachers' ratings as the measure of pupil achievement, had been selected. These could also lead to more or less random errors if, for example, teachers made the ratings at a time when they were tired or overstretched and did the task in a cursory way. Again, there are pretty obvious remedies (perhaps involving the provision of additional resources). *Observer bias* is also possible and, like participant bias, causes prob-lems in interpretation. It could be that teachers, in marking the tests, were consciously or unconsciously biasing the ratings they gave in line with their ideological commitment either in favour of or against the use of standard assessment tests. This is also a well-worked area methodologically, with pro-cedures including 'blind' assessment (the ratings being made by someone in ignorance of whether the pupil had been involved in standard assessment tests) and the use of two independent assessors (so that inter-observer agreements could be computed). Further details are given in chapter 11, p. 340.

*Construct validity*   If you have made a serious attempt to get rid of partici-pant and observer biases and have demonstrated the reliability of whatever measure you have decided on, you will be making a pretty good job of mea-suring something. The issue then becomes: does it measure what you think it measures? In the jargon – does it have construct validity?

There is no easy, single, way of determining construct validity. At its sim-plest, one might look for what seems reasonable, sometimes referred to as *face validity*. An alternative looks at possible links between scores on a test and the third measure suggested above – the pupils' actual educational achievement in their later life (i.e. how well does it predict performance on the criterion in question; this is called *predictive criterion validity*). These and other aspects of construct validity are central to the methodology of testing, which is discussed in detail in chapter 10, p. 292.

The methodological complexities of determining construct validity can lead to an unhealthy concentration on this aspect of carrying out an enquiry. For many studies there is an intuitive reasonableness to assertions that a certain approach provides an appropriate measure. Any one way of measuring or gathering data is likely to have its shortcomings, which suggests the use of multiple methods. One could use all three of the approaches to assessing educational achievement discussed above (achievement tests, teachers' ratings and 'certificate counting') rather than relying on any one measure. Similar patterns of findings from very different methods of gathering data increase confidence in the findings' validity. Discrepancies between them can be revealing in their own right. It is important to realize, however, that multiple methods do not constitute a panacea for all methodological ills. They raise their own theoretical problems; and they may in many cases be so resource-hungry as to be impracticable.

*Internal validity*    Let us say that we have jumped the preceding hurdle and have demonstrated satisfactorily that we have a valid measure of educational achievement. However, a finding that achievement increases *after* the introduction of the tests does not necessarily mean that it increased *because* of the tests. This gets us back to the consideration of causation which occupied us in chapter 2.

What we would like to do is to find out whether the treatment (introduction of the tests) actually caused the outcome (the increase in achievement). If a study can plausibly demonstrate this causal relationship between treatment and outcome, it is referred to as having *internal validity*. This term was introduced by Campbell and Stanley (1963), who provided an influential and widely used analysis of possible 'threats' to internal validity.

These threats are other things that might happen which confuse the issue and make us mistakenly conclude that the treatment caused the outcome (or obscure possible relationships between them). Suppose, for example, that the teachers of the primary school children involved in the study are in an industrial dispute with their employers at the same time that testing is introduced. One might well find, in those circumstances, a decrease in achievement related to the disaffection and disruption caused by the dispute, which might be mistakenly ascribed to the introduction of tests per se. This particular threat is labelled as 'history' by Campbell and Stanley – something which happens at the same time as the treatment. (There is the complicating factor here, in that a case might be made for negative effects on teaching being an integral part of the introduction of formal testing into a child-centred primary school culture, i.e. that they are part of the treatment rather than an extraneous factor. However, for simplicity's sake, let's say that the industrial dispute was an entirely separate matter.)

Campbell and Stanley (1963) suggested eight possible 'threats' to internal validity which might be posed by other, extraneous variables. Cook and Campbell (1979) developed and extended this analysis, adding a further four threats. All twelve are listed in box 5.1. The labels used for the threats are not to be interpreted too literally – mortality doesn't necessarily refer to the death of a participant during the study (though it might!). Not all threats are present for all designs. For example, the 'testing' threat is only there if a pre-test is given; and in some cases its likelihood, or perhaps evidence that you had gained from pilot work that a 'testing' effect was present, would cause you to avoid a design involving this feature.

In general design terms, there are two strategies to deal with these threats. If you know what the threat is, you can take specific steps to deal with it. For example, the use of comparison groups who have the treatment at different times or places will help to neutralize the 'history' threat. This approach of designing to deal with specific threats calls for a lot of forethought and is helped by knowledge and experience of the situation that you are dealing with. Moreover, you can hope to deal with only a fairly small number of pre-defined and articulated threats in this way. The alternative strategy, central to the design philosophy of true experiments as developed by Fisher (1935), is to use randomization, which helps offset the effect of a myriad of unforeseen factors. However, as Maxwell (1992) notes, 'This strategy of addressing particular threats to validity, or alternative hypotheses, *after* a tentative account has been developed, rather than by attempting to eliminate such threats through prior features of the research design is more fundamental to scientific method than is the latter approach (Campbell, 1988: Platt, 1964)' (p. 296, emphasis in original).

While true experiments are therefore effective at dealing with these threats, they are by no means totally immune to them. The threats have to be taken very seriously with quasi-experimental designs, and non-experimental fixed designs, and a study of the plausibility of the existence of various threats provides a very useful tool in interpretation. The interpretability of designs in the face of these threats depends not only on the design itself but on the specific pattern of results obtained (see p. 141 for an example).

If you rule out these threats, you have established internal validity. You will have shown (or, more strictly, demonstrated the plausibility) that a particular treatment caused a certain outcome. In critical realist terms 'caused' refers to the operation of one or more mechanisms whose operation you hypothesized when setting up the study. The validity threats can be thought of as mechanisms which can operate to affect the outcome; but which you are able to discount.

# Box 5.1

## Threats to internal validity

**1** *History*   Things that have changed in the participants' environments other than those forming a direct part of the enquiry (e.g. occurrence of major air disaster during study of effectiveness of desensitization programme on persons with fear of air travel).

**2** *Testing*   Changes occurring as a result of practice and experience gained by participants on any pre-tests (e.g. asking opinions about factory farming of animals before some intervention may lead respondents to think about the issues and develop more negative attitudes).

**3** *Instrumentation*   Some aspect(s) of the way participants were measured changed between pre-test and post-test (e.g. raters in observational study using a wider or narrower definition of a particular behaviour as they get more familiar with the situation).

**4** *Regression*   If participants are chosen because they are unusual or atypical (e.g. high scorers), later testing will tend to give less unusual scores ('regression to the mean'); e.g. in an intervention programme with pupils with learning difficulties where ten highest-scoring pupils in a special unit are matched with ten of the lowest-scoring pupils in a mainstream school, regression effects will tend to show the former performing relatively worse on a subsequent test. See further details on p. 142.

**5** *Mortality*   Participants dropping out of the study (e.g. in study of adult literacy programme – selective drop-out of those who are making little progress).

**6** *Maturation*   Growth, change or development in participants unrelated to the treatment in the enquiry (e.g. evaluating extended athletics training programme with teenagers – intervening changes in height, weight and general maturity).

**7** *Selection*   Initial differences between groups prior to involvement in the enquiry (e.g. the use of an arbitrary non-random rule to produce two groups ensures they differ in one respect which may correlate with others).

**8** *Selection by maturation interaction*   Predisposition of groups to grow apart (or together if initially different); e.g. use of groups of boys and girls initially matched on physical strength in a study of a fitness programme.

**9**   *Ambiguity about causal direction*   Does A cause B, or B cause A? (e.g. in any correlational study, unless it is known that A precedes B, or vice versa – or some other logical analysis is possible).

**10**   *Diffusion of treatments*   When one group learns information or otherwise inadvertently receives aspects of a treatment intended only for a second group (e.g. in a quasi-experimental study of two classes in the same school).

**11**   *Compensatory equalization of treatments*   If one group receives 'special' treatment, there will be organizational and other pressures for a control group to receive it (e.g. nurses in a hospital study may improve the treatment of a control group on grounds of fairness).

**12**   *Compensatory rivalry*   As above but an effect on the participants themselves – referred to as the 'John Henry' effect after the steel worker who killed himself through over-exertion to prove his superiority to the new steam drill; e.g. when a group in an organization sees itself under threat from a planned change in another part of the organization and improves performance).

(After Cook and Campbell, 1979, pp. 51–5.)

It is important to appreciate that 'validity threats are made implausible by *evidence*, not methods; methods are only a way of getting evidence that can help you rule out these threats' (Maxwell, 1996, p. 86, emphasis in original). The view that methods themselves can guarantee validity is characteristic of the discredited positivist approach and is itself untenable; whatever method is adopted there is no such guarantee. The critical realist assumption is that all methods are fallible: 'a realist conception of validity . . . sees the validity of an account as inherent, not in the procedures used to produce and validate it, but in its relationship to those things that it is intended to be an account *of*' (Maxwell, 1992, p. 281; original emphasis). See also House (1991).

The whole 'threat' approach sits well with a realist analysis, which is not surprising as Campbell was an avowed critical realist (see, however, House et al., 1989; House makes a case for his approach, particularly in Cook and Campbell, 1979, as being essentially eclectic, taking aspects from a whole range of theoretical positions).

## Generalizability

Sometimes one is interested in a specific finding in its own right. You may have shown, say, that a new group workshop approach leads, via a mechanism of increases in self-esteem, to subsequent maintained weight loss in obese teenagers at a residential unit. This may be the main thing that you are after if you are concerned only with whether or not the approach works with that specific group of individuals at the unit.

If, however, you are interested in what would happen with other client groups or in other settings, or with these teenagers when they return home, then you need to concern yourself with the generalizability of the study. Campbell and Stanley (1963) use the alternative term 'external validity'. Both this and 'generalizability' are in common use. Internal and external validity tend to be inversely related in the sense that the various controls imposed in order to bolster internal validity often fight against generalizability. In particular, the fact that the laboratory is the controlled environment *par excellence* makes results obtained there very difficult to generalize to any settings other than close approximations to laboratory conditions.

Given that your teenagers are a representative sample from a known population, then the generalization to that population can be done according to the usual rules of statistical inference. Generalizability to other settings or to other client groups has to be done on other, non-statistical, bases. LeCompte and Goetz (1982) have provided a classification of threats to external validity similar to that given for internal validity, which is listed in box 5.2. There are two general strategies for showing that these potential threats are discountable: *direct demonstration* and *making a case*. Direct demonstration involves you, or someone else who wishes to apply or extend your results, carrying out a further study involving some other type of participant, or in a different setting, etc. Making a case is putting forward a persuasive argument that it is reasonable for the results to generalize, by showing that the group studied,

---

## Box 5.2

### Threats to generalizability (external validity)

1  *Selection*  Findings being specific to the group studied.

2  *Setting*  Findings being specific to, or dependent on, the particular context in which the study took place.

3  *History*  Specific and unique historical experiences may determine or affect the findings.

4  *Construct effects*  The particular constructs studied may be specific to the group studied.

(After LeCompte and Goetz, 1982.)

or setting, or period is representative (i.e. it shares certain essential character-istics with other groups, settings or periods and hence the same mechanism is likely to apply in those also). This sorting out of the wheat of what is central to your findings from the chaff of specific irrelevancies can be other-wise expressed as having a theory or theoretical framework to explain what is going on.

Such a theory may be expressed in formal and explicit terms by the pre-senter of the findings. A study may be repeated with a different target group or in a deliberately different setting to assess the generalizability of its find-ings. As discussed in chapter 2, p. 42, there is a strong case, particularly with important or controversial findings, for attempting a replication of the origi-nal study. While in practice no replication is ever exact, an attempt to repeat the study as closely as possible which reproduces the main findings of the first study is the practical test of the reliability of your findings. Whether it is worth-while to devote scarce resources to replication depends on circumstances. Replication is nowhere near as common as it should be in social research. In consequence, we may well be seeking to build on very shaky foundations. The argument is sometimes put that as validity depends on reliability, then we should simply worry about the validity; if we can show that validity is accept-able then so, necessarily, is reliability. The problem here is that it becomes more difficult to disentangle what lies behind poor validity. It might have been that the findings were not reliable in the first place.

It is easy to guarantee unreliability. Carelessness, casualness and lack of commitment on the part of the enquirer help, as does a corresponding lack of involvement by participants. Reliability is essentially a quality control issue. Punctilious attention to detail, perseverance and pride in doing a good job are all very important, but organization is the key.

While validity and generalizability are probably the central elements in establishing the value and trustworthiness of a fixed design enquiry, there are many other aspects to which attention should be given. They include, in particular, objectivity and credibility.

## Objectivity

The traditional, scientific approach to the problem of establishing objectivity is exemplified by the experimental approach. The solution here is seen to be to distance the experimenter from the experimental participant, so that any interaction that takes place between the two is formalized – indeed, some experimenters go so far as not only to have a standardized verbatim script but even to have it delivered via a tape-recorder.

To some, this artificiality is lethal for any real understanding of phenomena involving people in social settings. An alternative is to erect an objective/

subjective contrast. 'Objective' is taken to refer to what multiple observers agree to as a phenomenon, in contrast to the subjective experience of the single individual. In other words, the criterion for objectivity is intersubjective agreement. This stance tends to go along with an involved rather than a detached investigator, and notions of 'triangulation' (see chapter 12, p. 371) where the various accounts of participants with different roles in the situation are obtained by investigators who, by combining them with their own perceptions and understandings, reach an agreed and negotiated account.

Formulated in terms of threats, objectivity can be seen to be at risk from a methodology where the values, interests and prejudices of the enquirer distort the response (experiment being for some the answer, and for others an extreme version of the problem). Relying exclusively on data from a single individual can similarly threaten objectivity. And again, enquiry carried out for an ideological purpose other than that of enquiry itself clearly threatens objectivity.

## Credibility

Shipman (1988) has suggested that we should go beyond the traditional concerns for reliability, validity and generalizability when considering the trustworthiness of research, and also ask the question: 'Is there sufficient detail on the way the evidence is produced for the credibility of the research to be assessed?'. We cannot satisfy ourselves about the other concerns unless the researcher provides sufficient information on the methods used and the justification for their use. This is a responsibility which has always been accepted by those using experimentation. It is explicitly required by the conventions of scholarly journal publishing that the report of an experiment in a journal article give sufficient detail about procedures, equipment, etc. for the reader to carry out an exact replication of the study.

This kind of requirement may be rejected as scientist by some practitioners using flexible designs, relying largely on qualitative data. However, it could be argued that there is a strong case for such research calling for an even greater emphasis on explaining the methods used and the warrant for the conclusions reached, because of the lack of codification of the methods of data collection or of approaches to analysis. This need is increasingly recognized by methodologists sympathetic to qualitative approaches (e.g. Miles and Huberman, 1984; Strauss, 1987; Marshall and Rossman, 1999). However, there is considerable debate about the applicability of concepts such as reliability and validity, and the possibility and appropriateness of objectivity, when assessing the trustworthiness of flexible qualitative research. The following chapter pays attention to this issue.

## Experimental Fixed Designs

*If, following your reading of the previous chapter, it appears possible that an experimental fixed design is likely to be appropriate for your project and its research questions, then perusal of this section should help in choosing a specific experimental design. However, before confirming that choice, it will be necessary to read later chapters of this book to help select appropriate methods of collecting data, and in particular to establish how you will analyse the data after they have been collected.*

To 'experiment', or to 'carry out an experiment' can mean many things. At one level of generality, to be experimental is simply to be concerned with trying new things and seeing what happens, what the reception is. Think of 'experimental' theatre, or an 'experimental' car, or an 'experimental' introduction of a mini-roundabout at a road junction. There is a change in something, and a concern for the effects that this change might have on something else.

However, when experimentation is contrasted with other research designs, a stricter definition is employed, usually involving the control and active manipulation of variables by the experimenter.

*Experimentation is a research strategy involving*

- *the assignment of participants to different conditions;*
- *manipulation of one or more variables (called 'independent variables') by the experimenter;*
- *the measurement of the effects of this manipulation on one or more other variables (called 'dependent variables'); and*
- *the control of all other variables.*

Note the use of the term *variable* (discussed above on p. 99). This is widespread within the experimental strategy, and simply denotes something which can vary. However, it carries within it the notion that there are certain specific aspects which can be isolated and which retain the same meaning throughout the study.

The experimental strategy is the prime example of a fixed research design. You need to know exactly what you are going to do before you do it. It is a precise tool that can map only a very restricted range. A great deal of preparatory work (either by you or by someone else) is needed if it is going to be useful. An experiment is an extremely *focused* study. You can handle only a very few variables, often only a single independent variable and a single dependent variable. These variables have to be selected with extreme care. You need to have a well-developed theoretical framework. The major problem in doing experiments in the real world is that you often have, at best, only a pretty shaky and undeveloped theory; you don't know enough about the thing you are studying for this selectivity of focus to be a sensible strategy. This need to know what you are doing before you do it is a general characteristic of fixed research designs, but experiments are most demanding in this respect because of their extreme selectivity.

## Experiments and the Real World

This book is primarily concerned with enquiry outside the laboratory. It is based on the premise that psychologists and others whose interests are primarily applied, and who are concerned with understanding and possibly influencing what is taking place in the real world, should take part in what Skinner (1963) refers to disapprovingly as the 'flight from the laboratory'. However, the notion that real world phenomena are best studied outside the laboratory needs justification.

Aronson and Carlsmith (1986) have distinguished two senses in which laboratory experimentation may lack realism (in a sense, incidentally, which has nothing to do with realist philosophy). One is *experimental realism*. In this sense, an experiment is realistic if the situation which it presents to the subject is realistic, if it really involves the subjects and has impact upon them. In the well-known Asch (1956) experiment on conformity, subjects made what seemed to them to be straightforward judgements about the relative length of lines. These judgements were contradicted by others in the room whom they took also to be subjects in the experiment. This study showed experimental realism in the sense that subjects were undergoing an experience which caused them to show strong signs of tension and anxiety. They appeared to be reacting to the situation in the same realistic kind of way that they would outside the laboratory.

However, it might be argued that the Asch study lacks what Aronson and Carlsmith term *mundane realism*. That is, the subjects were encountering events in the laboratory setting which were very unlikely to occur in the real world. Asch, following a common strategy in laboratory experimentation, had set up a very clearly and simply structured situation to observe the effects of group pressure on individuals. The real life counterpart, if one could be found, would be more complex and ambiguous, and in all probability would result in findings which were inconclusive. (The ethics of Asch's study are a different matter – see p. 65.)

Simplification of the situation, which is central to the experimental approach, may lead to clear results, but it does not protect against bias in them. The effects of two types of bias have been investigated in some detail. These are the *demand characteristics* of the experimental situation, and *experimenter expectancy* effects. In a very general sense, these are the consequences of the 'experimental units' (the participants) and the experimenters, respectively, being human beings (see Barber, 1976, for a thorough analysis of such 'pitfalls' in experimentation with humans).

Bias due to demand characteristics occurs because subjects know that they are in an experimental situation; know that they are being observed; know that certain things are expected or demanded of them (Orne, 1962). Hence the way in which they respond is some complex amalgam of the experimental manipulation and their interpretation of what effect the manipulation is supposed to have on them. Their action based on that interpretation is likely to be co-operative but could well be obstructive. Even in situations where subjects are explicitly told that there are no right or wrong answers, that one response is as valued as another, subjects are likely to feel that certain responses show them in a better light than others. There is evidence that persons who volunteer for experiments are more sensitive to these effects than those who are required to be involved (Rosenthal and Rosnow, 1975).

The classic ploy to counteract this type of bias is deception by the experimenter. Participants are told that the experiment is about $X$ when it is really about $Y$. $X$ is made to appear plausible and is such that if the participants modify their responses in line with, or antagonistically to, what the experimenter appears to be after, there is no systematic effect on the experimenter's real area of interest. As discussed in chapter 3 (p. 65), increasing sensitivity to the ethical issues raised by deceiving participants means that this ploy, previously common in some areas of social psychology, is now looked on with increasing suspicion.

Experimenter expectancy effects are reactive effects produced by the experimenters, who have been shown to bias findings (usually unwittingly) in the direction of what they expect to happen. Rosenthal and Rubin (1980) discuss the first 345 such studies. The effects can be minimized by decreasing the amount of interaction between subject and experimenter: using taped instructions, automated presentation of materials, etc. However, for many topics (apart from things like studies of human–computer interaction), this further attenuates any real world links that the laboratory experiment might possess. Double-blind procedures can also be used, where data collection is subcontracted so that neither the person working directly with the subjects, nor the subjects themselves, are aware of the hypothesis being tested.

Knowledge about determinants of laboratory behaviour (demand characteristics, etc.) can be of value in real life settings. Wells and Luus (1990), for example, conceptualize police identity parades as experiments, and make suggestions for improving them based on this knowledge and on general principles of experimental design (use of control groups, etc.).

# Field Experiments

The laboratory is essentially a place for maximizing control over extraneous variables. Move outside the laboratory door and such tight and comprehensive control becomes impossible. The problems of experimentation discussed in the previous section remain. Any special conditions marking out what is happening as 'an experiment' can lead to reactive effects. The classic demonstration of such effects comes from the well-known series of experiments carried out at the Hawthorne works of the Western Electric Company in the USA in the 1920s and 1930s (Roethlisberger and Dickson, 1939), and hence called the 'Hawthorne effect'. These studies, investigating changes in length of working day, heating, lighting and other variables, found increases in productivity during the study which were virtually irrespective of the specific changes; the workers were in effect reacting positively to the attention and special treatment given by the experimenters. Problems in carrying out field experiments are listed in box 5.3. There are gains, of course. Notwithstand-

---

## Box 5.3

### Problems in carrying out field experiments

Moving outside the safe confines of the laboratory may well be traumatic. Particular practical difficulties include:

*1 Random assignment*

There are practical and ethical problems in achieving random assignment to different experimental treatments or conditions (e.g. in withholding the treatment from a no-treatment control group). Random assignment is also often feasible only in atypical circumstances or with selected respondents, leading to questionable generalizability. Faulty randomization procedures are not uncommon (e.g. when procedures are subverted through ignorance, kindness, etc.). For small samples of the units being randomly assigned, sampling variability is a problem. Treatment-related refusal to participate or continue can bias sampling.

*2 Validity*

The actual treatment may be an imperfect realization of the variable(s) of interest, or a restricted range of outcomes may be insensitively or

---

imperfectly measured, resulting in questionable validity. A supposed no-treatment control group may receive some form of compensatory treatment, or be otherwise influenced (e.g. through deprivation effects).

### 3   Ethical issues

There are grey areas in relation to restricting the involvement to volunteers, the need for informed consent and the debriefing of subjects after the experiment. Strict adherence to ethical guidelines is advocated, but this may lead to losing some of the advantages of moving outside the laboratory (e.g. leading to unnecessary 'obtrusiveness', and hence reactivity, of the treatment). Common sense is needed. If you are studying a natural experiment where some innovation would have taken place whether or not you were involved, then the ethical considerations applying may be only those relating to the innovation (fluoridation of water supplies raises more ethical implications for users than an altered design of a road junction).

### 4   Control

Lack of control over extraneous variables may mask the effects of treatment variables, or bias their assessment. Interaction between subjects may vitiate random assignment and violate their assumed independence.

ing some degree of artificiality, and related reactivity, generalizability to the 'real world' (usually referred to as *external validity*) is almost self-evidently easier to achieve when the study takes place outside the laboratory in a setting which is almost real 'real life'. Note, however, that there are claims of good generalization of some findings from laboratory to field settings (Locke, 1986). Other advantages are covered in box 5.4.

Experimental designs as such are equally applicable both inside and outside laboratories. A crucial feature of so-called 'true' experiments (distinguishing them from 'quasi-experiments', which are discussed below) is *random allocation to experimental conditions*. If you can find a feasible and ethical means of doing this when planning a field experiment, then you should seriously consider carrying out a true experiment. Zhu (1999) suggests ways of overcoming some of the difficulties.

The advantage of random allocation or assignment is that it allows you to proceed on the assumption that you have equivalent groups under the two (or more) experimental conditions. This is a probabilistic truth; it allows you, among other things, to employ a wide battery of statistical tests of inference legitimately, but it does not guarantee that, in any particular experiment, the

---

### Box 5.4

## Advantages in carrying out experiments in natural settings

Compared to a laboratory, natural settings have several advantages:

#### 1   Generalizability

The laboratory is necessarily and deliberately an artificial setting, set apart from real life by the degree of control and isolation that applies. If we are concerned with generalizing results to the real world, the task is easier if experimentation is in a natural setting. Much laboratory experimentation is based on student participants, making generalization to the wider population hazardous. Although this is not a necessary feature of laboratory work, there is less temptation to stick to student groups when experiments take place in natural settings.

#### 2   Validity

The *demand characteristics* of laboratory experiments, where subjects tend to do what they think you want them to do, are heightened by the artificiality and isolation of the laboratory situation. Real tasks in a real world setting are less prone to this kind of game playing, so you are more likely to be measuring what you think you are measuring.

#### 3   Participant availability

It is no easy task to get participants to come into the laboratory. You have to rely on them turning up. Although it depends on the type of study, many real life experiments have participants in abundance, limited only by your energy and staying power – and possibly your charm.

---

two groups will in fact be equivalent. Indeed, no such guarantee is ever possible, although the greater the number of persons being allocated, the more confidence you can have that the groups do not differ widely.

An alternative way of expressing this advantage is to say that randomization gets rid (probabilistically at least) of the *selection* threat to internal validity discussed below in relation to quasi-experiments (see box 5.1). It provides a defence against the possibility that any change in a dependent variable is caused not by the independent variable but by differences in the characteristics of the two groups. The other potential threats to internal validity remain, and the discussion of the designs that follows is largely couched in terms of their adequacy, or otherwise, in dealing with these threats.

## Randomized Controlled Trials and the 'Gold Standard'

In many fields of applied research, the *randomized controlled trial (RCT)* is viewed as the 'gold standard', i.e. the method of choice if you seek to do quality research. It is a particular variant of true experimentation involving the use of a *control group*. Participants are *randomly assigned* to an experimental group, which follows the particular intervention (or whatever is the focus of the experiment) or to the control group (which does not receive any special treatment).

While there are some dissident voices even in its heartland of medical research (e.g. Johnson, 1998), the position of RCTs in social research is a matter of considerable controversy. They are anathema to many researchers working within qualitative design traditions. Even some of those who are happy with fixed design quantitative research have strong reservations about their use. They cite practical and ethical problems in setting them up, and the equivocal results commonly obtained when such problems are overcome.

The argument for RCTs is that they provide the best evidence for effectiveness, for whether something 'works'. In an age of accountability, the quest is for 'evidence-based' everything: medicine, health care, social services, education, etc. There is strong justification for requiring good evidence that scarce resources are being used to good effect. While the motivation may be largely financial, there is an ethical dimension. It is difficult to justify doing things with, to or for people if we do not know what their effects are – or at least, it would be if there are ways in which we can get reliable and valid assessments of these effects. RCTs are seen by their advocates as being able to do this. They provide evidence in numerical form which gives clear messages to managers and other decision-makers. Their design features are such that a well-run RCT generates highly trustworthy data. Why, then, do we not have the kind of 'experimenting society' envisaged by Donald Campbell (1988), where RCTs are the prime mechanism for ensuring the evolution of our institutions and services? Among the obstacles to achieving this utopian situation, four in particular deserve attention here.

First, *systematic enquiry (of whatever kind) is a minor player in developing and changing society*. It is both a frustration and a relief for social researchers to appreciate that it is rare for politicians and other decision-makers to be influenced by research outcomes (see chapter 7, p. 219). However, there are windows of opportunity when they may be receptive.

Second, *many social researchers are antipathetic to RCTs*. The rapid spread of qualitative research arose in part because of a distaste for quantitative, experimental approaches as being inappropriate for achieving a real understanding of social phenomena.

Third, there is a widespread view that *RCTs are not feasible*. In fact, while they can be difficult to set up, sufficient examples exist for this claim to be refuted. Oakley (2000, esp. chs 8–10) provides many examples (see also the 'Social, Psychological, Educational and Criminological Trials Register' noted below, p. 119).

Fourth, *social experiments, including RCTs, tend to yield equivocal results*. A major problem with real world field experiments involving people has been that they rarely produce clear-cut positive findings. Oakley (2000) provides a wide-ranging review of the (largely American) attempts at social experimentation carried out from the 1920s to the 1970s. The picture is depressing. The Negative Income Tax experiments demonstrated little impact on work disincentives; the Experimental Housing Allowance Program made little difference to housing consumption or housing stock; the Supporting Workers initiatives produced only small increases in employment or earnings; in the penal experiments, the minor effects on re-arrests in the LIFE study were reversed in the TARP experiments; in the Rand Corporation Health Insurance Study, cost-sharing insurance seemed to reduce health care use, but there was little evidence of any impact on people's health; the Youth Entitlement Program did not encourage young people to stay in school; and contracting out education to private firms failed to confirm the positive impact which had been claimed in an earlier non-experimental study. Some of the findings could even be put in the 'doing harm rather than good' category; these included the re-arrest figures in the TARP experiment, the results for sixteen-year-olds in the Youth Entitlement Program, and the apparently 'negative' effects on family breakup noted in the NIT experiments (p. 232). Details are provided in Oakley (2000, ch. 9).

The so-called 'golden age' of evaluation in the United States in the 1960s and 1970s, when there was a strong commitment to the evaluation of national programmes, produced a string of zero effects leading to considerable despondency among the evaluators and a backlash against systematic evaluation and controlled experimentation. It is now recognized that expectations were unrealistic. In some cases, sample sizes in the experiments were not large enough for statistically significant effects to be demonstrable. However, even well-designed evaluations of large-scale national interventions typically show very small overall effects (Peto, 1987).

If we accept the modest role for any form of systematic enquiry (except under particularly propitious circumstances), and that – from a mixture of prejudice and entirely reasonable considerations (including having different agendas, such as exploration of a new topic or seeking understanding rather than assessing outcomes) – some researchers will avoid RCTs, the main stumbling block appears to be the worrying inability of 'social' RCTs to come up with consistent positive findings.

It could be that the relative weakness of many findings generated by RCTs may be due to features associated with randomization; perhaps this in some way sets up an alienating situation which depresses performance in the experimental group and/or enhances performance in the control group. It appears more likely that experimenter effects (p. 98), or one or more of the threats to validity associated with quasi-experimental designs (see p. 105) may act to enhance the apparent size of any effects when RCTs are not used.

This lack of success in fields such as education, criminology, social work, and the evaluation of social programmes in a whole range of other fields can be contrasted with a clearly successful RCT movement within medicine and health care. Here various so-called 'Cochrane Centres' have produced critical summaries of the results of large numbers of RCTs organized by medical specialty and periodically updated (Cochrane, 1979: Cochrane Controlled Trials Register, 1999). Thus in the field of care in pregnancy and childbirth, extensive reviews have been produced, giving guidance not only about procedures which lead to desirable outcomes but also about those that should be avoided (Chalmers et al., 1989; Enkin et al., 1989; Health Committee, 1992). Several explanations have been suggested for the apparent failure of 'social' RCTs:

- *The interventions, approaches, procedures, etc.* are *ineffective*. It is unsurprising that many of the things studied by means of RCTs have little or no effect. Expecting, say, the provision of a leaflet on some aspect of child care to produce changes in behaviour or attitude change is highly optimistic. Even extensively resourced, large-scale social programmes or interventions often appear to be genuinely ineffective, at least as far as overall outcomes are concerned.

- *The design or implementation of the RCT is at fault.* RCTs can be subject to technical faults; for example, the sample size may not be sufficiently large to pick up any effects. In the field it may well be difficult to exert the degree of control necessary to ensure that the study is carried out properly. General sloppiness, including breakdown or subversion of the randomization procedures, can affect the chances of demonstrating any effects. Note that this could either increase or decrease the apparent size of the effect.

- *The methodology of the RCT is inappropriate.* Perhaps it is control group methodology, as traditionally conceptualized, that is the central problem. It may be unrealistic to expect a necessarily complex social programme or intervention to generate substantial overall effects irrespective of context, participant characteristics, etc.

*Note:* A register of reports and papers, including RCTs on social and educational interventions, known as the Social, Psychological, Educational and Criminological Trials Register (SPECTR) is currently under development by an international organization known as the Campbell Collaboration (Petrosino et al., 2000). It takes its title from Donald Campbell, the methodologist who did substantial work on assessing the validity of causal influences about the effects of interventions and was also an advocate of the 'experimenting society' (Cook and Campbell, 1979; Campbell, 1969).

## Realist Critique of Randomized Controlled Trials

Pawson and Tilley (1997, esp. chapter 2) elaborate the third explanation given above. They develop a swingeing criticism of RCTs in experimental evaluation and, by extension, their use in social research in general. For them, RCTs are inextricably linked to the discredited positivist view of science. As well as generating inconsistent findings, their concentration on outcomes does little or nothing to explain why an intervention has failed (or, in relatively rare cases, succeeded). Hence, they cannot yield the accumulation of findings that helps to build up understanding.

Experimentalists acknowledge the practical and ethical problems of achieving randomization of allocation to experimental and control groups in applied field experiments. To these perils Pawson and Tilley add causal problems. Allocation of participants to experimental or control groups by the experimenter removes that choice from the participants; but *'choice is the very condition of social and individual change and not some sort of practical hindrance to understanding that change'* (Pawson and Tilley, 1997, p. 36; emphasis in original). In their discussion of correctional programmes for prison inmates, they make the undeniable point that it is not the programmes themselves which work, but people co-operating and choosing to make them work.

The traditional solution to this problem is to run volunteer-only experiments. Volunteers are called for, then assigned randomly to one of the two groups. The assumption is made that motivation and co-operation will be the same in each of the groups. The reasonableness of this assumption will depend on the specific circumstances of the experiment. Pawson and Tilley illustrate, through an example of what they consider to be quality experimental evaluation research (Porperino and Robinson, 1995), the way in which participants' choice-making capacity cuts across and undermines a volunteer/non-volunteer distinction:

> The act of volunteering merely marks a moment in a whole evolving pattern of choice. Potential subjects will consider a program (or not), volunteer for it (or

not), co-operate closely (or not), stay the course (or not), learn lessons (or not), retain the lessons (or not), apply the lessons (or not). Each one of these decisions will be internally complex and take its meaning according to the chooser's circumstances. Thus the act of volunteering for a program such as 'Cog Skills' might represent an interest in rehabilitation, a desire for improvement in thinking skills, an opportunity for a good skive, a respite from the terror or boredom of the wings, an opening to display a talent in those reputedly hilarious role-plays, a chance to ogle a glamorous trainer, a way of playing the system to fast-track for early parole, and so on. (p. 38)

They back up this intuitive understanding of how prisoners find their way on to programmes by a detailed re-analysis of the findings. Their overall conclusion is that such volunteer-only experiments encourage us to make a pronouncement on whether a programme works without knowledge of the make-up of the volunteers. The crucial point is that 'programs tend to work for some groups more than others, but the methodology then directs attention away from an investigation of these characteristics and towards . . . the battle to maintain the equivalence of the two subsets of this self-selected group' (p. 40).

## A way forward?

We have, then, a serious dilemma. On the one hand, the messages that come from RCTs are undoubtedly invested with considerable value by many audiences. As we appear to be approaching a situation where governments and other decision-making bodies are more receptive to evidence from research findings, why not use RCTs? On the other hand, the track record for RCTs in social research is unfortunately very poor. Even Oakley (2000), in arguing for their use, accepts the continuing equivocal nature of their findings, while putting forward some proposals for improving them. We are in danger of repeating the cycle of enthusiasm–disillusion experienced by educational experimenters in the 1920s and 1930s and evaluation research in the USA in the 1960s and 1970s.

A possible way forward is via the realist mantra of establishing 'what works, for whom, and in which contexts' rather than looking for overall effects of social programmes, interventions, etc. Establishing the likely operative mechanisms for different groups or types of participants in particular situations and settings renders it feasible to set up circumstances where large effects are obtained. In other words, the experiment is retained as the tool for obtaining quantitative confirmation of something that we already know to exist (or have a strong intuition or hunch as to its existence).

How is this actually done? Pawson and Tilley (1997), discussing these matters largely in the context of large-scale evaluative research, advocate the use of sub-group analysis. With large numbers of participants, it becomes feasible to set up contrasts between sub-groups illustrating and substantiating the differential effects of mechanisms on different sub-groups.

For the small-scale studies on which this text focuses, and in real world settings where relevant previous work may be sparse or non-existent, there is much to be said for a *combined strategy design*, with an initial flexible design stage that is primarily exploratory in purpose. This seeks to establish, both from discussions with professionals, participants and others involved in the initial phase, and from the empirical data gathered, likely 'bankers' for mechanisms operating in the situation, contexts where they are likely to operate, and the characteristics of participants best targeted. The second, fixed design, phase then incorporates a highly focused experiment or other fixed design study. An RCT may be the design of choice for this second phase under some circumstances:

- when the sponsor of the research, and/or important decision-makers, consider the evidence from an RCT to be required (either for their own purposes or to help in making a case to others), *and*
- when the establishment of randomized experimental and control groups is feasible practically and ethically, *and*
- when it appears unlikely that there will be differential effects on the experimental or control groups unconnected to the intervention itself (e.g. persons within the control group become disaffected or disgruntled because of their non-selection for the experimental group).

Note that the sub-group for which a particular mechanism is considered likely to be operative (as established in the initial phase) should form the basis for the pool of volunteers from which the experimental and control groups are randomly formed. Where feasible, similar restrictions can be placed on the contexts so that they are equivalent for the two groups.

If one or other of the three circumstances does not obtain, then other designs can be considered. If randomization can be achieved, then a true experiment involving two or more comparison groups (rather than an experimental and a control group) has attractions. This may be the case, for example, when the initial work indicates that a particular enabling mechanism is likely to operate in one context but not in a different one, or that a disabling mechanism operates in the second. This avoids problems in establishing 'non-intervention' control groups.

Where there are problems, of whatever kind, in achieving randomization, quasi-experimental designs remain feasible. A control group design might be used, with efforts being made to ensure as far as possible that the experimental and control groups are closely equivalent (particularly in aspects identified during the initial phase as being of relevance to the operation of the mechanisms involved; this might be done, for example, by using selected participants for the two groups for whom a particular mechanism appears salient). Quasi-experimental designs can be used in situations where a mechanism is considered to be likely to be operative with one set or sub-group of participants but not with a second sub-group, or where an additional disabling mechanism is thought to be operative in the second sub-group. The initial exploratory phase is used not only to build up a picture of the likely enabling and disabling mechanisms, but also to find a way of typifying or categorizing the best ways in which participants might be grouped to illustrate the operation of these mechanisms. Randomized allocation of participants is, of course, not possible when a comparison between different sub-groups is being made.

Single case designs lend themselves well to a realist reconceptualization. The strategy of thoroughly analysing and understanding the situation so that reliable and reproducible effects can be achieved bears a striking resemblance to the methodology developed by the experimental psychologist B. F. Skinner (Sidman, 1960), even though the terminology and underlying philosophy are very different (see the discussion on p. 146). Similarly, the various non-experimental fixed designs can be viewed through realist eyes. In particular, they lend themselves to the type of sub-group analyses advocated by Pawson and Tilley (1997).

The designs discussed below should be looked at through the critical realist perspective considered here. While they bear more than a passing resemblance to traditional positivist-based experimental and non-experimental designs (and can be used in this traditional manner by those who have not yet seen the realist light), there are major hidden differences. As discussed above, the participants involved in the different groups, the situations, circumstances and contexts, and the aspects of an intervention or programme that are targeted are all carefully selected and refined in the interests of obtaining substantial clear differential effects. This is simply a rephrasing of the statement that fixed designs are theory-driven with which this chapter opened.

A highly focused study can be set up following an initial exploratory phase where hunches and hypotheses about the likely mechanisms and contexts and those participants for whom the mechanisms will operate are investigated. Alternatively, it might be based on an approach modelled on earlier work; or on your own intimate experience of the working of a programme or intervention; or on discussions with those who have that experience and understanding. It is worth noting that this is the common approach taken in the natural sciences. The actual experiment to test a theory is the culmination of much prior thought and exploration, hidden in the textbook rationalizations of the scientific method and the conventions of experimental report-writing.

A successful experiment with clear differential outcomes is supporting evidence for the causal mechanisms we proposed when designing the study, and a contribution to understanding where, how, and with whom they operate.

## True Experiments

A small number of simple designs are presented here. Texts on experimental design give a range of alternatives, and of more complex designs (e.g. Kirk, 1995; Maxwell and Delaney, 1999). Carlsson et al. (1997) and Diaper (1990) are examples of studies using this type of design (see also box 4.1, p. 84).

> *Often those involved in real world experimentation restrict themselves to the very simplest designs, commonly the 'two group' design given below. However, the main hurdle in carrying out true experiments outside the laboratory is in achieving the principle of random allocation. Once this is achieved there may be merit in considering a somewhat more complex design.*

Box 5.5 provides an overview of the main true experimental designs considered in this section.

### The post-test-only, two group RCT design

Participants are randomly assigned to the experimental treatment group or to a comparison group, as explained in box 5.6. If the comparison group is not subjected to any specific treatment (a 'no treatment' control), this is one version of the randomized control trial (RCT). The size of the effect of the treatment is assessed by comparing the results of the two post-tests.

This is probably the simplest true experimental design. Several possible threats to internal validity can be ruled out, as well as the *selection* threat covered by random allocation. *Maturation* (e.g. effects of development, ageing, fatigue) can be ruled out if both groups are tested at the same time after random allocation. Similarly, *history* can be eliminated if both groups are involved with the experiment over the same period, as can *instrumentation* if both groups were tested or observed using the same instrument.

Minor variants of the design are possible involving two or more treatment groups, as shown in box 5.7. Here the difference between the two post-tests provides an assessment of the differential effects of the two treatments. It could in fact be argued that the single treatment design is better represented in this way, as any comparison group will have something happening to it in the

# Box 5.5

## Overview of a range of true experimental designs

*Note*: The defining characteristic of a *true* experimental design is random allocation of participants to the two (or more) groups of the design

1   *Two group designs*

a   *Post-test-only randomized controlled trial (RCT)*   Random allocation
of participants to an *experimental group* (given the experimental
'treatment') and a 'no treatment' *control group*. Post-tests of the two
groups compared.

b   *Post-test-only two treatment comparison*   Random allocation of participants to *experimental group 1* (given experimental 'treatment' 1),
or to *experimental group 2* (given experimental 'treatment' 2). Post-
tests of the two groups compared.

c   *Pre-test post-test randomized controlled trial (RCT)*   Random
allocation of participants to an *experimental group* (given the experimental 'treatment') and a 'no treatment' *control group*. Pre-test
to post-test changes of individuals in the two groups compared.

d   *Pre-test post-test two treatment comparison*   Random allocation of
participants to *experimental group 1* (given experimental 'treatment'
1), or to *experimental group 2* (given experimental 'treatment' 2).
Pre-test to post-test changes of individuals in the two groups
compared.

2   *Three- (or more) group simple designs*
It is possible to extend any of the above two group designs by including
additional experimental groups (given different experimental 'treatments').
The RCTs retain a 'no treatment' *control group*.

3   *Factorial designs*
Two (or more) independent variables (IVs) involved (e.g. 'type of music'
and 'number of decibels'). Each IV studied at two (or more) 'levels'.
Random allocation of participants to groups covering all possible combinations of levels of the different IVs. Can be post-test only or pre-test
post-test.

4   *Parametric designs*
Several 'levels' of an IV covered with random allocation of participants to
groups to get a view of the effect of the IV over a range of values. Can be
post-test only or pre-test post-test.

**5**  *Matched pairs designs*
Establishing pairs of participants with similar scores on a varaible known
to be related to the dependent variable (DV) of the experiment. Random
allocation of members of the pairs to different experimental groups (or to
an experimental and control group). This approach can be used in several
two group designs. Attractive, but can introduce complexities both in
setting up and interpretation.

**6**  *Repeated measures designs*
Designs where the same participant is tested under two or more experimental treatments or conditions (or in both an experimental and control
condition). Can be thought of as the extreme example of a matched pairs
design.

---

## Box 5.6

### The post-test-only, two group RCT design

**1**  Set up an 'experimental group' and a 'comparison group' using random
assignment.

**2**  The experimental group gets the 'treatment'; the comparison group
gets no special treatment.

**3**  Give 'post-tests' (i.e. after the experimental group's 'treatment') to
both groups.

---

## Box 5.7

### The post-test-only, two group design, used to compare two treatments

**1**  Set up 'experimental group 1' and 'experimental group 2' using random
assignment.

**2**  Experimental group 1 gets 'treatment 1'; experimental group 2 gets
'treatment 2'.

**3**  Give 'post-tests' (i.e. after the 'treatment') to both groups.

period between allocation and observation. More complicated designs could involve two or more treatment conditions.

### The pre-test-post-test two group RCT design

This design incorporates an additional set of observations (pre-tests) before the experimental treatment. If a 'no treatment' control is employed, this is another version of the randomized controlled trial (RCT), as shown in box 5.8. While there are several advantages of the pre-tests, there are also disadvantages. The advantages are fairly obvious. There is a direct check on the effectiveness of random allocation in producing groups which are equivalent on the measure chosen. If the groups prove not to be equivalent, it is possible to apply a statistical adjustment to the post-treatment observations which may give a fairer assessment of the size of the effect of the treatment. The design also gives the opportunity of using the pre–post differences in individual participants as a basis for assessing the effect of the treatment. This provides a means of taking into account individual differences and hence can provide a more sensitive measure of treatment effects.

The main disadvantage, apart from the additional work involved in carrying out the pre-tests, is that they may in some way sensitize those taking part, so that their subsequent post-tests are affected (the 'testing' threat to internal validity). This is of particular concern if there is a differential effect between treatment and control groups, as this may well be mistaken for an effect of the treatment itself. There is no easy way of determining whether or not this has taken place beyond assessing its plausibility in each individual study.

---

## Box 5.8

### The pre-test, post-test, two group RCT design

1   Set up an 'experimental group' and a 'comparison group' using random assignment.

2   Give 'pre-tests' (i.e. before the experimental group's 'treatment') to both groups.

3   The experimental group gets the 'treatment'; the comparison group gets no special treatment.

4   Give 'post-tests' (i.e. after the experimental group's 'treatment') to both groups.

---

As with the first design, variants are possible, for example, using two or more treatment groups, or two or more treatment groups and a control group.

## Factorial designs

Factorial designs involve more than one independent variable. Such variables necessarily have more than one value or level (in the simplest form, this would be the presence or absence of the variable – perhaps a certain level of noise, or no noise at all). The factorial design involves all possible combinations of the levels of the different independent variables. Thus a relatively simple factorial experiment with, say, three independent variables, one having two levels, one with three, and one with five, would have thirty (two, times three, times five) combinations of treatment levels.

As things can easily get out of control with this number of combinations, let us restrict ourselves to the simple, and common, two by two design, represented in box 5.9. This is 'two by two' in the sense that there are two independent variables, each of which has two levels. The four resulting treatments represent all possible combinations of levels of the independent variables. This design enables one to assess the size of the effect, separately, of each of the independent variables (known as its 'main effect') and also whether the effect of one variable differs from one level to another of the second variable. If there is such a change of effect, this is known as an 'interaction' between the variables, as exemplified in figure 5.2.

---

## Box 5.9

### A post-test only factorial design

1  Set up four experimental groups using random assignment.

2  Experimental group 1 gets the treatment with both independent variables at level 1;

Experimental group 2 gets the treatment with independent variable A at level 1 and independent variable B at level 2;
Experimental group 3 gets the treatment with independent variable A at level 2 and independent variable B at level 1;
Experimental group 4 gets the treatment with independent variable A at level 2 and independent variable B at level 2.

3  Give post-tests to all four groups.

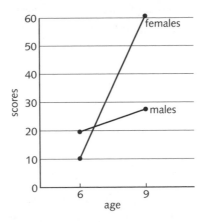

**Figure 5.2** Example of an interaction. The difference between male and female scores is not constant: it depends on age. i.e. the effect of one variable (gender) depends on the level of the second variable (age).

The simple factorial design is effectively an extension of the first, simple two group design. It would be possible to incorporate pre-testing into the design, as in the pre-test post-test design.

## Parametric designs

A parametric design involves incorporating a range of several levels or values of an independent variable into the experiment so that a fuller picture of its effect can be obtained. A simple parametric design is shown in box 5.10. It is, of course, possible to include a 'no treatment' comparison, and/or pre-tests, into the design.

## Designs involving matching

In its simplest form, the *matched pairs design*, matching involves testing participants on some variable which is known to be related to the dependent variable on which observations are being collected in the experiment. The results of this test are then used to create 'matched pairs' of subjects, that is, participants giving identical or very similar scores on the related variable.

Random assignment is then used to allocate one member of each pair to the treatment group and one to the comparison group. In this simplest form, the design can be considered as an extension to the simple two group

---

## Box 5.10

### A single-variable, post-test only, parametric design

**1** Set up a number (say five) of experimental groups using random assignment.

**2** Experimental group 1 gets the treatment at level 1 of the independent variable;

Experimental group 2 gets the treatment at level 2 of the independent variable;
Experimental group 3 gets the treatment at level 3 of the independent variable;
Experimental group 4 gets the treatment at level 4 of the independent variable;
Experimental group 5 gets the treatment at level 5 of the independent variable.

**3** Give post-tests to all five groups.

---

design, but with randomization being carried out on a pair basis rather than on a group basis. The principle can be easily extended to other designs, although of course if there are, say, four groups in the design, then 'matched fours' have to be created and individuals randomly assigned from them to the four groups.

While the selection and choice of a good matching variable may pose difficult problems in a field experiment, it is an attractive strategy because it helps to reduce the problem of differences between individuals obscuring the effects of the treatment in which you are interested. Generally, we need all the help we can get to detect treatment effects in the poorly controlled field situation, and matching can help without setting strong restrictions on important variables (which could have the effect of limiting the generalizability of your findings). To take a simple example, suppose that age is a variable known to be strongly related to the dependent variable in which you are interested. It would be possible to control for age as a variable by, say, working only with people between 25 and 30 years old. However, creating matched age pairs allows us to carry out a relatively sensitive test without the conclusions being restricted to a particular and narrow age range.

In practice, it is often difficult to come up with a good matching variable. In this aspect, as in so much of experimental design, the need for careful pre-planning and thought, and in particular, exploration of the topic or subject of interest through other approaches, is crucial.

There are other possible disadvantages of matching beyond the purely practical one of finding a good matching variable. The observation or measurement necessary to establish someone's position on a matching variable may be very similar to pre-testing. Hence there are the issues about whether or not the testing affects the person's subsequent performance in the experiment itself. When deciding whether the 'testing for matching' is likely to make someone approach the experiment in a different way – and in particular whether 'treatment' participants are differentially affected from 'control' participants – each situation has to be considered carefully and individually. Finding out a person's age and using that for matching purposes, particularly if it is collected among other demographic information, is unlikely to have this kind of effect. Having, say, some form of 'anxiety' test prior to a relatively stressful experimental treatment could well sensitize participants and affect their subsequent performance.

## Designs involving repeated measures

The ultimate in matching is achieved when an individual's performance is compared under two or more conditions. Designs with this feature are known as *repeated measures* designs. We have come across this already in one sense in the 'before and after' design – although the emphasis there is not on the before and after scores per se, but on the relative difference between them in the treatment and comparison groups as a measure of the treatment effect.

These are very seductive designs, but they do suffer from severe problems. Their attraction lies not only in the near-perfection of the matching – the person undergoing the two or more treatments or whatever in the experiment has the same heredity, environment, age, personality, gender, etc., etc., but also in your getting more data from fewer subjects. The problems stem from the central fact that the individual has more than one involvement in the experiment. Almost inevitably, this introduces a possible *order effect*. One treatment is undergone first, the other second. It may be that whatever is first results in a tendency to a superior performance to that which comes after – perhaps some kind of 'fatigue' effect. Or there can be the reverse tendency – some kind of 'practice' effect. Additionally, there may be some specific effect on the second treatment, resulting from the particular nature of whatever is done first – usually referred to as a 'carry-over' effect. This may be a short-term effect, say, resulting from some drug treatment, or longer-term, such as being led to approach a problem in a different way.

Order effects can be minimized by careful attention to detail. Practice effects can be reduced by incorporating substantial pre-experimental practice; fatigue effects by ensuring that the demands within the experiment are unlikely to tax the subjects. Likely carry-over effects will be highly specific to the types of treatment used, as will the approach to minimizing them, although in general this calls for increasing the time interval between treatments. Notwithstanding your best efforts, it is impossible to ensure that order effects are not present. An obvious strategy is to ensure that different subjects carry out the treatments in different orders. One approach is to determine randomly, for each participant, which treatment they undergo first, which second, and so on if there are more than two treatments. In its pure form, randomization will not ensure that the order effect is balanced, in the sense that equal numbers of subjects follow the different orderings. Any particular randomization exercise may have different numbers in the groups, although if the exercise were carried out repeatedly, they would tend to equality.

The solution more usually advocated for dealing with order effects is *counter-balancing*. This means adopting some system whereby participants are randomly assigned to different orders of carrying out the treatments so that the order effect is balanced out. This is illustrated, for the simple two group design, in box 5.11. The change from a pure randomization approach to a counter-balancing one may seem minimal, but it has substantial implications for the type of analyses which are possible and appropriate. Technically, this type of factorial design is called a *mixed design*: that is, it includes both a 'between subjects' independent variable (i.e. one where there are different groups of participants for the different treatments), as well as a 'repeated measures' independent variable. More complex designs involve more than one of each type of variable.

Box 5.12 gives some suggestions for choosing among true and randomized experimental designs when working outside the laboratory. Cook and Campbell (1979) have discussed some of the real world situations which are conducive to carrying out randomized experiments. Box 5.13 is based on their suggestions.

---

## Box 5.11

### A simple repeated measures design, using counter-balancing

1  Set up two experimental groups using random assignment.

2  Group 1 gets treatment 1 followed by treatment 2. Group 2 gets treatment 2 followed by treatment 1.

3  Both groups are tested after they have received the first treatment (whichever that is), and after the second treatment.

# Box 5.12

## Considerations in choosing among true experimental designs

**1** *To do any form of true experimental design you need to be able to carry out random assignment to the different treatments.* This is normally random assignment of *persons* to treatments (or of persons to the order in which they receive different treatments, in repeated measures designs). Note, however, that the unit which is randomly assigned need not be the person; it could be a group (e.g. a school class), in which case the experiment, and its analysis, is on classes, not individuals.

**2** *Use a matched design when*:

a   you have a matching variable which correlates highly with the dependent variable;
b   obtaining the scores on the matching variable is unlikely to influence the treatment effects; and
c   individual differences between subjects are likely to mask treatment effects.

**3** *Use a repeated measures design when*:

a   order effects appear unlikely;
b   the independent variable(s) of interest lend themselves to repeated measurement (subject variables such as sex, ethnic background or class don't – it is not easy to test the same person as a man and as a woman);
c   in real life, persons would be likely to be exposed to the different treatments; and
d   individual differences between subjects are likely to mask treatment effects.

**4** *Use a simple two group design when*:

a   order effects are likely;
b   the independent variable(s) of interest don't lend themselves to repeated measurement;
c   in real life, persons would tend not to receive more than one treatment; and
d   persons might be expected to be sensitized by pre-testing or being tested on a matching variable.

5   *Use a before–after design when*:

a   pre-testing appears to be unlikely to influence the effect of the treatment;
b   there are concerns about whether random assignment has produced equivalent groups (e.g. when there are small numbers in the groups); and
c   individual differences between subjects are likely to mask treatment effects.

6   *Use a factorial design when*:

a   you are interested in more than one independent variable; and
b   interactions between independent variables may be of concern.

7   *Use a parametric design when*:

a   the independent variable(s) have a range of values or levels of interest; and
b   you wish to investigate the form or nature of the relationship between independent variable and dependent variable.

There are occasions when one starts out with a true experiment but along the way problems occur, perhaps in relation to assignment to conditions, or to mortality (loss of participants) from one or other group; or it may turn out that you don't have the time or resources to carry out what you originally intended. Such situations may be rescuable by reconceptualizing what you are proposing as one of the quasi-experiments discussed below.

## Quasi-experiments

The term 'quasi-experiment' has been used in various ways, but its rise to prominence in social experimentation originates with a very influential chapter by Campbell and Stanley in Gage's *Handbook of Research on Teaching*. This was republished as a separate slim volume (Campbell and Stanley, 1963). For them, a quasi-experiment is:

> *a research design involving an experimental approach but where random assignment to treatment and comparison groups has not been used.*

## Box 5.13

### Real life situations conducive to randomized experiments

**1**   *When lotteries are expected*   Lotteries are sometimes, though not commonly, regarded as a socially acceptable way of deciding who gets scarce resources. When done for essentially ethical reasons, it provides a good opportunity to use this natural randomization for research purposes.

**2**   *When demand outstrips supply*   This sets up a situation where randomized allocation may be seen as a fair and equitable solution. There are practical problems. Do you set up waiting lists? Or allow re-application? Cook and Campbell (1979) advocate using the initial randomization to create two equivalent no-treatment groups, as well as the treatment group. One no-treatment group is told that their application is unsuccessful, and that they cannot reapply. This group acts as the control group. The second no-treatment group is permitted to go on a waiting list, they are accepted for the treatment if a vacancy occurs, but data from them are not used.

**3**   *When an innovation cannot be introduced in units simultaneously*   Many innovations have to be introduced gradually, because of resource or other limitations. This provides the opportunity for randomization of the order of involvement. Substantial ingenuity may be called for procedurally to balance service and research needs, particularly when opportunities for involvement arise irregularly.

**4**   *When experimental units are isolated from each other*   Such isolation could be temporal or spatial – or simply because it is known that they do not communicate. Randomization principles can then be used to determine where or when particular treatments are scheduled.

**5**   *When it is agreed that change should take place but there is no consensus about solutions*   In these situations, decision-makers may be more receptive to arguments in favour of a system of planned variation associated with random allocation.

**6**   *When a tie can be broken*   In situations where access to a particular treatment is based upon performance on a task (e.g. for entry to a degree or other course), there will be a borderline. It may be that several persons are on that border (given the less than perfect reliability of any such task, this is more accurately a border region than a line). Randomization can be used to select from those at the border who then form the treatment and no-treatment control groups.

7 *When persons express no preference among alternatives* In situations where individuals indicate that they have no preference among alternative treatments, their random assignment to the alternatives is feasible. Note that you will be comparing the performance on the treatments of those without strong preferences, who may not be typical.

8 *When you are involved in setting up an organization, innovation, etc.* Many opportunities for randomization present themselves if you as researcher can get in on the early stages of a programme, organization or whatever. It would also help if guidelines for local and national initiatives were imbued with a research ethos, which would be likely to foster the use of randomization.

(After Cook and Campbell, 1979, pp. 371–86.)

Campbell and Stanley's main contribution to this topic was to show the value and usefulness of several such designs. More generally, they have encouraged a flexible approach to design and interpretation, where the particular pattern of results and circumstances under which the study took place interact with the design to determine what inferences can be made. Their concern is very much with the *threats to validity* present in such studies (see p. 105), and with the extent to which particular threats can be plausibly discounted in particular studies. Quasi-experimental approaches have considerable attraction for those seeking to maintain a basic experimental stance in work outside the laboratory.

The position taken by most writers on the topic (e.g. Judd et al., 1991) is that quasi-experiments are a second-best choice: a fall-back to consider when it is not possible to randomize allocation. Cook and Campbell (1979), however, prefer to stress the relative advantages and disadvantages of true and quasi-experiments, and are cautious about advocating randomized experiments even when they are feasible. They recommend considering all possible design options without necessarily assuming the superiority of a randomized design – and with the proviso that, if a randomized design is chosen then it should be planned in such a way as to be interpretable as a quasi-experimental design, just in case something goes wrong with the randomized design, as it may well do in the real world.

Box 5.14 provides an overview of the main types of quasi-experimental designs covered in the following section. Harrison et al. (1999), King and Kennedy (1999) and Monnickendam and Markus (1996) are examples of studies using quasi-experimental designs (see also box 4.1, p. 84).

# Box 5.14

## Overview of a range of quasi-experimental designs

*Note*: A *quasi-experimental design* follows the experimental approach to design but does not involve random allocation of participants to different groups. The following list outlines a few commonly used designs.

1   *Pre-experimental designs*

a   *Single-group post-test-only.*
b   *Post-test only non-equivalent groups* i.e. use of groups established by some procedure other than randomization (e.g. two pre-existing groups).
c   *Pre-test post-test single group design.*

These designs should be avoided owing to difficulties in interpreting their results (though they may be of value as part of a wider study, or as a pilot phase for later experimentation).

2   *Pre-test post-test non-equivalent group designs*
Two (or more) groups established on some basis other than random assignment. One of these might be a control group. Interpretation of findings more complex than with equivalent true experimental designs.

3   *Interrupted time series designs*
In its simplest (and most common) form, involves a single experimental group on which a series of measurements or observations are made before and after some form of experimental intervention. Requires a dependent variable on which repeated measures can be taken and an extended series of measurements.

4   *Regression-discontinuity designs*
All participants are pre-tested and those scoring below a criterion value are assigned to one group (say an experimental group); all those above that criterion are assigned to a second group (say a control group). The pattern of scores after the experimental intervention provides evidence for its effectiveness.

## Quasi-experimental designs to avoid – the 'pre-experiments'

Quasi-experimental designs are essentially defined negatively – as not true experimental designs. They include several which are definitely to be avoided, although these so-called 'pre-experimental' designs continue to get used, and even published. Three of them are presented here (in boxes 5.15, 5.16 and 5.17) to enable you to recognize and avoid them, and also because the reasons why they are problematic present useful methodological points.

The third of these, what I have termed the 'pre-test post-test single group' design, is commonly found, and it is important to stress that the deficiencies covered here concern its nature *as an experimental design*. If the concern is simply to determine whether there is an increase of performance after a treatment, or even to assess its statistical significance, there are no particular problems. The difficulty is in possible validity threats. They may be very appropriate and useful as pilot studies, to determine whether something is worth doing an experiment on.

## Quasi-experimental designs to consider

It is possible to get at a feasible quasi-experimental design by considering the main problems with the previous two designs – the 'post-test only non-

---

### Box 5.15

### Designs to avoid, no. 1: the one group post-test-only design

*Scenario*   A single experimental group is involved in the treatment and then given a post-test.

*Disadvantages*   As an experiment, where the only information that you have is about the outcome measure, this is a waste of time and effort. Without pre-treatment measures on this group or measures from a second no-treatment control group, it is virtually impossible to infer any kind of effect.

*Improvements*   Either improve the experimental design *or* adopt a case study methodology.

*Note*: This is not the same thing as a case study. Typically, the case study has multiple *sources* of data (both qualitative and quantitative) extending over time, and there is also information about the context.

---

## Box 5.16

### Designs to avoid, no. 2: the post-test-only non-equivalent groups design

*Scenario*   As no. 1 but with the addition of a second non-equivalent (not determined by random assignment) group that does not receive the treatment, i.e.:

1   Set up an experimental and a comparison group on some basis other than random assignment.
2   Administer the treatment to the experimental group but not to the comparison group.
3   Do post-tests on both groups.

*Disadvantages*   It is not possible to determine whether any difference in outcome for the two groups is due to the treatment, or to other differences between the groups.

*Improvements*   Strengthen the experimental design by incorporating a pre-test, or by using random assignment to the two groups; or use case study methodology.

---

equivalent groups' design, and the 'pre-test post-test single group' design. With the former, we do not know whether or not the two groups differ before the treatment; with the latter, we do not know how much the group would have changed from pre-test to post-test in the absence of the treatment.

One tactic used to strengthen the design is, effectively, to combine the two designs into a 'pre-test post-test non-equivalent groups' design. A second tactic is to make additional observations:

- over time with a particular group, leading to the 'interrupted time-series' design, *and/or*
- over groups at the same time, leading to the 'regression-discontinuity' design.

Both these designs are discussed below.

*Pre-test post-test non-equivalent groups design*   This design is represented in box 5.16. The pattern of pre-test and post-test results has to be investigated to assess the effectiveness of the treatment. It is a general rule of quasi-experimental designs that it is necessary to consider not only the design of a

---

## Box 5.17

### Designs to avoid, no. 3: the pre-test post-test single group design

*Scenario*   As no. 1, but with the addition of measurement on the same variable before the treatment as well as after it; i.e. the single experimental group is pre-tested, gets the treatment, and is tested again.

*Disadvantages*   Although widely used, it is subject to lots of problems. It is vulnerable to many threats to validity – including *history* (other events apart from the treatment occurring between measures), *maturation* (developments in the group between measures), *statistical regression* (e.g. choice of a group 'in need' in the sense of performing poorly on the measure used, or some other measure which correlates with it, will tend to show an improvement for random statistical reasons unconnected with the treatment).

*Improvements*   Strengthen the experimental design, e.g. by adding a second pre-tested no-treatment control group.

*Note*: It may be possible on particular occasions to show that this design *is* interpretable. This may be because the potential threats to validity have not occurred in practice: for example, if you can isolate the group so that other effects do not influence it; or if you have information that there are no pre-treatment trends in the measures you are taking – although strictly that type of information turns this into a kind of time series design (see p. 142).

---

study, but also the context in which it occurs, and the particular pattern of results obtained, when trying to decide whether a treatment has been effective. Note the similarities with the realist approach, e.g. in the emphasis on context and the importance of detailed analysis of what actually happens in a study, the stress on 'what works, for whom, and in what circumstances'. This is not surprising as Cook and Campbell (1979, pp. 28–36) endorse a critical realist approach and seek to move beyond positivist notions of causation in their analysis.

Box 5.19 illustrates and discusses some possible patterns. Note that the issue is again one of ruling out possible threats to validity.

*Seeking equivalent groups through matching*   A common strategy in this type of design is to use one or more matching variables to select a comparison or control group. This is different from the matching strategy used in true or randomized experiments, where the experimenter matches participants and randomly assigns one member of the matched pair to the treatment group and

---

## Box 5.18

### Pre-test post-test non-equivalent groups design

**1**   Set up an experimental group and a comparison group on some basis other than random assignment.

**2**   Give pre-tests to both groups.

**3**   The experimental group gets the 'treatment'; the comparison group gets no special treatment.

**4**   Give post-tests to both groups.

---

one to the comparison group. Here the researcher tries to find participants who match the participants who are receiving a treatment. This approach is unfortunately subject to the threat to internal validity known as *regression to the mean*. While this threat is always present when matching is used without random assignment, it shows itself particularly clearly in situations where some treatment intended to assist those with difficulties or disadvantage is being assessed. Suppose that a comparison is being made of the achievements of a 'disadvantaged' with a 'non-disadvantaged' control group. The pre-treatment levels of the disadvantaged population will almost inevitably differ from those of the non-disadvantaged population, with the strong likelihood that those of the disadvantaged population tend to be lower. Hence in selecting matched pairs from the two populations, we will be pairing individuals who are pretty high in the disadvantaged group with individuals pretty low in the non-disadvantaged group. Figure 5.3 indicates what is likely to be going on.

Because pre-test scores are not 100 per cent reliable (no scores ever are), they will incorporate some random or error factors. Those scoring relatively high in their population (as in the selected disadvantaged group) will have some tendency to have positive error factors inflating their pre-test score. Those scoring relatively low in their population (as in the selected non-disadvantaged group) will have some tendency to have negative error factors reducing their pre-test score. On post-test, however, such random factors (simply because they are random) will be just as likely to be positive as negative, leading to the 'regression to the mean' phenomenon – namely, that post-test scores of originally extreme groups tend to be closer to their population means.

As can be seen from figure 5.3, the effect of this is to produce a tendency for the disadvantaged groups to score lower *even in the absence of any treatment effects*. Depending on the relative size of this effect and any treatment effect, there will appear to be a reduced treatment effect, or zero, or even a negative one.

# Box 5.19

## Possible outcomes of a pre-test post-test non-equivalent groups design in relation to threats to validity

*Outcome A*

*Situation*: Experimental group starts higher.
*Outcome*: Increase in experimental group. No change in comparison group.
*Issue*: Plausibility that causally irrelevant variables are affecting the experimental group but not the comparison group.

*Outcome B*

*Situation*: Experimental group starts higher.
*Outcome*: Increase in experimental group. Smaller increase in comparison group.
*Issues*: It appears that the comparison group may be changing – is the experimental group with the pre-test advantage changing (maturing) at a faster rate irrespective of the experimental treatment?

*Outcome C*

*Situation*: Experimental group starts lower.
*Outcome*: Increase in experimental group. No change in comparison group.
*Issues*: Regression may be a threat, depending on how the groups have been selected. It may be implausible that an experimental group with a pre-test disadvantage 'matures' more rapidly.

*Outcome D*

*Situation*: Experimental group starts lower.
*Outcome*: Increase in experimental group taking it above the comparison group at post-test. No change in comparison group.
*Issue*: A highly desirable pattern from the point of view of making causal inferences. The switching of the two groups from pre- to post-test permits many threats to be ruled out.

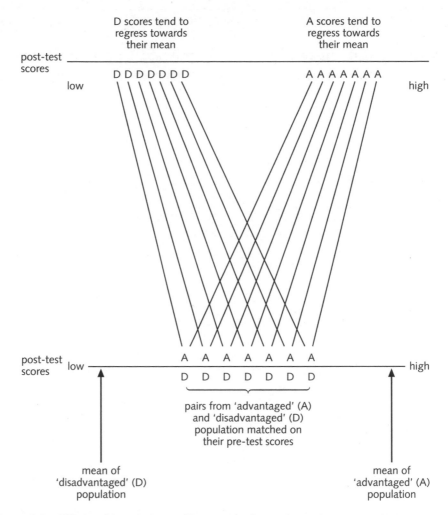

Figure 5.3 Effects of 'regression to the mean' when using extreme groups.

*Interrupted time-series design* In the simplest form of this design, there is just one experimental group, and a series of observations or tests before and after an experimental treatment. The time series approach is widely used in some branches of the social sciences (e.g. in economics) and has a well-developed and complex literature, particularly on the analysis of time series data (Franklin et al., 1996). Textbooks covering this field suggest rules of thumb for the number of data points needed in the before and after time series, typically coming up with figures of fifty or more.

This extent of data collection is likely to be outside the scope of the small-scale study targeted in this book. However, there are likely to be situations where, although fifty or so observations are not feasible, it is possible to carry out several pre- and post-tests. Certainly, some advantages accrue if even one additional pre- and/or post-test (preferably both) can be added. This is essentially because one is then gathering information about possible *trends* in the data, which help in countering several of the threats to the internal validity of the study.

With more data points, say five before and five after, the experimenter is in a much stronger position to assess the nature of the trend. Does the series appear to be stationary (i.e. show no trend to increase or decrease)? Or does it appear to increase, or decrease? And is this a linear trend, or is the slope itself tending to increase? And so on. Techniques for the analysis of such short time series are available, although not universally accepted (see chapter 13, p. 448). However, as with other quasi-experimental designs, their interpretation is based on a knowledge of the design itself in interaction with the particular pattern of results obtained, and contextual factors. Figure 5.4 illustrates a range of possible patterns of results.

Collecting data for a time series design can become a difficult and time-consuming task. The observations must be ones that can be made repeatedly without practical or methodological problems. Simple, non-obtrusive measures (e.g. of play in a school playground) are more appropriate than, say, the repeated administration of a formal test of some kind.

If pre-existing archive material of some kind is available, then it may be feasible to set up a time series design, even with an extended time series, at relatively low cost of time and effort for the experimenter. Increasingly, such material is gathered in conjunction with management information systems (see p. 361). However, very careful scrutiny will be required to establish its reliability and validity, and general usefulness, for research purposes. Generally it will have been gathered for other purposes (although if, as is sometimes the case, you are in a position to influence what is gathered and how it is gathered, this can be very helpful), which may well mean that it is inaccessible to you, or is systematically biased, or is being collected according to different criteria at different times, or by different people, or is inflexible and won't allow you to answer your research questions.

More complex time series designs are possible. For example, a non-equivalent comparison group can be added with the same series of pre- and post-treatment tests or observations being made for both groups. The main advantage of adding the control group is its ability to test for the 'history' threat. A 'selection–history interaction' is still possible, though: that is, that one of the two groups experiences a particular set of non-treatment-related events that the other does not. In general the plausibility of such a threat will depend on how closely comparable in setting and experiences the two groups are.

One way of discounting history-related threats is to use the group as its own control, and to take measures on a second dependent variable which

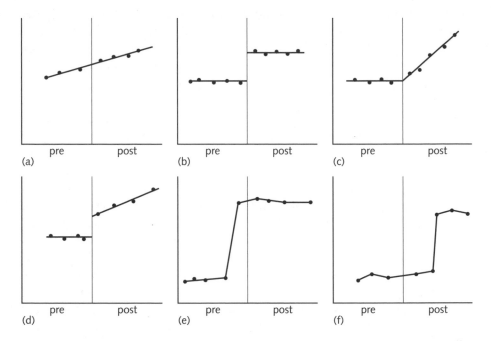

**Figure 5.4**   Patterns of possible results in a simple time series experiment. (a) No effect. Note that making single pre- and post-tests (or taking pre- and post-test averages) would suggest a spurious effect. (b) Clear effect. Stable pre and post – but at a different level. Several threats to validity still possible (e.g. history – something else may be happening at the same time as the treatment). (c) Again, clear effect, but of a different kind (move from stability to steady increase). Similar threats will apply. (d) Combines effects of (b) and (c). (e) 'Premature' and (f) 'delayed' effects. Such patterns cast serious doubts on the effects being causally linked to the treatment. Explanations should be sought (e.g. may get a 'premature' effect of an intervention on knowledge or skill, if participants are in some way preparing themselves for the intervention).

should not be affected by the treatment. Ross et al. (1970) used this design to analyse the effect of the introduction of the 'breathalyser' on traffic accidents. They argued that serious accidents should decrease, following the introduction of new legislation in Britain which brought in the 'breathalyser', *during the hours that pubs were open* (the 'experimental' dependent variable), but should be less affected during commuting hours when the pubs were shut (the 'control' dependent variable). They were able to corroborate this view, both by visual inspection of the time series and by statistical analysis.

Other time series designs involving the removal of treatment, and multiple and switching replications, have been used. A lot of the interest in these designs has been in connection with so-called 'single case' or 'single subject' research, particularly in the 'behaviour modification' field (e.g. Kratochwill, 1978).

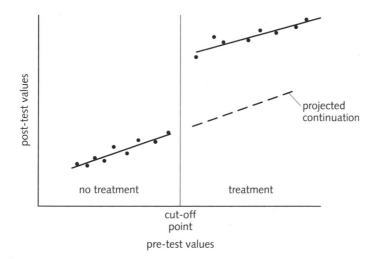

**Figure 5.5**    Illustrative outcome of a regression discontinuity design.

Although having their genesis in a very different area of the social sciences, time series designs show considerable similarities to *single case research designs* (see below).

*Regression discontinuity design*    This rather fearsomely named design is conceptually straightforward. As in the true experiment, a known assignment rule is used to separate out two groups. However, whereas with the true experiment this is done on a random basis, here some other principle is used. In probably its simplest form, all those scoring below a certain value on some criterion are allocated to, say, the experimental group; all those scoring above that value are allocated to the control group. Trochim (1984) gives details. Aiken et al. (1998) provide an example, in a study which also includes a randomized experiment and a non-equivalent control group design.

It might be, for example, that entry to some compensatory programme is restricted to those scoring below a particular cut-off point on some relevant test; or, conversely, that entrance scholarships are given to those scoring above some cut-off. Figure 5.5 illustrates a possible outcome for this type of design. As with other quasi-experimental designs, the pattern of outcome, design and context must be considered when seeking to interpret the results of a particular experiment.

There is a superficial similarity between the graphs obtained with this design and those for the time series design. Note, however, that, whereas the latter show time on the horizontal axis of the graph, the regression discontinuity design has pre-test scores along this axis. The issues are in both cases about trends in the data: are they present, do they differ and so on. 'Eyeballing' the data, i.e. inspecting them visually to assess this, forms a valuable part of the analysis, although most would argue that this examination needs to be supplemented by more formal statistical analysis. Conceptually, the analyses for the two designs are equivalent, although different statistical techniques have to be used.

## Concluding thoughts on quasi-experimental designs

Quasi-experimentation is more of a style of investigation than a slavish following of predetermined designs. The designs covered above should be seen simply as suggestions for starting points. If you are not in a position to do true experiments, then with sufficient ingenuity you ought to be able to carry out a quasi-experiment to counter those threats to internal validity that are likely to be problematic.

## Single Case Experiments

A distinctive approach to carrying out experiments originated in the work of B. F. Skinner (e.g. Skinner, 1938, 1974). It has subsequently been developed by his followers, variously known as (among other labels) Skinnerians, radical behaviourists or operant conditioners. Sidman (1960) has produced a very clear, though partisan, account of this approach, concentrating on the methodological issues and strategies involved. The work of Skinner arouses strong passions, and in consequence his approach to experimental design tends to be either uncritically adopted or cursorily rejected.

There is much of value here for the 'real world' investigator with a leaning to the experimental – mixed, as in Skinner's other work, with the unhelpfully polemical, the quirky and the rather silly. The approach is variously labelled, commonly as 'small-N', 'single subject' or 'single case' design. The last of these descriptions has the virtue, which would probably have been resisted by Skinner (Robson, 1985), of making the point that the 'case' need not necessarily be the individual person; it could, for example, be the individual school class, or the school itself. It does, however, carry the possibility of confusion with 'case study', which, as defined in this book, is a multimethod enterprise (though this may incorporate a single case experiment within it). Barlow et al. (1984) have coined the term 'time series methodology', which to some extent blurs the distinction between case study and single case experiment. It may be of considerable value to plan studies incorporating both of these traditionally divided approaches.

Having warned of the possibility of confusion with 'case study' we will stick, then, to 'single case experimental designs', while acknowledging that Barlow et al.'s term does make it clear that such designs depend crucially on *repeated measures on the same individuals over time, typically before, during and after an intervention.* Concentration on the individual rather than the group is crucial for Skinner. His search was for a methodology and technology which produced meaningful, reliable data at the level of the individual – and which didn't require the 'monstrous engines' of statistical testing to decide whether or not an effect was present. Franklin et al. (1996), as part of a detailed discussion of the design and analysis of single case experiments, cover the difficult area of the kind of statistical analyses which are appropriate for data from these types of experiment.

Box 5.20 gives an overview of the main types of single case design covered in this section. Many examples of studies using these designs can be found in the *Journal of Applied Behavior Analysis.* They include Engelmann et al. (1999); see also box 4.1, p. 84.

The design approach is in essence straightforward. Starting from the simplest, designs include the following.

## A–B design

Note that the terminology is different from that used in the previous designs, but is well established. This is essentially a *two-condition design.* The first condition (A) is referred to as the *base-line*; the second condition (B) corresponds to the treatment. Both conditions are 'phases' which extend over time, and a sequence of tests or observations will be taken in each phase.

The investigator looks for a clear difference in the pattern of performance in the two phases – this being an actual 'look', as typically the data are 'eye-balled' by Skinnerians, who have a principled antipathy to statistical analysis. A distinctive feature of the Skinnerian approach is that the base-line phase is supposed to be continued until stability is reached: that is, there is no trend over time. In practice, this is not always achieved. The restriction to a stable base-line obviously assists in the interpretation of the data, but even so, the design is weak and subject to several validity threats (e.g. history–treatment interaction). *Because of this, the design is probably best regarded as 'pre-experimental', with the same strictures on its use as with the other pre-experimental designs* considered in the preceding section on quasi-experiments (p. 137). The design can be strengthened in ways analogous to those employed in quasi-experimental design – effectively extending the series of phases either over time, or cross-sectionally over different base-lines.

The pragmatic question also arises whether the necessary base-line stability can in fact be achieved, although Skinnerians would consider it an essential

# Box 5.20

## Overview of a range of single case designs

*Note*: These designs call for a series of measures on a dependent variable (DV) (or, more rarely, on two or more such variables). Typically the study is repeated with a small number of participants to establish the replicability of the findings.

### 1   *A–B designs*
Base-line phase (A) of a sequence of observations prior to intervention followed by a second phase where the intervention is introduced (B) and a further sequence of observations. Effectiveness of intervention shown by difference in observations made in B from those made in A (note similarity to interrupted time series design).

### 2   *A–B–A designs*
As A–B but adding a third phase which reverts to pre-intervention base-line condition (A).

### 3   *A–B–A–B designs*
Addition of a second intervention phase (B) to A–B–A design. Avoids possible ethical problems of finishing with a return to base-line.

### 4   *Multiple base-line designs*

a   *Across settings*   A DV is measured or observed in two or more situations (e.g. at home and at school). Change is made from a base-line condition (A) to the intervention (B) at different times in the different settings.

b   *Across behaviours*   Two or more behaviours are measured or observed. Change is made from a base-line condition (A) to the intervention (B) at different times for the different behaviours.

c   *Across participants*   Two or more participants are measured or observed. Change is made from a base-line condition (A) to the intervention (B) at different times for the different behaviours.

Additional phases can be added leading to multiple base-line versions of the A–B–A and A–B–A–B designs.

feature of experimental control that conditions be found where there is stability. As with lengthy time series designs, this approach presupposes an observation or dependent variable where it is feasible to have an extended series of measures. Skinnerians would insist on the dependent variable being *rate of response*, but this appears to be more of a historical quirk than an essential design feature.

## A–B–A design

This improves upon the previous design by adding a *reversal* phase – the second A phase. The central notion is that the investigator removes the treatment (B) and looks for a return to base-line performance. Given a stable pretreatment base-line, a clear and consistent shift from this during the second phase, and a return to a stable base-line on the reversal, the investigator is on pretty strong ground for inferring a causal relationship.

The problems occur when this does not happen, particularly when there is not a return to base-line in the final phase. This leaves the experimenter seeking explanations for the changes that occurred during the second phase other than that they were caused by the treatment (B); or evaluating other possible explanations for the failure to return, such as carry-over effects from the treatment. The design is also open to ethical objections, particularly when used in an applied setting. Is it justifiable deliberately to remove a treatment when this appears to be effective? This is not too much of an issue when the goal of an enquiry is to establish or demonstrate some phenomenon, but when the intention is to help someone, many practitioners would have reservations about this design.

## A–B–A–B design

A simple, though not entirely adequate, answer to the ethical problems raised by the preceding design is to add a further treatment phase. In this way, the person undergoing the study ends up with the – presumed beneficial – treatment. Figure 5.6 provides an example.

Each sequential addition to the pattern of base-line and treatment phases, with regular and consistent changes observed to be associated with the phases, adds to confidence about the causal relationship between treatment and outcome. There is no reason in principle why this AB alternation should not continue as ABABAB – or longer. However, it does involve extra time and effort which could probably be better spent in other directions. The design does also still call for the treatment to be withdrawn during the sequence, and there are alternative designs which avoid this.

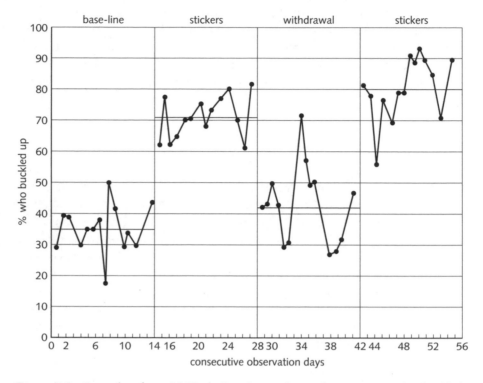

**Figure 5.6**  Example of an ABAB design: 'percentage of passengers who buckled up over 56 consecutive observation days, two weeks per consecutive base-line, intervention, withdrawal and intervention phase'.

*Note*: Group data are shown here rather than those for single subjects (which would not have been feasible in this study). This would be frowned upon by Skinnerian purists.

*Source*: Thyer and Geller (1987).

## Multiple base-line designs

The approach in this design involves the application of the treatment at different points in time to different base-line conditions. If there is a corresponding change in the condition to which the treatment is applied, and *no change in the other conditions* at that time, then there is a strong case that the change is causally related to the treatment.

Three versions of the design are commonly employed: multiple base-lines *across settings, across behaviours* and *across participants*.

- In the across settings design, a particular dependent variable (behaviour) of a participant is monitored in a range of different settings or situations and the treatment is introduced at a different time in each of the settings.

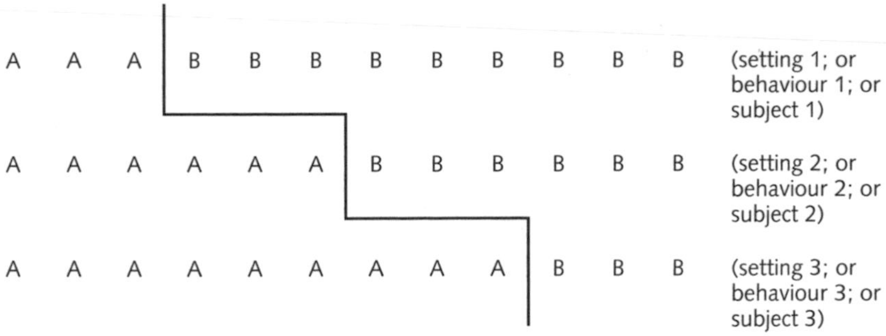

**Figure 5.7**   The multiple base-line design.

- In the across behaviours design, data are collected on several dependent variables (behaviours) for a particular participant and the treatment is applied at different times to each of the behaviours.
- In the across participants design, data are collected on a particular base-line condition for several participants and the treatment is applied at different times to the different participants.

The general approach is illustrated in figure 5.7 and a specific example given in figure 5.8.

## Further single case designs

Other designs have been used and are briefly explained here.

*Changing criterion designs*   A criterion for performance is specified as a part of the intervention. That criterion is changed over time in a pre-specified manner, usually progressively in a particular direction. The effect of the intervention is demonstrated if the behaviour changes to match the changes in criterion.

This design has not been widely used but appears attractive in interventions where the intention is to achieve a progressive reduction of some problem behaviour, or progressive increase in some desired behaviour. It is probably most useful for situations involving complex behaviours, or where the intention is to try to achieve some major shift from what the person involved is currently doing. Certainly the notion of 'successive approximations' which is built in to this design sits very naturally with the 'shaping of behaviour' approach central to Skinnerian practice and applicable by others.

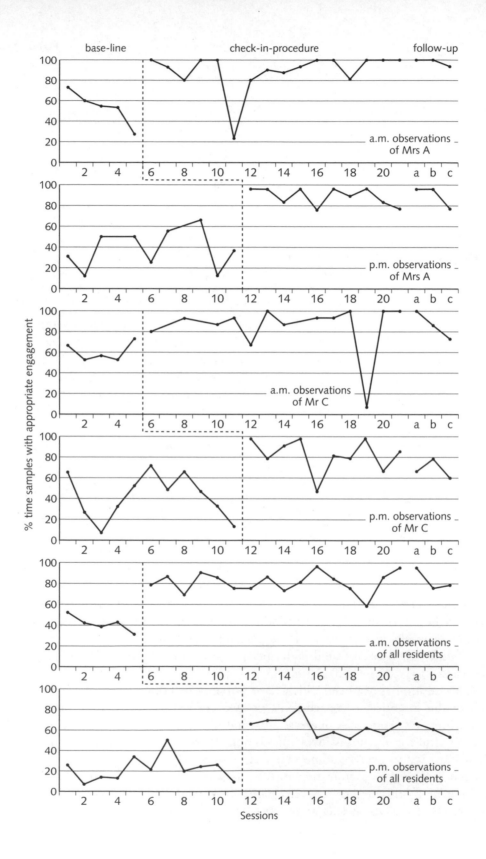

*Multiple treatment designs*    These involve the implementation of two or more treatments designed to affect a single behaviour. So, rather than a treatment being compared with its absence (which is effectively what base-line comparisons seek to achieve), there are at least two separate treatments whose effects are compared. In its simplest form, this would be ABC – i.e. a base-line condition (A), followed in sequence by two treatment conditions (B and C). This could be extended in several ways: ABCA or ABACA or ABACABCA, etc. The last pattern yields some kind of assessment of 'multiple treatment interference' – the extent to which there are sequence effects, where being exposed to one condition has a subsequent influence on the apparent effect of a subsequent condition.

There are several more complex variants. In one (known as a *multiple schedule design*), each treatment or intervention is associated in a consistent way, probably for a substantial number of times, with a particular 'stimulus' (e.g. a particular person, setting or time) so that it can be established whether or not the stimulus has consistent control over performance. An alternative (known variously as a *simultaneous treatment or alternating treatment design*) is for each of the settings to be balanced across stimulus conditions (persons, settings or times) so that each of the settings has been associated equivalently with each of the stimuli. This then permits one to disentangle the effects of the settings from 'stimulus' effects. Kazdin (1982) gives details. These designs have several advantages. As the main concern is for differential effects on the two conditions, the establishment of a stable base-line becomes less crucial. In the two latter variants, there is no need for treatment to be withdrawn or removed, and the relative effects of the different conditions can be determined without the need for lengthy successive involvement with different phases.

It is possible to generate what might be called 'combined designs' by putting together features from the individual designs considered above. For example, an ABAB design could be combined with a multiple base-line approach. Barlow et al. (1984) present a very helpful approach in terms of 'design elements' which can be combined in a variety of ways to generate tailor-made designs.

The general approach taken to design in single case experimentation bears some similarities to that taken in quasi-experimentation. There is concern for specific threats to validity which might make the study difficult or impossible

**Figure 5.8**    Example of a multiple base-line design. The percentage of time samples with appropriate engagement for Mrs A and Mr C, and mean aggregate data for all five residents. The dotted line indicates when each CNA was trained to conduct the check-in procedure.

*Source:* Figure 1 in Engelman et al. (1999).

to interpret, particularly in relation to causality. These are taken into account in developing the design. However, there is often substantially greater flexibility and willingness to modify the design than is found in other types of experimentation. It is common to review and possibly alter the design in the light of the pattern of data which is emerging. Decisions such as when to move from one phase to another are made in this way. The attraction of a combined design is that additional or changed design features (which can counter particular threats to validity) can be introduced reactively to resolve specific ambiguities.

This approach is foreign to the traditional canons of fixed design research, where a design is very carefully pre-planned and then rigidly adhered to. Interestingly, it has similarities to the flexible designs discussed in the next chapter.

There are also similarities between single case experimentation and the way in which experiments are carried out in some branches of the natural sciences, as discussed in chapter 2. Statistics play little part; the trick is so to set up the situation, through control of extraneous variables that would cloud the issue, so that the cause–effect relationship shines out for all to see; in realist terms ensuring the context is such that the mechanism(s) operate. It may be necessary to 'fine-tune' your study so that unforeseen eventualities can be accounted for. With sufficient experimental skill and understanding, you should be able to find out something of general importance about the specific focus of your study (whether this happens to be a person or a lump of iron). You will need to test it out on a few individuals just to assure yourself of typicality.

## Passive experimentation

Several types of study which appear to be cast as experiments, and which use the kind of language associated with experiments – referring, for example, to independent and dependent variables – do not have the *active manipulation of the situation by the experimenter* taken here to be a hallmark of the experimental approach. They are sometimes called passive experiments, but are discussed here under the heading of non-experimental fixed designs.

## Non-experimental Fixed Designs

*If, following your reading of the previous chapter, it appears possible that a non-experimental fixed design may be appropriate for your project and its research questions, then perusal of this section should help in choosing a specific non-experimental design. However, before confirming that choice, it will be necessary to read the chapters in part III of this book to help select appropriate methods of collecting data, and those of part IV to establish how you will analyse the data after it has been collected.*

This style of fixed design research differs from the experimental one in that the phenomena studied are not deliberately manipulated or changed by the researcher. Hence it is suitable in situations where the aspects of interest are not amenable to such changes, for whatever reason. These include variables or characteristics which:

- are not modifiable by the researcher (e.g. personal characteristics such as gender, age, ethnicity);
- should not be modified for ethical reasons (e.g. tobacco smoking, alcohol consumption);
- it is not feasible to modify (e.g. placement in a school or classroom).

As these constraints apply to a high proportion of the variables of likely interest in applied social research, such designs are of considerable importance to anyone intent on carrying out a fixed design study.

Dealing with things as they are, rather than as modified by the experimenter, has the advantage of not disturbing whatever it is that we are interested in. Non-experimental fixed designs are commonly used for descriptive purposes, and because of their fixed, pre-specified nature are not well adapted to exploratory work. They can be used when the interest is in explaining or understanding a phenomenon. Within the critical realist framework, they are useful in establishing cause in the sense of providing supportive evidence for the operation of mechanisms and for teasing out the particular situations and groups of people where enabling or disabling mechanisms have come into play. Within the realist approach, the specification of which mechanisms have operated in a *post-hoc* (i.e. after the study has taken place) manner is viewed as entirely legitimate. While prediction of the exact pattern of results may not be feasible because of the open nature of the systems which social research studies, this does not preclude an explanation of the particular pattern obtained.

Box 5.21 provides an overview of the main types of non-experimental fixed designs covered in this section.

## Relational Designs

Relational fixed designs, as the name indicates, measure the relationship between two or more variables. Do pupils from different ethnic backgrounds achieve differently in schools? Are there gender differences? What is the relationship between school characteristics and student achievement? They are

---

## Box 5.21

## Overview of a range of non-experimental fixed designs

*Note*: Non-experimental fixed designs follow the same general approach as that used in experimental designs but without the active manipulation of variables by the researcher characteristic of experimentation.

1   *Relational designs*
Measurements or observations are made on a range of variables. Relationships between the scores on the variables are analysed. Sometimes referred to as *correlational studies* as correlation is the main analytical technique.

a   *Cross-sectional designs*   All measures are taken over a short period of time. Widely used design typically used in conjunction with the *survey method*.
b   *Prediction studies*   Used to determine whether scores on one or more variables can be used to predict scores on one or more other variables. Hence the study has to extend over time to test these predictions.

2   *Comparative designs*
Two or more groups of participants are established and the main focus is on analysing differences between the groups.

3   *Longitudinal designs*
Use of repeated measures on one or more variables over an extended period of time where the main focus is on trends occurring over this period.

---

sometimes referred to as *correlational studies*. However, this tends to suggest that a particular statistical technique (the correlation coefficient) is to be used, whereas in fact there is a range of possibilities for analysis (discussed in chapter 13).

Relational research strategies are fixed in a very similar way to experimental research. The traditional approach is to start with theory, in some provisional form at least. In critical realist terms, this means having a pretty clear idea (e.g. from a previous study or from other sources) of likely mechanisms and the contexts in which they will operate. This theory is then used to identify the variables and possible relationships to be studied. Research questions are formulated prior to data collection. Similarly, decisions about the methods of data collection and analysis, and the sampling strategy determining who will be asked, are all finalized before data collection proper starts; and it is expected that, when these decisions have been made, they are kept to throughout the study.

## Category membership

The identification of membership of particular categories or groups in relational research can be difficult and complex. This may appear straightforward for a variable such as age. However, there are situations where even age can be problematic; say in a study of the drinking habits of young adults, or in cultures where date of birth may not be recorded or remembered. Gender, as a social construct, can raise category difficulties in particular cases. An area such as ethnicity bristles with complexities, particularly in multicultural societies (see Stanfield, 1993).

This is a particular problem in relational research. In flexible qualitative styles of research it is usually feasible to achieve the depth needed to deal with the complexities, but fixed design research necessarily has to simplify. Notwithstanding the difficulties, it would be unfortunate if relational research were not carried out in such fields. As Mertens (1998) comments, 'Discontinuing such research based on the rationale that our understanding of race, gender, and disability is limited needs to be weighed against the benefit associated with revealing inequities in resources and outcomes in education, psychology, and the broader society' (p. 90).

## Cross-sectional studies

In this design, the focus is on relationships between and among variables in a single group (i.e. there is no attempt to set up different groups of participants). The simple version, in which all measures are taken at the same time (or, in practice, over a relatively short period of time), commonly referred to as the *cross-sectional study*, is probably the most widely used design in social research. It is often employed in conjunction with the *survey method* of data collection, itself the most commonly used method. The pattern of relationships between variables may be of interest in its own right, or there may be a concern for establishing causal links. In interpreting the results of these studies, statistical and logical analysis effectively takes the place of the features of experimental design which facilitate the interpretation of true experiments.

The variables to be included in the study are those needed to provide answers to your research questions. These questions will, as ever, be governed by the purposes of your study and by the theory you have developed. Whereas the tradition in experimental research is to label these as independent variables (those which the experimenter manipulates) and dependent variables (those where we look for change), here they are usually referred to as *explanatory variables* and *outcome variables* respectively.

It is possible to include more explanatory variables in this design than is feasible in experimental and group comparison relational designs. However, this should not be taken as an excuse for a 'fishing trip'; just throwing in variables in the hope that something will turn up. To reiterate the principle: the variables are included because of their relevance to your research questions. There is also a technical criterion linked to the requirements of statistical analysis. A rule of thumb sometimes proposed is a minimum of fifteen participants per variable (e.g. Mertens, 1998, p. 95; see also discussion below on sample sizes, p. 161).

The choice of participants to make up the group is important. Again, your research questions effectively determine this. An issue is the homogeneity of the group. For example, while you may not be interested in this study in gender issues in themselves, you may consider it important to have both males and females in the group. It may be, however, that males and females are affected by different variables and hence there will be increased variability on the outcome variable. A solution here is to analyse the two genders separately, i.e. to perform a sub-group analysis.

When decisions have been made about the composition of the group, data can be collected. Typically quantitative, or quantifiable, data are collected, often using some type of test or scale for both explanatory and outcome variables.

## Prediction studies

The design can be used in a rather different way. Here the question is whether scores on one or more variables (the *predictor variables*) can be used to predict subsequent performance on one or more other variables (the *criterion variables*). Because these designs involve collecting data on the group at different points in time, they have a longitudinal dimension to them. However, they differ from longitudinal studies (as discussed below), which typically involve a series of repeated measures on the same variable(s) at different points in time.

## Analysing and interpreting relational designs

A variety of data analysis techniques can be used, including (but by no means limited to) correlational analysis. Chapter 13 (p. 450) gives examples. The techniques can be thought of as providing statistical control for factors controlled for in true experiments by employing a control group and randomization of allocation of participants to experimental and control groups. So, for example, a survey on attitudes to nuclear power might show gender differences. Frankfort-Nachmias and Nachmias (1992, p. 126) discuss an example from Solomon et al. (1989) where 59 per cent of men and 29 per cent of women support nuclear power. This analysis of differences in percentages (produced by 'cross-tabulation'; see chapter 13, p. 417) provides a kind of statistical equivalent to an experimental design which is of course not feasible due to the impossibility of randomly assigning individuals to be males or females!

Establishing the statistical significance of the relationship (perhaps using the Chi-square technique) between gender and attitude does not enable us to conclude that these variables are causally related. Nor does it, in itself, help in understanding what lies behind this relationship. In realist terms, we need to come up with plausible mechanisms and seek evidence for their existence. As Frankfort-Nachmias and Nachmias suggest, it may be that 'the women in the study may have been less knowledgeable about technological matters and therefore more reluctant to support nuclear power. Or perhaps women's greater concern with safety would lead them to oppose nuclear power more than men' (p. 127).

Further sub-division of the group allows one to control statistically for the effects of such variables, providing the relevant information (e.g. degree of knowledge) has been collected. Various statistical techniques such as path analysis, discussed in chapter 13, can be used to analyse the data in more detail. However, the interpretation, particularly in relation to causation, remains a challenging task and is an amalgam of theoretical, logical and statistical considerations.

## Comparative Designs

This design differs from the previous one in that a second, comparison, group is selected in addition to the originally defined one. As with relational designs, the terms *explanatory* and *outcome variables* are commonly used in preference to *independent* and *dependent variables*. The groups may be naturally occurring ones already in existence, or may be created specially for the study. Group selection raises the same issues about threats to internal validity as in experimental (particularly quasi-experimental) design (see p. 133). The threat of *differential selection* will arise if the groups differ in some ways other than those indicated by the *explanatory variable(s)*. Assuming random allocation to the two groups is not feasible, some other approach must be taken to guard against this threat. Possibilities include:

- *matching* on variables likely to be relevant;
- *using a statistical method of control* for existing differences (see chapter 13, p. 426);
- *using direct control*, e.g. by selecting participants only from a particular ethnic or socio-economic background;
- *analysing sub-groups.*

Measures will typically be made on other background or control variables (e.g. ethnicity) which may be of interest in their own right or as helping to understand what lies behind any differences found. They then form the basis for subsequent sub-group analyses.

While relational and comparative designs may seem very different, the difference is largely in the way the study is conceptualized. The example of gender differences in attitude to nuclear power was discussed above as a study involving a single group containing both males and females. The focus was on relations between gender and attitude. It could be viewed as based on separate groups of males and females. The focus is then on differences between the two groups.

Gender is a dichotomous variable (i.e. it has only two possible values). Other explanatory variables can take on a wide range of values. In studies involving these, instead of separate comparison groups differing on the variable of interest, there is a wide range of differences on that variable. Having separate and distinct comparison groups (two or more) can be thought of as a special case of that general situation. This approach effectively brings together both relational and comparative studies within the same framework. It also paves the way to the use of statistical techniques such as analysis of variance (and particularly in this context analysis of covariance, which permits the separation out of the effects of control variables) and multiple linear regression. Chapter 13, p. 426, provides an introductory account.

## Longitudinal Designs

Longitudinal designs involve repeated measures on the same variables for the same group or groups on an extended series of occasions. They can be either relational or comparative. Such studies might either precede or follow some intervention or other event and examine its effects over time. These designs are, in principle, very attractive. They avoid many of the difficulties in a cross-sectional study where such matters are handled retrospectively and depend on participants' recall of past events. However, they are difficult and complex to run, and typically call for considerable resources. Some of the problems include:

- *Sample attrition* This is when participants are lost to the study when follow-up measures are being made. It is greater the longer the time between measures.
- *Need to devise measures which can be used repeatedly* The nature and type of measure need to be appropriate for use on several occasions with the same persons. Threats to internal validity (e.g. testing, instrumentation – see p. 105) have to be considered.
- *Need for special methods of data analysis* The analysis must take note of the implications of there being repeated measures (Menard, 1991).

Ruspini (2000) provides a short and accessible review with extensive references.


## Sample Size in Fixed Designs

One of the most common questions asked by a novice researcher is 'What size of sample do I need?' The answer is not straightforward, as it depends on many factors. In some real world research, the question is answered for you by the situation. You may be working in an organization where the obvious thing is to survey everybody; or your resources may be so stretched that this sets the limits on the number of participants you can deal with. In such circumstances it is particularly important to have thought through how your data are to be analysed before proceeding. There are minimum numbers for statistical tests and procedures below which they should not be used. Hence, if you plan to use a particular test or procedure then this sets minimum numbers for your design. The 'rule of thumb' proposed by Mertens (1998), discussed earlier (p. 158), of about fifteen participants per variable in non-experimental relational designs, can be extended to the other fixed designs covered in the chapter (Borg and Gall, 1989). Note that in survey research, which typically seeks to incorporate more variables than experimental and other non-experimental designs, Borg and Gall recommend about 100 observations for each of the major sub-groupings in the survey, with twenty to fifty for minor sub-groupings. Cohen (1992) suggests more complex rules of thumb for a range of different statistical tests.

When the main interest, as in many surveys, is to generalize the findings to the population from which the sample is drawn, then issues such as the *homogeneity* of the population are important. If pilot work establishes considerable *heterogeneity*, this then indicates the need for a larger sample. Similarly, the more accurate you want the estimates from your study to be, the larger a sample is needed. There are statistical techniques for determining the relationship between sampling error and sample size. Formulae have been developed to assist in the choice of an efficient sample size when it is important to limit estimation errors to a particular level. Henry (1990, ch. 7) and Czaja and Blair (1996, pp. 126–44) give introductions. Lipsey (1990) provides a more detailed account and a useful general treatment of power analysis, which covers the factors that affect the sensitivity of a design in detecting relationships. Power analysis is applicable in experiments as well as in surveys (Kraemer, 1981; Still, 1982). Clark-Carter (1997) provides power tables to help in choosing sample sizes. These should be treated with care, as you need to be clear about the assumptions on which they are based. This is a matter on which it is advisable to seek assistance from a statistician if it is of importance in your study.

## Further Reading

Colman, A. M., ed. (1994) *Psychological Research Methods and Statistics*. London: Longman. Concise but wide-ranging. Coverage includes experimental, quasi-experimental and non-experimental designs; chapter on ethical issues.

Cook, T. D. and Campbell, D. T. (1979) *Quasi-experimentation: Design and Analysis Issues for Field Settings*. Chicago: Rand McNally. Definitive presentation of issues to do with the design of quasi-experiments. Includes discussion on design of true experiments in the field.

Franklin, R. D., Allison, D. B. and Gorman, B. S., eds. (1996) *Design and Analysis of Single Case Research*. Mahwah, NJ: Lawrence Erlbaum Associates. Wide-ranging coverage of principles and practice.

Kirk, R. E. (1995) *Experimental Design: Procedures for the Behavioral Sciences*, 3rd edn. Belmont, Calif.: Brooks/Cole. Comprehensive coverage of traditional experimental design.

Maxwell, S. E. and Delaney, H. D. (1999) *Designing Experiments and Analyzing Data: A Model Comparison Perspective*. Mahwah, NJ: Lawrence Erlbaum Associates. Advanced level experimental design text. Derives complex designs from underlying principles. Gives serious attention to the philosophical background, considering the implications of the failure of positivism.

Robson, C. (1994) *Experiment, Design and Statistics in Psychology*, 3rd edn. London: Penguin. Introductory treatment of the design and analysis of simple single-variable experiments.

Sapsford, R. and Jupp, V. (1996) Validating evidence. In R. Sapsford and V. Jupp, eds, *Data Collection and Analysis*. London: Sage. Concentrates on discussion of validity in relation to quantitative research.

# 6
# Flexible Designs

This chapter:

- reiterates the rationale for referring to 'flexible' research design rather than the more usual 'qualitative' research design;
- covers some general features of flexible design research and the researcher qualities it calls for;
- considers the place of reliability and validity in flexible design research and the ways in which researcher bias and threats to validity can be dealt with;
- concentrates on three traditions of flexible design research: case studies, ethnographic studies and grounded theory studies;
- examines the nature of case studies and discusses their design;
- discusses the ethnographic approach and how it might be used in real world studies;
- explains what is meant by a grounded theory approach and considers how a real world study might follow this approach;
- briefly reviews a range of other possible approaches, including the biographical (life history), phenomenological, hermeneutic and feminist research traditions.

## Introduction

It is now considered respectable and acceptable in virtually all areas of social research (including applied fields such as education, health, social work, and business and management) to use designs based largely or exclusively on methods generating qualitative data. This trend has developed to such an extent that some commentators warn about the dangers of 'methodolatry'

(Chamberlain, 2000) – the privileging of methodological concerns over other considerations in qualitative research. There are, however, still some isolated outposts, particularly in fields abutting medicine and in areas of experimental psychology, where such designs are considered illegitimate or inferior to traditional quantitative designs.

The position taken in this text is that for some studies and for certain types of research question, qualitative designs are indicated. For others, quantitative designs are needed. The qualitative/quantitative ways of labelling research designs are so well established that not to use them risks miscommunication. However, as already pointed out in chapter 2, their use is not entirely logical. In principle (and not uncommonly in practice), so-called qualitative designs can incorporate quantitative methods of data collection. All of these approaches show substantial flexibility in their research design, typically anticipating that the design will emerge and develop during data collection. By contrast, as discussed in the previous chapter, so-called quantitative approaches call for a tight pre-specification of the design prior to data collection. Hence my preference for referring to them as *flexible* and *fixed designs* respectively.

## General Features of Flexible Design Research

We first provide a general specification for the design of a flexible (qualitative) study and discussion of the issue of the reliability and validity of such designs. This is followed by accounts of three influential design traditions within flexible design research which appear to be of particular relevance for real world studies: *case studies, ethnographic studies* and *grounded theory studies*. Some of their key features are shown in box 6.1.

The chapter concludes with summaries of a range of other traditions within qualitative research.

Box 6.2 gives a flavour of the kind of characteristics to be found in a flexible design where serious attention has been given to the general norms and canons of this style of research. This should be seen in the context of the overall design framework developed in chapter 4 (figure 4.1, p. 82). In other words, thought and attention will have to be given to the *purpose(s)* of your research; to *theory*; to the *research questions* to which you seek answers; to the *methods* of data collection; and to the *sampling strategy* which will be needed to get these answers.

You don't try to get all of this cut and dried before starting data collection. The purpose or purposes of the study are likely to be pretty clear from the outset. However, at this stage you may not have much of an idea about what theoretical framework is going to be most helpful. Indeed, the grounded

## Box 6.1

## Comparing research traditions in qualitative research

|  | *Grounded theory* | *Ethnography* | *Case study* |
|---|---|---|---|
| *Focus* | Developing a theory grounded in data from the field | Describing and interpreting a cultural and social group | Developing an in-depth analysis of a single case or multiple cases |
| *Discipline origin* | Sociology | Cultural anthropology, sociology | Political science, sociology, evaluation, urban studies, many other social sciences |
| *Data collection* | Typically interviews with 20–30 individuals to 'saturate' categories and detail a theory | Primarily observation and interviews during extended time in the field | Multiple sources – documents, archival records, interviews, observations, physical artefacts |
| *Data analysis* | Open coding, axial coding, selective coding, conditional matrix | Description, analysis, interpretation | Description, themes, assertions |
| *Narrative form* | Theory or theoretical model | Description of the cultural behaviour of the group | In-depth study of a 'case' or 'cases' |

(Abridged from Cresswell, 1998, p. 65.)

theory tradition discussed below argues that you should seek to enter the field without theoretical preconceptions (something which many would regard as impossible to achieve). It is highly likely that your research questions will be initially underdeveloped and tentative. You obviously need to make some early decisions about methods of data collection, as if you don't, you will never get started. However, in these designs you don't have to foreclose on options about methods. Ideas for changing your approach may arise from your involvement and early data collection. Or, as you change or clarify the research questions, different means of data collection may be called for. Similarly, your sampling of who, where and what does not have to be decided in advance.

## Box 6.2

### Characteristics of a 'good' flexible design

**1**   Rigorous data collection procedures are used. Typically, multiple data collection techniques are used. Data are adequately summarized (e.g. in tabular form). Detail is given about how data are collected.

**2**   The study is framed within the assumptions and characteristics of the flexible (qualitative) approach to research. This includes fundamental characteristics such as an evolving design, the presentation of multiple realities, the researcher as an instrument of data collection and a focus on participants' views.

**3**   The study is informed by an understanding of existing traditions of enquiry; i.e. the researcher identifies, studies and employs one or more traditions of enquiry.

**4**   This tradition need not be 'pure', and procedures from several can be brought together. The beginning researcher is recommended to stay within one tradition initially, becoming comfortable with it, learning it, and keeping a study concise and straightforward. Later, especially in long and complex studies, features from several traditions may be useful.

**5**   The project starts with a single idea or problem that the researcher seeks to understand, not a causal relationship of variables or a comparison of groups (for which a fixed design might be indicated). Relationships might evolve or comparisons might be made, but these emerge later in the study.

**6**   The study includes detailed methods, a rigorous approach to data collection, data analysis and report writing. The researcher has the responsibility of verifying the accuracy of the account given.

**7**   Data are analysed using multiple levels of abstraction. Often, writers present their studies in stages (e.g. multiple themes that can be combined into larger themes or perspectives), or layer their analyses from the particular to the general.

**8**   The writing is clear, engaging, and helps the reader to experience 'being there'. The story and findings become believable and realistic, accurately reflecting the complexities of real life.

(After Cresswell, 1998, pp. 20–2.)

Again, you need to start somewhere, but the sampling strategy can and should evolve with other aspects of the design.

## Critical realism and flexible design

Within the realist framework it is held that theory, rather than data or the methods used to produce those data, is central to explaining reality. This is fully consonant with the view developed in this text that it is the research questions which drive the design of a study, whether it be flexible or fixed; and that these questions have to be linked to theory, whether pre-existing theory which is tested by the research, or new theory which is generated by the process of the research.

Hence a critical realist view has no problems with flexible design research, or with the use of qualitative data. As pointed out by Anastas and MacDonald (1994):

> Flexible or qualitative methods have traditionally included the researcher and the relationship with the researched within the boundary of what is examined. Because all any study can do is to approximate knowledge of phenomena as they exist in the real world (fallibilism) the process of study itself must be an object of study. Because all methods of study can produce only approximations of reality and incomplete understanding of the phenomena of interest as they exist in the real world, the findings of flexible method research can be seen as no more or less legitimate than those of any other type of study (p. 60).

## Researcher qualities needed for flexible design research

Doing flexible design research calls for flexible researchers. More generally, this approach to research makes great demands on the researcher *while carrying out the study*. It is commonly said that it involves the 'researcher-as-instrument' rather than relying on specialist tools and instruments (Chesney, 2001, analyses the 'dilemmas of self' that this involves). Certainly the quality of a flexible design study depends to a great extent on the quality of the investigator. It is not a 'soft' option in the sense that anyone can do it without preparation, knowledge of procedures or analytical skills. It *is* soft, however, in the sense that there are few 'hard and fast' routinized procedures, where all you have to do is to follow the formulae. This makes life harder rather than easier – though also more interesting.

Ideally, this kind of research calls for well-trained and experienced investigators, but other aspects are also important. Personal qualities such as having an *open and enquiring mind*, being a *'good listener'*, general *sensitivity* and *responsiveness to contradictory evidence* are needed. These are commonly regarded as skills central to the professional working with people in any capacity. Relevant professional experience of this kind is also likely to provide you with a firm grasp of the issues being examined in a particular study.

The professional or practitioner working with people as their job has much to contribute both *as* an investigator or *to* an investigator. As an investigator, probably carrying out 'insider' research, he will need a firm grasp of the material in this book, and experience (this can lead to 'Catch-22' problems – how do you get the experience without carrying out a study, and vice versa). Working in collaboration with someone who has the methodological skills and the experience is obviously one way forward. Box 6.3 provides an indication of the skills needed to be an effective flexible design researcher.

## Establishing Trustworthiness in Flexible Design Research

The trustworthiness or otherwise of findings from flexible, qualitative research is the subject of much debate. Fixed design experimentalists criticize the absence of their 'standard' means of assuring reliability and validity, such as checking inter-observer agreement, the use of quantitative measurement, explicit controls for threats to validity, and direct replication. Thus, for example, while the essential test of validity of a finding in the natural sciences is that it has been directly replicated by an independent investigator, this approach is not feasible when a flexible design is used (and is highly questionable in real world fixed design research involving people). One problem is that identical circumstances cannot be re-created for the attempt to replicate. As Bloor (1997) pus it: 'Social life contains elements which are generalizable across settings (thus providing for the possibility of the social sciences) and other elements that are particular to given settings (thus forever limiting the predictive power of the social sciences' (p. 37)).

Some researchers using qualitative, flexible designs deny the relevance of canons of scientific enquiry (e.g. Guba and Lincoln, 1989). Others go further and reject the notion of any evaluative criteria such as reliability and validity (Wolcott, 1994). Taking an extreme relativist stance, it is maintained that using such criteria privileges some approaches inappropriately.

Altheide and Johnson (1994) argue that fields in the humanities such as history and literature employ evaluative criteria such as elegance, coherence and consistency which provide more appropriate standards for qualitative studies. While they may appear imprecise to traditional positivistically inclined researchers, it is worth noting that even a notion so vague as elegance is used as a central criterion for the choice of one explanation over a rival in fields

---

### Box 6.3

## General skills needed by flexible design investigators

**1**   *Question asking*   Need for an 'enquiring mind'. Your task in fieldwork is to enquire why events appear to have happened or to be happening. This is something you ask yourself as well as others, and is mentally and emotionally exhausting.

**2**   *Good listening*   Used in a general sense to include all observation and sensing, not simply via the ears. Also 'listening' to what documents say. *Good* means taking in a lot of new information without bias; noting the exact words said; capturing mood and affective components; appreciating context. You need an open mind and a good memory. (Taping helps but is not a panacea.)

**3**   *Adaptiveness and flexibility*   These studies rarely end up exactly as planned. You have to be willing to change procedures or plans if the unanticipated occurs. The full implications of any changes have to be taken on board; e.g. you may need to change the design. Need to balance *adaptiveness* and *rigour*.

**4**   *Grasp of the issues*   The investigator needs to *interpret* information during the study, not simply record it. Without a firm grasp of the issues (theoretical, policy etc.) you may miss clues, not see contradictions, requirement for further evidence, etc.

**5**   *Lack of bias*   The preceding skills are negated if they are simply used to substantiate a preconceived position. Investigators should be open to contrary findings. During data collection, preliminary findings should be submitted to critical colleagues who are asked to offer alternative explanations and suggestions for data collection. See the following section on researcher bias (p. 172) and box 6.4.

---

such as theoretical physics, the very heartland of natural science. More generally, accepting that social science researchers of whatever persuasion can benefit from some understanding of methodology in the humanities need not be at variance with the aspiration of remaining within the scientific fold put forward in chapter 1. The problems of the relativist position outlined in chapter 2 suggest a need for evaluative criteria in flexible designs. However, given the inappropriateness of the methods and techniques used in fixed design research, it is clear that different procedures for ensuring trustworthiness are called for (Kirk and Miller, 1986).

## Note on terminology

The terms 'reliability' and 'validity' are avoided by many proponents of flexible, qualitative design. Lincoln and Guba (1985, pp. 294–301), for example, prefer the terms *credibility*, *transferability*, *dependability* and *confirmability*. This line was followed in the first edition of this text (Robson, 1993, pp. 403–7), where definitions and discussion of these alternative terms was provided. However, this attempt to rename and disclaim the traditional terms continues to provide support for the view that qualitative studies are unreliable and invalid (Kvale 1996, p. 73). As Morse (1999) puts it in a forceful journal editorial entitled 'Myth #93: reliability and validity are not relevant to qualitative inquiry':

> To state that reliability and validity are not pertinent to qualitative inquiry places qualitative research in the realm of being not reliable and not valid. Science is concerned with rigor, and by definition, good rigorous research must be reliable and valid. If qualitative research is unreliable and invalid, then it must not be science. If it is not science, then why should it be funded, published, implemented, or taken seriously? (p. 717)

While this argument goes over the top in apparently denying any value to non-scientific endeavours, it has force when we are seeking to characterize our research as scientific, following the arguments developed in chapter 1.

The problem is not so much with the apple-pie desirability of doing reliable and valid research, but the fact that these terms have been operationalized so rigidly in fixed design quantitative research. An answer is to find alternative ways of operationalizing them that are appropriate to the conditions and circumstances of flexible, qualitative enquiry.

## Validity

What do we mean by claiming that a piece of qualitative research is valid, that it has validity? It is something to do with it being accurate, or correct, or true. These are difficult (some would say impossible) things to be sure about. It is possible to recognize situations and circumstances which make validity more likely. These include the features of 'good' flexible design listed in box 6.1. Conversely, it is pretty straightforward to come up with factors likely to lead to invalid research. As with fixed, quantitative designs, they can be thought of as 'threats' to validity, and are discussed below.

An alternative, though related, tack is to focus on the credibility or trustworthiness of the research. The fact that some persons find it credible, or are prepared to trust it, is in itself a pretty weak justification. They may find it believable because it fits in with their prejudices. However, if the concern is with what might be appropriate bases for judging something to be credible, this returns us to consideration of what constitutes good quality research, and possible threats to validity.

## Threats to validity in flexible designs

Maxwell (1992) has presented a useful typology of the kinds of understanding involved in qualitative research. The main types are *description, interpretation* and *theory*. Each of the main types has particular threats to its validity (see also Elsworth, 1994, who presents a similar analysis, also from a realist perspective).

*Description* The main threat to providing a valid description of what you have seen or heard lies in the inaccuracy or incompleteness of the data. This suggests that audio- or video-taping should be carried out wherever feasible. Note that the simple fact that you have a tape does not mean that it must be fully transcribed. Where taping is not feasible, the quality of your notes is very important. These issues are discussed in detail in chapter 9, p. 289.

*Interpretation* The main threat to providing a valid interpretation is that of imposing a framework or meaning on what is happening rather than this occurring or emerging from what you learn during your involvement with the setting. This does not preclude a style of research where you do start with some kind of prior framework, but this must be subjected to checking on its appropriateness, with possible modification. Mason (1996) shows how you might go about demonstrating the validity of your interpretation:

> In my view, validity of interpretation in any form of qualitative research is contingent upon the 'end product' including a demonstration of how that interpretation was reached. This means that you should be able to, and be prepared to, trace the route by which you came to your interpretation . . . The basic principle here is that you are never taking it as self-evident that a particular interpretation can be made of your data but instead that you are continually and assiduously charting and justifying the steps through which your interpretations were made. (p. 150)

Note that Maxwell's notion of 'interpretation' refers specifically to interpretation of the meaning and perspective of participants, as in 'interpretive' research. He would consider the wider use of interpretation given here as not distinguishable from 'theory'.

*Theory*  The main threat is in not considering alternative explanations or understandings of the phenomena you are studying. This can be countered by actively seeking data which are not consonant with your theory. See the discussion of 'negative case analysis' below, and in chapter 14, p. 490.

Lincoln and Guba (1985) discuss various possible threats to the validity of flexible design research, dividing them into the three broad headings of *reactivity, respondent biases* and *researcher biases*. Reactivity refers to the way in which the researcher's presence may interfere in some way with the setting which forms the focus of the study, and in particular with the behaviour of the people involved. Respondent bias can take various forms, ranging from obstructiveness and withholding information – when, for example, the researcher is seen as a threat – to the 'good bunny' syndrome, when the respondent tries to give the answers or impressions which they judge that the researcher wants. Researcher bias refers to what the researcher brings to the situation in terms of assumptions and preconceptions, which may in some way affect the way in which they behave in the research setting, perhaps in terms of the persons selected for observation or interview, the kinds of questions asked, or the selection of data for reporting and analysis.

Phenomenological approaches to qualitative research (e.g. Crotty, 1998) stress the importance of reflexivity, i.e. an awareness of the ways in which the researcher as an individual with a particular social identity and background has an impact on the research process. They take the view that 'The ability to put aside personal feelings and preconceptions is more a function of how reflexive one is rather than how objective one is because it is not possible for researchers to set aside things about which they are not aware' (Ahern, 1999, p. 408). Ahern has produced a useful set of suggestions to help achieve what she terms 'reflexive bracketing', i.e. using reflexivity to identify areas of potential bias; these are summarized in box 6.4.

These issues are present in all research involving people. However, the nature of much flexible design research is such that they are often particularly problematic. There is typically a close relationship between the researcher and the setting, and between the researcher and respondents. Indeed, the notion of the 'researcher-as-instrument' emphasizes the potential for bias. Padgett (1998) presents a range of commonly used strategies to deal with these threats; they are summarized in box 6.5 and discussed below.

*Prolonged involvement*  Involvement over a period of years was a defining characteristic of ethnography in its traditional anthropological version. In most current studies following the ethnographic approach fieldwork is much more condensed, but a period of weeks or even months is still usual, much longer than is typical in fixed methods research. This relatively prolonged involvement is also typical of other styles of flexible design research. As indicated in box 6.5, this helps to reduce both reactivity and respondent bias. Researchers who spend a long time in the setting tend to become accepted and any initial

## Box 6.4

### Using reflexivity to identify areas of potential researcher bias

1  Write down your personal issues in undertaking this research, the taken-for-granted assumptions associated with your gender, race, socio-economic status, and the political milieu of your research. Finally, consider where the power is held in relation to your research project and where you belong in the power hierarchy.

2  Clarify your personal value systems and acknowledge areas in which you know you are subjective.

3  Describe possible areas of potential role conflict. Are there particular types of people and/or situations with or in which you feel anxious, annoyed, at ease? Is the publication of your findings likely to cause problems with a group of people? Consider how this possibly could influence whom you approach or how you approach them.

4  Identify gatekeepers' interests and consider the extent to which they are disposed favourably towards your project. This can help you prevent potential role conflicts.

5  Recognize feelings that could indicate a lack of neutrality. These include avoiding situations in which you might experience negative feelings, seeking out situations in which you will experience positive feelings.

6  Is anything new or surprising in your data collection or analysis? If not, is this cause for concern, or is it an indication of saturation? On occasion, stand back and ask yourself if you are 'going native'.

7  When blocks occur in the research process, re-frame them. For example, is there another group of people who can shed light on this phenomenon? Would an additional form of data collection, such as document analysis or diaries, give a greater insight?

8  Even when you have completed your analysis, reflect on how you write up your account. Are you quoting more from one respondent than another? If you are, ask yourself why.

9  Consider whether the supporting evidence in the literature really is supporting your analysis or if it is just expressing the same cultural background as yourself.

10  A significant aspect of resolving bias is the acknowledgement of its outcomes. Therefore, you might have to re-interview a respondent or reanalyse the transcript once you have recognized that bias in data collection or analysis is a possibility in a specific situation. It is also worth remembering that even if preconceptions and biases are acknowledged, they are not always easily abandoned.

(Abridged from Ahern, 1999, pp. 408–10.)

---

## Box 6.5

### Strategies for dealing with threats to validity

| | Threat to validity | | |
| --- | --- | --- | --- |
| Strategy* | Reactivity | Researcher bias | Respondent bias |
| Prolonged involvement | Reduces threat | Increases threat | Reduces threat |
| Triangulation | Reduces threat | Reduces threat | Reduces threat |
| Peer debriefing/ support | No effect | Reduces threat | No effect |
| Member checking | Reduces threat | Reduces threat | Reduces threat |
| Negative case analysis | No effect | Reduces threat | No effect |
| Audit trail | No effect | Reduces threat | No effect |

* See text for explanation of the strategies.
(After Padgett, 1998, p. 95.)

---

reactivity reduces. Similarly, it permits the development of a trusting relationship between the researcher and respondents where the latter are less likely to give biased information.

There can, however, be greater researcher bias with prolonged involvement. A positive or negative bias may build up. It may be difficult to maintain the researcher role over an extended period of time (the 'going native' threat); or developing antipathy might result in a negative bias.

*Triangulation*   This is a valuable and widely used strategy. As discussed in more detail in chapter 12 (p. 371), it involves the use of multiple sources to enhance the rigour of the research. Denzin (1988) has distinguished four types of triangulation:

- *data triangulation*: the use of more than one method of data collection (e.g. observation, interviews, documents);
- *observer triangulation*: using more than one observer in the study;
- *methodological triangulation*: combining quantitative and qualitative approaches;
- *theory triangulation*: using multiple theories or perspectives.

Triangulation can help to counter all of the threats to validity. Note, however, that it opens up possibilities of discrepancies and disagreements among the different sources. Thus interviews and documents may be contradictory; two observers may disagree about what has happened. Bloor (1997, pp. 38–41) argues that while triangulation is relevant to validity, it raises both logical and practical difficulties, e.g. when findings collected by different methods differ to a degree which makes their direct comparison problematic.

*Peer debriefing and support*    Peer groups (i.e. of researchers or students of similar status who are involved in flexible design research) can have a number of valuable functions. They can contribute to guarding against researcher bias through debriefing sessions after periods in the research setting. Such groups can also fulfil something almost amounting to a therapeutic function. This type of research can be extremely demanding and stressful for the researcher, and the group can help you cope.

*Member checking*    This involves returning (either physically or through correspondence, phone, e-mail etc.) to respondents and presenting to them material such as transcripts, accounts and interpretations you have made. It can be a very valuable means of guarding against researcher bias. It also demonstrates to them that you value their perceptions and contributions. There are potential problems; perhaps your interpretation is challenged, or a respondent gets cold feet and seeks to suppress some material. It is essential that you have a pre-agreed clear understanding with them about the rules governing such situations, and that you respect both the spirit and the letter of such agreements. However, a supine giving in to any criticism is not called for. Disagreements can usually be negotiated in a way which reflects both respondents' concerns and the needs of the study. Bloor (1997, pp. 41–8) discusses some of the complexities with examples.

*Negative case analysis*    This is discussed in more detail in chapter 14, p. 490. The search for negative cases is an important means of countering researcher bias. As you develop theories about what is going on, you should devote time and attention to searching for instances which will disconfirm your theory. You may do this using data you already have, or by collecting additional data. It is sometimes referred to as 'playing the devil's advocate', and you have a responsibility to do it thoroughly and honestly. Don't be too concerned that this procedure will lead to your ending up with a set of disconfirmed theories. In practice, it usually amounts to developing a more elaborated version of your theory.

*Audit trail*    The notion is that you keep a full record of your activities while carrying out the study. This would include your raw data (transcripts of interviews, field notes, etc.), your research journal (see p. 1), and details of your coding and data analysis (Lincoln and Guba, 1985, appendices A and B).

Maxwell (1996, pp. 92–6) and Miles and Huberman (1994; pp. 262–77) provide alternative, but overlapping, sets of strategies which might be considered. Note, however, that while using such strategies will undoubtedly help in ruling out threats to validity, there is no foolproof way of *guaranteeing* validity. Remember, too, that the strategies only help if you actually use them. Whereas in traditional fixed design research (particularly in true experimentation) threats to validity are essentially dealt with in advance as part of the design process, most threats to validity in flexible design research are dealt with after the research is in progress, using evidence which you collect after you have begun to develop a tentative account.

## Reliability in flexible designs

Reliability in fixed design research is associated with the use of standardized research instruments, for example formal tests and scales as discussed in chapter 10. It is also associated with the use of observation, where the human observer is the standardized instrument. The concern is whether the tool or instrument produces consistent results. Thinking in such terms is problematic for most qualitative researchers (Mason, 1996, chs 3 and 4). At a technical level, the general non-standardization of many methods of generating qualitative data precludes formal reliability testing. Nevertheless, there are common pitfalls in data collection and transcription including equipment failure, environmental distractions and interruptions, and transcription errors. Easton et al. (2000) suggest strategies to minimize the risk from these errors.

In a more general sense, researchers using flexible designs do need to concern themselves seriously with the reliability of their methods and research practices. This involves not only being thorough, careful and honest in carrying out the research, but also being able to show others that you have been. One way of achieving this is via the kind of audit trail described above.

## Generalizability in flexible designs

Maxwell (1992; 1996, p. 96) makes a useful distinction between *internal* and *external generalizability*. Internal generalizability refers to the generalizability of conclusions within the setting studied. External generalizability is generalizability beyond that setting. The former is an important issue in flexible designs. If you are selective in the people you interview, or the situations that you observe, in a way which, say, excludes the people or settings which you find threatening or disturbing, this is likely to bias your account.

External generalizability may not be an issue. A case study might just be concerned with explaining and understanding what is going on in a particular business, drop-in centre or whatever is the focus of the study. It very rarely involves the selection of a representative (let alone random) sample of settings from a known population which would permit the kind of statistical generalization typical of survey designs. However, this does not preclude some kind of generalizability beyond the specific setting studied. This may be thought of as the development of a theory which helps in understanding other cases or situations (Ragin, 1987; Yin, 1994), sometimes referred to as *analytic* or *theoretical generalization*: 'Here the data gained from a particular study provide theoretical insights which possess a sufficient degree of generality or universality to allow their projection to other contexts or situations' (Sim, 1998, p. 350).

## Research Traditions in Qualitative Research

Box 6.6 provides an overview of the approaches to flexible design research featured in this chapter (see also box 6.1, p. 165).

## Case Studies

In case study, the *case* is the situation, individual, group, organization or whatever it is that we are interested in. Case study has been around for a long time (Hamel, 1993, traces its history within social science). To some it will suggest the legal system, to others the medical one. Bromley (1986) points out that case study can be found in areas as disparate as administration, anatomy, anthropology, artificial intelligence, biochemistry, business studies, clinical medicine, counselling, criminology, education, gerontology, history, industrial relations, jurisprudence, management, military studies, personality, politics, psychiatry, social work and sociology. Note that there is some danger in using a well-worn term like 'case study', for all such terms carry 'excess baggage' around with them, surplus meanings and resonances from these previous usages.

The intention here is to provide guidance in carrying out *rigorous* case studies. This involves attention to matters of design, data collection, analysis, interpretation and reporting which form a major part of later chapters. Before getting on with this, however, let us be clear as to what we mean by case study,

---

## Box 6.6

## Overview of a range of approaches to flexible design research

*Note*: The approaches are based on existing traditions within qualitative research. The main focus of attention in this chapter is on case study, ethnographic studies and grounded theory studies, which are seen as particularly relevant in a real world context. Brief details on other approaches (*biographical* or *life history research*; *phenomenological research*; *symbolic interactionism*; *hermeneutics*; and *feminist perspectives*) are given at the end of the chapter.

### 1   Case study
A well-established research strategy where the focus is on a case (which is interpreted very widely to include the study of an individual person, a group, a setting, an organization, etc.) in its own right, and taking its context into account. Typically involves multiple methods of data colllection. Can include quantitative data, though qualitative data are almost invariably collected.

### 2   Ethnographic studies
Another well-established strategy where the focus is on the description and interpretation of the culture and social structure of a social group. Typically involves participant obervation over an extended period of time, but other methods (including those generating quantitative data) can also be used.

### 3   Grounded theory studies
A more recently developed strategy where the main concern is to develop a theory of the particular social situation forming the basis of the study. The theory is 'grounded' in the sense of being derived from the study itself. Popular in research on many applied settings, particularly health-related ones. Interviews are commonly used but other methods (including those generating quantitative data) are not excluded.

---

following the lead set by Robert Yin (1981; 1994), who has done much to resuscitate case study as a serious option when doing social research:

> *Case study is a strategy for doing research which involves an empirical investigation of a particular contemporary phenomenon within its real life context using multiple sources of evidence.*

The important points are that it is:

- a *strategy*, i.e. a stance or approach, rather than a method, such as observation or interview;
- concerned with *research*, taken in a broad sense and including, for example, evaluation;
- *empirical* in the sense of relying on the collection of evidence about what is going on;
- about the *particular*: a study of that specific case (the issue of what kind of generalization is possible from the case, and of how this might be done, will concern us greatly);
- focused on a *phenomenon in context*, typically in situations where the boundary between the phenomenon and its context is not clear; and
- undertaken using *multiple methods* of evidence or data collection.

The central defining characteristic is concentration on a particular case (or small set of cases) studied in its own right. However, the importance of the context or setting is also worth highlighting. Miles and Huberman (1994, p. 27) suggest that in some circumstances the term 'site' might be preferable, 'because it reminds us that a 'case' always occurs in a specified social and physical *setting*: we cannot study individual cases devoid of their context in a way that a quantitative researcher often does.'

Barrett and Cooperrider (1990), Brez and Taylor (1997), Oniskiw et al. (1999) and Pervin and Turner (1998) are examples of case studies carried out in different fields (see also box 4.1, p. 84). Note that while some commentators see case study as being essentially qualitative (e.g. Stake, 1995; Merriam, 1988), Yin (1994) gives examples using both quantitative and qualitative data collection methods.

## Taking case study seriously

Valsiner (1986) claims that 'the study of individual cases has always been the major (albeit often unrecognized) strategy in the advancement of knowledge about human beings' (p. 11). In similar vein, Bromley (1986) maintains that 'the individual case study or situation analysis is the bed-rock of scientific investigation' (p. ix). But he also notes, in an unattributed quotation, the common view that 'science is not concerned with the individual case' (p. xi). These widely divergent claims betray a deep-rooted uncertainty about the place and value of studying cases.

Case study was until recently commonly considered in methodology texts as a kind of 'soft option', possibly admissible as an exploratory precursor to some more 'hard-nosed' experiment or survey, or as a complement to such approaches, but of dubious value by itself. However, Cook and Campbell (1979) see case study as a fully legitimate alternative to experimentation in appropriate circumstances, and make the point that 'case study as normally practised should not be demeaned by identification with the one-group post-test-only design' (p. 96). The central point is that *case study is not a flawed experimental design; it is a fundamentally different research strategy with its own designs.*

It is useful to separate out criticisms of the practice of particular case studies from what some have seen as inescapable deficiencies of the strategy itself. As Bromley (1986) points out, 'case studies are sometimes carried out in a sloppy, perfunctory, and incompetent manner and sometimes even in a corrupt, dishonest way' (p. xiii). Even with good faith and intentions, biased and selective accounts can undoubtedly emerge. Similar criticisms could be made about any research strategy, of course. The issue is whether or not it is possible to devise appropriate checks to demonstrate what in experimental design terms are referred to as the reliability and validity of the findings (see the discussion above, p. 168).

## Can case study be scientific?

As discussed in chapter 2, the positivist 'standard view' of science has been comprehensively demolished, although its ghostly presence lingers on in the views and practices of many quantitatively inclined social researchers. Case study does not appear to present any special difficulties for the realist view of science, developed and defended in that chapter (see box 2.6, p. 32). The study of the particular, which is central to case study, is not excluded in principle. It is the aims and intentions of the study, and the specific methods used, that concern us. Carr and Kemmis (1986) reach very similar conclusions: 'What distinguishes scientific knowledge is not so much its logical status, as the fact that it is the outcome of a process of enquiry which is governed by critical norms and standards of rationality' (p. 121).

## Designing case studies

The 'case' can be virtually anything. The individual person as the case is probably what springs first to mind. A simple, single case study would just focus on that person, perhaps say in a clinical or medical context where the use of the term 'case' is routine. More complex, multiple case studies might involve several such individual cases. Case studies are not necessarily studies of individuals, though. They can be done on a group, on an institution, on a neighbourhood, on an innovation, on a decision, on a service, on a programme and on many other things. (There may be difficulties in defining and delimiting exactly what one means by the 'case' when the focus moves away from the individual person.) Case studies are, then, very various. Box 6.7 gives some indication of different types and of the range of purposes they fulfil.

Whatever kind of case study is involved (and the list in box 6.6 only scratches the surface), there is always the need, as in any kind of research, to follow a framework for research design such as that given in chapter 4 (figure 4.1, p. 82). The degree of flexibility of design will vary from one study to

---

## Box 6.7

### Some types of case study

**1** *Individual case study*  Detailed account of one person. Tends to focus on antecedents, contextual factors, perceptions and attitudes preceding a known outcome (e.g. drug use; immigrant status). Used to explore possible causes, determinants, factors, processes, experiences, etc., contributing to the outcome.

**2** *Set of individual case studies*  As above, but a small number of individuals with some features in common are studied.

**3** *Community study*  Study of one or more local communities. Describes and analyses the pattern of, and relations between, main aspects of community life (politics; work; leisure; family life; etc.). Commonly descriptive, but may explore specific issues or be used in theory testing.

**4** *Social group study*  Covers studies of both small direct contact groups (e.g. families) and larger, more diffuse ones (e.g. occupational groups). Describes and analyses relationships and activities.

**5** *Studies of organizations and institutions*  Studies of firms, workplaces, schools, trades unions, etc. Many possible foci, e.g. best practice; policy implementation and evaluation; industrial relations; management and organizational issues; organizational cultures; processes of change and adaptation; etc.

**6** *Studies of events, roles and relationships*  Focus on a specific event (overlaps with (3) and (4)). Very varied; includes studies of police–citizen encounters; doctor–patient interactions; specific crimes or 'incidents' (e.g. disasters); studies of role conflicts, stereotypes, adaptations.

(After Hakim, 1987, pp. 65–72; Whyte, 1984, and Yin, 1994, provide a range of other examples.)

another. If, for example, the main purpose is exploratory, trying to get some feeling as to what is going on in a novel situation where there is little to guide what one should be looking for, then your initial approach will be highly flexible. If, however, the purpose is confirmatory, where previous work has suggested an explanation of some phenomenon, then there is a place for some degree of pre-structure. There is an obvious trade-off between *looseness* and *selectivity*. The looser the original design, the less selective you can afford to be in data selection. Anything might be important. On the other hand, the danger is that if you *start* with a relatively tight conceptual framework or theoretical views, this may blind you to important features of the case, or cause you to misinterpret evidence. There is no obvious way out of this dilemma. Practicalities may dictate some pre-structuring, for example, if the project is on a very tight time-scale, as in much small-scale contract research.

## Holistic case studies

Yin (1994) differentiates between two versions of the single case study on the basis of the level of the unit of analysis. A study where the concern remains at a single, global level is referred to as *holistic*. This is typically (though not necessarily) how a case study of an individual would be viewed, but would also apply to, say, the study of an institution which remained at the level of the whole rather than seeking to look at and analyse the different functioning of separate sub-units within the institution.

Holistic case studies are appropriate in several situations. The *critical case* is a clear, though unfortunately rare, example. This occurs when your theoretical understanding is such that there is a clear, unambiguous and non-trivial set of circumstances where predicted outcomes will be found. Finding a case which fits, and demonstrating what has been predicted, can give a powerful boost to knowledge and understanding. This is the way in which experiment was used classically – the 'crucial experiment'. It is interesting to note that some of the most illustrious of this genre, for example, the verification of Einstein's theory of relativity by measuring the 'bending' of light from a distant star at a rare eclipse, are effectively case studies (being the study of a particular instance in its context) rather than experiments (in that no experimental manipulation of variables is possible).

The *extreme case* also provides a rationale for a simple, holistic case study. The extreme and the unique can provide a valuable 'test bed' for which case study is appropriate. Extremes include the 'if it can work here it will work anywhere' scenario, to the 'super-realization' where, say, a new approach is tried under ideal circumstances, perhaps to obtain understanding of how it works before its wider implementation.

## Multiple case studies

In many studies, it is appropriate to study more than a single case. A very common misconception is that this is for the purpose of gathering a 'sample' of cases so that generalization to some population may be made. Yin (1994) makes the useful analogy that carrying out multiple case studies is more like doing multiple experiments. These may be attempts at replication of an initial experiment; or they may build upon the first experiment, perhaps carrying the investigation into an area suggested by the first study; or they may seek to complement the first study by focusing on an area not originally covered. This activity, whether for multiple case studies or for multiple experiments (or for multiple surveys, for that matter, or even for multiple studies involving a range of different research strategies), is not concerned with statistical generalization but with *analytic generalization* (referred to above on p. 177). The first case study will provide evidence which supports a theoretical view about what is going on, perhaps in terms of mechanisms and the contexts in which they operate. This theory, and its possible support or disconfirmation, guides the choice of subsequent cases in a multiple case study. Findings, patterns of data, etc. from these case studies which provide this kind of support, particularly if they simultaneously provide evidence which does not fit in with alternative theories, are the basis for generalization.

Put simply, cases are selected where the theory would suggest *either* that the same result is obtained, *or* that predictably different results will be obtained. Given, say, three of each which fall out in the predicted manner, this provides pretty compelling evidence for the theory. This is an oversimplification because case studies and their outcomes are likely to be multifaceted and difficult to capture adequately within a simple theory. Support for the theory may be qualified or partial in any particular case, leading to revision and further development of the theory, and then probably the need for further case studies.

## Preparing to carry out a case study

An important feature of case study is that *if more than one investigator is involved, they typically take on essentially similar roles*. The tasks cannot be reduced to rigid formulae with division of function, as in survey research. All the investigators need an intelligent appreciation of what they are doing, and why. Hence it is highly desirable that all are involved in the first stages of conceptualization and definition of the research questions. Similarly, they should all be involved in the development of the case study plan.

The plan contains details of the data collection procedures to be used, and the general rules to be followed. Where there is a single investigator, the main purpose of the plan is to enhance the validity of the study, but it also acts as an aide-mémoire to the investigator. When a team is involved it also serves to increase reliability, in the sense of assisting all investigators to follow the same set of procedures and rules. Box 6.8 gives suggestions for the organization of the plan.

---

## Box 6.8

### The case study plan

It is highly desirable that an explicit plan is prepared and agreed by those involved *in the full knowledge and expectation that aspects of this may change as the work continues.*
    The following sections may be helpful.

**1** *Overview* Covers the background information about the project, that is the context and perspective, and why it is taking place; the issues being investigated and relevant readings about the issues.

**2** *Procedures* Covers the major tasks in collecting data, including:

a    access arrangements;
b    resources available;
c    schedule of the data collection activities and specification of the periods of time involved.

**3** *Questions* The set of research questions with accompanying list of probable sources of evidence and data matrices.

**4** *Reporting* Covers the following:

a    outline of the case study report(s);*
b    treatment of the full 'database' (i.e. totality of the documentary evidence obtained);
c    audience(s).*

* There may be several audiences, for which different reports (in style and length) are needed. Consideration of reports and audiences at this stage, and during the study, helps to guide the study. See chapter 15.

*Note*: The plan should communicate to a general intelligent reader what is proposed. It forms part of establishing the validity of the study.

---

## Pilot studies

A pilot study is a small-scale version of the real thing, a try-out of what you propose so its feasibility can be checked. There are aspects of case study research which can make piloting both more difficult to set up and, fortunately, less crucially important. It may be that there is only one case to be considered, or that there are particular features of the case selected (such as geographical or temporal accessibility, or your own knowledge of the case), such that there is no sensible equivalent which could act as the pilot.

In circumstances like these, the flexibility of case study gives you at least some opportunity to, as it were, 'learn on the job'. Or it may be that the initial formulation leans more towards the 'exploratory' pole of case study design, and later stages with the benefit of experience can have a more 'explanatory' or 'confirmatory' focus.

Yin (1994) distinguishes between 'pilot tests' and 'pre-tests'. He views the former as helping 'investigators to refine their data collection plans with respect to both the content of the data and the procedures to be followed'. For him, the pilot is, as it were, a 'laboratory for the investigators, allowing them to observe different phenomena from many different angles or to try different approaches on a trial basis' (p. 74). I prefer to regard these as case studies in their own right with an essentially exploratory function, where some of the research questions are methodological. What he calls the 'pre-test' is a formal 'dress rehearsal' in which the intended data collection plan is used as faithfully as possible, and is perhaps closer to the usual meaning of a pilot study.

## Every enquiry is a kind of case study

In one sense, all enquiries are case studies. They take place at particular times in particular places with particular people. Stressing this signals that the design flexibility inherent in the case study is there in all studies until we, as it were, design it out.

> *Many flexible design studies, even though not explicitly labelled as such, can be usefully viewed as case studies. They typically take place in a specific setting, or small range of settings, context is viewed as important, and there is commonly an interest in the setting in its own right. While they may not be multimethod as originally designed, the use of more than one method of data collection, when feasible, can improve many flexible design studies. Hence, even if you decide to follow one of the other flexible design traditions discussed below, you should find consideration of this section on case study of value.*

## Ethnographic Studies

An ethnography provides a description and interpretation of the culture and social structure of a social group. It has its roots in anthropology, involving an immersion in the particular culture of the society being studied so that life in that community could be described in detail. The ethnographer's task was to become an accepted member of the group, including participating in its cultural life and practices. Anthropologists initially focused on exotic cultures such as the Trobriand Islanders of New Guinea. Sociologists, initially at Chicago University, adapted the approach to look at groups and communities in modern urban society (Bogdan and Biklen, 1992), and it is currently widely used in social research (Atkinson and Hammersley, 1994). Fortier (1998) and Foster (1995) are examples of this type of ethnographic study (see also box 4.1, p. 84).

A central feature of this tradition is that people are studied for a long period of time in their own natural environment. Critics of the approach are concerned about researchers getting over-involved with the people being studied, perhaps disturbing and changing the natural setting, and hence compromising the quality of the research. However, the argument is that 'in order to truly grasp the lived experience of people from their point of view, one *has* to enter into relationships with them, and hence disturb the natural setting. There is no point in trying to control what is an unavoidable consequence of becoming involved in people's lives in this way' (Davidson and Layder, 1994, p. 165; emphasis in original). Hence it becomes necessary to try to assess the effects of one's presence.

The main purpose and central virtue of this approach is often considered to be its production of descriptive data free from imposed external concepts and ideas. Its goal is to produce 'thick description' (Geertz, 1973), which allows others to understand the culture from inside in the terms that the participants themselves used to describe what is going on. There is clear value in doing this for and about cultures where little is known, or where there have been misleading presumptions or prejudices about the culture of a group.

Some ethnographers display a general distrust of theorizing. However, there seems to be no reason why an ethnographical approach cannot be linked to the development of theory (Hammersley, 1985; Layder, 1993). Working within the ethnographic tradition is not an easy option for the beginner, for the reasons given in box 6.9.

## Using an ethnographic approach

Using an ethnographic approach is very much a question of general style rather than of following specific prescriptions about procedure. In process terms, it

---

## Box 6.9

### Difficulties in doing an ethnographic study

1   To 'do an ethnography' calls for a detailed description, analysis and interpretation of the culture-sharing group. This requires an understanding of the specialist concepts used when talking about socio-cultural systems.

2   For traditional ethnographies, the time taken to collect data is very extensive, extending over years. Some current approaches (sometimes referred to as 'mini-ethnographies') seek to cut this down drastically, but this creates a tension with the requirement to develop an intimate understanding of the group.

3   Ethnographies have typically been written in a narrative, literary style which may be unfamiliar to those with a social science background (conversely, this can be an advantage to those with an arts or humanities background). This may also be a disadvantage when reporting to some real world audiences.

4   Researchers have been known to 'go native', resulting in them either discontinuing the study, or moving from the role of researcher to that of advocate.

---

involves getting out into 'the field' and staying there – in classical ethnography, this meant for a period of years. This is highly unrealistic for virtually all real world studies, and hence this section focuses on the use of an ethnographic approach rather than on how to carry out a full-scale ethnography. Box 6.10 lists features of the ethnographic approach.

*Participant observation* is very closely associated with the process of an ethnographic study. Chapter 11 considers the different types of role the observer might take. Whatever degree of participation you adopt (ranging from that of full group member to one where you are involved solely as a researcher), observation is difficult, demanding and time-consuming. Box 6.11 lists reasons why you might feel you must work in this way.

Again, however, while it is undoubtedly true that virtually all ethnographic studies do use this type of observation, they can be eclectic in terms of methods, making use of whatever technique appears to be feasible. The feature which is crucial is that the researcher is fully *immersed* in the day-to-day lives of the people being studied.

The focus of an ethnographic study is a group who share a culture. The task is to learn about that culture; effectively, to understand their world as they do. Initially such studies were carried out by (cultural) anthropologists who studied societies and cultures very different from our own. Even when some

---

## Box 6.10

### Features of the ethnographic approach

**1** The shared cultural meanings of the behaviour, actions, events and contexts of a group of people are central to understanding the group. Your task is to uncover those meanings.

**2** To do this requires you to gain an insider's perspective.

**3** Hence, you need both to observe and study the group in its natural setting, and to take part in what goes on there.

**4** While participant observation in the field is usually considered essential, no method of data collection is ruled out in principle.

**5** The central focus of your study and detailed research questions will emerge and evolve as you continue your involvement. A priori theoretical orientation and initial research questions are not ruled out, but you should be prepared for these to change.

**6** Data collection is likely to be prolonged over time and to have a series of phases. It is common to focus on behaviours, events etc. which occur frequently so that you have the opportunity to develop understanding of their significance.

---

familiar group or sub-group within one's own society is the focus, the ethnographic approach asks the researcher to treat it as 'anthropologically strange'. This is a very valuable exercise, particularly for those carrying out 'insider research'. It provides a means of bringing out into the open presuppositions about what you are seeing.

### Ethnography and realism

Classically, ethnography was seen as a way of getting close to the reality of social phenomena in a way which is not feasible with the experimental and survey strategies. The Chicago sociologist Herbert Blumer talks about using ethnography to 'lift the veils' and to 'dig deeper', illustrating his realist assumptions (Hammersley, 1989).

However, as Atkinson and Hammersley (1994) note, there is a tension within the ethnographic research community on this issue. 'Central to the way in which ethnographers think about human social action is the idea that people *construct* the social world, both through their interpretations of it and through the actions based upon those interpretations' (Hammersley, 1992, p. 44,

---

## Box 6.11

### Reasons for using participant observation

Commit yourself to doing this only if the following fits you pretty closely.

1    You see interactions, actions and behaviours, and the way people interpret these, act on them, etc. as central.

2    You believe that knowledge of the social world can be best gained by observing 'real life' settings.

3    You consider that generating data on social interaction in specific contexts, as it occurs, is superior to retrospective accounts or their ability to verbalize and reconstruct a version of what happened.

4    You view social explanations as best constructed through depth, complexity and roundedness in data.

5    You are happy with an active, reflexive and flexible research role.

6    You feel it is more ethical to enter into and become involved in the social world of those you research, rather than 'standing outside'.

7    You can't see any alternative way of collecting the data you require to answer your research questions!

(Adapted and abridged from Mason, 1996, pp. 61–3.)

---

emphasis in original). Hammersley goes on to argue, persuasively, that this constructivist approach can be compatible with realism. However, this calls for an abandonment of the 'naïve' realism characteristic of early ethnography, where it was assumed that the phenomena studied were independent of the researcher, who could make direct contact with them and provide knowledge of unquestionable validity. He argues in favour of 'subtle' realism as a viable alternative to the relativist constructionist approach.

The key elements of subtle realism, elaborated in Hammersley (1992, pp. 50–4) are:

- defining knowledge as beliefs about whose validity we are reasonably confident (accepting that we can never be absolutely certain about the validity of any claim to knowledge);
- acknowledging that there are phenomena independent of our claims about them, which those claims may represent more or less accurately;
- an overall research aim of representing reality while acknowledging that such a representation will always be from a particular perspective

which makes some features of the phenomenon relevant and others irrelevant (hence there can be multiple valid and non-contradictory representations).

This represents a reprise, using rather different terminology, of the discussion in chapter 2, p. 34, where the case was made for adoption of the critical realist approach.

## Designing an ethnographic study

The framework for research design given in chapter 4 (figure 4.1, p. 82) is applicable for an ethnographic study. As with other types of study, you need to give serious consideration to the purposes of your work and to establishing some (probably very tentative) theoretical or conceptual framework. This gives you an initial take on possible research questions, which in themselves assist in the selection of data collection methods and sampling – in the sense of who you observe, where, when, etc. While you can assume that participant observation of some kind will be involved, it may be that you have research questions which call for an additional approach, or that additional methods will give valuable scope for triangulation.

An ethnographic approach is particularly indicated when you are seeking insight into an area or field which is new or different. It can help to provide valuable understanding which can then guide later research using other approaches. Remember that your initial research questions (and the other aspects of the framework you started out with) are highly likely to change and develop as you get involved.

There is no one specific design for an ethnographic study. Depth rather than breadth of coverage is the norm, with a relatively small number of cases being studied. Description and interpretation are likely to be stressed (Atkinson and Hammersley, 1994).

*While ethnography is a distinctive approach, it can be linked with either the case study or grounded theory approaches. A case study can be approached ethnographically; or an ethnographic study can be approached by means of grounded theory.*

## Grounded Theory Studies

A grounded theory study seeks to generate a theory which relates to the particular situation forming the focus of the study. This theory is 'grounded' in data obtained during the study, particularly in the actions, interactions and processes of the people involved. It is closely associated with two American sociologists, Barney Glaser and Anselm Strauss. Their highly influential text introducing this approach (Glaser and Strauss, 1967) has been followed by several more accessible introductions, including Glaser (1978) and Strauss and Corbin (1997; 1998).

Their approach was formulated in reaction to the sociological stance prevalent in the 1960s which insisted that studies should have a firm 'a priori' theoretical orientation. It has proved particularly attractive in novel and applied fields where pre-existing theories are often hard to come by. The notion that it is feasible to discover concepts and come up with hypotheses from the field, which can then be used to generate theory, appeals to many.

Grounded theory is both a strategy for doing research and a particular style of analysing the data arising from that research. Each of these aspects has a particular set of procedures and techniques. It is not a theory in itself, except perhaps in the sense of claiming that the preferred approach to theory development is via the data you collect. While grounded theory is often presented as appropriate for studies which are exclusively qualitative, there is no reason why some quantitative data collection should not be included. Indeed, the first studies reported in Glaser and Strauss (1967) made extensive use of quantitative data. In later years, differences built up between the two collaborators to the extent that Glaser (1992) took vigorous exception to the direction in which Strauss (and other colleagues) had taken grounded theory. Rennie (1998), in developing a rationale for grounded theory which reconciles realism and relativism, argues that Strauss and Corbin's approach effectively reverts back to the hypothetico-deductivism of traditional experimentalism, and that Glaser's procedures are more consistent with the objectives of the method.

Box 6.12 indicates some attractive features of grounded theory research; box 6.13 some problems in carrying it out.

## Carrying out a grounded theory study

A grounded theory study involves going out into 'the field' and collecting data. No particular type of 'field' is called for. Such studies have been carried out in a very wide range of settings. Glaser and Strauss initially worked in organizational contexts; interest in their studies of dying in hospitals (Glaser and Strauss, 1965, 1968) provided the stimulus for their first methodology text (Glaser and Strauss, 1967). Typical studies include ones on 'living with multiple sclerosis' (Davis, 1973); relationships between mothers and adult daughters (Henwood, 1993); and decision-making about pregnancy (Currie, 1988). Further examples are provided in box 4.1, p. 84.

Interviews are the most common data collection method. However, other methods such as observation (participant or otherwise) and the analysis of documents can be and have been used. Similarly, although grounded theory

---

### Box 6.12

## Attractive features of grounded theory research

**1**  Provides explicit procedures for generating theory in research.

**2**  Presents a strategy for doing research which, while flexible, is systematic and co-ordinated.

**3**  Provides explicit procedures for the analysis of qualitative data.

**4**  Particularly useful in applied areas of research, and novel ones, where the theoretical approach to be selected is not clear or is non-existent.

**5**  Wide range of exemplars of its use in many applied and professional settings now available.

---

### Box 6.13

## Problems in using grounded theory

**1**  It is not possible to start a research study without some pre-existing theoretical ideas and assumptions.

**2**  There are tensions between the evolving and inductive style of a flexible study and the systematic approach of grounded theory.

**3**  It may be difficult in practice to decide when categories are 'saturated' or when the theory is sufficiently developed.

**4**  Grounded theory has particular types of prescribed categories as components of the theory which may not appear appropriate for a particular study.

---

is typically portrayed as a qualitative approach to research, there is no reason in principle why some form of quantitative data collection cannot be used. Strauss and Corbin (1998) make the explicit point that grounded theory is a general method that can be used in both quantitative and qualitative studies.

Procedurally, the researcher is expected to make several visits to the field to collect data. The data are then analysed between visits. Visits continue until the *categories* found through analysis are 'saturated'. Or, in other words, you keep on gathering information until you reach diminishing returns and you are not adding to what you already have. (A category is a unit of information made up of events, happenings and instances – see below, p. 194.)

This movement back and forth – first to the field to gather information; then back to base to analyse the data; then back to the field to gather more information; then back home to analyse the data; etc. – is similar to the 'dialogic' process central to the hermeneutic tradition (see p. 196). It is very different from a traditional linear one-way model of research where you first gather all your data, then get down to the analysis. However, it is close to the common-sense approach which one might use when trying to understand something which is complex and puzzling.

Sampling in grounded theory studies is *purposive* (see p. 265). We do not seek a representative sample for its own sake; there is certainly no notion of random sampling from a known population to achieve statistical generalizability. Sampling of people to interview or events to observe is undertaken so that additional information can be obtained to help in generating conceptual categories. Within grounded theory this type of purposive sampling is referred to as *theoretical sampling*. That is, the persons interviewed, or otherwise studied, are chosen to help the researcher formulate theory.

The repeated comparison of information from data collection and emerging theory is sometimes referred to as the *constant comparative* method of data analysis. The process of data analysis in grounded theory research is systematic. A standardized form is given in Strauss and Corbin (1998) and summarized in box 6.14 (note, however, that Glaser, 1992, dissents quite violently from some elements of their formulation).

Further details of the analysis process are given in chapter 14, p. 492. A summary is presented here because of the intimate inter-relationship between design and analysis in a grounded theory study. It may also help you to appreciate that a grounded theory study is by no means an easy option and should not be undertaken lightly. It is, of course, possible to design a study which incorporates some aspects of grounded theory while ignoring others. For example, you may feel that the approach to coding is too prescriptive or restrictive. However, as with other research traditions, by working within the tradition you buy shelter and support from criticism – provided that the ways of the tribe are followed faithfully. And, somewhat less cynically, the fact that a group of researchers and methodologists have worked away at the approach over a number of years makes it likely that solutions to problems and difficulties have been found.

## Other Traditions of Flexible (Qualitative) Research Design

This section tries to give an indication of a range of other possible approaches which have been used, together with references which give further details. The

# Box 6.14

## Data analysis in grounded theory studies

The analysis involves three sets of coding:

**1** *Open coding* The researcher forms initial *categories* of information about the phenomenon being studied from the initial data gathered.

Within each category, you look for several sub-categories (referred to as *properties*), and then for data to *dimensionalize* (i.e. to show the dimensions on which properties vary and to seek the extreme possibilities on these continua).

**2** *Axial coding* This involves assembling the data in new ways after open coding. A *coding paradigm* (otherwise known as a *logic diagram*) is developed which:

* identifies a *central phenomenon* (i.e. a central category about the phenomenon),
* explores *causal conditions* (i.e. categories of conditions that influence the phenomenon),
* specifies *strategies* (i.e. the actions or interactions that result from the central phenomenon),
* identifies the *context* and *intervening conditions* (i.e. the conditions that influence the strategies), and
* delineates the *consequences* (i.e. the outcomes of the strategies) for this phenomenon.

**3** *Selective coding* This involves the integration of the categories in the axial coding model. In this phase, conditional *propositions* (or hypotheses) are typically presented.

The result of this process of data collection and analysis is a *substantive-level theory* relevant to a specific problem, issue or group.

*Note*: The three types of coding are not necessarily sequential; they are likely to overlap.

(After Strauss and Corbin, 1998.)

main principle for their inclusion has been that they may be useful for answering particular kinds of research question.

## Biographical or life history research

This may be thought of as a particular kind of case study where the 'case' studied is an individual person. The intention is to tell the story of a person's life. This is a well-established genre of literary endeavour covering virtually all kinds of different lives (historical, political, etc.) which may not aspire to be a form of social science research. However, there is no reason why biographical or life history research should not have the characteristics of a systematic study given in box 6.2.

One such format is the 'interpretive' biography (Denzin, 1989), where the intention is to interpret a person's life through telling their 'story'. Generally, this is done by using documents and records, together with interviews and conversations when the person is still alive. If possible, this is backed up by observation of the subject over a period of time, together with interviews with friends (and possibly enemies!) and colleagues.

The bases for selection of a subject can be many and varied. They include both lives of the 'great and the good' and those whose lives, otherwise unremarked, shed light on aspects of society and culture. Biography is, probably, an unlikely approach to be taken in a real world study. Apart from technical problems such as the extended time-scale needed to produce a rigorous and systematic study, it is doubtful that it will provide answers to research questions directly relevant to the kind of issues and problems which sponsors will fund.

Cresswell (1998, pp. 47–51) provides more detail and a wide range of references to different versions of the biographical approach.

## Phenomenological research

Phenomenological research focuses on the subjective experience of the individuals studied. What is their experience like? How can one understand and describe what happens to them from their own point of view? As the term suggests, at its heart is the attempt to understand a particular phenomenon. This might be, for example, the experience of a child with disabilities in a mainstream (or segregated) school classroom.

Phenomenology has its roots in the philosophy of Husserl (1977); see Stewart and Mickunas (1990) or Holstein and Gubrium (1994) for accessible introductions. It has been influential in several social sciences as well as applied fields such as nursing and the health sciences (Nieswiadomy, 1993). It has also had a major influence on the general development of qualitative methodology, and provides the philosophical basis for interpretive research strategies including ethnomethodology and conversational analysis (Holstein and Gubrium, 1994). There is also an extensive literature on psychological phenomenology and, in particular, how research can be carried out along these lines (e.g. Moustakas, 1994). However, there are considerable barriers in the way of a novice seeking to use this approach. There is a highly specialized vocabulary, and a solid grounding in some challenging philosophy is called for. Nevertheless, it is an approach which has much to offer in answering certain kinds of research question about subjective experience which may be highly relevant to some real world studies.

## Symbolic interactionism

Symbolic interactionism is an influential perspective within sociology and social psychology (e.g. Goffman, 1969; Berger and Luckman, 1967). While there are undoubtedly particular flexible research designs which employ this perspective explicitly, it is perhaps best viewed as a general and pervasive influence on the development of qualitative methodology. Box 6.15 lists some of the influences from this theoretical framework.

## Hermeneutics

Hermeneutics is the 'art and science of interpretation'. Its main initial use was by theologians in interpreting the Bible so that it was meaningful to a society very different from the one in which it was originally written. Bentz and Shapiro (1998, p. 105) cite the American use of hermeneutics in contemporary life in the interpretation of the US Constitution. A term such as 'freedom of speech' needs to be translated from an eighteenth-century context to today's situation. How, for example, do we apply the concept to speech broadcast via radio and television? Various levels of interpretation are called for. What were the writers' intentions? What has been the history of the concept? How have contextual changes led to a reinterpretation of the concept?

As all social science research involves interpretation, insights gained from hermeneutics are relevant to many aspects of the research process. Reason and Rowan (1981) point out that hermeneutics is just one example of the process whereby people make sense of their world. As all understanding takes place in time and a particular culture, a lesson from hermeneutics is that the pre-judgements we bring to this process are to some extent culturally pre-determined.

While hermeneutics was originally concerned with the interpretation of 'text' taken in a literal sense, it is now applied more widely to conversations,

---

## Box 6.15

### Principles of symbolic interactionism influential in the development of qualitative research

1   Social life is formed, maintained and changed by the basic meaning attached to it by interacting people, who interact on the basis of meanings they assign to their world; social life and objects become significant when they are assigned meanings.

2   Social life is expressed through symbols. Language is the most important symbolic system.

3   The purpose of social research is to study the structure, functions and meaning of symbolic systems.

4   The most appropriate method of social research is the *naturalistic* method, which incorporates two major procedures, *exploration* and *inspection* (Blumer, 1969; Wallace and Wolf, 1986). Exploration studies new areas, looks for details, and offers a clear understanding of the research question. Any method is useful here. Inspection, on the other hand, is an analytical method and contains a more intensive and more concentrated testing. (Blumer, 1969, called this type of approach *sympathetic introspection*.)

5   Data and interpretations depend on context and process and must be steadily verified and, when necessary, corrected.

6   Meanings are established in and through social interaction. They are learned through interaction and not determined otherwise.

7   Meanings are employed, managed and changed through interaction.

(After Sarantakos, 1998, pp. 49–50.)

---

interactions between people in different settings, and even fashion. The appropriateness of doing this is discussed by Giddens (1986).

When your main research task is the interpretation of text (considered in a broad sense), there are several hermeneutic strategies worth considering. For example, hermeneutics would maintain that the closer one is to the source of the text the more valid one's interpretation is likely to be (which is, of course, in sharp distinction to the positivist stance of 'distance' from the object being studied). Mothers of infants can interpret their language much more readily than outsiders.

A central feature is the 'dialogic' nature of hermeneutic enquiry. The text is returned to time and time again. Initial understandings are refined through interpretation; this then raises further questions, calling for a return to the text and revision of the interpretation. Throughout this process, one is trying to understand what it means to those who created it and to integrate that meaning with its meaning to us. Hermeneutics has contributed to qualitative research methodology the notion of an active involvement by the researcher in the research process.

It is a difficult method to follow, both procedurally and because of the tensions between being closely embedded in the context and process of explanation and the research need to be honest and balanced. As with other qualitative approaches, this dilemma can be addressed by providing detailed accounts of the research process so that it is possible to guard against suspicions of basing the interpretation on a selective and biased reading. A more detailed account and a range of examples are provided by Bentz and Shapiro (1998, pp. 105–14). Other examples include Little (1999) and von Post and Eriksson (1999). Draucker (1999) provides a critique of work in this area.

## Feminist perspectives and flexible designs

Some researchers adopting a feminist perspective reject quantitative methods and designs, and both positivism and post-positivism, as 'representations of patriarchal thinking that result in a separation between the scientist and the persons under study (Fine, 1992)' (Mertens, 1998, p. 162). For them flexible, qualitative designs are the only option. There is certainly an emphasis in these design traditions on non-exploitative research seeking an empathetic understanding between researcher and participants which chimes closely with feminist views. However, as Davidson and Layder (1994, p. 217) point out, feminist methodologists are not the only nor the first to advocate such approaches. Reinharz (1992), too, cautions against the assumption that research using qualitative methods is inherently feminist. She also describes the wide variety of viewpoints that feminists hold on the appropriateness of different methods and methodologies.

Hence the position taken here, following Davidson and Layder (1994), is that while the critique presented by feminist methodologists of traditional social science research has yielded important insights, and helped to strengthen the case for qualitative research, the claim for a distinctive feminist research methodology has not been substantiated.

## Sample Size in Flexible Designs

It is difficult to pre-specify the number of observation sessions, interviews, etc. required in a flexible design study. Although the terminology differs in the different traditions, the basic notion is that you keep going until you reach 'saturation'. This is when further data collection appears to add little or nothing to what you have already learned. It will take note of the fact that your continuing analysis and interpretation of the data you have already collected throws up conjectures, suggests new themes, etc. which may call for further data collection. It is also likely that in a real world study, external factors (such as having to complete by a given deadline) will limit what you can do.

Morse (2000) suggests that an estimate of the number of participants, observations, data sources etc. needed in a flexible study to reach saturation depends on several factors:

- *The scope of the study*    The broader the scope, the longer it takes. By all means, start pretty broad, but narrow down as soon as feasible. In this way you can keep the study within bounds, more focused, and probably of better quality.
- *The nature of the topic*    If the topic is obvious and clear, fewer participants are needed. If it is difficult to 'grab', or if participants find it difficult to talk about the topic, you need more.
- *Quality of the data*    'If data are on target, contain less dross, and are rich and experiential, then fewer participants will be required to reach saturation' (p. 4).
- *Study design*    Some study designs produce more data per participant than others (e.g. those where there are repeated interviews or the study unit is, say, the family, calling for interviews with all members of the family).
- *Research method*    If you are using, say, semi-structured interviews, producing a small amount of data per interview question, you need a large number of participants (of the order of thirty to sixty). Depth interviews producing much richer data can be fewer.

As Morse admits, 'Once all of these factors are considered, you may not be much further ahead in predicting the exact number, but you will be able to defend the estimated range presented in your proposal' (p. 3). In an earlier publication (Morse, 1994), she produced 'rules of thumb' for ethnographic and grounded theory studies, recommending approximately thirty to fifty interviews. This at the least provides some ammunition for those required to pre-specify a number as part of a project proposal (see also appendix A). Note that case studies are so various for it not to be sensible to give general suggestions.

## Further Reading

Cresswell, J. W. (1998) *Qualitative Inquiry and Research Design: Choosing among Five Traditions*. Thousand Oaks, Calif.: Sage. Even-handed exposition of the various options and approaches available to those wishing to design and carry out a flexible (qualitative) study.

Delamont, S. (1992) *Field Work in Educational Settings: Methods, Pitfalls and Perspectives*. London: Falmer. Practical, accessible and hugely enjoyable guide to doing qualitative research. Focus is on educational settings but much applies widely.

Hammersley, M. and Atkinson, P. (1995) *Ethnography: Principles in Practice*, 2nd edn. London: Routledge. Highly readable, systematic and coherent account of the ethnographic approach.

Lee, T. W. (1999) *Using Qualitative Methods in Organizational Research*. Thousand Oaks, Calif.: Sage. Broad review. Provides links to use of quantitative methods.

Lofland, J. and Lofland, L. H. (1995) *Analyzing Social Settings: A Guide to Qualitative Observation and Analysis*, 3rd edn. Belmont, Calif.: Wadsworth. Fully updated edition of classic manual of qualitative social research. Very clear and interesting.

Mason, J. (1996) *Qualitative Researching*. London: Sage. Very clear and accessible. Links principles and practice.

Miles, M. B. and Huberman, A. M. (1994) *Qualitative Data Analysis: An Expanded Sourcebook*, 2nd edn. Thousand Oaks, Calif.: Sage. Many useful ideas on design and analysis of case studies.

Padgett, D. K. (1998) *Qualitative Methods in Social Work Research: Challenges and Rewards*. Thousand Oaks, Calif.: Sage. Short, wide-ranging and practical, with focus on the needs of the social work researcher.

Silverman, D. (2000) *Doing Qualitative Research: A Practical Handbook*. London: Sage. A highly practical guide for those wanting to do qualitative research.

Stake, R. E. (1995) *The Art of Case Study Research*. Thousand Oaks, Calif.: Sage. Stimulating and readable text on (largely qualitative) case study.

Strauss, A. and Corbin, J. (1998) *Basics of Qualitative Research: Techniques and Procedures for Developing Grounded Theory*, 2nd edn. Thousand Oaks, Calif.: Sage. Provides just what the title claims.

Yin, R. K. (1994) *Case Study Research: Design and Methods*, 2nd edn. Thousand Oaks, Calif.: Sage. Key text on design and analysis of rigorous case studies.

# 7

# Designs for Particular Purposes: Evaluation, Action and Change

This chapter:

- stresses the ubiquity and importance of evaluation;
- discusses different forms of evaluation research;
- covers the planning and carrying out of evaluations;
- emphasizes their political dimension;
- introduces needs assessment and cost–benefit analysis;
- explains the distinctive features of action research;
- considers the place of research in producing social change, and some of the problems associated with doing this.

## Introduction

Much real world research in the social sciences has the main purpose of evaluating something. Real world researchers also often have an 'action' agenda. Their hope and intention is that the research and its findings will be used in some way to make a difference to the lives and situations of those involved in the study, and/or others. This takes us into the somewhat specialist fields of *evaluation research* and *action research*.

Researchers tend to bemoan the lack of influence that research has on practice. Some reasons for this ineffectiveness, and what might be done about it, are discussed in the following section. When practitioners get involved in research, they often want to change something linked to their practice. The chapter concludes with a discussion of roles they might take to achieve this, and how researchers might help them.

## Evaluation Research

*An evaluation is a study which has a distinctive purpose; it is not a new or different research strategy.*

The purpose of an evaluation is to assess the effects and effectiveness of something, typically some innovation, intervention, policy, practice or service. It is commonly referred to as *program evaluation* (the spelling reflecting that it started out as a largely North American activity). Fixed or flexible designs can be used, with either qualitative or quantitative methods, or some combination of both types.

A high profile is being given to evaluation in many different settings. There is an increasing expectation that real world enquirers will be able to carry out evaluation research. Carrying out such studies undoubtedly highlights and brings to the fore the 'real worldness' of the enterprise. Issues concerning clearances and permissions, negotiations with 'gatekeepers', the political nature of an evaluation, ethics, the type of report, etc., are not in themselves design issues, but they do set an important context for the choice of design. Evaluation is intrinsically a very sensitive activity where there may be a risk or duty of revealing inadequacy or worse. Your intentions may be misconstrued and your findings misused or ignored. There are also signs of weariness on the part of those being evaluated (Draper, 2001). The implication for those doing evaluations is that you have to think through very carefully what you are doing and why.

## The importance of evaluation

'Accountability' is now a watchword in the whole range of public services involving people, such as education, health and social services. This concern arises in part from political and ideological considerations, where it forms part of a drive to place public services within a framework similar to that governing private profit-making businesses. Irrespective of its origins, the notion that we should seek to understand and assess critically the functioning of services and programmes has much to commend it. The contentious issues are who does this, for whom, in what way and for what purposes.

Much of the enquiry that social scientists get involved with in the real world can be thought of as some kind of evaluation: *an attempt to assess the worth or value of some innovation, intervention, service or approach.* This is patently obvious in fields such as education, clinical practice and market research, but a high proportion of all applied non-laboratory work has an evaluative dimension to it.

Evaluation is not necessarily research. However, it profits from the kind of principled, systematic approach which characterizes research. Evaluation of this type is commonly referred to as *evaluation research*. It is a field which has grown rapidly since the 1960s, helped by the US government setting aside a proportion of the budget of the many social programmes initiated at that time for evaluation. Evaluations of such large-scale programmes have not been very conclusive, but have tended to show that they did not achieve their aims. There has been widespread criticism of the quality of many evaluations. Nevertheless, discussion of the problems and issues in carrying out large-scale evaluations has thrown up much of value for use in more manageable small-scale studies. Oakley (2000, chs 9 and 10) provides a detailed and balanced account of these issues.

The characteristics of real world enquiry discussed in chapter 1 above are present in evaluations in a very clear-cut way. For example, they are commonly commissioned by a client or sponsor, who will often have a direct interest in the thing evaluated. Hence, rather than deciding on the topic that interests them, evaluators have this determined by others, although the approach taken is likely to be the subject of negotiation between evaluator and client. Ethical issues abound. Whose interests are being served by an intervention? Who is the real client (is it the person funding the study, or those whom the service is intended to benefit)? How are vested interests taken into account? The evaluation, its results and how they are presented may affect people's jobs, education, health and sanity. Political issues are similarly inescapable. The type and style of evaluation chosen, as well as the criteria used, may mean a choice of the perspectives, values and goals of certain parties or participants rather than others.

Evaluations also highlight issues to do with change. The service, programme or other subject may well seek to produce or encourage change in those involved. A positive side of a topic having been chosen by the client or sponsor is that evaluation findings are more likely to influence the real world (or at least that bit of it represented by the programme or innovation being evaluated) than traditional research. This aspect is discussed in more detail in later sections on action research and change. The evaluation may indicate that changes are needed in the programme if it is to be effective. However, evaluation findings are likely to be just one of a complex set of influences on the future development of the programme. Evaluators need to communicate the results and their implications not so much to their peers in the scientific and evaluation community, who are likely to be both knowledgeable about and sympathetic to empirical enquiry, but to clients and decision-makers who are unlikely to be. This means that considerable thought has to be given to the communication process, and to the style and nature of evaluation reports. These topics are picked up again in the final chapter of this book.

The practical problems of doing real world research also loom large. Evaluation tends to work to short time-spans and tight deadlines. Participants may be difficult to contact, perhaps because they are busy, perhaps because they are keeping out of your way. 'Gatekeepers', such as middle management in a firm or a deputy headteacher in a school, may be obstructive. Administrators may decide to alter the system or context in important ways during the study. External events, ranging from national strikes to heavy snowstorms, may intervene.

## A note on possible subjects for an evaluation

The list is endless. Recently published examples include evaluations of:

- a juvenile offenders' 'halfway house' (Leon et al., 1999);
- a new night nursing service for elderly people suffering from dementia (Watkins and Redfern, 1997);
- a programme to reduce alcohol and other drug abuse among high-risk youth by increasing family resilience (Johnson et al., 1998);
- 'Safe in the Sun', a curriculum intervention for primary schools (McWhirter et al., 2000);
- a programme to reduce women's risk of multiple sexual victimization (Breitenbecher and Gidycz, 1998).

Indeed, once you get involved with evaluation, you appreciate the force of the 'Law of the Hammer' – give someone a hammer and it transforms their environment into a set of things to be hammered (Kaplan, 1964). Get into evaluation and everything seems to be a candidate for an evaluation.

The discussion in the rest of this chapter is couched mainly in terms of the evaluation of a 'programme'. This is for simplicity of presentation. Feel free to translate this into terms appropriate to whatever it is that you are called upon to evaluate. The concentration in this text is of course on human enquiry, on the 'people' aspects of the evaluation. In specific cases, it may be necessary to supplement this in various ways; for example, software evaluation will have a substantial additional technical agenda.

## Defining evaluation research

*The position taken here is that evaluation research is essentially indistinguishable from other research in terms of design, data collection techniques and methods of analysis.*

The realist approach advocated in chapter 2 is applicable to evaluations, particularly when the concern is for 'how' and 'why' a programme works (Pawson and Tilley, 1997). So-called 'theory-based evaluation' follows a very similar approach, though using different terminology (see Birckmayer and Weiss, 2000, for discussion of a range of examples).

Evaluation research can, and does, make use of flexible and fixed research strategies including virtually all of the variants discussed in the previous two chapters. It is sometimes claimed that the strongest evaluation studies follow an experimental strategy in making comparisons between at least two groups (one of which has received the new programme, service or whatever, while another has not). However, while the study of outcomes in this comparative way is often important, evaluations can sensibly target other aspects, such as whether or not a programme meets the needs of those taking part. Also, in practice, there are often severe problems in finding an appropriate control group, or in achieving random allocation to the different groups, and in securing effective isolation between them to avoid cross-contamination. There are also more fundamental critiques of the use of control group methodology in evaluation research (Pawson and Tilley, 1997), although it still has strong advocates (e.g. Oakley and Fullerton, 1996).

The flexibility in design and execution of the case study, together with the fact that most evaluations are concerned with the effectiveness and appropriateness of an innovation or programme in a specific setting (i.e. that it is a 'case' rather than a sample), make the case study strategy appropriate for many evaluations.

Evaluation is often concerned not only with assessing worth or value but also with seeking to assist in the improvement of whatever is being evaluated. Michael Quinn Patton, a prolific American evaluator, who writes more entertainingly than most in a field littered with turgid texts, considers that

> the practice of evaluation involves the systematic collection of information about the activities, characteristics and outcomes of programmes, personnel and products for use by specific people to reduce uncertainties, improve effectiveness, and make decisions with regard to what those programmes, personnel, or products are doing and affecting. (Patton, 1982, p. 15)

This definition would not be universally accepted, but is helpful in drawing attention to

- the need for *systematic* information collection;
- the *wide range of topics* to which evaluation has been applied;
- the point that, to be effective, the evaluation has to be *used* by someone;
- the *wide variety of purposes* of evaluations.

It also helps in broadening out the view of evaluation from an exclusive concern for the extent to which someone's objectives have been met. This is likely to continue to be an important aspect of the evaluation of many planned programmes with explicit objectives, but is clearly only a part of what an evaluation might concern itself with. Unplanned or unanticipated outcomes or processes may be very important, and would not be looked for. For example, Ross (1973), in surveying a number of evaluations of the effects of legal 'crackdowns', has shown a plethora of unsuspected results. Increasing penalties for speeding, instead of leading to the desired effects, resulted in substantially fewer arrests and a considerably greater proportion of those arrested being found 'not guilty'.

## Purposes of evaluation research

Box 7.1 lists a range of purposes, together with some questions associated with those purposes. This by no means exhausts the possibilities. Patton (1981) lists over 100 types of evaluation. He has also pointed out that evaluators may indulge in less than reputable types of activity, such as *quick-and-dirty evaluation* (doing it as fast as possible at the lowest cost); *weighty evaluation* (a thick report); *guesstimate evaluation* (what do we think is happening without collecting proper data); and *personality-focused evaluation* (are the programme staff nice, friendly, helpful, etc.).

Suchman (1967) produces a similar list of 'pseudo-evaluations', incorporating some possible covert motives of those funding evaluations. These include *eyewash* (emphasis on surface appearances); *whitewash* (attempts to cover up programme limitations or failures that have been discovered); *submarine* (the political use of evaluation to destroy a programme); *posture* (the ritualistic use of evaluation research without interest in, or intention to use, its findings – occurs when evaluation was a requirement for funding the programme); and *postponement* (using the need for evaluation as an excuse for postponing or avoiding action). While expressed in jocular fashion, these latter possibilities highlight the care that one should take before getting into the political situation which virtually all evaluations represent – see the section below on 'Carrying out an evaluation', p. 209.

## Formative and summative evaluation

The distinction between formative and summative evaluation is emphasized in several texts, and is covered here in some detail as experience suggests that clients with some knowledge of the jargon may tend to express their preferences in these terms. The distinction is primarily one of purpose.

# Box 7.1

## Some purposes of evaluation: likely questions posed by sponsor or programme staff

| | To find out if client needs are met | To improve the program | To assess the outcomes of a program | To find out how a program is operating | To assess the efficiency of a program | To understand why a program works (or doesn't work) |
|---|---|---|---|---|---|---|
| Likely questions posed by sponsor or program staff | What should be the focus of a new program?<br><br>Are we reaching the target group?<br><br>Is what we provide actually what they need? | How can we make the program better (e.g. in meeting needs; or in its effectiveness; or in its efficiency)? | Is the program effective (e.g. in reaching planned goals)?<br><br>What happens to clients as a result of following the program?<br><br>Is it worth continuing (or expanding)? | What actually happens during the program?<br><br>Is it operating as planned? | How do the costs of running the program compare with the benefits it provides?<br><br>Is it more (or less) efficient than other programs? | They are unlikely to seek answers to this – but such understanding may assist in improving the program and its effectiveness. |

*Note:* for 'program' read 'service', or 'innovation', or 'intervention' (or 'programme') as appropriate. (From Robson, 2000, table 1.1, p. 10.)

- *Formative evaluation* is intended to help in the *development* of the programme, innovation or whatever is the focus of the evaluation.
- *Summative evaluation* concentrates on *assessing the effects and effectiveness* of the programme. This is likely to cover the total impact of the programme; not simply the extent to which stated goals are achieved, but all the consequences that can be detected.

The distinction is not absolute. In particular, summative evaluation could well have a formative effect on future developments, even if it is presented after a particular 'run' of a programme or intervention. Most evaluations are neither totally negative nor totally positive, and typically carry within them strong implications for change.

It is obvious that formative evaluation needs to be carried out and reported on in time for modifications to be made as a result of the evaluation. There is a tension between doing something 'cheap and nasty' (and quick), of likely low reliability and validity, and better-quality work where the findings come too late to meet important decision points in the development of the project. This is one aspect of 'real world' working: you are also in 'real time'. The pace tends to be out of the control of the enquirer and in the hands of someone else. In all aspects of carrying out an evaluation, great attention has to be paid to feasibility. The design must take note of constraints on time and resources; on how information is to be collected; on the permissions and co-operation necessary to put this into practice; on what records and other information are available; and so on.

## Outcome and process evaluation

Similar aspects to those highlighted by the formative/summative distinction are sometimes expressed in terms of *process* and *outcome* respectively. The traditional view of evaluation restricted the questions asked to those concerning outcome. The task was seen as measuring how far a programme, practice, innovation, intervention or policy met its stated objectives or goals. This approach, while still considered a central feature by many, is now more commonly seen as only covering a part of what is needed.

Process evaluation is concerned with answering a 'how?' or 'what is going on?' question. It concerns the systematic observation and study of what actually occurs in the programme, intervention, or whatever is being evaluated. This may well be a crucial part of an evaluation as, without it, the nature of what is being evaluated may be obscure or misunderstood. The discrepancy between the 'official' view of what should be going on and what is actually taking place may be substantial. A new programme for, say, teaching reading may have timetabled daily individual sessions. Exigencies of the school's working, and a possible low priority accorded to the programme by a head or deputy, might mean that the majority of such sessions never take place. Or a school's emphasis on reading may be at the expense of time spent on writing: an unintended consequence of the programme. Generally, relying on an official account or label is dangerous.

Process evaluation provides a useful complement to outcome evaluation of either the *systems analysis* or *behavioural objectives* variety. The latter are essentially 'black box' approaches, concentrating on what goes into the box (i.e. the programme), and in particular on what comes out. A study of the intervening processes may help to shed light on this, and assist in determining the causal links involved. Such study of the processes involved may well be valuable in its own right, as well as in giving a better basis for the evaluation of outcomes. In some circumstances, the experiences and interactions provided by the programme may legitimately be the focus of interest, and prime criteria for judging its value.

## Carrying out an evaluation

Evaluations are things to avoid unless you have a good chance of doing them properly. Box 7.2 lists four criteria that should be satisfied before you commit yourself. The *utility* criterion emphasizes that usefulness is at the heart of an evaluation. Otherwise it becomes an essentially pointless activity. The aphorism that 'the purpose of evaluation is not to prove but to improve' expresses this view in strong terms.

---

### Box 7.2

### Features of evaluation

Any evaluation should meet the following criteria:

1  *Utility*   There is no point in doing an evaluation if there is no prospect of its being useful to some audience.

2  *Feasibility*   An evaluation should only be done if it is feasible to conduct it in political, practical and cost-effectiveness terms.

3  *Propriety*   An evaluation should only be done if you can demonstrate that it will be carried out *fairly* and *ethically*.

4  *Technical adequacy*   Given reassurance about utility, feasibility and proper conduct, the evaluation must then be carried out with technical skill and sensitivity.

---

Similarly, you have better things to do with your life than to get locked into a study where the results would be suppressed and not acted upon because of political sensitivity, or to accept a commission where the time and resources available preclude a serious and responsible study. You should similarly beware the 'submarine' – the study set up to legitimate the closure of a programme or service, or otherwise provide support for some already decided course of action. Obviously, anything which prejudices your position in this way is to be avoided.

And finally, a point also tied up with ethics, you have no business in getting involved in studies unless you can deliver as a technically adequate evaluator. Box 7.3 presents a checklist of some of the things that need to be thought about in planning an evaluation. Box 7.4 lists some of the relevant skills, and it will be clear that they mirror closely many of the topics covered in this text. Hence, although this section is itself quite short, it is fair to say that virtually all of the book is concerned with what to do when carrying out evaluations. The last skill, 'sensitivity to political concerns', looms particularly large in evaluations and is expanded upon below.

## The politics of evaluation

It is almost inevitable that an evaluation has a political dimension to it. Innovations, policies and practices will have their sponsors and advocates. Most will have critics and sceptics. Staff running programmes may have much to gain or lose from particular outcomes of an evaluation. Jobs may be on the line. A positive evaluation may lead to the expansion of a programme, to inflows of money and resources which can make major differences to the lives of clients involved.

Evaluations tend to focus on programmes which are in the political arena, whether at national or local level, or simply of concern in an individual business, school or other unit. Because of these policy implications, the existence and outcomes of an evaluation are likely to be of interest and concern to a whole range of 'stakeholders' – national and local government, both politicians themselves and bureaucrats; the agencies and their officials responsible for administering the programme; persons responsible for direct delivery; the clients or targets of the programme, and groups such as unions responsible for looking after their interests; possibly taxpayers and citizens generally. It would be highly unlikely for the interests of all of these groups to be identical, and one can usually guarantee that, whatever the results and findings of an evaluation, some will be pleased and others not.

This means, among other things, that carrying out an evaluation is not an activity for those particularly sensitive to criticism, or disturbed by controversy. Criticism may be both methodological (of the way the study has been carried

# Box 7.3

## Checklist for planning an evaluation

1  *Reasons, purposes and motivations*

- Is the evaluation for yourself or someone else?
- Why is it being done?
- Who should have the information obtained?

2  *Value*

- Can actions or decisions be taken as a result?
- Is somebody or something going to stop it being carried out?

3  *Interpretation*

- Is the nature of the evaluation agreed between those involved?

4  *Subject*

- What kinds of information do you need?

5  *Evaluator(s)*

- Who gathers the information?
- Who writes any report?

6  *Methods*

- What methods are appropriate to the information required?
- Can they be developed and applied in the time available?
- Are the methods acceptable to those involved?

7  *Time*

- What time can be set aside for the evaluation?
- Is this adequate to gather and analyse the information?

8  *Permissions and control*

- Have any necessary permissions to carry out the evaluation been sought and received?
- Is participation voluntary?
- Who decides what goes in any report?

9  *Use*

- Who decides how the evaluation will be used?
- Will those involved see it in a modifiable draft version?

- Is the form of the report appropriate for the designated audience (style/length)?

*And remember:*

- *Keep it as simple as possible* – avoid complex designs and data analyses.
- *Think defensively* – if it can go wrong it will, so try to anticipate potential problems.

(Adapted from Harlen and Elliott, 1982; see also Robson et al., 1988, p. 85.)

---

## Box 7.4

### Skills needed to carry out evaluations

There are many different kinds of evaluation which call for different mixes of skills. The following seem fundamental to most evaluations:

- writing a proposal;
- clarifying purposes of the evaluation;
- identifying, organizing and working with an evaluation team;
- choice of design and data collection techniques;
- interviewing;
- questionnaire construction and use;
- observation;
- management of complex information systems;
- data analysis;
- report writing, including making of recommendations;
- fostering utilization of findings;
- sensitivity to political concerns.

---

out) or political (of the findings); or the latter masquerading as the former. The main implication is that it pays to give meticulous attention to the design and conduct of the study, and to ensuring that the legitimate concerns of gate-keepers have been taken into account.

## Needs assessment

An innovatory programme is usually set up because of a perceived need which is not being met by current provision. Logically, the assessment of such needs should take place before the programme is set up and organized, and it would appear reasonable for this to be the responsibility of the programme planners. However, it is quite common for evaluators to be asked to advise on the needs assessment, or even carry it out themselves. Similarly, there are situations where those involved both run and evaluate the programme. Hence a note on the topic might be useful.

Needs assessment is the process whereby needs are identified and priorities among them established. It is fairly clear what is meant by 'needs' at a common-sense level, but it may help to regard them as arising when there is a discrepancy between the observed state of affairs and a desirable or acceptable state of affairs. Several approaches to needs assessment have been proposed (e.g. Baldwin, 1998; Reveire et al., 1996; Witkin and Altschuld, 1995). Box 7.5 outlines one possibility.

The danger of concentrating on 'accessible' needs must be acknowledged. As Judd et al. (1991, p. 408) point out, such technical decisions have

---

## Box 7.5

### Steps in carrying out a needs assessment

**1** *Identify possible objectives*   The first step involves collecting as comprehensive a set of potential objectives as is possible. These can be gleaned from a variety of sources, including the literature (if any), experts in the field and those likely to be involved in the programme in any capacity.

**2** *Decide on important objectives*   Select groups of participants representing important 'constituencies', e.g. likely consumers of the service or users of the programme, providers and managers or administrators. Get them to rate the importance of each of the potential objectives.

**3** *Assess what is currently available to meet the important objectives*   In some cases, this can be combined with the previous step by having respondents rate current availability, and if possible, give information about how needs are currently being met. Alternatively, information can be sought from records or through a small-scale survey.

**4** *Select final set of objectives*   Judgement must now be exercised in selecting a set of objectives which rate high on importance and low on current availability. Other criteria such as feasibility may also be incorporated. Different needs and objectives may be best addressed by different kinds of programme (e.g. it may be that the providers wish to develop a self-instructional training programme, but the needs assessment throws up objectives which can be best addressed by individual consultancy).

ideological consequences. They cite crime prevention programmes. If the events leading to crime are considered as a long causal chain, intervention at any point along that chain might reduce crime. This could range from intervening in the childhood experiences of potential delinquents, through providing job skills for the unemployed, to promoting better home security measures. Programmes focusing on the installation of door locks, security lighting and burglar alarms are much more accessible, with clear outcome measures; but they carry the ideological implication that reducing crime is about protecting potential victims.

## Cost–benefit evaluation

There is an increasing call for measuring the effectiveness of programmes in financial terms. Cost–benefit analysis attempts to compare the costs (the various inputs to a programme, such as staff, facilities, equipment, etc.) with the benefits accruing, with both measured in monetary terms (Bagley and Pritchard, 1998, and Shearn et al., 2000, provide examples from the social work and learning disabilities fields respectively). If the benefit to costs ratio exceeds one, this provides support for continuation or expansion of the programme. Other things being equal, a programme with a higher benefit to costs ratio is to be preferred to one with a lower ratio. The main difficulties in such an analysis are in deciding what to include in both costs and benefits, and then how to determine the amounts of money involved. Cost-effectiveness analysis is similar, but here the benefits are expressed in non-monetary terms (e.g. in terms of the academic qualifications achieved by those following an educational programme). Providing that an appropriate means of assessing non-monetary benefit is available, this can provide a simpler way of making relative judgements about programmes.

These analyses are complex and call for skills within the province of economics. An introduction is provided in Robson (2000, pp. 136–40) and more extended coverage in Yates (1996, 1998).

## What an evaluator needs

Virtually the whole of this book is relevant to the potential evaluator. You need to have an understanding of the issues involved in the initial development of a proposal, in the selection of a general research strategy, and of specific methods and techniques of collecting data. There has been a tendency in small-scale studies to equate evaluations with the use of questionnaires (as the sole method) but evaluation is a complex field where the benefits of multiple methods are particularly clear. Many evaluations collect both qualitative and quantitative data, and you need to know appropriate analysis and interpretation techniques. Reporting in a way that is understandable and helpful for those who have to act on the findings is crucial.

This section has sought to give some indication of where the very young science of evaluation research is at, and in particular to encourage an appreciation of the complexity and sensitivity of the evaluator's task. Your job is to select a research strategy and a method (probably, in most evaluations, several methods) of data collection and analysis. A thorough knowledge of the programme being evaluated is an essential precursor to your selection and subsequent sensitive use of the methods.

An open-minded exploration of the most suitable strategy and best methods for the task in hand is needed. *However, it is the usefulness of the data for the purposes of the evaluation, and not the method by which it is obtained*, which is central. As Jones (1985) puts it:

> If you can find out something useful about a program by talking to a few disgruntled employees, then talk to them. If the only way you can get the data you need is by participant observation, then participate and observe (and do not forget to take good notes). If you need a time series design with switching replications, then set it up and switch when the time comes. If you need archival data, then locate the necessary records and extract whatever you require. Use whatever you have in your toolbox that will get the job done. (p. 258)

Rigour and systematic data collection are important. Unfortunately, the quality of many evaluations is suspect. See, for example, McCulloch's (2000) analysis of the weaknesses of five different evaluations of the same community regeneration project.

## Action Research

As with evaluation research, action research is primarily distinguishable in terms of its purpose, which is to influence or change some aspect of whatever is the focus of the research. In this sense it is concerned with the emancipatory purpose of research, discussed in chapter 3. It adds the promotion of change to the traditional research purposes of description, understanding and explanation. *Improvement* and *involvement* are central to action research. There is, first, the improvement of a *practice* of some kind; second, the improvement of the *understanding* of a practice by its practitioners; and third, the improvement of the *situation* in which the practice takes place.

Collaboration between researchers and those who are the focus of the research, and their participation in the process, are typically seen as central to action research, the terms *participatory research* (Park, 1993) or *participatory action research* (Selener, 1997) being commonly used as synonyms.

Kurt Lewin first used the term 'action research' (Lewin, 1946). He viewed it as a way of learning about organizations through trying to change them. It has continued to be used to promote organizational change and development (e.g. Argyris et al., 1985; Wilkinson, 1996). Action research has been a popular approach to research in educational settings (e.g. Atweh et al., 1998). Its protagonists maintain that practitioners are more likely to make better decisions and engage in more effective practices if they are active participants in educational research. Action research developments in education were initially largely stimulated by professional researchers, particularly John Elliott and colleagues at the Centre for Applied Research in Education at the University of East Anglia (Elliott, 1991; Norris, 1990). There has subsequently been a tendency to de-emphasize the role of the external researcher and to stress the value of groups of practitioners carrying out their own enquiries into their own situation, though linked for mutual support in a loose network.

This educational variant of action research has come in for strong criticism from various quarters. Adelman (1989) considers much of educational action research to be 'inward looking and ahistorical' and of poor quality. In his view, the claims for action research as an 'alternative research paradigm, as a democratizing force and means of achieving informed, practical change arising from issues at the grass roots' are 'overbearing' (p. 179). Atkinson and Delamont (1985) have been severely critical of the way that this approach has developed in educational research, castigating its atheoretical posture and denial of the need for systematic methods.

Lewin, writing and working just after the Second World War, saw action research as a tool for bringing about democracy (it is interesting to note, as pointed out by Bentz and Shapiro, 1998, p. 128, that his initial studies were aimed at convincing homemakers through group discussions to use less meat in wartime, which is perhaps democratic in a somewhat limited sense). Later action researchers see action research more as an embodiment of democratic principles in research. Merging activism and research with the aim of empowering women has been central to the agenda of many feminist researchers (Reinharz, 1992). More generally, it has been seen as a means of fighting oppression and social injustice (Cancian, 1993; Stringer, 1996).

This close and collaborative relationship between researcher and researched fits well with the approach of flexible, qualitative design and is alien to that of fixed, quantitative design. However, the joint concern for action and research, particularly when this is carried through at all stages of the research, can cause serious problems. For example, if notions of collaboration and participation are taken seriously, then some power of decision about aspects of the design and data collection are lost by the researcher. This may well be a price worth paying, particularly if you have the skills to head participants off from non-feasible designs and inappropriate method. You are not just an investigator 'but a collaborator and a facilitator: the political nature, the participatory character, the emancipatory elements and the direct, committing and personal involvement of the researcher are at the front of the research activity' (Sarantakos, 1998; p. 113).

As with evaluation research, the technical aspects of action research do not differ in essentials from those of social research in general, in that the same range of methods of data collection are potentially available. While evaluation research can follow either fixed or flexible design strategies, depending on the purposes of the evaluation, there are, as indicated above, affinities between action research and the flexible, qualitative strategy. These lie in the close links between researcher and participants. However, the particular stress in both ethnographic and grounded theory on the 'researcher-as-instrument', and the consequential central role of the researcher's perceptions, are at some variance with the collaborative, democratic stance of action research. The flexibility of case studies in design and approach, as well as in the use of method, encourages their use as a model for action research.

## Links between evaluation research and action research

The focus of a piece of action research can be, and often is, an evaluation. Conversely, there are particular variants of evaluation which aspire to the same kind of goals as action research. These include *participatory evaluation* (Cousins and Earl, 1995) and *empowerment evaluation* (Fetterman et al., 1996).

## The action research cycle

A widely adopted version of action research views it as a spiral, or cyclical, process (Kemmis and Wilkinson, 1998, p. 21). This involves planning a change; acting and then observing what happens following the change; reflecting on these processes and consequences; and then planning further action and repeating the cycle. Bassey (1998) presents a more detailed specification of the various stages involved, given here as box 7.6. If, following these stages, the change is deemed insufficient, then the whole process could be repeated. As with most representations of what happens in research, this is an idealization and in practice unlikely to be as neat as suggested.

It might be argued that a participative collaborative style is more important than sorting out the complexities of various feedback loops in the cycle. As Fuller and Petch (1995) point out, it

---

## Box 7.6

## Stages of action research

**1** *Define the inquiry*   What is the issue of concern? What research question are we asking? Who will be involved? Where and when will it happen?

**2** *Describe the situation*   What are we required to do here? What are we trying to do here? What thinking underpins what we are doing?

**3** *Collect evaluative data and analyse it*   What is happening in this situation now as understood by the various participants? Using research methods, what can we find out about it?

**4** *Review the data and look for contradictions*   What contradictions are there between what we would like to happen and what seems to happen?

**5** *Tackle a contradiction by introducing change*   By reflecting critically and creatively on the contradictions, what change can we introduce which we think is likely to be beneficial?

**6** *Monitor the change*   What happens day-by-day when the change is introduced?

**7** *Analyse evaluative data about the change*   What is happening in this situation now – as understood by the various participants – as a result of the changes introduced? Using research methods, what can we find out about it?

**8** *Review the change and decide what to do next*   Was the change worthwhile? Are we going to continue it in the future? What are we going to do next? Is the change sufficient?

(Slightly modified from Bassey, 1998, pp. 94–5.)

---

involves collaboration with others more traditionally thought of rather demeaningly as the 'subjects' of research in the development of ideas about what to study; it may also include their active participation in carrying out the study and in interpreting results. Thus initial thoughts about researchable topics and priorities may have been developed collectively in formal or informal discussions with professional colleagues or with groups of users or carers. The latter may then be involved in collecting and analyzing data, or (perhaps more often) in discussions about the interpretations of findings and their dissemination. In this way, both the choice of topic and the processes of research are democratized, the research has wider ownership than the researcher alone, and there is an extra level of commitment both to its successful completion and to acting on the findings. (p. 6)

Issues involved in working in this way, and in a move towards practitioner research when there is an action agenda, are covered in appendix B.

## Intervention and Change

'How to get new educational programmes to work in practice has increasingly frustrated and mystified those involved in education over the past two decades' (Fullan, 1982, p. ix). Notwithstanding the failings and shortcomings of the approaches to implementing change, it appears that something of value can be gleaned from the substantial efforts which have been made both before and after he made this assertion. As Fullan (1982, 1991) points out, from this experience we now know, admittedly at a pragmatic and common-sense level, a considerable amount about what we should and should not do when seeking to implement change. Heller (1986) approaches this question from a consideration of users' needs. They need to be given *access* to the research findings, proposals, programme or whatever. They need to *seriously consider* them; there may well be 'deep-seated non-intellectual obstacles that prevent serious consideration of new findings or ideas'. They then need to *make a decision*, which may not be simple acceptance or adoption but could involve postponement until further work is done. If it has been decided to go ahead, then *implementation* is necessary. Heller stresses that things can go wrong at each of these stages.

Fullan's work, though focusing on change in educational settings, provides a useful general framework for both understanding and effecting change. He stresses that *change is a process, not an event*, and provides a set of general maxims which are presented, in abridged form, as box 7.7.

## Researchers and Practitioners

Practitioners such as nurses, social workers and teachers will not necessarily have expertise in the strategies, methods and analytical techniques needed to carry out research. Notwithstanding the obvious benefits that skills and experience bring, the underlying common-sense core to the practice of social research, as highlighted in this text, is not difficult to grasp. Such a grasp enables the interested practitioner to be directly involved in carrying out worthwhile studies – to become a 'practitioner–researcher'. Involving practitioners in research, whether through following an action research model or otherwise, provides an obvious means of facilitating change.

---

## Box 7.7

### Assumptions for those wishing to initiate change

1  Don't assume that your version of what the change should be is the one that could or should be implemented. You have to exchange your reality of what should be through interaction with others concerned.

2  Change involves ambiguity, ambivalence and uncertainty about the meaning of the change. Effective implementation is a process of clarification.

3  Some conflict and disagreement are not only inevitable but fundamental to change.

4  People need pressure to change (even in directions they desire) but it is only effective under conditions that allow them to react and interact. Re-socialization is at the heart of change (otherwise you need to replace the people involved!).

5  Effective change takes time. It is a developmental process that takes at least two years.

6  Lack of implementation isn't necessarily attributable to rejection or resistance. There are many other reasons, including insufficient resources or time elapsed.

7  Don't expect all, or even most, people or groups to change. Progress occurs by increasing the number of people affected.

8  You need a plan based on these assumptions and underpinned by a knowledge of the change process.

9  Change is a frustrating, discouraging business. If you are not in a position to make the above assumptions, which may well be the case, don't expect significant change, *as far as implementation is concerned.*

(Adapted and abridged from Fullan, 1982, p. 91.)

---

Appendix B discusses the relative roles of practitioner–researchers, researchers and consultants in carrying out real world research. It also gives practical advice on doing this.

### Further Reading

Iwaniec, D. and Pinkerton, J., eds (1998) *Making Research Work: Promoting Child Care Policy and Practice.* Chichester: Wiley. Focus on how research can be applied more effectively to policy and practice.

Pawson, R. and Tilley, N. (1997) *Realistic Evaluation*. London: Sage. Intentionally provocative and stimulating text advocating the realist approach within evaluation research.

Posovac, E. J. and Carey, R. G. (1997) *Program Evaluation: Methods and Case Studies*, 5th edn. Upper Saddle River, NJ: Prentice-Hall. Balanced, comprehensive and practical. Focus on programme improvement.

Robson, C. (2000) *Small-scale Evaluation: Principles and Practice*. London: Sage. Expanded version of the approach taken here.

Schratz, M. and Walker, R. (1995) *Research as Social Change: New Opportunities for Qualitative Research*. London: Routledge. Attempts to integrate action research, case study and other qualitative strategies within professional practice.

Selener, D. (1997) *Participatory Action Research and Social Change*, 2nd edn. Cornell Participatory Action Research Network. Ithaca, NY: Cornell University. Comprehensive overview of different approaches to participatory action research. Extensive bibliography.

Vaughan, R. J. and Buss, T. F. (1998) *Communicating Social Science Research to Policymakers*. Thousand Oaks, Calif.: Sage. Seeks to help researchers make a contribution to policy debates.

Weiss, C. H. (1997) *Evaluation: Methods for Studying Program and Policies*, 2nd edn. Upper Saddle River, NJ: Prentice-Hall. A very clear, wise, and well-written text.

# Part III
## Tactics: The Methods of Data Collection

Having decided on a focus for the research, the research questions to which you seek answers, and the overall research strategy that is appropriate for getting those answers, you now need to give thought to methods. How will you actually go about what a detective would call 'making enquiries'? In fact, when carrying out real world research, our options are essentially the same as those available to the detective. We can *watch* people and try to work out what is going on; we can *ask* them about it; and we can look out for fingerprints (as well as any other evidence they leave behind them).

Put in the more usual research language, watching becomes *observation*; asking becomes *interviewing*, using *questionnaires* and administering *tests*. Interviewing is usually taken as implying personal, face-to-face (or, in the case of telephone interviewing, increasingly common particularly in the United States, voice-to-voice) interaction. Questionnaires and tests may be administered in an interview, face-to-face situation, presented without direct, personal interaction – as in a postal survey. 'Looking for other evidence' covers a variety of methods, including *documentary analysis*.

Chapter 8 covers the development and use of questionnaires in the context of the sample survey. Interviews are covered in chapter 9, and tests and scales in chapter 10. Chapter 11 covers observational methods. Chapter 12 focuses on how existing documents of various types can provide data, gathers together a range of other possible methods, and considers issues involved in using multiple methods of data collection in a study.

## Selecting the method(s)

The selection of a method or methods is based on what kind of information is sought, from whom and under what circumstances. It is decided at an early stage in a fixed design project. Even in flexible designs, there is a need to make some initial decisions about how to collect data (or you never get started). However, in flexible designs, the nature and number of methods used can change as data collection continues.

## A   A rational choice?

The rational approach is to ask: given your research questions, and a decision on research strategy, what methods are most suitable? However, in practice, the choice of particular methods may well precede the choice of a research problem. As Walker (1985) puts it:

> Just as an instrumentalist will not change from playing the clarinet to playing the trumpet because a particular piece demands it, but will usually turn to another piece of music, searching for pieces that suit both the instrument and the player, so researchers generally give a lot of time and thought to the formulation of possible and potential research problems, looking for those that appear to fit their interests and preferred methods. (p. 47)

This phenomenon of 'methods in search of problems' rather than the reverse is a genuine one. In one sense it does not matter, provided that the methods fit the problem chosen. However, it can cause difficulties in real world research where the problem is presented to you and, if you do not have a good range of methods at your disposal, the choice might be between using an inappropriate method or turning the work away. The moral is to seek to get a broad grounding in all strategies and a broad range of methods, so that you are in a position to make a rational choice.

## B   What methods are available?

Many. Interviews and questionnaires, and direct observation of different kinds, tend to be the most popular. Experiments also use some form of controlled observation, but the actual technique is often specific to the particular field of study.

The following are simple rules of thumb for selecting methods:

- To find out what people do in public use *direct observation*.
- To find out what they do in private, use *interviews* or *questionnaires*.
- To find out what they think, feel and/or believe, use *interviews*, *questionnaires* or *attitude scales*.
- To determine their abilities, or measure their intelligence or personality, use *standardized tests*.

## C   Consider practicalities

Anything you propose to do must be feasible within the constraints of available time and resources. You may wish to carry out a participant observation study, but if it would take three months for you to be accepted and fully involved, then it is impracticable for a one-month maximum study period. A second-best alternative involving interviews may be called for.

Business confidentiality, or the stress it might cause, might rule out direct observation. Ethical considerations will similarly rule out some methods in some situations.

# 8
# Surveys and Questionnaires

This chapter:

- discusses the characteristics of surveys and their advantages and disadvantages
- compares self-completion, face-to-face and telephone interviews
- explains the various stages involved in carrying out a sample survey
- stresses the professionalism needed to carry out a high-quality survey
- outlines the development and use of questionnaires
- concludes with a discussion on the why and how of sampling.

## Introduction

Surveys are common. You will have to have led a very hermit-like existence not to have been asked to take part in some form of survey – which brand of washing powder or lager do you buy, and what other brands do you know? Who would you vote for if there were a national election next week? Do you think the government is doing a good job? And so on, and on. Similarly, the results of surveys of one form or another pepper the pages of newspapers and broadcast output. This week's top ten paperback fiction books; 'Latest British Social Attitudes Survey shows 9 per cent of people believe sex before marriage is always wrong'; 'Poll finds that 30 per cent of university students do part-time work'; 'Survey finds two-thirds of MBAs work more than 55 hours per week, and more than half want to spend more time with their families' – all these are in the newspaper I have in front of me.

Surveys have been with us for a long time. The Domesday Book, and efforts to assess the effects of the plague in London in the seventeenth century, provide notable landmarks. Tonkiss (1998) highlights their importance in the development of a science of society in the late eighteenth and early nineteenth centuries. Marsh (1982, ch. 1) gives a detailed and fascinating account as part of her defence of the strategy against critics of the use of surveys within sociology.

Much current use of surveys is highly instrumental, undertaken in the interests of better marketing and increased sales of some service or product. A substantial amount is academic in the sense of seeking to find out something about what is going on in society today. In either case, there is a high premium on 'getting it right'; that is, on getting an accurate and unbiased assessment of whatever it is that is being measured. In some fields, most notably in political polling, error can be glaringly obvious – when the predicted winner loses, or there is a wide discrepancy between polls purporting to measure the same thing. Often, however, there is no obvious reality test, and judgements of reliability and validity have to fall back on an analysis of how the survey was carried out.

Large-scale surveys are big business and require substantial time, effort and a range of personnel to carry out. Even the relatively small-scale survey likely to be feasible for readers of this text cannot be completed quickly, due to the various stages which have to be completed, as indicated in box 8.1. This refers to the situation where a small sample of, say, 200–300 people are involved in the main study. Rough estimates of 'person-days' have been given so that if, say, several interviewers are available, the actual period of time taken in the main data collection can be reduced (although time will be needed to train interviewers). Coding of data can take place as soon as some interviews have taken place.

A period of three to four months for the whole process is probably a realistic minimum. However, if you don't have that amount of time available, it's surprising what can be done by burning the midnight oil. Just don't try to leave out any of the activities; they are all important if you are to do a worthwhile study. This timetable assumes that no problems will occur (and they will; you just don't know in advance what they are going to be – bad weather, school holidays, industrial disputes, flu or other epidemics, and computer breakdowns are not unknown).

A survey using questionnaires sent by mail will have a rather different time schedule. The need for repeat mailings, reminders, etc., central to getting satisfactory response rates in a postal survey, takes up a substantial period of time.

## What Is a Survey?

*As discussed in chapter 5, p. 157, there is a sense in which surveys are more like a research strategy (i.e. an overall approach to doing social research) than*

---

## Box 8.1

### Steps in carrying out a small-scale interview-based questionnaire survey

| Activity | Estimated number of days (likely minimum) |
|---|---|
| 1   Development of research questions, study design (including sample selection for pre-tests and main study), and initial draft of questionnaire | 20 |
| 2   Informal testing of draft questionnaire | 5 |
| 3   Revise draft questionnaire | 3 |
| 4   Pre-test revised draft using interviews | 3 |
| 5   Revise questionnaire again (possible revision of design and main study sample) | 3 |
| 6   Carry out main data collection interviews | 30* |
| 7   Code data and prepare data files | 10 |
| 8   Analyse data and write report | 20 |

\* Depends on size of sample, whether telephone or face-to-face (and, if latter, on travelling time between interviews).

---

*a tactic or specific method. However, many of the concerns involved in doing a survey are not so much with questions of overall strategic design as with highly practical and tactical matters to do with the detailed design of the instrument to be used (almost always a questionnaire, largely or wholly composed of fixed-choice questions), determining the sample to be surveyed and ensuring high response rates.*

Box 8.1 is couched in terms of a survey carried out by *interviewers*: those persons armed with clip-boards and a questionnaire who stop you in the street or knock on the front door and ask if you would mind answering a few questions. However, other forms of survey are possible, including the self-administered *postal (mail) questionnaire* and, increasingly commonly, the *telephone survey*. Indeed, surveys are not necessarily restricted to the use of questionnaires. A traffic survey may be exclusively observational; a survey of the working life of lecturers in universities may rely on a weekly diary (leaving on one side for the moment the likely trustworthiness of such information if it is to be used to seek to demonstrate to their paymasters how hard-working they are).

Because of the ubiquity of surveys, it is likely that you will have a good common-sense appreciation of what the term means. It is, however, difficult to give a concise definition, precisely because of the wide range of studies that have been labelled as surveys. The typical central features are:

- the use of a fixed, quantitative design;
- the collection of a small amount of data in standardized form from a relatively large number of individuals;
- the selection of representative samples of individuals from known populations.

While this captures the large majority of surveys, there are examples where a considerable amount of data is collected from each individual; where the 'unit' involved is not an individual but some form of organization such as a school, firm or business; and, particularly in the latter case, where the number of 'units' sampled gets down to single figures. In such situations, you may be able to survey *all* the population rather than a sample (e.g. all the staff of an organization you are studying). Bryman (1989) provides the following definition: 'Survey research entails the collection of data on a number of units and usually at a single juncture in time, with a view to collecting systematically a body of quantifiable data in respect of a number of variables which are then examined to discern patterns of association' (p. 104).

He warns against taking the 'single juncture in time' too literally. Practicalities will often dictate that data are collected over a period of weeks or even months, but they are treated as if collection were simultaneous. In other words, this is a cross-sectional design. There is, however, nothing in principle against the use of surveys in longitudinal designs.

## Advantages and Disadvantages of the Survey

Researchers tend to have strong, frequently polarized, views about the place and importance of surveys. Some see the survey as *the* central 'real world' strategy. It may be that, in non-laboratory situations where experiments are often neither feasible nor ethically defensible, surveys give that reassuring scientific ring of confidence. Associated with surveys is a satisfyingly complex set of technological concerns about sampling, question-wording, answer-coding, etc.

Mishler (1991, ch. 1) stresses the differences between asking and answering in naturally occurring, contextually grounded conversations and the question–response process in survey interviews. His view is that many of the routine procedures of this kind of research represent efforts to bridge this gap. An essential feature of survey interviewing is that it is organized social discourse; but, 'by adopting an approach that is behavioral and antilinguistic, relies on the stimulus-response model, and decontextualizes the meaning of responses, researchers have attempted to avoid rather than to confront directly the inter-related problems of context, discourse and meaning' (p. 27).

At a practical level, others view surveys as generating large amounts of data often of dubious value. Falsely prestigious because of their quantitative nature, the findings are seen as a product of largely uninvolved respondents whose answers owe more to some unknown mixture of politeness, boredom and a desire to be seen in a good light than to their true feelings, beliefs or behaviour. As is often the case, such caricatures are not without foundation. Surveys have also suffered from being viewed as necessarily positivistic, a view comprehensively demolished by Marsh (1982, esp. ch. 1).

The reliability and validity of survey data depend to a considerable extent on the technical proficiency of those running the survey. If the questions are incomprehensible or ambiguous, the exercise is obviously a waste of time. This is a problem of *internal validity*, where we are not obtaining valid information about the respondents and what they are thinking, feeling, doing, etc.

The problem of securing a high degree of involvement by respondents to a survey is more intractable. This is particularly so when it is carried out by post, but is also difficult when the survey is carried out face-to-face (remember that nearly all surveys carried out by interviewers involve fleeting interactions with total strangers – it is asking a great deal of the interviewer to establish a rapport with each and every respondent so that they are fully involved). Securing involvement is in part also a technical matter (a poorly designed and printed, lengthy questionnaire administered just before Christmas to workers in an organization who are currently trying to meet a seasonal deadline is unlikely to get a good response), but it has to be accepted as a likely hazard of the strategy per se.

If the sampling is faulty, this produces a *generalizability* or *external validity* problem such that we cannot generalize our findings. Another type of external validity problem occurs if we seek to generalize from what people say in a survey to what they actually do. The lack of relation between attitude and behaviour is notorious – see, for example, Hanson (1980), who, in a review of forty-six studies, found twenty which did not demonstrate a positive relationship between attitudes and behaviour. Reliability is more straightforward. By presenting all respondents with the same standardized questions, carefully worded after piloting, it is possible to obtain high reliability of response.

Notwithstanding all these caveats, a good, competently run survey is something all generalist real world social researchers should be able to offer. Surveys provide the sort of data which are not difficult for an intelligent lay audience to understand, particularly an audience which is scientifically literate. Lindblom and Cohen (1979) make a strong case that, of the various forms of 'usable knowledge' those carrying out professional social enquiry might provide, the humble survey may well be the most influential. Zeisel (1984) presents the somewhat back-handed, but realistic, compliment that

> the apparent exactness and rigorousness of statistical analysis [of survey data] is a useful device to win arguments with people who do not understand the value of qualitative knowing in scientific research. This is an important characteristic of the method when research results are to be used in a court of law, in a political setting, in applied design – in any competitive decision-making situation. (pp. 160–1)

Hakim (1987) makes a related point in referring to the main attractions of the sample survey as its *transparency* (or *accountability*): in other words, that

> the methods and procedures used can be made visible and accessible to other parties (be they professional colleagues, clients, or the public audience for the study report), so that the implementation as well as the overall research design can be assessed. (p. 48)

To this end, a standardized language is used to refer to the sampling procedures employed. Questionnaires, code-books, introductory letters, analyses of non-response, etc. are expected to be included in the report. Increasingly, raw survey data are deposited in data archives, permitting both checking and further analysis by other workers. This standard of professionalism found in quality survey work mirrors that expected in experimental studies, and is now recognized as calling for serious attention in flexible designs with largely qualitative data.

Box 8.2 lists some of the advantages and disadvantages of the survey.

## Why a Survey?

Surveys are almost always carried out as part of a non-experimental fixed design. While this can be for *any* of the research purposes, whether exploratory, descriptive, explanatory or emancipatory, surveys are not well suited to carry-

# Box 8.2

## Advantages and disadvantages of questionnaire-based surveys

*Disadvantages*

*General to all surveys using respondents*

1   Data are affected by the characteristics of the respondents (e.g. their memory; knowledge; experience; motivation; and personality).

2   Respondents won't necessarily report their beliefs, attitudes, etc. accurately (e.g. there is likely to be a social desirability response bias – people responding in a way that shows them in a good light).

*Postal and other self-administered surveys*

3   Typically have a low response rate. As you don't usually know the characteristics of non-respondents, you don't know whether the sample is representative.

4   Ambiguities in, and misunderstandings of, the survey questions may not be detected.

5   Respondents may not treat the exercise seriously, and you may not be able to detect this.

*Interview surveys*

6   Data may be affected by characteristics of the interviewers (e.g. their motivation; personality; skills; and experience). There may be interviewer bias, where the interviewer, probably unwittingly, influences the responses (e.g. through verbal or non-verbal cues indicating 'correct' answers).

7   Data may be affected by interactions of interviewer/respondent characteristics (e.g. whether they are of the same or different class or ethnic background).

8   Respondents may feel their answers are not anonymous and be less forthcoming or open.

*Advantages*

*General to all surveys using respondents*

1   They provide a relatively simple and straightforward approach to the study of attitudes, values, beliefs and motives.

**2**   They may be adapted to collect generalizable information from almost any human population.

**3**   High amounts of data standardization.

*Postal and other self-administered surveys*

**4**   Often this is the only, or the easiest, way of retrieving information about the past history of a large set of people.

**5**   They can be extremely efficient at providing large amounts of data, at relatively low cost, in a short period of time.

**6**   They allow anonymity, which can encourage frankness when sensitive areas are involved.

*Interview surveys*

**7**   The interviewer can clarify questions.

**8**   The presence of the interviewer encourages participation and involvement (and the interviewer can judge the extent to which the exercise is treated seriously).

*Notes*: Advantages 4 and 5 may be disadvantages if they seduce the researcher into using a survey when it may not be the most appropriate strategy to answer the research question(s).
The telephone survey is a variation of the interview survey which does not involve face-to-face interaction and has rather different advantages and disadvantages (see p. 253).

ing out exploratory work. There is nothing to stop you asking a wide range of largely open-ended questions in an attempt to explore some area, but it is likely to be an inefficient and ineffective procedure, taking a great deal of time to analyse. Surveys work best with standardized questions where it is possible to be confident that the questions mean the same thing to different respondents, a condition which is difficult to satisfy when the purpose is exploratory. The requirement is that you know what kind of information you want to collect.

Many, probably most, surveys are carried out for descriptive purposes. They can provide information about the distribution of a wide range of 'people characteristics', and of relationships between such characteristics. For example, a political party might be interested in voters' views about their policies, and on how such views are related to, say, age, gender, income, region of the country, etc. At a local level, there may be a need to find the relative degree of support for or opposition to alternative development plans.

It is possible to go beyond the descriptive to the interpretive, that is, to use the survey to provide explanations of the phenomena studied and the patterns of results obtained. Details of possible approaches to analysis are provided in chapter 13. Surveys can be used to get at causal relationships, but this is not an easy or a straightforward undertaking – essentially because of the non-experimental design used, but also because the information acquired is typically in the form of correlations; and, as will no doubt be burned into the brain of anyone who has followed even an elementary course in statistics, correlation does not imply causation. What is required is a sophisticated analysis of the detailed pattern of correlations.

Suppose we are interested in the jobs into which pupils from different ethnic backgrounds go after leaving school; and that we want not only to see who goes to what kind of job, but also to interpret this information. When we try to explain why there is a differential involvement of, say, Pakistani, Afro-Caribbean and white youths in particular types of employment, we might find from a survey that there are differences in educational attainment among the groups from different ethnic backgrounds and, further, that this attainment is related to occupational type. It is not legitimate simply to make the connection that differences in educational attainment are the cause of the differential pattern of occupation for the pupils from different educational backgrounds. Leaving aside practical problems such as how jobs can be classified, and the more intractable measurement problem of ensuring that tests of educational attainment are 'culture-free' (that is, that they do not introduce biases related to ethnic background – which itself constitutes a threat to the internal validity of the study), it is patently obvious that the different ethnic groups are likely to differ in a host of other ways apart from their educational attainment. Differential encouragement from the home; family income; parental and friends' occupations; careers advice (or the lack of it); attitudes of potential employers – these are just a few of the possibilities.

Explanation and interpretation depend on incorporating into the study information on a substantial number of such variables and then analysing the pattern of correlations, seeing where relationships are strong and where they are weak or non-existent. From this, you seek to tell the most convincing story that you can; in realist terms, what mechanisms are operating in which contexts. What goes into the pot, that is, which variables you seek information on, is determined by pilot work where potential mechanisms are suggested (perhaps involving semi-structured interview, focus groups or other methods of data collection) and by previous studies, as well as by any theoretical framework or contenders for mechanisms that you have developed.

## Approaches to Survey Data Collection

Most surveys involve the use of a questionnaire. There are three main ways in which this questionnaire is administered:

- *Self-completion* Respondents fill in the answers by themselves. The questionnaire is often sent out by post, permitting large samples to be reached with relatively little extra effort.
- *Face-to-face interview* An interviewer asks the questions in the presence of the respondent, and also completes the questionnaire.
- *Telephone interview* The interviewer contacts respondents by phone, asks the questions and records the responses.

Responses are usually sought from individuals, although that individual might be responding on behalf of a group or organization. Self-completion survey questionnaires can be administered on a group basis (e.g. by gathering all students in a school into a hall and asking them to complete the survey at the same time). This is essentially for administrative convenience and efforts would be made to ensure that individual responses were received.

The format and appearance of the questionnaire will vary depending on the method of data collection selected. Box 8.3 summarizes features of the three approaches.

### Resource factors

While all forms of data collection call for a substantial investment of time and effort in developing the questionnaire, the self-completion version is substantially lower in cost to administer than face-to-face interviews. In its usual postal version, the costs are essentially those of postage (though this does involve the provision of stamped addressed envelopes, reminders, etc. – see below, p. 249). If the questionnaires are being administered in a group setting, you don't even have the cost of stamps. Interviews involve an interviewer for the whole time; in a face-to-face situation travel time can add very substantially to the time and cost involved.

The data collection period is shortest in telephone interviews. It is feasible to carry out a substantial number of these per interviewer on each working day, though some repeat calls will be needed. A substantial amount of time is taken up in postal questionnaires by the necessity of sending out reminders and repeat questionnaires to non-respondents. However, where a self-completion questionnaire is administered in a group setting and all members of the sample are present, the process can be completed in an hour or so.

## Box 8.3

## Comparison of approaches to survey data collection

| Aspect of survey | Self-completion questionnaire | Face-to-face interviews | Telephone interviews |
|---|---|---|---|
| **Resource factors** | | | |
| Cost | **LOW**[a] | High | Low/medium |
| Length of data collection period | Long | Medium/long | **SHORT** |
| Distribution of sample | **MAY BE WIDE** | Must be clustered | **MAY BE WIDE** |
| **Questionnaire issues** | | | |
| Length of questionnaire | Short | **MAY BE LONG** | Medium |
| Complexity of questionnaire | Must be simple | **MAY BE COMPLEX** | **MAY BE COMPLEX** |
| Complexity of questions | Simple to moderate | **MAY BE COMPLEX** | Short and simple |
| Control of question order | Poor | **VERY GOOD** | **VERY GOOD** |
| Use of open-ended questions | Poor | **GOOD** | Fair |
| Use of visual aids | Good | **VERY GOOD** | Not usually possible |
| Use of personal/family records | **VERY GOOD** | Good | Fair |
| Rapport | Fair | **VERY GOOD** | Good |
| Sensitive topics | **GOOD** | Fair | Fair/**GOOD** |
| **Data-quality issues** | | | |
| Sampling frame bias | Usually low | **LOW** | **LOW** (with RDD[b]) |
| Response rate | Difficult to get high | Medium/**VERY HIGH** | Medium/high |
| Response bias | Medium | **LOW** | **LOW** |
| Control of response situation | Poor | **GOOD** | Fair |
| Quality of recorded response | Poor | **GOOD** | Fair |

[a] Entries in bold capitals indicate particularly the type of survey which has an advantage for a particular aspect
[b] Random Digit Dialling (see p. 241).
(Abridged and adapted from Czaja and Blair, 1998, Exhibit 3.1, p. 32.)

The geographical distribution of the sample can be wide for both self-completion questionnaires and telephone interviews, but to make face-to-face interviews feasible in resource terms it is necessary to limit the study to a particular area.

## Questionnaire issues

The questionnaire length, and hence the time taken to complete it, can be greatest in face-to-face interviews. When a self-completion questionnaire is used, its complexity has to be kept to a minimum. You also lose control of question order in this situation; respondents can answer the questions in any order, which may have effects on the answers given.

Although surveys rely very largely on closed questions (where there is a choice among a number of fixed alternatives), some open-ended questions (where respondents are free to answer as they wish) can be successfully introduced in face-to-face interviews, and to a lesser extent in telephone interviews. It is also feasible, when in the face-to-face situation, to include the use of visual aids, for example cards with lists from which the respondent chooses. It may be necessary for some surveys to obtain information about personal or family records, perhaps ages of family members. Self-completion questionnaires, particularly when completed in the family setting, permit respondents to seek out the information before completing the question.

A skilled interviewer should be able to achieve good rapport with nearly all interviewees in the face-to-face situation. This is somewhat more difficult when the telephone is used, and the self-completion questionnaire has to rely on the quality of its presentation. Conversely, the lack of direct contact means that self-completion questionnaires, and to a somewhat lesser extent telephone interviews, are better at dealing with sensitive topics.

## Data-quality issues

There are no major differences in bias in the sampling frame (a list of the population from which a sample is drawn; see below, p. 240) among the different approaches, although both telephone and face-to-face interview situations make it relatively easy to check that the respondent falls within the population of interest. A low response rate is a serious and common problem with self-completion questionnaires and, as discussed below, every effort should be made to get the rate up to an acceptable level. Self-completion questionnaires can be subject to response bias; for example, people with reading and/or writing difficulties are less likely to respond. These skills are not called for in the interview situation.

The interviewer has good control of the response situation particularly when across the table from the respondent. However, there is essentially no control of this with self-completion questionnaires; we don't even know for certain whether the person completing the questionnaire is who they say they are. Similar considerations apply to the quality of recorded response.

## Carrying Out a Sample Survey

The various activities involved in carrying out a sample survey (listed in box 8.1) can be divided into six main stages: initial design and planning; designing the questionnaire; pre-testing it; final design and planning; data collection; and analysis and reporting.

### Initial design and planning

The context is that the general purposes of your proposed study, what is feasible and, in particular, the research questions you are seeking to answer, will have led you to a non-experimental fixed design. Some form of survey using a questionnaire is highly likely to be the method of choice.

The most straightforward task for a survey is to answer questions of the 'how many?', 'how much?', 'who?', 'where?' and 'when?' types. It can provide an estimate of the number or proportion of people who hold a certain belief (e.g. that physical punishment of children by parents should be illegal) or engage in a particular behaviour (e.g. who have, as a parent of a child under five years, punished the child physically during the past twelve months).

This kind of descriptive information can be of value in its own right in helping to gauge public opinion, perhaps as a precursor to introducing or changing legislation. It can also be used to answer research questions or test hypotheses derived from theories: for example, the hypothesis that 'non-parents are more likely than parents to support all physical punishment of children by parents being made illegal,' arising from a 'realities of parenting' mechanism that the experience of parenting leads to an awareness of the need for physical punishment in particular contexts. This is, in principle, something which can be addressed by means of a survey.

Here, as in many surveys, it would be necessary to collect information about specific sub-groups in the population, in this case parents and non-parents. Showing, even from a well-designed and carried out survey, that a higher proportion of non-parents support legislation (and even if it is statistically significant) does not in itself provide convincing evidence for the 'realities of parenting' mechanism. Collecting additional information – on, for example, the gender of the respondents; their actual amount of involvement in the bringing up of young children (some non-parents may have substantial involvement; some 'bringing up the children is the mother's job' fathers may have very little); age, number and gender of children; attitude of parents to this issue before they were parents – permits more sophisticated analyses and tests of causal models to be conducted, as discussed in chapter 13, p. 432.

The importance of a theoretical framework for surveys seeking to move beyond description to explanation cannot be over-estimated. Whether expressed in terms of a set of possible mechanisms and the contexts in which they operate, or in other terms, they prevent the survey questionnaire degenerating into a fishing trip where questions are added simply because 'it seemed a good idea at the time'.

While most surveys target the individual, this is not an essential feature. We may be interested in groups, organizations or other units. Schools, hospitals, social services departments, etc. in the United Kingdom are surveyed to assess aspects of their performance (e.g. school attendance rates; hospital waiting lists) to generate league tables of various kinds and to 'name and shame' those whose performance is judged unsatisfactory.

*Population*   An early design decision concerns the population from which the sample of respondents is to be drawn. An important consideration is the geographical area to which we wish to generalize the results. This is governed largely by the research questions and the resources available. It may be necessary to modify your research questions, perhaps making them more geographically specific, to make the survey feasible within the resources available. As indicated in box 8.3, this is only a major issue with surveys where the questionnaire is administered by interviewers.

For many surveys, the target age range of participants requires consideration. An 'adult' population could be 21 years or older, but depending on the particular focus of the survey younger eligible ages might be appropriate. Obviously, the wider the age range covered in the population, the fewer of each age for a given sample size. As the confidence that can be placed in a finding increases with the number of persons on which it is based, it is sensible to use a restricted age range (e.g. 20–29 years inclusive) if this ties in with your research questions – or if the questions can be modified without doing violence to your overall aims.

*Sampling frame*   The sampling frame is the source of the eligible population from which the survey sample is drawn. For a survey of people in an organization, this could be all those on the payroll. For general population surveys, telephone directories have often been used, though a moment's thought will reveal some of their inadequacies (e.g. not everyone has a phone; it is usually based on households rather than individuals; people may be ex-directory). Random-digit dialling (RDD) techniques, discussed below on p. 253, overcome some of these difficulties, although they obviously still don't reach those without a telephone. Voters' lists are sometimes used, but are likely to be both dated and incomplete.

If a reasonably adequate sampling frame can be obtained, this puts you in the position of being able to draw a (reasonably adequate) random sample, i.e. a sample where all members of the population of interest have an equal chance of being selected for the sample. The advantages of doing this are substantial and are discussed below (p. 260).

When there is not a perfect match between the sampling frame and the population of interest, questions arise about the size and nature of the discrepancy between them and how this will bias the estimate of the variable(s) we are interested in. Suppose RDD is used; a bias may be introduced by households without telephones. In countries such as the United States, the percentage without telephones is overall very low. There is considerable demographic variability – in 1988, the proportions were: overall 6 per cent; African American households 16 per cent; those living below poverty index 27 per cent (Thornberry and Massey, 1988; cited in Czaja and Blair, 1996, pp. 16–17). For other countries, percentages without telephones are typically substantially higher. With low non-telephone percentages, little bias will be produced by their exclusion. With higher values, the potential for bias increases and it may be worthwhile to visit sufficient homes to contact enough non-telephone households to obtain an estimate of the likely bias. Decisions about this depend on your research questions. If you are, say, interested in the views of poor people, or are focusing on topics where they are likely to have different views from the more affluent, it would be inadvisable to rely on a telephone-based survey.

## Designing the questionnaire

This section covers general issues of survey questionnaire design. Issues specific to the design of self-completion and interview-based (both face-to-face and telephone) data collection are covered at the end of the section.

It is worth stressing that the questions for the questionnaire are *not* produced by you sitting down and trying to think of some interesting things to ask; or even by getting a group together to do this. The survey questions should be designed to help achieve the goals of the research and, in particular, to answer the research questions. Czaja and Blair (1996, p. 53) present a model (based upon Tourangeau and Rasinski, 1988, and Presser and Blair, 1994) of how the survey questions fit into the overall survey process, shown here as figure 8.1. The model is useful because it not only emphasizes the

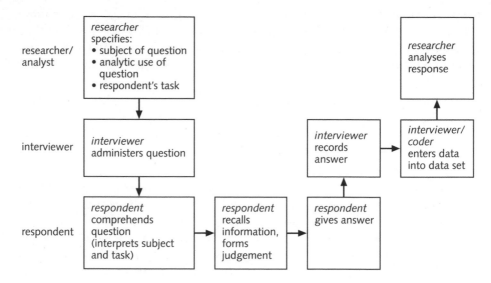

**Figure 8.1**   Model of the survey data collection process.
*Source*: Czaja and Blair (1996).

researcher's task of linking research questions to survey questions (their 'ana-lytic use') but also stresses the respondent's tasks, which involve interpreting the question, recalling information which is relevant to it, deciding on an answer and reporting that answer to the interviewer (who may or may not be the same person as the researcher). This helps us to appreciate that a good questionnaire not only

- provides a valid measure of the research questions, but also
- gets the co-operation of respondents, and
- elicits accurate information.

Respondents must be able to understand the questions in the way that the researcher intends, have accessible the information needed to answer them, be willing to answer them, and actually answer in the form called for by the question. A major part in the art and craft of producing a survey questionnaire is in writing it in such a way that respondents understand what you want from them, and are happy to give it to you, while the questions at the same time remain faithful to the research task.

*The researchers' task*   The researchers' central task is to link research questions and survey questions. Returning to the example about physical punishment of children, the research question

*Are non-parents more likely than parents to support all physical punishment of children by parents being made illegal?*

is clearly inappropriate as an actual survey question. If we were to ask the question and get, say, 57 per cent agreeing, 23 per cent disagreeing and 20 per cent 'don't know' responses, any assessment based on these results would be very dubious. Respondents cannot very well report about the views of parents and non-parents in general. Even if they could, the question is indirect, asking for their views about the views of others.

An obvious improvement is to ask

*Should all physical punishment of children by parents be made illegal?*
*(1)   Yes*
*(2)   No*
*(3)   Don't know,*

targeting the question on a sample of parents and non-parents. In this form, they are asked what they think rather than judging the opinions of others.

Reflecting further on this, or doing some type of pre-testing, might raise possible criticisms of this form of the question:

- Respondents may not understand what is meant by 'physical punishment', nor even by the exact meaning of 'made illegal'.
- Respondents may have different views of what is meant by 'physical punishment'.
- Respondents may consider that, under some specific circumstances, particular forms of physical punishment should be legal.
- 'Don't know' is not appropriate here; they are asked about their views or opinions, not their knowledge ('no opinion' or 'not sure' would be preferable).

These illustrate common issues in drafting questionnaires. The language of the question may have to be changed so that it is both understandable and unambiguous to respondents.

Suppose the question is rephrased as

*Should parents be allowed to smack their children?*

This certainly gets rid of the relatively complex and possibly ambiguous terms 'physical punishment' and 'made illegal'. However, in trying to ensure that it is clear and understandable, we have moved a long way from the research question. It also limits and restricts; smacking is only one form of punishment.

Criticisms of initial attempts at survey questions often result in an appreciation that the single question won't do; that multiple questions may have to replace it. In this example, it may be necessary to include coverage of different forms of punishment, and different circumstances. The exercise of writing survey questions may lead to your revisiting your research questions. When you get down to working out exactly what you are going to ask people, it may become clear to you that you are really interested in something rather different from what you originally thought. Here, for example, mature reflection may suggest that you should focus on the morality of physical punishment rather than its legality.

*The respondents' task*    As shown in the model in figure 8.1, the respondent has first to understand the question, which is why its wording is so important. When the self-completion format is used, respondents are on their own; you can't help them other than by the written instructions and the questions themselves. Many surveys ask respondents to remember and report things: 'How many times during the last month have you . . .', 'When did you last . . .', etc. An important part of pre-testing is to find out whether they can remember the information you are asking for. If you make the task too difficult, not only will the quality of the answers be low but you are likely to make the task uninviting, leading to low response rates.

The set of possible fixed-alternative responses should be *accurate, exhaustive, mutually exclusive* and *on a single dimension*:

- *accurate* means that they link to the central point of the question; if the question relates to the value of something, you don't have responses of 'very interesting', etc.;
- *exhaustive* means that all possible options are covered (include 'other' if necessary, but try by pre-testing to include most possibilities, so that its use is kept to a minimum);
- *mutually exclusive* means that only one of the possible responses applies (note, however, that a format is sometimes used where respondents are asked to select each of the responses that apply; e.g. the newspapers that they read regularly);
- a set of responses including 'very useful', 'useful', 'boring' and 'very boring' relates to more than *one dimension*.

A wide variety of ways of presenting the response alternatives has been used. Perhaps the most common is the numerical scale, as in figure 8.2 below, question 14 (p. 248). Graphic responses can also be used. The simplest form is a line joining two opposing adjectives, say 'bad' and 'good', the respondent indicating the strength of their response by a mark on the line; the distance of the mark from an end of the line can then be measured. An alternative graphic approach uses a set of 'smiley' faces spaced in a line, with the mouth line at one extreme a U shape indicating happiness and the other an inverted U for sadness. Respondents indicate their feelings to the question by marking or indicating the relevant face.

Various techniques and approaches, including Likert scales and the semantic differential, used in connection with the development of tests and scales, can also be used in survey questionnaires. For more details on these techniques see chapter 10.

*The questions*    The central part of the survey questionnaire is devoted to the survey questions which derive from your research questions. Their wording, as has already been pointed out, is crucially important. Box 8.4 provides suggestions for avoiding the most obvious problems. Further details are given in more specialized texts (e.g. Oppenheim, 1992; de Vaus, 1991; Sapsford, 1999).

*Designing self-completion questionnaires*    Figure 8.2 gives a simple example of a self- completion questionnaire. Cut down open-ended questions to a minimum with this type of questionnaire unless you can afford to spend a lot of time on analysis or have only a small number of responses to deal with. The desire to use open-ended questions appears to be almost universal in novice survey researchers, but is usually rapidly extinguished with experience. Pilot work using interviews and open-ended questions can provide suggestions for closed alternatives.

There is much that one can do to increase the likelihood of getting a high response rate, as set out in box 8.5 (p. 249). Note the emphasis given to the

---

## Box 8.4

### Checklist to help avoid problems in question wording

1    *Keep the language simple* Avoid jargon. Seek simplicity but avoid being condescending.

2    *Keep questions short* Long and complex questions are difficult to understand.

3    *Avoid double-barrelled questions* Double-barrelled questions ask two questions at once (e.g. 'Is your key worker caring and supportive?'). Split into separate questions.

4    *Avoid leading questions* Leading questions encourage a particular answer (e.g. 'Do you agree that . . . ?').

**5** *Avoid questions in the negative*   Negatively framed questions are difficult to understand; particularly when you are asked to agree or disagree (e.g. 'Marijuana use should not be decriminalized: Agree/Disagree.' 'Marijuana use should remain illegal' avoids the problem).

**6** *Ask questions only where respondents are likely to have the knowledge needed to answer*   'Do you agree with the government's policy on foreign aid?' is unsatisfactory if respondents don't know what it is. Either tell them, or ask a preliminary filter question to establish whether they know what the policy is. Then ask only those who said 'yes'.

**7** *Try to ensure that the questions mean the same thing to all respondents*   Meanings and terms used may vary for different age groups, regions, etc.

**8** *Avoid   a prestige bias*   This occurs when a view is linked with a prestigious person before asking the respondent's view.

**9** *Remove ambiguity*   Take great care with sentence structure.

**10** *Avoid direct questions on sensitive topics (in interview situations)*   Several indirect strategies are possible (e.g. using numbered cards with the alternatives; respondent gives relevant number).

**11** *Ensure the question's frame of reference is clear*   When asking for frequency of an event, specify the time period.

**12** *Avoid creating opinions*   Respondents don't necessarily hold opinions on topics. Allow a 'no opinion' alternative.

**13** *Use personal wording if you want the respondents' own feelings, etc.*   Impersonal wording gives their perception of other people's attitudes (use it if that is what you are after).

**14** *Avoid unnecessary or objectionable detail*   It is unlikely that you will want precise income or age; use income or age groupings.

**15** *Avoid prior alternatives*   Give the substance of the question first, then the alternatives. Not the reverse.

**16** *Avoid producing response sets (particularly in interview situations)*   With 'agree/disagree' questions, some people tend to agree regardless of their real opinion ('acquiescence response set') or provide answers making themselves look good ('social desirability response set'), e.g. inflate their income or decrease their alcohol consumption. Seek to put people at their ease and avoid giving the impression that some answers are normal or unusual.

(Adapted and abridged from de Vaus, 1991, pp. 83–6.)

# Consumer behaviour and green attitudes

**First some facts about you**

1. Sex      Male ☐      Female ☐

2. Age group

   16–24 ☐      25–34 ☐      35–49 ☐      50–64 ☐      65+ ☐

## Now some questions about the things you buy

3. Of the following household items, which brands do you normally buy?

   Toilet roll _____

   Washing powder _____

   Washing-up liquid _____

   Household cleaners/polishes _____

   Nappies _____

4. With regard to the goods just mentioned, which of the following things would you say influenced you when choosing what to buy?

   Quality ☐                          Reliability ☐

   Reputation ☐                       Advertising ☐

   Presentation/Packaging ☐          Brand name ☐

   Cost ☐                            'Environmental friendliness' ☐

   Ethics (e.g. animal testing) ☐

5. Do you have any insulation in your home?

   None ☐      Loft ☐      Cavity ☐

6. Does anyone in your household run a car?

   Yes ☐      No ☐

   If Yes, do any of them run on unleaded petrol?

   Yes ☐      No ☐

7. How often do you use any of the following?

   |              | Always | Sometimes | Never |
   |--------------|--------|-----------|-------|
   | Bottle banks | ☐ | ☐ | ☐ |
   | Recycled paper | ☐ | ☐ | ☐ |

8. Does the use of artificial additives and preservatives affect what foods you buy?

   Yes ☐      No ☐

9. With reference to any issues have you, during the past 5 years, done any of the following?:

   Signed a petition ☐                    Been a member of a political party ☐

   Written to an M.P. ☐                   Been part of a demonstration ☐

   Been a member of a pressure group ☐

P.T.O

*continued*

**Figure 8.2**  Example of a self-completed questionnaire.

## Now some opinions about the following statements

10. The following is a set of statements about attitudes to green issues.
For each statement please say whether you agree strongly, agree, are neutral,
disagree or disagree strongly with it. Tick the appropriate box.

|  | Strongly agree | Agree | Neutral | Disagree | Strongly disagree |
|---|---|---|---|---|---|
| Britain should not allow its air pollution to cause acid rain in Scandinavia. | ☐ | ☐ | ☐ | ☐ | ☐ |
| There is too much panic about running out of resources. | ☐ | ☐ | ☐ | ☐ | ☐ |
| Manufacturers shouldn't make things that are harmful to the environment. | ☐ | ☐ | ☐ | ☐ | ☐ |
| Recycling is just a fad. | ☐ | ☐ | ☐ | ☐ | ☐ |
| Countries with rain forests are entitled to chop them down to sell their timber. | ☐ | ☐ | ☐ | ☐ | ☐ |
| Live for today. Don't worry about tomorrow. | ☐ | ☐ | ☐ | ☐ | ☐ |
| Industries should stop damaging the countryside, even if prices must rise to pay for it. | ☐ | ☐ | ☐ | ☐ | ☐ |
| Being 'Green' is just another youth craze. | ☐ | ☐ | ☐ | ☐ | ☐ |
| The government should invest more money into looking at alternatives to nuclear power. | ☐ | ☐ | ☐ | ☐ | ☐ |

## Just a few more facts about you

11. What is your occupation? Please give details

12. What is the income level of your household?

£5,000–9,999 ☐    £10,000–14,999 ☐    £15,000–19,999 ☐    £20,000 and over ☐

13. Educational qualifications

None ☐    GCSE ☐    A-levels ☐    Degree ☐    Other (please give details) ☐

14. What point in this scale best indicates your political views?
Circle the appropriate number.

**Left**    1    2    3    4    5    6    7    **Right**

# Thank you very much for your cooperation

Source Gibbs, n.d.

**Figure 8.2** *Continued.*

---

## Box 8.5

### Factors in securing a good response rate to a postal questionnaire

**1** The appearance of the questionnaire is vital. It should look easy to fill in, with plenty of space for questions and answers.

**2** Clarity of wording and simplicity of design are essential. Give clear instructions (e.g. 'put a tick').

**3** Arrange the contents to maximize co-operation, e.g. ensure that early questions don't suggest to respondents that the enquiry is not for them. If there are attitude questions, interpose them throughout the questionnaire to vary the response required.

*Design and layout*

**4** Coloured pages (e.g. different colour for instructions) can clarify the structure.

**5** Answering by putting ticks in boxes is familiar to most respondents. Circling pre-coded answers can confuse.

**6** Sub-lettering questions (e.g. 5a, 5b, etc.) can help in grouping questions on a specific issue.

**7** Repeat instructions if confusion is possible.

**8** Initial questions should be easy and interesting. Middle questions cover the more difficult areas. Make the last questions interesting to encourage return of the questionnaire.

**9** *Wording of questions is of crucial importance. Pre-testing is essential.*

**10** A brief note at the end can:

a ask respondents to check that they have not accidentally omitted to answer any questions;
b solicit an early return of the questionnaire;
c thank them for their help; and
d offer to send an abstract of the findings.

*Initial mailing*

**11** Use good-quality envelopes, typed and if possible addressed to a named person.

**12**  Use first-class postage, stamped not franked if possible.

**13**  Enclose a stamped addressed envelope for return of the questionnaire.

**14**  For 'home' surveys, Thursday is the best day for sending out; for organizations, Monday or Tuesday.

**15**  Avoid a December mailing.

*Covering letter*

**16**  This should indicate the aim of the survey and convey its importance; assure confidentiality; and encourage reply. If serial numbers or other codings are used, say why.

**17**  Tailor it to the audience (e.g. a parent survey might stress its value for child care).

**18**  Give the name of the sponsor or organization carrying out the survey on the letterhead and in the body of the letter.

**19**  Pre-survey letters, advising respondents of the forthcoming questionnaire, can increase response rate.

*Follow-up letter*

**20**  *This is the most productive factor in increasing response rates. All the above suggestions in the previous section apply here too.*

**21**  Emphasize the importance of the study and the value of the respondent's participation.

**22**  Conveying disappointment and surprise at non-response can be effective.

**23**  Don't suggest that non-response is common.

**24**  Enclose a further copy of the questionnaire and another stamped addressed envelope.

*Further follow-ups*

**25**  These are subject to the law of diminishing returns but are worthwhile. Three reminders are commonly recommended. They can increase response rates by a further third.

*Use of incentives*

**26**  Incentives accompanying the initial mailing appear to be more effective than rewarding the return of completed questionnaires (e.g. through a prize draw). They should be a token rather than a payment, e.g. a ball-point pen.

covering letter and to the various follow-up activities. The latter are crucial in achieving an acceptable response rate. For some populations you may need to be creative; for example, Lensing et al. (2000) were able to increase the response rate in a survey of physicians (a notoriously difficult group) by offering the option of receiving and returning a survey by fax.

*Response rate*   Non-response is a very serious issue for those using postal self-completion surveys. A low response rate on other types of survey is just as serious but easier to avoid. Obviously, if people have not responded we do not know what their response would have been, unless we can find out by other means (e.g. interviewing those who didn't respond to a postal questionnaire). The 'other means' tend to be very time-consuming, but unless we can do something along these lines, we have little basis for assuming that responders and non-responders are similar. While rates of about 70 per cent are quoted by some authors (e.g. Gay, 1992), it has been demonstrated by simulation techniques that even moderate differences between respondents and non-respondents call for a response rate of about 90 per cent if biased estimates are to be avoided (Jones, 1995; cited in Mertens, 1998, p. 130).

*Designing interview-based surveys*   Much of the general advice on interviewing covered in the following chapter is relevant to those involved in interview-based surveys, whether face-to-face or telephone-based. The distinctive feature of these interviews is that they are highly structured. Such structured interviews can be used for other purposes than for surveys, but they are most commonly found in this context. In effect, they involve you using essentially the same type of instrument as that for a self-completion survey. There is a fixed set of questions with pre-specified and standardized wording. The response alternatives are also typically fixed and pre-specified, although it is common to have a small number of questions where the answer is open-ended (typically of the 'any other comment on this that you would like to make' variety).

The questionnaire in an interview-based survey is more usually referred to as the *interview schedule*. It covers:

- what the interviewer says by way of introduction;
- introductions to particular questions, or groups of questions;
- the questions (word for word);
- the range or set of possible answers (sometimes referred to as 'prompts');
- response codes;
- possible 'skips' in sequence (e.g. where a 'yes' answer is followed by a particular question, a 'no' answer by a 'skip' to a different question);
- closing comments;
- reminders to the interviewer about procedure.

It is helpful to distinguish those parts of the schedule which are an 'aide-memoire' to the interviewer from those which are to be said to the respondent (e.g. by having them in different colours, or by having one group in lower-case and the other in CAPITALS).

The codes for different responses are usually circled directly, during the interview, by the interviewer to assist in subsequent analysis. Any apparently open-ended questions are often provided with a set of pre-categorized responses, and it is the interviewer's responsibility to decide in which of these categories the actual response lies. Either this is done during the interview, or a verbatim response is recorded during the interview and the coding carried out as soon as possible afterwards. The set of pre-categorized responses is developed during pilot work, as discussed below on p. 254. The self-completion questionnaire shown above as figure 8.2 could be used, with minimal adaptation, for an interview-based survey.

When specialist interviewers are used in a project, it is helpful to have a separate *interview guide.* This gives detailed instructions on procedure, to try to ensure that this is standardized across different interviewers. Often there will also be training sessions with the same aim. For the relatively small-scale project on which this text focuses, and in particular where the researcher(s) are also doing the interviewing, a separate interview guide may not be necessary. Sufficient procedural instructions can be incorporated in the interview schedule. However, it is crucial that these details of procedure are not lost, and are incorporated in the report eventually arising from the interviews. Box 8.6 gives general advice appropriate for all structured interviews, whether for surveys or for other purposes.

*Comparing self-completion and interview-based surveys*   The crucial procedural difference between self-completion questionnaires and interview-based surveys is of course that while the respondent fills in the self-completion questionnaire, the interviewer completes the interview schedule. This may seem a straightforward difference, but it has complex ramifications. The presence of the interviewer opens the door for factors to do with the interviewer: skills, experience, personality and degree of involvement in or alienation from the research, to name but a few. When several interviewers are employed in a project, it is easy to show that factors such as these can have major effects on the responses of interviewees. With single interviewers, such effects are still present but their effects are virtually impossible to gauge. Interactions between interviewer and interviewee can also be influential; differences or similarities in class, ethnic origin, gender, age and status can affect rapport and the extent to which the interviewee seeks to please, or reacts against, the interviewer. Ways of dealing with these problems are discussed in the section on *interviewer effects* in chapter 9, p. 273.

---

## Box 8.6

### General advice for interviewers carrying out structured interviews

1 *Appearance* Dress in a similar way to those you will be interviewing. If in doubt, err on the side of neatness and neutrality.

2 *Approach* Be pleasant. Try to make the respondent comfortable.

3 *Familiarity with questionnaire/interview schedule* View yourself as an actor, with the interview schedule as your script. Know it thoroughly.

4 *Question wording* Use the exact wording of questions and keep to their sequence.

5 *Fixed-alternative response questions* Allow only the standard alternatives.

6 *Open-ended response questions* Either code immediately or record the answers exactly for later coding. Don't make cosmetic adjustments, correct or fabricate.

---

The self-completion questionnaire has its own problems. The researcher is ignorant of many of the factors influencing the choice of response to a question. While there are ways of assessing a respondent's consistency, for example, by including different forms of the same question at different points in the questionnaire, these are themselves problematic as it is well documented that small and seemingly innocuous changes in wording can sometimes have substantial effects on response. It is virtually impossible to determine whether or not the respondent is giving serious attention to the questions, or regarding the exercise as a tedious chore to be completed in a perfunctory manner. An interview permits the assessment of this type of factor, and gives the possibility of differentiating respondents on this basis. Also, because of the fact of person-to-person interaction in the interview, involvement, and hence the quality of data, is likely to be greater than with the impersonal questionnaire.

The refusal rate for interviews (particularly personal face-to-face ones) is typically very much smaller than the non-response rate for postal questionnaires. As pointed out above (see p. 251), good planning can increase the response rate for questionnaires, but this remains a major problem.

*Issues specific to telephone-based survey interviews* Telephone-based surveys are becoming increasingly common. They provide a means of capitalizing on many of the advantages of interview-based surveys while substantially reducing the time and resources involved in running face-to-face interviews by cutting out the travel requirement. With more people choosing to have ex-directory phone numbers, problems arise in the use of telephone directories to establish the sampling frame (p. 240) and this increases the attractiveness of *random digit dialling* (*RDD*) techniques. This is a way of selecting numbers for a telephone survey, where some of the last digits of the phone number are generated randomly.

Box 8.7 lists some of the aspects to consider in carrying out a telephone survey.

## Pre-testing

The draft questionnaire is best pre-tested informally, initially concentrating on individual questions. Colleagues, friends and family can usually be cajoled into reading them through and providing (hopefully) constructive comments on wording. Are the questions clear, simple, unambiguous?

A second stage uses respondents from the groups of interest. This can be done on an individual basis, asking them to give any thoughts that occur to them when the question is read out. The intention is to help the researcher understand the meaning of the question to respondents, and how they arrive at their response, to help improve the wording. It is an approach widely used by cognitive psychologists, known as *protocol analysis* (Ericsson and Simon, 1993) – see chapter 12, p. 367. An alternative is to use *focus groups* to help improve not only question wording but other aspects of the survey (e.g. length of questionnaire, wording of covering letter). Details on the size, composition and running of these groups are given in chapter 9 (p. 284).

A formal pre-test can now be run as a miniature pilot version of the real thing; that is, your best shot at the procedures, questionnaire and covering materials. The number of respondents to aim for depends on a variety of factors, including the sub-groups you are interested in (e.g. males and females; ethnic groups; ages), and the resources you have available, but you should aim for at least twenty. It is highly likely that you will need to revise both questionnaire and procedures as a result of this exercise. If anything other than very minor changes are made, a second formal pre-test should be run. Even with limited resources, you should allow for the possibility of this second pre-test. If the first pre-test throws up major problems, it is back to the drawing board and further informal testing before a second pre-test. You keep on with this process until you have overcome any problems that have arisen.

With self-completion postal surveys (where it is usually feasible to have a relatively large pre-test), a low response rate to the first pre-test rings warning bells. It is worth expending considerable time and effort on doing something

# Box 8.7

## Planning and conducting telephone surveys

**1** It is usually a good idea to send a letter before calling, unless you are using a 'random digit dialling' (RDD) strategy, in which case you would not necessarily know the names and addresses of respondents.

**2** Provide a brief explanation of your purpose, who you are, and what your expectations are.

**3** Make sure that you are talking to the right person! You may find that your initial contact would prefer to refer you to someone else who would be more appropriate for your purposes.

**4** Once you are sure that you are talking to the right person, make sure that this is a good time to talk. If not, schedule an appointment for a follow-up call. And be sure to return the call at the appointed time.

**5** Try to keep the phone time to a short duration. On the basis of pilot testing, you should be able to give the respondent a rough estimate of the amount of time that the survey will take.

**6** Establish rapport and move quickly. Be organized.

**7** Use an appropriate tone of voice (friendly and conversational). Sound enthusiastic, fresh, and upbeat. If you get tired, take a break. (No one wants to continue in a survey if you are asking questions with your head down on the desk from fatigue.)

**8** Speak at an appropriate speed (sometimes, matching the respondents' speed will increase their comfort level).

**9** Keep a log of calls made and their outcomes (e.g., busy, no answer, completed, follow-up appointment made) and date and time your notes.

**10** Before conducting the survey, be sure to rehearse.

**11** Set hour-by-hour goals (e.g. I want to make five, ten or twenty phone calls each hour). With a large telephone survey, it is easy to start feeling that you are not getting anywhere, so set your goals and you will see that you are making progress if you keep with it.

**12** You can tape-record a phone call, but you must inform the respondent that you are doing so.

(Abridged and adapted from Mertens, 1998, pp. 131–2.)

about this. You may be able to find out what lies behind this by contacting non-respondents. Or run focus groups to try to find what the obstacles are and how they might be overcome. If a second pre-test also gives low rates, you should consider changing to an interview-based (probably telephone) approach.

## Final design and planning

After implementing the suggestions from pre-testing, your main task with the questionnaire is editorial. Make sure there are no spelling mistakes, and that the layout is professional with appropriate spacing and clear presentation.

At this stage, you make final decisions about the sampling plan and the coding procedures to be used. You should also ensure that you know the main analyses of the data that you are going to use (see chapter 13, p. 450). It is foolish in the extreme to spend considerable resources in designing and running the survey if you don't analyse it in a way that is both technically acceptable and helps to answer your research questions. If you haven't checked this in advance, you are likely to end up with something unanalysable.

## Data collection

Your main task is to keep on top of things, making sure that the practicalities are being attended to and the carefully worked-out plan followed. Book-keeping should be meticulous, so that you know when the various things have happened. In postal surveys this includes dates of posting of materials and follow-ups, recording of return questionnaires, etc. In interview-based studies, it includes dates of all contacts and resulting action, etc. This monitoring role lets you see if problems are arising so that you can do something about them early.

The returned questionnaires should be checked immediately they are received. If sections have been missed by, say, turning over two pages, or entries are illegible or inconsistent (e.g. if someone replies to both the questions following 'If YES please . . .' and 'If NO please . . .'), then this is picked up and a second contact made to try to resolve the problem.

The section on 'practicalities' on p. 376 covers further issues relating to this phase.

## Analysis: coding of responses

Codes are symbols, usually numbers, which are used to identify particular responses, or types of response, in questionnaires and similar instruments.

They help in organizing, quantifying and analysing your data (see chapter 13, p. 393). For example, the answer to a question about a respondent's sex might be coded as '1' for female, and '2' for male. The numbers are arbitrary; they could be reversed or different ones used, provided the coding is consistent.

*Closed questions* With closed questions, there should be little difficulty in coding. The range of possible responses will have been checked and, if necessary, modified during piloting. Numerical symbols are assigned to the various answer categories, and analysis can proceed directly. From the point of view of analysis, it is preferable to include the codes on the questionnaire. For example:

*At which of the following ages did your* father *finish his full-time education?*

*Please tick the appropriate box.*     |   *official*
                                                       |   *use only*

|  | | |
|---|---|---|
| *14 or younger* | __1 | \| |
| *15* | __2 | \| |
| *16* | __3 | \| |
| *17 or 18* | __4 | \| |
| *19 or 20* | __5 | \| |
| *21* | __6 | \| |
| *22 or over* | __7 | \| |

*(The code is included in the box to help the analyst; the code of the box ticked is written by the analyst in the right-hand column.)*

You are free to assign any meaning that you wish to a coding digit (or digits) – *provided that the meaning is consistent within a particular coding scheme.* The code can be arbitrary (e.g. yes = 1; no = 2) or can be the actual number (e.g. age in years = 27 or whatever). It is preferable to have a code for non-response (e.g. 0 or −1) rather than leaving a blank. Whether or not this needs to be discriminated from (and hence separate codes used for) 'don't know', 'not sure', etc., will depend on the particular survey.

*Open questions* Coding of responses here involves combining the detailed information contained in the response into a limited number of categories that enable simple description of the data and allow for statistical analysis. The main purpose is to simplify many individual responses by classifying them into a smaller number of groups, each including responses that are similar in content. *This process inevitably involves some loss of information.*

    Coding of open questions should be based on a substantial, representative sample (say fifty cases) selected from the total set of responses. It should not be based solely on early responses, as these may well be unrepresentative, and it may prove necessary subsequently to develop a revised set of coding categories, which leads to wasteful recoding of those already analysed.

The standard procedure has been to copy all the responses to a particular question on a (large) sheet of paper, headed by the text of the question, and with each response preceded by the case number (i.e. the code given to that person's questionnaire). The object is then to try to develop a smallish set of categories (say eight to ten) into which these responses can be sorted. This is not an easy exercise. It is largely driven by the nature of the responses and the themes and dimensions they suggest. However, one should also bear in mind the purposes of the survey in general and of that question in particular, and try to ensure that the coding categories are such that a minimum of relevant information is lost. The number of categories that it is sensible to use is in part dependent on the overall number of cases in the sample and on the detail of the statistical analysis you wish to carry out.

This process has the effect of turning the answers to open questions to a defined set of standard responses. It is sometimes used at the pilot stage of a questionnaire study to produce a set of categories for closed questions.

## Diaries

A diary, considered as a research tool, is a kind of self-administered questionnaire. As such, it can range from being totally unstructured to a set of responses to specific questions. Diaries are tantalizingly attractive because they appear, on the surface, to provide the means of generating very substantial amounts of data with minimal amount of effort on the part of the enquirer. They can also serve as a proxy for observation in situations where it would be difficult or impossible for direct observation to take place – as with Coxon's (1988) use of sexual diaries for mapping detailed sexual behaviour.

The diary, however, places a great deal of responsibility on the respondent. Unstructured diaries leave the interpretation of the task very much with the pen of the respondent. There is evidence (e.g. Bourgue and Back, 1982) in favour of using a specific set of questions, which ask about the respondent's activities at given times. But even simplifying and structuring the task in this way produces data which are prone to bias.

Even when the situation provides no obvious distorting factors of this kind, there are worries. The kind of enthusiastic involvement that one would seek carries with it dangers of misreporting (perhaps to please the enquirer), or even of changing the behaviour to be reported on (perhaps to show the diarist in a good light). These are phenomena potentially present in any enquiry where the respondents know they are involved in an enquiry, but they are sufficiently bothersome here to cast doubt on the use of the diary as the *sole* method in an investigation. Bourgue and Back (1982), for example, combined a structured diary approach with direct observation, and conducted cross-checks against formal timetabled activity in a way that gave confidence about the reliability and validity of the diary method in the situation in which they were using it.

Burgess (1981) has argued for the use of diaries as precursor to interviewing, especially as a means of generating the list of questions to be covered in the interview. This approach was used by Zimmerman and Wieder (1977), who go so far as to suggest that this dual tactic of diary followed by interview can fulfil many of the purposes of participant observation when the latter is precluded by resource considerations. The type of question asked will, as with other techniques, be dictated by the purpose of your study. Box 8.8 gives suggestions for the development of a diary form (see Gullan et al., 1990, for an example).

Variants of the diary method have been used. One attempts to combine the keeping of a diary with the 'critical incident' approach (e.g. Bryman, 1989). This attempts to separate out, and to get people to notice, specific happenings that they consider to be important. Thus, in a managerial context, these might be whatever is crucial or critical in achieving a satisfactory outcome in a particular task. Respondents are then asked to rate these incidents according to their difficulty and importance to the job.

---

## Box 8.8

### Notes for guidance in developing a diary form

1  Think of it as a questionnaire. You need to devote the same amount of care and preparation (and piloting) as you would for other questionnaires.

2  Because the diary involves self-completion of a series of forms, co-operation is vital. You need to ensure that respondents know *what* they have to do; *why*, and *when*.

3  As with other questionnaires, include an item only if you know what you are going to do with it. You should be clear, before you start the study proper, how the items relate to your research questions, and how you will analyse them subsequently.

4  In a study extending over time, do not assume that 'things are going on all right'. Check, preferably by a personal contact.

5  General considerations about confidentiality, anonymity, feedback of results, permissions, etc. apply.

---

The 'reflective journal' (e.g. Northcott and Brown, 1998), where participants are asked to provide an account of their experiences in a particular setting
or situation, and a reflection on that experience, can be viewed as an unstructured variant of a diary.

## Sampling in Surveys – and Elsewhere

Sampling is an important aspect of life in general and enquiry in particular.
We make judgements about people, places and things on the basis of fragmentary evidence. Sampling considerations pervade all aspects of research and
crop up in various forms no matter what research strategy or investigatory
technique we use. The discussion here focuses on survey sampling, where it is
closely linked to the *external validity* or *generalizability* (see chapter 5, p. 106)
of the findings: the extent to which what we have found in a particular situation at a particular time applies more generally.

The idea of 'sample' is linked to that of 'population'. *Population refers to
all the cases.* It might be, for example, all adults living in the United Kingdom;
or all children attending schools in Texas; or all privately run homes for the
elderly in Paris. The last example illustrates that 'population' is being used in
a general sense – it isn't limited to people. The concept can be further stretched
to include units that are not 'people-related' at all: for example, populations
of situations (e.g. all possible locations in which someone might be interviewed), or of events or of times. It is unusual to be able to deal with the
whole of a population in a survey, which is where sampling comes in. *A sample
is a selection from the population.*

Non-'people-related' sampling is, in practice, very important (e.g. sampling
places and times – deciding, for example, where, when and how interviews
take place), and is discussed further in the context of flexible designs (see
chapter 6, p. 164). However, particular attention needs to be given to the
selection of the 'people sample' in planning a survey. This is because the
dependability of a survey is crucially affected by the principles or system used
to select respondents – usually referred to as the 'sampling plan'.

There are some circumstances where it is feasible to survey the whole of a
population. A national census attempts to do just that, of course, and while it
hardly qualifies as the small-scale study targeted in this book, there are occasions when the population of interest is manageably small – say, the line managers in an organization; or the pupils in a particular school; or patients in a
hospital; or clients of a particular local social service. It should not be assumed,
however, that a full census is necessarily superior to a well-thought-out sample
survey. There are trade-offs requiring careful thought. Will you actually be able
to carry out the full set of interviews, or would it be preferable to do a smaller

number of longer, more detailed ones? Can you in fact reach (virtually) everybody? The 'hard-to-get' may differ from the rest in important ways that you should know about. If you are sampling, you might be able to devote more time and resources to chasing them up.

The various types of sampling plan are usually divided into ones based on *probability samples* (where the probability of the selection of each respondent is known), and on *non-probability samples* (where it isn't known). In probability sampling, statistical inferences about the population can be made from the responses of the sample. For this reason, probability sampling is sometimes referred to as *representative sampling*. The sample is taken as representative of the population. In non-probability samples, you cannot make such statistical inferences. It may still be possible to say something sensible about the population from non-probability samples – but not on the same kind of statistical grounds.

## What size of sample?

While probability samples allow you to generalize from sample to population, such generalizations are themselves probabilistic. The larger the sample, the lower the likely error in generalizing. The discussion in chapter 5, p. 161 refers to this issue.

## Probability samples

*Simple random sampling*   This involves selection at random from the *sampling frame* (see p. 240) of the required number of persons for the sample. A lottery method, random number tables (as found in many statistics books) or a computer can be used. If properly conducted, this gives each person an equal chance of being included in the sample, and also makes all possible combinations of persons for a particular sample size equally likely. Note that each person is chosen at random, as compared with systematic sampling where only the first one is (see below). You can't produce a simple random sample without a full list of the population.

Detailed examples of procedures for this, and the other forms of probability sampling, are given in Baker (1988, pp. 146–56).

*Systematic sampling*   This involves choosing a starting point in the sampling frame at random, and then choosing every *n*th person. Thus, if a sample of fifty is required from a population of 2,000, then every fortieth person is chosen. There would have to be a random selection of a number between one and forty to start off the sequence. For the sample to be representative, this method relies on the list being organized in a way unrelated to the subject of the survey. Although this may seem to be a simple and straightforward way of drawing a probability sample, it has certain statistical peculiarities. Whereas the initial chance of selection of any person is the same, once the first person has been chosen, most persons will have no chance of inclusion and a few will be automatically selected. Similarly, most combinations of persons are excluded from the possible samples that might be chosen. This might be important if the ordering in the list is organized in some way (possibly unknown to yourself).

Both random and systematic sampling require a full list of the population. Getting this list is often difficult. Hence, if there is any possibility of ordering in the list messing up your systematic sample, you may as well go for a random sample as the extra effort involved is minimal.

*Stratified random sampling*  This involves dividing the population into a number of groups or *strata*, where members of a group share a particular characteristic or characteristics (e.g. stratum A may be females; stratum B males). There is then random sampling within the strata. It is usual to have *proportionate sampling*: that is, where the numbers in the groups selected for the sample reflect the relative numbers in the population as a whole (e.g. if there are equal numbers of males and females in the population, there should be equal numbers in the samples; if 80 per cent of the population are from one ethnic group and 20 per cent from another group, then one sample should be four times the other in size). It may sometimes be helpful to have *disproportionate sampling*, where there is an unequal weighting. This would allow you to 'oversample' a small but important stratum, or to ensure that there is at least some representation of certain 'rare species', even to the extent of including all examples of them. Also, if it is known (perhaps from pilot work) that there is greater variation in response from one particular stratum, then this is an indication to include a disproportionately large number from that stratum in the overall sample.

Sampling theory shows that, in some circumstances, stratified random sampling can be more efficient than simple random sampling, in the sense that, for a given sample size, the means of stratified samples are likely to be closer to the population mean. This occurs when there is a relatively small amount of variability in whatever characteristic is being measured in the survey *within* the stratum, compared to variability across strata. The improvement in efficiency does not occur if there is considerable variability in the characteristic within the stratum. So, for example, if females tend to give similar measures, ratings or whatever in a particular survey, and males also tend to give similar ratings to other males, but show overall differences from females, there would be advantage in stratifying the sample by gender.

It is possible to combine stratification with systematic sampling procedures. However, the same criticisms apply to systematic sampling as discussed above, and there seems little or no reason to prefer them to stratified random samples.

*Cluster sampling*   This involves dividing the population into a number of units, or *clusters*, each of which contains individuals having a range of characteristics. The clusters themselves are chosen on a random basis. The sub-population within the cluster is then chosen. This tactic is particularly useful when a population is widely dispersed and large, requiring a great deal of effort and travel to get the survey information. Random sampling might well generate a perversely scattered sample, and as usual it is likely to be the most distant and difficult to reach who are not there when you call, necessitating a second difficult visit. It may also be that permission has to be negotiated to interview respondents, and doing this on what is effectively a one-to-one basis for all respondents will be particularly time-consuming.

An example might involve schoolchildren, where there is initially random sampling of a number of schools, and then testing of all the pupils in each school. There are problems in generalizing to the population of children. Strictly, statistical generalization should be limited to the population of schools (i.e. the clustering variable). This method has the valuable feature that it can be used when the sampling frame is not known (e.g. when we do not have a full list of children in the population, in the above example).

*Multistage sampling*   This is an extension of cluster sampling. It involves selecting the sample in stages, i.e. taking samples from samples. Thus one might take a random sample of schools, then a random sample of the classes within each of the schools, then from within the selected classes choose a sample of children. As with cluster sampling, this provides a means of generating a geographically concentrated sampling. The generalizability issue is the same as for cluster sampling, but judicious use of sampling at appropriate stages enables one to tailor the scale of the project to the resources available.

It is possible to incorporate stratification into both cluster and multistage sampling. Judging the relative efficiencies of these more complicated forms of sampling, and their relationship to the efficiency of simple random sampling, is difficult, and if you are expending considerable resources on a survey it is worth seeking expert advice.

## Non-probability samples

In probability sampling, it is possible to specify the probability that any person (or other unit on which the survey is based) will be included in the sample. Any sampling plan where it is not possible to do this is called 'non-probability sampling'.

Small-scale surveys commonly employ non-probability samples. They are usually less complicated to set up and are acceptable when there is no intention or need to make a statistical generalization to any population beyond the sample surveyed. They can also be used to pilot a survey prior to using a probability sample approach for the main survey. They typically involve the researcher using his judgement to achieve a particular purpose, and for this reason are sometimes referred to as *purposive samples*, although it is perhaps more useful to restrict the use of the term as indicated below.

A wide range of approaches has been used. The first two, quota and dimensional sampling, are basically trying to do the same job as a probability sample, in the sense of aspiring to carry out a sample survey which is statistically representative. They tend to be used in situations where carrying out a probability sample would not be feasible, where for example there is no sampling frame, or the resources required are not available. Their accuracy relies greatly on the skill and experience of those involved.

*Quota sampling*   Here the strategy is to obtain representatives of the various elements of a population, usually in the relative proportions in which they occur in the population. Hence, if socio-economic status were considered of importance in a particular survey, then the categories 'professional/managers and employers/intermediate and junior non-manual/skilled manual/semi-skilled manual/unskilled manual' might be used. Interviewers would be given a quota of each category (with examples to assist them in categorization). Within the category, convenience sampling (see below) is normally used. The interviewer will, for example, seek to interview a given number of unskilled manual workers, a given number of semi-skilled manual workers, etc., by, say, stopping passers-by, and will continue until his quota for the day is complete. The common use of the term 'representatives' in quota sampling has to be looked at with some care. They are representative only in number, not in terms of the type of persons actually selected.

All such means of gathering quota samples are subject to biases. Careful planning, experience and persistence can go some way to addressing obvious biases. If, for example, home visits are involved, avoiding houses where there is a Rottweiler or other large dog, or there are no curtains, or apartments where the lift is out of order, etc. may be understandable behaviour on the part of the sensitive interviewer, but militates against representativeness in householders in the sense of all householders having an equal chance of appearing in the sample.

*Dimensional sampling*   This is an extension of quota sampling. The various dimensions thought to be of importance in a survey (perhaps established by pilot work) are incorporated into the sampling procedure in such a way that at least one representative of every possible combination of these factors or dimensions is included. Thus a study of race relations might identify ethnic group and length of stay in this country as important dimensions. The sampling plan could consist of a table or matrix with 'ethnic group' and 'length of stay' constituting the rows and columns. Refinements of this approach involve selection of particular combinations of the dimensions (e.g. 'Kenyan Asians' with '10–15 years residence'), either because of their particular importance, or because of an inability through lack of time and resources to cover all combinations.

The critical comments made about quota sampling apply with equal force to dimensional sampling.

*Convenience sampling*   involves choosing the nearest and most convenient persons to act as respondents. The process is continued until the required sample size has been reached.

> *Convenience sampling is sometimes used as a cheap and dirty way of doing a sample survey. You do not know whether or not findings are representative.*

This is probably one of the most widely used and least satisfactory methods of sampling. The term 'accidental sample' is sometimes used but is misleading as it carries some suggestion of randomness, whereas in fact all kinds of largely unspecifiable biases and influences are likely to influence who gets sampled. There are sensible uses of convenience sampling, but they are more to do with getting a feeling for the issues involved, or piloting a proper sample survey.

Sampling is used in many contexts other than a sample survey. The following approaches tend to be used in other types of fieldwork, particularly in case studies and where participant observation is involved.

*Purposive sampling*   The principle of selection in purposive sampling is the researcher's judgement as to typicality or interest. A sample is built up which enables the researcher to satisfy her specific needs in a project. For example, researchers following the 'grounded theory' approach (Glaser, 1992; Strauss and Corbin, 1997, 1998) carry out initial sampling, and from analysis of the results extend the sample in ways guided by their emerging theory (this is sometimes referred to as 'theoretical sampling'). The rationale of such an approach is very different from statistical generalization from sample to population. It is commonly used within other flexible designs as well.

*Snowball sampling*   Here the researcher identifies one or more individuals from the population of interest. After they have been interviewed, they are used as informants to identify other members of the population, who are themselves used as informants, and so on. Snowball sampling is useful when there is difficulty in identifying members of the population, e.g. when this is a clandestine group. It can be seen as a particular type of purposive sample.

## Other types of sample

Other types of sample may be used for special purposes. They include the following.

*   *Time samples*   Sampling across time, for example in a study of the char-acteristics of the persons who use a particular space at different times of the day or week (can be probabilistic or non-probabilistic, depending on how it is organized). Commonly used in observational studies.
*   *Homogeneous  samples* Covering a narrow range or single value of a particular variable or variables.
*   *Heterogeneous  samples* A deliberate strategy of selecting individuals varying widely on the characteristic(s) of interest.
*   *Extreme case samples*   Concentration on extreme values when sampling, perhaps where it is considered that they will throw a particularly strong light on the phenomenon of interest.
*   *Rare element samples*   Values with low frequencies in the population are over-represented in the sample; the rationale is similar to the previous approach.

## Representative sampling and the real world

The exigencies of carrying out real world studies can mean that the require-ments for representative sampling are very difficult, if not impossible, to fulfil. Sampling frames may be impossible to obtain. A doctor may not be prepared to provide you with a list of patients, or a firm a list of employees. Or what you get hold of may be out of date, or otherwise incorrect. This leads to 'inel-igibles' – persons on the sampling frame who are not part of your target population. Conversely, 'eligibles' may not get into the frame. This slippage between what you have and what you want causes problems with representa-tiveness and lowers your sample size.

Non-response can be a very serious problem and it is worth giving consid-erable time and effort to reducing it (see the suggestions on p. 249). The basic issue is that those who do not participate may well differ from those who do, but it is extremely difficult to allow for this. It is worth stressing that even if you get everything else right (perfect random sample from perfect sampling frame), anything other than a very high response rate casts serious doubts on the representativeness of the sample you actually achieve. And once you fall below that rate, it is not so much a question of the rate you get but the (unknown) degree of difference between responders and non-responders that matters. It would be entirely feasible for a response rate of 30 per cent to lead to a more representative sample than one of 60 per cent.

There are things that you can do. In a postal survey it is possible to compare late returners of questionnaires with earlier ones, or those responding after one, or two, reminders with those responding without prompting. If you know some characteristics of the population, you can check to see whether the sample you obtained is reasonably typical of the population on these variables (Oliver, 1990, attempts to excuse a 36 per cent response rate on these grounds). In any survey where there is differential responding between categories (say, a particularly low rate from Asian females or top executives) you can compare their responses with those from other categories. Or you can make a real effort with a random sub-set of the non-respondents and try to turn them into respondents, then compare these with previous respondents. However, these are only palliatives, and the real answer is that if representativeness is crucial for you, then you so set up your study that virtually everyone responds.

But probability sampling and statistical inference are not all. Bryman (1989, pp. 113–17) shows that in practice few instances of survey research in organization studies are based on random samples. He quotes from Schwab:

> Of course we all know that almost all of the empirical studies published in our journals [organizational studies] use *convenience*, not probability samples . . . Thus if one took generalization to a population using statistical inference seriously, one would recommend rejecting nearly all manuscripts submitted. (Schwab, 1985, p. 173)

It may be that they should try harder. There will continue to be situations where probability samples are feasible. The theoretical basis for their use is clear and well developed. What is clearly inappropriate is to play one game (convenience or other purposive sampling) according to the rules of another (probability sampling). If it is not feasible to work with probability samples, or if it is not possible to achieve adequate response rates, then the argument has to follow different lines. Even if statistical generalization is not legitimate, it may be feasible to use the kind of theoretical generalization discussed in the context of flexible design research (see chapter 6, p. 176).

## Further Reading

Czaja, R. and Blair, J. (1996) *Designing Surveys: A Guide to Decisions and Procedures.* Thousand Oaks, Calif.: Pine Forge. Up to date with detailed discussion of telephone surveys. Covers both practical guidelines and the underlying logical principles.

de Vaus, D. A. (1991) *Surveys in Social Research*, 3rd edn. London: UCL Press/Allen & Unwin. Short text covering design and practicalities. Very clear.

Dillman, D. (2000) *Mail and Internet Surveys: The Tailored Design Method*, 2nd edn. Chichester: Wiley. Full coverage of survey design and practice, including extensive treatment of internet surveys.

Hakim, C. (1987) *Research Design: Strategies and Choices in the Design of Social Research*. London: Allen & Unwin. See chapter on 'Ad Hoc Sample Surveys' for discussion of design of small surveys.

Hoinville, G., Jowell, R. and Associates (1985) *Survey Research Practice*, 2nd edn. London: Gower. Excellent text on the practical aspects of survey design and execution.

Marsh, C. (1982) *The Survey Method: The Contribution of Surveys to Sociological Explanation*. London: Allen & Unwin. Though primarily methodological, its interest is wider than the subtitle suggests. Very extensive annotated bibliography.

Mishler, E. G. (1991) *Research Interviewing: Context and Narrative*. Cambridge, Mass.: Harvard University Press. Presents a powerful critique of the survey research interview. Suggests that the standard approach of decontextualizing questions and response leads to problems in analysis and interpretation.

Sapsford, R. (1999) *Survey Research*. London: Sage. Useful discussion of applied research in constrained circumstances and with limited resources. Also of the practicalities of sampling in the real world.

Turner, C. F. and Martin, E., eds (1986) *Surveying Subjective Phenomena*, 2 vols. New York: Russell Sage. Detailed reference on central methodological concerns of survey research.

# 9
# Interviews

This chapter:

- discusses different types of interviews, differentiating them in terms of amount of structure
- considers the circumstances under which the different types are appropriate
- reviews the advantages and disadvantages of interviews
- provides general advice for interviewers, including the kinds of questions to avoid
- covers the phases of an interview
- gives particular attention to semi-structured interviews, including interview schedules
- reviews issues involved in running group interviews
- details advantages and disadvantages of focus groups
- concludes by reviewing the skills needed by interviewers

## Introduction

Interviewing as a research method typically involves you, as researcher, asking questions and, hopefully, receiving answers from the people you are interviewing. It is very widely used in social research and there are many different types. A commonly used typology distinguishes among structured, semi-structured and unstructured interviews. The different types can link to some extent to the 'depth' of response sought. The extreme example of a highly structured format is the survey interview discussed in the previous chapter. This is effectively a questionnaire with fixed questions in a pre-decided order and standardized wording, where responses to most of the questions have to be selected from a small list of alternatives. Less structured approaches allow the person interviewed much more flexibility of response, and at the other extreme is the 'depth interview' (Miller and Crabtree, 1999), where the respondent is largely free to say whatever they like on the broad topic of the interview, with minimal prompting from the researcher. Interviews are commonly one-to-one and face-to-face, but they can take place in group settings and, as discussed in the previous chapter, the telephone is increasingly being used because of the savings in time and resources it permits.

Interviews can be used as the primary or only approach in a study, as in a survey or many grounded theory studies. However, they lend themselves well to use in combination with other methods, in a multimethod approach. A case study might employ some kind of relatively formal interview to complement participant observation. An experiment could often usefully incorporate a post-intervention interview to help incorporate the participant's perspective into the findings.

The last chapter covered interview-based survey questionnaires. This chapter focuses on a range of other types of interview where open-ended questions are the norm. A typical scenario envisaged is the small-scale enquiry where you, working as a student, teacher, social worker, applied social researcher or whatever, are wanting to carry out a study with limited resources and time, perhaps alone, perhaps with a colleague or some part-time assistance, possibly concerned with some situation in which you are already an actor. In these situations, such interviews can be a powerful tool, though they are not without potential problems – practical, theoretical and analytical, among others.

## Types and Styles of Interviews

A commonly made distinction is based on the degree of structure or standardization of the interview:

- *Fully structured interview*  Has predetermined questions with fixed wording, usually in a pre-set order. The use of mainly open-response questions is the only essential difference from an interview-based survey questionnaire.
- *Semi-structured interview*  Has predetermined questions, but the order can be modified based upon the interviewer's perception of what seems most appropriate. Question wording can be changed and explanations given; particular questions which seem inappropriate with a particular interviewee can be omitted, or additional ones included.
- *Unstructured interviews*  The interviewer has a general area of interest and concern, but lets the conversation develop within this area. It can be completely informal.

Semi-structured and unstructured interviews are widely used in flexible, qualitative designs. King (1994) refers to them as *qualitative research interviews* and suggests guidelines for the situations in which they might be used, presented as box 9.1.

Powney and Watts (1987, ch. 2) prefer a different typology, making a basic distinction between *respondent interviews* and *informant interviews*. In respondent interviews, the interviewer remains in control (or at least that is the interviewer's intention) throughout the whole process. All such interviews are necessarily structured to some extent by the interviewer. In this type, or style, of interview, the central point is that the intention is that 'interviewers rule'; their agenda is what matters. Both fully and semi-structured interviews are typically, in this sense, respondent interviews.

In informant interviews (sometimes referred to as *non-directive*, in reference to the interviewer's role), the prime concern is for the interviewee's

---

## Box 9.1

### Circumstances in which a qualitative research interview is most appropriate

1  Where a study focuses on the meaning of particular phenomena to the participants.

2  Where individual perceptions of processes within a social unit – such as a work-group, department or whole organization – are to be studied prospectively, using a series of interviews.

3  Where individual historical accounts are required of how a particular phenomenon developed – for instance, a new shift system.

4  Where exploratory work is required before a quantitative study can be carried out. For example, researchers examining the impact of new technology on social relationships in a workplace might use qualitative interviews to identify the range of different types of experience which a subsequent quantitative study should address.

5  Where a quantitative study has been carried out, and qualitative data are required to validate particular measures or to clarify and illustrate the meaning of the findings. For instance, people with high, medium and low scores on a new measure of stress at work might be interviewed to see whether their experiences concur with the ratings on the measure.

(From King, 1994, pp. 16–17.)

perceptions within a particular situation or context. From the point of view of the interviewer, such a session will almost inevitably appear unstructured, as he is unlikely to be privy to the interviewee's agenda. However, it could be much more structured as far as the interviewee is concerned.

Interviews can, of course, be used for purposes other than research. Aldridge and Wood (1998), for example, discuss the use of investigative interviews in the context of child care and child abuse. There are very substantial overlaps in the two approaches, in that in both cases the essential purpose is to seek answers to questions: research questions and questions of guilt or innocence respectively.

## Question focus

Distinctions are commonly made among seeking to find out what people know, what they do, and what they think or feel. This leads, respectively, to questions concerned with *facts*, with *behaviour*, and with *beliefs* or *attitudes*.

Facts are relatively easy to get at, although errors can occur due to lapses in memory or to response biases of various kinds (age may be claimed to be less than it is by the middle-aged; inflated by the really aged). The best responses are obtained to specific (as opposed to general) questions about important things, in the present or recent past. The same rules apply to questions about behaviour, and of course the respondent is often in a uniquely favourable position to tell you about what they are doing or have done. Beliefs and attitudes form a very important target for self-report techniques, but are relatively difficult to get at. They are often complex and multidimensional, and appear particularly prone to the effects of question wording and sequence. These problems point to the use of multiple questions related to the belief or attitude and can be best attacked by the construction of appropriate scales (see chapter 10).

## Advantages and Disadvantages of Interviews

The interview is a flexible and adaptable way of finding things out. The human use of language is fascinating both as a behaviour in its own right, and for the virtually unique window that it opens on what lies behind our actions. Observing behaviour is clearly a useful enquiry technique, but asking people directly about what is going on is an obvious short cut in seeking answers to our research questions.

Face-to-face interviews offer the possibility of modifying one's line of enquiry, following up interesting responses and investigating underlying motives in a way that postal and other self-administered questionnaires cannot. Non-verbal cues may give messages which help in understanding the verbal response, possibly changing or even, in extreme cases, reversing its meaning. To make profitable use of this flexibility calls for considerable skill and experience in the interviewer. The lack of standardization that it implies inevitably raises concerns about reliability. Biases are difficult to rule out. There are ways of dealing with these problems, but they call for a degree of professionalism which does not come easily. Nevertheless, although the interview is in no sense a soft option as a data-gathering technique (illustrating once more that apparently 'soft' techniques, emphasizing qualitative data, are deceptively hard to use well), it has the potential of providing rich and highly illuminating material.

Interviewing is time-consuming. The actual interview session itself will obviously vary in length. Anything under half an hour is unlikely to be valuable; anything going much over an hour may be making unreasonable demands on busy interviewees, and could have the effect of reducing the number of persons willing to participate, which may in turn lead to biases in the sample that you achieve. Above all, don't say that it will take half an hour and then keep going for an hour and a half. It is up to you to terminate the interview on schedule, and you have the professional responsibility of keeping this, as well as all other, undertakings that you make. The reverse phenomenon is not unknown: that of the interviewee so glad to have a willing ear to bend that you can't escape. How you deal with this depends very much on your own 'closure' skills. Remember that, just as you are hoping to get something out of the interview, it is not unreasonable for the interviewee to get something from you.

All interviews require careful preparation – making arrangements to visit, securing necessary permissions – which takes time; confirming arrangements, rescheduling appointments to cover absences and crises takes more time. Notes have to be written up; tapes, if used, must be transcribed, in full or in part (allow something like a factor of ten between tape time and transcription time unless you are highly skilled: i.e. a one-hour tape takes ten hours to transcribe fully). Subsequent analyses are not the least of your time-eaters. As with all other techniques, time planning and time budgeting is a crucial skill of successful enquiry in the real world.

## General Advice for Interviewers

The interview is a kind of conversation, something that we have all had experience in doing. However, interviewing does demand rather different emphases in the social interaction that takes place from those in ordinary conversation.

Your job as interviewer is to try to get interviewees to talk freely and openly. Your own behaviour has a major influence on their willingness to do this.

To this end you should:

- *Listen more than you speak*    Most interviewers talk too much. The interview is not a platform for the interviewer's personal experiences and opinions.
- *Put questions in a straightforward, clear and non-threatening way*    If people are confused or defensive, you will not get the information you seek.
- *Eliminate cues which lead interviewees to respond in a particular way*    Many interviewees will seek to please the interviewer by giving 'correct' responses ('Are you against sin?').
- *Enjoy it (or at least look as though you do)*    Don't give the message that you are bored or scared. Vary your voice and facial expression.

It is also essential that you *take a full record of the interview*. This can be from notes made at the time and/or from a recording of the interview. Experienced interviewers tend to have strong preferences for one or other of these approaches. McDonald and Sanger have given a detailed account of their relative advantages and disadvantages (Walker, 1985, pp. 109–16 provides a summary). The literature (discussed in Hoinville et al., 1985) suggests that various kinds of questions should be avoided; these are summarized in box 9.2.

## Content of the Interview

In interviews which are to a greater or lesser extent pre-structured by the interviewer, the content, which can be prepared in advance, consists of

- a *set of items (usually questions)*, often with alternative subsequent items depending on the responses obtained;
- suggestions for so-called *probes* and *prompts*;
- and a proposed *sequence for the questions* which, in a semi-structured interview, may be subject to change during the course of the interview.

### The items or questions

Three main types are used in research interviews: *closed* (or *fixed-alternative*), *open* and *scale* items. Closed questions, as the fixed-alternative label suggests,

---

## Box 9.2

### Questions to avoid in interviews

*Long questions*   The interviewee may remember only part of the question, and respond to that part.

*Double-barrelled (or multiple-barrelled) questions*, e.g. 'What do you feel about current pop music compared with that of five years ago?' The solution here is to break it down into simpler questions ('What do you feel about current pop music?'; 'Can you recall any pop music from five years ago?'; 'How do you feel they compare?').

*Questions involving jargon*   Generally you should avoid questions containing words likely to be unfamiliar to the target audience. Keep things simple to avoid disturbing interviewees; it is in your own interest as well.

*Leading questions*, e.g. 'Why do you like Huddersfield?' It is usually straightforward to modify such questions, provided you realize that they are leading in a particular direction.

*Biased questions*   Provided you are alert to the possibility of bias, it is not difficult to *write* unbiased questions. What is more difficult, however, is not (perhaps unwittingly) to lead the interviewee by the manner in which the question is asked, or the way in which you receive the response. Neutrality is called for, and in seeking to be welcoming and reinforcing to the interviewee, you should try to avoid appearing to share or welcome their views.

---

force the interviewee to choose from two or more fixed alternatives. Open questions provide no restrictions on the content or manner of the reply other than on the subject area (e.g. 'What kind of way do you most prefer to spend a free evening?'). Scale items, which may well not be in question form, ask for a response in the form of degree of agreement or disagreement (e.g. strongly agree/agree/neutral/disagree/strongly disagree). Logically they are of the closed or fixed-alternative type, but are sometimes regarded as a separate type.

As open-ended questions are probably more commonly used in interviews than in other settings, it is appropriate to discuss them here.

The advantages of open-ended questions are that they

- are flexible;
- allow you to go into more depth or clear up any misunderstandings;

- enable testing of the limits of a respondent's knowledge;
- encourage co-operation and rapport;
- allow you to make a truer assessment of what the respondent really believes;
- can produce unexpected or unanticipated answers.

The disadvantages lie in the possibilities for loss of control by the interviewer, and in particular in being much more difficult to analyse than closed ones.

## Probes

A probe is a device to get interviewees to expand on a response when you intuit that they have more to give. The use of probes is something of an art-form and difficult to transmit to the novice interviewer. Sometimes the interviewer may be given instructions to probe on specific questions. There are obvious tactics, such as asking 'Anything more?' or 'Could you go over that again?' Sometimes when an answer has been given in general terms, a useful probe is to seek a personal response, e.g. 'What is your own personal view on this?' There are also very general tactics, such as the use of

- a period of silence;
- an enquiring glance;
- 'mmhmm . . .';
- repeating back all or part of what the interviewee has just said.

Zeisel (1984, pp. 140–54) gives an extended analysis of different types of probe.

## Prompts

Prompts suggest to the interviewee the range or set of possible answers that the interviewer expects. The list of possibilities may be read out by the interviewer, or a 'prompt card' with them on can be shown (e.g. a list of names of alcoholic drinks for a question on drinking habits). All prompts must be used in a consistent manner with different interviewees (and by different interviewers, if more than one is involved), and form part of the interview record.

## The sequence of questions

A commonly used sequence is as follows:

1   *Introduction*   Interviewer introduces herself, explains purpose of the interview, assures of confidentiality, asks permission to tape and/or make notes.
2   *'Warm-up'*   Easy, non-threatening questions at the beginning to settle down both of you.
3   *Main body of interview*   Covering the main purpose of the interview in what the interviewer considers to be a logical progression. In semi-structured interviewing, this order can be varied, capitalizing on the responses made (ensure 'missed' topics are returned to unless this seems inappropriate or unnecessary. Any 'risky' questions should be relatively late in the sequence so that, if the interviewee refuses to continue, less information is lost.
4   *'Cool-off'*   Usually a few straightforward questions at the end to defuse any tension that might have built up.
5   *Closure*   Thank you and goodbye. The 'hand on the door' phenomenon, sometimes found at the end of counselling sessions, is also common in interviewing. Interviewees may, when the recorder is switched off or the notebook put away, come out with a lot of interesting material. There are various possible ways of dealing with this (switch on again, reopen the book, forget about it) but in any case you should be consistent, *and* note how you dealt with it.

## Carrying Out Different Types of Interview

### Structured interviews

In virtually all respects the procedures and considerations for carrying out structured interviews are the same as those discussed for survey interviews in the previous chapter (p. 251). However, you do need to ensure that responses to open-ended questions are captured word for word. The easiest way of ensuring this is by taping the interview. As always, the consent of the interviewees must be obtained and the practicalities of recording have to be sorted out (see p. 376).

Structured interviews of this kind do not fit easily into flexible design studies. They are more likely to be contributing to a fixed design alongside other methods. While no one form of data analysis is called for, content analysis (which effectively transforms the data into quantitative form) is commonly used: see chapter 12 (p. 351).

## Semi-structured interviews

This type of interview is widely used in flexible designs, either as the sole method or in combination with others. In Powney and Watts's (1987) terminology, this is still a respondent interview. Interviewers have their shopping list of topics and want to get responses to them, but they have considerable freedom in the sequencing of questions, in their exact wording, and in the amount of time and attention given to different topics.

The *interview schedule* can be simpler than the one for the structured interview (p. 251). It will be likely to include the following:

- introductory comments (probably a verbatim script);
- list of topic headings and possibly key questions to ask under these headings;
- set of associated prompts;
- closing comments.

It is common to incorporate some more highly structured sequences (e.g. to obtain standard factual biographical and other material). One strategy is to have the different topics and associated questions and prompts on a series of cards. The interviewer will have an initial topic but will then be to some extent guided by the interviewee's responses as to the succeeding sequence of topics. Cards can be put on one side when they have been covered. Notes should be made during the interview, even if it is also being taped (in part as a fail-safe in case of a taping problem). Allow a substantial amount of space for each topic as you won't know in advance how much material you will obtain in any particular area. The prompts may not be necessary, but they provide a useful structure for organizing your notes. Box 9.3 gives an example of an interview schedule for semi-structured interviews.

## Unstructured interviews

One type of unstructured interview is non-standardized, open-ended and in-depth. It has been compared to a lengthy, intimate conversation; as a research tool, it is not an easy option for the novice. Ely et al. (1991) give a graphic account of what is involved, with related references.

Lofland and Lofland (1995), who prefer the term 'intensive interviewing', stress the importance of an interview *guide* when working in this way:

## Box 9.3

### Example of interview schedule for semi-structured interview

Thank you for being willing to take part in a follow-up interview to the previous survey. Can I first of all assure you that you will remain completely anonymous and no records of the interview will be kept with your name on them.

1    Can I first ask you if you are now in employment?

If *yes* take details of:

a    Job
b    How person came to hear of job
c    Application procedure
d    Selection procedure
e    Why this one was successful in contrast to previous attempts
f    What problems did the person experience in previous attempts? (Probe until topic exhausted)
g    Advance to 2.

If *no* take details of:

a    Last job applied for
b    How person came to hear about job
c    Application procedure
d    Selection procedure
e    Why was this one unsuccessful?
f    If person not interviewed, ask above questions about the last job that got as far as interview. If none, ask above questions about the one they felt they got nearest to
g    What problems does the person in general experience in relation to finding work? (Probe until topic exhausted)
h    Advance to 2.

2    What careers advice have you received:

a    At school?
b    From local careers service?
c    From any other source including informal sources?

3    How would you evaluate that advice? (Ask in relation to all sources identified in 2.)

4    Have you taken part in any of the services for the unemployed provided locally? (Probe this and explain but do not prompt with examples at this stage.)

**5**   How would you evaluate these services? (Ask in relation to all sources identified in 4.)

**6**   Take respondents through the following list and ask them if they are aware of the service, what is provided, if they have had direct experience, and if they had, how they would rate that experience. (Omit from the list any services already covered in 4 and 5 above.)

a      Adult training
b      Youth training
c      Training Access Points
d      Worklink
e      Kirklees Community Enterprise Training Agency (KCETA)
f      Start-up business units
g      Business Access Scheme
h      Workers' co-operatives
i      Careers and Education Advice Service for Adults (CEASA)
j      Careers service
k      Redundancy counselling.

**7**   What kinds of services could be provided that would help you personally to get a job (or would have made it easier if in employment)? Probe and direct to less obvious areas such as child minding and transport – pick up on factors mentioned in 1 and 2 above – but do not neglect more obvious direct services.

**8**   Have you been helped by any informal organizations? Probe on community-based initiatives, job clubs, local support networks, etc. Do not neglect simply the help and advice of relatives, friends and neighbours.

**9**   How do the factors identified in 8 compare to help received through formal services? Probe in what ways better, similar, worse or different.

**10**   Do you have a regular routine to organize your time for the week? Probe the extent to which this includes finding employment or perhaps precludes it. NB if now employed ask in relation to time when unemployed.

**11**   Do you find your present income adequate and fair? If in employment contrast with time when out of employment.

**12**   Some people see the society we live in as a ladder to climb to greater rewards: others see it as divided between the haves and have-nots. How do you see society? Probe on social imagery.

**13**   Thank you very much for helping us and giving up your time. Can I finally ask you if you think there is any aspect of your experience of looking for work that has not been covered in this interview?

(From Cliff et al., n.d.)

a guide is *not* a tightly structured set of questions to be asked verbatim as written, accompanied by an associated range of preworded likely answers. Rather, *it is a list of things to be sure to ask about when talking to the person being interviewed* . . . You want interviewees to speak freely in their own terms about a set of concerns you bring to the interaction, plus whatever else they might introduce. (p. 85, emphasis in original)

They also reproduce an excellent set of self-instructions for introducing oneself prior to an intensive interview, given here as box 9.4. These were originally developed by Davis to introduce himself to persons with handicaps, but are of general relevance.

McCracken (1988) advocates the use of what he calls the *long interview*. By this he means not simply an interview which takes a long time, but an ethnographic style which might be substituted for participant observation in situations where the latter is impossible because of time or other constraints (see chapter 6, p. 186).

---

## Box 9.4

### Introducing yourself: a list of self-instructions

**1**    Explain purpose and nature of the study to the respondent, telling how or through whom he came to be selected.

**2**    Give assurance that respondent will remain anonymous in any written reports growing out of the study, and that his responses will be treated in strictest confidence.

**3**    Indicate that he may find some of the questions far-fetched, silly or difficult to answer, for the reason that questions that are appropriate for one person are not always appropriate for another. Since there are no right or wrong answers, he is not to worry about these but to do as best he can with them. We are only interested in his opinions and personal experiences.

**4**    He is to feel perfectly free to interrupt, ask clarification of the interviewer, criticize a line of questioning, etc.

**5**    Interviewer will tell respondent something about himself – his background, training, and interest in the area of enquiry.

**6**    Interviewer is to ask permission to tape-record the interview, explaining why he wishes to do this.

(From Davis, 1960; see also Lofland and Lofland, 1995, pp. 84–5.)

A further type of unstructured interview is the *informal interview*. This is where one takes an opportunity that arises to have a (usually short) chat with someone in the research setting about anything which seems relevant. In an ethnographic-style study, this might arise after a period of observation to try to seek clarification about the meaning or significance of something that took place. It is not appropriate as the main data collection method but, used in conjunction with other methods, can play a valuable part in virtually all flexible design research. It is not usually feasible to tape-record such interviews (getting out the recorder, asking permission etc. is highly likely to get rid of the spontaneity and informality) but it is important that you make a detailed note of the interaction as soon as possible afterwards.

## Telephone interviews

These were discussed in the previous chapter (p. 253) in the context of surveys, but can be used more widely. They share many of the advantages of face-to-face interviewing: a high response rate; correction of obvious misunderstandings; possible use of probes, etc. Rapport may be more difficult to achieve, but this is compensated for by evidence of smaller interviewer effects and a lower tendency towards socially desirable responses (Bradburn and Sudman, 1979). The lack of visual cues may cause problems in interpretation. The major advantage, particularly if the sample to be reached is geographically dispersed, is the lower cost in terms of time, effort and money. They can be safer as well: you won't get physically attacked over the phone.

## Informant Interviews

Informant interviews are not simply casual conversations. In one version, known as the *non-directive interview*, the direction of the interview and the areas covered are totally in the control of the informant (the interviewee). Carl Rogers (1945) has used this approach widely in therapeutic settings, and it has had a considerable influence on interviewing style. However, there are important differences between clinical and research purposes. In Rogerian therapy, the interview is initiated by the client, not the therapist; the motivation, and hence the purpose of the interview, is to seek help with a problem, and the extent to which it is helpful is the index of success. Because of this, Whyte (1984) has claimed that a genuine non-directive interviewing approach is not appropriate for research. Powney and Watts (1987, p. 20) suggest that Piaget's type of clinical interviewing, as used in his studies of cognitive development (e.g. Piaget, 1929, 1930), where he is insistent that the child must determine the content and direction of the conversation, fits better into research purposes. There is a certain irony here, as experimental psychologists, while recognizing Piaget's theoretical contributions, have been very dismissive of his methodology.

An approach which allows people's views and feelings to emerge, but which gives the interviewer some control, is known as the *focused interview* (Merton et al., 1956). It can be used where we want to investigate a particular situation, phenomenon or event (e.g. a youth training programme, an X-ray unit or a TV programme). Individuals are sought who have been involved in that situation (e.g. they are all in an open prison and have been subjected to a 'short, sharp, shock' treatment).

The first task is to carry out a *situational analysis*, by means of observation, documentary analysis or whatever. Typically this covers:

- the important aspects of the situation to those involved;
- the meaning these aspects have for those involved; and
- the effects they have on those involved.

An interview guide is then developed covering the major areas of enquiry and the research questions. The interviews concentrate on the subjective experiences of those involved. This approach demands considerable experience and skill on the part of the interviewer and great flexibility. In particular, the probe is a crucial aspect. Zeisel (1984, ch. 9) provides detailed and useful suggestions.

## Group Interviews

Interviews can take place in a group context as well as one-to-one. Group interviews can fall into any of the types previously discussed and, in particular, may be highly structured, semi-structured or unstructured. Fontana and Frey (1994) give details of five different types. The more common versions have a substantial degree of flexibility and are effectively some form of hybrid with characteristics of a discussion as well as of an interview. Even though general topics, and sometimes specific questions, are presented by the researcher, the traditional interview format of alternate question and answer is both difficult to maintain and eliminates the group interaction which can be a particular strength of the group interview.

The generic term 'group interview' has tended recently to be used interchangeably with 'focus group' because of the latter's popularity, even though it has specific characteristics, as discussed below.

## Focus groups

Focus groups originated in market research in the 1920s, arising from
the recognition that many consumer decisions were made in a social, group
context (Bogardus, 1926). They are now widely used by political parties
seeking to assess the likely response to proposed policies, and are currently a
very popular method of data collection in many fields of applied social research.
Johnson (1996) argues from a critical realist perspective that they have considerable potential to raise consciousness and empower participants. Focus
groups show signs of taking over from questionnaires as the automatic stock
response to the question 'What method should we use?' This is in part because
they share with postal questionnaires the advantages of being an efficient way
of generating substantial amounts of data, and apparently being easy to carry
out. However, as with questionnaires, these perceived advantages are offset by
considerable disadvantages. For example, it is difficult or impossible to follow
up the views of individuals; and group dynamics or power hierarchies affect
who speaks and what they say. A particular problem is when one or two persons
dominate. Focus groups are not easy to conduct well. Box 9.5 lists some of
the advantages and disadvantages.

A focus group (sometimes referred to as a *focus group interview* – which
emphasizes the fact that this is a particular type of interview) is a group

---

## Box 9.5

### Advantages and disadvantages of focus groups

*Advantages*

1   A highly efficient technique for qualitative data collection since the
amount and range of data are increased by collecting from several people
at the same time.

2   Natural quality controls on data collection operate; for example, participants tend to provide checks and balances on each other and extreme
views tend to be weeded out.

3   Group dynamics help in focusing on the most important topics and it
is fairly easy to assess the extent to which there is a consistent and shared
view.

4   Participants tend to enjoy the experience.

5   The method is relatively inexpensive and flexible and can be set up
quickly.

**6**   Participants are empowered and able to make comments in their own words, while being stimulated by thoughts and comments of others in the group.

**7**   Contributions can be encouraged from people who are reluctant to be interviewed on their own, feel they have nothing to say or may not usually participate in surveys.

**8**   People who cannot read or write or who have other specific difficulties are not discriminated against.

**9**   Facilitation can help in the discussion of taboo subjects since less inhibited members may break the ice or provide mutual support.

### Disadvantages

**1**   The number of questions covered is limited. Typically fewer than ten major questions can be asked in an hour.

**2**   Facilitating the group process requires considerable expertise.

**3**   The interview process needs to be well managed or the less articulate may not share their views, extreme views may predominate, and bias may be caused by the domination of the group by one or two people.

**4**   Conflicts may arise between personalities. Power struggles may detract from the interview and there may be conflicts of status within the procedure.

**5**   Confidentiality can be a problem between participants when interacting in a group situation.

**6**   The results cannot be generalized as they cannot be regarded as representative of the wider population.

**7**   The live and immediate nature of the interaction may lead a researcher or decision-maker to place greater faith in the findings than is actually warranted.

(Adapted and abridged from Robinson, 1999, pp. 909–10.)

interview on a specific topic; which is where the 'focus' comes from. It is an open-ended group discussion guided by the researcher, typically extending over at least an hour, possibly two or more. Opinion varies on the optimum size of the group. Figures of eight to twelve are usually thought suitable (Stewart and Shamdasani, 1990), although smaller group sizes have been used.

There is debate about whether the groups should be homogeneous (e.g. a study of the client perspective on the working of a health service might consist of a group of people who have recently used the service) or heterogeneous (e.g. a study within a firm might include shop-floor workers, secretarial staff, managers, etc.). The pros and cons of the two approaches are presented as box 9.6. Market researchers traditionally brought together groups of strangers on the assumption that this would lead to a greater focus on the designated topic. However, this is not feasible for many real world research projects. Mac-Dougall and Fudge (2001) provide highly practical advice on the planning and recruiting of samples for focus groups, based on a synthesis of the literature and their research experience.

Complex studies can have several different focus groups. Brown (1999) describes several studies using focus groups in clinical research. A typical study involved a total of seven focus groups, consisting of two groups of senior citizens, two informal carer groups and three health care provider groups,

---

## Box 9.6

### Homogeneous or heterogeneous groups?

*Homogeneous groups*

Have a common background, position or experience, which

- facilitates communication;
- promotes an exchange of ideas and experiences;
- gives a sense of safety in expressing conflicts or concerns;
- may result in 'groupthink' (unquestioning similarity of position or views).

*Heterogeneous groups*

Differ in background, position or experience, which

- can stimulate and enrich the discussion;
- may inspire other group members to look at the topic in a different light;
- may risk power imbalances;
- can lead to lack of respect for opinions expressed by some members;
- can lead to a dominant participant destroying the group process.

(Derived from Brown, 1999, p. 115.)

representing each of the three primary care areas – medical, home-based and public health.

*Uses of focus groups*    Focus groups can be, and have been, used as the primary data collection method in a study. Examples include examining risk-taking behaviour in relation to HIV infection (Kitzinger, 1994); the information concerns of partners of women with breast cancer (Rees et al., 1998); the fear of crime among lower socio-economic status Latina women in New York (Madriz, 1998); respect for elders in current Singapore society (Mehta, 1997); and facilitating self-help in young persons with arthritis (Barlow and Harrison, 1996). They are, however commonly used in conjunction with other methods: for example, with observation and individual interviews (Cash et al., 1999), or with questionnaires (Sloan, 1999).

Other uses include the focus group as a precursor to the development of a more structured instrument. Hyland et al. (1994), for example, used them to help in the construction of a quality of life questionnaire. The reverse sequence is also possible, for example using focus groups to amplify and understand the findings from a survey (Evason and Whittington, 1997). Further discussion on different types of multimethod study is presented in chapter 12.

*The moderator role*    The person running a focus group is usually referred to as the *moderator* (sometimes the *facilitator*). The terms signal two aspects of their role: to moderate in the dictionary sense of regulating, or keeping within measures or bounds; to facilitate in the sense of helping the group to run effectively.

These are not easy tasks, and call for considerable skills and experience if they are to be done well. A balance between an active and a passive role is needed. 'The moderator has to generate interest in and discussion about a particular topic, which is close to his or her professional or academic interest, without at the same time leading the group to reinforce existing expectations or confirm a prior hypothesis' (Sim, 1998, p. 347). Acting as a moderator for a focus group run for research purposes may be particularly difficult for some professionals. Those from helping and caring professions must appreciate that it is not being run for therapeutic purposes: they are not running a support group, although it may be that participants get a great deal from the experience (Brown, 1999; Brown et al., 1993).

There are considerable advantages in having a second researcher or other person involved in the running of the group. These include:

- it provides coverage of both the substantive area of interest and focus group experience (often not possible to combine in a single person);

- a second person can make notes on who is speaking (difficult to determine if audio-taping is used; video-taping can be obtrusive);
- the second person can note non-verbal interactions and
- can give feedback on the moderator's performance (e.g. talking too much; over-prompting; inhibiting discussion; allowing one person to dominate; etc.).

*Data collection in focus groups*   Audio-taping is generally recommended, although there are some situations where this may affect the working of the group (perhaps because of the sensitivity of the topic, or the characteristics and expectations of group members). It is good practice to have written notes made even if the session is recorded. Groups are notoriously difficult to get good recordings from, recorders fail, etc. This is a task for the second researcher; keeping the session going well is a sufficiently demanding task for the moderator.

*Data analysis and interpretation*   This should follow the general principles and processes for qualitative data analysis discussed in chapter 14. As with other flexible designs generating qualitative data, analysis and interpretation of data from focus groups must take account of the context and circumstances in which the data are gathered.

The group context leads to some issues which are relatively specific to focus groups. Group dynamics obviously play a major part in what happens during the session, and hence in determining the data you obtain (Cohen and Garratt, 1999 argue for the use of insights from group work theory and practice, as possessed by social workers and other 'helping and caring' professionals). It is dangerous to interpret an absence of dissenting voices as indicating consensus. Silence may indicate consent, but it could reflect an unwillingness to express dissent. In this connection advantages have been claimed for *computer-mediated focus groups* (Walston and Lissitz, 2000), where all communication occurs at the computer, much as in an internet chat room (note that this has similarites to the Delphi Method discussed in chapter 3, p. 57; see also Adler and Ziglio, 1996).

*Problematic methodological issues*   Much of the literature on focus groups is methodologically naïve. This perhaps reflects its roots in market research, where concerns have tended to be highly practical; the literature focuses on how to do it, rather than worrying overmuch about the warrant for the assertions made and conclusions drawn. Some aspects needing consideration from a research perspective are listed in box 9.7. See also Kidd and Parshall (2000), who suggest procedures for enhancing the rigour of analysis, and the reliability and validity of focus group findings.

> ## Box 9.7
>
> ## Methodological issues arising from focus groups
>
> 1   The skills and attributes of the moderator and the manner of data recording will exert a powerful influence on the quality of the data collected in a focus group.
>
> 2   Focus groups explore collective phenomena, not individual ones. Attempts to infer the latter from focus group data are likely to be unfounded.
>
> 3   Focus group data may be a poor indicator of a consensus in attitudes, though they may reveal a divergence of opinion and the extent to which certain issues recur across groups.
>
> 4   Focus groups can reveal the nature and range of participants' views, but less so their strength.
>
> 5   Generalization from focus group data is problematic. If feasible it will be theoretical generalization (see p. 176) rather than empirical or statistical generalization.
>
> 6   Focus groups tap a different realm of social reality from that revealed by one-to-one interviews or questionnaire studies. Each of these methods should be selected in terms of its relative appropriateness for the research question concerned, and should not be expected to fulfil objectives for which it is methodologically unsuited.
>
> (Derived from Sim, 1998, p. 351.)

## Analysis of Interview Data

The ways in which research interviews have been reported have not in general been noteworthy for their standards of rigour or detail. Typically, accounts are strong on content and its interpretation, much weaker on providing sufficient information to judge the reliability and validity of those accounts.

### Taping and transcribing

Whenever feasible, interviews should be audio-taped (exceptions include informal interviews where taping is likely to be intrusive). The tape provides a permanent record and allows you to concentrate on the interview. Whether or not you make a full transcript of the tape depends on the resources at your disposal, the number of tapes to be transcribed and the way you will analyse the data.

Kvale (1996, ch. 10) discusses what he terms the '1,000 Page Question': 'How shall I find a method to analyze the 1,000 pages of interview transcript?' His answer is simple. The question is posed too late. As discussed earlier in relation to fixed designs (chapter 6), it is too late to start thinking about analysis after the interviewing is done. In flexible design research, the implications for analysis of amassing large amounts of interview (or any other) data have to be thought through before you commit yourself to the data collection. It makes little sense to have mounds of data that you have neither the time nor resources to deal with. Kvale reformulates the 1,000 page question in various ways, including:

- How shall I conduct my interviews so that their meaning can be analysed in a coherent and creative way?
- How do I go about finding out what the interviews tell me about what I want to know?
- How can the interviews assist in extending my knowledge of the phenomena I am investigating?

An alternative to full transcription is to be selective, picking out relevant passages, and noting the tape counter numbers where there are particular quotations, examples, etc.

Chapters 13 and 14 provide a discussion of the issues involved in analysing interview data, covering quantitative and qualitative aspects respectively.

## Skills in Interviewing

You don't become a good interviewer just by reading about it. Skills are involved which require practice, preferably under 'low risk' conditions where it is possible to receive feedback on your performance.

The skills involved in structured interviews are relatively low-level. Is the script being kept to? Are standard questions being asked in the same way to all interviewees? Are the 'skips' depending on particular answers carried out correctly? Are all interviewees responded to in the same way? And so on. The less the degree of structure in the interview, the more complex the performance required from the interviewer.

It is highly desirable that the pilot (or a pre-pilot) stage includes explicit interviewer assessment and training. Clearly, if you are totally alone as a researcher, this may be problematic, but it is possible to ask the interviewees in the pilot to comment on your performance as well as on the interview schedule. A recording (audio or video) will facilitate the interviewer's evaluation of their performance.

If you are working with colleagues, then mutual (constructive) assessment of each other's interview performance is feasible. This type of feedback information is not only helpful for training purposes but also helps in the general task of viewing the interview situation as a complex social interaction whose characteristics have to some extent to be captured by the analysis.

## Further Reading

Aldridge, M. and Wood, J. (1998) *Interviewing Children: A Guide for Child Care and Forensic Practitioners.* Chichester: Wiley. Very practical and helpful guide for practitioners in these fields. Not primarily research interview focused, but contains much of relevance to researchers interviewing children.

Fontana, A. and Frey, J. H. (2000) The interview: from structured questions to negotiated text. In N. K. Denzin and Y. S. Lincoln, eds, *Handbook of Qualitative Research*, 2nd edn. Thousand Oaks, Calif.: Sage. Useful overview of a wide range of types of interview.

Kvale, S. (1996) *InterViews: An Introduction to Qualitative Research Interviewing.* Thousand Oaks, Calif.: Sage. Very comprehensive review of both the theoretical underpinnings and practical aspects of qualitative research interviewing.

Krueger, R. A. and Casey, M. A. (1998) *Focus Groups: A Practical Guide for Applied Research*, 3rd edn. Thousand Oaks, Calif.: Sage. Good coverage of the practical issues in planning and running focus groups.

Mishler, E. G. (1991) *Research Interviewing: Context and Narrative.* Cambridge, Mass.: Harvard University Press. Challenging critique of the standard approach to the survey interview. Advocates alternative methodologies based on narrative analysis.

Weiss, R. (1994) *Learning from Strangers: the Art and Method of Qualitative Interview Studies.* New York: Free Press. Excellent introduction to actually carrying out qualitative interviews.

# 10
# Tests and Scales

This chapter:

- discusses the common use of tests and scales to measure attitudes
- reviews the Likert, Thurstone, Guttman and Semantic Differential approaches to scaling
- stresses the advantages of using existing tests whenever feasible
- briefly reviews a selection of widely used tests
- and warns about the difficulties in developing your own test

Psychologists and other social scientists have developed a substantial range of self-report measuring instruments to assess people's abilities, propensities, views, opinions and attitudes – to name but a few. Most widely known by the lay public is the IQ or intelligence test, but there are also tests of attainment, of creativity and of personality. They are, in many cases, versions of structured interviews or of self-completion questionnaires, though not usually referred to as such.

Technically, such tests provide a *scale* on which we can assess, usually quantitatively, the individual's performance or standing on the attribute in question. There are other measurement scales where the function is not to test, but to gain some insight into what people feel or believe about something. Most common is *attitude measurement*. This is singled out here partly because it is common – many social scientists want to measure people's attitudes: to the environment, to abortion, to Europe, to single-parent families, etc. *The same principles apply to the development of many other scales.*

## Attitude Measurement

The term 'attitude' is somewhat slippery. It falls in the same kind of sphere as opinion, belief or value, but views differ as to how these different terms are interrelated. Lemon (1973) provides a clear analysis for those who wish to take this further, but also suggests that the term's widespread usage derives in part from this very fuzziness; each worker has been able to tailor it to suit their own purposes.

There is a substantial technology and associated mystique about attitude measurement. Central to this is the belief that it is not possible to assess something like attitude by means of a single question or statement. For example, suppose someone strongly disagreed with the statement: 'Economic aid should be given to countries in eastern Europe.' By itself, this could not be taken as indicating an unsympathetic attitude to those countries' situation. The respondent might feel that such assistance would act against their interests, perhaps by inhibiting necessary changes in their economy. Answers to a range of statements can help in teasing out such issues. Having a set of ten or twenty items is another form of *triangulation*: the response to each gives something of a 'marker' on the respondent's attitude, and putting the responses together enables us to build up a much fuller picture. The problems arise in selecting the items or statements and in working out how to put together the responses.

## Arbitrary scales

It is still distressingly common to see scales cobbled together by assembling an arbitrary group of statements which sound as if they would be relevant, with similarly 'off the top of the head' ratings assigned to different answers, and a simple addition of these ratings to obtain some mystical 'attitude score'. Put like this, the deficiencies are obvious. We need some form of systematic procedure so that we can demonstrate that the different items are related to the same attitude. Similar justification is needed for the assignment of numbers of some kind to particular answers.

## The summated rating (or Likert) scale

The summated rating approach is very widely used. It has the added advantage of being relatively easy to develop. It was originally devised by Likert in the 1930s (Likert, 1932) and scales developed by this method are commonly termed *Likert scales*. Box 10.1 gives procedural details and box 10.2 an example of such a scale.

Items in a Likert scale can look interesting to respondents, and people often enjoy completing a scale of this kind. This can be of importance, not only because if they are interested they are likely to give considered rather than perfunctory answers, but also because in many situations people may, not unreasonably, just not be prepared to co-operate in something that appears boring.

# Box 10.1

## Developing a summated rating (Likert) scale

**1** *Gather together a pool of items that appear to be related to or important to the issue* This can be done by reading round the issue, borrowing from existing scales and 'brainstorming'. Items should reflect both a positive and a negative stance to the issue. Extreme positive and extreme negative statements should be avoided as they may be insensitive to individual differences in attitude (we want to discriminate between individuals – extreme statements may get everyone giving the same response). There should be about the same number of positive and negative statements.

**2** *Decide on a response categorization system* The most common is to have five fixed-alternative expressions, labelled 'strongly agree', 'agree', 'undecided', 'disagree' and 'strongly disagree'.[a] Weights of 1, 2, 3, 4 and 5 are assigned to these alternatives, with the direction of weighting depending on whether the statement is positive or negative (e.g. 5 for a 'strongly agree' with a positive statement, and 'strongly disagree' with a negative statement).

**3** *Ask a large number of respondents to check their attitudes to the list of statements* The list should be in random order with positive and negative statements intermingled. The respondents should be a representative sample from the population whose attitude you wish to measure.

**4** *Obtain a total score for each respondent* This is done by summing the value of each of the responses given (e.g. 'agree' to positive item scores 4; 'strongly disagree' with negative item scores 5; 'neutral' to either scores 3; 'agree' to negative item scores 2; etc.). Rank the respondents according to total score obtained.

**5** *Select items for final scale using 'item analysis'* Each item (i.e. statement) is subjected to a measurement of its *discriminative power* (DP): that is, its ability to discriminate between the responses of the upper quartile (25 per cent) of respondents, and the responses of the lower quartile (25 per cent) – see worked example below. Items with the highest DP indices are chosen for the final scale. A typical scale would consist of 20–30 items.

*Notes*: There are alternative techniques for selecting the items for the final scale (e.g. each statement can be correlated with the overall score – those items with the highest correlations are retained). Scales can be tested for validity and reliability using the methods covered in Loewenthal (1996, pp. 91–130).
[a] alternatives are possible (e.g. 3, 4, 6 or 7 alternatives – odd numbers permit a neutral mid-point which is usually considered desirable); different labels for the alternatives may be used where appropriate (e.g. 'almost always', 'frequently', 'occasionally', 'rarely', and 'almost never').

*Calculating the discriminative power (DP) of items*

**1**   Suppose the scale is tested on a sample of sixty respondents. The upper quartile will thus consist of the fifteen respondents (25 per cent of sixty) with the highest total scores; the lower quartile the fifteen respondents with the lowest total scores.

**2**   The distribution of scores (i.e. number of 1s, 2s, 3s, 4s and 5s) for the upper quartile group is tabled for each item.

**3**   The distribution of scores (i.e. number of 1s, 2s, 3s, 4s, and 5s) for the lower quartile group is tabled for each item.

**4**   Weighted totals and means are calculated separately for the upper and lower quartile groups, for each item:

*Example for one item*

| Weighted group | Number in group | Item scores 1 2 3 4 5 | Weighted total | Weighted mean |
|---|---|---|---|---|
| Upper | 15 | 0 1 2 7 5 | $(1.2) + (2.3) + (7.4)$ $+ (5.5) = 61$ | 61/15 = 4.07 |
| Lower | 15 | 3 8 3 1 0 | $(3.1) + (8.2) + (3.3)$ $+ (1.4) = 32$ | 32/15 = 2.13 |

**5**   The index of discriminative power (DP) for an item is the difference between the weighted means.

For the example above, DP = 4.07 − 2.13 = 1.94.

However, even though the items may look arbitrary and similar to those in magazine self-rating exercises, the systematic procedures used do help to ensure that the scale has internal consistency and/or the ability to differentiate among individuals.

## The equal appearing interval (or Thurstone) scale

In this approach, which was systematized by Thurstone and Chave (1929), a small number of items form the final scale with each of them representing a particular scale value with respect to the attitude, ranging from highly favourable through neutral to highly unfavourable.

## Box 10.2

### Example of Likert scale –
### generalized expectancy for success scale

Highly improbable          1 2 3 4 5          Highly probable

In the future I expect that I will:

1    find that people don't seem to understand what I am trying to say
2    be discouraged about my ability to gain the respect of others
3    be a good parent
4    be unable to accomplish my goals
5    have a successful marital relationship
6    deal poorly with emergency situations
7    find my efforts to change situations I don't like to be ineffective
8    not be very good at learning new skills
9    carry through my responsibilities successfully.
10   discover that the good in life outweighs the bad
11   handle unexpected problems successfully
12   get the promotions I deserve
13   succeed in the projects I undertake
14   not make any significant contributions to society
15   discover that my life is not getting much better
16   be listened to when I speak
17   discover that my plans don't work out too well
18   find that, no matter how I try, things just don't turn out the way I
     would like
19   handle myself well in whatever situation I'm in
20   be able to solve my own problems
21   succeed at most things I try
22   be successful in my endeavours in the long run
23   be very successful in working out my personal life
24   experience many failures in my life
25   make a good impression on people I meet for the first time
26   attain the career goals I have set for myself
27   have difficulty dealing with my superiors
28   have problems working with others
29   be a good judge of what it takes to get ahead
30   achieve recognition in my profession

(From Fibel and Hale, 1978.)

The development of a Thurstone scale is considerably more cumbersome and difficult than the development of a Likert scale. Perhaps for this reason it is less frequently used, and summary details only are given in box 10.3. If, having read the summary given, you think that you are in a position to follow the Thurstone approach, you will find further details in Anastasi (1988).

The practical problem with this approach, in addition to the considerable amount of labour involved if it is done thoroughly, is in getting hold of the

---

## Box 10.3

## Development of an equal-appearing interval (Thurstone) scale – summary only

**1** *Collect a large number of statements relating to the attitude in question* Similar sources can be used to those suggested in Likert scaling (reading around the topic, consulting published scales, brainstorming, etc.). However, it is important to have several very extreme positive and very extreme negative statements in the set.

**2** *Give the statements to 50–100 'judges'* Judges are asked to work independently, and to rate each of the statements on an 11-point scale according to the degree of favourableness it shows towards the attitude (11 most favourable, 6 neutral and 1 most unfavourable). Judges are asked *not* to rate in terms of their own attitude, simply to try to rate in terms of favourableness.

**3** *Find the scale value of each statement* The median rating for each statement is computed. The amount of variability in rating for each is also calculated.

**4** *Select a number of statements spread evenly along the scale* Statements are selected from those with low variability in rating across judges. A second standardization is sometimes introduced at this stage by getting a sample from the population on which the scale is to be used to respond to each item on a yes/no basis (usually agree/disagree). Items which show good *discriminating power* (as with the Likert scale) between those having favourable and unfavourable attitudes are selected for the final scale. The items selected should cover the full range of scale values, and should be evenly spread along the scale. A typical scale includes 10–30 items.

*Note*: The items are presented in randomized order when the scale is used. Respondents are asked if they agree or disagree with the various items. The attitude measure is the median of the scale values that the respondent agrees to.

requisite number of 'judges'. There is nothing magic about the suggested number of 50–100 judges, and having a somewhat smaller number is unlikely seriously to affect the liability and validity of the scale. However, getting this kind of number of individuals who can and will make a conscientious assessment of the favourableness of a set of 100 or more items to a particular attitude is no easy undertaking. It is also important to ensure that these judges themselves have a wide range of attitudes as, although they are asked to discount their own attitude when rating items, there is evidence that judges' attitudes have a substantial effect on the ratings (e.g. Hovland and Sherif, 1952).

Although, in their traditional format, Likert and Thurstone scales differ in the type of response asked for, hybrids are possible. For example, Eysenck and Crown (1949) constructed a scale along Thurstone principles and then administered it in the Likert fashion ('strongly agree', 'agree', etc.). The advantage of this approach is that it enables one to find out not only those statements which the respondent endorses, but also the strength or emphasis with which they hold the opinion.

## The cumulated (or Guttman) scale

Critics of both Thurstone and Likert scales have pointed out that they may contain statements which concern a variety of dimensions relating to the attitude of concern. For example, a scale on attitudes to nuclear power stations could include ethical and moral statements, statements concerning the economic consequences of developing nuclear power, a health dimension, an environmental aspect, etc., etc. Combining statements relating to several dimensions on the one scale may well reflect the underlying structure of the attitude, but will make it difficult to interpret cumulative scores.

Approaches to determining the structure of attitudes fall into two broad categories: *phenomenological* – such as repertory grid technique (see below, p. 366); and *mathematical* – as in factor and cluster analysis (see chapter 13). The Guttman approach (Guttman, 1944) overcomes this complexity by seeking to develop a unidimensional scale.

In this type of scale, items have a cumulative property. They are chosen and ordered so that a person who accepts (agrees with) a particular item will also accept all previous items. An analogy is sometimes made with high-jumping. If someone has cleared the bar at 2 metres, we can be confident that they would also do so at 1.8 metres, 1.6, 1.4, 1.2, etc. Box 10.4 summarizes the steps needed to develop a Guttman scale and box 10.5 shows how the analysis is carried out. Additional details can be found in Dawes and Smith (1985).

---

# Box 10.4

## Developing a cumulated (Guttman) scale

**1** *Collect a large number of apparently relevant and usable statements* The approach is the same as with the Thurstone scale.

**2** *Administer the statements to a standardization group* Members of the group have to answer in a yes/no (agree/disagree) fashion.

**3** *Carry out a scalogram analysis of the standardization group's responses* This involves attempting to arrange the responses into the 'best' triangular shape – as demonstrated in box 10.5.

**4** *Apply the scale to respondents* The attitude measure is usually the total number of items accepted or agreed to.

---

There are obvious attractions in the simplicity of a scale which gives a unidimensional assessment of attitude, so that one feels that the score obtained gives much firmer ground for subsequent interpretation and analysis than the multidimensional complexity of the other approaches we have discussed. The other side of this is that it is best adapted to measuring a well-defined and clear-cut dimension, so that items reflecting unidimensionality can be generated without undue difficulty.

## Semantic differential scales

A widely used type of scale, the *semantic differential scale* (Osgood et al., 1957) takes a very different approach. It is concerned with assessing the subjective meaning of a concept to the respondent, instead of assessing how much they believe in a particular concept. The scale is designed to explore the ratings given along a series of bipolar rating scales (e.g. bad/good; boring/exciting). Factor analyses have shown that such ratings typically group together into three underlying dimensions – activity, evaluation and potency. In this sense, it provides a kind of attitude scale.

*Activity* refers to the extent to which the concept is associated with action (dimensions might be 'fast', 'active', 'exciting', etc.). *Evaluation* refers to the overall positive meaning associated with it ('positive', 'honest', 'dependable', etc.). *Potency* refers to its overall strength or importance ('strong', 'valuable', 'useful', etc.). A list of appropriate adjective pairs is generated for the particular

## Box 10.5

### Guttman's scalogram analysis – example

In practice, the analysis will be based on a substantially greater number of items and participants in the standardization group than those included here. The principles are the same.

**1** *List items and participants in order of the total number of 'agrees'* (x = agrees; o = disagrees).

| Subject | 3 | 6 | 7 | 1 | 9 | 8 | 10 | 2 | 5 | 4 | Total for item |
|---------|---|---|---|---|---|---|----|---|---|---|----------------|
| Item 5 | x | x | x | x | x | x | x | x | x | x | 10 |
| Item 7 | o | x | x | x | x | x | x | x | x | x | 9 |
| Item 8 | o | o | x | o | x | x | x | x | x | x | 7 |
| Item 9 | o | x | o | x | x | x | x | x | x | x | 8 |
| Item 12 | o | o | x | x | o | x | x | x | x | x | 7 |
| Item 1 | o | o | o | o | x | x | x | x | x | x | 6 |
| Item 15 | o | o | o | x | o | x | x | o | x | x | 5 |
| Item 2 | o | o | o | o | x | o | x | x | x | x | 5 |
| Item 11 | o | o | o | o | x | o | o | x | x | x | 4 |
| Item 6 | o | x | o | o | o | o | o | x | o | x | 3 |
| Item 14 | o | o | o | o | o | o | o | x | x | x | 3 |
| Item 10 | o | o | o | x | o | o | o | o | o | x | 2 |
| Item 3 | o | o | o | o | o | o | o | o | x | x | 2 |
| Item 4 | o | o | o | o | o | x | o | o | o | o | 1 |
| Item 13 | o | o | o | o | o | o | o | o | o | x | 1 |
| Total for subject | 1 | 4 | 4 | 6 | 7 | 8 | 8 | 10 | 11 | 14 | |

**2** *Select those items which give the closest approximation to a triangular shape, i.e. to this pattern*:

```
x x x x x
o x x x x
o o x x x
o o o x x
o o o o x
o o o o o
```

This will involve some trial and error, and possible reorderings of the columns (i.e. the participants) when rows are removed.

| Subject | 3 | 6 | 7 | 1 | 8 | 10 | 9 | 2 | 5 | 4 | Total |
|---|---|---|---|---|---|---|---|---|---|---|---|
| Item 5 | x | x | x | x | x | x | x | x | x | x | 10 |
| Item 7 | o | x | x | x | x | x | x | x | x | x | 9 |
| Item 8 | o | x | o | x | x | x | x | x | x | x | 8 |
| Item 9 | o | o | x | o | x | x | x | x | x | x | 7 |
| Item 1 | o | o | o | o | x | x | x | x | x | x | 6 |
| Item 2 | o | o | o | o | o | x | x | x | x | x | 5 |
| Item 11 | o | o | o | o | o | o | x | x | x | x | 4 |
| Item 14 | o | o | o | o | o | o | o | x | x | x | 3 |
| Item 3 | o | o | o | o | o | o | o | o | x | x | 2 |
| Item 13 | o | o | o | o | o | o | o | o | o | x | 1 |
| Total for subject | 1 | 3 | 3 | 3 | 5 | 6 | 7 | 8 | 9 | 10 | |

**3** *Assess the reproducibility of the responses (i.e. the extent to which the participants' pattern of responses is predictable from their total score*  This amounts to the same thing as the divergence from the perfect triangular shape. Guttman proposes a 'coefficient of reproducibility' which he suggests should be at least 0.9 if the scale is to be used. The coefficient $R = 1 - e/nk$, where

$e$ = number of errors,
$n$ = number of respondents, and
$k$ = number of items.

In the example, there are 2 errors (both with subject 7; with a score of 3 the subject would have been expected to agree with item 8 and disagree with item 9). Hence $R = 1 - 2/100 = 0.98$.

**4** *Administer the test to a fresh set of respondents and replicate the results to an acceptable degree of reproducibility*  This step is important (and unfortunately often omitted) as the initial selection of a relatively small set of items from a long list will inevitably capitalize on chance to some extent. It may be necessary to incorporate substitute items at this stage, which then necessitates further replication.

---

## Box 10.6

### Example of a semantic differential scale

*Instructions*   For each pair of adjectives place a cross at the point between them which reflects the extent to which you believe the adjectives describe policemen.

| clean | : | : | : | : | : | : | : | : | dirty |
| honest | : | : | : | : | : | : | : | : | dishonest |
| kind | : | : | : | : | : | : | : | : | cruel |
| helpful | : | : | : | : | : | : | : | : | unhelpful |
| fair | : | : | : | : | : | : | : | : | biassed |
| delicate | : | : | : | : | : | : | : | : | rugged |
| strong | : | : | : | : | : | : | : | : | weak |
| stupid | : | : | : | : | : | : | : | : | intelligent |
| unreliable | : | : | : | : | : | : | : | : | reliable |
| heavy | : | : | : | : | : | : | : | : | light |
| foolish | : | : | : | : | : | : | : | : | wise |
| passive | : | : | : | : | : | : | : | : | active |
| energetic | : | : | : | : | : | : | : | : | lazy |
| boring | : | : | : | : | : | : | : | : | exciting |
| valuable | : | : | : | : | : | : | : | : | useless |
| impulsive | : | : | : | : | : | : | : | : | deliberate |

---

concept you are trying to measure. However, broadly similar lists can be used in many contexts. Sources of lists include Osgood et al. (1957) and Valois and Godin (1991). Box 10.6 gives an example of a semantic differential scale.

*Using the scale*   The scale is administered to the chosen sample of respondents in a standard fashion. It is scored simply by summing the ratings given to each adjective pair on a scale of 1–7 (or whatever the number of alternatives have been given). Average ratings can be computed, and comparisons between subgroups in the sample are feasible. To take it further, it is necessary to carry out a factor analysis (see chapter 13, p. 433) to assess the relationship of the different adjective pairs, and link them to the evaluative dimensions.

## Other Scaling Techniques

There are several other possibilities, including the following.

## Q-sorts

This is a technique used to measure the relative position or ranking of an individual on a range of concepts. Stephenson (1980) describes an example where a four-year-old girl was asked to sort a number of postcard pictures of other little girls. The sorting is done successively on different criteria, e.g. 'most like me'; 'like me according to my mother'; 'like me according to my teacher', etc. The technique has been most often used with individuals or with small numbers, as the analysis becomes extremely complex with large numbers.

## Sociometric scales

A technique used to describe relationships between individuals in a group. In its simplest form, it requires members of a group to make choices among other members of a group (e.g. whom they like). It is a versatile technique and has been used with groups ranging from pre-school children to prisoners. The technique is straightforward and results can be displayed in the form of 'sociograms' which give a diagrammatic representation of the choices made. Dane (1990, pp. 282–5) gives a simple introduction.

## Using Existing Tests and Scales

The development of tests for assessing some aspect or other of human functioning is a complex and burgeoning enterprise. It could well be that a useful measure in a study is provided by scores on an attainment test (e.g. in relation to reading) or that other indices (such as scores on a test of intelligence) provide valuable supplementary evidence. Considerable use is also made of tests seeking to assess aspects of personality, such as the Eysenck Personality Questionnaire (EPQ), Minnesota Multiphasic Personality Inventory (MMPI), and Sixteen Personality Factor test (16PF).

It is crucial that any such tests are professionally competent. One way to achieve this is by picking an existing test 'off the shelf'. The prime source of information on existing British and American tests is the series known as the *Mental Measurement Yearbooks* (see e.g. Impara and Plake, 1998). These are regular publications (also available on CD-ROM) detailing available tests, with information extracted from their manuals, reviews and references to papers and theses in which they have been used. If a test appears to be suitable you can then send off for the test and its associated manual. Note that each edition of the yearbook is an update, and you will need to consult earlier editions for previously published tests This will give details on the reliability and validity of the test, and the test norms (i.e. the results of standardizing the test by using it with a given sample, so that you have a comparative base-line to assist in interpreting the scores you obtain).

Other strategies you might use in finding an appropriate test include:

- asking colleagues and others working in the same field if they know of anything suitable
- consulting CD-ROM and on-line data bases (see chapter 3, p. 51) using a key word search
- consulting the catalogues of test publishers (listed in the *Mental Measurement Yearbooks*). You will have to pay for such tests, including the manual, and there may be restrictions on who can use them.

A small selection of some widely used tests is presented as box 10.7.

Kline (1990) provides a useful set of suggestions for 'selecting the best test'. Many tests are now available in a computer-based version (French, 1990) which can cover both the administration of the test and its analysis. Beaumont and French (1987) discuss a range of these, including verbal and non-verbal IQ, personality and aptitude tests. It is unlikely to be cost-effective for you to tool up to use a computer-assisted test for a small one-off enquiry, but there may be opportunities for making use of facilities developed for other purposes. It should also be borne in mind that tests with a cumbersome or complex scoring procedure which has previously inhibited their use (such as the MMPI) become much more feasible with computer analysis.

## Developing Your Own Test

An alternative is, of course, to develop your own test. Don't do this unless you are prepared to devote considerable time and resources to the exercise. It also means that you lose the opportunity of making comparisons with other studies, which may be feasible when using an existing test. Rust and Golombok (1999) provide an excellent guide to the main stages of test construction, and show how to tailor a test for specific purposes. Suhonen et al. (2000) and Walsh-Daneshmandi and MacLachlan (2000) provide accounts of the development of instruments for the measurement of individual care in adult hospital patients, and the assessment of environmental risk perception, respectively.

The middle way is to change an existing instrument so that it better fits your needs. This is preferable to starting from scratch, but you should remember that the existing reliability, validity and norms will not then apply, and will

# Box 10.7

## Some widely used tests and scales

1 *STATE MEASURES* enable you to assess the relatively short-term effect of something that has happened; e.g. of having been involved with a research study or some other intervention.

a   *Multiple Affect Adjective Check List (MAACL)* – Zuckerman and Lubin (1963)
    Assesses depression, anxiety and hostility. One-hundred-plus item checklist; quick to do and well-researched.

b   *Beck Depression Inventory (BDI)* – Beck and Steer (1987)
    Widely used measure of depression. Quick to use and very well researched. Expensive and raises some ethical issues because of its use of intrusive (threatening) questions.

c   *Hospital Anxiety and Depression Scale (HAD)* – Zigmond and Snaith (1983)
    Quick and relatively cheap. Provides independent assessment of anxiety and depression. Appropriate for community as well as hospital samples.

d   *State Self-Esteem Scale (SSES)* – Heatherton and Polivy (1991)
    Relatively new and not yet widely used measure of state self-esteem in adults.

2 *TRAIT MEASURES* assess relatively stable dispositions (e.g. personality, intelligence). A large number of such tests are available. Many are restricted and require special training before they can be used.

e   *Eysenck Personality Inventory (EPI)* – Eysenck and Eysenck (1964) and *Eysenck Personality Questionnaire (EPQ)* – Eysenck and Eysenck (1975)
    Very widely used and researched measures. Quick, no special training required. Main traits are *neuroticism (N)* and *extraversion–introversion (E)*. Also incorporates a *Lie (L)* scale. Loewenthal (1996, p. 76) reviews several technical problems with the *N* scale.

f   *Minnesota Multiphasic Personality Inventory (MMPI)* – Hathaway and McKinley (1967)
    Most widely used personality test. Large number of items but easy to score.

g   *Myers–Briggs Type Indicator* – Myers and McCaulley (1985)
    Widely used in occupational psychology to advise people the types of occupation they are best fitted for. Special training required.

h   *Sixteen Personality Factors Questionnaire (16PF)* – Cattell (1965)
    Also widely used. Quick and easy to complete and score. Results in a personality profile. Loewenthal (1996, p. 77) recommends its use as a quick measure of intelligence which also provides personality information.

**i**　　*Wechsler Adult Intelligence Scale (WAIS)* – Wechsler (1955) and
**j**　　*British Ability Scales (BAS)* – Elliott (1983)
　　　　Two widely used individually administered tests of intelligence.
　　　　Require lengthy sessions and special training. Normally the province
　　　　of educational and clinical psychologists.
**k**　　*Group Test of General Intelligence (AH4)* Heim (1970)
　　　　Relatively rapid group intelligence test. Other versions (AH5 and
　　　　AH6) cover adults of high ability.
**l**　　*Jenkins Activity Survey* – Jenkins et al. (1979)
　　　　Measures 'Type A' behaviour, the so-called 'coronary-prone person-
　　　　ality' (i.e. a person who is competitive, impatient, with a sense of
　　　　urgency and drive for success). Popular and easy to use and score.
　　　　Findings based on the scale are controversial, although its reliability
　　　　and validity appear acceptable.

**3　ATTITUDE MEASURES**, as indicated earlier in the chapter (p. 292),
form one of the most common areas where scales have been developed.
Attitudes are usually regarded as being concerned with feelings. In this
respect, the researcher is interested in whether the person has a positive or
negative emotional response. They are sometimes viewed as synonymous
with beliefs, but here the researcher's concern is more with whether the
person considers something to be true or false.

Examples include:

**m**　　*California F* – Adorno et al. (1950)
　　　　Traditional measure of *authoritarianism*. Measures beliefs and atti-
　　　　tudes, and to some extent personality. Dated, and subjected to much
　　　　criticism, but still widely used.
**n**　　*Wilson-Patterson C* – Wilson and Patterson (1968)
　　　　Measure of *conservatism* in social attitudes and beliefs. Easy to admin-
　　　　ister and score.
**o**　　*Religious Life Inventory* – Batson et al. (1993)
　　　　One of several measures of religious beliefs and related matters

**4　OTHER MEASURES** A wide range of other measures, not falling
under the previous headings, have been developed. Loewenthal (1996, pp.
81–6) gives details of measures of *social desirability* (useful in assessing
possible response biases); *stress*; *values*; *social support*; *locus of control* (the
extent to which people feel that events are caused by internal or external
factors); and *health*.

*Note*: **PROJECTIVE TESTS**, most famously the *Rorschach* ('inkblot') personality
test, are popular in some circles. However, their validity is very suspect.
(Derived from Loewenthal, 1996, pp. 72–86, who gives further details and
references.)

have to be re-established. If the material is copyright, modification will require the permission of the copyright holder. The easiest and most common modification is to shorten the test by omitting items. If data are available from the original development of the test, it may be possible to use them to re-establish validity and reliability. You may, alternatively, wish to change the response options (e.g. from seven to five alternatives, perhaps to fit in with other questionnaire items). Changes of question wording are tricky, because of the major effects that apparently minor changes can have on responding, but there may be justification in moving from general questions to more specific ones, or in modifying a test targeted for one professional group to be appropriate for a different one. In this connection, the use of a sample very different from the one on which the test was standardized will call for new validation of the test.

## Tests and scales based on observation rather than self-report

We have dealt here with a very similar agenda of issues to those faced in the development of a structured direct observation instrument (chapter 11, p. 325). There are considerable overlaps. In a self-report situation, respondents are effectively acting as observers of their own behaviour. Direct observation by the researcher reduces potential biases and distortions arising from this process, but it is obviously limited to those things that can be directly observed. Thoughts and feelings, beliefs and attitudes need self-report. Low-frequency and private behaviours are best approached in this way as they would be expensive and obtrusive to observe directly.

## Further Reading

American Psychological Association (2001) *Finding Information about Psychological Tests.* <http:www.apa.org/science/findingtests.pdf>. Accessed 22 June 2001. A Highly practical guide for locating and using both published and unpublished texts.

Bellack, M. S., Hersen, M. et al., eds (1998) *Behavioral Assessment: A Practical Handbook*, 4th edn. Boston, Mass.: Allyn and Bacon. Wide-ranging compendium of assessment techniques.

Kline, P. (2000) *Handbook of Psychological Testing*, 2nd edn. London: Routledge. Very comprehensive and authoritative. Standard text for occupational and educational psychologists. Last section challenges conventional psychometrics and suggests innovative approaches.

Loewenthal, K. M. (1996) *An Introduction to Psychological Tests and Scales.* London: UCL Press. Short and very clear introduction to the construction of simple self-report measures. Detailed suggestions for finding existing tests. Appendices on the use of computer packages to assess reliability and validity.

Oppenheim, A. N. (1992) *Questionnaire Design, Interviewing and Attitude Measurement*. London: Pinter; New York: Basic. Very clear presentation of the logic and skills of scale construction.

Rust, J. and Golombok, S. (1999) *Modern Psychometrics: The Science of Psychological Assessment*, 2nd edn. London: Routledge. Useful introduction. Includes practical step-by-step guide to the development of a test.

# 11
# Observational Methods

This chapter:

- discusses the advantages and disadvantages of direct observation
- considers its role in real world research
- focuses on the very different approaches of structured observation and participant observation
- analyses different participant observer roles and considers their implications
- considers how to get started; then the collection and recording of data
- reviews observational biases which have to be taken into account
- discusses structured observation and coding schemes
- recommends the use of an existing coding scheme whenever feasible
- considers the practicalities of recording
- concludes by describing ways of assessing the reliability of structured observation

## Introduction

As the actions and behaviour of people are central aspects in virtually any enquiry, a natural and obvious technique is to watch what they do, to record this in some way and then to describe, analyse and interpret what we have observed. Much research with people involves observation in a general sense. The typical experiment, whether in the laboratory or in the field, incorporates a form of controlled observation. However, we use a rather more restricted definition here, sticking primarily to *direct observation* as carried out by the human observer.

Fundamentally different approaches to the use of observational methods in enquiry have been employed. Two polar extreme types are *participant observation* – an essentially qualitative style, originally rooted in the work of anthropologists and particularly associated with the Chicago school of sociology; and *structured observation* – a quantitative style which has been used in a variety of disciplines. Participant observation is a widely used method in flexible designs, particularly those which follow an ethnographic approach. Structured observation is almost exclusively linked to fixed designs, of both experimental and non-experimental types. Both styles call for a heavy investment of time and effort and should not be used without careful consideration of their resource implications in a real world study.

Concentration on these two approaches has tended to eclipse a third one, which may be styled *unobtrusive observation*. Its defining characteristic is that it is non-participatory in the interests of being *non-reactive*. It can be structured but is more usually unstructured and informal.

## Advantages and Disadvantages of Observation

### Advantages

A major advantage of observation as a technique is its directness. You do not ask people about their views, feelings or attitudes; you watch what they do and listen to what they say. Thus, for example, in an evaluation of an intervention aiming to reduce sun exposure and develop sun-protection habits in primary school children (Milne et al., 1999), observation is the obvious method to use in assessing its effectiveness.

Data from direct observation contrasts with, and can often usefully complement, information obtained by virtually any other technique. Interview and questionnaire responses are notorious for discrepancies between what people say that they have done, or will do, and what they actually did, or will do. For example, Auge and Auge (1999) found that the scale of drug use by professional bodybuilders assessed by direct observation substantially exceeded estimates from earlier surveys. As Agnew and Pyke (1982) put it, 'on a questionnaire we only have to move the pencil a few inches to shift our scores from being a bigot to being a humanitarian. We don't have to move our heavyweight behavior at all' (p. 129). Or as Montaigne, over 400 years ago, observed, 'Saying is one thing; doing is another.' These inherent difficulties in the reliability and validity of such data, arising from deficiencies in memory and the wish to present oneself in a favourable light (the 'social desirability response bias'), among many other factors, were discussed in chapter 8 (p. 233).

Observation also seems to be pre-eminently the appropriate technique for getting at 'real life' in the real world. It is, of course, possible to observe through one-way glass in a laboratory or clinic, or set up some other situation and observe that; but direct observation in the field permits a lack of artificiality which is all too rare with other techniques. It can also reveal substantial differences from observations carried out in more contrived settings (Handen et al., 1998).

## Disadvantages

Observation is neither an easy nor a trouble-free option. There is a major issue concerning the extent to which an observer affects the situation under observation. It is commonly claimed that this can be overcome – for example, by seeking to ensure that the observed are unaware of being observed, at one extreme; or by their being so accustomed to the presence of the observer that they carry on as if she were not there, at the other extreme (Gittelson et al., 1997, provide empirical evidence on the size of these reactivity effects and how they can be controlled).

There is a logical problem here. How do we know what the behaviour would have been like if it hadn't been observed? And, moreover, whether one takes on a very detached or very involved role as an observer, or something in between, there are related methodological and ethical problems. Virtually total detachment can come across as anti-social and itself cause reactions from those observed. To be highly involved risks compromising your researcher role.

A practical problem with observation is that it tends to be time-consuming. The classic participant observation study, deriving from social anthropology, demands an immersion in the 'tribe' for two or three years. There is a trend toward a more 'condensed field experience' based on observation (Stenhouse, 1982) which has become popular in applied fields such as education, but this still requires a large time commitment. More structured approaches, normally requiring the use of some kind of observation schedule, can reduce the actual observation time substantially, but there is a correspondingly increased time investment required in developing such an instrument from scratch. Even on those rare occasions when an existing observation schedule developed by a previous worker is suited to your task, acquiring proficiency in its use can take much time and effort.

## Observation in Real World Research

Observation, in part because it can take on a variety of forms, can be used for several purposes in a study. It is commonly used in an *exploratory phase*, typically in an unstructured form, to seek to find out what is going on in a situation as a precursor to subsequent testing out of the insights obtained. For this purpose, the *unobtrusive observation* approach is most appropriate.

Observation can be also used as a *supportive* or *supplementary method* to collect data that may complement or set in perspective data obtained by other means. Suppose that the main effort in a particular study is devoted to a series of interviews; observation might then be used to validate or corroborate the messages obtained in the interviews. For example, Rose (1998) compared the relationship between direct observation and daily diaries in a study of staff and learning-disabled residents in community homes. It is not unusual, however, for observation to be the *primary method* in a particular study, especially though not exclusively when the main intention is descriptive. Or it could be used in a multimethod case study or other type of flexible design, where additional methods, such as documentary analysis, supplement the observational data.

Unobtrusive observation also has a potential role in experimental research. By watching what participants do in the experimental situation, it may be possible to gain valuable insights. The use of observation as a technique in survey and other types of non-experimental research is fairly unusual. Simple structured observational techniques could, however, be used to substitute for, or complement, the widely used interview or questionnaire in some situations.

## Approaches to Observation

In prospect it may seem very straightforward, but the actual experience of being put in a situation with the instruction 'Observe!' is daunting even to the experienced enquirer. There seems to be either so much, or so little, going on. And how does one characterize and capture it?

As with all enquiry, the driving force behind the use of observation for enquiry purposes is the research question or questions, even though these may be very broad, general and loosely phrased in an exploratory study. Leading on from this is the type of information which will be most helpful in answering these research question(s). There is a major divide here between *narrative accounts* and *coded schedules*. The former, typified by the reports arising from classic participant observation, are regarded by some as 'humanistic' rather than 'scientific' (see e.g. Bakeman and Gottman, 1997, pp. 2–3). However, as discussed in earlier chapters, the intention in this text is to welcome such endeavours within a broad notion of science, with the stipulation that adequate attention be given to rigour in matters of reliability and validity.

It may also be worth stressing at this point that narrative accounts, though traditionally almost exclusively dependent on single-method qualitative approaches, need not be so. A narrative account can be constructed from quantitative, structured schedule data, and it is encouraging to note multimethod case studies incorporating participant observation being advocated by anthropologists (e.g. Fetterman, 1989).

## Classifying observational methods

The preceding discussion highlights one important dimension of difference in approaches to observation: the degree of *pre-structure* in the observation exercise. This can be dichotomized as *formal* or *informal observation*. Informal approaches are less structured and allow the observer considerable freedom in what information is gathered and how it is recorded. They would include note-taking and generally gathering information from informants. This kind of information is relatively unstructured and complex, and requires the observer to perform difficult tasks of synthesis, abstraction and organization of the data. Formal approaches impose a large amount of structure and direction on what is to be observed. The observer has only to attend to these pre-specified aspects; everything else is considered irrelevant for the purposes of the study. High reliability and validity are easier to achieve with these approaches, but at the cost of a loss of complexity and completeness by comparison with the informal route.

A second dimension, in practice by no means independent of the formality/structure dimension, concerns the *role* adopted by the observer in the situation observed. Specifically, this relates to the extent of *participation* in that situation. As indicated above, we will concentrate here on the two extreme positions on this dimension, where the intention is either to participate fully, effectively to become a part of the group or whatever is being studied, or to be a 'pure' observer, seeking to be an unnoticed part of the wallpaper. These two 'ideal types' carry with them very different methodological and philosophical views about the nature and purposes of observation. The participant observer will tend to use flexible designs and qualitative, unstructured approaches. The pure observer might use qualitative approaches, but has tended towards fixed-design and quantitative, structured methods. While the pure observer typically *uses* an observation instrument of some kind, the participant observer *is* the instrument.

## Participant Observation

A key feature of participant observation is that the observer seeks to become some kind of member of the observed group. This involves not only a physical presence and a sharing of life experiences, but also entry into their social and 'symbolic' world through learning their social conventions and habits, their use of language and non-verbal communication, and so on. The observer also has to establish some role within the group.

This may sound warning bells of subjectivity and general 'bad science' to those trained in traditional views of experimental design and quantitative analysis. However, it can be argued persuasively that, when working with people, scientific aims can be pursued by explaining the meaning of the experiences of the observed through the experiences of the observer. This arises from a perspective that the social world involves subjective meanings and experiences constructed by participants in social situations. The task of interpreting these meanings and experiences can only be achieved through participation with those involved (Manis and Meltzer, 1967).

Whether or not one is prepared to accept this view as recognizably science, it is still possible to use the touchstones established in chapter 2 as typifying the scientific approach. In particular, the necessary bases of reliability and validity can be achieved. Similarly, objectivity can be approached through a heightened sensitivity to the problem of subjectivity, and the need for justification of one's claims. Admittedly, by no means all of the studies published which use participant observation pay serious attention to these canons. Several are more appropriately judged in terms of journalism or literature. This is not intended as a dismissive statement. If the intention is polemical, or to throw light on the human condition, then it would be crass scientific hegemony to claim that science is the only, or the best, means of persuasion or illumination.

There are, however, particular benefits from playing the science game, as already rehearsed. The claim made here is that by giving particular attention to reliability and validity, participant observation, along with other essentially qualitative techniques, can be scientific.

Participant observation, even in an abbreviated version where the involvement is measured in weeks or even days rather than the years of the classical anthropological model, places a considerable burden on the shoulders of the observer. Richards and Postle (1998) discuss these challenges in relation to social work settings. Such a period of observation can be extremely involving, as graphically illustrated by Waddington (1994) in a candid account of his doctoral study of a five-month brewery strike.

The primary data are the interpretations by the observer of what is going on around him. The observer *is* the research instrument, and hence great sensitivity and personal skills are called for if worthwhile data are to be collected. Lincoln and Guba (1985) warn that 'one would not expect individuals to function adequately as human instruments without an extensive background of training and exposure' (p. 195). With participant observation, it is difficult to separate out the data collection and analysis phases of an enquiry. Analysis takes place in the middle of collection and is used to help shape its development. This kind of approach revisits, at the level of method or technique, issues raised in connection with research strategy when flexible designs were discussed in chapter 6. Box 11.1 gives an indication of situations where you might consider using participant observation in a small project.

---

## Box 11.1

### When participant observation might be useful in a small project

1  *With small groups*   You need to be able to get to know virtually all the people involved in a way that would not be feasible in a large group.

2  *For events/processes that take a reasonably short time*   That is, unless you can afford to give up a major slice of your life to the study. Even then the 'information overload' would be horrendous.

3  *For frequent events*   Participant observation is in general more easily handled in situations where there is repetition of the central activities fairly frequently (e.g. it's easier to study an office with a daily routine than a merger between two businesses – though the latter could well incorporate some participant observation within a multimethod case study).

4  *For activities that are accessible to observers*   This is an obvious point, but don't forget that direct observation can be supplemented by interviews or informal discussions with group members.

5  *When your prime motivation is find out what is going on*   The wealth of information available in a participant observation study is such that you can probably find supporting evidence for virtually any initial hypothesis. Hence it is a dangerous (though seductive) technique for those simply wishing to confirm their pre-judgements.

6  *When you are not short of time*   Even a small participant observation study takes up a lot of time, both day-to-day (writing up adequate field notes) and in terms of the 'immersion' you need to get anywhere. It is difficult to budget this time in advance.

What is referred to in this book as flexible design is sometimes termed participant observation (or even field studies, or qualitative research). My quarrel with these usages is that their 'participant observation' is likely to include other methods in addition to observation, such as interviews and the use of documents and other artefacts; that 'field study' appears to refer to where the study takes place rather than to the kind of study it is; and similarly that 'qualitative' appears to refer to the kind of data collected rather than the methods or strategies used in their collection. However, tradition may well be stronger than logic.

Participant observers can either seek to hide the fact that they are carrying out some kind of enquiry, or make it clear from the start what their purpose is in participating. Both roles have their problems, as discussed below.

## The complete participant

The complete participant role involves the observer concealing that she is an observer, acting as naturally as possible and seeking to become a full member of the group. Festinger et al. (1956), in a widely known study, infiltrated a group of persons who believed a prediction of the imminent destruction of the world on a known day. Similar studies have been carried out of criminal fraternities and military training units. Clarke (1996) describes such covert observation in a mental health secure unit claiming to be a therapeutic community and found conflicts between 'carers' and 'controllers' (who saw their role as custodial). In each case, a justification for keeping the group in ignorance of the researchers' real purposes was made in terms of the group's likely refusal to co-operate if these purposes were revealed. A subsidiary consideration was that the behaviour under observation would change if it were known that someone was prying into it.

There are obvious and strong ethical objections to this stance. Entering into a situation with the deliberate and planned intention to deceive is regarded as indefensible by many researchers and is becoming increasingly rare. There are enough problems in carrying out real world enquiry without being saddled with that particular guilt. There are also methodological problems with the complete participant role. The tendency to 'go native' (a problem shared by anthropologists and colonial administrators) is probably greatest when observation and recording have to be covert activities. In the research context, this refers to the situation where the role you have adopted in the group takes over to the extent that the research perspective is lost. Great care has to be taken that your activities are appropriate to the role, or suspicions and consequent distortions may be produced. Postponing recording until one is safely alone heightens the danger of seriously incomplete and selectively biased accounts; and there is always the risk that your true purpose will be discovered.

Increasingly, the position taken by Kirby and McKenna (1989) is being adopted:

It is essential that as a participant who is also a data gatherer, the researcher recognize the obligation to inform those in the setting about the research (i.e. what sort of research it is, for what purposes, and who is involved). Research from a *covert* or *manipulative* perspective is not generally acceptable. (p. 78, emphasis in original)

*These considerations suggest that you should avoid taking on the 'complete participant' role. If it appears impossible to carry out the enquiry if your research purpose were to be revealed, you are strongly recommended to seek the advice of experienced participant observers, and to ensure that your study falls within the appropriate code of conduct (see page 65).*

## The participant as observer

A feasible alternative is the participant-as-observer role. The fact that the observer *is* an observer is made clear to the group from the start. The observer then tries to establish close relationships with members of the group. This stance means that as well as observing through participating in activities, the observer can ask members to explain various aspects of what is going on. It is important to get the trust of key members of the group (key either because of their position, or because of personal qualities, such as openness or interest in the ways of the group). Maintaining the dual role of observer and participator is not easy; acceptance will be heavily dependent on the nature of the group and the interaction of particular features of the observer with the group. Variables such as age, class, gender and ethnic background can be important in particular circumstances.

Intuitively, it would appear that this role would have more of a disturbing effect on the phenomena observed than that of the complete participant, and several experienced participant observers have documented this (e.g. Whyte, 1984). However, one effect may be that members of the group, particularly key informants, are led to more analytical reflection about processes and other aspects of the group's functioning. There are situations, for example in the evaluation of an innovatory programme, where this can be of positive benefit.

One possible strategy for the participant as observer is to *evoke* a particular situation or behaviour from members of the group. Essentially this involves setting up a situation which has meaning for the group and then observing what happens. There are potential ethical problems here, and also the danger of artificiality. The group may perhaps do something, or do something in a different way, to please or placate the 'important' observer. This kind of active involvement borders on carrying out an informal field experiment, or, viewed in a different light, can be seen as a kind of simulation or role-play exercise.

It may also be possible to take advantage of the roles ascribed to one in a situation to gather information in a more active fashion. For example, when you work as a participant observer in some schools, particularly those for younger children or for children with special educational needs, the children commonly view you as something akin to a teacher. They are not surprised to be quizzed by you on any and every aspect of their school life. Similarly, the researcher in hospitals is likely to be classified as some sub-species of the 'helping and caring' staff, providing potential insights into patient relationships with such staff.

The special case of observing a group of which you are already a member carries obvious advantages and disadvantages. Your knowledge of the group's ways may well be extensive, but there is a corresponding problem in achieving anything approaching objectivity if you are already a native. Similarly, existing relationships with individuals can short-circuit a lengthy process of development of trust; but it may prove difficult for others to see you in your new role as observer, and there may be an artificiality and hesitancy in seeking to get shared understandings explicit and out into the open. In settings where there is a strong hierarchical structure, such as a school or hospital, a higher-status member may look askance at being observed or questioned by a lower-status member. There is further discussion of issues raised by this kind of 'insider' research on p. 533.

## The marginal participant

In some situations it may be feasible and advantageous to have a lower degree of participation than that envisaged in the preceding sections. This can be done by adopting the role of a largely passive, though completely accepted, participant – a passenger in a train or bus, or a member of the audience at a concert or sports meeting. Your likely familiarity with such roles helps, but it can also get in the way of the observer role. Conscious attention to active and open-minded observation is needed. Roles permitting note-taking are advantageous (e.g. student in a library, lecture theatre or seminar). Zeisel (1984) warns against assuming that while *you* know what role you are playing, others automatically come to the same conclusion: 'the marginal observer assumes when watching an informal football game in the park that he is taken to be a casual spectator. Meanwhile the football players think he is a park attendant about to tell them to stop playing on the grass' (p. 119).

Careful attention to dress and behaviour can help with such problems. 'Props' can be useful, such as bringing along a child if you are observing in a children's playground. Zeisel also suggests that you can test assumptions about how you are perceived by others by slightly changing your normal behaviour to see how people in the situation respond.

Some marginal roles are effectively indistinguishable from that of the 'complete observer' – someone who does not take part in the activity, and whose status as a researcher is unknown to the participants.

## The observer-as-participant

This is someone who takes no part in the activity, but whose status as researcher is known to the participants (Gold, 1958). Such a state is aspired to by many researchers using systematic observation. However, it is questionable whether anyone who is known to be a researcher can be said not to take part in the activity – in the sense that their role is now one of the roles within the larger group that includes the researcher.

## Getting started

Actually getting into, and getting to be a part of, the group that you are interested in can loom large as a problem. There is a real worry that you might 'blow it' by unintentional insensitivity or crassness. Anthropology abounds with horror stories of choosing as one's sponsor someone disliked or mistrusted by the rest of the group; Barley (1989) provides an engaging account of these issues. If, as may well be the case, you already have links with the group, these may provide what Lofland (1971) refers to as 'pre-existing relations of trust'.

There are differing views as to how much work you should have done before starting observation. The classic view of many researchers using participant observation, typified by Whyte (1951), is that the theory should emerge from the observation and that hence you need a minimum of initial theoretical orientation. Jones (1985) makes a useful distinction between the 'how' and the 'what and why' questions in this respect. In participant observation, our central research questions are likely to be 'hows': How does the teacher control the class? How does a committee come to decisions? Clues about these things should be gathered during and as a result of the observation. The 'whats' and the 'whys', primarily factual things like the context, details of the setting and its history, can profitably be found out ahead of time.

The immersion process of actually getting 'into' the group can be both confusing and stressful. Have faith: what may initially seem to be total chaos will, with time, reveal pattern, structure and regularity. 'Getting started' issues are picked up again in general terms in marked pages on 'Arranging the Practicalities' (p. 376).

## Collecting data

The basic task of the participant observer is to observe the people in the group, unit, organization or whatever is the focus of the enquiry, while being involved with them. Accounts are collected from informants. However, to give form and precision to the data, the observer often has to *ask questions* about the situation and the accounts that are given. These are both questions to oneself, and, more sparingly, explicit questions to group members.

This may seem to go against the notion of direct observation, and be more akin to interviewing. The distinction is blurred, but in participant observation you are much less likely to have 'set-piece' interviews and much more likely to have opportunistic 'on the wing' discussions or informal interviews with individuals. None the less, interviewing skills are very useful to the participant observer (see chapter 9).

It is common practice to start with *descriptive observation*. The basic aim here is to describe the setting, the people and the events that have taken place. Spradley (1980) distinguishes nine dimensions on which this descriptive data may be collected, explained in box 11.2. An early task is to develop a detailed portrait using this descriptive approach. This is the initial *story* or *narrative account* based on the events with which you have been involved. There is a similarity here to the approach of the investigative journalist who is after the 'story'. The Chicago school which pioneered the serious use of participant observation within sociology (see Hammersley, 1989, for a detailed and interesting account) had direct roots in journalism. The big difference between

---

## Box 11.2

### Dimensions of descriptive observation

| | | |
|---|---|---|
| 1 | *Space* | layout of the physical setting; rooms, outdoor spaces, etc. |
| 2 | *Actors* | the names and relevant details of the people involved |
| 3 | *Activities* | the various activities of the actors |
| 4 | *Objects* | physical elements: furniture etc. |
| 5 | *Acts* | specific individual actions |
| 6 | *Events* | particular occasions, e.g. meetings |
| 7 | *Time* | the sequence of events |
| 8 | *Goals* | what actors are attempting to accomplish |
| 9 | *Feelings* | emotions in particular contexts |

the researcher and the journalist (assuming that the latter is wanting to do a responsible job and trying to get to the bottom of the story) is that the researcher has to go beyond the story. This next stage involves developing a set of concepts, a theoretical framework, properly grounded in the detail of the story, which helps you to understand, and explain to others, what is going on.

Particular dimensions may loom large in some studies. Considering these dimensions, in the light of the research questions which led you to choose this group or setting in the first instance, is likely to lead to a greater focusing of the questions. This *focused observation* might be on a specific dimension or dimensions, or on themes which cross the dimensions. For example, Burgess (1983), in a study of a comprehensive school, used his descriptive observations, within a general theoretical framework derived from symbolic interactionism, to focus his questions on such topics as:

> How do teachers define the Newsom course? How do pupils define and re-define the course? What strategies, negotiations and bargains are used by the teachers and pupils? To what extent do activities in the Newsom department influence work within the core courses which Newsom pupils attend? (p. 209)

Terms such as 'negotiation', 'strategy' and 'bargain', led him to an understanding of the concepts which were used by the participants to come to terms with the situations in which they were located (see Burgess, 1983, pp. 115–35 for an extended discussion).

Stated in somewhat more formal terms, the process involved in participant observation has been regarded as an example of *analytic induction* (Johnson, 1998). This is summarized in box 11.3.

> *Observation and analysis are intertwined here. This is characteristic of flexible designs (which are likely to use participant observation), as discussed in chapter 6. There is more detailed coverage of the analysis of the qualitative data produced through participant observation in chapter 14.*

## Recording in participant observation

In principle, the fact that one is a participant does not preclude or prescribe any approach to recording, provided that the group knows and accepts that you have this role and task of observer. However, some approaches, for example, the use of taping, could inhibit the group and your participation in its activities. It may be the case that a group *for its own purposes* wishes to have its activities observed and analysed (possibly stimulated in this desire by your presence in their midst as a researcher – a beneficial 'Hawthorne'-like effect). In this case your role in participating is that of observer.

---

## Box 11.3

### The process of analytic induction

1   Formulate a rough definition of the phenomenon of interest.

2   Put forward an initial hypothetical explanation of this phenomenon.

3   Study a situation in the light of this hypothesis, to determine whether or not the hypothesis fits.

4   If the hypothesis does not fit the evidence, then *either* the hypothesis must be reformulated, *or* the phenomenon to be explained must be redefined so that the phenomenon is excluded.

5   Repeat with a second situation. Confidence in your hypothesis increases with the number of situations fitting the evidence. Each negative one requires either a redefinition or a reformulation.

*Note*: Situations should be selected to maximize the chances of discovering a decisive one. In this way weaknesses are more quickly exposed. 'Situation' is used as a general term to indicate an instance, phenomenon, case, aspect (or whatever) that is observed.

---

By the nature of the activity, it is not possible to be prescriptive about the recording of unstructured observation, even if this were desirable. Issues to do with the use of recording devices are the same as those discussed in the context of interviews (see chapter 9, p. 289). Box 11.4 discusses some of the issues involved.

## Observational biases

The human instrument as used in participant observation has a lot going for it. It is very flexible and can deal with complex and 'fuzzy' situations which give even powerful computers a headache. It does have deficiencies as an instrument, though. Knowing what distortions and biases we are likely to introduce in our observation should help in counteracting them.

Such effects are the stock-in-trade of many psychologists in the fields of memory, perception and social interaction, although the extent to which this knowledge is transferred to colleagues engaging in observational tasks is questionable. The following is very much a layperson's guide to a complex area:

## Box 11.4

### Issues in recording participant observation

**1**   Even with the most unstructured observation it is crucial to have a system which allows you to capture information unambiguously and as faithfully and fully as possible.

**2**   Where possible, a record is made of observation *on the spot, during the event*. This may be very condensed, using abbreviations, etc. Its main purpose is to remind you of what happened when you are writing up detailed notes. Baker (1988, p. 24) refers to these records as 'memory sparkers': who was there; any unusual details of the physical scene; important/interesting verbatim comments; incongruencies (it may help to ask yourself questions – why did he do that? etc.).

**3**   The record must as a matter of routine be gone through shortly after-wards to add detail and substance and to ensure that it is understandable and says what you intended it to say.

**4**   Getting this full record right may take as long as the original obser-vation did. Lofland and Lofland (1995, pp. 93–5) suggest five types of materials to be included in the record:

- *Running descriptions*   Specific, concrete, descriptions of events who is involved, conversations. Keep any inferences out (e.g. 'A was trying to get B to . . .').
- *Recalls of forgotten material*   Things that come back to you later.
- *Interpretive ideas*   Notes offering an analysis of the situation. You need both notes addressing the research question, and ones which will add supportive or elaborative material.
- *Personal impressions and feelings*   Your subjective reactions.
- *Reminder to look for additional information*   Reminder to check with A about B, take a look at C, etc.

You will need a system to mark and separate out these different types of material (e.g. round brackets, square brackets, double brackets, etc.).

**5**   Notebook computers, if available, can be very effective in producing these records actually in the field. In any case, there is considerable advan-tage in getting the record on to a computer using word-processing or spe-cialist text analysis software. This enables multiple copies of typescripts to be generated easily, for record and analysis purposes; or the computer file can be analysed directly. The organization and analysis of this kind of qualitative data are covered in chapter 14.

6   If you feel that this on-the-spot recording interferes with your observation, or alternatively when your participating role gets in the way, then notes should be made as soon as feasible afterwards. It may be worthwhile developing facility in the use of a mnemonic system (see e.g. Yates, 1966), which can have a dramatic effect on the number of items recallable. Inevitably, however, notes made after the event are subject to greater distortion, particularly when there are intervening events.

7   A good basic rule is that you should always prepare the detailed notes of the full report within twenty-four hours of the field session, and certainly never embark on a second observation session until you are sure that you have sorted out your notes for the first one.

- *Selective attention* All perceptual processes involving the taking in of information by observation and its subsequent internal processing are subject to bias. Attention, the concentration on some aspects of our surroundings rather than others, is an essential feature of coping with the overwhelming complexity of those surroundings. Our *interests*, *experience* and *expectations* all affect what we attend to. Features of the situation we are observing will also have differential salience – in the sense that some are likely to stand out and be more likely to be attended to. At a simple level, if you can see a person's face, then you are more likely to attend to what they say than to someone with their back to you. The basic message is to *make a conscious effort to distribute your attention widely and evenly*. There are sampling techniques, commonly used in systematic observation, which can assist you to do this and which could be used in some participant observation situations without doing violence to the approach.
- *Selective encoding* Expectations inevitably colour what you see, and in turn affect the encoding and interpretation of this. This is a rapid, usually unconscious, set of processes and hence, difficult to guard against. Related to this is the 'rush to judgement', where something is categorized on the basis of initial and very partial information. Later information, which might have been used to modify the judgement, is as a result not taken into account. Hence, *try to start with an open mind – and keep it open*.
- *Selective memory* The longer you wait after the event in constructing a narrative account, the poorer such an account will be in terms of its accuracy and completeness, and the more it will be in line with your pre-existing schemas and expectations. The moral is clear. *Write up field notes into a narrative account promptly*.

- *Interpersonal factors* In the early stages of a participant observation, because of your own insecurity and other factors, you may focus on, and interact with, only a few of the group members, perhaps those who seem welcoming and easy to get on with. This is probably inevitable, but carries with it the potential for bias. Those who welcome you may do so because they don't get on with other members of the group. Perhaps they are marginal or disaffected members. As you get to know more about the group, you should be able to avoid this, but there is still the danger of your developing relationship with the more friendly and helpful members affecting your picture of the whole. There are still the likely biasing effects of your own presence. The general strategy is to *seek to recognize and discount all biases.*

## Structured Observation

Readers who worry about such things will appreciate that making the divide in this chapter between 'participant' and 'structured' observation lacks a little in logic. The former covers the dimension of the observer's participation in the situation, the latter the degree of structure that is used in observation. As discussed previously, participant observers have primarily used qualitative techniques, and in some senses their work could be labelled unstructured or unsystematic. However, to my ears at least, this carries a somewhat pejorative tone which I consider to be unwarranted. In fact, good participant observation *is* systematic, but more in terms of the logical inference system used than the degree of pre-structure of observational categories. It is, of course, possible to have non-participant observation which is unstructured. The *ethological approach* (Tinbergen, 1963), for example, starts with careful, exploratory, observation seeking a detailed and comprehensive description of the animal's (or human's) behaviour.

Structured observers tend to take a detached, 'pure observer', stance. For them, structured observation is a way of quantifying behaviour. There have been important developments in the use of quantitative systematic observation which deserve wider recognition (e.g. Sackett, 1978; Bakeman and Gottman, 1997).

### Coding schemes

Coding schemes contain predetermined categories for recording what is observed. They range from simply noting whether or not a particular behaviour has occurred, to complex multicategory systems. Other forms of structured observation are possible – you can, for example, ask observers for global ratings of what they have seen over the whole of a session (or even based on an extended period). Barlow et al. (1984, pp. 134–8) give examples. Such global ratings are effectively *rating scales*, and are dealt with in chapter 10, p. 293.

> *The key features of much structured observation are the development of a coding scheme and its use by trained observers.*

The start is, as always, from some research question. Researchers then need to define important concepts and devise ways in which they can be measured. And, of course, they need to concern themselves with reliability and validity. An essential feature is that the reliability of the measuring instrument used, the coding scheme, depends crucially on the skills of the observer. Hence a major, and often very time-consuming, task is to train observers so that they produce essentially the same set of codes when confronted with a particular instance or sequence of behaviour.

Achieving adequate inter-observer reliability is primarily a technical matter, calling for a knowledge of the characteristics of a usable coding scheme and adequate time spent in training observers. It may be worth stressing the likely congeniality of structured observational work to the frustrated experimentalist, yearning for the relative certainties and simplified complexities of laboratory-based experimental work, and thwarted by the exigencies of the real world. The 'instrument makers' have now developed this type of observational methodology to a fine art, particularly in connection with sequential interaction.

## Checklists and category systems

A distinction is sometimes made between observation systems based on checklists, and those based on category systems. Rob Walker (1985) uses the term *category system* for 'systems that, unlike checklists, use a relatively small number of items, each of which is more general than a typical checklist item, but which attempts to use the system to maintain some sort of more-or-less continuous record' (p. 136). Checklists are seen as providing a long series of items which can be recorded as present or absent. The distinction is blurred in many cases, and the general term 'coding scheme' will be used here.

## Experimentation and coding schemes

Structured observation is commonly used in field experiments, particularly in obtaining measures on the dependent variable(s). Simple coding schemes are likely to be used. It is not unusual for the 'observation' to be carried out by an automatic device (e.g. a microswitch which detects a particular kind of behaviour, such as whether or not a child is sitting at a desk).

## Possible bases for a coding scheme

We have to decide what type of activity is going to be observed. A widely used system, which seems to be adaptable to a range of research questions, is derived from Weick (1968). It is summarized in box 11.5.

## Observer effects

Moving away from the laboratory, with its comforting screens and one-way mirrors, tends to leave the observer exposed to the observed. The extent of this exposure depends on the setting, the group involved and the research task. It is probably not too difficult to carry out unobserved systematic observation in the stands of a soccer ground, if one can select a good vantage point, even without access to the high-definition police video camera carrying out its own observation task. It is well-nigh impossible to achieve the same degree of invisibility in a secondary school classroom.

---

## Box 11.5

### Possible bases for the development of codes

There is a wide range of possibilities, including:

1  *Non-verbal behaviours*  Bodily movements not associated with language.

2  *Spatial behaviours*  The extent to which individuals move towards or away from others.

3  *Extra-linguistic behaviours*  Covers aspects of verbal behaviour other than the words themselves. This includes speaking rates, loudness and tendency to interrupt or be interrupted.

4  *Linguistic behaviours*  Covers the actual content of talking and its structural characteristics.

(Smith, 1975, pp. 203ff, provides examples of the use of these dimensions.)

---

However, even when it is possible to carry out a study without the knowledge of the observed, ethical issues could well be involved once more. These are largely a matter of common sense, and of consideration of the principles underlying 'codes of practice' (see chapter 3, p. 65). If a multimethod approach is used, where structured observation is supplemented by the use of other methods, then, given that the other available methods tend almost always to depend on the knowledge and co-operation of the persons involved, we have a practical reason for disclosure to support the ethical one.

Once the observed persons know that this is happening, then the observer is inevitably, to some extent, a participant in the situation, and the observation becomes potentially reactive (i.e. potentially changing the thing observed). The two main strategies used to minimize such 'observer effects' are *minimal interaction* with the group, and *habituation* of the group to the observer's presence. Minimal interaction is achieved through such obvious strategies as avoiding eye contact, the use of simple behavioural techniques such as not reinforcing attempts at interaction from the group (e.g. by smiling or otherwise responding positively when they do this), and planning your position in the environment to be 'out of the way'. Habituation involves one's repeated presence in the setting so that, particularly when you are an unrewarding, minimal interactor, it is no longer noticed.

It is never logically possible to be completely sure that your presence has not in some way changed what you are seeking to observe, but there are several indicators which provide some reassurance:

- The pattern of interaction stabilizes over sessions.
- Different observers code essentially identical patterns for different sessions.
- Members of the group appear to accept your presence to the extent that they do not seek interaction.
- Group members say that your presence doesn't affect what is going on. (It is helpful here to check this with different 'constituencies' present. A teacher may say that nothing has changed, whereas pupils may claim that lessons are better prepared!)

It is worth noting that in some circumstances an essentially non-interacting observer may be of more continuing interest and disturbance than one who gives a friendly smile or nod from time to time. It may also be more 'natural' and less disturbing to take up an explicit role in the situation. In work in special school classrooms, for example, we have found it profitable sometimes to take the role of 'teaching assistant', thus providing a natural entrée to interaction with the child about events in the classroom, while not precluding periods of busy, non-interacting, systematic observation.

## Deciding on a Coding Scheme

As with participant observation, it is likely that the first phase of a study which ends up using structured observation study will be exploratory, and that this exploration will occur prior to the choice of a coding scheme. The need for a coding scheme arises when it has been decided (at least tentatively) that structured observation, probably alongside other techniques, is to be used. The research question(s) will (after a period of unstructured observation and, probably, after gathering supporting information from other sources such as interviews and questionnaires), suggest how the processes you wish to study might be captured by various observational categories.

In certain circumstances, it may be appropriate to start, as it were, even further back than this, that is, to regard the initial exploratory observation sessions as essentially fulfilling a *hypothesis generation* function. The style advocated for this phase is essentially the 'analytic induction' approach (see p. 490).

### The use of existing coding schemes

Given that the development of a coding scheme is a difficult and time-consuming task, and that there are already in existence a multiplicity of such schemes, one solution seems obvious: take one off the shelf. Furthermore, the concern sometimes expressed that researchers in the social sciences often seem more interested in paddling their own canoes rather than doing their bit by adding another brick to the grand collective scientific enterprise indicates that more replication of studies would not come amiss.

However, the position advocated here, which is the mainstream methodological view, is that the research question comes first. Sort that out, and refine it through pilot work; that then leads you to the specification of the coding scheme. You may well find considerable difficulty in getting hold of an existing coding scheme that does the job you want it to.

This should not, however, stop you from seeking one using the search techniques discussed in chapter 3, p. 51. Even if any instruments that you come across are not directly usable, you are likely to get valuable ideas about different possible approaches. Box 11.6 shows the widely used system devised by Flanders (1970) for analysing teacher and pupil behaviour in the classroom. Of the ten categories, seven refer to aspects of teacher talk, and two to student or pupil talk, with the tenth being a 'residual' category. An interval coding system is used, where coders are expected to code every three seconds. Figure 11.1 shows a typical recording sheet. Each row represents one minute of time

# Box 11.6

## Categories used in Flanders interaction analysis (IA) system

**1** *Teacher accepts student feeling* Accepts and clarifies an attitude or the feeling tone of a pupil in a non-threatening manner. Feelings may be positive or negative. Predicting and recalling feelings are included.

**2** *Teacher praises student* Praises or encourages pupil action or behaviour. Jokes that release tension, but not at the expense of another individual; nodding head, or saying 'Mm hm?' or 'Go on' are included.

**3** *Teacher use of student ideas* Clarifying, building or developing ideas suggested by a pupil. Teacher extensions of pupil ideas are included, but as the teacher brings more of his ideas into play, switch to category 5.

**4** *Teacher questions* Asking a question about content or procedure, based on teacher ideas, with the intention that a pupil will answer.

**5** *Teacher lectures* Giving facts or opinions about content or procedures, expressing *his* own ideas, giving *his* own explanation, or citing an authority other than a pupil.

**6** *Teacher gives directions* Directions, commands or orders to which a pupil is expected to comply.

**7** *Teacher criticizes student* Statements intended to change pupil behaviour from non-acceptable to acceptable pattern; bawling someone out; stating why the teacher is doing what he is doing; extreme self-reference.

**8** *Student response* Talk by pupils in response to teacher. Teacher initiates the contact or solicits pupil statement or structures the situation. Freedom to express own ideas is limited.

**9** *Student-initiated response* Talk by pupils which they initiate. Expressing own ideas; initiating a new topic; freedom to develop opinions and a line of thought, like asking thoughtful questions; going beyond the existing structure.

**10** *Silence or confusion* Pauses, short periods of silence and periods of confusion in which communication cannot be understood by the observer.

(From Flanders, 1970, p. 34.)

Minute
1       5 5 5 5 5 5 5 5 4 4 4 4 8 8 2 3 3 3 3 5
2       5 5 5 6 6 6 6 6 8 8 1 1 6 6 0 0 7 7 7 7 7
3       5 5 5 5 5 5 5 5 5 5 5 5 5 5 5 5 5 5 5 5
4       5 5 0 0 0 0 7 7 0 0 7 7 4 4 4 4 8 8 3 3
5       4 4 4 8 8 2 2 2 3 3 3 5 5 5 5 9 9 7 7 7
6
7
8
9
10

**Figure 11.1**   Sample recording sheet for Flanders interaction analysis.

*Note*: Category '10' is coded as '0' for ease of coding.

(twenty three-second intervals) and hence the sample would allow for ten minutes' coding. The first five minutes have been completed, illustrating the fact that the appropriate category has to be inserted in the matrix for each coding interval. This obviously requires the coder to have fully memorized and internalized the coding system.

This system has been used in a very large number of studies (see examples in Croll, 1986) and attempts have been made to categorize classrooms through a variety of indices which can be derived from the analysis. These include proportions of teacher talk to student talk, the extent to which pupils initiate interactions (category 9 as a proportion of all pupil talk), etc. The very short time interval makes this what is termed a 'quasi-continuous' schedule; three seconds is seen as short compared with the processes that go on in classrooms. A particular use has been the study of 'interaction matrices' looking at pairs of observations, where the matrix shows how many times a particular type of utterance is followed by other types (Croll, 1986, ch. 5 gives an example). Examples of studies using standardized observation schedules include Stratton and Mota (2000) – a children's activity rating scale; Gilloran et al. (1993) – quality of care in psychogeriatric wards; and McColl et al. (1996) – consultations at a sexually transmitted disease clinic.

## Developing your own scheme

The use of an initial exploratory observational stage in helping to clarify and focus your research questions has been described above. The first version of the coding scheme which emerges from this process should incorporate those behaviours and distinctions which you think are important in providing answers to these questions. It is not possible to give a 'cook-book' set of procedures for this process. However, box 11.7 suggests a number of things which may be of help and box 11.8 gives an example.

It may be useful to have more than one coding scheme in a study. Bryman (1989, pp. 207–9) describes an influential study of managerial work by Mintzberg (1973) which used three: a *chronological record*, categorizing the

---

## Box 11.7

### Considerations in developing a coding scheme

*If there is an existing scheme which appears appropriate, consider using or adapting it.*

The categories should be devised to provide information relevant to the research questions in which you are interested (your preliminary exploratory observation should help in clarifying the question). To be straightforward and reliable in use, it will help if they are:

1   *Focused*   Looking only at carefully selected aspects of what is going on. Simply because you can observe it doesn't mean that you have to code it; ask yourself: 'What use will the data be?'

2   *Objective*   Requiring little inference from the observer.

3   *Non context-dependent*   The observer's task is more difficult if the category to be used in coding an event depends on the context in which it occurs (however, if such contextual information is essential to answer the research question, then the observer will have to live with it).

4   *Explicitly defined*   Through a detailed definition of each category, with examples (both of what falls within the category and what doesn't).

5   *Exhaustive*   Covering all possibilities so that it is always possible to make a coding (to be compatible with (1) above it may be necessary to have a large 'residual' or 'dump' category).

6   *Mutually exclusive*   A single category for each thing coded (if the system has both (5) and (6) characteristics it is commonly referred to as an MEE system – a *Mutually Exclusive and Exhaustive system*). Note, however, that in some situations it may be simpler to have an event multiply categorized.

7   *Easy to record*   Just ticking in a box rather than requiring recall of which of a large number of categories to use. Observers will, though, need to be completely familiar with the category system if they are to use it properly.

---

## Box 11.8

### Example of use of observational schedule

Barton et al. (1980) studied naturally occurring interactions between staff and residents in a home for the elderly. They developed an observational schedule with five categories:

1 *Independent behaviour*   A resident's carrying out of bathing, dressing, eating, grooming or toileting tasks (or parts of such tasks) without assistance. Can be self-initiated or initiated by others.

2 *Dependent behaviour*   A resident's request for, or acceptance of, assistance in bathing, dressing, eating, grooming or toileting.

3 *Independence-supportive behaviour*   Staff verbal encouragement of, or praise for, a resident's execution of personal maintenance tasks without help, *and* staff discouragement of, or scolding for, a resident's request for assistance or non-attempts of execution of self-maintenance tasks.

4 *Dependence-supportive behaviour*   Staff assistance in a resident's personal maintenance, praise for a resident's acceptance, *and* discouragement of a resident's attempts to execute personal maintenance tasks without help.

5 *Other behaviour*   Staff or resident behaviour that is not related to personal maintenance tasks.

(From Barton et al., 1980.)

---

types of activities in the manager's working day, and their beginning and end times; a *mail record*, covering the nature of mail received, how it is dealt with, and the mail generated (this is largely a documentary analysis but involves observational coding of the kind of attention given to each item of mail – read, skimmed etc.); and a *contact record*, detailing the meetings, calls and tours of the chronology record, categorizing their purposes and initiators.

Examples of studies involving the development of a structured observation schedule include Fitzpatrick et al. (1996) – instrument to measure nurse behaviour in the clinical setting; Singh et al. (1997) – rating family-friendliness of care sytems for children with emotional and behavioural disorders; Hofer et al. (1999) – observation of adolescent daughters' disputes with mothers; and Muijs and Reynolds (2000) – classroom observation of mathematics teaching.

## Coding Sequences of Behaviour

Your use of the coding scheme depends on the type of data you wish to collect. This in turn depends on the research questions you are seeking to answer.

It may be that simple frequency measures will suffice. This is adequate if all that is necessary is to compare frequencies; say, the relative frequencies of staff's 'dependence-supportive' and 'independence-supportive' behaviours when using Barton et al.'s (1980) schedule. However, in many studies, the concern is when, and under what circumstances, different behaviours occur. Is residents' independence behaviour followed by staff independence-supportive behaviour? Is staff reliance on dependence-supportive behaviour associated with trends in residents' behaviour? Because of this common need for sequence information, the rest of this section focuses on the use of coding schemes for observing behaviour sequences.

A central issue concerns the 'unit' which is to be coded. The two main alternatives are to base this either on *time* or on an *event*. In the former, a particular time interval is coded (e.g. as 'child talking to mother'). In the latter, observers wait for a particular event to occur and note what type of event it was. One can also distinguish between 'momentary events' and 'behavioural states'. Momentary events are relatively brief and separate events (such as a child's smile), and the likely interest is in when they occur, and how frequently. Behavioural states are events of appreciable duration (such as a baby sleeping), and in addition to 'when', and 'how often', the likely concern is with 'for how long'. Obviously, there is not a strict dichotomy between the two – all events take some time to complete. Technically it is now straightforward, using event recorders, or computers effectively functioning as event recorders, to store the times of occurrence of momentary events, and the start and end times of behavioural states.

### Event coding

Events can be recorded in a variety of ways. Essentially, the observer responds whenever the event occurs, using either pencil and paper or some more complex recording instrument. Alternatives are shown in figure 11.2. Tallying events with a simple checklist will often be sufficient. This provides frequency data, both in absolute terms (i.e. how many times each event has occurred) and relatively (i.e. the relative frequency of different events). The sequence record adds the order in which different events occur, hence providing information about transitions (i.e. which events follow which). Adding a time-line gives information about the time interval between similar events and times for the various transitions. It obviously contains within it the simple sequence

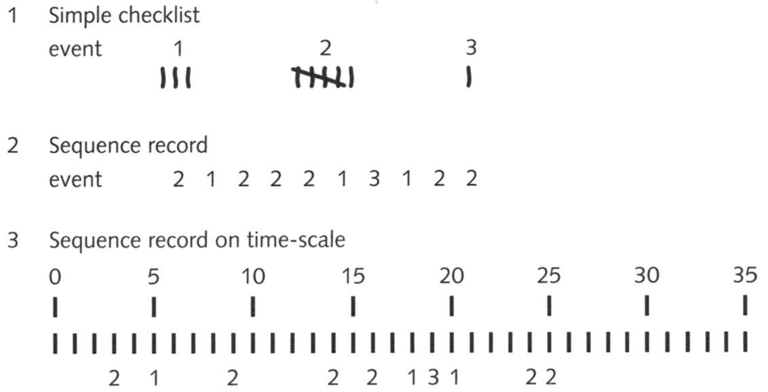

1   Simple checklist
    event        1                    2                    3
             Ⅲ (            ＴＨＬＩ                Ｉ

2   Sequence record
    event        2  1  2  2  2  1  3  1  2  2

3   Sequence record on time-scale

| 0 | 5 | 10 | 15 | 20 | 25 | 30 | 35 |
|---|---|----|----|----|----|----|----|
| Ｉ | Ｉ | Ｉ | Ｉ | Ｉ | Ｉ | Ｉ | Ｉ |

ＩＩＩＩＩＩＩＩＩＩＩＩＩＩＩＩＩＩＩＩＩＩＩＩＩＩＩＩＩＩＩＩＩＩＩＩ

          2   1      2        2  2  1 3 1      2 2

**Figure 11.2**   Alternative ways of coding events.

information, and the frequency information can be computed from both the last two records, so it could be argued that there is virtue in always recording both sequence and time. However, this does give the observer a more complex task, and the general principle is still that the type of recording should be determined by what information is needed to answer the research questions.

## State coding

While simple checklists and sequence records (usually indicating 'change of state' – e.g. from 'asleep' to 'awake') may sometimes be useful, it is usual to include time information giving the duration of particular states. Electronic recording devices make it straightforward to record start (onset) and finish (offset) times for the states being coded. This information produces a record equivalent to that shown in figure 11.3. In practice, the onset of a particular state will probably be coded by pressing a key or button on a keyboard, and its offset in a similar way.

Many coding schemes have codes which are *mutually exclusive and exhaustive* (MEE). This means that the definitions of states are such that if one state occurs, it is not logically possible for it to do so at the same time as any other (mutual exclusion), and that the total set of possible states covers all eventualities (exhaustiveness). Such MEE schemes have considerable advantages when it comes to analysis. Box 11.9 gives a simple example.

For recording, there is also the practical advantage that only 'onset' times need be recorded – as each 'onset' necessarily means the 'offset' of some other state (illustrated in figure 11.4).

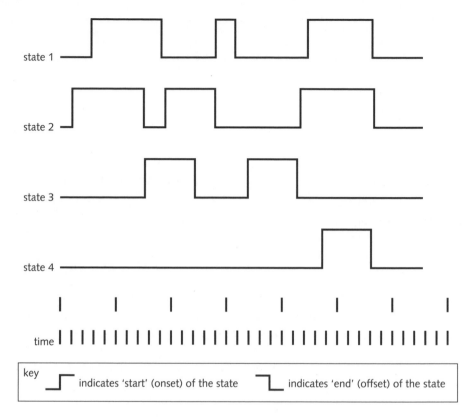

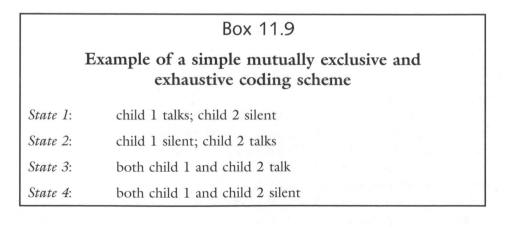

**Figure 11.3**   Record of 'onset' and 'offset' of states.

## Box 11.9

### Example of a simple mutually exclusive and exhaustive coding scheme

*State 1*:        child 1 talks; child 2 silent

*State 2*:        child 1 silent; child 2 talks

*State 3*:        both child 1 and child 2 talk

*State 4*:        both child 1 and child 2 silent

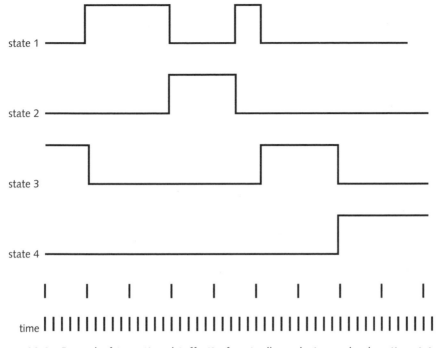

**Figure 11.4** Record of 'onset' and 'offset' of mutually exclusive and exhaustive states.

## Interval coding

Interval coding is triggered by time rather than by events. The observation period is divided into a number of intervals, say of ten or fifteen seconds in duration. The job of the observer is to note down information about what happened during the interval. This can be done in various ways, but a common strategy is to code with the category which best represents what occurred during that interval (e.g. the most frequent event, or the dominant state – the state present during the greater part of the interval).

This can be coded with pencil and paper using a simple sequence record (as in figure 11.2 above) or a specially designed sheet incorporating the time intervals can be used (as in figure 11.5 below). More complicated schemes may be called for. A commonly used variation is to have different types of coding for different time intervals. For example, general coding is carried out for five successive ten-second intervals, and the next ten seconds is used in a different way (say, counting the number of children in the group who are 'on task').

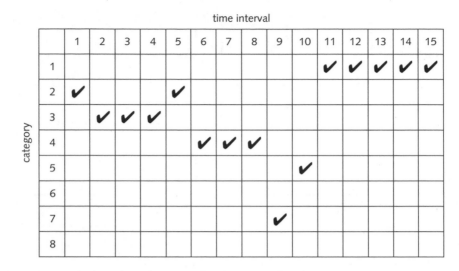

**Figure 11.5**   Coding sheet for interval coding (pencil and paper).
Note that a mutually exclusive and exhaustive scheme is in use.

This type of interval coding can be made easier to carry out by means of a 'bug in the ear': that is, a simple device which gives a click audible only to the observer at the end of each interval. Special pieces of equipment are available for this purpose, but it is a simple matter to use a cassette recorder on which the time intervals have been recorded, together with an earpiece. It is also possible to record additional 'aide-memoire' information on the tape to help the observer.

Interval coding, though widely used, is not without its critics. Distortion can be introduced into the data if the interval chosen is not shorter than the shortest duration typically encountered for a codable state. Bakeman and Gottman's advice is that

> when simplicity and low cost of instrumentation matter more than accuracy, or when the interval is shorter than most codable events and observers prefer checking or categorizing intervals to recording onset times, then an interval coding strategy probably makes sense. For all other cases, some variant of event coding should probably be used. (Bakeman and Gottman, 1997, pp. 48–9)

## Time sampling

In time sampling, some principle is used to select the time intervals during which coding takes place. These are interspersed with intervals where there is no coding (or a different form of coding, as in the example given in the preceding section). The principle may be random – random number tables can be used to select the time intervals in seconds, minutes or whatever, from, say, the end of one coding interval to the start of the next. Or some regular sequence may be used – say five minutes 'on' followed by fifteen minutes 'off'. This approach is sometimes used when the 'off' non-observing intervals are used actually to make the recording.

Careful thought must be given to assessing whether the type of sampling used leads to a representative picture of the phenomenon under observation. General sampling principles, as discussed in chapter 8, p. 260, apply. Time sampling can be a useful and efficient way of measuring how much time is spent within the various categories of the coding scheme. It is likely to be a poor way of collecting sequential information, however, because of the gaps between observation periods.

## Cross-classifying events

In situations where you have acquired a substantial appreciation of what is going on and hence are in a position to focus your observation sharply on certain kinds of events, an alternative approach to classification may be valuable.

Suppose you are interested in what happens when a child misbehaves in the classroom – say when he takes something from another child. Observers might be asked to note not only the occurrence of this behaviour, but specific aspects of what the two children were doing immediately before the incident, what kind of a disturbance occurred, and how it was settled. If mutually exclusive and exhaustive sets of codes can be devised for each of these phases, it becomes possible to cross-classify this event. Analysis can then subsequently show what is likely to lead to what and hence aid in its understanding.

## Reliability and Structured Observation

When using structured observation, the observation schedule *as used by the observer* is the instrument, and an important question is: How good an instrument is it? Reliability and validity raise their heads once more. Validity concerns are essentially similar to those raised by any method of investigation (as discussed in chapter 5, p. 101), but an assessment of the reliability of data obtained from structured observational schedules has attracted particular specialist approaches. Hops et al. (1995) discuss these methodological issues in the context of the development of the LIFE (living in familial environments) coding system.

Problems occur if the observer-instrument shows variation at different times, or if different observer-instruments vary from each other. Hence there are two kinds of reliability: *intra-observer reliability* (sometimes called *observer consistency*) and *inter-observer reliability* (or *inter-observer agreement*).

### Observer consistency

This is the extent to which an observer obtains the same results when measuring the same behaviour on different occasions (e.g. when coding the same audio- or video-tape at an interval of a week).

### Inter-observer agreement

This is the extent to which two or more observers obtain the same results when measuring the same behaviour (e.g. when independently coding the same tape).

It is highly desirable to have more than one observer in any study involving structured observation. With a single observer, even if he shows high consistency, it may be that he is using the observation schedule in a totally idiosyncratic fashion. Demonstrating good inter-observer agreement defends against this, and indeed goes some way towards showing validity. Even if a study is predominantly single-observer, it is often possible to enlist the help of a colleague who will devote the time necessary to learn to use the schedule and observe a proportion of the sessions to be coded.

Both observer consistency and inter-observer agreement are measured by the same means. Several indices have been developed. They involve the calculation either of the degree of correlation between the two sets of measurements, or of the agreement (sometimes called concordance) between them. There is some disagreement as to the relative merits of these two approaches. Martin and Bateson (1986) consider that 'an index of concordance need only be used if there is some reason why agreement over each occurrence of the behaviour is an important issue, or if the behaviour is measured on a nominal scale' (p. 92). However, Bakeman and Gottman (1997) feel that this kind of agreement is generally valuable, particularly in sequential analyses involving coding over time. They advocate the use of concordance measures, such as Cohen's Kappa, which correct for chance agreement. There would be advantages in comparing results obtained in different studies and with different instruments if there were some standardization in this area. Box 11.10 illustrates the computation of an index of concordance and of Cohen's Kappa with

# Box 11.10

## Measuring inter-observer agreement

1   *Draw up the 'confusion matrix'*  Suppose that the coding schedule has five different categories (A, B, C, D and E) and that there are 100 occasions when coding has taken place. With two observers, an *agreement* takes place when they both use the same code for the same occasion. If they use different codes, then that is a *disagreement*. The pattern of agreements and disagreements can be shown on a two-dimensional matrix (often referred to as a 'confusion matrix').

|              |   | Observer two |    |    |    |       |
| ------------ | - | - | - | - | - | ----- |
| Observer one | A | B | C | D | E | Total |
| A            | 8  | 0  | 0  | 0  | 0  | 8   |
| B            | 2  | 21 | 1  | 0  | 0  | 24  |
| C            | 1  | 0  | 18 | 2  | 1  | 22  |
| D            | 0  | 0  | 0  | 24 | 6  | 30  |
| E            | 1  | 0  | 0  | 1  | 14 | 16  |
| Total        | 12 | 21 | 19 | 27 | 21 | 100 |

Note that scores on the diagonal from top left to bottom right indicate agreement between the two observers; scores off this diagonal indicate their disagreement.

2   *Calculate the proportion of agreement* $(P_0)$  This is given by

(number of agreements)/(number of agreements + number of disagreements)

which in this case is $\dfrac{8 + 21 + 18 + 24 + 14}{100}$ or 0.85.

NB *The index of agreement (or concordance)* is simply this proportion expressed as a percentage (i.e. in this case, 85 per cent).

3   *Calculate the proportion expected by chance* $(P_c)$  Probability theory shows that if the probability of the first observer using, say, code A is $P_{1A}$, and the probability of the second observer using the same code is $P_{2A}$, then the probability of their both using the same code by chance is simply the product of these two separate probabilities (i.e. $P_{1A} \times P_{2A}$ or $0.08 \times 0.12$). Hence the total chance proportion for all five codes is

$$P_c = (0.08 \times 0.12) + (0.24 \times 0.21) + (0.22 \times 0.19) + (0.30 \times 0.27)$$
$$+ (0.16 \times 0.21)$$
$$= 0.262.$$

**4** *Calculate Cohen's Kappa* $(K)$   This is given by the formula

$$K = \frac{P_o - P_c}{1 - P_c}$$

In the example,

$$K = \frac{0.850 - 0.262}{1 - 0.262} = 0.797.$$

Note that the value of Kappa, while still quite high, is noticeably smaller than the uncorrected proportion of agreement.

There are ways of assessing the significance of Kappa (see Bakeman and Gottman, 1997). However, as with other statistics, statistical significance is not everything and, particularly with large samples, it is possible to achieve statistical significance with proportions which show little agreement between the observers. Fliess (1981) has suggested the following 'rules of thumb':

Kappa of 0.40–0.60: 'fair';
Kappa of 0.60–0.75: 'good';
Kappa of above 0.75: 'excellent'.

simple data. Bakeman and Gottman (1997, pp. 62–4) give an extended discussion with examples and further references.

Construction of the 'confusion matrix' has the advantage that it shows very clearly where the two observers are differing in their judgements. This can be valuable at the training stage to highlight these confusions. It may be that further training is needed, or that some attention has to be given to the definitions of the categories.

With some coding schedules, the 'units' being coded are non-problematic and different observers will have no problems in recognizing them. Suppose you simply have to categorize each complete contribution that a child and an adult make to a conversation. It is easy to determine whether it is the child or the adult speaking; the difficulty comes when you have to decide how to code that utterance. However, if you have a scheme where each of the contributions each makes has to be split up into different sequential units ('gives instruction', 'provides model', 'gives praise', etc.), the transition points between the units may well be a source of disagreement between observers. In this situation it is necessary first to establish to satisfactory inter-observer agreement on the unit boundaries (which can be done in a similar way to that for the coding schedule itself – Bakeman and Gottman, 1997, pp. 68–71) before going on to the main task of assessing agreement on the categories.

## Reactivity of assessing inter-observer agreement

Just as there is the problem that the observer may change the thing observed, so the observer's observing may be affected by testing for inter-observer agreement. Taplin and Reid (1973) looked at the effects of different ways of monitoring the reliability of observation. They monitored observers continuously but told different groups different things. The poorest performance in terms of reliability was from observers who did not think that they were being monitored. Intermediate performance came from those who knew that they were being monitored on specific occasions. The best performance came from those under the impression that they were being monitored covertly on randomly selected occasions. The implications are clear. It is desirable not only to have inter-observer agreement checks, but also for observers to know this – but not to know which sessions will be checked. This is, of course, easier to organize when analysis takes place via a video or other tape than when sessions are coded live.

## 'Observer drift'

The kinds of threats to validity discussed in chapter 5 in the context of fixed designs (see p. 105) rear their heads again when structured observation is used. 'Instrumentation' is a particular problem. This is caused by possible changes in the measuring instrument, and refers here to changes in the way that the observer uses the schedule; it is usually termed 'observer drift'. Increased familiarity with use of the instrument may well make it easier to 'see' examples of particular categories, or there may be subtle differences in the ways in which category definitions are interpreted over time. Inter-observer agreement checks go some way to minimizing these effects, as the drift is likely to be individual and idiosyncratic. Intra-observer checks, perhaps by returning periodically to the rating of training examples, can also be used.

## Expectancy effects

Observers coding behaviour after some intervention may well expect to see 'positive' changes compared to the pre-intervention situation. This is a classic Rosenthal-type expectancy situation (Rosenthal, 1976; Rosenthal and Rubin, 1980), particularly when the observer is also the person with a stake in the outcome of the study. Again, inter-observer agreement tests will give some safeguard, although (unconscious?) collusion can occur. 'Blind' coding of various kinds should be considered. If there are comparison groups, observers may not be told to which group the individual observed belongs. It might be feasible for observers to be 'blind' as to whether they are watching a pre- or post-treatment session. A system where one observer is closely involved in that particular trial and knows exactly what is going on, but a second trained observer (who may be closely involved in another trial) is 'blind' to these features, can sometimes be set up.

The use of video-tape provides other solutions. Pre- and post-treatment sessions can be coded in a random sequence after all the data have been collected. However, even if considerable care is taken, it is virtually impossible to eliminate all clues (clothing, decorations, leaves on trees, etc.). Taped material has other advantages, particularly in giving the opportunity of multiple viewing, but its use should be carefully thought through, piloted and time-budgeted. The tape necessarily captures only one perspective of the events and it is very tempting to accumulate large quantities of to-be-coded tapes.

## Further Reading

Foster, P. (1996) Observational research. In R. Sapsford and V. Jupp, eds, *Data Collection and Analysis*. London: Sage. Clear summary of both approaches.

Apart from the above, there is little overlap between the participant observation and structured observation literatures, and so the rest of this Further Reading section is presented in two separate parts.

*Participant observation*

Adler, P. A. and Adler, P. (1987) *Membership Roles in Field Research*. Newbury Park, Calif.: Sage. Insightful analysis of the difficulties encountered in different roles (peripheral, active and complete membership).

Bogdewic, S. P. (1999) Participant observation. In B. F. Crabtree and W. L. Miller, eds, *Doing Qualitative Research*. Thousand Oaks, Calif.: Sage. Short, clear, review.

Emerson, R. M., Fretz, R. I. and Shaw, L. L. (1995) *Writing Ethnographic Fieldnotes*. Chicago: University of Chicago Press. Deals very clearly with ethnographic data collection, and the analysing and writing up of results.

Lofland, J. and Lofland, L. (1995) *Analyzing Social Settings: A Guide to Qualitative Observation and Analysis*, 3rd edn. Belmont, Calif.: Wadsworth. Very readable book with good discussion of both methodological issues and practicalities.

Nason, J. and Golding, D. (1998) Approaching observation. In G. Symon and C. Cassell, eds, *Qualitative Methods and Analysis in Organizational Research: A Practical Guide*. London: Sage. Short account emphasizing that observation is part of other methods of data collection.

Whyte, W. F. (1984) *Learning from the Field: A Guide from Experience*. Newbury Park, Calif., and London: Sage. Discussion and dissection of issues in field work with focus on participant observation.

*Structured observation*

Bakeman, R. and Gottman, J. M. (1997) *Observing Interaction: An Introduction to Sequential Analysis*, 2nd edn. Cambridge: Cambridge University Press. Straight-forward, clear and detailed. Essential reading for anyone doing a structured observational study involving process-oriented aspects of behaviour. Very practical. Sections on recording, assessing agreement, representing and analysing the data.

Gottman, J. M. and Bakeman, R. (1998) Systematic observational techniques or building life as an observational researcher. In Gilbert et al., eds, *Handbook of Social Psychology*, 4th edn. Oxford: Oxford University Press. Useful complement to Bakeman and Gottman (1997).

Martin, P. and Bateson, P. (1993) *Measuring Behaviour: An Introductory Guide*, 2nd edn. Cambridge: Cambridge University Press. Based on biology/animal behaviour but of general relevance. Covers wider range than Bakeman and Gottman in less detail. Excellent annotated reference section.

Sackett, G. P., ed. (1978) *Observing Behavior*, vol. 2: *Data Collection and Analysis Methods*. Baltimore: University Park Press. Slim volume covering wide range of methodological aspects of using structured observation (e.g. category definition, sampling, analysis, recording and reliability).

# 12

# Additional Methods of Data Collection

This chapter:

- focuses on a range of approaches to the collection of data additional to those covered in the previous four chapters
- concentrates on a major group of methods known variously as unobtrusive measures or indirect observation, including documentary analysis, content analysis and archival analysis
- points out their drawbacks when used as the sole method of investigation
- stresses the advantage that they are typically non-reactive (i.e. using them does not have an effect on the thing you are studying)
- emphasizes their use as a complement to other methods as a means of providing triangulation
- provides brief reviews of a range of other possible approaches, including simulation, discourse analysis, repertory grids, protocol analysis, meta-analysis, and feminist research methods
- concludes with a discussion of some of the practicalities, advantages and problems of using multiple methods in an enquiry.

## Unobtrusive Measures

We are becoming increasingly conscious of the effects that humans have on their environment, particularly in relation to pollution: 'ozone holes', radio-active waste and so on. One particular class of such effects covers the artefacts that people make and leave behind them: things created 'on purpose', ranging in time from prehistoric cave paintings, through medieval cathedrals to styro-foam containers for take-away pizzas. There is a general case to be made that humans reveal something of themselves through such productions: that such things contain clues about the nature of society's lifestyles.

Whether unintended outcome or intentional creation, the 'things' that people produce provide opportunities for the real world enquirer. Eugene Webb and his colleagues Donald Campbell, Richard Schwartz and Lee Sechrest (Webb et al. 1981, 2000) have sensitized social scientists to a wide range of what they term 'unobtrusive measures'. These are things which might, through ingenuity and inference, be considered as indices of some aspect of human behaviour. Their most often-quoted example is of the floor tiles around the hatching-chick exhibit at Chicago's Museum of Science and Industry, which needed replacing at six-weekly intervals, while tiles in other parts of the museum did not need to be replaced for years. This 'selective erosion' provided an index of the relative popularity of exhibits.

Webb and colleagues distinguished between such *erosion measures* and *accretion measures*. The latter, for example, might be counting empty spirit bottles in rubbish bins as a measure of the level of home consumption of alcohol in a town that was officially 'dry'. Both types are *trace measures* – the physical effects of interaction which remain after that interaction. They are sometimes referred to as 'behavioural by-products' (Barlow et al., 1984). For example, weight as a by-product of eating has been used as a measure in studies of obesity (Mahoney et al., 1973). Box 12.1 gives a range of examples, illustrating the wide variety of possibilities. In each of the examples, there are likely to be problems in making the suggested inferences.

## Accretion measures

An accretion is something extra or added, the build-up of a product or residue. Apart from analyses of different types of garbage (Rathje and Murphy, 1992), particularly popular with archaeologists but less so with social scientists (could it be to do with the stench dissipating over time?), examples include litter and graffiti. Litter has been used as an index of usage patterns in public places. Graffiti have been related to territoriality, for example in areas of Belfast. Usage is a popular focus for accretion measures – the number of date stamps in a library book; or mileage logged by a car or van; or persons through a turnstile. However, some evidence on virtually any phenomenon is there for the taking. For example, the 'internal mail' envelopes that land in my pigeon-hole, with their sequentially completed and crossed out addressees in their little boxes on the envelopes, suggests a potential tool for getting at communication patterns within an institution.

## Erosion measures

Erosion refers to deterioration or wear, something being worn down or removed totally. Again, usage is the most obvious focus, with wear giving measures of interaction patterns, relative popularities, etc.

---

## Box 12.1

### A variety of unobtrusive measures

- The diameter of a circle of children as an index of fear induced by a ghost-story-telling session.
- Dilation of the pupil of the eye as an index of fear or interest.
- Degree of clustering of white and black students in lectures as an index of racial attitudes.
- Distortion in the size of drawings of Santa Claus as an index of children's interest in Christmas.
- Time spent in front of a display as an index of its popularity.
- Number of times books are borrowed from a library (or bought from bookstores) as indices of their popularity.
- Weight of food left on plate compared to initial weight as an index of acceptability of food in an institution.
- Settings of car radios when brought in for service as an index of relative popularity of different stations.
- Amount and type of graffiti in pairs of male and female public toilets as an index of gender differences.
- Differences in amount of litter as an index of the relative effectiveness of different anti-littering strategies.

(Taken, in part, from Webb et al. 2000, pp. 2–3.)

---

Box 12.2 lists some advantages and disadvantages of 'trace' measures. It is probably a fair assessment that physical trace measures have only a small part to play in research involving humans; certainly few social scientists make serious use of them currently. Page (2000) regards their use as something of a 'lost art'. They do have, though, a strong potential contribution to a multiple-method approach. Looked at in this light, many of their disadvantages dissolve, and their non-reactivity can provide useful validation for other, more central, methods.

## Using Documents

Although the use of physical trace measures has never achieved much more than curiosity value in the social sciences, there has been substantial interest in the analysis of a particular kind of artefact: the *document*. By this is meant,

---

## Box 12.2

### Advantages and disadvantages of 'trace' measures

*Advantages*

1   They are unobtrusive and non-reactive. That is, the enquirer does not need to be in direct contact with the person(s) producing the trace, and hence there is no reason why the behaviour should be influenced by the enquiry.

2   They can provide valuable cross-validation of other measures, either in support or disconfirmation of them.

3   They encourage ingenuity and creativity on the part of the enquirer.

*Disadvantages*

1   The person(s) responsible or the trace and/or the population from which they come may be difficult or impossible to specify.

2   Similarly, it may not be reasonable to assume that all persons involved make equivalent contributions to the trace (a single person may make a substantial contribution through repetitive involvement).

3   Apparent link between cause and effect (e.g. usage and trace) may be mediated by other factors (e.g. softness of ground).

4   Ethical difficulties of researching without people's knowledge or consent (likely to depend on the case – a study of whisky bottles or letters in rubbish bins is more ethically dubious than footpath wear patterns).

---

primarily, the written document, whether this be a book, newspaper or magazine, notice, letter or whatever, although the term is sometimes extended to include non-written documents such as films and television programmes, pictures, drawings and photographs.

A common approach to documentary analysis is *content analysis*, the quantitative analysis of what is in the document. It differs from the techniques that we have considered so far in that it is indirect. Instead of directly observing, or interviewing, or asking someone to fill in a questionnaire for the purposes of our enquiry, we are dealing with something produced for some other purpose. It is an *unobtrusive measure* (see preceding section) which is non-reactive, in that the document is not affected by the fact that you are using it. Note that it is, of course, possible to analyse the contents of documents or other materials which have been collected directly for the purposes of your research. In this case, it is not an unobtrusive technique. The fact that a person is filling in, say, a diary for the project may in some way alter their behaviour; in other words, there is a possible reactive effect.

Content analysis has been defined in various ways. Krippendorff's (1980) definition, that 'content analysis is a research technique for making replicable and valid inferences from data to their context' (p. 21), while perhaps over-inclusive in not making clear that we are dealing with certain kinds of data (those coming from documents of various kinds), does have the virtue of stressing the relationship between content and context. This context includes the *purpose* of the document as well as institutional, social and cultural aspects. It also emphasizes that reliability and validity are central concerns in content analysis.

It is possible to do other things with documents over and above analysing their contents. Such approaches, for example focusing on the authenticity of the document, or the intentions of the writer, are derived from the methods of historians. They are essentially concerned with the problems of selection and evaluation of evidence. Barzun and Graff (1977) provide a view of research from the perspective of the historian which constitutes a very valuable extension to the methodological education of any social scientist.

The checklist of criteria suggested by Gottschalk et al. (1945, p. 35), in relation to the use of personal documents in history, anthropology and sociology, covers important concerns relevant to the accuracy of all documents:

- Was the ultimate source of the detail (the primary witness) *able* to tell the truth?
- Was the primary witness *willing* to tell the truth?
- Is the primary witness *accurately reported* with regard to the detail under examination?
- Is there any *external corroboration* of the detail under examination?

Content analysis is in several senses akin to structured observation. This similarity is particularly evident when structured observation is carried out on a recording of the situation observed. A video-recording of such a session appears to be a very similar kind of artefact to, say, a video-recording of a television programme. The main difference is that in the former case, the intention is to obtain a closely equivalent picture to that which the 'live' observer would have seen in the situation. Focus and direction will be selected with the needs of the observer in mind. The edited picture making up the TV programme appears under the direction of the programme-maker, who has her own agenda, which is unlikely to include the needs of the content analyst.

This illustrates a general problem in content analysis. The material to be analysed is not only unstructured, or at least not structured with the needs of the observer in mind; it will in general be a document with a purpose. And that purpose is important in understanding and interpreting the results of the analysis. A distinction is sometimes made in documentary analysis between *witting* and *unwitting evidence*. Witting evidence is that which the author intended to impart. Unwitting evidence is everything else that can be gleaned from the document.

## Content Analysis

Content analysis came to prominence in the social sciences at the start of the twentieth century, in a series of quantitative analyses of newspapers, primarily in the United States. Campaigns against 'cheap yellow journalism' were bolstered by statistical studies showing how 'worthwhile' news items were being increasingly dropped in favour of gossip, sports and scandals (Krippendorff, 1980, pp. 13–15 provides details). This type of content analysis was subsequently extended to radio, and then to television, and continues unabated in, for example, studies of advertising, and of pornography and violence in the media.

Similar studies have attempted to assess bias in school textbooks, and the depiction of favourable or unfavourable attitudes to blacks, females and homosexuals, both in textbooks and in other publications. While the main interest has probably continued to be in the field of mass communications, content analysis has more recently been used in a wide variety of areas. In particular, the approach discussed here can be readily adapted for use in the analysis of qualitative interview and questionnaire data (e.g. in the coding of open-ended questions in surveys) and of direct observation (typically through coding of tapes and transcripts).

Documents themselves cover a very wide range, including for example:

- minutes of meetings;
- letters, memoranda, etc.;
- diaries;
- speeches;
- newspapers;
- magazine articles.

Particular contexts generate specific types of document. In social work and medical settings various types of case record can be of importance. Studies involving schools or other educational establishments might include:

- written curricula;
- course outlines, and other course documents;
- timetables;
- notices;
- letters, and other communications to parents.

Remember also that 'document' is taken to include such non-written forms as:

- films;
- television programmes;
- comic strips and cartoons;
- photographs.

These require somewhat different approaches to analysis from those discussed below, although the basic principles remain the same (see Fetterman, 1989; and Walker and Adelman, 1975, specifically on using photographs).

The main focus in this text is on the use of content analysis as a secondary or supplementary method in a multimethod study. This does not preclude carrying out a study based solely on content analysis, but this involves substantial difficulties and deficiencies (see box 12.4 below on 'Advantages and disadvantages of content analysis'). On the other hand, it is often possible to 'acquire' copies of documents of a variety of types in conjunction with interviews and observations. (One useful attribute for a real world researcher is a jackdaw mentality, where you are always on the lookout for such things – you need to seek and get permission to use them, but it is rarely refused.) They can be used for triangulation purposes, or to provide something of a longitudinal dimension to a study when a sequence of documents is available extending back in time.

## How to carry out a content analysis

As with virtually all the techniques covered in this text, content analysis is *codified common sense*, a refinement of ways that might be used by laypersons to describe and explain aspects of the world about them.

*Start with a research question*   Once again, the effective starting point for the process is the research question. Perhaps: 'Is there a greater emphasis on sex and violence in the mass media now than there was ten years ago?' A different research question might derive from the comment, commonly heard in listeners' responses to radio programmes, that there is political bias in radio

programmes. For example, the BBC Radio 4 *Today* programme seems particularly adept at generating near-apoplexy in politically committed listeners.
Note here that, while the communication here is initially 'on the air', in practice any study of the programme's content will be likely to be based on a transcript of what is heard. It is likely, however, that an audio-tape will also be
helpful, enabling you to judge from intonation whether a particular comment
is to be taken in a sarcastic or ironic sense.

There may be occasions when you have documents but no properly formulated notion of what you are looking for (e.g. at an early, exploratory, phase
of the study when the research questions have not been properly developed).
In many methodology texts, this so-called 'fishing trip' is severely frowned
on; for example, 'content analysis cannot be used to probe around a mass of
documents in the hope that a bright idea will be suggested by probing. Content analysis gets the answers to the question to which it is applied' (Carney,
1973, p. 284). However, in the context of a flexible design, this is an entirely
appropriate strategy. (Note that this would be an example of a flexible design
where the data collected are essentially quantitative.) It is in the tradition of
exploratory data analysis discussed in chapter 13, p. 399. Obviously, the choice
of data is determined by what you want to know, your tentative research questions. But to suggest that there is a difference in value between the research
of one enquirer who starts out with the question, and that of another who
gets the idea for the question from peeking at the data, verges on the metaphysical. Either there is good evidence about the question from the data, or
there isn't.

*Decide on a sampling strategy*   It is usually necessary to reduce your task to
manageable dimensions by *sampling* from the population of interest. General
principles of sampling apply, as discussed in chapter 8, p. 260. Thus, in the case
of the *Today* programme, it might be considered appropriate to take a random
sample of, say, twenty programmes from those transmitted over a three-month
period. Or, possibly, some form of stratification might be considered – perhaps
ensuring that all presenters of the programme are equally represented in the
sample. A different approach would be to have as one's sample all the programmes transmitted over an extended period, but to focus, from the point
of view of the analysis, on a small part of the content, say, on references to a
particular incident or type of incident.

There may be situations where the relevant documents are so rare or
difficult to get hold of that sampling in this sense is inappropriate.

*Define the recording unit*   In addition to deciding on categories, it is necessary to select a recording unit. The unit most commonly used is probably the
*individual word*. In the simplest version, all occurrences of the word would
be treated as equal, and counts of them made and compared. A somewhat

more sophisticated approach would differentiate between the different senses of words that have multiple meanings (e.g. 'right' as 'correct', or as 'non-left') and code phrases constituting a semantic unit (e.g. 'ice cream' or 'Houses of Parliament'). It is also possible to use *themes, characters* (i.e. the actors or individuals mentioned in the document, as in the analysis of the fiction example in box 12.3 below), *paragraphs* or *whole items* as the recording unit.

Other possibilities suggest themselves for particular tasks. For example, when analysing newspaper or magazine content, these might be:

- number of stories on a topic;
- column inches;
- size of headline;
- number of stories on a page;
- position of stories within the page or paper as a whole;
- number and/or type of pictures.

For some purposes, it may be necessary to examine the *context* in which a recording unit is set in order to categorize it. Although you may have fixed on the word as recording unit, if you are interested in coding whether a treatment is positive or negative, favourable or unfavourable, it is likely that you will have to take into account the sentence in which the word appears.

There is some argument in content analysis circles about the degree of inference which coders should be called upon to make when categorizing items. This is sometimes expressed in terms of *manifest content* and *latent content*, corresponding essentially to low- and high-inference items respectively. Manifest items are those which are physically present (e.g. a particular word); latent content is a matter of inference or interpretation on the part of the coder. At its simplest, this may just require a judgement of warmth, favourableness etc., but some might require use of a complex personality typology. As with other techniques of data collection, it is obviously likely to be more straightforward to achieve reliable results with low-inference systems. However, the research question should determine the type of system you are using, and it may well be that a high-inference system is appropriate. This then puts greater stress on ensuring that you can demonstrate reliability through the use of independent coders, or by some other means such as triangulating with data obtained through other sources.

*Construct categories for analysis*   It is difficult to give helpful general comments here, as there is such a wide range of possible types of research question for which content analysis might be used. Holsti (1969) lists several types of categories. Thus, in looking at what is said in the document, categories might be concerned with:

- *Subject matter*  What is it about?
- *Direction*  How is it treated, e.g. favourably or not?
- *Values*  What values are revealed?
- *Goals*  What goals or intentions are revealed?
- *Methods*  What methods are used to achieve these intentions?
- *Traits*  What are the characteristics used in describing people?
- *Actors*  Who is represented as carrying out the actions referred to?
- *Authority*  In whose name are statements made?
- *Location*  Where does the action take place?
- *Conflict*  What are the sources and levels of conflict?
- *Endings*  In what way are conflicts resolved (e.g. happily)?

As with structured observation systems, it is highly desirable that these categories are *exhaustive* and *mutually exclusive*. The former ensures that everything relevant to the study can be categorized (even if you have to resort to a 'dump' category for things that you don't know how to deal with). The latter means that anything to be analysed can be categorized in one way only; if it is categorized in one particular way, it can't also be categorized as something else.

The categories also have to be *operationalized*; that is, an explicit specification has to be made of what indicators one is looking for when making each and any of the categorizations. *Sorting out the categories is the most crucial aspect of the content analysis.* As Berelson (1952) points out, 'since the categories contain the substance of the investigation, a content analysis can be no better than its system of categories.' Box 12.3 gives examples of category systems.

---

## Box 12.3

### Examples of category systems

1  To answer questions about characteristics of heroines in fiction targeted at adolescents

*physical characteristics*
height
weight
'vital statistics'
age
hair colour
eye colour (etc.)

*social characteristics*
ethnic background
socio-economic class
occupation
housing
income
religion (etc.)

*emotional characteristics*
warm
aloof
stable
anxious
hostile (etc.)

**2**   To answer questions on trends in contents of newspapers

*domestic news*
political
ecological
crime
transport (etc.)

*foreign news*
European
American
Russian
Chinese
Third World (etc.)

*cultural*
music
theatre
art
opera (etc.)

*sport*
*business and financial*
*television and radio*
*children's and young people's items*
*women's items*
*cartoons*
*advertisements (etc.)*

(All of the above could be sub-categorized.)

*Test the coding on samples of text and assess reliability*   This is the best test of the clarity and lack of ambiguity of your category definitions. It is highly likely that this process will lead to the revision of your scheme. With human (as against computer) coding, at least two persons should be involved at this stage. When the scheme appears workable, tests of reliability should be made (these are formally equivalent to the tests carried out when assessing the inter-observer agreement of structured observation schedules – see chapter 11, p. 340). If the reliability is low, further practice is necessary, and it may also be necessary to revise the coding rules. The process should be repeated until the reliability is acceptable. If computer coding has been used, it is necessary to check for errors in computer procedures (see p. 393).

*Carry out the analysis*   In formal terms, the analysis is equivalent to the set of activities you carry out when using and analysing a structured observation schedule. The statistical analysis of the data obtained can follow exploratory data analysis procedures or more conventional approaches (see chapter 13). The most common approach is to relate variables from the content analysis to other 'outside' variables (e.g. gender of the persons producing the documents, or type of school from which they come). More complex procedures involve the use of factor analysis, as either an exploratory or a confirmatory tool, to identify themes in texts; and the subsequent use of techniques such as analysis of variance to outside variables.

Box 12.4 lists advantages and disadvantages of content analysis.

## Computers and content analysis

Content analysis can be extremely laborious and time-consuming. It is a field where computerization has led to substantial benefits. Analyses which would have been beyond the resources of small-scale research can now be completed routinely, given access to a computer and specialized software. The text can be easily manipulated and displayed in various ways (e.g. showing all sentences, or other units, containing a particular word or phrase). The availability of optical character recognition (OCR) devices can translate a document directly into a computer file without the necessity for typing.

A major methodological bonus if you are using computer-aided content analysis is that the rules for coding the text have to be made completely explicit, or the computer will not be able to carry out the task. Once these rules have been established and written into the software (itself no mean task), then it is possible to work through a range of documents and achieve results which are formally compatible with each other. At the same time, once the development stage has been completed, and any 'bugs' removed from the

---

## Box 12.4

### Advantages and disadvantages of content analysis

*Advantages*

- When based on existing documents, it is *unobtrusive*. You can 'observe' without being observed.
- The data are in permanent form and hence can be subject to re-analysis, allowing reliability checks and replication studies.
- It may provide a low cost form of longitudinal analysis when a run or series of documents of a particular type is available.

*Disadvantages*

- The documents available may be limited or partial.
- The documents have been written for some purpose other than for the research, and it is difficult or impossible to allow for the biases or distortions that this introduces (note need for triangulation with other accounts/data sources to address this problem).
- It is very difficult to assess causal relationships. Are the documents causes of the social phenomena you are interested in, or reflections of them (e.g. in relation to pornography and/or violence in the mass media)?

---

system, the computer provides perfect coder reliability in applying the rules built in to the program.

This does not mean that all problems have been solved. Little matters of validity, interpretation and explanation remain. You also still face the inescapable fact that content analysis is concerned with *data reduction*. You throw away much of the information in a document in order to see the wood through the trees. Weber (1985) provides a good review of ways in which the computer can help in carrying out content analysis and these related ground-clearing tasks. Box 12.5 highlights some of these approaches. More complex multivariate data analysis techniques are also facilitated by using computers. Weber (1985, pp. 58–64) presents an extended analysis and interpretation of an example using factor analysis. However, he stresses the need to return to the document to validate the interpretation of themes derived from such statistical results. Fan (1997) discusses a range of possibilities in computer content analysis of text in a journal issue devoted to the topic.

## Box 12.5

### Computer aids to content analysis

**1** *Key-word-in-context (KWIC) list* Provides a list of contexts in which any selected 'key word' appears. This would give the location of each use of the key word and, say, the ten preceding and ten following words. KWIC lists are equivalent to *concordances*, which are much used in literary analysis and biblical study. They sensitize the analyst to variations in use and meaning of particular words, possibly suggesting the need to separate out different uses in the content analysis. They similarly draw attention to phrases or idioms which might be dealt with as separate units.

**2** *Word frequency list* Provides lists of words in the document, ordered according to the number of times that they appear; together with the frequencies themselves. Usually the (say) twenty highest-frequency words are listed. Specific words such as 'a', 'an', 'the', 'is', 'are', etc. can be omitted. Can be used for comparative purposes with different documents, but needs treating with care. For example, use of pronouns and synonyms can decrease apparent frequencies; lumping together the different meanings of a word increases them. More sophisticated programs can 'disambiguate' such meanings through syntactical and other cues.

**3** *Category counts* Providing the rules can be fully and explicitly specified, there is no problem in the computer moving from word counts to category counts, which is the central activity in content analysis. Although more complex approaches can be used, comparison of simple percentages of use is often all that is needed.

**4** *Combined criteria list* It is feasible not only to search documents for the occurrence of particular words or content analysis categories, but also to have more complex criteria for searching (e.g. for joint occurrences of two words or phrases in a sentence or passage). These are sometimes termed *collocations*. Such co-occurrences can be selected on the basis of your research questions.

*Note*: These techniques can be used for any data in the form of written text. The computer doesn't mind if this comes from a document or the transcript of an interview.

## Using Data Archives

An archive is simply a record, or set of records. Some records are in the form of documents containing text, as covered in the preceding section. Others may contain quantitative statistical information. Such archives share an important feature with the documents just discussed, in that they have been produced for some other purpose than for your use as a researcher. They will have been collected and paid for by someone else (though there is also the possibility of revisiting a study you carried out previously, with a view to carrying out a different or extended analysis). The ten-yearly National Census is an archetypal example, but there are many recurrent and one-off surveys (e.g. the Current Population Survey, General Household Survey, British Social Attitudes Survey, American General Social Survey, British Workplace Industrial Relations Survey, British Crime Survey, and others; Hakim, 1987, ch. 7, provides details).

There are clear advantages and disadvantages associated with such data. It is possible to tap into extensive data sets, often drawn from large representative samples, well beyond the resources of the individual researcher. Recent data sets should have good documentation, including full code-books describing the variables and codes that have been used, and easily accessible recording methods. The disadvantages flow from the fact that even those surveys carried out for research purposes are unlikely to be directly addressing the research question you are interested in. Useful on-line sites include 'The Data Archive' (http://www.data-archive.ac.uk/) which holds over 4,000 datasets from government, academic researchers, opinion poll organizations, etc. worldwide, and CASS (The Centre for Applied Social Surveys – http://www.natcen.ac.uk/cass) which provides access to questionnaires from major surveys and associated commentary to assist survey design.

It is, of course, perfectly possible to focus one's research solely on the *secondary analysis* of such data. This is defined by Hakim (1982) as 'any further analysis of an existing data set which presents interpretations, conclusions or knowledge additional to, or different from those presented in the first report' (p. 1). This can be an attractive strategy as it permits you to capitalize on the efforts of others in collecting the data. It has the advantage of allowing you to concentrate on analysis and interpretation. Baker (1988, pp. 254–60) discusses the issues involved and presents examples.

Archival research is not limited to the re-analysis of survey data. Bryman (1989, ch. 7) gives varied examples from the field of organization studies. A frequently quoted study is by Grusky (1963), who analysed the performance of sports teams in relation to turnover of personnel such as team coaches and managers. Later studies have followed related themes – in part, one suspects, because sports performance is an area where there is a surfeit of published statistical information. Fielding and Fielding (2000) argue that as qualitative data are costly to collect and analyse, and commonly only a small proportion of such data are the subject of final analysis and publication, secondary analysis could be used with advantage. They demonstrate this approach by using secondary analysis to evaluate classic studies of crime and deviance. Qualidata, the Economic and Social Research Council's Qualitative Data Archival Resources Centre, is a repository of much useful data: see <http://www.essex.ac.uk/qualidata>.

## Using administrative records and management information systems

Many small-scale real life studies concern organizations, such as an office, school or hospital. A feature they all have in common is the collection of records and other information relating to their function. Such records can form a valuable supplementary resource, and it is often possible to obtain access to them. The usual ethical principles apply in relation to confidentiality, and there may be particular problems associated with information collected for one purpose being used for a different one.

The records are, however, unlikely to provide direct answers to the questions we are interested in when carrying out research. Indeed, they may form a tempting distraction, with pages of descriptive statistics on individual measures, and cross-tabulations between measures, amassed to little or no purpose. Simply to know that there are 73 per cent of males on an innovatory programme, or that 23 per cent of the males and 48 per cent of the females are from low-income families, carries little meaning in its own right. The issue is: *What light can this information throw on our research questions?* We may be interested in answering questions on recently introduced crèche facilities, or different access arrangements, and this kind of routine data may in such circumstances be of direct value. Nevertheless, a thorough exploratory study of existing data may suggest questions, or act as a starting point for unforeseen lines of enquiry. It is well worth while spending a fair amount of time looking at and playing with data from record systems. Patterns may suggest themselves and trends emerge which had not previously occurred to you.

Typically it will be necessary to rearrange the data in various ways, so that, for example, you can compare data over different time periods. Your research questions assist in selecting from what can easily be a data mountain. If, as is increasingly the case, these routine systems have been computerized, your task *may* be simplified. It is, for example, usually relatively easy to provide suitably anonymized extracts from computer records. Previously it would have been necessary to go through filing cabinets and record cards to obtain the information you need. This carries the possibility of introducing transcription errors, and may also require that the researchers have access to confidential or private records. Access to computer records should be subject to strict controls, and any necessary clearances must be obtained. Remember, however, that there is no guarantee at all that the computer system designed to cope with routine data collection has the flexibility to deliver the comparisons or selections that you need.

Hakim (1987, ch. 4) discusses the design of studies based exclusively on administrative records. She makes the point that they have to be designed 'back to front'. That is, instead of designing the study and then collecting the data, the researcher starts by finding out what data are available in the set of records and then identifies a possible research model. The situation is rather different in a multimethod case study. If administrative records are available, they are examined to see what additional corroboration or light they can throw on the case. If they don't help with your research questions, then either don't use the administrative records, or consider whether it makes sense to modify what you are after in the light of what they can tell you.

Box 12.6 lists some issues to be taken into account when using administrative records from management information systems; box 12.7 gives an example of their use. Caputo (1988) and Bronson et al. (1988) provide useful background on the use of management information systems, covering theoretical and practical (including computer) aspects respectively.

## Brief Review of Additional Approaches

This section briefly covers some specialized techniques worth considering for particular tasks. Some of the approaches (e.g. repertory grids) are embedded within a theoretical view of the person and the world they live in, to the extent that it could be dangerous to view them as 'off-the-peg' techniques usable without buying into the theory. Others, while regarded by some commentators as methods of investigation, might be better thought of as different research strategies (e.g. simulation) or as analytic techniques (e.g. meta-analysis). In short, they are a mixed bag. They by no means exhaust the possibilities. Smith (cited in Rob Walker, 1985, pp. 60–6) presents a catalogue of thirty-eight distinct and different methods, with pen-picture and basic references.

### Simulation

Simulations attempt to carry over the essential structural elements of some real world phenomenon into a relatively well controlled environment. They imitate the processes of a system to try to see how it works. Although some experi-

---

## Box 12.6

### Issues in using administrative records for research purposes

**1**  *The quality of the data must be assessed*   Generally, information central to the activities of an organization will be of better quality than more peripheral items. Check on what actually happens (e.g. are large batches of forms filled in cursorily long after the event?). Find the views of the persons entering the data. If they think that 'the yellow form always goes into the dustbin' (actual quotation from a social worker), then they are unlikely to fill them in conscientiously.

**2**  *Careful study of existing record systems may allow you to avoid unnecessary duplication in data collection*   Informants in studies are often busy people and it is highly desirable to minimize the extra load you put on them for the purposes of research. Even though an existing question may not be asking for exactly what you had in mind, it may provide you with a close enough approximation of the information you need. It is sometimes feasible to add temporary 'research' questions to standard administrative forms.

**3**  *Sampling from administrative records may well be needed*   A variety of approaches may be possible (e.g. time samples, sampling of individuals, sampling of items).

*Note*: As administrative records often give information on a rigidly defined set of topics over considerable periods of time, they lend themselves to some form of time series analysis (see chapter 13, p. 448).

---

ments in which a few variables are manipulated are sometimes thought of as simulations, the more common usage tries to capture the whole of the pattern, which is likely to involve a myriad of variables. The focus is on what happens when the phenomenon, one hopes with all its essential characteristics, is transposed to a more controlled setting. In this sense, they represent a half-way house between the decontextualized artificiality of the laboratory setting and the sometimes intractable and inaccessible real world setting.

Suppose one is interested in the working of juries in legal cases. This is very difficult to examine in a real 'real life' setting, which is not open to the investigator. Simulation of the jury room, and the task, is feasible – though much work in this field has been criticized because of its artificiality in following the experimental approach of manipulating single variables such as the attractiveness of the defendant.

---

## Box 12.7

### Example of the use of administrative records in an evaluation

The evaluation focused on the effects and effectiveness of a widely used training package on the use of behavioural techniques in the education of persons with severe learning difficulties (the EDY package; see Foxen and McBrien, 1981).

A main aspect of the evaluation involved a substantial postal survey of persons who had completed the course, and their instructors. The second main aspect involved a series of case studies of the use of the package in a range of different settings.

The instructors of persons who had successfully completed the course had been, since its inception, invited to send in a request form to the sponsoring institution. Provided their performance reached certain criteria, they were then sent an official certificate. The request form incorporated useful information which was analysed as part of the evaluation. This included biographical and career information which established the representativeness of this sample in relation to the survey sample.

There were also indices of the trainees' performance at an early stage and on completion of the course. It was appreciated that the 'demand characteristics' of this situation on the instructors might lead to their decreasing the former scores and increasing the latter ones. Nevertheless, useful corroborative information was gained. For example, high pre-intervention scores, in connection with some of the skills covered in the course, supported evidence from the case studies and assisted in framing recommendations for the revision of the course.

(From Robson et al., 1988.)

---

Simulations commonly require participants to play an explicit role. This calls attention to our expectations about how someone fulfilling a particular role will behave. As Harré and Secord (1972) put it, humans in social situations are 'rule-following agents'. A notorious example is the simulated prison cell block investigated by Zimbardo and his colleagues (Haney et al., 1973). Students were paid to role-play 'prisoners' and 'guards' under very realistic conditions. Prisoners, for example, were actually arrested by local police; handcuffed, searched, cautioned, etc. The study was terminated less than halfway through its planned duration because of the strong effects that it had on both prisoners (including extreme depression and anxiety) and guards (enjoyment of the power in their roles). Ethical criticisms are obvious, as well as the concern about the adequacy of the simulation in representing the reality of prison life. Note that this is a different issue from whether or not the participants take the situation seriously and are fully involved, which is a common problem in simulations. This feature can be employed with advantage when the simulation is used as a teaching tool, and in intervention studies where the intention is to modify behaviour.

Simulation can be viewed as an alternative research strategy (e.g. Kern, 1991), or as a means of implementing a case study, as it can involve different methods of investigation. The Zimbardo study, for example, used various checklists and personality tests, diaries, questionnaires and direct observation. Veitch and Newsham (2000) provide an example of a simulation set up as an experiment, where comparison is made between a simulated office in which participants can set the working conditions (e.g. workplace lighting and temperature) with one in which, though working under identical conditions, participants were given no choice in determining them.

Suggested reading is provided at the end of the chapter.


## Discourse analysis

A great deal of research based on humans, particularly approaches which generate qualitative data, focuses on language. There are, however, researchers interested in language as such – how it is used and with what consequences. To the outsider, this might appear as a topic area rather than a method in itself, but it is claimed that because language has such a central role in social life, the study of it provides the key to understanding our social functioning. In these approaches, it is not only the substance of what is said (which forms the basis for conventional analyses) that is important, but the styles and strategies of the language users – how they say things.

The term discourse analysis (sometimes *conversational analysis*) is used, but unfortunately there is little agreement as to its usage. For some, it covers all research concerned with language in its social and cognitive context (van Dijk, 1985). Others focus on the variations in the use of language of different social groups (e.g. Milroy, 1980). The variants likely to be of greatest value in the type of enquiry covered in this text are not primarily linguistic but more social-psychological (e.g. Potter and Weatherell, 1987). Typically, they call for a very detailed analysis of small fragments of discourse and require a good understanding of the theoretical framework for the analysis.

Virtually any social text can be used as a basis for this type of analysis, including existing documentation, individual and group discussion and interview transcripts. Note, however, that the perspective differs from the traditional one in important respects. With interviews, for example:

the interview is no longer seen as a means of measuring the genuine views of a participant but as a means of exploring the varied ways of making sense, or accounting practices, available to participants. The concern is at the level of language or discursive practices, rather than with the individual interviewee. (Marshall, 1994, p. 95)

Suggested reading is provided at the end of the chapter.

## Repertory grid techniques

George Kelly proposed a theory of personality based on the notion of *personal constructs* (Kelly, 1970; Salmon, 1994). Personal constructs are the dimensions we use to make sense of, and extend, our experience of the world. He views humans as effectively acting as scientists in their day-to-day activities, seeking to understand the course of events in which they are involved. We evaluate the phenomena making up our world through a limited number of constructs which we have found helpful in creating our personal view. This is clearly a constructivist approach (see chapter 2, p. 27), but Stevens (1998) claims that it is compatible with a realist stance.

Kelly suggests that these personal constructs are bipolar (e.g. on a dimension from 'good' to 'bad'; or from 'makes me feel angry' to 'makes me feel pleased'). Repertory grid techniques are ways of eliciting these constructs and have been widely used, both by followers of Kelly and by others who simply find them useful. Kelly's use of the technique required a subject to complete a set of cards showing the names of a number of significant persons in their life (e.g. 'mother', 'best friend'). They were then asked to provide an important way in which two of the persons differed from the third – perhaps that two were 'kind' and one was 'cruel'. This was repeated several times to elicit a range of such constructs, which then constituted how that subject interpreted the behaviour of people important in her life. A grid could then be constructed, displaying the matrix of constructs against 'elements' (persons).

Such grids have been used in clinical and counselling sessions and are finding their way into research studies. Examples include Howkins and Ewens (1999), who studied the professional socialization of nurses; Burke (1997), who sought to assess homosexual stress; Fournier (1997), who studied graduates' patterns of career development; Botterill and Crompton (1996), who carried out case studies of the experiences of US tourists visiting Britain; and Lynch (1995), who elicited personal constructs about smoking from a group of adolescents (demonstrating that individuality, rather than social and image constructs, appeared to be of far greater significance than indicated in the research literature using other approaches).

A current debate concerns how far it is necessary to stay with 'elicited' constructs, which are necessarily idiosyncratic to the individual, and often difficult to deal with in research, or whether it is possible to work with 'provided' constructs. Although this seems to go against the basic tenet of the Kellian approach, it has been advocated by some of his followers (e.g. Bannister and Mair, 1968 – who do, however, point out the dangers of provided constructs).

A range of different types of grid has been developed. Approaches such as 'laddering', which look at the location of individual constructs within the overall construct system, have also been used (Butt, 1995). A tension can increasingly be detected between the technology of 'gridding' (for which several computer packages are now available) and the philosophical roots of Kelly's view of personality.

Suggested reading is provided at the end of the chapter.

## Verbal protocols

A verbal protocol (or 'think aloud') is the name given to a self-report by a person about 'what they are doing, what they are about to do, what they hope to achieve, etc. with respect to a particular task or behaviour' (Johnson and Briggs, 1994, p. 61). Green (1995) provides a short, clear introduction. It provides a means of gathering information about how people approach a problem or task and the mental processes they adopt when doing this. The technique can provide rich, qualitative information about how people conceptualize their actions in specific situations.

This technique has been popular in fields such as software evaluation, where there is increasing concern about the usability of materials. This is partly because it can provide rapid feedback in a cost-effective manner (Wright and Monk, 1991). Two main variants have been used: in one, participants are asked to verbalize about the task while carrying it out; in the other, this is done immediately after the task is completed. If the former is used, the demands of the technique should not be so onerous that they interfere with performance of the task. This type is best suited to tasks which the person can complete at their own pace. Difficulties can arise in getting participants to produce a detailed commentary. The instructions given to them, and the type and amount of any prompts to be used, need careful consideration.

The technique has been somewhat controversial, possibly because it has been used in fields more accustomed to quantitative data. It is likely to be of particular use where people interact with complex systems, as in human–computer interaction and software design (Sonnentag, 1998), but is worth considering in any situations where greater insight and understanding of what is going on will be gained by having those involved tell you about it. Examples include Fowler (1997), who used the technique to examine the strategies used by experienced home help nurses when planning nursing care; Barber and Roehling (1993), who investigated the process of deciding whether or not to apply for jobs; and Cacioppo et al. (1997), who review several uses in psychotherapy research.

Suggested reading is provided at the end of the chapter.

## Meta-analysis

Meta-analysis is a process used in summarizing the results of a number of different studies (Sutton et al., 1999). It is an analysis of the analysis (hence a meta-analysis). It can be viewed as a method of doing research, although it is more usually regarded as an analytic technique. It may well be a sensible use of the time and resources of even a small-scale enquirer to put together findings from previous work in a heavily researched area, rather than carry out one more empirical study.

Meta-analysis should be distinguished from the *research review* (which has the more synoptic aim of putting together and evaluating different kinds of findings in a particular field of interest) and *secondary analysis* (concerned with extending the analysis of, or carrying out a different analysis on, existing data).

Most work has been carried out on the meta-analysis of quantitative studies, particularly of experiments. The aim here is to provide an integrated study of research results on a specific question, giving particular attention to the size of effects and to statistical significance. Rosenthal and Rubin's study, summarizing the first 345 studies on experimenter expectancy, provides a good example (Rosenthal and Rubin, 1980). More recent studies include Milton and Wiseman (1999) on mass-media tests of extrasensory perception, representing over 1.5 million trials in eight studies with an overall cumulative outcome which doesn't differ from chance expectation; Quinn et al. (1999), who investigated the effects of social skills interventions for students with emotional and behavioural disorders, showing respectable overall effect sizes; and DeRubeis et al. (1999), who found no difference in outcomes for cognitive behaviour therapy and medication with severely depressed outpatients.

Considering the large numbers of studies on such topics as the effects of psychotherapy on patients, or of class size on student learning, we should surely be reaching some overall conclusions; or perhaps the lack of any such conclusions will begin to throw serious doubt on the type of social research which has been carried out. Statistical methods have been developed which go beyond a simple summing of significant and non-significant results, although they do have quite restrictive assumptions. The technique is also reliant on material from all relevant studies being published and available. The bias in favour of positive results in the publication policies of some journals also causes problems. Finally, the quality of the studies included is obviously of importance – garbage in, garbage out! Smith and Egger (1998) review some unresolved issues in the use of meta-analysis.

Meta-analysis can also be used in conjunction with a literature review in order to assess the influence of different research designs and other methodological factors on results obtained by different studies in the same area (e.g. Crain and Mahard, 1983, on the effect of school desegregation on the educational achievements of black children).

Some attempts have been made to extend meta-analysis to studies incorporating qualitative data (e.g. Yin, 1989, pp. 123–4).

Suggested reading is provided at the end of the chapter.

## Feminist research methods

Chapter 2 covered the contribution of feminist approaches to methodology (p. 28). The feminist view is that accepted ways of carrying out research (particularly positivistic, quantitative approaches) are dominated by males and miss many of the issues specific to women. Such research is regarded as a form of exploitation arising from the differential relationship between the researcher and respondent, particularly when the former is male and the latter female (Oakley, 1981). Theories, which influence the ways in which questions are framed and data are collected and analysed, even if not inherently male, distort the experiences of women in the accounts that are collected.

This is also taken as support for specific feminist research methods that are qualitative and non-positivist (e.g. Roberts, 1981). Reinharz (1992) has, however, taken the view that, while there are distinct methodological practices that have been associated with feminist research, there is no one method that is solely owned by feminist researchers, nor is there a method that is in principle unusable by feminist researchers. Similarly, Mason (1997), in the context of social work research, rejects the view that there is a 'best' method for upholding feminist principles. Oakley (1998) has sought to rehabilitate quantitative methods and to integrate a range of methods in the task of creating an emancipatory social science. This debate has been side-stepped to some extent by Reinharz (1992), who has produced a useful compendium focusing on the diversity of methods actually used by feminist social scientists. She includes chapters on quantitative 'feminist survey research and other statistical research formats' and 'feminist experimental research', as well as the more qualitative approaches such as semi-structured and unstructured interviewing which are undoubtedly central to much feminist research practice. Nevertheless, feminist researchers have been in the forefront of devising innovative methods and of adapting existing ones. Examples include:

- *Correspondence* Using communication by letter between researchers and respondents (Letherby and Zdrodowski, 1995).
- *Story/dialogue* Structuring group dialogue around stories addressing particular themes relevant to practice (Labonte et al., 1999).

- *Focus groups*   Seen as a means of addressing the feminist critique of traditional methods (Wilkinson and Unger, 1999; Wilkinson, 1998).
- *Life histories; biographies*   As a means of revealing the key role of complex subjectivity and emotion in the development of feminist consciousness (Henwood, 1997).
- *Conversation analysis*   Seen as having potential for feminist researchers (Kitzinger, 2000).

See also Gergen et al. (1999) and Reinharz (1992, ch. 12), who review a wide selection of methods congenial to feminist research.

The stance taken in this book, while not accepting the full feminist critique, is that there is considerable virtue for real world research in taking on board feminist proposals – particularly in acknowledging the emotional aspects of doing real world research, and the value of emphasizing commitment as against detachment.

Suggested reading is provided at the end of the chapter.


## Using Multiple Methods


Even when the overall research strategy has been decided, a research question can, in almost all cases, be attacked by more than one method. As emphasized earlier, it is often the personal preferences of investigators, influenced by their past experiences, which dictate to them that they should use a particular strategy such as an experimental approach, or a grounded theory study. Similarly, specific methods may be selected simply because they are familiar. However, while there are questions for which, say, the structured interview seems the obvious tool to choose, it does not usually take much ingenuity to come up with a totally different approach which might be used.

There is no rule that says that only one method must be used in an investigation. Using more than one can have substantial advantages, even though it almost inevitably adds to the time investment required. Studies may combine methods producing quantitative data with others yielding qualitative data. Examples of such designs include Kopinak (1999), Tolson et al. (1999) and Winchester (1999); see also box 4.1, p. 84. One important benefit of multiple methods is in the reduction of *inappropriate certainty*. Using a single method and finding a pretty clear-cut result may delude investigators into believing that they have found the 'right' answer. Using other, additional, methods may point to differing answers which remove specious certainty. Unfortunately, such conflicting results across methods do add to confusion and uncertainty. Partisans of particular methods, or particular findings, may be convinced of the rightness of their opposing positions. There is also the general problem that, in so far as such conflicting findings get publicized and disseminated, they tend to reinforce lay views about the unreliability of social science research. Brewer and Hunter (1989) discuss strategies for minimizing these potential problems.

The main advantage of employing multiple methods is commonly cited as permitting *triangulation*. Triangulation, in surveying, is a method of finding out where something is by getting a 'fix' on it from two or more places. Analogously, Denzin (1988) suggested that this might be done in social research by using multiple and different *sources* (e.g. informants), *methods*, *investigators* or *theories*. For example, Nee and Taylor (2000) make use of both prison-based and 'natural environment' interviews with burglars, and draw comparisons between experimental and ethnographic studies. Foster (1997) advocates 'conceptual' triangulation by means of parallel fixed and flexible design strategies.

It is impossible to avoid the confounding effects of methods on our measurements. With a single method, some unknown part or aspect of the results obtained is attributable to the method used in obtaining the result. Hence it is argued that because we can never obtain results for which *some* method has not been used to collect them, the only feasible strategy is to use a variety of methods. (Blaikie, 1991, is one of several critics of this approach, arguing that it is inappropriate to combine methods based on different theoretical positions.) On this model, we should choose methods which are very different from each other to get a better estimate of 'the' answer. Using a logic equivalent to that of classical test theory, the error due to methods is regarded as tending to average out when multiple methods are used.

Multiple methods can help in other ways. Rather than focusing on a single, specific research question, they may be used to address different but complementary questions within a study. This focuses on the use of different methods for alternative tasks. A common example occurs when initial exploratory work is done by means of unstructured interviews, and subsequent descriptive and explanatory work employs a sample survey.

Multiple methods can also be used in complementary fashion to enhance interpretability. For example, in a primarily quantitative study, the interpretation of statistical analyses may be enhanced by a qualitative narrative account. Conversely, a qualitative account may be the major outcome of a study, but it can be enhanced by supportive quantitative evidence used to buttress and perhaps clarify the account. Hartley and Chesworth (2000) compare the results from qualitative and quantitative methods in a study of essay writing, showing that each has advantages and disadvantages. Two or more quantitative, or two or more qualitative methods could also be combined (see Bradford, 1990, who rated the behaviour of children during X-ray procedures on a systematic observation schedule, and followed the families up, assessing them on a number of psycho-social variables). Box 12.8 summarizes a range of ways in which qualitative and quantitative methods can be combined.

## Box 12.8

## Approaches to combining qualitative and quantitative methods

**1** *Triangulation* Checking the results of a qualitative method with those of a quantitative method (or vice versa).

**2** *Qualitative method used to facilitate fixed research design* Helps to provide information on context and participants; acts as a source of hypotheses; aids scale construction.

**3** *Quantitative method used to facilitate flexible research design* Quantitative method (e.g. survey) used to help select participants in a flexible design.

**4** *Provision of a general or more complete picture* Quantitative method used to fill a gap in a flexible design study (e.g. when the researcher can't be present because of other research commitments); when the research questions raise issues which can't be addressed by purely qualitative, or purely quantitative, methods.

**5** *Structure and process* Broadly speaking, fixed design research is more effective at getting at 'structural' aspects of social life, while flexible design research is more effective in dealing with processes. Combining them allows both aspects to be covered.

**6** *Researcher and participant perspectives* Fixed designs are typically focused on the researcher's perspective. Flexible designs can follow the participants' perspectives. A combined study can deal with both aspects.

**7** *Adding statistical generalizability* Flexible design research rarely permits statistical generalizability. Employing an additional qualitative method may permit some generalization.

**8** *Facilitating interpretation* Fixed designs are well adapted to establishing relationships between variables, but are typically weak in establishing the reasons for them. Qualitative methods can help in developing explanations.

**9** *Relations between macro and micro levels* Qualitative methods tend to focus on the small-scale, micro, aspects of social life. Quantitative methods are often concerned with more large-scale, macro aspects. Combining the two can help to integrate both levels.

**10**  *Stage of the research*   Different methods may be appropriate at different stages of the research process (for example, a fixed design study may be preceded by, or followed by, the use of qualitative methods).

**11**  *Hybrids*   One way to combine the two approaches is to use qualitative methods in a fixed design, or quantitative methods in a flexible design. For example, qualitative methods might be employed in a quasi-experimental design.

(Summarized from Bryman 1992, pp. 59–61.)

The *complementary purposes* notion can be used to assess the plausibility of threats to the validity of the primary research technique used. This is a tactic used particularly in the context of quasi-experimental approaches (see chapter 5, p. 133). The basic notion is that the particular pattern of findings and context of a specific quasi-experimental design may leave its interpretation open to particular 'threats'. So, for example, in a time series design, some persons may drop out of a treatment group during the course of a study (the 'mortality' effect). Interviews might be undertaken, both from this group and from those continuing, to assess whether there are differences between those who drop out and those who continue.

The basic message is that you need not be the prisoner of a particular method or technique when carrying out an enquiry. There is much to be said for multimethod enquiry. The main disadvantage (apart from the possibility that the methods produce conflicting results which need interpretation) is the time and resources needed to use each of the methods to a professional standard.

## Further Reading

Brannen, J., ed. (1992) *Mixing Methods: Qualitative and Quantitative Research.* Aldershot: Avebury. Mainly concerned with the issues involved in combining qualitative and quantitative approaches, but also includes a helpful set of case studies of various examples of mixing methods.

Greene, J. C. and Caracelli, V. J., eds (1997) *Advances in Mixed-Method Evaluation: The Challenges and Benefits of Integrating Diverse Paradigms.* San Francisco: Jossey-Bass. Similar agenda to Brannen (1992) but with analysis of illustrative cases from evaluation research.

Hakim, C. (1982) *Secondary Analysis in Social Research: A Guide to Data Sources and Methods with Examples.* London: Allen & Unwin. Very useful introduction to, and appraisal of, the uses of secondary analysis.

Krippendorff, K. (1980) *Content Analysis: An Introduction to its Methodology.* Newbury Park, Calif.: Sage. Comprehensive introduction with detailed suggestions for carrying out an analysis.

Lee, R. M. (2000) *Unobtrusive Measures in Social Research.* Buckingham: Open University Press. Essentially an updated version of Webb et al. (1966), written in a similarly engaging style. Includes useful section on unobtrusive measures and the internet.

Roberts, C. W., ed. (1997) *Text Analysis for the Social Sciences: Methods for Drawing Statistical Inferences from Texts and Transcripts.* Hove: Lawrence Erlbaum Associates. Interesting set of papers with wide range of suggested approaches.

Scott, J. (1990) *A Matter of Record.* Cambridge: Polity. Issues in documentary research. Useful appraisal grid for analysis of documentary evidence.

Tashakkori, A. and Teddlie, C. (1998) *Mixed Methodology: Combining Qualitative and Quantitative Approaches.* Thousand Oaks, Calif.: Sage. Practical guide to both mixed model and mixed method studies.

Webb, E. J., Campbell, D. T., Schwartz, R. D. and Sechrest, L. (2000) *Unobtrusive Measures*, rev. edn. Thousand Oaks, Calif.: Sage. Compendium of possible unobtrusive measures. Ingenious and wide-ranging. Covers ethics, and limitations of the measures. Note that while referred to as a revised edition, it is a reissue of the classic text first published in 1965. A second edition was published in 1981 by Houghton Mifflin.

*Further reading for 'additional approaches'*

In addition to the suggested reading for specific methods given below, these collections include introductions to several 'new paradigm' and other methods.

Morgan, G., ed. (1983) *Beyond Method: Strategies for Social Research.* Newbury Park, Calif.: Sage.

Reason, P. and Rowan, J., eds (1981) *Human Inquiry: A Sourcebook of New Paradigm Research.* New York: Wiley.

Smith, J. A., Harré, R. and Van Langenhove, L., eds (1998) *Rethinking Methods in Psychology.* London: Sage.

*Simulation*

Bryman, A. (1989) *Research Methods and Organisation Studies.* London: Unwin Hyman. Pages 214–20 cover uses of simulation in organizational research (including in-basket tests, simulating organizations and computer simulation).

Cohen, L., Manion, L. and Morrison, K. (2000) *Research Methods in Education*, 5th edn. London: Routledge/Falmer. Chapter on role-playing, setting it in the context of role-play as a substitute for deception in social psychological studies. Concentrates on role-play in educational settings, with examples.

Gilbert, N. and Troitzch, K. G. (1999) *Simulation for the Social Scientist.* Buckingham: Open University Press. Practical text on techniques of computer simulation.

Yardley, K. (1998) Role play. In J. A. Smith., R. Harré and L. Van Langenhove, eds (1998) *Rethinking Methods in Psychology*. London: Sage. Advice on how role-play can be made to work as a research method.

### Discourse analysis

Coulthard, M. (1977) *An Introduction to Discourse Analysis*. London: Longman. General introduction covering both social and cognitive aspects.

Gill, R. (1996) Discourse analysis: practical implementation. In J. T. E. Richardson, ed., *Handbook of Qualitative Research Methods for Psychology and the Social Sciences*. Leicester: BPS Books. Practical account on how to do it, with case study example.

Potter, J. and Wetherell, M. (1987) *Discourse and Social Psychology: Beyond Attitudes and Behaviour*. Newbury Park, Calif., and London: Sage. Accessible introduction to the theory and application of discourse analysis within social psychology. Wide range of examples.

### Repertory grid techniques

Burr, V. and Butt, T. (1992) *Invitation to Personal Construct Psychology*. London: Whurr. Very readable short introduction.

Cohen, L., Manion, L. and Morrison, K. (2000) *Research Methods in Education*, 5th edn. London: Routledge/Falmer. Chapter 19 provides a clear summary.

Fransella, F. and Bannister, D. (1977) *A Manual for Repertory Grid Technique*. London: Academic Press. Straightforward introduction to using grids.

### Verbal protocols

Ericsson, K. A. and Simon, H. A. (1984) *Protocol Analysis: Verbal Reports as Data*. Cambridge, Mass.: MIT Press. Key text to the principles of using verbal protocols.

Gilhooly, K. and Green, C. (1996a) Protocol analysis: theoretical background. In J. T. E. Richardson, ed., *Handbook of Qualitative Research Methods for Psychology and the Social Sciences*. Leicester: BPS Books. This, along with:

Gilhooly, K. and Green, C. (1996b) Protocol analysis; practical implementation. In J. T. E. Richardson, ed., *Handbook of Qualitative Research Methods for Psychology and the Social Sciences*. Leicester: BPS Books, provides a clear introduction to both the background and how to do it.

Johnson, G. I. and Briggs, P. (1994) Question-asking and verbal protocol techniques. In C. Cassell and G. Symon, eds, *Qualitative Methods in Organizational Research: A Practical Guide*. London: Sage. Short introduction focusing on organizational research.

### Meta-analysis

Hunter, J. E., Schmidt, F. L. and Jackson, G. B. (1982) *Meta-analysis: Cumulating Research Findings across Studies*. Newbury Park, Calif.: Sage. Thorough review of quantitative meta-analysis in the context of organizational research.

Noblitt, G. W. and Hare, R. D. (1988) *Meta-ethnography: Synthesizing Qualitative Studies*. Newbury Park, Calif., and London: Sage. Interesting attempt to apply meta-analysis to studies with qualitative data.

Rosenthal, R. (1984) *Meta-analytic Procedures for Social Research*. Newbury Park, Calif.: Sage. Accessible general coverage of quantitative meta-analysis.

*Feminist research methods*

Eichler, M. (1988) *Nonsexist Research Methods: A Practical Guide*. London: Unwin Hyman. Provides a systematic approach to identifying, eliminating and preventing sexist bias in social science research.

Hollway, W. (1989) *Subjectivity and Method in Psychology: Gender, Meaning and Science*. Newbury Park, Calif., and London: Sage. Attempts to show how 'psychology can be done differently'. Uses her work on subjectivity and gender difference to illustrate her feminist methodology.

Maynard, M. and Purvis, J., eds (1994) *Researching Women's Lives from a Feminist Perspective*. London: Taylor & Francis. Wide-ranging set of readings.

Reinharz, S. (1992) *Feminist Methods in Social Research*. Oxford: Oxford University Press. Compendium of wide range of methods used by feminist researchers. Extensive bibliography.

## Arranging the practicalities

### A   You need to know what you are doing before starting the data collection

Persevering to this stage should have got you fully equipped with a focus for your enquiry and some related research questions, which may be quite specific and concrete but are more likely to be relatively tentative. You will have given thought to the most appropriate research strategy and have sorted out the methods and techniques you need to implement this strategy.

Perhaps. This is the rational, sequential version of the enquiry process. However, there is a 'reconstructed logic' to the process, mirroring that of the scientific paper (Silverman, 1985, p. 4). Buchanan et al. (1988), in a paper which should be required reading for anyone contemplating real world research, emphasize the necessarily opportunistic flavour to much real world research. For example,

> a friend made a casual enquiry about our research . . . he suggested that we study his own company . . . We then discussed what the company would be prepared to let us do, and the research design was settled over a mixed grill and two pints of beer . . . the following week, after a couple of telephone calls and an exchange of letters, we met the manager responsible . . . It became clear that we should interview the head of the new word-processing section . . . our first interview with him started there and

then . . . the manager suggested that as the computer system was to be shut down on Wednesday . . . we could come back tomorrow . . . and interview our first batch of video typists. He also asked if we would like to see the minutes of the working party that had decided to install the system, and he produced from the drawer figures charting the performance of the company's typists since 1975. (pp. 54–5)

They stress that the published account (Buchanan and Boddy, 1982) implies that the research questions were based on a prior assessment of the literature, with the research strategy and methods being selected as most appropriate in this context. In fact there was no opportunity to carry out a formal literature review, explore other possible methods, or design and pilot interview schedules. In other words, enquiry in the real world is very much the 'art of the possible'. *They were able to carry out the study successfully because of a prior familiarity with the literature and the field, which helped frame the research questions, and their experience in carrying out similar studies.*

There are several 'insider accounts' of research projects which make very valuable reading for anyone seeking to carry out a project. These include Burgess (1984) and Bryman (1988b), the latter of whom provides many other examples. Luttrell (2000) reflects on the key decisions she made while carrying out ethnographic research. Deem (1996) provides an autobiographical account of her career as a researcher, emphasizing that, as in the progress of a research project, 'What has occurred has frequently been contingent, rarely linear, sometimes accidental and often serendipitous' (p. 6).

Such accounts reveal the fact that *experienced researchers can and do make a variety of mistakes*, including false starts and initial over-ambitiousness requiring substantial refocusing of the study. Novice researchers should take considerable heart from this. Such mistakes do not indicate that you are no good as a researcher; more that you are human. The accounts highlight the 'luck' or 'serendipity' factor (the 'happy knack of making fortunate discoveries'). It is also clear that the move from the traditional distant, uninvolved relationship between researcher and participant which is called for in most qualitative flexible design studies heightens the emotional dynamics of the research relationship, and is likely to generate considerable anxiety in the researcher (Berg, 1988). The emotional ante is raised for all concerned when sensitive topics are the focus of the study (Sutton and Schurman, 1988).

This injection of reality into the discussion does not indicate that consideration of the earlier sections of this text is a waste of time. The matters covered need to be internalized before you are in a position to follow this free-form approach. There are similarities to what Martin (1981) calls the 'garbage can' model of research. Here the four elements of research – theory, methods, resources and solutions – swirl about in the garbage can or decision space of the research project. Each influences the others, and the assumption of a sequence of steps in the research process is discarded.

*continued*

## B   Negotiating access

Much real world research takes place in settings where you require *formal* agreement from someone to gain access. Issues about access vary to a considerable extent with the kind of task you are carrying out and the nature of the organization concerned. Horn (1996) discusses the problems she encountered when researching the police force. In contrast to this experience, Punch (1986, p. 79) found much greater freedom when studying the Amsterdam police than in a study of a progressive private school. For more or less pure researchers, the task agenda is set by their perceptions of what is important in the academic discipline, say, in the development of a theoretical position, or in response to recent research. Thus it is the researcher's agenda that is important, and the access issue is essentially persuading people to let you in. If you are clear about your intentions, perhaps with a pretty tight, pre-structured design, then the task is probably easier initially, in that you can give them a good indication of what they are letting themselves in for. With a looser, more emergent design, there may be more difficulties as you are to some extent asking them to sign a 'blank cheque', as it is impossible to specify in advance exactly what you will do.

Studies with a more applied focus simplify some access problems and make others more complex, and more sensitive. If the study looks at 'practice' in some professional, industrial or business situation, there is the considerable advantage that you can legitimately present the study as relating to, and probably arising from, the concerns of practitioners. When you have been asked to do the study by persons from the institution or organization concerned, then at first sight this seems to solve problems of access. However, the investigator might, legitimately or not, be seen as a 'tool of management' supporting the squeezing of more blood out of the workers, or, conversely, as a dangerous agitator upsetting labour relations. In particular, studies with an overt 'change' approach are, almost by definition, disturbing. Even in a 'commissioned' study, you are very likely to want to observe and collect information from persons who were not party to the request for you to be involved.

Several researchers stress the need to be flexible and opportunistic. Buchanan et al. (1988) recommend using friends, relatives and contacts wherever possible. This is not always feasible, and for some styles of research may lead to sampling problems. However, they stress that in real world enquiry, the contest between what is theoretically desirable and practically possible must be won by the practical.

It is helpful to regard the negotiation of access as a continuing process rather than a single event. The checklist in box ATP.1 gives an indication of the things you might consider.

Much of this is common sense and simply requires you to be sensitively alert to requirements of the situation. Given that you are inevitably going to trespass upon other people's time, and are probably giving them extra work to do, for you to be there in good faith you must believe, and do all you can to ensure, that they get something out of it. This can be at many levels. People often derive considerable satisfaction from talking about what they are doing to a disinterested but sympathetic ear. Taking part in a study can lead to respondents reflecting on their

---

## Box ATP.1

### Checklist on negotiating access

**1**   Establish points of contact, and individuals from whom it is necessary to get permission.

**2**   Prepare an outline of the study.

**3**   Clear any necessary official channels by formally requesting permission to carry out the study. Permission may be needed at various 'levels'.

**4**   Discuss the study with 'gatekeepers' (e.g. manager, head-teacher). Go through study outline (purposes, conditions – including consent and participation). Attempt to anticipate potentially sensitive issues and areas.

**5**   Discuss the study with likely participants. Go through outline as above. May be with a group or with individuals, depending on circumstances.

**6**   Be prepared to modify the study in the light of these discussions (e.g. in respect of timing, treatment of sensitive issues).

---

experience in a way they find helpful. Stebbins (1987) makes helpful suggestions about 'fitting in', agreeing with Lofland and Lofland (1984) that you need to 'have enough knowledge about the setting or persons you wish to study *to appear competent to do so'*. Lofland and Lofland (1995) have an extensive and wise section on 'getting in' (ch. 3, pp. 31–45), which is well worth studying if this is likely to be a problem. Hall and Hall (1996, p. 61) provide a useful set of suggestions to help structure an initial discussion with members of an organization, oriented particularly towards the student researcher. In arguing for a formal contract to be drawn up in collaboration with all parties at the outset, Grinyer (1999, p. 3) suggests that it should cover the following issues:

- What happens if the research focus changes?
- Are there limitations on the type of data to be collected and their subsequent use?
- Who approves any publications?
- Who controls dissemination of the findings?
- Does the client see material before publication?
- Who owns the intellectual property rights?
- Can the client use the researcher's name and institution?
- What are the ethical implications and issues?
- How will the project be evaluated?
- Will the parties involved be continuously informed of the progress of the research?

*continued*

Such questions arise in most real world research and are not exclusive to 'contract' research.

There is a distinction between what is formally necessary to gain access, and what may be necessary over and above this to gain support and acceptance. The 'system' may not require you to get formal approval from a deputy head in a school, but if she is hostile to the study, it is not difficult for her to subvert it by, say, changing the timetabling arrangements. Formalities are necessary, not only to get you in, but also to refer back to if something goes wrong. People forget what they have agreed to, particularly if they had not thought through some of its implications. It can help to remind them of their agreed conditions, although they should be able to withdraw from the study if they wish.

Box ATP.2 gives a specification for a 'fully informed consent' form and box ATP.3 an example.

---

# Box ATP.2

## Specification for 'fully informed consent' form

You should prepare this form in advance of any contact with respondents, containing at a minimum:

**1** The name, address and telephone number of the person and/or agency seeking the consent.

**2** A statement of the purpose of the enquiry, sufficient to convey to the respondents what their role will be, and how the information collected will be used.

**3** Specific information on consent and participation, as follows:

a    intention to maintain confidentiality and anonymity;

b    measures to be taken to prevent data being linked with a specific informant and to limit access to data;

c    a note that the respondent has the right to withdraw from the study at any time;

d    a note that participation is entirely voluntary unless the respondent has already agreed, as a part of a prior contract, to participate in legitimate studies.

**4** A sign-off space for the participant in which they acknowledge having read and agreed to the previous stipulations as a condition of signing, with a space for the date.

**5** If the investigator intends to quote respondents, the consent form should also provide a second sign-off space in which that consent is specifically given.

**6** A copy of the signed consent form should be provided to the respondent.

## Box ATP.3

### Example of 'informed consent' form

*(To be read out by researcher before the beginning of the session – interview, experiment, etc. One copy of the form to be left with the respondent; one copy to be signed by the respondent and kept by the researcher.)*

My name is_____. I am doing research on a project entitled _____.
The project is sponsored by _____.
I am [X is] directing the project and can be contacted at

_____

_____

_____

(address and telephone number) should you have any questions.
Thank you for agreeing to take part in the project. Before we start I would like to emphasize that:

– your participation is entirely voluntary;
– you are free to refuse to answer any question;
– you are free to withdraw at any time.

The interview [or whatever] will be kept strictly confidential and will be available only to members of the research team. Excerpts from the interview/individual results may be made part of the final research report, but under no circumstances will your name or any identifying characteristics be included in the report.

Please sign this form to show that I have read the contents to you.

_____ (signed)
_____ (printed)
_____ date
Please send a report on the results of the project:

        YES                NO              (circle one)

Address for those requesting a research report

_____

_____

_____

*(Researcher to keep signed copy and leave unsigned copy with respondent.)*

There is evidence that the reduction in sample size which may result from this procedure has little or no biasing effect on the findings (Dent et al., 1997). The option of withdrawing from the study at a later time, without prejudice, is particularly necessary when relatively loose, emergent, designs are used. In these circumstances, it may not be possible to foretell all that is involved when the respondent is first approached for consent.

*A note on access and the 'insider'*  It is increasingly common for researchers to carry out a study directly concerned with the setting in which they work. Teachers look at their own local authority, school or even classroom; social workers or 'health' personnel seek to evaluate or otherwise study some aspect of the service they are providing; the personnel department of a firm investigates its own interviewing procedures.

There are clear practical advantages to this kind of 'insider' research. You won't have to travel far. Generally you will have an intimate knowledge of the context of the study, both as it is at present and in a historical or developmental perspective. You should know the politics of the institution, not only of the formal hierarchy but also how it 'really works' (or, at least, an unexamined common-sense view of this). You will know how best to approach people. You should have 'street credibility' as someone who will understand what the job entails, and what its stresses and strains are. In general, you will already have in your head a great deal of information which it takes an outsider a long time to acquire.

The disadvantages are, however, pretty substantial. Adding the role of researcher to that of colleague is difficult both for yourself and for your co-workers. Interviewing colleagues can be an uncomfortable business, particularly in hierarchical organizations if they are higher in status than yourself. Supposing that you obtain confidential information, appropriately enough within the conditions of confidentiality of the research. Is this going to affect your working relationship with colleagues? If you make mistakes during the study, you are going to have to live with them afterwards. More fundamentally, how are you going to maintain objectivity, given your previous and present close contact with the institution and your colleagues?

Given this mixture of advantage and disadvantage, there is much to be said in favour of using mixed insider–outsider research teams. Thomas et al. (2000) describe an example and discuss the issues involved.

Grady and Wallston (1988, pp. 29–31) discuss these issues in the context of health care settings, but they identify principles that are of general application:

- *Try to foresee likely conflicts*  For example, collecting data about drug and alcohol abuse by pregnant teenagers called for a non-reactive researcher; the same person as 'helping professional' appreciated the consequences of the abuse.
- *Make a plan to deal with them*  In the abuse example, non-reaction might be construed as acknowledgement that the behaviour was not harmful, or that

no help was available, and so a procedure was developed to provide appropriate referrals at the end of the interview session when base-line data had been collected.

- *Record your responses*  It helps to have a full log with notes made after each session so that they can be subsequently scrutinized for possible contaminating effects on the research.
- *Where possible, get the collaboration of researcher colleagues from outside the situation*  They will help you to maintain the researcher stance.

## C  Get yourself organized

As soon as is feasible, you need to work out schedules for the arrangement and timing of sessions for observation, interviewing, etc. The extent to which this is pre-plannable depends very much on the style of your enquiry, but even with a flexible design, you are likely to be pressed for time and need (flexible) plans. Use calendars or wall charts to draw up timed and sequenced activity lists or flow charts. Howard and Sharp (1996) suggest techniques useful for complex projects, including network analysis and control charts.

## D  Pilot if at all possible

The first stage of any data gathering should, if at all possible, be a 'dummy run' – a pilot study. This helps to throw up some of the inevitable problems of converting your design into reality. Some methods and techniques necessarily involve piloting in their use (e.g. in the development of a structured questionnaire or a direct observation instrument). Fixed design studies can and should be piloted on a small scale in virtually all circumstances. Most flexible designs can incorporate piloting within the study itself. The effort needed in gaining access and building up acceptance and trust is often such that one would be reluctant to regard a case study or ethnographic study simply as a pilot. Of course, if things go seriously wrong, for whatever reason, or it appears that the situation is not going to deliver in relation to your research questions, then it is better to transfer your efforts elsewhere.

## E  Work on your relationships

Formal approval from the boss may get you in, but you then need informal agreement and acceptance from informants, respondents or participants in order to gather worthwhile data. This is largely a matter of relationships. You have to establish that you can be relied on to keep promises about confidentiality, etc. It is assumed that you are not proposing to deceive them, and so you can share with them the general aims of your study and genuinely get over the message that you are there because you feel they can contribute.

*continued*

## F   Don't just disappear at the end

It helps you, and everybody concerned, if your initial negotiations set a period for your involvement and a date for your departure. It can be difficult to leave, particularly when things have gone well and you are an accepted part of the scene. There will almost always be more data that it would be desirable to collect. However, in real world enquiry, cutting your coat to fit a fixed length of cloth is often part of the reality, and it helps to concentrate your efforts.

Make sure that people know that you are going. Honour your commitments. Keep your bridges in good order so that you can return if necessary -- and so that you haven't spoiled things for later researchers.

## G   Don't expect it to work out exactly as you planned

'Trouble awaits those unwary souls who believe that research flows smoothly and naturally from questions to answers via a well organized data collection system' (Hodgson and Rollnick, 1989, p. 3). It is as well to appreciate this from the start in real world research or you will be in for a dispiriting shock. Measles plays havoc with your carefully planned school sessions, or unseasonal snow cuts you off. Strikes shut down the plant or, even more frustrating, a 'work to rule' or 'withdrawal of goodwill' closes it to you. Communication channels do not function. The hospital you phoned yesterday to confirm an appointment denies your very existence. Hodgson and Rollnick provide a serious set of suggestions on 'how to survive in research' in a jocular manner. This includes a list of aphorisms well worth taking on board ('Getting started will take at least as long as the data collection'; 'A research project will change twice in the middle'; etc.) and a set of maxims for keeping going, based on the practices of Alcoholics Anonymous (e.g. 'one day at a time': don't be overwhelmed by the size of the task; focus on smaller goals).

Having some flexibility built in and a 'forgiving' design (where it is possible to substitute one case or activity for another) helps. Experimental designs, sabotaged by breakdowns in sampling procedures or some other reason, can be sometimes patched up as quasi-experimental equivalents. Hakim (1987, ch. 10) provides a very useful section on 'trading down to a cheaper design' to cope with reductions in resources or time available.

# Part IV
## Dealing with the Data

The central, totally indispensable, part of a real world enquiry is the collection of data. No data – no project. The specifics of data collection are bound up with the different methods of investigation. Whatever methods are used, there is a need for a systematic approach to the task – a need probably, paradoxically, at its greatest in so-called 'soft' methods such as participant observation and unstructured interviewing. Once you have data, the next step is analysis.

### Collecting the data

Collecting the data is about using the selected methods of investigation. Doing it properly means using these methods in a systematic, professional fashion. The chapters in part III covered the issues raised in the use of specific methods. At this stage you need to ask yourself the following questions:

#### A   Have you explored thoroughly the choice of methods?

There is no general 'best method'. The selection of methods should be driven by the kind of research questions you are seeking to answer. This has to be moderated by what is feasible in terms of time and other resources; by your skills and expertise; and possibly, in commissioned research, by the predilections of the sponsor.

#### B   What mix of methods do you propose to use?

The virtues of multimethod enquiry have been emphasized in the previous chapter (p. 370). All methods have strengths and weaknesses and you are seeking to match the strength of one to the weakness of another, and vice versa. If it is impracticable to use more than one method, don't worry – many studies are still monomethod. Don't give up too easily, though – it is often possible to devote a small fraction of your effort to a complementary method. This might be an unstructured interview session at the end of an experiment. Or, perhaps, two or three mini case studies based on observation, interview and document analysis – linked to a questionnaire survey.

## C   Have you thought through potential problems in using the different methods?

You don't choose methods unless you have the skills and personality characteristics they call for (I would pay a fairly substantial amount not to have to do a telephone survey involving 'cold' calling). Nor if they would be unacceptable in the setting involved. Nor if they raise ethical concerns. Pilot work almost always brings out problems: better then than in the middle of a fixed design study.

## D   Do the methods have the flexibility that you need?

You don't do fixed design research unless you have a clear idea about what you are doing before the main data collection starts. If you don't, you use some type of flexible design. The methods themselves in flexible design study need to have a corresponding flexibility (e.g. relatively unstructured observation and interview). This does not preclude a move on to a confirmatory phase at a later stage of the study using more structured instruments.

## E   Whatever methods you use, data collection calls for commitment

You have to care: both about the substantive area, and about your responsibilities as a researcher. This dual commitment is crucial. Care solely about getting answers to the research questions, and particularly about 'helping', and you are in danger of losing objectivity and the ability to appraise the evidence fairly. Caring only about doing a good piece of research may lead to the degree of detachment rightly castigated by feminist methodologists (see p. 369). And you need high commitment not only to do a quality job, but also to get you through the inevitable bad times while you are doing it.

## Analysing and Interpreting the Data

After data have been collected in an enquiry, they have at some stage to be analysed and interpreted. The model traditional in fixed design research is for this to take place after all the data are safely gathered in. It is, however, central to flexible design research that you start this analysis and interpretation when you are in the middle of the enquiry. Analysis, at whatever stage, is necessary because, generally speaking, data in their raw form do not speak for themselves. The messages stay hidden and need careful teasing out. The process and products of analysis provide the bases for interpretation. It is often the case that, while in the middle of analysing data, ideas for interpretation arise (which is a disadvantage of relying on the now virtually ubiqitous, and immensely useful, computer packages for analysis of quantitative data).

Analysis, then, is not an empty ritual, carried out for form's sake between doing the study and interpreting it. Nor is it a bolt-on feature which can be safely ignored until all the data are collected. If you do this, you are likely to end up with an unanalysable mish-mash of quantitative data which no known test or procedure can redeem. Or a mountain of qualitative data which keeps you awake at night wondering what to do with it.

Hence, as emphasized in part II, thinking about how the analysis *might* be carried out forms an integral part of the design process for any investigation. A particular disposition of your resources which, say, gets more data from a smaller number of respondents, or fewer data from a greater number of respondents, might make all the difference between there being a straightforward path of analysis and a highly dubious one. If you have thought through such an analysis, that is then available as a 'banker'. You can then, with confidence, explore the data when they are in, and see if there are alternative or additional messages you can get from them.

The intention here is to sensitize you to analysis issues and to cover a range of ways of dealing with both quantitative and qualitative data. *The aims are primarily to set out guidelines and principles to use in selecting appropriate procedures, and to discuss how the results obtained from these procedures might be interpreted.*

Little attempt is made to cover computational aspects. The advent of powerful computers and statistical packages removes the need for factual knowledge about formulae or for craft skills in performing complex calculations. No doubt inertia in the presentation of courses, and remnants of the puritan ethic, will force further generations of students through these satisfyingly labour-intensive hoops. However, there are more profitable ways of spending your time than doing something which a computer can do better, and more quickly. This does not gainsay, as mentioned above, the value to interpretation of really getting to know your data by playing about with them. And this is also something with which the computer can help.

## Preparing for analysis

You have collected some, or all, of your data. You now need to understand them. Data come in all sorts of shapes and sizes – audio- and video-tapes, sets of instrument readings or test results, responses to questionnaires, diary entries, reports of meetings, documents, etc., etc. Many of them are either words or numbers – or can, without too much difficulty, be turned into words or numbers. And some features of the words can be captured in numbers. So we have *qualitative analysis* (for words, and other data which come in a non-numerical form) and *quantitative analysis* (for numbers, and other data that can be transformed into numbers). Much real world study produces both, and it is important that you are able to deal competently with the two kinds.

## A    Seek advice about quantitative analysis

A vast technology on the carrying out of quantitative (or statistical) analysis exists, and it would be foolish to expect everyone carrying out an enquiry to have all of it at their fingertips. There is a tendency to gain some familiarity with a narrow range of approaches and then be determined to use them. This means either inappropriate analyses or severe restrictions on the type of research questions you can tackle (the analytic equivalent of the one-track methods person who tackles everything with a questionnaire). The technique of 'analysis of variance', as used by some experimental psychologists, provides a case in point.

A more extreme, though not uncommon, response is to shun all things quantitative and stick solely to qualitative analyses. Although this may be presented in terms of ideological objection to positivistic quantitative approaches, suspicion remains that there may be other blocks to the use of statistics.

One solution is to get advice from a consultant or other person familiar with a wide range of approaches to the quantitative analysis of social research data, and to get that advice at the design stage of your project, *not after you have collected the data*. The advice should also, in many cases, home you in on a computer package which will do the analytical work for you. All this does not mean that you come naked to the consultant's table. It is important that you have at least an intuitive grasp of the kinds of approaches that might be taken, so that you know what is being talked about. Chapter 13 seeks to do that job. Even if you are on your own with no consultant available, it will sensitize you to a range of possibilities which, with further reading, you should be able to implement.

## B    You are going to have to do much of the qualitative analysis for yourself

Qualitative analysis has now, like horticulture, moved out of the 'muck and magic' phase. It was commonly held that there was some ineffable mystique whereby the methods could only be used by experienced researchers admitted to the magic circle after a lengthy apprenticeship. Following Merton et al.'s insistence (1956, p. 17) that this is no 'private and incommunicable art', serious attempts have been made to show that qualitative analysis can be systematized and made widely accessible. These approaches are discussed in chapter 14.

However, while there are helpful routines and procedures, they are less technical and differentiated than much statistical analysis – closer to codified common
sense. It will undoubtedly be helpful to get external help and support to carry out
qualitative analysis from someone with experience in this field. This, however, is
more concerned with getting feedback on the processes you are using, and checking the warrant for the interpretations you are making. There are computer packages to facilitate the process, but they in no sense do the job of analysis for you
in the way that a statistical package does.

# 13
# The Analysis of Quantitative Data

## with Darren Langdridge

This chapter:

- stresses the advantages of using a software package when analysing quan- titave data, and your likely need for help and advice when doing this
- shows how to create a data set for entry into a computer
- distinguishes between exploratory and confirmatory data analysis
- explains statistical significance and discusses its controversial status
- advocates greater reliance on measures of effect sizes
- suggests how to explore, display and summarize the data
- discusses ways of analysing relationships between various types of data and a range of statistical tests that might be used
- does the same thing for analysing differences between data
- shows how SPSS (the Statistical Package for the Social Sciences) can be used to carry out these analyses
- discusses issues specific to the analysis of quasi-experiments, single-case experiments and non-experimental fixed designs

## Introduction

You would have to work quite hard in an enquiry not to generate at least some data that were in the form of numbers, or could be sensibly turned into numbers of some kind. Hence, techniques for dealing with such quantitative data are an essential feature of your professional tool-kit. Their analysis covers a wide range of areas, from simple organization of the data to complex statistical analysis. This chapter does not attempt a comprehensive treatment of all aspects of quantitative data analysis. Its main aim is to help you appreciate some of the issues involved so that you have a feeling for the questions you need to ask when deciding on an appropriate kind of analysis.

## Three assumptions

*1   You are likely to be using one or more of the excellent software packages now available for personal computers*   If you have only a very small amount of quantitative data, it may be appropriate for you to carry out analyses 'by hand' (or with the help of an electronic calculator). However, the drudgery and potential for error in such calculation, and the ease with which the computer can perform such mundane chores for you, suggest strongly that you make use of the new technology if at all possible. The power, speed and storage capacity of modern personal computers, and the features and capabilities of current software packages, should enable you to cope with the statistical requirements of the kinds of projects dealt with in this book.

Perhaps the most popular software package for statistical analysis in the social sciences is SPSS (the Statistical Package for the Social Sciences – available in both Windows and Macintosh versions). However, for simple statistical texts, you may not require such specialist software; spreadsheet software such as Excel can perform a range of statistical tasks (Pelosi et al., 1998). This chapter provides examples of the ways in which SPSS for Windows v. 10 deals with analysis, and shows how the results of the main analyses are presented. Earlier versions of SPSS for Windows produce similar output.

A number of books have been produced which specifically concentrate on quantitative data analysis using SPSS for Windows. If you are using SPSS without specialist assistance, you should get hold of one of them, as it is not feasible in a general text to provide the detailed help you will need. These include Bryman and Cramer (1997), Foster (2001) and Brace et al. (2000). Each of these texts provides an accessible, well-thought-through introduction to the use of SPSS for Windows for the statistical analysis of data. Gray and Kinnear (1998) provide a corresponding manual for the Macintosh version.

SPSS is, of course, not the only package available. If you are familiar with a different one, and/or have a statistical adviser experienced in its use, use it.

*2   You have some prior acquaintance with the basic concepts and language of statistical analysis*   If not, you are recommended to spend some time with one of the many texts covering this material at an introductory level (e.g. Robson, 1994).

*3   You will seek help and advice in carrying out quantitative data analysis*   The field of quantitative data analysis is complex and specialized, and it is unreasonable to expect everyone carrying out real world enquiry to be a statistical specialist. It is, unfortunately, a field where it is not at all difficult to carry out an analysis which is simply wrong, or inappropriate, for your data or your purposes. The negative side of readily available analytic software is that it becomes much easier to generate elegantly presented rubbish (remember GIGO – garbage in, garbage out).

Preferably, such advice should come from an experienced statistician sympathetic to the particular difficulties involved in 'human' enquiry. It should be sought at the earliest possible stage in the *design* of your project. Inexperienced non-numerate researchers often have a touching faith that enquiry is a linear process in which first they collect the data and then the statistician shows them the analysis to carry out. It is, however, all too easy to end up with unanalysable data, which, if they had been collected in a somewhat different way, would have been readily analysable. In the absence of personal statistical support, you should be able to use this chapter to get an introduction to the kind of approach you might take. The references provided should then help with more detailed coverage.

## Organization of the chapter

The chapter first covers the creation of a 'data set' as a necessary precursor to using SPSS or other software for data analysis. Suggestions are then made about how you might carry out various types of statistical data analysis appropriate for different research designs and tasks.

# Creating a Data Set

The point has already been made that you should be thinking about how your data are to be analysed at the design stage of your project. This is important not only to ensure that what you collect is analysable, but also to simplify as much as possible the actual process of analysis.

If you are to make use of a software package for analysis, then the data must be entered into the computer in the form required by the software. This may be done in different ways:

1   *Direct automatic entry*   It may be feasible for the data to be generated in such a way that entry is automatic. For example, you may be using a structured observation schedule with some data collection device (either a specialized instrument or a notebook computer) so that the data as collected are directly usable by the analysis software.

2   *Creation of a computer file which is then 'imported' to the analysis software*   It may be easier for your data to be entered into a computer after collection. For example, a survey might use questionnaires which are 'optically readable'. Respondents or the person carrying out the survey fill in boxes on the form corresponding to particular answers. The computer can directly transform this response into data which it can use. Such data form a computer 'file' which is then 'imported' into the particular analysis software being used. This is feasible with SPSS, although you may need assistance to ensure that the transfer takes place satisfactorily.

3   *Direct 'keying' of data into analysis software*   For much small-scale enquiry, automatic reading or conversion of the data into a computer file will be either not possible or not economically justifiable. There is then the requirement for manual entry of data into the analysis software. The discussion below assumes that you will be entering the data in this way.

Whichever approach is used, the same principle applies – try at the design stage to capture your data in a form which is going to simplify this entry process. Avoid intermediate systems where the original response has to be further categorized. The more times data are transferred between coding systems, the greater the chance of error. *Single-transfer coding* (i.e. where the response is already in the form which has to be entered into the computer) is often possible with attitude and other scales, multiple-choice tests, inventories, checklists and many questionnaires. In a postal or similar survey questionnaire, you will have to weigh up whether it is more important to simplify the task of the respondent or the task of the person transferring the code to the computer. Box 13.1 shows possible alternatives.

The conventions on coding are essentially common sense. Suggestions were made in chapter 8 (p. 257) about how this might be dealt with in relation to questionnaires. Note that it is helpful to include the coding boxes on the questionnaire itself, conventionally in a column on the right-hand side of each page.

The data sets obtained from other types of enquiry will be very various. However, it is almost always possible to have some sensible arrangement of the data into *rows* and *columns*. Typically, each row corresponds to a *record* or *case*. This might be all of the data obtained from a particular respondent. A record consists of *cells* which contain data. The cells in a column contain the data for a particular *variable*. Box 13.2 presents a simple example derived from a survey-type study. A similar matrix would be obtained from a simple experiment where, say, the columns represent scores obtained under different experimental conditions.

---

## Box 13.1

### Question formats requiring (a) single-transfer coding and (b) double-transfer coding

a      How many children are there in your school?

| under 40 | 40–49 | 50–59 | 60–69 | 70–79 | 80–89 | 90–100 | over 100 |
|----------|-------|-------|-------|-------|-------|--------|----------|
| code   1 | 2     | 3     | 4     | 5     | 6     | 7      | 8        |

enter code (  )

b      How many children are there in your school?

(please circle)

under 40   40–49   50–59   60–69   70–79   80–89   90–100   over 100

(response has then to be translated into appropriate code).

---

## Box 13.2

### Faculty, entry points, degree classification and income two years after graduating of a sample of students

| Student | Faculty | Sex | Entry points | Degree class | Income (£) |
|---------|---------|-----|--------------|--------------|------------|
| 1  | A  | F | 14 | 2.1  | 14,120 |
| 2  | EN | M | 6  | 2.2  | 15,900 |
| 3  | EN | M | 5  | Fail | 11,200 |
| 4  | ED | F | 10 | 2.2  | 21,640 |
| 5  | S  | M | 4  | 2.1  | 25,000 |
| 6  | B  | F | 13 | 2.1  | 11,180 |
| 7  | A  | F | 16 | 2.1  | 12,600 |
| 8  | EN | M | 6  | 3    | 9,300  |
| 9  | ED | M | 5  | 3    | 2,200  |
| 10 | EN | M | *  | 2.2  | 17,880 |

*Key*: A = Arts; B = Business; ED = Education; EN = Engineering; S = Sciences; M = Male; F = Female; * = missing data
*Note*: Data are fictitious, but modelled on those in Linsell and Robson, 1987.

## Entering the data into the analysis software

The details of the procedure for entering this data set into the computer vary according to the particular software you are using. With early versions of SPSS this was quite complex, but later versions are very straightforward to use, particularly if you are familiar with the operation of spreadsheets.

*Columns*   Each column in the 'data view' window represents a variable in your data. You should define how each column is labelled and what kind of data will be entered in the cells of a column. Various types of data can be dealt with, including *integers* (whole numbers), *real numbers* (numbers with fractional parts; e.g. 10.34) and *categories* (e.g. 'gender', which has the *elements* 'male' and 'female').

Creating a data set with SPSS simply involves defining the characteristics for each column in the data set. This is done simply by double-clicking on the 'var' label at the top of each column. SPSS v. 10 differs from previous versions in the way that you define the characteristics of your data. Data are entered in the 'Data View' window but each variable is defined (in terms of type of data, missing values etc.) in the 'Variable View' window (you move between these windows by clicking on either the 'Data View' or 'Variable View' at the bottom left of the screen).

*Rows*   Each row in the 'Data View' window represents a record or case. In the example these are the data for an individual student. When the columns have been defined (in the 'Variable View' window), all you have to do is start entering the data, cell by cell, one column or case at a time. Figure 13.1 shows the result of doing this: a simple reformulation of the data table from box 13.2.

*Missing data*   'The most acceptable solution to the problem of missing information is not to have any' (Youngman, 1979, p. 21). While this is obviously a counsel of perfection, it highlights the problem that there is no really satisfactory way of dealing with missing data (see Huisman, 2000, for some suggestions). In social research, it may well be that the reason why data are missing is in some way related to the question being investigated. Those who avoid filling in the evaluation questionnaire, or who are not present at a session, may well have different views from those who responded. So it is well worth spending considerable time, effort and ingenuity in seeking to ensure a full response. Software normally has one or more ways of dealing with missing data when performing analyses, and it may be necessary to investigate this further as different approaches can have substantially different effects on the results obtained.

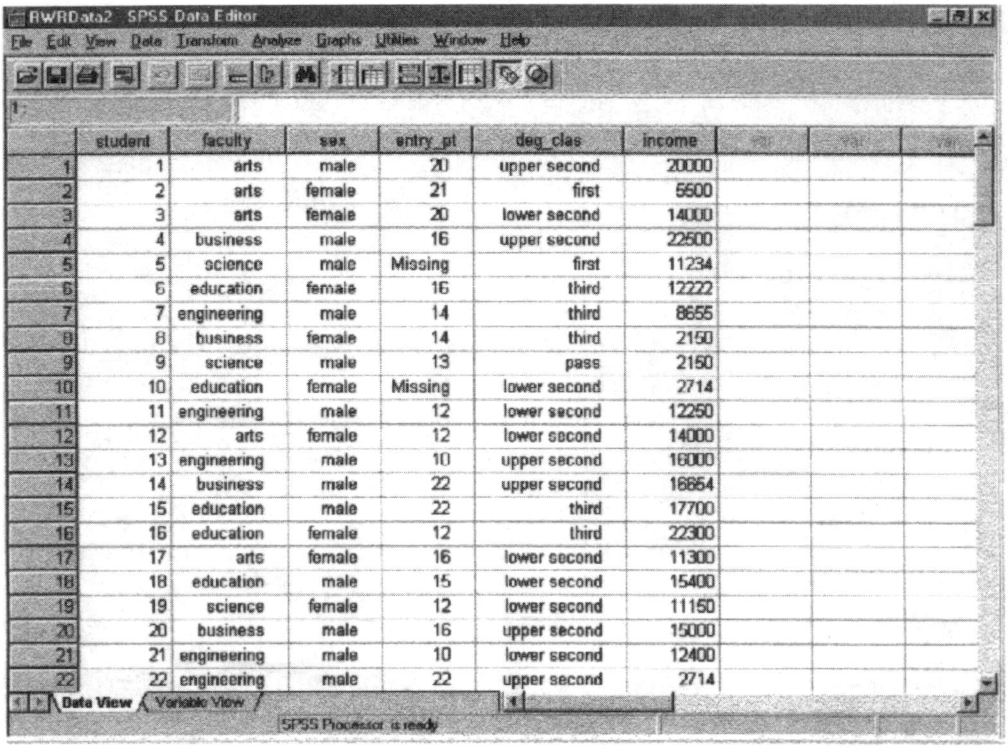

| | student | faculty | sex | entry_pt | deg_clas | income |
|---|---|---|---|---|---|---|
| 1 | 1 | arts | male | 20 | upper second | 20000 |
| 2 | 2 | arts | female | 21 | first | 5600 |
| 3 | 3 | arts | female | 20 | lower second | 14000 |
| 4 | 4 | business | male | 16 | upper second | 22500 |
| 5 | 5 | science | male | Missing | first | 11234 |
| 6 | 6 | education | female | 16 | third | 12222 |
| 7 | 7 | engineering | male | 14 | third | 8655 |
| 8 | 8 | business | female | 14 | third | 2150 |
| 9 | 9 | science | male | 13 | pass | 2150 |
| 10 | 10 | education | female | Missing | lower second | 2714 |
| 11 | 11 | engineering | male | 12 | lower second | 12250 |
| 12 | 12 | arts | female | 12 | lower second | 14000 |
| 13 | 13 | engineering | male | 10 | upper second | 16000 |
| 14 | 14 | business | male | 22 | upper second | 16654 |
| 15 | 15 | education | male | 22 | third | 17700 |
| 16 | 16 | education | female | 12 | third | 22300 |
| 17 | 17 | arts | female | 16 | lower second | 11300 |
| 18 | 18 | education | male | 15 | lower second | 15400 |
| 19 | 19 | science | female | 12 | lower second | 11150 |
| 20 | 20 | business | male | 16 | upper second | 15000 |
| 21 | 21 | engineering | male | 10 | lower second | 12400 |
| 22 | 22 | engineering | male | 22 | upper second | 2714 |

**Figure 13.1** Data table in SPSS for Windows (part only).

Technically, there is no particular problem in coding data as missing. There simply needs to be a signal code which is used for missing data, and only for missing data. Don't get in the habit of using 0 (zero) to code for missing data, as this can cause confusion if the variable in question could have a zero value, or if any analytic procedure treats it as a value of zero. Ninety-nine or –1 are frequently used. SPSS will show the value that you have specified as missing data and deals with it intelligently (e.g. by computing averages based only on the data present).

It is worth noting that a distinction may need to be made between missing data where there is no response from someone, and a 'don't know' or 'not applicable' response, particularly if you have catered for possible responses of this type by including them as one of the alternatives.

## Cleaning the data set after entry

Just as one needs to proof-read text for errors, so a computer data set needs to be checked for errors made while 'keying in' the data. One of the best ways of doing this is for the data to be entered twice, independently, by two people. Any discrepancies can then be resolved. This can be very time-consuming but is worthwhile, particularly if substantial data analysis is likely.

A valuable tip is to make use of 'categorical' variables whenever feasible. So, in the data set of box 13.2, 'degree class' has the categories 'first, 'upper second', etc. The advantage is that the software will clearly show where you have entered an invalid value (especially if you specify that you want 'value labels' to be viewed).

While this eliminates several potential mistakes, it is, of course, still possible to enter the wrong class for an individual. The direct equivalent of proof-reading can be carried out by checking the computer data set carefully against the original set. Simple *frequency analyses* (see below, p. 403) on each of the columns (variables) are helpful. This will throw up any instances where 'illegal', or highly unlikely, codes have been entered. For continuous variables *box plots* can be drawn, and potential 'outliers' highlighted (see p. 410).

*Cross-tabulation*   This involves counting the codes from one variable that occur for each code in a second variable. It can show up more subtle errors. Suppose that the two variables are 'withdrew before completing degree' and 'class of final degree'. Cross-tabulation might throw up one or two students who appeared to have withdrawn before completion, but were nevertheless awarded a classified degree. These should then be checked, as while this might be a legitimate result (perhaps they returned) it could well be a miscoding. Cross-tabulation is easy when the variables have only a few values, as is the case with most categorical variables. However, it becomes very tedious when continuous variables such as age or income, which can take on many values, are involved. In this circumstance, scatterplots (see below, p. 419) provide a useful tool. These are graphs in which corresponding codes from two variables give the horizontal and vertical scale values of points representing each record. 'Deviant' points which stand out from the general pattern can be followed up to see whether they are genuine or miscoded.

*The 'cleaned' data set is an important resource for your subsequent analyses. It is prudent to keep a couple of copies, with one of the copies being at a separate physical location from the others. You will be likely to modify the set in various ways during analysis (e.g. by combining codes); however, you should always retain copies of the original data set.*

## Starting Data Analysis

Now that you have a data set entered into the computer, you are no doubt itching to do something with it. Data analysis is commonly divided into two broad types: exploratory and confirmatory. As the terms suggest, exploratory analysis explores the data, trying to find out what they tell you. Confirmatory analysis seeks to establish whether you have actually got what you expected to find (for example on the basis of theory, such as predicting the operation of particular mechanisms).

With all data sets, and whatever type of research design, there is much to be said for having an initial exploration of the data. Try to get a feeling for what you have got, and what it is trying to tell you. Play about with it. Simple graphical displays help: charts, histograms, graphs, pie-charts, etc. Get summaries in the form of means and measures of the amount of variability, etc. Details on what is meant by these terms, and how to do it, are presented later in this chapter. Acquiring this working knowledge is particularly useful when you are going on to use various statistical tests with SPSS. Statistical packages will cheerfully and quickly produce complex nonsense if you ask them the wrong question or misunderstand how you enter the data. A good common-sense understanding of the data set will help to protect you against this.

Exploratory approaches of various kinds have been advocated at several points during this book. They are central to much flexible design research. While these designs mainly generate qualitative data, strategies such as case study commonly also result in quantitative data which we need to explore to see what has been found, and to help direct later stages of data collection.

Much fixed design research is exclusively quantitative. The degree of pre-specification of design and of pre-thought-about possible analyses called for in fixed design research means that the major task in data analysis is confirmatory: i.e. we are seeking to establish whether our predictions or hypotheses have been confirmed by the data. Such *confirmatory data analysis* (CDA) is the mainstream approach in statistical analysis.

However, there is an influential modern approach to quantitative analysis known as *exploratory data analysis* (EDA), advocated by Tukey (1977) – see also Velleman and Hoaglin (1981) and Lovie and Lovie (1991). Tukey's approach and influence come in at two levels. First, he has proposed several ingenious ways of displaying data diagramatically. These devices, such as 'box plots', are non-controversial, deserve wider recognition and are discussed below (p. 410). The more revolutionary aspect of the EDA movement is the centrality it places on an informal, pictorial approach to data. EDA is criticized for implying that the pictures are all that you need, that the usual formal statistical procedures involving tests, significance levels, etc. are unnecessary. However, Tukey (1977) does acknowledge the need for CDA. In his view, it complements EDA and provides a way of formally testing the relatively risky inductions made through EDA.

To a large extent, EDA is simply regularizing the very common process whereby researchers make inferences about relationships between variables after an enquiry which their study was not designed to test formally – or which they had not expected prior to the enquiry – and providing helpful tools for that task. It mirrors the suggestion made in chapter 5 (p. 97) that while, in fixed design research, strong pre-specification is essential and you have clear expectations of what the results will show (i.e. the task of analysis is primarily confirmatory), this does not preclude additional exploration.

In practice the EDA/CDA distinction is not clear cut. As de Leeuw puts it (in Van de Geer, 1993), there is a view that

> The scientist does all kinds of dirty things to his or her data . . . and at the end of this thoroughly unrespectable phase he or she comes up (miraculously) with a theory, model, or hypothesis. This hypothesis is then tested with the proper confirmatory statistical methods. [This] is a complete travesty of what *actually* goes on in all sciences some of the time and in some sciences all of the time. There are no two phases that can easily be distinguished. (emphasis in original)

> *The treatment in this chapter is influenced by EDA and seeks to follow its spirit. However, there is no attempt to make a rigid demarcation between 'exploring' and 'confirming' aspects.*

While SPSS is more concerned with confirmatory analysis and not particularly oriented to EDA approaches, it is possible to use it to generate box plots and many other displays. Display techniques have, of course, been around before 1977 and EDA. Several of these are presented in the following sections.

## The significance test controversy

For many social scientists, quantitative analysis is virtually synonymous with significance testing. The whole point and purpose of the exercise is taken to be answering the question: 'Have we got a significant result?' 'Is $p < 0.05$?' This refers to *statistical significance*. (I am grateful to a reviewer, Joe Maxwell, who pointed out the potentially misleading treatment of statistical significance in a draft version of this text. The following discussion leans heavily on material which he kindly provided.)

The probability that a significance test gives you is not the probability that a result is due to chance (as is commonly claimed). What a $p$ value actually tells you is something that sounds very similar to this statement, but is in fact quite different. It tells you how likely it would be that you would get the difference you did (or one more extreme), by chance alone, if there really is no difference, in the population from which you drew your sample, between the categories represented by your groups. (This assumption of 'no difference' is referred to as the 'null hypothesis'). In other words, a statistical significance test 'tests' the plausibility that the null hypothesis – no difference between the population means – is true; if your result would be very unlikely if the null hypothesis were true, this makes it less plausible that the null hypothesis is true.

Thus, the result of a statistical significance test tells you nothing directly about the actual population to which you want to make inferences; it simply helps you to rule out one possible validity threat to your result – namely, that the result could be due to random variation in your sample, rather than to real differences in the population. If your $p$ value is small rather than large, this makes it less likely that your result is due to chance variation rather than to a real difference, other things being equal. However, the 'other things being equal' is very important, because the actual likelihood that your result is due to chance is not completely expressed by the $p$ value, but must also take into account the likelihood of other possible explanations for the result. For example, suppose you pull a coin out of your pocket or purse, flip it ten times, and get ten heads. This is an extremely unlikely occurrence (less than one chance in a thousand, or $p < 0.001$) if it's a fair coin (one that has an equal likelihood of coming up heads or tails – the null hypothesis). However, my judgement would be that it's still more likely that this particular result is due to chance than it is that the coin is biased. If it came up heads fifty times, the latter possibility becomes somewhat more plausible. Both explanations are unlikely, and if no other explanations can be put forward, then the more improbable it is that your result could have happened by chance if you have a fair coin. Hence the more likely it is that the alternative explanation of bias, however implausible, is true.

Statistical significance testing is both deeply entrenched in practice and highly controversial. Meehl (1978) goes so far as to conclude that reliance on statistical significance was one of the 'worst things that ever happened in the history of psychology' (p. 817). Haig (1996) considers that 'It is a major professional embarrassment that researchers continue to employ such tests in the face of more than three decades of damning criticism' (p. 201), citing Gigerenzer (1993), Meehl (1990), Morrison and Henkel (1970) and Oakes (1986) in support of this view.

One problem is that statistical significance is not related to the size or importance of an effect or relationship, which is in many cases what we are really interested in. The chance of obtaining a statistically significant result increases as the sample size increases, because, for example, you then get a more sensitive test of any difference between the experimental and control groups in an RCT. But there is always likely to be some difference between the two conditions. Hence the common injunction to 'use a larger number of participants' may buy statistical significance at the expense of real life triviality. Paradoxically, if one is relying on statistical significance, there is much to be said for keeping the sample small so that only robust effects are going to be picked up.

Readers who wish to work out their own position on this controversy might review the interestingly titled 'What If There Were No Significance Tests?' (Harlow et al., 1997) and Hagen (1997) to get a flavour of the debate.

> *Because significance testing is expected by many audiences, including sponsors and journal editors* (see, however, Rigby, 1999, for an example of an editor who takes an opposing view), *it is advisable to give measures of statistical significance. However, because of the various criticisms, you should not rely solely on them. Providing additional information on the direction and size of the effect or relationship found in a study is highly recommended.*

Depending on the type of study, this additional information might be based on differences in means, correlation coefficients and/or regression coefficients (each of these is discussed later in the chapter in connection with different analyses).

These are simply ways of summarizing aspects of the data, i.e. summary or descriptive statistics (p. 407). Hence they do not carry with them the positivistic conceptual baggage associated with some uses of significance testing. With a realist approach, statistical analysis is used to confirm the existence of mechanisms whose operation we have predicted in the contexts set up in an experi-ment or other study. Large effect sizes provide confidence in their existence; hence they are what you are looking for. Significance levels play a subsidiary role, their inclusion perhaps lacking something in logic but sanctioned by convention.

## Measuring effect sizes

There are two main approaches to measuring the size of an effect produced in a study:

- evaluating the *'proportion of variance explained'* (PVE) by means of various statistics based on measures such as the square of the correlation between two variables (e.g. *R* squared; eta squared; and omega squared);
- calculating *standardized measures of differences in statistics* such as the standardized differences in means.

These are covered later in the chapter in relation to particular types of analysis. There is further discussion of the PVE approach on p. 423, and of the standardized difference approach on p. 437.

## Exploring the Data Set

### Frequency distributions and graphical displays

A simple means of exploring many data sets is to recast them in a way which counts the frequency (i.e. the number of times) that certain things happen, or to find ways of displaying that information. For example, we could look at the number of students achieving different degree classifications. Some progress can be made by drawing up a *frequency distribution*. Figure 13.2 shows the 'drop-down menus' and resultant dialogue box you need to select for SPSS to produce a frequency distribution. Figure 13.3 shows the 'output window' produced by SPSS following any statistical analysis, and figure 13.4 shows the frequency tables produced by SPSS. They simply give the number of students (referred to in SPSS as the 'frequency') with each class of degree, the percentage and a few other statistics (e.g. mean, median and mode) which will be discussed later. The table labelled 'degree class' in figure 13.4 can, alternatively, be presented as a *histogram* (figure 13.5).

The chart can be shown with either frequencies or percentages on the vertical axis; be sure to indicate which you have used. The classes of degree are ordered (here shown from first 'downward', going from left to right). For some other variables (e.g. for faculties), the ordering is arbitrary.

A distinction is sometimes made between histograms and *bar charts*. A bar chart is a type of histogram where the bars are separated from each other, rather than being joined together. The convention has been that 'joined-up' histograms are only used for continuous variables (i.e. where the bar can take on any numerical value and is not, for example, limited to whole number values). Figure 13.5 shows a variable 'degree class' which takes on only a limited number of values and so, following this convention, the bars are shown as separated.

*Pie charts* provide an alternative way of displaying this kind of information (see figure 13.6).

Bar charts, histograms and pie charts are probably preferable ways of summarizing data to the corresponding tables of frequency distributions. They are more quickly and easily understood by a variety of audiences (see Spence and Lewandowsky, 1990, for a review of relevant empirical studies). Note, however, that with continuous variables (i.e. ones which can take on any numerical value, not simply whole numbers), both frequency tables and histograms may lose considerable detailed information. This is because of the need to group together a range of values for a particular row of the frequency table or bar of the histogram. In all cases, there will be a trade-off between decreasing the complexity of the display and losing information.

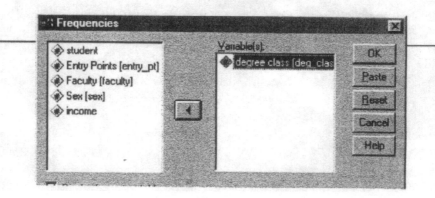

**Figure 13.2** Calculating frequencies using SPSS for Windows.

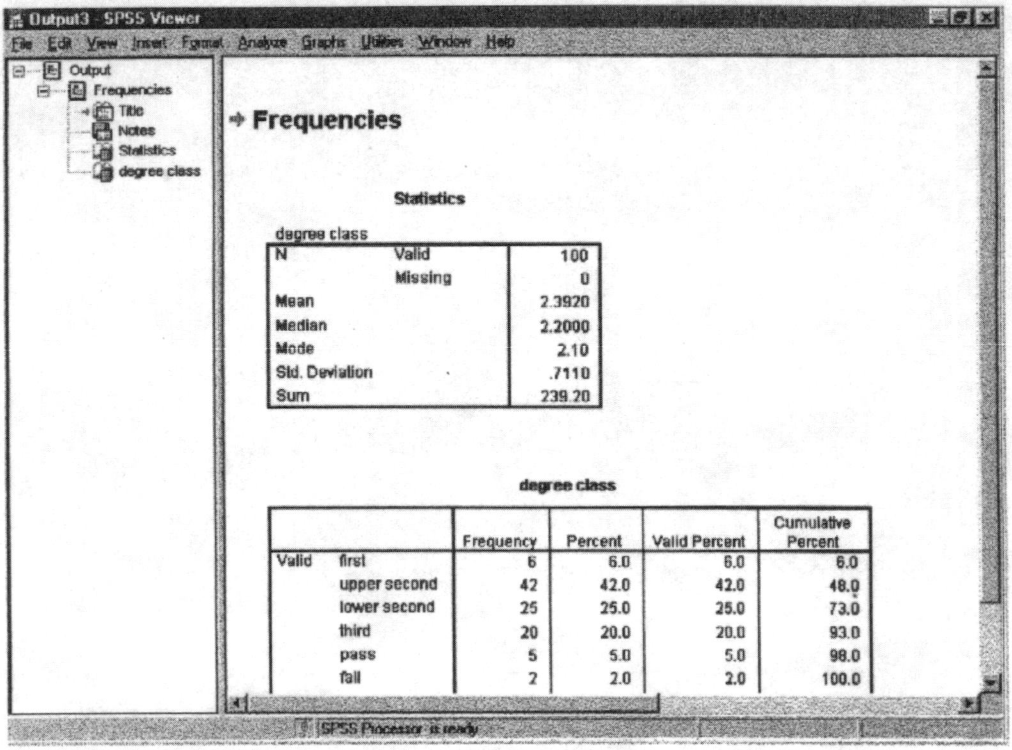

**Figure 13.3** Example output window in SPSS for Windows.

**Statistics**

degree class

| N | Valid | 100.00 |
|---|---|---|
| | Missing | 0.00 |
| Mean | | 2.3920 |
| Median | | 2.2000 |
| Mode | | 2.10 |
| Std. Deviation | | 0.7110 |
| Sum | | 239.20 |

**Degree class**

| | | Frequency | Percent | Valid Percent | Cumulative Percent |
|---|---|---|---|---|---|
| Valid | first | 6 | 6.0 | 6.0 | 6.0 |
| | upper second | 42 | 42.0 | 42.0 | 48.0 |
| | lower second | 25 | 25.0 | 25.0 | 73.0 |
| | third | 20 | 20.0 | 20.0 | 93.0 |
| | pass | 5 | 5.0 | 5.0 | 98.0 |
| | fail | 2 | 2.0 | 2.0 | 100.0 |
| | Total | 100 | 100.0 | 100.0 | |

**Figure 13.4** Example of frequency distribution and statistics (distribution of students across 'degree class') from SPSS for Windows.

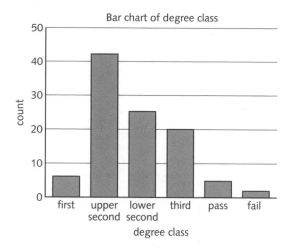

**Figure 13.5**   Bar chart showing distribution of students across 'degree class'.

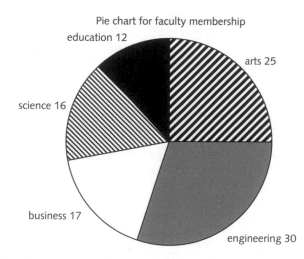

**Figure 13.6**   Pie chart showing relative numbers of students in different faculties.

There are EDA display techniques, such as the *stem and leaf display* (see Marsh, 1988, for a particularly clear account), which do not involve this loss of information. However, they suffer from the difficulty that their meaning is not intuitively obvious, and requires explaining to a lay audience. An alternative summarizing display is the *boxplot*. This, and some further techniques of graphical display, are returned to later in the chapter, following the discussion on summary statistics below (see p. 407).

Graphs (line charts) are well known ways of displaying data. SPSS provides a wide range of ways of generating and displaying them, although the quality of output many not be high enough for some needs. Specialized graphics packages commonly have a range of such displays available. Increasingly, professional standard displays are expected in presenting the results of projects. Apart from assisting communication, they transmit positive messages about the quality of your work. It is a matter of judgement whether or not any package to which you have access provides output of a quality adequate for presentation to a particular audience.

Marsh (1988) gives detailed, helpful and down-to-earth suggestions for hand-produced material in appendices on 'Good Table Manners' (pp. 139–42) and 'Guide to Effective Plotting' (pp. 196–8). Tufte (1983) provides a fascinating compendium for anyone who needs to take graphical display seriously.

## Summary or descriptive statistics

Summary statistics (also commonly known as 'descriptive statistics') are ways of representing some important aspect of a set of data by a single number. The two aspects most commonly dealt with in this way are the *level* of the distribution and its *spread* (otherwise known as *dispersion*). Statistics summarizing the level are known as *measures of central tendency*. Those summarizing the spread are called *measures of variability*. The *skewness* (asymmetricality) and other aspects of the shape of the distribution which are also sometimes summarized are considered below in the context of the normal distribution (see p. 414).

*Measures of central tendency*   The notion here is to get a single figure which best represents the level of the distribution. The most common such measure to the layperson is the 'average', calculated by adding all of the scores together and then dividing by the number of scores. In statistical parlance, the figure obtained by carrying out this procedure is referred to as the *arithmetic mean*. This is because 'average', as a term in common use, suffers from being imprecise – some other more-or-less mid-value might also be referred to as average. There are, however, several other measures of central tendency in use, some appropriate for special purposes. Box 13.3 covers some of them.

*Measures of variability*   The extent to which the data values in a set of scores are tightly clustered or relatively widely spread out is a second important feature of a distribution for which several indices are in use. Box 13.4 gives details of the most commonly used measures.

In common with many statistics packages, SPSS provides a very wide range of summary statistics (some of which are listed with brief descriptions

---

## Box 13.3

### Measures of 'central tendency'

The most commonly used are:

- *Mean* (strictly speaking, this should be referred to as the *arithmetic mean*) – this is the average, obtained by adding all the scores together and dividing by the number of scores.
- *Median* – this is the central value when all the scores are arranged in order of size (i.e. for eleven scores it is the sixth). It is also referred to as the '50th percentile' (i.e. it has 50 per cent of the scores below it, and 50 per cent above it).
- *Mode* – the most frequently occurring value.

Statistics texts give formulae and further explanation.

---

## Box 13.4

### Measures of variability

Some commonly used measures are:

- *Range* – difference between the highest and the lowest score.
- *Inter-quartile range* – difference between the score which has one-quarter of the scores below it (known as the 'first quartile', or '25th percentile') and that which has three-quarters of the scores below it (known as the 'third quartile', or '75th percentile').
- *Variance* – a measure of the average of the squared deviations of *individual* scores from the mean.
- *Standard deviation* – square root of the variance.
- *Standard error* – a measure of the standard deviation of the *mean* score.

Statistics texts give formulae and further explanation.

---

in figure 13.7). Essentially, what is provided is an optional menu of ways of summarizing any column within your data table.

## Further graphical displays for single variables

It is possible to incorporate summary statistics into graphical displays in various ways. SPSS provides a number of ways of doing this.

**Statistics**

Entry points

| N | Valid | 97.00 |
|---|---|---|
| | Missing | 3.00 |
| Mean | | 16.14 |
| Std. Error of Mean | | 0.40 |
| Median | | 16.00 |
| Mode | | 14.00 |
| Std. Deviation | | 3.91 |
| Variance | | 15.29 |
| Skewness | | 0.266 |
| Std. Error of Skewness | | 0.245 |
| Kurtosis | | −0.941 |
| Std. Error of Kurtosis | | 0.485 |
| Range | | 16.00 |
| Minimum | | 10.00 |
| Maximum | | 26.00 |
| Sum | | 1566.00 |
| Percentiles | 25 | 13.00 |
| | 50 | 16.00 |
| | 75 | 20.00 |

**Figure 13.7**   Summary descriptive statistics produced by SPSS for Windows.

All the measures of central tendency given in box 13.3, and the measures of variability in box 13.4, can be given by SPSS (you have to work out the 'inter-quartile range' as the difference between the 25th percentile and the 75th percentile). Additionally you can get, for example, percentiles. The 25th, 50th and 75th percentiles are given. The 25th percentile is the score that has 25% of the scores below it. The 50th percentile is another name for the median. For skewness and kurtosis see figure 13.12. The other information given should be self-evident.

*Standard deviation error bars*   SPSS will generate a display showing the mean value as a dot, above and below which extends an 'error bar'. This represents one standard deviation unit above and below the mean. Typically, about two-thirds of the observed values will fall between these two limits (see the discussion of the normal distribution below, p. 414).

This is often a useful way of displaying the relative performance of subgroups, and more generally of making comparisons. A similar-looking display is used to show the *confidence intervals* for the mean. These are limits within which we can be (probabilistically) sure that the *mean* value of the population from which our sample is drawn lies: 95 per cent limits (i.e. limits within which we can be 95 per cent sure) are commonly used, but others can be obtained. Figure 13.8 shows error bar charts for both one standard deviation and 95 per cent confidence intervals. The display makes clear both the similar

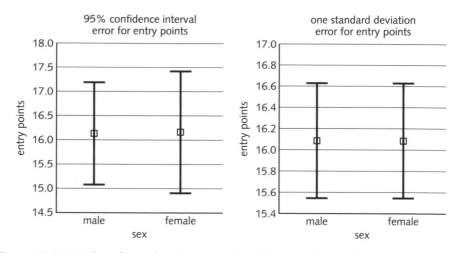

**Figure 13.8**   Display of error bar charts produced by SPSS for Windows.

variability in male and female scores, and the relatively small difference in means compared with variability.

*Box plots and whiskers*   Figure 13.9 shows the general meaning of the box and its upper and lower 'whiskers'; figure 13.10 provides an example.

The plot is based on medians and other percentiles, rather than on means and standard deviations. Unfortunately, SPSS does not readily generate the circles representing individual scores above the 90th percentile and below the 10th percentile as shown in figure 13.9. Emphasizing them in this way (which you will have to plot by hand), helps in deciding whether there is justification in omitting them, or otherwise treating them differently from the rest of the data. The term *outlier* is commonly used for a value which is inconsistent from the others on objective grounds. For example, an error might be made in entering the data set where separate entries of '2' and '7' get entered together as '27'. If no obvious reason of this kind can be unearthed, then the treatment is problematic. Criteria for rejection of extreme values based solely on their degree of extremeness have been proposed (e.g. Marsh, 1988, p. 108). Lovie (1986) provides a very helpful summary of the issues. Barnett and Lewis (1984) give a comprehensive review.

Many statistical procedures are very sensitive to the presence of outliers. For example, one advantage of the median over the mean as a measure of central tendency is its lack of such sensitivity. EDA has been much interested in outliers, both in their own right and in the study of measures which are robust (i.e. relatively unaffected) in their presence.

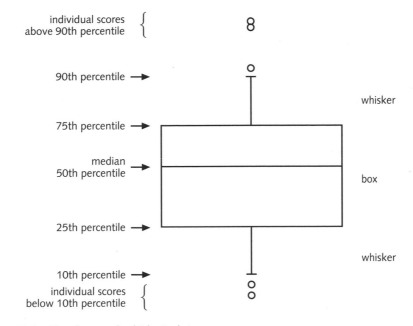

**Figure 13.9** The 'box and whisker' plot.

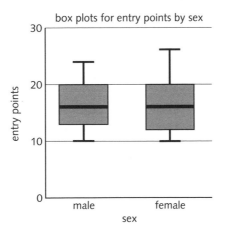

**Figure 13.10** Example of 'box and whisker' output.

## Manipulating the data

Marsh (1988, p. 42) states that 'data . . . is produced, not given'. This stance rejects our classical heritage in two ways. The derivation of data is 'things given', and the word is plural – one datum; two or more data. Taking the latter point first, it appears that most people now use data as a singular noun. However, in a field where the term is used frequently, such as the reports of enquiry, you may be perceived as ignorant of the 'correct' usage if you follow the popular trend. Not wanting to put you in that position, we propose to play the pedant and stick to the plural use.

The 'produced, not given' point is important. Many of the data that we collect are actually produced during the enquiry itself. They tend not to be things lying around that we pick up. We often have a very active hand, not only in what is collected, but in how it is collected. The actual numbers that we subject to analysis are very much formed by a process of selection and choice – at a very simple level, for example, do we use grams, kilograms, ounces, pounds, tons, . . . ?

This basic choice will have been made at the time that the data are collected. In the example of units of weight just raised, this would probably now be metric, with the specific unit chosen to avoid very large, or very small, numbers (e.g. 5 grams rather than 0.005 kilograms; 2.3 kilograms rather than 2,300 grams). There is still the possibility of manipulating the data subsequently, so that it is easier to analyse, or so that attention can be focused on features of interest, or so that it is easier to compare two or more sets of data. As in many aspects of enquiry, this process is driven by your research questions. Are there things that you can do with your data that can help give clearer answers to these questions?

It perhaps needs saying that 'manipulating data' in this sense is nothing to do with 'How to Lie with Statistics' (Huff, 1973). 'Massaging' the data to give a biased or downright untruthful message should have no place in the kind of enquiry covered in this book. The prime safeguard is your own honesty and integrity, but this should be supported by detailed reporting. Sufficient detail should be included to enable the sceptical reader to follow the trail from the collected data, through whatever you do to it, to the interpretation and conclusion.

## Scaling data

The earlier section on descriptive statistics emphasized two aspects of a set of data: its *level* and its *spread*. The two simplest ways of scaling data involve these aspects directly.

*Adding or subtracting a constant*   A straightforward way of focusing attention on a particular aspect of the data is to add or subtract a particular constant amount from each of the measurements. The most common tactic is to
subtract the arithmetic mean from each score. Scores transformed in this way
are referred to as *deviations*:

deviation = (individual score) − (mean score)

This has the advantage of making clear how far each score is from the mean,
though with the possible disadvantage that about half the deviation scores will
have minus signs associated with them. A similar tactic can be used when the
median, or some other measure of central tendency has been employed.

*Multiplying by a constant*   This is sometimes referred to as *scaling* or *rescal-
ing* the variable. It is what you do when changing from weight in imperial
measure (pounds, ounces, etc.) to metric (kilograms, grams). This tactic is particularly useful in comparing different sets of data which have initially been
measured on different scales. For example, the prices of goods or services in
different European countries could be better compared by transforming them
all into the standard 'euro', or into one particular currency.

*Other transformations*   There are many other things that you can do. *Taking
logarithms*, or *taking a power* (e.g. *square, square root, reciprocal*) are tactics
commonly used when the distribution of the scores is asymmetrical or in some
other way inappropriate for the type of statistical analysis proposed. Details are
given in Marsh (1988, ch. 11). SPSS allows you to carry out these transformations and almost every other possible way of transforming data that you
could imagine.

*Standardizing data*   One way of manipulating data is very commonly used.
It involves combining the two approaches covered above, i.e. subtracting the
mean (or other measure of central tendency) and dividing by the standard
deviation (or other measure of spread).

$$\text{standardized score} = \frac{(\text{individual score} - \text{mean score})}{(\text{standard deviation})}$$

Expressed in terms of symbols, this becomes

$$\text{standardized score} = \frac{X - \overline{X}}{SD}$$

or

$$\text{standardized score} = \frac{\text{(individual score} - \text{median score)}}{\text{(semi-inter-quartile range)}}$$

which in terms of symbols becomes

$$\text{standardized score} = \frac{X - M(X)}{dQ}$$

This standardization gives the mean (or median) of the standardized distribution of 0, and its standard deviation (or semi-inter-quartile range) as 1. Distributions that have been standardized in this way are much easier to compare, and in some circumstances combine, than unstandardized ones. This transformation is available in SPSS. It is also possible to display a standard score frequency distribution, which also aids comparisons between distributions.

## The normal distribution

There are theoretical distributions for which the shape is completely determined once the mean and standard deviation are known. The so-called *normal* (or *Gaussian*) distribution is the best known of these. An example is shown as figure 13.11. Many distributions of scores obtained in practice are reasonable approximations to the normal distribution. To find if this is the case for a particular set of scores, they are first standardized as shown above and then

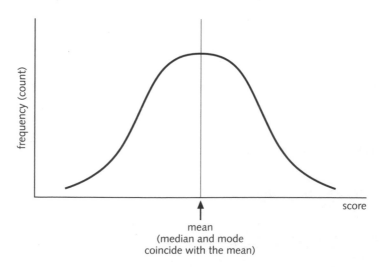

**Figure 13.11** The theoretical 'normal' distribution.

scrutinized to see whether the proportion of cases falling at different distances from the mean are as predicted from tables showing the theoretical distribution.

For example, the expectation is that:

- 68 per cent of cases are within one SD of the mean,
- 95 per cent of cases are within two SDs of the mean, and
- 99.7 per cent are within three SDs of the mean.

Further details, and appropriate tables, are in many statistics texts (Robson, 1994, provides a simple account). It is possible to test the 'goodness of fit' of your data to the normal distribution by using a version of the Chi-square test (see below, p. 418).

Whether or not a distribution of scores can reasonably be represented as normal is then of value in describing, summarizing and comparing data. However, don't fall into the trap of thinking that 'only "normal" is normal'. Data won't necessarily fall into this pattern. This is no major disaster; your job is to seek to understand what you have got, playing about with the scale if this seems to help. Such transformations may bring the distribution closer to normal, but that in itself may not further your understanding.

The normal distribution also has a part to play if one wants to go on to carry out formal statistical tests on the data. Many of the more commonly used tests are based on the assumption that a normal distribution is involved. Often these tests are *robust* in the sense that deviations from normality do not appear to have much effect on the outcome of the test. However, there are 'distribution free' tests (commonly called 'non-parametric' tests) available (Siegel and Castellan, 1988; Meddis, 1984) which do not make assumptions about the shape of the distributions involved.

*Skewness* As can be seen from figure 13.11, the normal distribution is symmetrical about its centre (which is where the mean, median and mode coincide). In practice, a distribution may be 'skewed', as shown in figure 13.12.

'Negative' skew suggests that the majority of extreme observed values are less than the mean; 'positive' skew that the majority of extreme observed values are above the mean. A simple indication of this can be obtained by comparing the mean and median values. If the median is less than the mean, this suggests that over 50 per cent of the values are below the mean, and hence to compensate the right hand or upper tail of the distribution must extend further – indicating positive skew. SPSS provides a measure of the skewness of a distribution. The normal distribution (being symmetrical) would have a value of 0, while significant positive values indicate a distribution with a long right tail and significant negative values indicate a distribution with a long left tail.

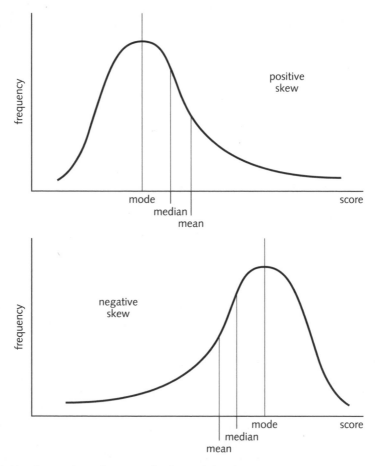

**Figure 13.12**   Positively and negatively skewed distributions.

*Note*: SPSS provides an index of *skewness* (see figure 13.7). For symmetrical distributions this is 0; it takes on positive values for positive skew and vice versa. A *kurtosis* is also provided. This is an index of the 'peakiness' of the distribution. See statistics texts for details.

## Analysing Relationships between Two Variables

Having considered how one might deal with individual variables, let us switch the focus to one of the main concerns in carrying out social research – looking for relationships between variables. Here we will limit ourselves to relations between two variables.

To say that there is a relationship between two variables means that the distribution of scores or values on one of the variables is in some way linked to the distribution of values on the second variable – that, say, higher scores on one variable for that case (person, perhaps) tend to occur when there are higher scores on the second variable for that case. An example would be the relationship between smoking and lung cancer; those who smoke are more likely to develop lung cancer.

## Cross-tabulation

Cross-tabulation is a simple and frequently used way of showing whether or not there is a relationship between two variables. It is an extension of the use of frequency tables as discussed in connection with the analysis of single variables. Take once more the data on students presented in box 13.2. Let us say that we are interested in the relationship between faculty and the relative number of male and female students, i.e. between the variables 'faculty' and 'sex'. Figure 13.13 presents these data in what is usually called a 'contingency

**Sex\* Faculty Crosstabulation**

| | | Faculty | | | | | |
|---|---|---|---|---|---|---|---|
| | | arts | engineering | business | science | education | Total |
| Sex male | Count | 3.0 | 29.0 | 9.0 | 10.0 | 4.0 | 55.0 |
| | Expected Count | 13.8 | 16.5 | 9.4 | 8.8 | 6.6 | 55.0 |
| | % within Sex | 5.5% | 52.7% | 16.4% | 18.2% | 7.3% | 100.0% |
| | % within Faculty | 12.0% | 96.7% | 52.9% | 62.5% | 33.3% | 55.0% |
| | % of Total | 3.0% | 29.0% | 9.0% | 10.0% | 4.0% | 55.0% |
| female | Count | 22.0 | 1.0 | 8.0 | 6.0 | 8.0 | 45.0 |
| | Expected Count | 11.3 | 13.5 | 7.7 | 7.2 | 5.4 | 45.0 |
| | % within Sex | 48.9% | 2.2% | 17.8% | 13.3% | 17.8% | 100.0% |
| | % within Faculty | 88.0% | 3.3% | 47.1% | 37.5% | 66.7% | 45.0% |
| | % of Total | 22.0% | 1.0% | 8.0% | 6.0% | 8.0% | 45.0% |
| Total | Count | 25.0 | 30.0 | 17.0 | 16.0 | 12.0 | 100.0 |
| | Expected Count | 25.0 | 30.0 | 17.0 | 16.0 | 12.0 | 100.0 |
| | % within Sex | 25.0% | 30.0% | 17.0% | 16.0% | 12.0% | 100.0% |
| | % within Faculty | 100.0% | 100.0% | 100.0% | 100.0% | 100.0% | 100.0% |
| | % of Total | 25.0% | 30.0% | 17.0% | 16.0% | 12.0% | 100.0% |

**Chi-Square Tests**

| | Value | df | Asymp. Sig. (2-sided) | |
|---|---|---|---|---|
| Pearson Chi-Square | 42.389[a] | 4 | 0.000 | [a]0 cells (.0%) have |
| Likelihood ratio | 50.558 | 4 | 0.000 | expected count less |
| Linear-by-Linear Association | 0.562 | 1 | 0.454 | than 5. The minimum |
| N of Valid Cases | 100.0 | | | expected count is 5.40 |

**Figure 13.13**   Cross-tabulation and results of a chi-square analysis of 'sex by faculty'.

table' in the form produced by SPSS. There are five faculties (five levels of the variable 'faculty') and two sexes (two values of the variable 'sex') and hence ten (five times two) possible combinations of levels of the variables. The boxes in the table, corresponding to each of these combinations, are referred to as *cells*. The total for each row and each column is given at the end or margin of the row or column. These totals are called the *row marginals* and *column marginals* respectively.

SPSS also provides information on 'percentages of row totals' and 'percentages of column totals' as shown in figure 13.13. The row total presentation shows the way in which females (and males) are distributed across the faculties, labelled as 'counts'. The column total presentation shows the relative percentages (or proportions) of males and females in different faculties (e.g. the proportion of males in the science faculty). The contingency table, viewed in terms of percentages, helps to highlight any relationships between the two variables. Here the low percentage of females in the engineering faculty is a striking, though unsurprising, feature.

## Chi-square tests

The lower, smaller, table in figure 13.13 labelled 'Chi-Square Tests' provides the results from a number of statistical tests. The top one of these, referred to as 'Pearson Chi-Square' is a test commonly used in contingency and other tables, usually just as 'Chi-square'. Note that SPSS also provides the results of two other tests – 'Likelihood Ratio' and 'Linear-by-Linear Association'. This illustrates a common feature in SPSS and other statistical packages. The results often include, apart from the test you are interested in, several others you may never have heard of, although you can limit the number of test results it throws at you by checking the box only for those you are interested in. Don't worry about this.

Chi-square, in a contingency table, is a measure of the degree of association or linkage between the two variables. The more that there is a tendency for the relative number of males and females to vary from faculty to faculty, the greater is Chi-square. It is based on the differences or discrepancies between the frequencies in the different cells (the 'counts') and those that you would expect if there was no association at all between the two variables (i.e. the ratio of males to females is the same in all faculties). These latter are known as the 'Expected' counts and are shown in the main table in figure 13.13.

It is possible to assess the so-called *statistical significance* of relationships in contingency tables. This concept, and some of the problems in its use, were discussed earlier in the chapter on p. 400. The chi-square ($\chi^2$) test is commonly used to assess the statistical significance of such relationships in contingency tables. The probability in this example is somewhat cryptically labelled as 'Asymp. Sig. (2-sided)' and is here given as '.000'. This does not mean that it is actually zero (sorry about this) but that it is smaller than 0.0005; i.e. zero if only three decimal places are given. This is clearly very much smaller than the conventional 0.05; and hence statistically significant. (Incidentally, 'df' refers to 'degrees of freedom', a somewhat esoteric statistical concept linked to the number of cells in the contingency table, which you would need if you were to look up the statistical significance of the value of chi-square in statistical tables.)

Statisticians warn against the use of chi-square when one or more *expected* frequencies fall below a particular value, usually taken as 5 in small tables. Fisher's Exact Test is a substitute which can be used in circumstances where the expected frequencies are too low for chi-square (see Siegel and Castellan, 1988). SPSS computes Fisher's Exact Test for you as an addition when the expected values fall below this limit.

A chi-square analysis, if statistically significant (as in the present case), indicates that *overall* there is a relationship between the two variables (here 'faculty' and 'sex') which is unlikely to be explained by chance factors. In two-by-two contingency tables (where both variables have only two values), statisticians formerly used a formula incorporating a 'correction for continuity' (sometimes referred to as 'Yates' correction') for computing chi-square. This is now considered to be inappropriate (Richardson, 1990). SPSS provides both chi-square and a 'corrected' value when analysing two-by-two tables, producing an appropriately adjusted chi-square. You are recommended to ignore the corrected value.

*Using chi-square to test for 'goodness of fit'* Chi-square can also be used to compare frequencies on a single variable to see how closely they 'fit' to those expected or predicted on some theoretical basis. A common theoretical expectation is for all frequencies to be the same; or perhaps it may be desired to test the goodness of fit to the frequencies expected if the data were normally distributed. The difference in terms of computation is that these expected frequencies have to be supplied, rather than being generated automatically from the observed frequencies. An example is given on p. 438.

## Scattergrams

A scattergram (also known as a scatterplot or scatter diagram) is a graphical representation of the relationship between two variables. It makes sense only when it is possible to order the values for each of the variables in some non-arbitrary manner. Hence, in the data set of box 13.2, it would be reasonable to draw a scattergram for, say 'degree class' against 'entry points'; but not for 'faculty' against 'entry points'. This is because any particular ordering of the faculties along an axis is arbitrary, and the apparent graphical relationship between the variables will vary with the ordering.

Figure 13.14 presents two scattergrams showing, the relationship between 'entry points' and 'income' for a sample of graduates. It shows the position of each person on the two variables. For example, the far right point on the scattergram corresponds to someone who gained 26 entry points and has an income of about £18,000. Various techniques are available to deal with overlap of data points; the figure 13.14(b) shows an example.

Scattergrams are a powerful pictorial device, giving a clear picture of the nature and strength of the relationship between the variables. They have their limitations, however. Many types of data are not readily amenable to display in this way, particularly when there are very few values on one or both of the variables. Nevertheless, unless you have data where the ordering of values is arbitrary, you should always consider the feasibility of drawing a scattergram for two-variable data. It is possible to produce contingency tables from the same data, summarizing by taking appropriate intervals along the variables when they have many values.

Multiple groups (strata) are often shown together on scattergrams to facilitate comparisons between sub-groups. Figure 13.15 shows one of way of doing this with SPSS.

## Correlation coefficients

Measures of correlation (i.e. of the co-relationship between two variables) are referred to as correlation coefficients. They give an indication of both the strength and the direction of the relationship between the variables. The commonly used coefficients assume that there is a linear relationship between the two variables. Figure 13.16 demonstrates this in the idealized form of the 'perfect' linear correlation. However, perfection is not of this world. Certainly, you are very unlikely to get that degree of 'tightness' in the relationship with data concerning humans and their doings. Figure 13.17 illustrates the kind of picture you are likely to see if there is a strong linear correlation. As you can see, the points fall within a cigar-shaped 'envelope'. The thinner the cigar, the stronger the relationship. With weaker correlations, the cigar is fatter; an essentially zero correlation shows no discernible pattern in the scattergram.

SPSS will compute a Pearson's correlation coefficient ($r$). Other coefficients are available. SPSS can calculate the Spearman rank correlation coefficient and Kendall's rank correlation coefficient (known as Kendall's Tau). As their labels suggest, they are both used with data in the form of ranks, or orderings of data (what is first, second, etc.). The data may have been collected in this form, perhaps through participants expressing their preferences for different objects

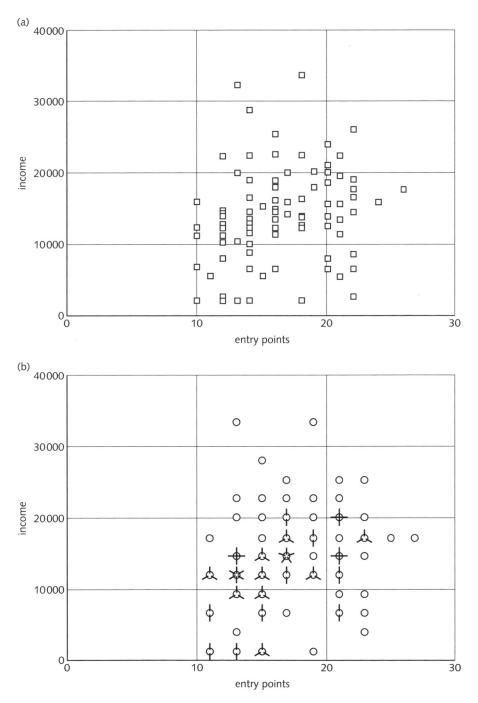

**Figure 13.14** Scattergrams of 'entry points by income'.

The second part, (b), shows 'sunflower' display to deal with overlap of points. ('Sunflowers' are points with 'petals'. A single data point is shown, as usual, as a circle. For two or more data points there is a corresponding number of 'petals'.)

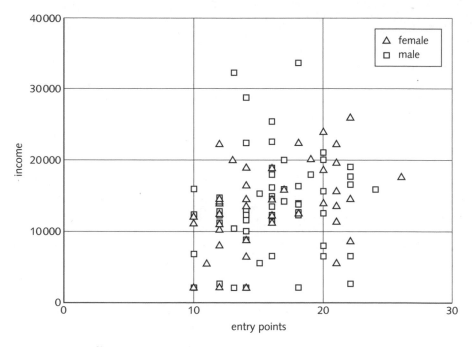

**Figure 13.15**  Differentiation of sub-groups in a scattergram.

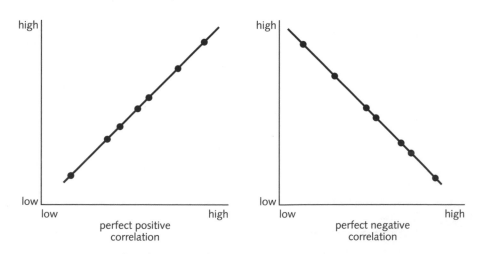

**Figure 13.16**  A 'perfect' linear correlation.

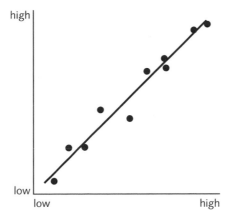

**Figure 13.17**   Example of a high positive correlation.

or situations, or may have been collected in other forms and subsequently converted into ranks. They do not assume normal distribution of the data and
hence may be used when that assumption, on which the Pearson coefficient
is based, is dubious. They are, however, measures of linear correlation
(see below). The Spearman coefficient is effectively a Pearson coefficient
performed on the ranks and is preferred by some on that ground, but most
analysts appear to prefer Kendall's Tau, possibly because it deals with ties more
consistently.

*Proportion of variance explained (PVE)*   While the correlation coefficient is a
measure of the relationship between the variables, it is difficult to assess the
strength of this relationship (real 'significance' or importance, rather than
statistical significance) from the correlation coefficient.

The square of the correlation coefficient ($r^2$) is a useful index as it corresponds to the proportion of the variation in values of one of the variables which
can be predicted from the variation in the other variable. Broadly speaking, if
this is low (say, less than 0.3 – but this will depend on circumstances), then it
is unlikely to be profitable to exert much further time and effort in investigating the relationship. High values might suggest carrying out a subsequent
regression analysis (see below).

*Measuring the statistical significance of a correlation*   The statistical significance (see p. 400) of correlation coefficients is commonly computed and is
indicated by SPSS with an asterisk (with further information about the level
of significance at the bottom of the table) for the Pearson, Spearman and
Kendall's Tau coefficients.

The given probability is that a relationship of at least this size could have arisen by chance. It is important to appreciate that the size of correlation coefficient which reaches a particular statistical significance (conventionally $p = 0.05$ being taken as the largest acceptable probability for this type of significance) is very strongly affected by the size of the sample of data involved. Thus for twenty pairs of scores the value of the Pearson correlation coefficient is 0.44 (two-tailed test – see below, page 438); for fifty it is 0.28; for 100 less than 0.2; and for 500 less than 0.1. This again illustrates the point that *statistical* significance has little to do with significance as commonly understood. Certainly, with a large sample such as 500, you can achieve statistical significance when less than 1 per cent of the variability in one variable is predictable from variation in the other; 99 per cent comes from other sources!

The message is that if the statistical significance of a correlation is to be quoted, make sure that the size of the correlation (and/or of its square as a measure of the proportion of variance explained) and of the sample also get quoted.

*Non-linear relationships between variables*   It is perfectly possible to have some form of non-linear relationship between two variables. One virtue of the scattergram is in highlighting such non-linearities, in part because they are likely to call for discussion and explanation. They should also give a warning against using statistical techniques which assume linearity. *Curvilinear* relationships might be found. The envelope, instead of being cigar-shaped, might be better represented by a banana or boomerang, as in figure 13.18.

This is one situation where the data transformations discussed earlier in the chapter (p. 412) may be of value, as the appropriate transformation might

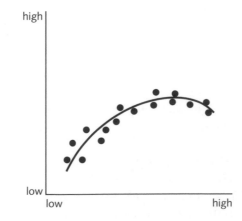

**Figure 13.18**   Example of a curvilinear relationship.

convert the relationship in figure 13.18 to something closely approaching linearity – and hence more amenable to statistical analysis. Even if this transformation does 'work' in that sense, there may be consequent problems of interpretation. To know that there is a strong linear correlation between one variable and, say, the square of another variable may be of descriptive and even predictive value, but may still defy your attempts at understanding. However, finding that a reciprocal transformation works, such that a non-linear relationship involving 'time elapsed' as one variable becomes linear when a 'rate' measure (i.e. reciprocal of time) is used, may well be readily interpretable.

*Lines of 'best fit'*   It is possible to draw a line of best fit on a scattergram. This can be estimated by drawing a line having roughly equal numbers of points above and below it, and making each point as near to the line as possible (using the minimum, i.e. perpendicular, distance from the line in each case).

There are systematic means of drawing such a line, which should be employed if it is to be used in any formal way. One approach which is commonly used is *linear regression*. This involves finding the line for which the squared deviation of individual points from the line (in the vertical, i.e. the $Y$ dimension) is a minimum. This can be routinely performed by many computer packages, including SPSS. There are alternative ways of deriving these lines (see e.g. Marsh, 1988, pp. 188–92, who advocates 'resistant lines'). When data are 'well behaved' (reasonably normal distributions with no problematic 'outliers'), linear regression is probably preferable, if only because of the ease with which the task can be completed.

The 'line of best fit', when obtained by one of the above means, is a powerful and useful way of summarizing the linear relationship between two variables. All straight lines can be expressed by a simple algebraic formula, one form of which is

$$Y = bX + a,$$

Where $Y$ and $X$ are the two variables (conventionally, when there are dependent and independent variables, $Y$ is the dependent variable and $X$ the independent variable); and $a$ and $b$ are constants which typify the particular line of best fit. The constant $a$ is known as the *intercept* and is the point where the line cuts the vertical or $Y$ axis; $b$ is known as the *slope*. This is shown diagrammatically in figure 13.19.

In addition to providing an elegant way of summarizing the data, the line of best fit (or the coefficients $a$ and $b$, which amount to the same thing) can be used for predictive purposes – for example, in the present case to give an estimate of the likely increase in income over a specified number of years.

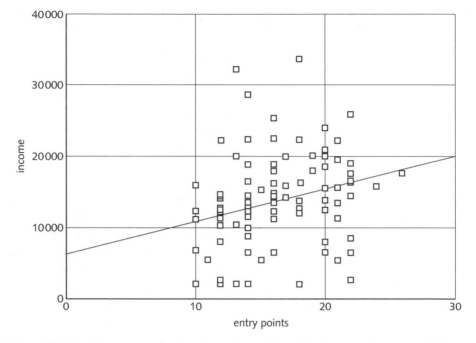

**Figure 13.19**   Fitting a 'regression line' for relationship between 'entry points' and 'income'.

There is a difficulty with the data in that the amount of variability of the points around the regression line is not constant. It appears to increase with higher values of entry points and income. This not uncommon feature goes by the somewhat fearsome name of *heteroscedasticity* and, strictly, violates one of the assumptions on which Pearson's correlation coefficient is based. Again, this is a situation where possible transformations of the data might be attempted.

## Analysis of covariance

It is worth mentioning here a technique which combines regression with analysis of variance methods (discussed later in the chapter; see p. 441). It is a technique introduced by Ronald Fisher in the 1930s for the statistical, as against experimental, control of the effects of one or more uncontrolled variables. Suppose we are concerned with comparing three methods of teaching some part of the curriculum. Each method is used with a different randomly assigned group and tests of achievement administered. The groups may differ in intelligence, and it appears likely that their performance on the test correlates with intelligence. If measures of intelligence are available, they can be used as a *covariate* in the analysis to adjust for the effect of intelligence and produce a corrected measure of the effects of the three methods. Many statistical texts provide further details (see e.g. Dancey and Reidy, 1999).

There are major interpretational problems with this approach. Any statistical adjustment of this kind is based on assumptions that are quite difficult to justify. The approach is certainly no substitute for seeking control of extraneous variables directly in the enquiry. Nevertheless it is used, and there are specialist applications where it is of value. It is available in SPSS.

## Analysing Relationships among Three or More Variables

Establishing a relationship between two variables is important but not necessarily the end of the matter as far as analysis is concerned. If an experimental design has been used, this may be adequate in demonstrating a causal link between the two variables, although often experimental designs are more sophisticated, involving multiple variables which call for different approaches to analysis. Multivariate analyses which are concerned with the *joint* effects of multiple variables are covered later in this section. We will, however, first consider approaches which look at the effects of taking into account a third variable on the relationship between two variables.

### Three-variable contingency tables: the 'elaboration' approach

With non-experimental strategies, it is often essential to explore the effects of other variables when seeking to understand the basis of a two-variable relationship. One set of techniques is known as 'elaboration analysis. It has been widely used in the analysis of data from surveys and other non-experimental designs. Marsh (1982, pp. 84–97) gives a very clear account of the logic of the approach. It involves the following steps:

a    establish a relationship between two variables;
b    subdivide the data on the basis of the values of a third variable;
c    review the original two-variable relationship for each of the sub-groups;
d    compare the relationship found in each sub-group with the original relationship.

The third variable is referred to as the *test* (or *control*) *variable*. The original relationship between the two variables, where the third variable is not being held constant at a particular value, is called the *zero-order relationship*. The relationship that is found for a particular value of the test variable is known as a *partial relationship*.

The pattern of effects of the test variable on the zero-order relationship can help in interpreting and understanding what is going on. Possibilities include the following:

*Partial relationships essentially the same as zero-order relationship*   This is a *replication* of the original relationship showing the lack of effect of the control variable.

*Partial relationships reduced essentially to zero*   The interpretation depends on your view of the logical link between the test variable and the original variables. It can be *either* (a) an *antecedent variable*, that is, a logically prior variable affecting both the original variables directly, *or* (b) an *intervening variable* affect*ed by* the original independent variable, and affect*ing* the original dependent variable.

If the test variable is antecedent, then this suggests that the original zero-order 'relationship' was *spurious*. There is no causal relationship between the two original variables, the apparent link being the effect of the test variable.

If the test variable is intervening, then we have made progress in *interpreting* the way in which the initial independent variable is affecting the dependent variable. We are strengthened in the view that the original relationship was causal and have some understanding as to how the causal process is working.

Clearly, it is crucial that one can differentiate between antecedent and intervening variables. For example, suppose that a study of Russia suggests that the economic collapse in the early 1990s was a causative factor in the revival of religious observance. Here a likely third variable is the breakdown of the Communist system. Considering the time sequence, and intuitively, it seems more plausible that the Communist breakdown was an antecedent variable affecting both the economy and religious observance, than that the economic collapse led to the Communist breakdown which then acted as an intervening variable. Hence the conclusion is that the apparent link between economic collapse and religious revival is spurious.

*Differential effects on different partial relationships*   (e.g. one reduced essentially to zero, another virtually unchanged). This indicates a *moderated relationship*. In the example given it means that we have specified the conditions under which the original relationship occurs. This pattern is commonly referred to as an *interaction* between the two original variables (particularly in the context of analysis of variance; see p. 445).

*Partial relationships substantially stronger than zero-order relationship*   Test variables are normally used only when there is a sizeable original relationship. However, it is feasible in some circumstances that a weak original relationship is strengthened when a test variable is introduced. Rosenberg (1968) referred to control variables having this effect as *suppressor* variables. It is even possible for the direction of the original relationship to be changed through use of a test variable. Rosenberg (1968, pp. 94–5) cites the hypothetical example of an original relationship between social class and attitudes toward civil rights – with the working classes being somewhat stronger civil rights supporters than the middle classes. Using the test variable of race, he found the opposite in the partial relationships, with slightly stronger middle-class support among whites, and very substantially greater middle-class support among blacks. Race is then a distorter variable (the reversal being possible because of the widely differing proportions of middle and working class in the black and white groups).

This approach to data analysis is simply a somewhat more complex version of the use of contingency tables, which were covered earlier. It provides a way of testing out, and possibly modifying, the conceptual model you developed when designing the study (see chapter 3, pp. 63–5); or, in other words, identifying the causal links. In realist terms, this amounts to specifying which mechanisms are in operation. Moderated relationships, as discussed above, provide evidence for the contexts in which the mechanism operates.

The real world is complex, and analysis may well not generate patterns as clear-cut as those discussed above. Thus the original relationship may, with an antecedent test variable, drop to a fraction of its original value without approaching zero. This would tend to suggest a more complex situation where the original relation is partially spurious and the test variable is having some causative influence. In practice, it is likely that multiple causation is the norm for many of the phenomena which interest us, and that models which allow for multiple independent variables are to be preferred (see below).

It is possible to extend this type of analysis to four or even more variables (i.e. to two or more test variables) but it rapidly becomes unwieldy, particularly when there are several categories on each variable. Unless large amounts of data have been collected, the data base for each sub-group becomes very small. The choice of test variables for elaboration analysis is obviously of central importance as it is possible to include only very few of them. They have to be pre-specified at least to the extent that you have collected the necessary data (some of the variables on which data have been collected can, of course, be omitted at the analysis stage). The message for small-scale studies is to keep the conceptual model simple. As repeatedly emphasized in chapter 5, if you are carrying out fixed design research with a view to understanding and explaining a phenomenon, you don't do this unless and until you have established a clear and simple conceptual framework.

## Using partial correlations

Essentially the same type of logical analysis can be carried out using partial correlation coefficients, rather than proportions in contingency tables. This amounts to examining the correlation between two variables and then seeing how, if at all, it changes when one or more other variables are held constant.

In the three-variable case, the correlation matrix is first calculated; this gives each of the three possible correlations between the variables. A partial correlation matrix is then calculated. Interpretation of the relationship between the variables is based on the pattern of correlations and the logical potential link between the test variable and the two original variables (e.g. antecedent or intervening).

The partial correlation approach cannot be used when testing for a 'moderated' relationship (see above, p. 427), because this depends on comparing the relationship for different categories of the test variable and the partial correlation effectively gives you a single averaged figure. There are also problems in computing the correlation coefficients if one of the variables has a small number of categories or values.

## Multiple regression

Multiple regression is multiple in the sense that it involves a single dependent variable and two or more independent variables (or, in the terminology more commonly used in non-experimental research, a single response variable and more than one explanatory variable). It is a flexible, widely used approach which has been made readily accessible through computer packages.

Taking the simplest possible case, for multiple regression, of one dependent variable and two independent variables, the regression equation (refer back to page 425) is

$$y = a + b_1 x_1 + b_2 x_2$$

where $y$ is the dependent variable, $x_1$ and $x_2$ are the two independent variables, $a$ is the intercept, and $b_1$ and $b_2$ the regression coefficients for the two independent variables. The regression coefficient gives you the change in the dependent variable for each unit change in that independent variable, *with the effect of any of the independent variables controlled* ('partialled out').

While multiple regression can be used in the same way as linear regression, to give a line of best fit and to provide predictions through substitutions of different values of $x_1$ and $x_2$, its main use is to provide an estimate of the

**Model Summary**

| Model | R | R Square | Adjusted R Square | Std. Error of the Estimate |
|---|---|---|---|---|
| 1 | 0.401[a] | 0.161 | 0.143 | 6168.34 |

[a] Predictors: (Constant), degree class, Entry Points

**ANOVA[b]**

| Model | | Sum of Squares | df | mean square | F | Sig. |
|---|---|---|---|---|---|---|
| 1 | Regression | 6.84E + 08 | 2 | 34222640.2 | 8.994 | 0.000[a] |
| | Residual | 3.58E + 09 | 94 | 38048475.88 | | |
| | Total | 4.26E + 09 | 96 | | | |

[a] Predictors: (Constant), degree class, Entry Points
[b] Dependent Variable: INCOME

**Coefficients[a]**

| Model | | Unstandardized Coefficients | | Standardized Coefficients | t | Sig |
|---|---|---|---|---|---|---|
| | | B | Std. Error | Beta | | |
| 1 | (Constant) | 19547.724 | 4984.736 | | 3.922 | 0.000 |
| | Entry Points | 136.985 | 190.995 | 0.080 | 0.717 | 0.475 |
| | degree class | –3315.685 | 1056.706 | –0.352 | –3.138 | 0.002 |

[a] Dependent Variable: INCOME

**Figure 13.20**   Results of a multiple regression analysis.

relative importance of the different independent variables in producing changes in the dependent variable. To do this, it is necessary to convert the regression coefficients to allow for the different scales on which they have been measured. When this is done, they are referred to as *standardized regression coefficients* or *beta weights*. They then tell you how many standard deviation units the dependent variable will change for a unit change in that independent variable. Figure 13.20 provides an example of the output obtained from SPSS.

The printout incorporates several useful statistics, as follows.

R-*squared*   This is the *multiple coefficient of determination*, a measure of the proportion of the variance in the dependent variable which is explained by the independent variables in the equation. In the example, as $R^2$ is 0.16, the proportion of variance explained is 16 per cent. An 'adjusted $R^2$' is also produced. This will be smaller than $R^2$ and is adjusted in the sense that it takes into account the number of independent variables involved and would normally be preferred to the unadjusted value.

t-*value of coefficients*   This presents a test of whether or not the associated beta coefficient is significantly different from zero. The probability value is given in each case.

*Standard error of coefficients*   This is a measure of the accuracy of the individual regression coefficients (see p. 425). This information is useful in assessing the likely accuracy of predictions based on the regression equation.

Note that the ANOVA table refers to 'analysis of variance'; this is discussed later in the chapter (p. 441).

This discussion merely scratches the surface of multiple regression and its possibilities as an analytic tool. If a major concern is in *developing* a model, effectively in deciding on an appropriate regression equation, then an option known as *stepwise regression* is worth considering. This starts with the simplest possible model and then step-by-step examines the implications of adding further independent variables to the equation.

If you already have an explicit model which you are testing, *hierarchical* (or *stepwise*) *multiple regression* is preferable. This involves entering the variables into the analysis in an order determined by your model.

You are strongly recommended to seek advice when considering using multiple regression, as not only is it complicated, but it is particularly easy to do something silly and inappropriate with the packages available. It is worth noting, however, that multiple regression can be used with a wide variety of types of data. In particular, it can be used with categorical variables such as 'gender' and 'faculty' in the example we have been using. The apparent difficulty here is that the ordering of categories is essentially arbitrary for such variables, and, particularly when there are more than two categories for a variable, the ordering chosen would affect the result obtained. This can be handled by the use of so-called 'dummy variables'. It involves coding particular categories as 'present' (say, coded '1') or absent (say, coded '0'). Bryman and Cramer (1990, pp. 240–1) give details. Alternatively, *logistic regression* may be used for both continuous and categorical data as long as you have (or can produce) a categorical dependent variable (see Field, 2000 for a thorough discussion).

## Multivariate analyses

Multivariate analyses, strictly speaking, involve more than one dependent or response variable and possibly additional explanatory variables (Ryan, 1997). This excludes multiple regression, although it is commonly referred to as a multivariate technique. The focus here is on two widely used approaches: factor analysis and structural equation modelling. A wide variety of other multivariate techniques exist (including *cluster analysis* and *path analysis*); these are covered in statistics texts such as Stevens (1997) and Tabachnick and Fidell (1996).

*Factor analysis*   Factor analysis is an approach to making sense of a large number of correlations between variables. It has similarities with regression analysis but differs in that the variables all have equal status; no single variable is designated as the dependent or criterion variable. Factor analysis starts with a matrix of correlations.

Matrices of this type, particularly when they contain up to 100 or so variables, are very difficult to interpret. Factor analysis aids in this process by pointing to clusters of variables which are highly intercorrelated. The 'factors' referred to are hypothetical constructs developed to account for the intercorrelations among the variables. Factor analysis seeks to replace a large and unwieldy set of variables with a small and easily understood number of factors. Suppose that your correlation matrix arises from a fifty-item questionnaire on aggression and aggressiveness. You find, say, that there are strong intercorrelations among twelve items concerning aggression towards family and friends, and similar intercorrelations among nine items concerning aggressiveness towards people in authority, but no other strong clusters. This then provides good evidence that two factors are important in understanding your results.

The technique is widely used in the development of tests and scales (see e.g. Loewenthal, 1996). It allows you to assess the extent to which different test items are measuring the same concept (strong intercorrelations), or whether their answers to one set of questions are unrelated to their answers on a second set. Hence we get an assessment of whether the questions are measuring the same concepts or variables.

Factor analysis is typically used as an exploratory tool. An alternative version referred to as 'confirmatory factor analysis' (Long, 1983) assesses the extent to which the solution obtained matches a hypothesized pattern and is therefore useful when we are testing a conceptual structure where we have predicted the operation of specific mechanisms. Exploratory factor analysis starts with the correlation matrix. For it to be worthwhile to carry out the analysis, the matrix should show a substantial number of significant correlations (either positive or negative).

The number of respondents should exceed the number of variables. When the interest is not simply to describe the factors summarizing the relations between variables, but to try to get a reliable estimate of these underlying factors, then minima of five times the number of participants to the number of variables have been suggested. There are many versions of factor analysis including canonical, alpha, image and maximum likelihood factoring, but the most commonly used are *principal-components analysis* (strictly speaking, a form of regression analysis) and *principal-axis factoring* (sometimes simply referred to as 'factor analysis'). Accounts of the process are found in Tabachnik and Fidell (1996), and in specialized texts such as Loewenthal (1996) and Child (1990).

SPSS provides most factor analysis options you are likely to need. Bryman and Cramer (1997) provide details of the procedures to be followed and the kinds of output obtained when the SPSS is used to carry out principal-components and principal-axis analyses.

*Structural equation modelling*　Structural equation modelling (or SEM), sometimes called covariance structure modelling, is a multivariate data analysis technique that takes a confirmatory structural approach to the analysis of some phenomena. Hypothesized models are typically causal with observations on multiple variables. SEM combines elements of both multiple regression and exploratory factor analysis in that it provides a way of modelling the structural (i.e. regression) relationships between factors (or 'latent variables'). An hypothesized model can be tested statistically in a simultaneous analysis of the entire system of variables to assess its fit to the data. If the 'goodness of fit' (of the model to the data) is good enough, then the hypothesized model represents a plausible account of the relationships between variables; if it is inadequate, then the model is rejected.

There are several elements to structural equation modelling that make it attractive. First, unlike many older multivariate techniques, SEM is confirmatory rather than exploratory (although there is the potential for post-hoc exploratory work), thus enabling researchers to test hypotheses. Secondly, SEM incorporates measurement error into the specified model. It is often not readily apparent, for example, how much of the magnitude of parameter estimates in regression is affected by measurement error. SEM, through multiple measurement of latent variables, provides explicit estimates of these error parameters. Finally, as mentioned above, SEM allows the researcher to explore the relationships between unobserved (or latent) variables in addition to observed variables. Latent variables are generally better understood as theoretical or abstract constructs that have to be estimated through one (or preferably more) observed measures. The best-known procedure for examining the relationships between observed and latent variables is factor analysis (discussed above). However, in contrast to the factor analytic model, SEM enables the researcher to test structural (i.e. regression) relationships between factors.

SEM has become increasingly popular in the social sciences for the analysis of non-experimental data. Quintana and Maxwell (1999) give an extensive non-technical account of its use. Much of the popularity is due to the development of increasingly accessible and reliable software packages. Byrne (1989) provides an excellent introduction to SEM using LISREL. Byrne (1994) is an accessible guide to using EQS (one of the easier SEM packages to use). There is also a useful chapter on SEM in Tabachnik and Fidell (1996).

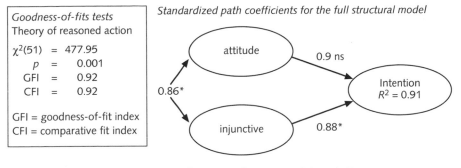

| Goodness-of-fits tests |
| Theory of reasoned action |
| $\chi^2(51)$ = 477.95 |
| $p$ = 0.001 |
| GFI = 0.92 |
| CFI = 0.92 |
| GFI = goodness-of-fit index |
| CFI = comparative fit index |

Standardized path coefficients for the full structural model

* Coefficient significant at $p < 0.01$ or better.

**Figure 13.21**   Results from a structural equation modelling analysis.

Figure 13.21 shows some of the results (presented in a simplified form) from a test of the theory of reasoned action (Ajzen and Fishbein, 1980) in respect of the intention to have a child (from Langdridge et al., forthcoming). In simple terms, the theory of reasoned action (TRA) states that a person's attitude towards a behaviour and their perception of what important others think they should do regarding the behaviour (subjective norm) should both predict their intention to perform that behaviour. The results shown here concern the application of the TRA to people's intentions to have a child at some time in the future.

For a structural equation model to be considered acceptable, it should ideally show a non-significant chi-square statistic (yes – non-significant with SEM – for reasons dealt with in detail by Byrne, 1989, 1994) and high (>0.90) values for other fit indices (such as the GFI and CFI). The chi-square is significant. However, as mentioned earlier in this chapter, the significance of statistics like chi-square is highly dependent on sample size, and this study had a large (N = 897) sample. The other fit indices (CFI and GFI), which are independent of sample size, show a good fit to the data. As the overall model fit is satisfactory it is appropriate to examine the path coefficients of the structural model. It can be seen that only the injunctive norm measure significantly predicts the intention to have a child. However, this one measure alone accounts for 91 per cent of the variance in the intention to have a child at some time in the future ($R^2 = 0.91$).

## Analysing Differences

So far, this chapter has focused on displaying, describing and summarizing quantitative data; and on analysing relationships among data. We now turn to what has, traditionally, been viewed as the major task when analysing quantitative data. Are there *differences* between the scores, values or observations obtained under one condition and those obtained under another condition (or conditions)?

Looking for differences and looking for relationships are really two ways of viewing the same thing. Asking whether there are differences between the performance of three groups taught by different methods is essentially equivalent to asking whether there is a relationship between teaching method and performance.

It is to answer questions of difference that many of the *tests of statistical inference* have been developed. The basic logic behind such tests is not difficult, although its working out in specific tests can be complex. The test is commonly used to make decisions about the state of affairs in some 'population' as compared with the actual sample of scores or observations that we have obtained. For example, suppose we want to find out whether the ratio of men to women in a particular sample is such that we can consider it representative of a specific population where the ratio of men to women is known. If there is a fifty–fifty split in the population but there are no women in a sample of twenty, then common sense might be unwilling to regard this as a representative sample, and perhaps cast doubts upon the randomness of the procedure used to select the sample. However, even if we decide that the sample was not drawn from the fifty–fifty population, we could be wrong. A sample of twenty consisting of twenty women is in fact just as likely to occur as any other specific sample (the analogy often drawn is with tossing coins – it is possible to have a sequence of twenty heads in a row; and that sequence is just as likely as any other specific sequence such as HTTHTTTHHTHHTHTTTHH). There are, however, many possible ways in which one could end up with, say, eleven males and nine females, but in fact only one sequence which gives all twenty females. It is then possible to come to the decision (based on probabilities) that the sample didn't come from the population when it in fact did, an error known as a *type one error*.

Statistical tests provide ways of assessing this type of error. In situations like the one above, the term *statistical significance*, already used in connection with tests mentioned earlier in the chapter, simply refers to the probability of making a type one error. The convention has also been mentioned of setting this at a probability of 0.05 (i.e. 5% or 1 in 20). However, the fact that many computer programs including SPSS typically generate exact probability figures for the chance of making a type one error, rather than saying that it is 'less than 0.05', means that there is an increasing tendency for such exact probabilities to be quoted.

There is also a *type two error*: that is, the probability of deciding that the sample came from the population when in fact it did not. There is an inverse relationship between the two types of error, in the sense that we can reduce our chances of making a type one error by setting the significance level at a very low probability (say 0.001, or 1 in 1,000). However, setting the decision line at this point produces a corresponding increase in the chances of making a type two error.

As stressed earlier in the chapter, significance testing is both strongly entrenched and highly controversial (see p. 400). The strategy recommended there, and reiterated here when analysing differences, is to follow the pragmatic line of quoting significance levels, but supplementing these with summary statistics such as means and standard deviations, and with measurements of effect sizes.

## Measuring effect sizes

What is needed is a statistic which is, unlike statistical significance, independent of sample size. When looking at the difference between the means of two sets of scores, this can be achieved by dividing the difference in means by the standard deviation in the population from which they come. So one obtains a difference expressed in standard deviation units; e.g. the difference in means is 0.6 standard deviations.

There are some underlying complexities. The population standard deviation is rarely known, and a standard deviation estimated from the sample of scores available usually has to be substituted. Details of how this can be done are provided in texts concentrating on statistical analysis (e.g. Clark-Carter, 1997). There is also the issue of what constitutes a large enough difference to be taken note of. Cohen (1988) provides guidelines suggesting that a value of 0.2 is small; 0.5 is medium; and 0.8 is large. The use of *confidence intervals*, as discussed on p. 409, is another possibility. Confidence intervals are routinely computed by SPSS. Effect sizes can be derived from the information about means and standard deviations given by SPSS. Details are given in Dancey and Reidy (1999).

Rosnow and Rosenthal (1996) have suggested some convenient statistical procedures for the computation of both effect sizes and confidence intervals for several statistics. Note that, while the title of their paper suggests their use by research 'consumers', they are equally applicable to researchers.

## Single group tests

In most situations we are concerned with comparing the scores or values obtained under one condition with those obtained under another condition during the enquiry. However, you might want to compare what you have obtained with some expectation arising outside the study to see whether there is a difference. SPSS incorporates two tests of this kind.

*Chi-square as a test of 'goodness of fit'*   This test has already been mentioned (p. 418). In SPSS, you select 'Nonparametric tests' and then 'Chi-square'. Figure 13.22 shows the output from a chi-square goodness of fit test on faculty distribution from SPSS. Here the question is whether or not the 'observed' figures differ sufficiently from an equal distribution across the faculties for this to be unlikely to be due to chance factors alone. The probability figure ('Asymp. Sig') here is 0.030; i.e. less than 0.05 and hence statistically significant.

*One-group* t-*test*   The *t*-test is a very widely used test used to compare two means. In this version, the comparison is between a mean obtained from the particular sample of scores that you have obtained under some condition and a hypothesized population mean. For example, we might wish to test whether the mean of the entry points given in the data set of box 13.2 (sample mean = 16.14) differs significantly from the overall mean of entry points for the corresponding national intake (population mean = 16.50). Figure 13.23 presents the results of this analysis in SPSS, showing that this difference in means does not approach statistical significance.

   The probability value given here is referred to as '2-tailed'. It is possible to opt for either '1-tailed' or '2-tailed' probabilities. '2-tailed' is simply concerned with establishing the probability of a difference between the two means. With '1-tailed' the hypothesis is that the difference will be in a particular direction (hence referred to as a 'directional' hypothesis). '2-tailed' probabilities should be selected unless there is a strong a priori reason (e.g. from your model or other theory about what is happening) for expecting the difference to be in a

**Faculty**

|  | Observed N | Expected N | Residual |
|---|---|---|---|
| arts | 25 | 20.0 | 5.0 |
| engineering | 30 | 20.0 | 10.0 |
| business | 17 | 20.0 | −3.0 |
| science | 16 | 20.0 | −4.0 |
| education | 12 | 20.0 | −8.0 |
| Total | 100 | | |

**Test Statistics**

|  | Faculty |
|---|---|
| Chi-Square[a] | 10.700 |
| df | 4.0 |
| Asymp. Sig. | 0.030 |

[a] 0 cells (.0%) have expected frequencies less than 5. The minimum expected cell frequency is 20.0

**Figure 13.22**   Chi-square as a test of 'goodness of fit'.

**One-Sample Statistics**

|  | N | Mean | Std. Deviation | Std. Error Mean |
|---|---|---|---|---|
| entry points | 97 | 16.14 | 3.91 | 0.40 |

**One-Sample Test**

| | Test Value = 16.5 | | | | | |
|---|---|---|---|---|---|---|
| | | | | | 95% Confidence Interval of the Difference | |
| | 7 | df | Sig. (2-tailed) | Mean Difference | Lower | Upper |
| entry points | –0.896 | 96 | 0.373 | –0.36 | –1.14 | 0.43 |

**Figure 13.23**   One-group *t*-test.

particular direction. Recall that details of the means and of effect sizes should be given. Statistics texts give detailed explanations.

## Two group tests

Many of the questions we are interested in when carrying out a study producing quantitative data boil down to whether there are differences between the scores obtained under two conditions, or by two groups. Do mature students admitted without standard entry qualifications get poorer degrees than 18-year-old standard entrants? Do patients suffering from low back pain get better more quickly when treated by chiropractic than by drugs? And so on.

*Two group t-tests*   The *t*-test is very commonly used to compare the means of two groups. It comes in two versions. The *paired two-group* t-*test* (sometimes called the *dependent samples* t-*test*) should be used when there are pairs of scores. This would be the case, for example, if the same person provided a score in each of the conditions. The *unpaired two-group* t-*test* (otherwise known as the *independent samples* t-*test*) applies where there is no such basis for putting together pairs of scores. Figure 13.24 gives an example of the SPSS output from an independent samples *t*-test.

Recall, once again, that it is good practice, when recording the results of such tests, to include not only the *t*-value and its statistical significance (the probability value, which must be lower than 0.05 for conventional significance) but also the means and standard deviations of the two sets of scores and the effect size. Incidentally, a minus sign for the value of *t* is not of importance, and does not affect its significance. It simply indicates that the mean of whatever has been taken as the first set of scores is less than that for the second

**Group Statistics**

| | Sex | N | Mean | Std. Deviation | Std. Error Mean |
|---|---|---|---|---|---|
| INCOME | male | 55 | 14008.00 | 7127.98 | 961.14 |
| | female | 45 | 13296.00 | 6157.01 | 917.83 |

**Independent Samples Test**

| | | Levene's test for Equality of Variances | | t-test for Equality of Means | | | | |
|---|---|---|---|---|---|---|---|---|
| | | F | Sig | t | df | Sig. (2-tailed) | Mean Difference | Std. Error Difference |
| INCOME | Equal variances assumed | 0.490 | 0.486 | 0.528 | 98.0 | 0.599 | 711.91 | 1348.65 |
| | Equal variances not assumed | | | 0.536 | 97.691 | 0.593 | 711.91 | 1328.98 |

**Figure 13.24**   Results of an independent samples *t*-test.

group of scores. The 'df' which occurs in this and many other printouts, refers to 'degrees of freedom'. It is also worth noting that SPSS automatically provides Levene's test for equality of variances. As you might expect, this tells you if you have a statistically significant difference in the variances (concerned with the distribution of scores about the mean) of the two groups. If there is no significant difference (as in this case), you can use the output for 'equal variances assumed', and if there is a significant difference, use the output for 'equal variances not assumed'.

*Nonparametric equivalents to the* t-*test*   SPSS, in common with many statistical packages, provides a range of 'nonparametric' tests. Parametric tests (of which the *t*-test is an example) are ones that have been based in their derivation on certain assumptions as to the nature of the distributions from which the data come (usually that they are normal). Nonparametric tests are based on other principles and do not make this kind of assumption. Proponents of parametric tests argue that they are more *efficient* (in the sense that they will detect a significant difference with a smaller sample size than the corresponding non-parametric test); that it is possible to carry out a greater range and variety of tests with them; and that they are *robust* (meaning that violations of the assumptions on which they are based, e.g. about the normality of the distribution from which the data samples are drawn, have little or no effect on the results they produce).

Advocates of nonparametric tests counter with the arguments that their tests tend to be easier to use and understand and hence less prone to mindless regurgitation; that because they are based on fewer assumptions they are usable in a wider variety of contexts; that the best of such tests are virtually identical in efficiency to parametric ones in situations where the latter can legitimately be used – and obviously preferable in other situations; and that there is now an adequate range of tests to deal with virtually any situation (Meddis, 1984).

We suggest a pragmatic approach, driven mainly by the kind of data you are likely to have to deal with, and the range of tests to which you have access through computer packages. Unless your data are obviously non-normal, or are in the form of ranks (i.e. first, second, etc. – nonparametric test typically work on ranks, and scores are first transformed into ranks when they are computed), then use a parametric test if one is available. With computer packages, we do not need to worry about the amount of computation required.

The *Mann–Whitney U test* is a nonparametric equivalent of the unpaired two-group *t*-test. The *Wilcoxon signed-rank test* is a nonparametric equivalent of the paired two-group *t*-test. Computation is straightforward and the SPSS output in both cases provides 'z-scores' (standardized scores expressed in standard deviation units) and associated probabilities. If there are ties in the scores, a corrected z-score is also provided and should be used. Strictly, the tests should not be used if there is a substantial proportion of ties.

SPSS can also carry out two further nonparametric tests which, in the version used in SPSS, are appropriate for use for the same type of situation as a Mann–Whitney U test. These are the *Kolmogorov–Smirnov test* and the *Wald–Wolfowitz Runs test*. They are not widely used.

## Three (or more) group tests

It is not uncommon, in experiments, to have three or more conditions. You may wish, for example, to compare the effects of 'high', 'medium' and 'low' stress levels on performance in some situation. It would be possible to take these conditions in pairs and carry out three separate *t*-tests. However, there are techniques which allow this to be done in a single, overall, test. It is necessary to separate out the 'independent samples' and 'paired samples' designs in the same kind of way as was done with the *t*-test.

*Analysis of variance (single-factor independent samples)* This situation requires the simplest version of a very widely used, and extremely versatile, technique known as analysis of variance. Figure 13.25 shows the format of data referred to. In SPSS terminology this is simply called a 'One-Way

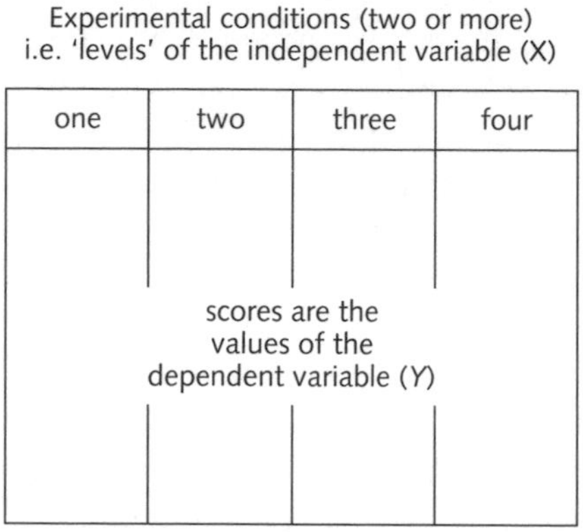

Experimental conditions (two or more)
i.e. 'levels' of the independent variable (X)

| one | two | three | four |
|---|---|---|---|
| | | | |

scores are the
values of the
dependent variable (Y)

**Figure 13.25**   Format of single-factor independent samples analysis of variance.

ANOVA'. Figure 13.26 illustrates the type of output generated by SPSS for this design; very similar output is produced by other packages.

The key finding here is that *there is no overall difference between the means under the different conditions*. This is shown by the $F$-test result and its associated probability, which exceeds the 0.05 level. This would be reported as:

> *The difference between groups is not significant ($F = 0.226$, $p = 0.923$; with 4 and 95 df).*

*If* there is a significant overall difference between the groups, various additional statistics are available helping to pinpoint which of the differences between particular pairs of means are contributing to this overall difference. Figure 13.26 includes one of these, the *Scheffé F-test*. Others are the *Fisher PLSD test*, and the *Dunnett t-test*. They are alternative ways of dealing with the problem of assessing significance level when a sequence of similar tests are carried out on a data set. Effectively, what 'significant at the 5 per cent level' implies is that if you carry out, say, twenty tests you would expect one of the twenty (5 per cent) to be significant even if there is no real effect and only random factors are at work. Any of the three tests could be used, but the Scheffé test is probably the most 'conservative' (i.e. giving the most stringent criteria for significance) and hence is the safest bet. Any significant difference between two conditions is indicated by an asterisk – but should only be reported as such if the overall $F$-test is significant.

As with $t$-tests, it is helpful not only to report the results of the statistical test but also to give the summary statistics, such as the means, standard devia-

**ANOVA**

INCOME

| | Sum of Squares | df | Mean Square | F | Sig. |
|---|---|---|---|---|---|
| Between Groups | 41702340 | 4 | 10425584.95 | 0.226 | 0.923 |
| Within Groups | 4.38E+09 | 95 | 46131195.93 | | |
| Total | 4.42E+09 | 95 | | | |

Dependent Variable: INCOME
Scheffe

| (I) Faculty | (J) Faculty | Mean Difference (I–J) | Std.Error | Sig. | 95% Confidence Interval | |
|---|---|---|---|---|---|---|
| | | | | | Lower Bound | Upper Bound |
| arts | engineering | –343.01 | 1839.28 | 1.000 | –6121.39 | 5435.37 |
| | business | 461.54 | 2135.15 | 1.000 | –6246.34 | 7169.43 |
| | science | 1424.66 | 2174.50 | 0.980 | –5406.86 | 8256.18 |
| | education | –570.20 | 2385.27 | 1.000 | –8063.88 | 6923.49 |
| engineering | arts | 343.01 | 1839.28 | 1.000 | –5435.37 | 6121.39 |
| | business | 804.56 | 2061.87 | 0.997 | –5673.12 | 7282.23 |
| | science | 1767.67 | 2102.60 | 0.950 | –4837.95 | 8373.29 |
| | education | –227.18 | 2319.91 | 1.000 | –7515.53 | 7061.16 |
| business | arts | –461.54 | 2135.15 | 1.000 | –7169.43 | 6246.34 |
| | engineering | –804.56 | 2061.87 | 0.997 | –7282.23 | 5673.12 |
| | science | 936.11 | 2365.76 | 0.997 | –6469.27 | 8395.49 |
| | education | –1031.74 | 2560.83 | 0.997 | –9076.99 | 7013.51 |
| science | arts | –1424.66 | 2174.50 | 0.980 | –8256.18 | 5406.86 |
| | engineering | –1767.67 | 2102.60 | 0.950 | –8373.29 | 4837.95 |
| | business | –963.11 | 2365.76 | 0.997 | –8395.49 | 6469.27 |
| | education | –1994.85 | 2593.74 | 0.964 | –10143.47 | 6153.76 |
| education | arts | 570.20 | 2385.27 | 1.000 | –6923.49 | 8063.88 |
| | engineering | 227.18 | 2319.91 | 1.000 | –7061.16 | 7515.53 |
| | business | 1031.74 | 2560.83 | 0.997 | –7013.51 | 9076.99 |
| | science | 1994.85 | 2593.74 | 0.964 | –6153.76 | 10143.47 |

**Figure 13.26**   Results of a single independent samples analysis of variance.

tions and confidence intervals under the different conditions. This applies when reporting any analysis of variance findings and helps you, and the reader, to appreciate what the analysis means.

*Kruskal–Wallis test*   This is a nonparametric equivalent to the above analysis of variance. It is simpler to compute manually, but with computer assistance there seems little reason to prefer it unless the data are in a form for which a parametric test is unsuitable.

Experimental conditions (two or more)
i.e. 'levels' of the independent variable (X)

| | one | two | three | four |
|---|---|---|---|---|
| participant 1 | | | | |
| participant 2 | | | | |
| participant 3 | scores are the values of the dependent variable (Y) | | | |
| participant 4 | | | | |

**Figure 13.27**   Format of single-factor repeated measures analysis of variance.

*Analysis of variance (single-factor repeated measures)*   The only difference between this design and the previous analysis of variance is that there is a basis for pairing individual scores across the conditions (usually because the same person produces a score under each condition, i.e. there are 'repeated measures'). Figure 13.27 gives an example. The output generated by SPSS is complex, including several esoteric statistics. See Field (2000) for a detailed discussion.

*Friedman test*   This is a nonparametric equivalent to the paired samples analysis of variance discussed above. Again, it is relatively simple to compute manually but with computer assistance there seems little reason to prefer it when the data are in a form for which a parametric test is suitable.

## Testing differences when two (or more) independent variables are involved

As discussed in chapter 5, it is feasible to have two or more independent variables in an experiment, commonly in what are called factorial designs (p. 127). There is a plethora of different analyses for the many different designs. The following account simply covers some main issues.

*Simple two-variable (or factor) analysis of variance*   Figure 13.28 illustrates the form of the data with this design, and Figure 13.29 gives corresponding output from SPSS. The analysis permits an assessment of the effect of each

two independent variables (*A,B*)

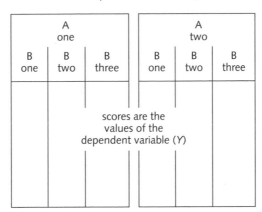

**Figure 13.28**   Format for simple two-variable analysis of variance.

variable separately (the 'main effect' of variables A and B) and also of any possible 'interaction' (or AB effect) between the two variables (refer back to chapter 5, p. 127). In the case of the example shown in figure 13.29, significant effects were found for sex and attractiveness of student on the score they received for their class presentation. If the interaction is significant, this means that the effect of one variable differs at different levels of the second variable. It is then not legitimate to talk about A or B having an overall effect. It can be seen in the example in figure 13.29 that the variables 'sex' and 'attractiveness' show a significant interaction. In realist terms it may be evidence that a mechanism is operating for one gender but not for the other.

The pattern of results should be examined carefully. It helps to display any significant interaction graphically, as in the graph in figure 13.29.

Note that while ANOVA analysis generally assumes that there is the same number of scores in each cell (called a 'balanced' model), SPSS can also cope with differing numbers in the cells (an 'unbalanced' model).

*Two-variable (or factor) analysis of variance with repeated measures* A frequently used complication of the above design is for there to be repeated measures. Thus, participants may not be simply tested once under a particular combination of levels of the two variables, but may be given a series of trials. See Field (2000) for further discussion and examples using SPSS.

**Tests of Between-Subjects Effects**

Dependent Variable: Presentation score (out of 20)

| Source | Type III Sum of Squares | df | Mean Square | F | Sig. |
|---|---|---|---|---|---|
| Corrected Model | 428.083[a] | 3 | 142.694 | 31.857 | 0.000 |
| Intercept | 853.333 | 1 | 853.333 | 190.512 | 0.000 |
| SEX | 158.700 | 1 | 158.700 | 35.431 | 0.000 |
| ATTRACT | 252.300 | 1 | 252.300 | 56.327 | 0.000 |
| SEX*ATTRACT | 83.333 | 1 | 83.333 | 18.605 | 0.001 |
| Error | 71.667 | 16 | 4.479 | | |
| Total | 1281.000 | 20 | | | |
| Corrected Total | 499.750 | 19 | | | |

[a.] R Squared = 0.875 (Adjusted R Squared = 0.830)

**1. SEX**

Dependent Variable:
Presentation score (out of 20)

| SEX | Mean | Std. Error |
|---|---|---|
| male | 9.542 | 0.683 |
| female | 3.792 | 0.683 |

**2. Attractiveness**

Dependent Variable:
Presentation score (out of 20)

| Attractiveness | Mean | Std. Error |
|---|---|---|
| attractive | 10.292 | 0.683 |
| not attractive | 3.042 | 0.683 |

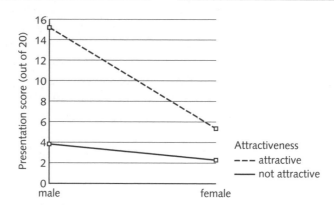

**Figure 13.29**   Results of a two-way independent samples analysis of variance.

## Testing differences when two (or more) dependent variables are involved

The above analyses are all limited to dealing with a single dependent variable. In studies with more than one, it is possible simply to repeat the analysis for each dependent variable in turn. However, there are advantages in carrying out a single, global analysis. One version of this is called *multivariate analysis of variance* (MANOVA). The analysis and its interpretation are complex and should not be undertaken without advice. MANOVA is available on SPSS. Bryman and Cramer (1997) provide a basic introduction. Field (2000) provides more detailed coverage.

## Quantitative Analysis and Different Fixed Design Research Strategies

This chapter has not attempted to make one-to-one correspondences between the different fixed design research strategies and particular techniques of quantitative analysis. Ways of displaying, summarizing and manipulating data are essentially common to all strategies. Many of the ways of exploring relationships among the data are applicable to each of them. There are, admittedly, problems of interpretation when tests of significance are used in the absence of random sampling, but they do not so much preclude their use in quasi-experiments, or non-experimental fixed designs, as require the analyst to think very carefully about interpretation.

There are strong links between some analytical approaches and particular research strategies, which have been referred to at various points in the chapter. Analysis of variance was developed to deal with the analysis of the true experiment. Correlation matrices and associated techniques such as factor analysis are commonly used in surveys and similar non-experimental settings. However, labelling each test as appropriate only for a specific strategy would be as unnecessarily restrictive as insisting that a particular method of data collection, such as direct observation, should only be used in an experiment – when it could well play a part in a case study, or even in a survey.

It may be helpful, nevertheless, to highlight issues in the analysis of data from two types of experimental study likely to be of real world interest (quasi-experiments and single-case experiments) and in the analysis of surveys and other non-experimental designs.

### The analysis of quasi-experiments

Three possible quasi-experimental designs were recommended for serious consideration in chapter 4: the pre-test post-test non-equivalent groups design, the interrupted time series design and the regression discontinuity design (pp. 138–46). The three designs require differing approaches to their analysis.

*Pre-test post-test non-equivalent groups design*   This is a very common design and it is not unusual (though incorrect) for researchers to treat it as a true experiment in both description and analysis. The non-equivalence of the groups means that there are possible selection effects that may bias the results. Several techniques are available which attempt to separate out the treatment effect (i.e. the effect of the independent variable on the dependent variable) from the effect of selection differences. The most frequently used approaches are:

a   simple analysis of variance;
b   analysis of variance with blocking or matching of participants;
c   analysis of variance based on 'gain' scores (e.g. difference between pre and post scores);
d   analysis of covariance (with either single or multiple covariates).

Reichardt (1979) provides details of each of these approaches, and of the difficulties they raise. He concludes that 'any one of these statistical methods could be biased enough so that a useful treatment might look harmful and a harmful treatment could look benign or even beneficial' (p. 197). His recommendation, in line with the general approach taken in this text, is not that we give up and regard the statistical procedures as worthless, but that we give them a relatively minor role – by seeking to eliminate, or at least trying to reduce, the effect of selection and other threats through the *design* of the study rather than relying on the statistical analysis removing their effects. One interesting approach is to try to 'bracket' the effect of a treatment by using a variety of different but reasonable techniques of analysis (see Cook et al.'s 1975 evaluation of the *Sesame Street* TV series for an example).

*Interrupted time series design*   The approaches to the analysis of this design which are generally regarded as satisfactory (e.g. the use of autoregressive integrated moving average models – ARIMA models – as developed by Box and Jenkins, 1976) require a minimum sequence of about fifty data points, and preferably over 100 of them. Series of this length tend to be very rare in small-scale studies, although if anyone manages to generate this amount of data, the discussion by Glass et al. (1975), provides useful suggestions.

For smaller amounts of data, the use of repeated measures analysis of variance has been advocated. This assumes that the data are independent – that is, that with events occurring in time, those close together in time are no more closely correlated with each other than those further apart in time – which is a very dubious assumption. Another form of 'bracketing' technique has been proposed by Greenhouse and Geisser (1959) to deal with this issue.

Similar data patterns to those found in interrupted time series designs occur with single-case designs, and hence the forms of analysis suggested for single-case designs may be appropriate in some cases (see Gorman and Allison, 1996; and the next section).

*Regression discontinuity design*    In contrast to the two previous designs, there is a satisfactory and readily accessible means of analysing data from this design. The recommended approach is to use the analysis of covariance, with the pre-test as the single covariate. Reichardt (1979, pp. 202–5) gives details.

## The analysis of single-case experiments

The simple form of single-case experiment involves a single independent variable and a single dependent variable (traditionally the *rate* of some response, although this is not a necessary feature). Hence it might have been dealt with earlier together with other two-variable situations. However, there are major differences of ideology about purposes and procedures of analysis between single-case experimenters and others that warrant their separate consideration.

Researchers using single-case designs have avoided statistical analysis and relied upon 'eyeballing' the data – looking at a comparison, in graphical form, of the participant's performance (sometimes called 'charting') in the different phases of the study. They tend to claim that if statistical techniques were needed to tease out any effects, then the effects were not worth bothering about (see Sidman, 1960, for a clear exposition of the ideas underlying this methodology). This argument has undeniable force, though we will see that, as usual, things are more complicated than they may at first appear. It arose in part because of the applied focus of many single-case studies (see the *Journal of Applied Behavior Analysis* for examples), where the distinction is commonly made between *clinical significance* and *statistical significance*. As discussed previously (p. 400) the latter refers to the unlikeliness that a result is due to chance factors. Clinical significance means that a treatment has produced a substantial effect such that, for example, a person with problems can now function adequately in society.

However, while Skinner and his fellow experimenters working with rats or pigeons in the laboratory were able to exert sufficient control so that stable base-lines could be obtained from which the performance in subsequent phases could be differentiated, this has, not surprisingly, proved more difficult in applied 'field' studies with humans. This once again illustrates the difference between 'open' and 'closed' systems (see chapter 2, p. 39). Some researchers with 'applied' interests have questioned the wisdom of ignoring non-dramatic changes, particularly in exploratory work (e.g. Hersen and Barlow, 1976). They argue that we should determine whether changes are reliable, and then subsequently follow them up. It has also been demonstrated that the reliability of 'eye-balling' as a technique can leave a lot to be desired, with different individuals reaching different conclusions as to what the data were telling them (e.g. DeProspero and Cohen, 1979).

These factors have led to an increasing interest in, and use of, statistical tests of significance in single-case studies, although this is still a controversial area. Gorman and Allison (1996) provide an up-to-date account; see also Kazdin (1982, ch. 10). The techniques advocated are themselves the subject of controversy, largely for the same reason encountered in considering time series quasi-experimental designs, namely, the lack of independence of successive data points obtained from the same individual. Again, the sequence of data points obtained in most real world single case-experiments is insufficient to use standard time series approaches, but they provide a good solution if extensive data are available. Additional possibilities include the following:

- t-*tests and analysis of variance*   Used to assess whether there is a significant change between two phases ($t$), or among a number of phases (ANOVA). Assumes that there is independence in the observations.
- *Randomization tests*   Can only be used if the different experimental conditions can be randomly assigned over time, e.g. on a weekly basis.
- $R_A$ *test of rank*   Used in multiple base-line designs, with the intervention being applied to the different base-lines in randomized order. Minimum of four base-lines needed to give possibility of a significant result.
- *Split-middle test*   Basically a descriptive technique that can be used with most single-case designs, but can incorporate statistical significance through use of the binomial test. Needs several equally spaced observations over a number of phases.

Further details on these tests and their application, together with references, are provided in Kazdin (1982, appendix B).

## The analysis of surveys

Surveys, and many other non-experimental designs, in their simplest form produce a two-dimensional rows and columns matrix coding data on a range of variables from a set of respondents. As ever, your research questions drive the form of analysis which you choose. If the study is purely descriptive, the techniques covered in the section on 'Exploring the Data Set' (p. 403) may be all that you need. Frequency distributions, graphical displays such as histograms and box plots, summary statistics such as means and standard deviations, will go a long way towards providing the answers you need. You may need to go on to analyse relationships using contingency tables and correlation coefficients and/or analysing differences through *t*-tests and other statistics.

With studies seeking to explain or understand what is going on, you should still start with this exploratory, 'know your data' phase. However, when you have some conceptual model, possibly expressed in terms of mechanisms, which provides the basis for the research questions you will need to take the analysis further following a more confirmatory style.

This may involve the testing of some specific two-variable relationships. The 'elaboration' approach (discussed on p. 427) can help to clarify the meaning of relationships between variables. More sophisticated analyses such as multiple linear regression perform a similar task in more complex situations. Modelling techniques such as SEM (p. 434) provide ways of quantifying and testing the conceptual model.

*Causation in surveys and other non-experimental designs*  Catherine Marsh (1982) accepts that 'the process of drawing causal inferences from surveys is problematic and indirect' (p. 69). Writing from a realist perspective, she provides a very clear account of some ways of going about this difficult task (Marsh, 1982, ch. 3). Recall that the traditional positivist view of causation, known as 'constant conjunction', was found in chapter 2 to be seriously wanting. Following realist precepts, we are concerned to establish a causal model which specifies the existence of a number of mechanisms or processes operating in particular contexts.

How can surveys help in doing this? Obviously correlations can be computed, but the injunction that 'correlation does not imply causation' should be etched deeply on the cortex of anyone who has followed a course in statistics. The temptation to get SPSS to cross-tabulate 'ALL' against 'ALL' (i.e. asking it to crunch out relationships between all the variables and then cherry-picking the significant ones) should be resisted. Working with a 5 per cent significance level means that we expect on average one in twenty of the results to be significant due to chance factors. While there are ways of dealing with the problem of chance correlations (e.g. by splitting the cases randomly into two equal sub-sets, exploring the correlations obtained with the first, then checking with the second), you still need to make ad hoc arguments to explain your pattern of findings.

One approach, simple in principle, involves the *'elaboration'* strategy discussed above and earlier in the chapter (p. 427). If you have a thought-through proposed causal model involving a small number of possible mechanisms, it can be tested in this way. Unfortunately, this process rapidly becomes unwieldy as more variables are included in the model. By going back and forth between model and data, gradually elaborating the model, it may be feasible to build up a more complex model. This process need not be totally 'pure'. While the unprincipled fishing trip is not a good way of developing a causal model, further development of the model based in part on hunches and insights that occur during analysis is well within the spirit of exploratory data analysis. Marsh (1988) summarizes the task as follows:

> In the absence of an experiment, a statistical effect of one variable on another cannot just be accepted as causal at face value. If we want to show that it is not *spurious*, we have to demonstrate that there are no plausible *prior variables* affecting both the variables of interest. If we want to argue that the *causal mechanism is* fairly direct, we have to control for similar intervening variables. (p. 238, emphases added)

Marsh (1988, esp. chs 12–15) gives an excellent account of the use of elaboration and related techniques to establish causation. It is stressed here as still being of value in small-scale real world study when data on a restricted set of variables have been collected, and the model to be tested is necessarily simple.

More generally, the more powerful multivariate techniques accessible via SPSS, in particular structural equation modelling (SEM), as discussed on p. 434, have tended to replace the type of sequential logic required when using elaboration. As a confirmatory data analysis approach, it provides a clear means of testing conceptual models.

*A note on interactions*   Formally, an interaction is when the effect of one variable on a second one depends on the value of a third variable. They were discussed earlier in the chapter in the context of two-variable analyses of variance (p. 444). When such interactions exist – and they are extremely common in social research – they mean that any generalizations we seek to make about causal processes are limited. This is a serious obstacle to positivistic researchers, who seek universal laws. However, it is entirely consistent with the critical realist view that mechanisms do not operate universally and that the research task is to specify the contexts in which they do work.

## A realist reminder on the analysis and interpretation of experiments

The realist view of experimentation, as discussed in chapter 5 (p. 120), is fundamentally different from the traditional positivist one. The main remaining similarity is in the active role taken by the experimenter. It is her responsibility so to set up and manipulate the situation that predicted mechanisms are given the chance to operate. This calls for a considerable degree of prior knowledge and experience of the phenomenon or situation studied, so that a conceptual map or model can be developed with some confidence. This predicts likely mechanisms, the contexts in which they may work, and for whom they will work.

Viewing experiments in this light does not, in general, either preclude or privilege any of the experimental designs covered in chapter 5, nor any of the analyses covered in this chapter. There may well be situations, as discussed by Pawson and Tilley (1997, pp. 34–54) where the nature of likely causal agents is such that, for example, randomized allocation to different conditions changes the nature of the phenomenon of interest. Hence control group methodology is inappropriate. Careful attention to such possible distortions is needed at the design stage.

Assuming the choice of an appropriate design, the question becomes one of deciding whether we have good evidence for the operation of the predicted mechanisms. In most cases this boils down to deciding whether an obtained relationship or difference (typically of means) provides that evidence. While it will in many cases be feasible to generate statistical significance values, they need to be taken with even more than the usual pinch of salt (see p. 400). This is because they have been derived within the positivistic conceptualization of experimental design. While it seems intuitively reasonable that, irrespective of this heritage, a lower probability value for the statistical significance of a difference gives greater confidence in the reality of that difference, it is difficult to go much further than that. Recall, however, that the advice throughout has been to place greater reliance on measures of effect sizes based on statistics such as confidence intervals and standardized differences in means (p. 402). Armed with these and graphical displays, you then have to judge the quality of the evidence.

## Further Reading

Bryman, A. and Cramer, D. (1997) *Quantitative Data Analysis with SPSS for Windows: A Guide for Social Scientists*. London: Routledge. This and:

Foster, J. J. (2001) *Data Analysis Using SPSS for Windows. New Edition: Versions 8–10*. London: Sage are two clearly presented, non-technical introductions to quantitative analyses using SPSS.

Byrne, B. M. (1994) *Structural Equation Modeling with EQS and EQS/Windows: Basic Concepts, Applications, and Programming*. Thousand Oaks, Calif.: Sage. Clear introduction to the structural equation modelling approach.

Marsh, C. (1988) *Exploring Data: An Introduction to Data Analysis for Social Scientists*. Cambridge: Polity. Very clear and detailed exposition of exploratory data analysis (EDA) approaches. Concentrates more on analysis of large-scale studies, but much of value here.

Maxwell, S. E. and Delaney, H. D. (1999) *Designing Experiments and Analyzing Data: A Model Comparison Perspective*. Mahwah, NJ: Lawrence Erlbaum Associates. Definitive analysis of variance text for those who wish to understand the underlying logic. Shows how this provides a framework for understanding more complex techniques such as structural equation modelling. Follows a realist approach.

Myers, J. L. (1979) *Fundamentals of Experimental Design*, 2nd edn. Boston: Allyn & Bacon. Essentially an analysis of variance book. Clear and adopts an approach usable for virtually all ANOVAs.

Pilcher, D. M. (1990) *Data Analysis for the Helping Professions: A Practical Guide*. Newbury Park, Calif.: Sage. Part I gives guidelines on selection of statistical procedures. Part II gives illustrations of how the analysis can be done, covering an unusually wide range of tests.

Siegel, S. and Castellan, N. J. (1988) *Nonparametric Statistics for the Behavioral Sciences*, 2nd edn. New York: McGraw-Hill. Second edition of widely used book on nonparametric statistics. Deservedly popular.

Tabachnik, B. G. and Fidell, L. S. (1996) *Using Multivariate Statistics*, 3rd edn. New York: HarperCollins. Accessible introduction to a complex topic.

# 14

# The Analysis of Qualitative Data

This chapter:

- considers approaches to the systematic analysis of qualitative data
- stresses the central role of the person doing the analysis, and warns about some deficiencies of the human as analyst
- discusses the advantages and disadvantages of using specialist computer software
- provides an introduction to the use of the NUD*IST package
- explains the Miles and Huberman approach to analysis which concentrates on reducing the bulk of qualitative data to manageable amounts and on displaying them to help draw conclusions
- reviews particular features of the analysis of data arising from the three main flexible design strategies: case studies, ethnographic studies and grounded theory studies
- briefly summarizes some alternative approaches

## Introduction

Qualitative data have been described as an 'attractive nuisance' (Miles, 1979). Their attractiveness is undeniable. Words, which are by far the most common form of qualitative data, are a speciality of humans and their organizations. Narratives, accounts and other collections of words are variously described as 'rich', 'full' and 'real', and contrasted with the thin abstractions of number. Their collection is often straightforward. They have a quality of 'undeniability' (Smith, 1975) which lends verisimilitude to reports.

The 'nuisance' refers to the legal doctrine that if you leave an attractive object, such as an unlocked car, where children can play with it, you may be liable for any injuries they sustain. Naïve researchers may be injured by unforeseen problems with qualitative data. This can occur at the collection stage, where overload is a constant danger. But the main difficulty is in their analysis.

There is no clear and accepted single set of conventions for analysis corresponding to those observed with quantitative data. Indeed, many 'qualitative' workers would resist their development, viewing this enterprise as more of an art than a science. For those who do wish to work within the kind of scientific framework advocated in this book, and who wish to persuade scientific or policy-making audiences, there are ways in which qualitative data can be dealt with systematically. This chapter seeks to provide an introduction to that task.

If you are using a multimethod approach, it may well be that one or more of the methods generates qualitative data. Some such data, say from documents or, possibly, open responses in questionnaires, may be best dealt with by the kinds of techniques discussed in chapter 12 under the heading of 'content analysis'. Other verbal data are likely to be very various and to need different treatment. In the typology of research strategies that has been adopted in this text, the various types of flexible designs are the prime generators of large amounts of such complex qualitative data.

Qualitative data may, however, be useful in supplementing and illustrating the quantitative data obtained from an experiment or survey. Small amounts of qualitative data used as an adjunct within a largely quantitative fixed design study will not justify detailed and complex analysis. Often the need is simply to help the account 'live' and communicate to the reader through the telling quotation or apt example. However, when methods generating qualitative data form the only, or a substantial, aspect of the study, then serious and detailed attention needs to be given to the principles of their analysis.

## Two assumptions

*1   If you have a substantial amount of qualitative data you will use some kind of software package to deal with it*   A word-processing package can do much to reduce the sheer tedium of qualitative data analysis. For anything other than a small amount of data, the amount of drudgery you can avoid, and the ease with which you can relate to the data, make the use of a computer near to essential. There are also specialist qualitative data analysis packages which aid the process even more. This chapter covers one such package which is now widely used – NUD*IST (a somewhat provocative acronym simply referring to 'Non-numerical, Unstructured Data Indexing, Searching and Theorizing').

*2    Unless you already have experience yourself, you will be helped or advised by someone who does have experience in this type of analysis*    The dominant model for carrying out qualitative analysis has in the past been that of apprenticeship. Without accepting all the implications of such a model (which tends, for example, to include a principled inarticulacy about process), there is undoubted value in expert advice. The help provided by software is very different from that in quantitative analysis. There the 'expert's' role is largely to point you towards an appropriate test and to ensure that you understand the outcome. In qualitative data analysis, both the experienced person and the computer help you through a not very well specified process.

## Types of Qualitative Analysis

Tesch (1990, p. 58) lists forty-six labels that qualitative researchers have used to describe their approach. She reduces these to four basic groupings, where the interest is in:

a    the characteristics of language;
b    the discovery of regularities;
c    the comprehension of the meaning of text or action; and
d    reflection.

Crabtree and Miller (1992) produce a different typology, more closely linked to the method of data analysis used:

a    quasi-statistical methods;
b    template approaches;
c    editing approaches; and
d    immersion approaches.

In each case this constitutes a progression from more to less structured and formal. The final groupings, 'reflection' or 'immersion', are ones whose proponents are particularly resistant to any systemization of their analytical process. Box 14.1 provides further details using the latter typology.

Quasi-statistical approaches rely largely on the conversion of qualitative data into a quantitative format and have been covered under the heading of content analysis in chapter 12, p. 351). Because of the difficulties in reconciling the 'immersion' approach with accepted canons of what is implied by taking a scientific approach (see chapter 2, p. 18), this is not pursued further here.

## Box 14.1

### Different approaches to qualitative analysis

*1   Quasi-statistical approaches*

- Use word or phrase frequencies and inter-correlations as key methods of determining the relative importance of terms and concepts.
- Typified by *content analysis.*

*2   Template approaches*

- Key codes are determined either on an a priori basis (e.g. derived from theory or research questions) or from an initial read of the data.
- These codes then serve as a template (or 'bins') for data analysis; the template may be changed as analysis continues.
- Text segments which are empirical evidence for template categories are identified.
- Typified by *matrix analysis,* where descriptive summaries of the text segments are supplemented by matrices, network maps, flow charts and diagrams.

*3   Editing approaches*

- More interpretive and flexible than the above.
- No (or few) a priori codes.
- Codes are based on the researcher's interpretation of the meanings or patterns in the texts.
- Typified by *grounded theory* approaches.

*4   Immersion approaches*

- Least structured and most interpretive, emphasizing researcher insight, intuition and creativity.
- Methods are fluid and not systematized.
- Close to literary/artistic interpretation and connoisseurship (i.e. calling for expert knowledge and targeted at a similarly skilled audience).
- Difficult to reconcile with the scientific approach.

(Based, in part, on Drisko, 2000.)

This leaves the template and editing approaches, which together cover the kinds of systematic approaches to qualitative data analysis likely to be most useful with the flexible designs covered in this text. Whatever approach is taken, the researcher has the responsibility of describing it in detail. You have to be able to demonstrate how you got from the data to your conclusions. In other words, the reliability and validity of your interpretation is a serious concern, to which we return below on p. 483.

## The importance of the quality of the analyst

The central requirement in qualitative analysis is clear thinking on the part of the analyst. As Fetterman (1989) puts it, in the context of an ethnographic stance, the analysis is as much a test of the enquirer as it is a test of the data: 'First and foremost, analysis is a test of the ability to think – to process information in a meaningful and useful manner' (p. 88) Qualitative analysis remains much closer to codified common sense than the complexities of statistical analysis of quantitative data. However, humans as 'natural analysts' have deficiencies and biases corresponding to the problems that they have as observers (see chapter 11, p. 322). Some of these are listed in box 14.2. This chapter suggests ways of adopting a more systematic approach which will help to minimize these human deficiencies. However, there is an emphasis on *interpretation* in dealing with much qualitative data which precludes reducing the task to a defined formula. Hence, the suggestions made in this chapter are more in the nature of guides to possible approaches than tight prescriptions.

## Common features of qualitative data analysis

While the possible approaches to analysis are very diverse, there are recurring features. Miles and Huberman (1994, p. 9) give a sequential list of what they describe as 'a fairly classic set of analytic moves':

- giving codes to the initial set of materials obtained from observation, interviews, documentary analysis, etc.;
- adding comments, reflections, etc. (commonly referred to as 'memos');
- going through the materials trying to identify similar phrases, patterns, themes, relationships, sequences, differences between sub-groups, etc.;
- taking these patterns, themes, etc. out to the field to help focus the next wave of data collection;
- gradually elaborating a small set of generalizations that cover the consistencies you discern in the data;
- linking these generalizations to a formalized body of knowledge in the form of constructs or theories.

---

## Box 14.2

### Deficiencies of the human as analyst

**1**  *Data overload*   Limitations on the amount of data that can be dealt with (too much to receive, process and remember).

**2**  *First impressions*   Early input makes a large impression so that subsequent revision is resisted.

**3**  *Information availability*   Information which is difficult to get hold of gets less attention than that which is easier to obtain.

**4**  *Positive instances*   There is a tendency to ignore information conflicting with hypotheses already held, and to emphasize information that confirms them.

**5**  *Internal consistency*   There is a tendency to discount the novel and unusual.

**6**  *Uneven reliability*   The fact that some sources are more reliable than others tends to be ignored.

**7**  *Missing information*   Something for which information is incomplete tends to be devalued.

**8**  *Revision of hypotheses*   There is a tendency either to over- or to under-react to new information.

**9**  *Fictional base*   The tendency to compare with a base or average when no base data is available.

**10**  *Confidence in judgement*   Excessive confidence is rested in one's judgement once it is made.

**11**  *Co-occurrence*   Co-occurrence tends to be interpreted as strong evidence for correlation.

**12**  *Inconsistency*   Repeated evaluations of the same data tend to differ.

(Adapted and abridged from Sadler, 1981, pp. 27–30.)

---

## Using Computer Software for Qualitative Data Analysis

The single constant factor reported by qualitative researchers is that their studies generate very large amounts of raw data. A small ethnographic study is likely to generate many pages of field notes including records of observations, informal interviews, conversations and discussions. This is likely to be supplemented by copies of various documents you have had access to, notes on your own thoughts and feelings, etc., etc. A multimethod case study will produce a similar range and amount of material. Even a strictly limited grounded theory study relying solely on interviews leaves you with twenty or more tapes to be transcribed and subsequently analysed.

Before getting on with any of Miles and Huberman's 'analytic moves', you need to ensure that you know what data you have available and that they are labelled, stored and, if necessary, edited and generally cleaned up so that they are both retrievable and understandable when you carry out the analysis. The first analytic task of coding the materials (i.e. deciding that a particular part or segment of, say, an interview transcript falls into the category of 'requesting information' or 'expressing doubt') involves not only assigning that code but also having a way of seeing it alongside other data you have coded in the same way.

In the pre-computer era, these tasks were accomplished by means of file folders containing the various sources of data, markers and highlighters, and copious photocopying. One strategy was to make as many photocopies of a page as there were different codes on that page, then to file all examples of a code together. It is clear that much of the drudgery of this task can be eliminated by using a word processor. Many data sources will either be directly in the form of computer files or can be converted into them without difficulty. It may be feasible to enter field notes directly into a notebook computer. An interview tape can be entered into the word processor as it is being transcribed. Incidentally, if you have to do this yourself, there is much to be said for the use of speech recognition software for this task (listen to each sentence on the tape through headphones, then repeat it out loud to activate speech recognition). Similarly, if you have access to a scanner with optical character recognition (OCR) software, it is now straightforward to convert many documents into word processor files. There are, however, some types of data for which this will not be feasible (e.g. handwritten reports and very long documents).

Word processors are a boon in storing, organizing and keeping track of your data. Obviously, you need to observe good housekeeping practices and should take advice on how you can survive possible hard disk crashes, loss, theft, fire, etc. Essentially, this means having multiple copies of everything, regularly kept up to date in more than one location, and in both paper and computer file versions. Word processors can also help with the coding task through 'copy' and 'paste' functions. In this way, it is easy to build up files containing all instances of a particular coding while retaining the original file with the original data to which codes have been added.

The live issue is whether you go beyond this to use one of the many specialist software packages designed to help with qualitative data analysis. Box 14.3

---

# Box 14.3

## Advantages and disadvantages of specialist qualitative data analysis (QDA) computer programs

### Advantages

- They provide an organized single location storage system for all stored material (also true of word processing programs).
- They give quick and easy access to material (e.g. codes) without using 'cut and paste' techniques.
- They can handle large amounts of data very quickly.
- They force detailed consideration of *all* text in the database on a line-by-line (or similar) basis.
- They help the development of consistent coding schemes.

### Disadvantages

- Proficiency in their use takes time and effort.
- There may be difficulties in changing, or reluctance to change, categories of information once they have been established.
- Particular programs tend to impose specific approaches to data analysis.

*Note*: Different programs do different things; see Weitzman and Miles (1995). (Adapted and abridged from Cresswell, 1998, pp. 155–6.)

---

covers some general advantages and disadvantages in their use (see also Fielding and Lee, 1998; and Catteral and Maclaran, 1998). Typically, these packages are of little help in the detailed examination of small amounts of data, as for example in conversation analysis and some types of discourse analysis (Seale, 2000, pp. 162–3).

Weitzman and Miles (1995) distinguish five types of software, though they make the point that most programs are actually a blend or combination of these general types. They are:

- *text retrievers*, which specialize in finding all instances of words, phrases or other strings of characters; some have features useful for content analysis (e.g. counting and displaying words in their context);
- *textbase managers*, which are good at organizing a large number of files, sorting them, making systematic sub-sets of the text and then providing for search and retrieval;

- *code and retrieve programs*, which help you divide texts into segments, attach codes to them, and then find and display all chunks with a given code (or combination of codes);
- *code-based theory builders*, which have the same type of code and retrieve capabilities as the previous type but also include specific features intended to support theory-building (e.g. help to make connections between codes and build higher-order codes, to formulate and test propositions implying that a particular conceptual structure fits the data);
- *conceptual network-builders*, which also help build and test theory but work via systematically built graphic networks developed from your data and concepts.

Several examples of each type are reviewed and evaluated by Weitzman and Miles, though this is a rapidly changing field where new versions and new packages regularly become available.

Stanley and Temple (1996) compared a widely used word processing package (Word for Windows) with five then current specialist programs (The Ethnograph, askSAM, ETHNO, NUD*IST, and InfoSelect) and concluded that:

> qualitative researchers should consider using a good word-processing package as their basic analytic aid, and that only if they want to do something that this package cannot do should they then consider using a dedicated package. That is, for many researchers, the facilities provided in a good word-processing package will be sufficient to the analysis required. (p. 167)

(Note, conversely, that the authors of NVivo claim that the word processing facilities in NVivo are sufficient to write your paper, report, etc. in that program.) The essential downside to using specialist software is the time and effort needed to become proficient in its use. This is difficult to quantify, but can be reduced by involvement in hands-on workshops. The position taken here (influenced by the increasing user-friendliness of such packages) is that while the effort may not be worthwhile if you are concerned only with a small, one-off qualitative project, you should definitely make the effort if the project is large, or collaborative, or other qualitative projects are on the cards.

NUD*IST has been selected for discussion in this chapter, mainly because of its current wide penetration in this market but also because, although it can be used as a theory-generation program and was initially designed for grounded theory, it is not rigidly tied to a particular view of qualitative data analysis. It is classified by Weitzman and Miles (1995) as a 'code-based theory builder', which, as indicated above, implies that it can also be used just for coding and retrieving. An alternative program covering the same general areas and with several attractive features is ATLAS/ti (Windows only: www.scolari.co.uk). Alexa and Zuell (2000) review fifteen currently available packages for those who want to look further.

## An Overview of the NUD*IST Approach

The intention here is to try to give a general feel for what NUD*IST does and how you use it. Later sections of the chapter cover its use in the different contexts of the analysis of data from the three main flexible designs covered in this text (grounded theory studies, ethnographic studies and case studies). The versions current at the time of writing are NUD*IST 5 for Windows, and NUD*IST 4 for Macintosh. The program includes sample data sets and tutorials, and has a good manual, all of which you should work through; see also Gahan and Hannibal (1998). It is highly desirable to have the help and support of someone with experience in its use, and attendance at a practical workshop will prove useful. The listserv 'qual-software' maintained by the CAQDAS Networking Project at the University of Surrey, UK (www.soc.surrey.ac.uk/caqdas) carries regular postings about workshops in many parts of the world. Meadows and Dodendorf (1999) give a clear and detailed example, based on a project on midlife women's health, of the use of NUD*IST.

A new package from the same stable as NUD*IST, known as NVivo, is available. It follows the same basic approach but has several clear advantages over NUD*IST (Richards, 1999; Gibbs, 2001).

## The document system ('Document Explorer')

This is the means by which your various sources of data are made available to the program. It can deal with *imported documents* (where the actual texts are made available to the computer) and with *external documents* (where a reference to the document, rather than the document itself, is held within the computer). Imported documents are things like transcriptions of interviews and summaries of conversations. In fact, anything which you can transform into a computer text file can be imported (an advantage of NVivo is that video-tapes, audio-tapes, etc. can also be imported). External documents might include handwritten field notes, video-tapes, books, etc. These can be linked into the program (for example, you can code your field notes and then keep a reference to the position of each coding), but you will have to return to the original document to examine its content when doing the analysis.

Documents imported into NUD*IST have to be saved as 'plain text' files; this means that any special word-processing formatting (such as the use of italics or underlining) is removed. Document introduction in NUD*IST 5 is much easier than in earlier versions. Further preparation is not essential but can be helpful. You may wish to include a *header* to the document (for an interview this might be, say, the time and place, and name of interviewee). Headers have to be preceded by an asterisk (*) and followed by a 'hard' carriage return (i.e. entered via the use of the return or new-line key rather than the computer's start of a new line automatically). They are not searchable by the program. This means that if you do wish to have the potential for coding or searching for some feature, it must be included in the body of the text.

You can also, if you wish, split the document into *sections* by the use of *sub-headings*. A subheading starts with an asterisk as the first character in the line; a section consists of the subheading and all the text that follows it until the next subheading is indicated by the use of an asterisk at the start of a line. This is a useful feature for many documents and enables you to identify things like the speaker in an interview, or question numbers, which can help in various searches.

*The text unit*   You have to decide on the basic unit of text appropriate for the analysis of an imported document. The end of a unit and start of a new one is indicated by using a hard carriage return (producing the paragraph symbol in Word and other word-processing packages). A paragraph with one or more sentences (perhaps representing a reply to a question in an interview) is a common unit; however, you might choose to use a single sentence, or a line, or even an individual word as your unit; in each case, this is indicated by a hard carriage return at the end of a unit. If individual words are chosen as the unit the document, with a single word on each line, is unwieldy to deal with and has the effect of stripping a word from its context. Hence NUD*IST is not well adapted to this fine-grained analysis. You can have paragraphs in the document as a default choice, but insert extra hard carriage returns at points such as sentence ends, or phrase ends, if you wish to. ATLAS/ti and NVivo permit 'free form coding' (you simply select each piece of text you wish to act as a unit).

External documents can be divided in a similar manner and can have text units of varying lengths and types (e.g. a page in a field notebook; or the tape counter number for an untranscribed audio- or video-tape). You specify the number of text units in a document when integrating it into NUD*IST and can code these units as you would those in an imported document. While you can't retrieve the text itself, the text unit numbers can be looked up in the documents themselves.

## The index system ('Node Explorer')

This system provides a tool for thinking about your data, and for developing and exploring ideas about the data. Gahan and Hannibal (1998, p. 9) view the document and index systems as two separate metaphorical bags sitting alongside each other. The document bag contains your data in a variety of documents which are mostly complex, messy and pretty chaotic. The index bag has nothing in it to start with. You put into it things which appear to you to be likely to help in analysing and understanding your project. These include categories, themes and labels which express characteristics of things in the data; your first attempts at developing theories about what is going on. In other terms, your coding of the data goes into the index bag.

*Coding in NUD\*IST is the process of indexing your text so that the coding scheme can be used as an index for retrieving text.* The codes are (somewhat confusingly – though you get used to it) referred to as *nodes.* This is because NUD\*IST encourages you to develop a hierarchical 'tree' structure, where the nodes are the points in the tree where branching takes place, as illustrated in figure 14.1. It is, however, up to you how the nodes are organized. They can be entirely unstructured, or be in a flat non-hierarchical structure; or some may be left free-floating while others are linked in a tree. As you proceed with the analysis and exploration of the data, it is likely that at least some degree of structure will develop. You can construct a node tree without indexing or coding any text at the nodes, for example if you have a pre-existing template to use.

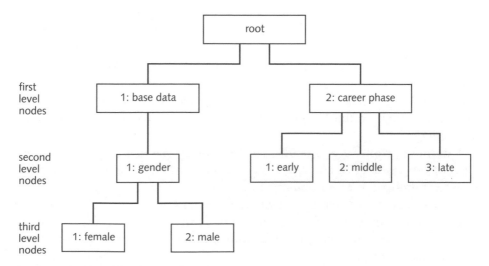

**Figure 14.1** Example of a simple index tree.

It is worth stressing that nodes can represent anything you want. For example, as well as categories or concepts they can refer to individuals, or specific contexts, or to a case. As discussed below, one node in a grounded theory study might concern all the demographic information about those interviewed; or, in an ethnographic study, a node might relate to descriptive information about the culture being studied. A particular text unit can be coded in more than one way.

Whenever you create a new node, NUD*IST will ask you to specify its position in the index tree hierarchy, or to create it as a free node. If, as is likely at the initial stages, you are not sure about this or haven't thought about it, don't let the program bully you. You can leave a node, or all nodes for that matter, as free nodes for the time being, and assign them a place in a developing hierarchy at a later stage.

*Note*: The top of the tree in NUD*IST is referred to as the *root, or first, level*! The next, lower, level in the hierarchy is the second level, etc. This is the reverse of the way in which trees grow; and also of how we usually think of hierarchies (although a familiar usage in computer file organization).

## Making memos in NUD*IST

The making of memos plays an important part in the practice of qualitative flexible design research generally and is central to the analysis of qualitative data. Traditionally, this is carried out in field notebooks, on odd pieces of paper, etc. Memos provide ways of capturing insights and surmises occurring both in the field and when analysing the data, which can all too easily be lost if not written down straight away. Miles and Huberman (1994) suggest ways of systematizing this process, which is also integral to the grounded theory school; see p. 473 below.

Traditional paper-based approaches to taking memos can still be used with NUD*IST through the 'external document' route. Or, if the notes can either be produced as a word processed or other computer file, or can be transformed into one, they can be internal fully searchable documents. There are other possibilities with NUD*IST:

- *Adding memos to nodes and documents*   Nodes can have memos linked to them. These can provide your initially tentative feeling for what that category, theme or whatever is about, and can be changed and developed. The contents of memos cannot be searched. Memos can be integrated into the system by cutting and pasting as an 'annotation' (see below). You can, in a similar way, add memos to documents.
- *Annotations to documents*   Short memos in the form of text units can be added to documents wherever you think appropriate and can be

coded as 'annotations'. They are the equivalent of the marginal notes commonly added to interview and other transcripts. All such annotations, or a selection from them, can be reviewed later.

- *Appendices to documents*  Thoughts about a document can often be most usefully gathered together as an appendix to the document itself rather than as a separate document. They can be added to and developed throughout the project.

## Linking the document and index systems

You can work with either the document or the index system. Any document can be searched, either manually line by line, or automatically, for a particular word or phrase. The index system can be reviewed to find out the nodes you have created and to organize them as your ideas develop. Some or all of these nodes are likely to have arisen from your reading of the documents. However, if you have a strong a priori conceptualization of the project, it is feasible to set up a template for the index system independent of any links with the document system.

In either case, the drawing of connections between the document and index systems is central to the analysis. This is likely to be an iterative process involving going back and forth between the two systems. Working within the document system, you code text units at one or more nodes (note that not every text unit needs to be coded at a node). Much time can be saved on repetitive coding tasks involving commonly occurring features by the use of automated coding. Within the index system, you can browse all the text units you have coded at a particular node. You can think about them, perhaps recode some of them, or split them into two or more sub-categories (i.e. create new nodes at the next level of the hierarchy). You can easily return to the document system to view particular text units in context to help in this process.

*Interactive coding*  NUD*IST encourages coding and categorizing directly from the computer screen. With a document in view, you look through it and, if you get an idea about how a particular text unit or units might be categorized, you simply ask NUD*IST to code it for you. It can be coded either at an existing node or at a new one that you name. You can specify it as a 'free node' (i.e. you are not sure how it might fit into a hierarchy with other nodes at this stage) or give it an 'address' (i.e. where it fits into the hierarchy).

Other text units coded in the same way (i.e. at that node) can be examined. Doing this, you might want to rename the node; perhaps change or add to the memo linked to it; or annotate the document. You can also see which other nodes, if any, have coded this text unit, which may give you ideas about merging or separating out nodes, starting or changing the tree structure, etc.,

etc. This is a very interactive process and helps you to stay close both to your data and to the conceptual structure you are building.

*Off-screen coding*   You may prefer to do coding on paper away from the computer. It is straightforward to obtain a paper copy of all or part of an imported document (this is referred to as a *report* in NUD*IST-speak). The report should have line numbers, which will make it easy to tell NUD*IST what text units to code at which nodes. All that is needed is to mark up codes against text units on the page. On returning to NUD*IST, you tell it the coding for each of the text units, indicating where each node fits into the tree structure, or leaving it as a free node. The same procedure is of course used with external documents which have not been imported into the program.

It is advisable to play about with the two types of coding, possibly treating the same document in both ways. Some people find actually doing it on the computer screen inhibits creativity and playfulness, and the paper report less daunting. Others feel just the reverse.

*Text searches*   A further way in which NUD*IST can foster the process of linking the document and index systems and of developing ideas from the data, is by the use of a variety of searches of documents. Text searches look for strings or patterns of characters. A *string search* simply finds every text unit in which a particular sequence of characters occurs, usually a word (e.g. 'age') or phrase (e.g. 'bogus asylum seeker'). Various restrictions can be placed on the search which can help to make it more likely that the 'hits' are linked to a particular concept (e.g. selecting 'whole word or phrase only' cuts out 'page', 'outrage', etc. from the 'age' search). Searches can also be restricted to nodes. *Pattern searches* go for patterns or combinations of characters rather than the exact match of a string search. Typical examples include searches for words with similar meanings (e.g. 'help' and 'assistance') and different forms of a word (e.g. 'help', 'helped', 'helping').

All finds of text searches are saved in a special 'text searches' part of the Node Explorer. Text searches provide references simply to the text units found; that is, they do not provide the context for the unit. Context can be provided by 'spreading' the results of a find, which provides a specified number of additional text units around each of the finds. This is referred to as *system closure* in NUD*IST. The found text, including any spread-to text, is coded at the new node, placed in the 'text searches' (or 'index searches' in the case of an index search) area of the Node Explorer. This means that the text found as a result of a search can be used to do further analyses such as further searches. The node can be renamed and moved to the node tree, or it can be merged with an existing node. The node can also be used to restrict the scope of further searches. If, after due consideration, you are sure that it doesn't help with the analysis, then delete it.

*Index searches*  These are a particularly strong feature of NUD*IST and are of particular value when you want to move beyond simply establishing a set of categories, and what there is in each of them, to explore interrelationships between categories. As a simple example, you may have set up two or more separate nodes which you may suspect actually refer to the same category or concept. Doing a 'union' search gathers all the text units coded at the different nodes together and lets you easily explore whether or not they are effectively the same thing. If you decide that this is the case, the results of this search can be used to merge them together. As a different example, you might be interested in contextual relationships between codes, perhaps whether text units with a particular coding are closely followed (say within three text units) by a particular second coding.

There are five groups of searches with seventeen types overall, as listed in Box 14.4. They permit asking and getting answers to many different kinds of questions about the data. Using index searches forces you to be precise about the questions you are asking the data. They can also reveal problems and inconsistencies in your coding, perhaps indicating that your definition of a node has in effect changed as you are going through different documents.

Each index search automatically creates a new node which is placed in the 'Index Search' part of the index system (i.e. the Node Explorer). Like other nodes, these can be browsed and can be used to develop new nodes which can be inserted into the Index Tree system (or left as free nodes); see the discussion above on text searches. As a result of carrying out a number of index searches you may well decide to make major modifications to your index system. This is particularly likely if you are following a grounded theory

---

## Box 14.4

## Index system searches in NUD*IST

*Collation operators*

- *Intersect*  Finds all text units coded at *all* of the nominated nodes.
- *Union*  Finds all text units coded at *any* of the nominated nodes. This is useful for merging nodes.
- *Less*  Finds all text units coded at one node but not at a second one.
- *Just one*  Finds all text units coded at just one of the nominated nodes.
- *Overlap*  Finds all text units coded at two nominated nodes if there is some overlap of units. It is a union where there is at least one intersection.

*Negation operator*

- *Not in*   Finds data not indexed at a node. Can be restricted to find data not coded at a nominated node in a subset of all the data.

*Contextual operators*

- *At least*   Finds all text units coded at the nominated nodes in a section or a document if at least *x* nodes have references in that section or document.
- *If inside*   Finds all text units for a node if the units fall inside units of another node.
- *If outside*   Finds all text units for a node if the units enclose units of another node.
- *Near*   Finds all text units coded at a node within a specified range of text units coded at another nominated node.
- *Followed by*   Finds sequences where text coded at a nominated node is followed by text coded at a second nominated node.

*Restrictive operators*

- *Including documents from*   Finds all text units coded at a nominated node included in documents coded by another nominated node. It can be further restricted to exclude documents coded at other nominated nodes.
- *Excluding documents from*   Finds all text units coded at a node excluding documents coded at another nominated node. It can be further restricted to exclude documents coded at other nominated nodes.

*Tree structured operators*

- *Inherit*   Searches for and merges text coded at all the nodes directly above a specified node in a hierarchy into a new single node. The specified mode itself isn't merged.
- *Collect*   Searches for and merges text coded at all the nodes directly below a specified node in a hierarchy into a new single node. The specified mode itself is also merged.
- *Matrix*   Provides a cross-tabulation of the contents of nodes below a particular node in relation to the contents of nodes below a second node at the same level of the hierarchy.
- *Vector*   Provides a single dimensional matrix relating a node to the contents of nodes below a second node at the same level of the hierarchy.

approach where the theory (in the form of the index system) arises from your interaction with the data.

### Displaying data with NUD*IST

A range of tools is provided which help you see and appreciate the results of your analysis, both while it is in process and when you have finished it. As indicated above, you can ask for a 'report' about any of the nodes. This will provide you with all the text units which have been coded at that node and, optionally, headings and sub-headings. You can, additionally or alternatively, also view associated memos and a summary covering things like the definition you have given for the node and other descriptive data. Reports such as this, which are editable text files, form a valuable resource for your own report of the project. Telling quotations and other extracts can be used to illustrate your account and to provide evidence for claims you are making.

Data can also be obtained from NUD*IST in tabular form. For example, the result of a matrix or vector index search can be generated as a file providing displays of the type proposed by Miles and Huberman (1994). The index tree itself (or particular parts of it) also provides a valuable graphic display.

### Summary

The account presented here necessarily only scratches the surface of the various features of what is a sophisticated and complex analytic tool. If you think it may be for you, there is no substitute for actual hands-on experience. A combination of working through Gahan and Hannibal (1998), the tutorials provided with NUD*IST, use of the extensive 'help' functions, attendance at a practical workshop and (if at all possible) assistance from an experienced user, should get you going.

## Approaches to Qualitative Data Analysis in Different Design Traditions

The following sections provide further detail on the analysis of qualitative data when working within the three flexible design traditions on which this text focuses: case studies, ethnographic studies and grounded theory studies. Some consideration is also given to alternative approaches.

The approach taken when following the grounded theory line is unusual in that there are available quite tight specifications for the rules of the game, terminology, procedures, etc. (even though there are lively disagreements among grounded theorists about their appropriateness). Ethnographers appear to have much less concern about setting cut-and-dried rules for the way in which data analysis should take place, but there are important considerations to be taken into account when doing the analysis, arising from the purpose and focus of ethnographic studies. And just as case studies can be extremely various, so have been the approaches taken to the analysis of the data they generate (which are likely to be quantitative as well as qualitative).

## Case Study Data Analysis

The fact that a study is a case study does not, in itself, call for a particular approach to the analysis of the qualitative data which it produces. A case study could be approached as an exercise in the generation of grounded theory; or it could be thoroughly ethnographic, with the major concern being to gain an understanding of the culture of whatever constitutes the case.

*If you wish to take a grounded theory or an ethnographic approach to the case study you are recommended to consult the respective section below.* Each of these approaches has particular concerns which you should bear in mind and which take precedence over the fact that your study concerns a particular case. Neither of them is likely to devalue the importance of context central to case study.

This section focuses on case studies which are neither exclusively ethnographic nor grounded theory studies. Box 14.5 provides a varied set of such studies where the account gives details of the approach to analysis. Note that NUD*IST has specific tools for dealing with cases.

### The Miles and Huberman approach

Miles and Huberman (1994) provide an invaluable general framework for conceptualizing qualitative data analysis. It is particularly useful in case studies, but can be used more widely. The intention here is to provide sufficient detail for you to appreciate their approach and terminology so that you can see whether it is likely to be appropriate for your purposes. If that seems to be the case, you are strongly advised to refer directly to their text for the analysis. Don't be put off by its size; it should be used selectively as a sourcebook.

Philosophically, their position is firmly entrenched in realism, hence permitting a consistency of the realist view through from design (as discussed in chapter 6) to analysis. Their approach can come across as heavily structured. It forms a safe haven for more quantitatively oriented researchers who accept

---

# Box 14.5

## Examples of case study analyses

*Asmussen and Cresswell (1995)*   Exploratory qualitative case study of a campus response to a student gunman. Emergent design, context-dependent study and inductive data analysis. Use of semi-structured interviews, observational data, documents and visual materials.

*Lam (2000)*   Single case study of a Chinese immigrant teenager's written correspondence with a transnational group of peers on the internet, using ethnographic and discourse analytic methods.

*MacMillan and McLachlan (1999)*   Interesting combination of the 'potentially incompatible approaches' of content analysis and discourse analysis in a single case study on education news in the press using NUD*IST.

*Silverman (2000, ch. 11)*   Case study of decision-making in a child heart clinic. Use of Miles and Huberman (1994) techniques together with ethnographic and grounded theory aspects.

*Smith (1995, 1997)*   Qualitative case study on identity change during pregnancy and the transition to motherhood. Longitudinal multimethod study involving interviews, diaries, use of a standard free-response test and repertory grids.

*Wulfhorst (2000)*   Study of the effects on a community of living near a hazardous waste management facility using ethnographic, interview and content analysis.

---

the necessity of 'going qualitative' but are concerned that they will have to leave their scientific principles behind if they do so.

Those from qualitative traditions, while accepting that in the current research climate their procedures may need greater codification, can find the Miles and Huberman language unsympathetic and aversive. You are urged nevertheless to give them a fair trial; many of the things they suggest can translate into practices with which you are already familiar. However, the approach is not for everyone, and it may be that there are procedures within the grounded theory and ethnographic sections which you find more congenial.

## Realist data analysis and causation

The Miles and Huberman approach is realist in the sense discussed in chapter 2. They hold that phenomena (including social phenomena) 'exist not only in the mind but also in the objective world – and that some lawful and reasonably stable relationships are to be found among them' (1994, p. 4). The explanations they seek to provide via their techniques flow from an account of how structures produced the observed effects:

> We aim to account for events, rather than simply to document their sequence. We look for an individual or a social process, a mechanism, a structure at the core of events that can be captured to provide a *causal description* of the forces at work. (p. 4, emphasis in original)

This calls both for causal explanation and for evidence showing that each entity is an instance of that explanation. So what is needed is not only the explanatory structure or mechanisms, but also a knowledge of the particular set of circumstances. Hence this approach moves away from the deductive logic of positivist approaches to the use of inductive methods.

The view of causation that they espouse is the realist generative one advocated in chapter 2 rather than the standard positivist successionist view. They reject the conventional wisdom that classical experimental control designs are to be preferred when seeking causal attributions. As they point out, 'Seeing that an experimental group had effect X and that controls did not tells us nothing about what went on in the "black box". We don't understand how or why it happened, and can only guess at the mechanisms involved' (p. 147).

Their claim is that qualitative analysis can, however, be a very powerful method for assessing causality:

> Qualitative analysis, with its close-up look, can identify *mechanisms*, going beyond sheer association. It is unrelentingly *local*, and deals with the *complex* network of events and processes in a situation. It can sort out the *temporal* dimension, showing clearly what preceded what, either through direct observation or *retrospection*. It is well equipped to cycle back and forth between *variables* and *processes* – showing that 'stories' are not capricious, but include underlying variables, and that variables are not disembodied, but have connections over time. (p. 147, emphases in original)

Note that, in the terminology adopted in this text, 'qualitative analysis' is shorthand for 'analysis of the (largely qualitative) data obtained when using flexible designs'.

## Components of data analysis

Miles and Huberman view analysis as consisting of three concurrent 'flows of activity': data reduction, data display, and conclusion drawing/verification.

*Data reduction*   Qualitative data can easily become overwhelming, even in small projects. Hence you need to find ways of keeping the data manageable. This process starts before any data are collected, when you focus the study and make sampling decisions about people to interview, places to visit, etc. During and after data collection, you have to reduce the data mountain through the production of summaries and abstracts, coding, writing memos, etc. Miles and Huberman emphasize that this is a part of analysis and not a separate activity. Decisions about what to select and to summarize, and how this is then to be organized, are analytic choices.

*Data display*   The mantra is: 'You know what you display.' Qualitative data are typically in the form of (large amounts of) text. This brings to the fore many of the deficiencies of the human as analyst listed in box 14.2, producing hasty, partial and unwarranted conclusions. Better means of organizing and displaying the information are needed, and may be found in the use of matrices, charts, networks, etc. These are also ways of achieving data reduction. They have a vital function both during data collection and afterwards, so that you get a feel for what the data are telling you, what justified conclusions can be drawn and what further analyses are called for.

*Conclusion drawing and verification*   You start to draw conclusions about what things mean from the start of data collection, noting patterns and regularities, positing possible structures and mechanisms, etc. These are then firmed up during and after the data collection. Miles and Huberman stress that this should be accompanied throughout by a verification process: that is, you are testing their validity and reliability. Is an explanation plausible? Can you find evidence confirming it? Can a finding be replicated in another data set?

These three flows of activity, together with the activity of collecting the data itself, form a continuous iterative process. For example, coding a data set (data reduction) will lead to ideas of how the data may be displayed, which may help form a tentative conclusion about the operation of a mechanism, or for changing the display or coding system. Note that this has its counterpart in quantitative analysis. Data reduction is achieved through descriptive and summary statistics; data display through graphs and tables of correlations; conclusion drawing through the use of inferential statistics, test of significance, etc. (The results of such quantitative analyses, of course, supplement the qualitative analysis if you have multiple methods in a case study yielding both quantitative and qualitative data.). The difference is that while the quantitative analysis techniques are fully codified and largely non-contentious, qualitative data analysis is more fluid and contested.

## Methods for data reduction and display

The following suggestions are arranged in rough sequence from those which should be started early in your involvement with the analysis to ones appropriate for later, and from simple to more complex. They are described here in fairly general and flexible terms. Miles and Huberman (1994) give more prescriptive versions which are invaluable for larger projects involving several workers and a substantial amount of pre-planning, but may well be over-formalized for a small-scale study.

*Session summary sheet*   Shortly after a data collection session (e.g. an interview or observation session) has taken place and the data have been processed, a single sheet should be prepared which summarizes what has been obtained. It is helpful if this sheet is in the form of answers to summarizing and focusing questions (e.g. who was involved; what issues were covered; relevance to research questions; new hypotheses suggested; implications for subsequent data collection).

*Document sheet*   A similar sheet should be prepared for each document collected. This clarifies its context and significance, as well as summarizing the content of lengthy documents. The session summary and document sheets assist in data reduction, which is, of course, viewed as part of the analysis process. Note that both session summary and document sheets can be entered as document headers in NUD*IST.

*Development of coding categories*   Qualitative data rapidly cumulate, and even with regular processing and summarizing, it is easy to get overwhelmed. The material is unstructured and difficult to deal with. Coding provides a solution. A code is a symbol applied to a section of text to classify or categorize it. Codes are typically related to research questions, concepts and themes. They are retrieval and organizing devices that allow you to find and then collect together all instances of a particular kind.

Miles and Huberman (1994) distinguish between first- and second-level coding. First-level coding is concerned with attaching labels to groups of words. Second-level or pattern coding groups the initial codes into a smaller number of themes or patterns. The development of pattern codes is an integral part of first-level coding, where you need to be continually asking yourself, 'What seems to go with what?' and elaborating on and checking these hunches. You will probably start with a very small number of potential patterns, modify and add to them during the course of analysis, and finally be left with a small number once more as various 'runners' are disconfirmed by the data. The work that you do in creating these codes is central to developing an understanding of your data. It lays the foundation for your subsequent analysis. Further details on coding are given below in the section on grounded theory analysis (p. 492), where a somewhat different terminology is used.

*Memoing*   A memo can be anything that occurs to you during the project and its analysis. A particularly important type gives ideas about codes and their relationships as they strike you while coding. The length is not important; they are simply attempts either to link data together, or to suggest that a particular piece of data falls within a more general category. They should be adequately labelled so that they can be sorted and retrieved. Memoing is a useful means of capturing ideas, views and intuitions at all stages of the data analysis process.

A wide range of types of memo have been suggested, including:

a   initial, orienting memo;
b   preliminary memo;
c   memo 'sparks';
d   memo that opens an attack on new phenomena;
e   memo on a new category;
f   initial discovery memo;
g   memo distinguishing between two or more categories;
h   memo extending the implications of a borrowed concept;
i   additional thoughts memo;
j   integrative memo; and
k   organizing, summary memo.

The memo is also an important part of grounded theory analysis (see p. 492).

*The interim summary*   This is an attempt to summarize what you have found out so far and highlight what still needs to be found out. It is recommended that this is done before you are halfway through the time you have available for data collection. The summary should cover not only what is known but also the confidence you have in that knowledge, so that gaps and deficiencies can be spotted and remedied. *Flexible designs enable you to do this in a way which would not be feasible in a fixed design study; but to capitalize on this flexibility, you must force yourself to find the time to do this interim summary while you can still take advantage of its findings to direct and focus the later phases of data collection.* The summary can also usefully incorporate a *data accounting sheet* which lists the different research questions and shows, for different informants, materials, settings, etc., whether adequate data concerning each of the questions have been collected.

*Data displays*   The summary and document sheets discussed above, while having the primary function of data reduction, are also ways of displaying your

| CONDITIONS | EXAMPLES[a] | HOW IMPORTANT[b] | WHY IMPORTANT[c] |
|---|---|---|---|
| commitment understanding materials training etc. | | | |

[a] Specific illustrations, marked with A or U for administrator or user, respectively.
[b] Rating – very, quite, somewhat, or not important.
[c] Explanations of reasons for importance of condition, given by respondent (A or U) or researcher (R).

**Figure 14.2**   Checklist matrix on preparedness (alternative format 3).
*Source*: Miles and Huberman (1994).

data. Miles and Huberman present a large range of other suggestions for ways of displaying data, both within a single case and across different cases. Some are for exploring and describing the data, others for explaining and predicting. Miles and Huberman consider two main types: *matrices* (i.e. tables with rows and columns) and *networks* (i.e. a set of boxes or 'nodes' with links between them). Figure 14.2 and figure 14.3 give simple examples. Tufte (1990) is a wonderful source-book of other ideas for 'envisioning' information. Box 14.6 provides suggestions for the use of matrices; boxes 14.7 and 14.8 present typologies of matrices and networks respectively.

When there are several persons involved in data analysis and collection, it is important that they are all involved in the preceding exercises. While it may be possible in surveys to get much of the routine work carried out by 'hired hands' who follow fully standardized procedures, the importance of the sensitivity and judgement of the 'human instrument' precludes this tactic in a case study. All workers on a case study have essentially similar roles. It is crucial that there are shared understandings about the process of analysis, so that, for example, the codings are carried out in the same way. Cross-checking should be carried out in as many ways as possible. Formal meetings will be needed.

## Methods for drawing conclusions

These are some of the tactics you might use for drawing meaning from data displays. Qualitative researchers appear to have little difficulty in making sense of their data and generating conclusions. Indeed, humans in general organize

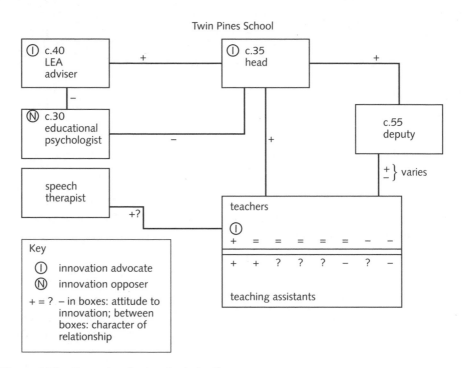

**Figure 14.3**   Example of a 'context chart'.

*Source*: Miles and Huberman (1994).

and interpret the complex and messy world around them as a part of every-day life. The issue is more whether or not these conclusions are valid and correct, referred to here as verification.

Miles and Huberman (1994, pp. 245–6) list the following thirteen tactics for generating meaning:

1   *Noting patterns, themes and trends.*
2   *Seeing plausibility*   Do the trends, patterns and conclusions make sense?
3   *Clustering*   Grouping events, places, people, processes, etc. together if they appear to have similar patterns or characteristics.
4   *Making metaphors*   Metaphors are rich, data-reducing and pattern-making devices which help to connect data with theory.
5   *Counting*   Helps to enable you to see what's there by counting frequency of occurrence of recurrent events.
6   *Making contrasts and comparisons*   Establishing similarities and differences between and within data sets.
7   *Partitioning variables*   Splitting variables may help in finding more coherent descriptions and explanations.

---

## Box 14.6

### Rules of thumb for matrix data entry

1   The conclusions drawn from a matrix depend on the quality of the original data collected and the thoughtfulness with which they are entered into the matrix.

2   Keep entries as 'thick' as feasible, giving context, details, intentions, meanings, etc.

3   Data entry inevitably involves much selection and condensation. Give decision rules about how this was done, including bases for making judgements and degree of confidence in the data. Maintain this as a log throughout data entry.

4   Show missing or ambiguous data explicitly in the matrix.

5   Ensure that you can locate sources of entries in the original data.

6   Be prepared to revise the format of the matrix as further data are added.

7   Get a colleague to review a completed matrix at an early stage together with the decision rules and links to original data. Such auditing procedures can be very time-consuming and it is probably only feasible to do this on a selective basis. They are, however, crucial to establishing the trustworthiness of your procedures.

(Adapted and abridged from Miles and Huberman, 1994, pp. 241–2.)

---

8   *Subsuming particulars into the general*   Linking specific data to general concepts and categories.

9   *Factoring*   Attempting to discover the factors underlying the process under investigation.

10   *Noting relations between variables*   Using matrix displays and other methods to study interrelationships between different parts of the data.

11   *Finding intervening variables*   Trying to establish the presence and effects of variables intervening between observed variables.

12   *Building a logical chain of evidence*   Trying to understand trends and patterns through developing logical relationships.

13   *Making conceptual/theoretical coherence*   Moving from data to constructs to theories through analysis and categorization.

---

## Box 14.7

### Different types of matrix

1  *Checklist matrix*   Uses data which can be combined into an index or scale.

2  *Time-ordered matrix*   Columns are arranged in time sequence. A specific version of this is known as an *event listing*, where concrete events, sorted into categories, are arranged into time sequence.

3  *Role-ordered matrix*   Rows represent data from sets of individuals occupying different roles (e.g. doctor/nurse/administrator/patient).

4  *Conceptually clustered matrix*   Columns are arranged to bring together items 'belonging together' (e.g. relating to same theme).

5  *Effects matrix* Displays data on outcomes (i.e. on dependent variable(s)).

6  *Case dynamics matrix*   Columns concern issues, what happens in connection with them (e.g. who does what), and outcomes.

*Note*: There are also several variants, including hybrids.

---

## Box 14.8

### Some different types of networks

1  *Context charts*   Show interrelationships between roles, groups, organizations, etc. which provide the context for the case studied.

2  *Event flow networks*   Show events (e.g. experiences, incidents) ordered by time and sequence.

3  *Activity records*   Display a specific recurring activity (e.g. a classroom lesson) as a sequential pattern with specific actions each assigned to a link.

4  *Decision modelling*   Flow chart giving sequential decisions made.

5  *Conceptually ordered tree diagrams*   Shows how phenomena are classified (e.g. by an individual) and sub-categorized.

6  *Cognitive map*   Displays a person's representation of concepts about a particular domain or area of interest, showing the relationships between them.

7  *Causal network*   Consists of boxes showing the most important variables or factors in a study, with arrows showing the relationships between them.

While many of these tactics simply represent a labelling of common practices, several, such as 'factoring' and the 'variable-speak' tactics, reveal Miles
and Huberman's direct translation of concepts from quantitative analysis into
qualitative analysis. Several qualitative researchers may well view this as inappropriate. However, there is no requirement to take these tactics en bloc.

## Methods for verification

Box 14.9 lists tactics you might use for testing and confirming the findings.

---

### Box 14.9

### Assessing the quality of qualitative data analysis: tactics suggested by Miles and Huberman

*Assessing data quality*

1   *Checking for representativeness*   There are many pitfalls to the gathering of representative data. The informants, and the events or activities
sampled, may be non-representative. Safeguards include the use of random
sampling where feasible; triangulation through multiple methods of data
collection; constructing data display matrices; and seeking data for empty
or weakly sampled cells. Your analysis may be biased, not only because you
are drawing inferences from non-representative processes, but also because
of your own biases as an information processor (see p. 460). Auditing
processes by colleagues help guard against this.

2   *Checking for researcher effects*   These come in two versions: the effects
you have on the case, and the effects your involvement with the case have
on you. They have been discussed previously (p. 311).

3   *Triangulation*   Again discussed earlier (p. 371). Not a panacea, and it
has its own problems. (What, for example, do you do when two data sources
are inconsistent or conflicting? Answer: you investigate further, possibly
ending up with a more complex set of understandings.) However, it is very
important: 'triangulation is not so much a tactic as a way of life. If you self-
consciously set out to collect and double-check findings, using multiple
sources and modes of evidence, the verification process will largely be built
into data collection as you go' (Miles and Huberman, 1994, p. 267).

4   *Weighting the evidence*   Some data are stronger than others and you
naturally place greater reliance on conclusions based on the former. Stronger

data are typically those you collect first-hand; which you have observed directly; which come from trusted informants; which are collected when the respondent is alone rather than in a group setting; and which arise from repeated contact.

## Testing patterns

**5**   *Checking the meaning of outliers*   These are the exceptions, the ones that don't fit into the overall pattern of findings or lie at the extremes of a distribution. Outliers can be people, cases, settings, treatments or events. Don't be tempted to hide or forget them.

**6**   *Using extreme cases*   These are outliers of a particular type, defined in terms of being atypical situations or persons rather than by the data they provide, which may or may not be atypical. An innovation which failed in a school where the circumstances appeared close to ideal seemed to be linked to the unexpressed resistance of the deputy headteacher responsible for timetabling, hence suggesting a key factor.

**7**   *Following up surprises*   Surprises can be salutary. You may well be surprised because something is at variance with your (possibly implicit and not thought through) theory of what is going on. This then provides the opportunity to bring that theory to the surface, possibly to revise it, and to search for evidence relevant to the revision.

**8**   *Looking for negative evidence*   This is the tactic of actively seeking disconfirmation of what you think is true. While this is in principle straightforward, you are likely to have some reluctance to spending a large amount of effort on this activity. Miles and Huberman (1994, p. 271) make the helpful suggestion of giving a colleague your conclusions and free access to your original data with a brief to try to find evidence which would disconfirm your conclusion. If they manage to do this then your task is to come up with an alternative, broadened, or elaborated explanation.

## Testing explanations

**9**   *Making if–then tests*   Testing possible relationships: i.e. if one condition obtains or is the case, look to see if a second one is. If it is, we are on the way to understanding what is going on and can make further similar tests. If it isn't true, we have to make other conjectures.

**10**   *Ruling out spurious relationships*   If you appear to have established a relationship, consider whether there may be a third factor or variable which underlies, influences or causes the apparent relationship. In the relationship between guardsmen fainting on parade and the softness of the tar in the asphalt of the parade ground, it appears highly likely that the temperature is providing an intervening causal link rather than noxious fumes from the tar having a direct effect. Note that this is essentially the same tactic discussed above under the heading of 'finding intervening variables' but used for a different purpose. It can also be thought of as finding rival explanations for a relationship.

**11** *Replicating a finding* If a finding can be repeated in a different context or data set, then it is more dependable. Given that once you find a relationship or develop a theory there is a strong tendency for you to find confirming evidence (and to ignore disconfirming evidence), it is even better if someone else, not privy to your findings, confirms it. Note that this is a particular type of triangulation.

**12** *Checking out rival explanations* It is good practice to try to come up with one or more rival explanations which could account for all or part of the phenomena you are studying. Keeping these 'in play' while you are analysing and gathering further data helps to prevent the premature closure effect discussed above.

**13** *Getting feedback from informants* This process of 'member checking' performs several useful functions. It honours the implicit (or preferably explicit) contract between researcher and informant to provide feedback about the findings. It also provides an invaluable means of corroborating them. While problems of jargon and terminology may need to be attended to, you should be able to present findings in a way that communicates with informants and allows them to evaluate the findings in the light of their superior experience of the setting.

## NUD*IST and case study data analysis

Reviewing the sections on the Miles and Huberman approach to case study data analysis and the preceding discussion on using NUD*IST should make it clear that it is straightforward to incorporate this approach into NUD*IST. It permits and simplifies the production of:

*   *session summary sheets* as imported documents which can be appended to the document containing data from the session (if short, probably better as part of a document header);
*   *document sheets* as imported documents which can be appended to each document (if short, probably better as part of a document header);

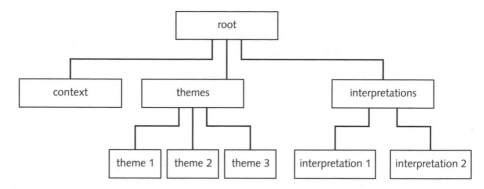

**Figure 14.4**  A generalized version of an index tree for case study analysis.

- *interim summaries* as free-standing imported documents, incorporating data accounting sheets;
- *codes* through adding and defining nodes; first- and second- ('pattern') level codes can be represented and positioned within the tree structure generated by NUD*IST;
- *memos* of whatever kind can be incorporated in NUD*IST and linked to nodes or documents; and
- *data displays* in the form of *matrices* of various kinds can be easily generated and modified.

Graphic displays are limited in NUD*IST to the *tree network*. Figure 14.4 gives a generalized version of an index tree for case studies. Case nodes can also be used to restrict the scope of searches, and hence analyses.

A major bonus is that when you have invested the time and effort required to become familiar with NUD*IST and to get all your data together with the coding and memos into the system, it encourages thorough, detailed and systematic exploration. Through devices such as index system searches, the various tactics for conclusion drawing and verification can be tried out. There is a close affinity between the systematic, explicit and principled stance to analysis advocated by Miles and Huberman and the approaches encouraged by the use of a software package such as NUD*IST.

## Data Analysis in Ethnographic Studies

Studies using ethnographic approaches can also be case studies, and can be analysed using the techniques discussed in the previous section. Ethnographic studies could be, and not infrequently are, analysed using grounded theory. However, you may be interested in research outcomes other than the generation of theory, such as the development of descriptions and explanations. Nevertheless, the general approach of grounded theory analysis, and in particular the iterative process whereby data analysis feeds into subsequent data collection with this then stimulating further analysis, is a feature of the analysis of virtually all ethnographic studies. Hence, using the techniques described in the following section on grounded theory in a relatively relaxed manner (e.g. not necessarily using the terminology of open coding, axial coding, etc.), is a viable approach. Similarly, if your study can reasonably be conceptualized as a case study, and you find the Miles and Huberman approach congenial, the preceding section provides detailed suggestions for analysis. Box 14.10 provides a varied set of ethnographic studies where the account gives details of the approach to analysis.

The ethnographic approach is typically exploratory. It is a method of discovery, well suited to the study of the unfamiliar, the new and the different. Wolcott (1994) suggests three steps in the analysis and transformation of the data in an ethnographic study: *description of the culture-sharing group*; *analysis of themes of the culture*; and *interpretation*. To do this, your three main tasks are:

- *Thinking*   A vast array of complex information has to be made sense of. There is no substitute for knowing the data well, and thinking about it

---

## Box 14.10

### Examples of ethnographic analyses

*Chapple and Nofziger (2000)*   Small exploratory ethnographic study investigating bingo players and bingo playing in a south-western US town.

*Karp (1993)*   Development of a typology of responses by patients to the prescription of anti-depressant drugs.

*Porter (1993)*   Ethnographic study of how racism affects occupational relationships between nurses and doctors using participant observation. Critical realist perspective.

*Simpson (2000)*   Interpretive ethnography of young people's use of spaces in a record store in Tampa, Florida.

*Wolcott (1974)*   Primarily descriptive study of the workings of a committee involved in selecting the principal of an elementary school.

and what it might be telling you. Any thoughts that occur can form the basis of memos, linked to the data source or to your analysis.

- *Developing categories*  You need categories to impose some kind of order on the data; where you get them from is up to you. They may come from your interaction with the data (perhaps from the participants themselves), as in grounded theory; or from your prior experience with this setting or similar settings; or from 'the literature' (i.e. concepts developed by previous researchers). If you want to move beyond description and explanation of the particular setting or case studied you may wish to develop a *typology* (Hammersley and Atkinson, 1995, pp. 215–17).
- *Progressive focusing*  As analysis and data collection continue, the research questions should be developed and clarified. The research itself should become progressively more focused, a process described by Hammersley and Atkinson (1995, p. 206) as a characteristic 'funnel' structure. As Wolcott (1994) suggests, there is also a shift from an initial concern for describing events and processes to interpretation.

Some more specific ways of accomplishing these tasks include:

- *Looking for patterns*  Establishing patterns of thought, action and behaviour; understanding of a culture is acquired through observing and analysing the patterns of everyday life.
- *Key events*   In every social group, there will be key or focal events which can be used to analyse a culture. They provide a lens through which it can be viewed, and in many cases a metaphor for their way of life or social values.
- *Triangulation*  Testing one source or set of information against another.

Even if you are not following the Miles and Huberman (1994) approach directly, two of their central techniques are well worth considering:

- *Visual representations*  Maps, flowcharts and organizational charts provide useful tools helping to crystallize and display complex information.
- *Matrices*  Two-dimensional arrays of information help in comparing, contrasting and cross-referencing data.

And finally:

- *Crystallization*   If the gods smile on you, your study will have moments when things fall into place. Such crystallizations range from the mundane to the 'earth-shattering epiphany' (Fetterman, 1989, p. 101) after which nothing is the same.

It is also worth emphasizing that ethnographic studies typically provide access to large amounts of written records of different kinds, the analysis of which provides evidence for patterns and opportunities for triangulation with observational and interview data; and that, in some ethnographic studies, quantitative data may be collected which can be subjected to statistical analysis.

## Bases for developing categories

As indicated above, the important initial analytical task of developing categories has been approached quite eclectically in ethnographic studies. Hammersley and Atkinson (1995, p. 214) suggest that 'one should use whatever resources are available which help to make sense of the data.' In this, as in other respects, there are differences among ethnographers: some take more of a purist line and some theoretical approaches are ruled out (e.g. Fielding and Fielding, 1986; Silverman, 1993).

The categories, and underlying concepts, are likely in the early stages of analysis to be imprecise and relatively poorly defined. They may be pretty mundane and descriptive. Blumer (1954) distinguishes between such 'sensitizing concepts' and 'definitive concepts'. The latter are based on precise definitions and have a position within an explicit model. When you have some confidence in the set of categories as providing a description of the group, although not yet at the stage where a definitive status has been achieved, the next step is to explore their inter-relationships.

While grounded theory views this as a purely inductive process which is driven by the data, the more usual ethnographic stance is wider. Clearly the data, and your understanding of relationships within the data, constitute an invaluable resource. However, pre-existing theory, previous empirical research, your own expectations and hunches can also play a part. Hammersley and Atkinson (1995, p. 214) cite work by Bensman and Vidich (1960) where ten different theoretical positions were used to provide the focus for their analysis, each time asking the question: 'What in [these] theories would permit us to comprehend the data?'

## Realism, theory and ethnographic studies

As discussed in chapter 6, early ethnography adopted a 'naïve' realist position which was subjected to lethal constructivist criticism (see p. 29). The more sophisticated 'subtle' realism advocated by Hammersley (1992, pp. 50–4), is largely in line with realism as discussed in some detail in chapter 2, and appears to provide a defensible approach to the analysis of ethnographic studies. Note, however, that, as pointed out by Porter (1993, p. 595), there are differences between subtle and critical realism. In particular, the former is concerned with understanding the perspectives of others rather than judging them, whereas Bhaskar (1989) asserts that critical realism entails evaluation, which he sees as an essential part of social research.

It is worth emphasizing that, in addition to asserting a 'real' status for the concepts and categories established by an ethnographic study, there is also a concern for underlying mechanisms and structures and the conditions under which they operate. On this view, ethnographic studies are capable of testing causal relationships, although the view of causation is generative rather than based on the successive logic central to positivistic science (p. 19).

Ethnographic studies can also be used both to develop and to test theories, although many of them are content to stay at a descriptive level. The approach taken to do this is known as *analytic induction* (discussed in connection with participant observation in chapter 11; see box 11.3, p. 322). It stresses the importance of maximizing the chances of discovering a decisive *negative* case ('case' here can be taken here as an aspect, facet, phenomenon or whatever). Thus, when developing theory, the suggestion is that one should go out of one's way to look for negating evidence.

Kidder (1981) has produced a systematized version, known as *negative case analysis*. This involves continuously revising and refining a hypothesis until it accounts for all known cases without exception. She cites as an example a study by Cressey (1953), summarized in box 14.11.

Kidder suggests that negative case analysis replaces statistical analysis in qualitative research. This kind of inductive analysis violates the canons of conventional hypothesis-testing approaches by forming hypotheses to fit the data rather than finding data to test the hypotheses. However, her argument is that with abundant data, resulting from having made many observations and recorded many instances, the conclusions can be convincing. Her version insists on *zero* exceptions. Lincoln and Guba (1985, p. 312) consider that this is too rigid a criterion, equivalent to the perfect statistical finding, significant at the 0.000 level. They suggest that in practice, even if the final theory were true, there would be likely to be apparent exceptions (e.g. due to people lying, or practising unconscious deception, or forgetting) which one may be unable to uncover; and hence that a theory which fits a good proportion of the cases gives substantial evidence of its acceptability.

For any version of these explanation-building approaches to be rigorous, substantial safeguards have to be built into the process. You need to be punctilious in documenting the initial statement and its changing versions, together with the rival explanations, and the chain of evidence which leads you to your

## Box 14.11

### Example of negative case analysis

1   The initial version of the theory is:

Embezzlement occurs when someone has learned in connection with the business or profession in which he is employed that some forms of violation of trust are merely technical and are not really illegal or wrong. Conversely, that if this definition has not been learned, then violations do not occur.

2   Interviews with imprisoned embezzlers made it clear they knew it was illegal. Theory changed to:

Embezzlement occurs when the holder of a position of trust defines a need for extra funds or extended use of property as an emergency which cannot be met by legal means.

3   Some interviewees said they had taken money without an emergency; others said they had at times been confronted by an emergency but had not taken money. Theory changed to:

Embezzlement occurs when persons in positions of trust conceive of themselves as having incurred financial obligations which are not socially sanctionable and which must be satisfied by private means.

4 ' Checking against previous and subsequent interviews revealed instances in which nothing existed that could be considered a financial obligation, and others in which non-sanctionable obligations had existed without embezzlement. Theory changed to:

Embezzlement occurs not only for the reason cited in the previous version, but also because of present discordance between the embezzler's income and expenditure.

5   Further study of the interview records revealed instances where the conditions existed but embezzlement had not occurred. Theory changed to its final version:

Trusted persons violate that trust when they see themselves as having a financial problem which is non-shareable, are aware that this problem can be secretly resolved by violation of the position of trust, and are able to apply to their own conduct in that situation verbalizations which enable them to adjust their conception of themselves as users of the entrusted funds or property.

This was tested against all the data gathered previously and new data, no negative cases being found.

(Adapted from Kidder, 1981, p. 243.)

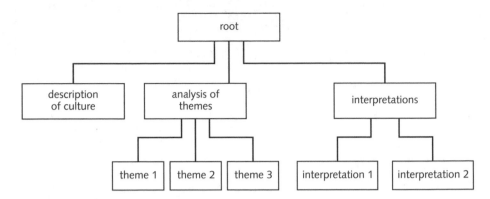

**Figure 14.5**   A generalized version of an index tree for an ethnographic study.

conclusions. The use of standardized data display and summary devices is recommended.

## NUD*IST and the analysis of ethnographic studies

NUD*IST obviously provides a means of getting together in one location each of the data sets you acquire, either as imported or external documents. Similarly, the coding, as it is developed, can be incorporated into the index system. Memos of various kinds representing your thoughts and ideas can be included in either document or index systems.

A simple way of proceeding is to set up a tree diagram within NUD*IST which mimics the structure and steps for analysis proposed by Wolcott (1994), shown as figure 14.5.

## Data Analysis in Grounded Theory Studies

Many analyses of flexible design studies have been influenced by grounded theory. They typically reference the work of either or both of the originators of the approach, Barney Glaser and Anselm Strauss (Glaser and Strauss, 1967), which was discussed in chapter 6. However, while some of these analyses follow the detailed prescriptions and terminology discussed in the following sections, others are much more 'in the general style of' a grounded theory approach.

## The aim of grounded theory analysis

The aim is to *generate* a theory to explain what is central in the data. Your task is to find a central core category which is both at a high level of abstraction and grounded in (i.e. derived from) the data you have collected and analysed. This is done in three stages:

1    find conceptual categories in the data;
2    find relationships between these categories;
3    conceptualize and account for these relationships through finding core categories.

It is achieved by carrying out three kinds of coding:

*    *open coding* to find the categories;
*    *axial coding* to interconnect them; and
*    *selective coding* to establish the core category or categories (Strauss and Corbin, 1998).

Throughout the analysis, theory is built through interaction with the data, making comparisons and asking questions of the data. It is sometimes referred to as the *method of constant comparison* (Pidgeon and Henwood, 1996, pp. 92–4).

## Open coding

Here data (interview transcripts, field notes, documents, etc.) are split into discrete parts. The size of the part chosen is whatever seems to be a unit in the data: perhaps a sentence, or an utterance, or a paragraph. The question asked is: 'What is this piece of data an example of?' The code applied is a label. It is provisional and may be changed. A piece of data may have several codes (labels), i.e. it may be considered to fall within more than one conceptual category. Labels can be of whatever kind that seems appropriate, including descriptive (e.g. 'accepting advice'), 'in vivo' (i.e. a direct quotation from the data), or more inferential.

These conceptual categories arise from the data. Using pre-determined coding categories and seeking to fit data into such categories is against the spirit of grounded theory. However, this distinction is somewhat metaphysical as the 'conceptual baggage' you bring to your data (whether derived from a pre-existing theory or from analysis of data collected earlier) will inevitably have some influence on what you are likely to 'see' in the data.

Open coding is essentially interpreting rather than summarizing. It is about teasing out the theoretical possibilities in the data. There is much to be said for doing it in a small group. This will enhance the ideas pool about what the data are examples of, and it will assist in keeping individuals 'on task'. Is a particular code really grounded in the data? Is the central purpose of open coding being kept in mind?

While carrying out open coding, you should bear in mind any ideas that occur from working with the data about relationships between the categories, and even first thoughts about the core category. This can be encouraged by stepping back from the data from time to time and getting an overall feel for what is going on. As with other approaches to flexible design, this initial analysis will be taking place before data collection is complete. There is no requirement to code all the data fully at this stage, but you do need to have done a substantial amount of coding and to have a good appreciation of what you have captured overall in the various data sets arising from the interviews, field notes, etc. In an ideal world, you will have got to the stage where the various categories are 'saturated'. That is, you have squeezed as much conceptual juice as you can out of the data so that continuing analysis is giving severely diminished returns in the new categories and insights that it is yielding.

## Axial coding

Axial, or *theoretical*, coding is about linking together the categories developed through the process of open coding. Glaser and Strauss, the begetters of grounded theory (Glaser and Strauss, 1967), now have diverging views about the approach to be taken when trying to establish these relationships. Strauss and Corbin (1998) work within an exclusively interactionist paradigm, where axial coding is viewed as leading to an understanding of the central phenomenon in the data in terms of its context, the conditions which gave rise to it, the action and interaction strategies by which it is dealt with, and their consequences. Glaser (1992) takes a more purist grounded line. He argues that the axial codes, and the form that they take, should emerge from the data rather than being forced into any particular pre-determined format.

Whichever line is taken, axial coding is about putting together again in some way the data which have been effectively split apart into categories by open coding. As Mertens (1998) puts it:

During this phase, you build a model of the phenomena that includes the conditions under which it occurs (or does not occur), the context in which it occurs, the action and interactional strategies that describe the phenomena, and the consequences of these actions. You continue to ask questions of the data; however, now the questions focus on relationships between the categories. (p. 352)

If you are simply concerned with exploring or describing the phenomena being studied, this completes the analysis. However, grounded theory, as the term suggests, seeks to go further. For this, you need to go on to selective coding.

## Selective coding

In this third stage, selective coding, you select one aspect as the *core category* and focus on it. The basis for doing this arises from axial coding, which provides you with a picture of the relationships between various categories. In doing this you should begin to get a feeling for what the study is about, in what way you can understand and explain the overall picture. This may well involve limiting the study to the major relationships which fit with this conceptualization.

In grounded theory, there must be a central integrating focus to those aspects which remain in the study. If more than one remain, the notion is that they have to be integrated into a single one at a higher degree of abstraction. This must remain grounded in the data but is abstract and integrated as well as being highly condensed. The core category is the centrepiece of your analysis. It is the central phenomenon around which the categories arising from axial coding are integrated.

Strauss and Corbin (1998) approach this task via the *story line*. This starts as a description of what axial coding has produced. You have to move from this descriptive account to a conceptualization of the story line. In other words, you are seeking a core conceptual category which enables you to understand the story line.

## Doing a grounded theory style analysis

The preceding section is intended to give the 'flavour' of a full grounded theory analysis. Studied in conjunction with one or more of the examples cited in box 14.12 it should be of assistance to anyone wanting to carry out an analysis following a general grounded theory style.

It is, however, more or less bereft of the theory behind grounded theory. Substantial further reading, as indicated at the end of this chapter, is called for if you wish to get on top of this preparatory to doing a genuine grounded theory analysis. Punch (1998, pp. 210–21) provides a helpful introduction. He also cites Denzin's warning that, just as grounded theory is being widely adopted in many areas of social research,

> it is being challenged by a new body of work coming from the neighboring fields
> of anthropology and cultural studies . . . [They] are proposing that postmodern

---

## Box 14.12

### Examples of grounded theory analyses

*Chenitz and Swanson (1986)*   Set of grounded theory studies on a range of nursing topics.

*Drisko (1998)*   Application of grounded theory in the social work context of an evaluation of family preservation programmes.

*Glaser and Strauss (1965, 1968)*   The two original grounded theory studies, focusing on the process of dying in hospitals.

*Madill et al. (2000)*   Discussion of two simple studies using grounded theory to analyse interviews with relatives of individuals diagnosed as schizophrenic. Comparison of analyses carried out using realist, contextualist and radical constructionist epistemologies.

*Morrow and Smith (1995)*   Grounded theory study of survival from, and coping with, childhood sexual abuse, leading to development of visual model.

*Wuest (2000)*   Feminist grounded theory study of women's caring. Focuses on the 'emerging fit' with existing research on health care relationships.

---

ethnography can no longer follow the guidelines of positivist social science. Gone are words like theory, hypothesis, concept, indicator, coding scheme, sampling, validity, and reliability. In their place comes a new language; readerly texts, modes of discourse, cultural poetics, deconstruction, interpretation, domination, the authority of the text, the author's voice, feminism, genre, grammatology, hermeneutics, inscription, master narrative, narrative structures, otherness, post-modernism, redemptive ethnography, semiotics, subversion, textuality, tropes. (Denzin, 1988, p. 432)

This is a reprise of an earlier theme in this book: the demise of positivism and the challenge of interpretive, constructivist and relativist voices (see chapter 2, pp. 17–29). The argument put forward there was not to deny the value of this new body of approaches, but to insist that there were continuing virtues in maintaining a broad scientific approach for real world enquiry; and that critical realism provides a viable means of doing this in a post-positivist scientific era. Admittedly, some of the language and terminology traditional in grounded theory harks back to an earlier era; but there appears to be no basic incompatibility between grounded theory and realism. The approach is one way of finding out underlying structures and mechanisms, and realism has no quarrel with theory being generated from analysis of the data gathered in a study.

## NUD*IST and grounded theory analysis

A prime aim in the initial and subsequent development of NUD*IST has been to facilitate grounded theory analysis (Richards and Richards, 1994). A particularly helpful feature for grounded theory analysis is the flexibility of the index system as theory develops, new categories emerge and you see the need to change the relationships between categories. This can be easily achieved with NUD*IST.

As with other approaches, grounded theory is based upon coding (indexing) and memoing. In the course of the analysis you will produce an ever-expanding system of memos about the data. The coding system will initially expand rapidly when open coding is proceeding. The tree structure will build up as notions about relationships between codes occur to you. Figure 14.6 provides a generalized version, based on Cresswell (1998, p. 160) following the coding process recommended by Strauss and Corbin (1998). There is likely to be a phase of major change both to the coding and the structure as axial and eventually selective coding predominate. And as the core concept becomes clear, so the coding structure will simplify. NUD*IST greatly facilitates this sequence and helps you keep tabs on the various stages you have gone through to achieve the end result.

## Alternative Approaches to Qualitative Analysis

As discussed in chapter 6, there is a wide range of other traditions of flexible research design additional to the three types selected as particularly appropri-

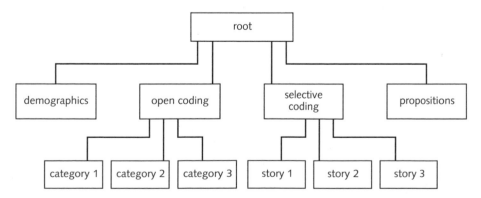

**Figure 14.6**   A generalized version of an index tree for a grounded theory study.

ate for real world research. Of those covered in that chapter, the *phenomeno-logical* tradition has a detailed and fully developed approach to analysis. Cresswell (1998, pp. 147–50) provides an introduction and Moustakas (1994) a detailed account. There are also specific strategies for analysing text central to *hermeneutic* research. See Bentz and Shapiro (1998, pp. 105–20), who provide references.

There are many other possibilities including *narrative, discourse, account* and *attributional analyses* (see chapters in Hayes, 1997). The reader still unsure about which route to take may well find inspiration in Coffey and Atkinson (1996), where a single data set is analysed using a range of different strategies including different versions of *narrative analysis*, linguistic or *semiotic analyses*, types of *textual analysis*, and interpretive or *hermeneutic* goals.

## Further Reading

Coffey, A. and Atkinson, P. (1996) *Making Sense of Qualitative Data: Complementary Research Strategies*. Thousand Oaks, Calif.: Sage. Covers a wide range of alternative strategies for transforming and analysing qualitative data. Very useful if you are not sure which approach to take.

Gibbs, G. (2001) *Qualitative Data Analysis: Explorations with NVivo*. Buckingham: Open University Press. Very thorough, accessible and well-structured guide to the use of NVivo.

Glaser, B. (1992) *Basics of Grounded Theory Analysis: Emergence versus Forcing*. Mill Valley, Calif.: Sociology Press. Accessible text providing a 'purist' grounded theory approach.

Hammersley, M. and Atkinson, P. (1995) *Ethnography: Principles in Practice*, 2nd edn. London and New York: Routledge. Chapter 8 provides a clear account of the process of analysis in ethnographic studies.

Miles, M. B. and Huberman, A. M. (1994) *Qualitative Data Analysis: An Expanded Sourcebook*, 2nd edn. Thousand Oaks, Calif.: Sage. Invaluable and updated collection of techniques to assist in the systematic analysis of qualitative data. Oriented to large-scale studies but much of relevance.

Pidgeon, N. and Henwood, K. (1996) Grounded theory: practical implementation. In J. T. E. Richardson, ed., *Handbook of Qualitative Research Methods for Psychology and the Social Sciences*. Leicester: BPS Books. Short, practical and accessible account of how to carry out grounded theory analysis.

Silverman, D. (2000) *Doing Qualitative Research: A Practical Handbook*. Thousand Oaks, Calif., and London: Sage. Part III provides a very practical guide to analysing qualitative data. Large number of examples and case studies.

Strauss, A. (1987) *Qualitative Analysis for Social Scientists*. Cambridge: Cambridge University Press. Provides a systematic approach to the analysis and interpretation of qualitative data along 'grounded theory' lines.

Tesch, R. (1990) *Qualitative Research: Analysis Types and Software Tools*. London: Falmer. Makes a useful distinction between structural and interpretational analysis types, and shows how the computer can be used with each of them.

Weitzman, E. A. and Miles, M. B. (1995) *Computer Programs for Qualitative Data Analysis: a Software Sourcebook*. Thousand Oaks, Calif.: Sage. Clear, user-friendly and very comprehensive review. Inevitably somewhat dated in this very rapidly changing field, but likely to be of continuing use for several years.

Yin, R. K. (1994) *Case Study Research: Design and Methods*, 2nd edn. Thousand Oaks, Calif.: Sage. Chapter 5 provides helpful advice on strategies for the analysis of case study data.

# 15
# Reporting on the Enquiry

This chapter:

- emphasizes the importance of considering your intended audience when writing a report
- stresses the difference between writing for academic and other audiences
- covers conventions of the traditional scientific journal format
- considers approaches to the reporting of flexible (qualitative) design studies, giving particular attention to alternative styles of case study report
- stresses the special nature of evaluation reports
- discusses issues in writing for clients, and alternative presentations for different purposes
- concludes with advice on writing.

## Introduction

Consideration of the form that a report of your enquiry might take brings to the fore, once again, the implications of a 'real world' focus. This highlights the notion of *audience*. Who is the report for? What are you seeking to achieve by reporting to them?

### Reporting what you have found

*A   Reporting is an essential part of the enquiry process*

For an enquiry to count in research terms it must be made public. Reporting is the way you do this.

### B   The appropriate format for the report depends on the nature and purpose of the enquiry

If you have academic intent, it is likely that a conventional journal format is appropriate. For other purposes, other formats may well communicate better.

### C   You need not be limited to a single type of report

Real world research often seeks to inform and influence several different audiences. It is unlikely that the same style of report will be best suited to all of them. There is nothing (apart from the effort involved) to stop you producing several different reports. They don't (all) have to be written reports.

### D   Real world enquiry calls for professional standards of reporting and presentation

This applies if you are simply seeking to inform. It is even more important if you want the report and findings to be acted on in some way.

Writing for academic audiences almost always has to follow strict rules. The conventions and expectations in report writing for academic audiences for fixed (quantitative) designs and flexible (qualitative) designs differ considerably. They are therefore considered separately here. When reporting to other audiences, the central issue is the format and approach which best gets your message to them.

## Ethics and reporting

Several parties or stakeholders are likely to be concerned with what is reported, and with how it is reported. You have both an interest in, and a responsibility for, ensuring that the results of your study get into the 'public domain' (to publish is, literally, to make public). 'Publish or perish' may be over-dramatic, but it is inescapable that if your role permits you to carry out enquiry, a likely index of your work and worth will be the quantity and quality of the reports that you produce.

Participants in the research may well be concerned with how they appear in the report, and whether their interests, individually or collectively, are affected by publication. Can you keep to the assurances of anonymity and confidentiality that you gave them? Surveys and experiments are usually straightforward in this respect. But flexible design projects, such as case studies, where the context is important, pose problems. Obviously, it is possible to use pseudonyms for persons and settings, but this may not guarantee anonymity (particularly internally), while further changes that you make to seek disguise may distance your report from the reality it is trying to describe or under-stand. The basic stance usually adopted is to take reasonable precautions to ensure anonymity, and then publish.

When the study has been carried out for sponsors, they also have concerns. How are they, and/or whoever they represent, being portrayed? Will the report be used by others to criticize, compete with or undermine them? Can they stop you (discussed below)? 'Gatekeepers' will be interested in the out-comes of any approval they gave for the study to take place. Are they going to get hassle from others as a result?

*Misrepresentation, plagiarism and assistance from others*   A more straight-forward set of issues concerns your own ethical standards when reporting. You should, of course, try to produce an honest and truthful account of what you have done. Claiming to do work which you have not done, or exagger-ating its extent, or fabricating results or findings is unforgivable, as it strikes at the heart of trust in research. If suspected, it should be investigated thoroughly (with protection for the 'whistle-blower'), and if substantiated should be severely punished. Instances of such cheating are, unfortunately not unknown (see p. 506), and pressures to publish may well increase their incidence.

A basic rule is that you should not try to pass off someone else's work or ideas as your own. It is highly unlikely, and in most cases highly undesirable, that you will have carried out a research project without in some sense having assistance from others. In any report, this assistance should be acknowledged. Typically, this is done by formal referencing of previously published material or by explicit acknowledgement of ideas or advice from colleagues or others. Above all, you do not copy material from others without making this clear. Similarly, if you are doing a replication study (which may well be very valu-able), this has to be made clear.

In some situations, such as presenting material for an academic award, there will be an expectation that the research itself is 'all your own work', which you may be called on to certify. In many real world settings, this is unrealistic: parts of the data collection may have been carried out on a group basis; or some stakeholders may have contributed in various ways; or you may have received support from a statistician for statistical analysis; or you may be reporting on part of a larger study where it is necessary for you to also include the work of colleagues to make what you have done understandable. You should make clear to the reader exactly what contribution you have made, so that a judge-ment can be made about its value.

A convention of academic reporting is that quoting a reference implies that you have read it yourself rather than seen it quoted by someone else (where you use 'cited by' and give the full reference to the work doing the citing). Observing this convention would help stop the transmission of mistakes and misattributions through generations of such references.

*Sexist language*   Sexist language is offensive to many as, in the language of the legal definition, the male term is simply assumed to 'embrace the female'. It can also be ambiguous, as in the use of 'businessman' (as a generic term in the sense of covering females as well as males), when it is then not clear whether or not only male individuals are being referred to. Empirical studies have shown that the use of sexist language does make a difference in the inferences that readers draw (Adams and Ware, 1989; Pearson, 1985).

Several sets of guidelines exist aiming to sensitize people to the forms that sexist language takes and suggesting non-sexist alternatives. For example, the BSA's 'Guidelines on Anti-Sexist Language' (British Sociological Association, 1989a) include:

| *sexist* | *anti-sexist* |
|---|---|
| man/mankind | person, people, human beings |
| man-made | synthetic, artificial, manufactured |
| manpower | workforce, staff, labourpower |
| manhours | workhours |
| forefathers | ancestors |
| master copy | top copy, original |

There is a set of corresponding issues concerning racist language; see e.g. British Sociological Association (1989b).


## Reporting Fixed Design (Quantitative) Research

There is a conventional model for the format of written reports on fixed design, quantitative research in academic journals. If you do not follow the model, you are very unlikely to get published in such journals. Broadly speaking, the same conventions apply to reporting of quantitative research in professional journals, although some which are specifically aimed at practitioners may adopt a more relaxed stance. There are other ways of disseminating findings to fellow researchers and professionals, most notably through conference papers (and other conference activities such as 'poster sessions', where you display a summary of your research and stand by the posters to answer questions and discuss the work with interested conference members) and seminar papers. There is sometimes an unexamined assumption that these latter types of activities should mimic the journal paper in style. However, you may well communicate more effectively face-to-face by adopting one of the other formats covered later in the chapter.

The student on a degree or postgraduate course is commonly required to follow the scientific paper format for all quantitative reports. Similar expectations exist for dissertations produced by doctoral and other research students. There is a strong case for students being required to gain skills in other kinds of presentation. Report writing for academic audiences is likely to be a high-frequency activity for only a small minority of students in their subsequent careers. Many more will have to produce reports for other audiences.

## The Scientific Journal Format

Almost all journals require contributors to follow a specific format and to keep within certain areas of subject content and limits of length. Instructions are given, usually on one of the inside covers of the journal, and may include reference to a 'style manual' such as that published by the American Psychological Association (1994). A good strategy is to peruse recent journal issues and seek a suitable model.

The traditional writing style expected has been impersonal, in the past tense and in the passive voice (as in 'subjects were asked to complete all questions'). This is understandable as an attempt to demonstrate the scientific credentials of the activity, but can lead to a dryness and lack of impact in the writing. Several journals do not now require the passive impersonal style (e.g. 'We found that . . .' is accepted in place of the traditional 'It was found that . . .'). Conversely, too much authorial intrusion, with 'I did this and then I . . .', sounds naïve, at least to my ear. Continued use of the past tense for things that have already happened (for previous studies referred to, and also what *was* done in the one you are reporting on), does however seem justified.

Calling those who have taken part in the study 'subjects' has also been criticized, in part as suggesting an inappropriate role – that they are 'subjected' to various things. The term 'participant' is now recommended by the APA and the British Psychological Society (BPS). In some contexts, 'respondent', 'informant' or just 'person' may be appropriate. Sexist language should be avoided, as discussed above (p. 503) and in chapter 3 (p. 73). Box 15.1 presents a checklist of areas commonly covered in a report produced in journal format.

Reminders about pitfalls in the use of the term 'significant' in quantitative research (discussed in chapter 13, p. 400, are perhaps worth repeating here. Significance in the '$p < 0.05$' sense should always be reported as 'statistical significance' rather than just 'significance'. The 'importance', or 'clinical significance', of a finding is another thing entirely. The common conclusion following a non-statistically significant finding in a small-scale experiment that

---

Box 15.1

## Checklist of areas covered in report for scientific journal

1    *Title* Summarizing the main topic of the report.
2    *Abstract* A concise summary, typically in about 150 words.
3    *Introduction*

a    explains nature of study;
b    describes background and previous work;
c    gives design and the research questions with rationale for choice;
d    notes ethical issues* raised by the study and procedures followed to address them.

4    *Method* A detailed account of procedures used which would enable the reader to repeat the study:

a    participants
       i   number
       ii  selection process
       iii characteristics
       iv  means of handling refusals/non-returns;
b    apparatus/materials
       i   description of tests/scales/observation schedules, etc.
       ii  development procedures for new instruments
       iii scoring/coding procedures;
c    procedure
       i   observers/interviewers, etc.: characteristics and training
       ii  reliability and validity of instruments/procedures
       iii description of setting
       iv  verbatim instructions to participants
       v   duration, number and timing of sessions.

5  *Results*

a    methodological checks (e.g. showing matching of two groups);
b    quantitative data analysis
       i   descriptive statistics
       ii  exploratory data analysis
       iii confirmatory data analysis;
c    qualitative data analysis;
d    tables, graphs and figures (appropriately interspersed);
e    summary statement.

6   *Discussion*

a   answers to research questions;
b   relationship to earlier findings;
c   implications;
d   suggested improvements; questions raised; suggestions for further research.

7   *Notes and references*

a   text of notes (indicated by superscript numbers in the article itself);
b   list of references cited in the article, in standard format.

* Ethical issues are not mentioned in the guidelines for some journal reports. They should be.
*Note*: Check the *specific* requirements of the journal to which you propose to send your paper.

'the study should be replicated on a larger scale', with the implicit or explicit inference that a statistically significant result would thereby be obtained, is a truism. Achievement of statistical significance is a direct function of sample size; if you wish to obtain statistical significance, simply run a large enough study!

To make progress as a professional enquirer or researcher, writing accounts in this format is a 'real world' activity for you. Reputation, progress and research money are strongly related to the number and quality of articles accepted for publication in reputable, refereed journals. And rightly so. The conventions of this style of publication, with detailed and explicit concern for descriptions of procedure and analysis, together with the system of anonymous review by peers, provide important safeguards of the quality of the collective scientific endeavour. Scandals where the system breaks down, because of fraud, delusion or collusion, are not unknown. Broad and Wade (1985) discuss a range of examples. The alleged fraud within psychology perpetrated by Sir Cyril Burt (Hearnshaw, 1979) has been the subject of much controversy, with the British Psychological Society delivering an 'open verdict' (British Psychological Society, 1992; see also Joynson, 1989; Mackintosh, 1995; Butler and Petrulis, 1999). The system within science, in principle though not always in practice, should be self-correcting because of the principle of the replicability of findings (maverick findings are highly likely to be checked by others, and faked results will not replicate).

There are potential difficulties and tensions in reporting applied studies to both academic and other audiences. Many concentrate on specific settings, persons or organizations, selected because of practical concerns rather than through some representative sampling procedure. Such studies may be difficult to fit into the traditional format. In particular, you must ensure that problems in the interpretation of statistical findings produced by such sampling are made explicit in your report. Further details on the 'scientific journal' format for reporting case studies are presented in a later section of this chapter (p. 511).

## Reporting Flexible Design (Qualitative) Research

There is little consensus on the format for reporting qualitative research in academic or professional journals. Again, the best advice is to study carefully any guidelines included in the journals which interest you, and the actual reports printed in recent volumes. Several 'qualitative' journals have an explicit policy of encouraging alternative formats.

### General features

Commentators, such as Stainback and Stainback (1988), suggest the need for 'deep and valid description' and 'well-grounded theories emerging from a wide variety of data'. Mertens (1998) adds to this 'contextual meaning'; i.e. an 'attempt to understand the social and cultural context in which the statements are made and the behaviors exhibited', including 'a description of relevant contextual variables, such as home, community, history, educational background, physical arrangements, emotional climate, and rules' (p. 361). Padgett (1998) encapsulates the task concisely: 'Our basic goal is to produce a report that is scholarly, trustworthy, and readable' (p. 104).

Miles and Huberman (1994) have produced a set of guidelines which are sufficiently general to cover many types of qualitative research, given as box 15.2. Box 15.3 provides a checklist which, if followed, would cover most of the aspects typically found in a report of a qualitative-design study. Silverman (2000, part 5: 'Writing Up') gives detailed and very helpful consideration of this task.

Working in this way produces a conventionally structured, mainstream report of a qualitative study. There are additional features of the research which might be included in the report, and alternative possible structures. If, for example, you are working in a field or area where quantitative research is the norm, it may be politic to provide a detailed defence of the legitimacy of a qualitative approach. However, in most areas there is now sufficient

---

## Box 15.2

### Guidelines for qualitative reports

1   The report should tell us what the study was about or came to be about.

2   It should communicate a clear sense of the social and historical context of the setting(s) where data were collected.

3   It should provide us with what Erickson (1986) calls the 'natural history of the inquiry', so we see clearly what was done, by whom and how. More deeply than in a sheer 'methods' account, we should see how key concepts emerged over time; which variables appeared and disappeared; which codes led into important insights.

4   A good report should provide basic data, preferably in focused form (vignettes, organized narrative, photographs or data displays) so that the reader can, in parallel with the researcher, draw warranted conclusions.

5   Finally, researchers should articulate their conclusions, and describe their broader meaning in the worlds of ideas and action they affect.

(After Miles and Huberman, 1994, p. 304.)

---

experience of qualitative research for this to be unnecessary (though there is still, as with quantitative designs, a need to justify why specific methods or approaches have been taken in relation to their appropriateness for the research questions, as in point 3(e) of box 15.3).

Punch (1986) considers that the reader ought to know more about the 'muddy boots and grubby hands' aspect of doing fieldwork, by including in the report such things as the

- problems encountered getting into and out of the field;
- micro-politics of the site and the role played by your study;
- conflicts, ambiguities and more sordid understandings (!) gained during fieldwork.

Wolcott (1990) argues against a free-standing literature review chapter early in the report. He suggests that it is better 'to draw upon the literature selectively and appropriately as needed in the telling of [the] story' (p. 17). Also, to the extent that a grounded theory approach has been adopted, there is a case for introducing and discussing theories arising from the literature towards the end of a study.

Box 15.3

## Checklist of sections in a report of a qualitative study

1   *The first pages* A short but crucially important part of the report; it includes:

a   *The title* It is worth giving considerable attention to the wording of the title; it 'sells' the report. You will have some kind of working title (perhaps from your initial proposal) from the start, but don't be afraid to revise it. Note any ideas for titles as memos. Finalize the title as late as you can. A two-part title structure is common: something capturing the essence of the study followed by a more descriptive subtitle.

b   *The abstract* This needs to cover the research problem or topics; why it is worth studying; what data have been obtained; the methods used; the main findings; and their implications. If a word limit is specified keep to it; if not 150 words is typical.

c   *The list of contents* If this is a mess, it signals that the report is likely to be one. It needs to be very clear and logically set out. There are different views and preferences about the number of levels of sub-headings and whether they should be numbered, but you definitely need to have some within chapter headings to help the reader find their way around.

d   *The introduction* Explains what the report is about, why this topic was chosen and what approach you are taking; outlines your research questions; and gives a short explanation of the structure of the report.

2   *The literature review chapter(s)* This is important for demonstrating your academic credentials (it is much less important for non-academic audiences). While the writing of such a review can be an important early task, it will need to be rewritten after completion of data analysis. You can thus ensure that everything in the review is directly relevant to your study. It should include:

a   what is already known about the subject of the study;
b   your evaluation of this previous work;
c   the relationship of your work to these earlier studies.

3   *The methodology chapter* Many different approaches are possible. You should give information about:

a   the kinds of data you have obtained;
b   why these data were selected;
c   how the data were obtained, including issues of access and consent;

d    the methods used to collect the data;

e    why these methods were used;

f    the approach taken to data analysis;

g    discussion of the reliability, validity and generalizability of the data;

h    the decisions made during the course of the study, including changes of focus and direction;

i    ethical issues raised by the study and the procedures followed to address them.

4    *The data chapter(s)* In real world empirical studies, these form the heart of the report. The central purpose of such studies is to collect data and analyse them. Remember that in flexible design studies, the analysis goes hand-in-hand with data gathering. As data and analysis are so intimately interconnected, it is not generally advisable to have separate chapters on data and analysis. You may well need two or more chapters to cover different facets or aspects of the study. Each one should contain:

a    *Introduction* Explain the topic covered in the chapter, how it relates to the research questions, and how the chapter is organized.

b    *Main section* This contains a logical sequence of points, for each of which the case is made through references to specific data. The reader must be able to see how and why you have made each interpretation.

c    *Conclusion* Ties the chapter together by explaining what has been achieved, and how and where in the report issues arising will be dealt with.

5    *The final chapter* It is not uncommon for a researcher to be so exhausted by this stage of writing the report that they simply provide a cursory summary of findings from the data chapter, finishing with the formulaic 'more research needs to be done'. You need to finish with much more of a 'bang', perhaps covering:

a    *The research questions that you have answered, and what the answers are* In flexible design studies these may be very different from the questions you started with.

b    How what you have found links to previous knowledge as discussed in the literature review.

c    Lessons to be learned from the *conduct* of the study (remember that you should learn something not only substantively about the topic of the study, but also about how to do studies – you are not expected to be perfect, but you are expected to learn).

d    Implications for practice and/or policy.

e    Specific suggestions for further research.

(Suggested report structure based on Silverman, 2000, pp. 221–53.)

The most common means of organizing the data chapters is probably through a discussion of the research questions one by one and the evidence you have from the data about how they might be answered. Again, this does not sit easily with an inductive, grounded theory approach. It is also, to a greater or less extent, a reconstructed account of what you eventually made of the data, likely to lose any feeling for the process of the analysis. An alternative, but similar version is advocated by Strauss and Corbin (1998). The 'analytic story' emerging from a grounded theory analysis is placed up-front in this approach. The remainder of the account is devoted to spelling out in detail and substantiating this story.

## Reporting on Case Studies

Case studies can be written up in many different ways. As with the design and analysis of any flexible design study, reporting is not a once-only event tagged on to the end of the process. Yin (1989, p. 127) advocates composing parts of the report (e.g. the bibliography) at an early stage, and drafting and redrafting other parts of the report (e.g. the methodological section) rather than waiting for the end of the data analysis process.

*As many real world studies following an ethnographic or grounded theory approach are also case studies (see chapter 6, p. 185), the discussion below applies to them too. See Emerson et al. (1995, ch. 7) for a useful general discussion on 'writing an ethnography', and Strauss and Corbin (1998, ch. 15) for discussion on writing up grounded theory studies.*

### The 'scientific journal' case study format

Use of this standard approach for structuring research reports is feasible with many case studies, and has the advantage that it is familiar to the person steeped in the traditions of laboratory-based enquiry. It is similarly the style of presentation least likely to raise hackles in academic circles. Conversely, it is unlikely to be the most appropriate format in communicating to other audiences.

The 'issue/methods/findings/conclusions' structure provides the broad framework. Lincoln and Guba (1985, p. 362), advocate the use of case study reporting as a way of getting some order into qualitative field research reports (which have previously been characterized variously by Lofland, 1971, p. 109, as showing 'democratic pluralism', 'chaos' or 'anarchy'). They suggest two-part structure, with a main report consisting of:

a    an explanation of the focus of the case study (e.g. problem, issue, policy option, topic of evaluation),

b    a description of the context or setting in which the enquiry took place, and with which it was concerned,

c    a description and analysis of the data obtained, and

d    a discussion of the outcomes of the enquiry,

followed by a methodological appendix containing a description of:

e    the credentials of the investigator(s), to include training and experience, together with a statement about the methodological predispositions and any biases towards the problem or setting,

f    the methods employed and the nature of the design as finally implemented, and

g    the methods used to enhance and assess trustworthiness.

Lincoln and Guba also stress the need for assessing each of these considerations at several different times in the study so that the report incorporates what was *intended* in respect of each of them and what was actually *implemented*.

## Other formats for case study reports

These formats are based on Yin (1989, pp. 132–41), who cites examples of published case studies following the different formats.

*The suspense structure*   Here, there is an inversion of the normal sequence as presented above. The main findings are presented in the initial chapter. The rest of the report is devoted to building up to this conclusion, showing what was done in the study, the picture that emerged, and how alternative explanations had to be discarded, so that that particular outcome was reached. It has considerable merit in explanatory studies (probably most people read the main findings first anyway!) as a presentational device.

*The narrative report*   A classic case study report format is the straightforward account of the case. This might be bolstered by tables, figures and photographs, but the story is essentially told in continuous prose without the kind of analytic sub-divisions found in the previous format. Multiple case studies are handled by having a section for each individual case, with a separate section for consideration of cross-case considerations.

A variant replaces the narrative by a series of questions and answers bringing out the findings from the study, which can be supplemented by an abbreviated narrative. Repetition of the same questions across cases permits easy comparisons in a multiple case study. Alternatively, multiple case studies can be presented in a narrative form where the organization is issue-based rather than case-based. This type of account can be supplemented by abbreviated summaries of individual cases.

*The comparative structure*    Here the same case is examined two or more times sequentially, each time in terms of a different explanatory or descriptive framework. The purpose is to demonstrate, or to give the reader sufficient information to judge, which of the explanations or descriptions best fits the data.

*The chronological structure*    Evidence is presented in the report in chronological sequence. Its chief virtue is in explanatory studies, where the emphasis on temporal order assists in the teasing out of cause–effect relationships. Insistence on strict chronology as being the only organizational principle can, however, in anything but very simple case studies, provide a confusing and unnecessarily muddled account.

*Theory-generating structures*    Here the structure serves to support a theoretical case that is being made. Each succeeding section establishes a further part of, or link in, the argument, so that the totality provides a convincing case for a particular theoretical formulation. It can be used for either explanatory or exploratory case studies. This approach demands considerable powers of exposition and analytic grasp if it is not only to be theoretically convincing but also to demonstrate a rigorous approach to data analysis and interpretation.

*Unsequenced structures*    This structure, where the sequence of the different sections is of little or no importance, may be appropriate for descriptive case studies. Several important and frequently quoted descriptive case studies – e.g. the Lynd and Lynd (1929) 'Middletown' study – are unsequenced. A problem is that with this type of very open structure, it may be difficult to know, or establish, whether important areas have been omitted.

These structures may suggest ideas for presentation of particular kinds of case study to different audiences. A well-written narrative account, totally bereft of tables of data, possibly presented in question and answer form, may communicate best to the manager, or social worker, or lay audience. More technical details can be included as appendices.

Many applied studies can legitimately seek to reach multiple audiences through multiple forms of publication. The sponsor, the wider practitioner and lay audiences can receive appropriate treatment(s), while the scientific audience can be reached through thesis and journal article.

## Writing for Non-Academic Audiences: The Technical Report

Many real world projects involve carrying out an enquiry for someone, whom we will refer to here as the client. Evaluations, for example, often come into this category. The client may be an outside agency of some kind which has given you financial and other assistance to do a project, probably on a contractual basis. Or the enquiry might be a normal part of your job, which you have been asked to do by your boss, section head or manager, where she is the client. Or, again within your job, it might be a part of your professional responsibility to carry out projects, largely on your own initiative. In this latter case, and to some extent in the previous ones, the clients may be thought of as the persons forming the focus of the study: for example, staff and children in schools, or nurses, doctors and patients in hospitals.

The nature of report for a sponsor or superior, which we will refer to as a *technical report*, is very much conditioned by their requirements and expectations. For some, the required report is very much along the lines of the 'scientific journal article' model. For other clients, this may be totally inappropriate. In case studies, the alternative formats considered in the previous section deserve serious consideration.

The Rowntree Trust (n.d.), a major British funder of social research, has a strong position on dissemination. It requires projects to be of value to policy-makers, decision-takers and practitioners, and is hence concerned to ensure that research findings

> are presented in a form which can be grasped quickly by influential people who are normally too busy to read long reports or books. The Trust attaches importance to reports which are short, to the point and written in plain English. Compact summaries of research findings are likely to provide the basis of the Trust's Dissemination activities. . . . it seriously doubts whether scholarly publications ever represent an effective means of communication with policy makers and practitioners, certainly in the short term. (p. 10)

In contract research, the type, length and date of presentation of the final report are usually specified in the terms of the contract itself. The issue here is whether you can live with these terms. They are frequently standard, but may be negotiable. The degree of control that the sponsors have over content and publication should be clarified in the initial contract. Some may expect a power of veto, and modification or exclusion of things they object to (e.g. Jenkins, 1984). Others simply expect consultation at a draft stage. The issue may be not so much about your report to them, but whether they seek restrictions on further reports to other audiences. This is a particularly contested area with evaluation studies, largely because of the likely sensitivity of the findings for both sponsors and other parties. There are no general answers here, apart from making sure that you know where you stand before you get into the project, and feeling that you can live with the constraints both practically and ethically. The sponsors should appreciate, however, that they are paying for your expertise and that your concern is to 'tell it as it is'. If they seek to muffle or distort that message, then to an extent they are wasting their money.

## Practicalities of technical report writing

*Find out what is expected*   Ask. Some clients will want everything included, perhaps in an adaptation of the 'scientific journal' format but with minimal use of jargon, particularly of statistical terminology. Others may simply want major findings. Implications and suggested courses of action may either be specifically required, or specifically excluded. It often helps to check the form, style and length of any similar reports for the same sponsor – ask to see any they thought to be particularly helpful, good models, etc. Be ruthless on length; do not exceed what they have asked for.

*Provide an 'executive summary'*   This is a short (usually one-page), punchy summary, outlining the problem, methods used, results and conclusion.

*Put as much material as possible into appendices*   Any supplementary materials which you feel should be included, but which are not crucial to understanding what has been done, should be put in appendices. Put them in a separate volume if they are likely to make the report appear off-puttingly large; alternatively, you may want them in the same volume to emphasize how much work you have done with the client's money. Their main function is to provide additional detail for readers with specialized interests. Typical appendix items would be

- detailed tables, charts and statistical analyses (summary charts would usually be in the main report);
- copies of instruments and documents used (e.g. questionnaires, coding and other instructions, observation schedules, form letters);
- glossary of terms, including acronyms, used (also explained on first use in the main body of the report).

*Make sure that the presentation of the report is to a professional standard*   The sponsor has the right to expect professionalism in presentation of the report, just as much as in your carrying out and analysing the study. Anyhow, good presentation aids communication. See the general comments on writing and presentation below (p. 519).

## Special features of evaluation reports

A distinctive feature of many evaluation reports is the emphasis on *recommendations*. Box 15.4 provides suggestions on the writing of effective recommendations (i.e. ones likely to be acted on).

## Alternative Forms of Presentation

Applied research may be most effectively communicated to some audiences through forms different from a written report. Alternatives include oral presentations, audio-visual ones of various kinds and literary forms other than the report. They are thought of here mainly as supplementary ways of communicating what you have done. They are additional to the written report in which you demonstrate the rigour and quality of your study.

It is increasingly common for the culmination of a piece of funded research with an applied focus to involve not simply a technical report and journal publication, but also oral presentations to both the funding body and other audiences. For some studies, there may be the need for workshop sessions with practitioner groups, where the implications of the study for action form the bases of practical sessions. This begins to take us into wider dissemination issues, which were discussed in chapter 7 (p. 203).

Practical constraints will often have a major influence on these alternative forms of presentation. You may have fifteen minutes with the board of directors, or the team of community workers in a particular area; or a one-day in-service training course for practitioners; or a four-page A5 supplement to a newsletter sent out to proprietors of private residential homes for the elderly. Each of those would present a substantial, and different, presentational challenge.

Comments are made below on a few possibilities. The suggestions are all obvious and owe more to common sense than systematic analysis, but the abysmal quality of many presentations indicates that they may be helpful.

---

### Box 15.4

### Recommendations in evaluation reports

1   *The most important aspects are that recommendations should:*

a      *be clearly derived from the data;* and
b      *be practical* (i.e. *capable of implementation*).

2   It is helpful to distinguish:

a   *findings* – information about the situation;
b   *interpretations* – explanations offered about the findings;
c   *judgements* – values brought to bear on the data; and
d   *recommendations* – suggested courses of action.

Patton (1982) describes exercises designed to develop skills in making these distinctions. He suggests taking a set of data and writing a final section of the report in which the findings, interpretations, judgements and subsequent recommendations are summarized *in one place*. The reasonableness of a recommendation depends on its being logically backed up by a set of findings, a reasonable interpretation of the findings and a judgement applied to them. Criteria for the making of judgements should be made explicit. Interpretations are necessarily speculative, and may be the subject of dispute. Resolution should be sought through discussion, and returning to the findings, to ensure that interpretations are grounded in these findings.

3   The process of generating recommendations takes time. A carefully carried out evaluation can be ruined by seeking to produce recommendations under severe time pressure. There should be the opportunity to discuss provisional recommendations with those holding a stake in the evaluation.

4   Consider presenting recommendations as a *set of options*. Given a list of findings, there may be several reasonable interpretations and different value positions which will generate a whole range of options. Each should be fully documented, showing fairly how the findings, interpretations and judgements support the option.

5   The nature of recommendations should be negotiated with decision-makers, or whoever form the audience for the report, at an early stage. This will have implications for the kind of evaluation carried out and the questions addressed. Note that it is possible that decision-makers may not want the evaluator to present recommendations but simply to deliver findings, with or without analysis and interpretation.

6   The people who will make use of the evaluation information should be closely involved in generating the recommendations. They are more likely to act on things that they have thought out for themselves than on ideas foisted on them by an outside evaluator. From your point of view as an evaluator, they are a valuable resource enabling you to escape being over-influenced by your own prejudices. This does mean that they will have to be prepared to invest time and effort in making the progression from facts to recommendations. Getting them in the way of doing this may have spin-offs way beyond the particular evaluation.

## Oral presentations

Possibilities include the use of overhead projectors, slides and flip-charts to get over information via different media. Professional standards here are just as important as with the report and are easy to achieve using presentational packages such as PowerPoint. Particular attention should be given to the quality and legibility of lettering, its size being such that it is easily read by all those present. A handout which complements the oral presentation is helpful. Mere repetition in the handout of what is said is a waste of time and opportunity.

## Alternative literary presentations

A greater degree of creativity in this respect seems to have been shown by evaluators than those doing other types of study, although there seems to be no reason why they should not be used more widely. Approaches include the following.

*Pamphlet production*   The task of compressing an account of a project into a short pamphlet for a general audience is daunting. Emphasis should be on the findings and on implications for action. Jargon should be ruthlessly excised. An attractive, uncluttered layout with strong headings is needed, and judicious use should be made of photographs, drawings and simple tables. Resist the temptation to get in as many words as you can. Give an indication of what the interested reader can do to follow up the topic by providing references to other publications and an address.

This kind of short document is one way in which you can fulfil promises made to participants to let them know about the outcome of the project. The full report is not usually suitable for this purpose, although it should normally be available on request. 'Member checking' and the production of 'negotiated accounts' represent a very different kind of activity and responsibility to participants, and must be completed prior to publication of any final reports (see chapter 14, p. 483).

*News releases*   One way of reaching a wider audience is through newspapers, and radio and television stations. For a small-scale study, the local and possibly regional media are the likely targets. A short news release, usually on one side of A4, written in a lively style with an eye-catching heading, is required. Regard it as a further boiling down of the pamphlet described in the previous section. Give a telephone contact number and try to prepare for questions, so that you can avoid injudicious quotations.

A problem is that you do not have control over what is written. Busy journalists are likely to use at least parts of the release verbatim – a likelihood enhanced by your lively writing – but they will be prone to inserting their own distortions and (mis)interpretations. While it may be wisest not to seek publicity for studies carried out in some sensitive areas, there is a general responsibility to help promote the better information of the general public that all who carry out real world research should recognize.

## Writing Skills

The actual activity of writing receives scant attention in most books on the doing of research. It is similarly rarely dealt with explicitly on research methods courses – apart from that form of summative evaluation of reports of investigations otherwise known as marking or assessment. There is research relevant to this kind of writing. Hartley (1985) provides a practical guide, which, although oriented towards instructional material such as textbooks, contains much of relevance to anyone seeking to communicate through writing. It is, incidentally, very readable! As with other skills, writing benefits from practice, particularly if detailed and early feedback can be provided by a constructive colleague.

### The first draft

The importance of having a clear sense of audience has already been stressed in relation to style, length and general approach. If you have followed the suggestions for a structured approach to design, data collection and analysis made in earlier chapters, you should have a substantial base of material for the report. The advice, stressed in connection with flexible design studies, of starting to write parts of the report while still involved with data collection, could usefully be generalized to other research strategies. Even so, there has to be a period towards the end of a study where the major task is writing – putting it all together, and getting out the 'first draft'.

There are major individual differences in preferred approach to this task (Hartley and Branthwaite, 1989). The word processor has much to commend it, particularly in the ease with which amendments to drafts can be made, both in content and in sequence. Many users report a liberating effect with proficiency in word processing, where a more 'playful' writing style emerges, with lower barriers to both starting (the 'blank page' phenomenon) and continuation. However, it is important that you possess a good working knowledge of the system and its features, and absolutely crucial that you stick to good 'housekeeping' principles, including regular saving of what you have typed, backing up of copies of computer files, and the equally regular printing out of drafts of what you have produced.

Notwithstanding its advantages, there is no rule which says that you must use a word processor if you are to produce a good report. If you can best deliver when writing longhand, or speaking into a dictating machine, then go ahead. *What is essential is that you allow yourself sufficient uninterrupted time for the activity.* And go for 'prime time'. Writing is difficult, and you should devote to it the time of the day when you are at your most effective. For many people, this is the first two or three working hours in the day, but it could well be in the evening or some other time. A regular schedule helps.

Interruptions reduce efficiency. Try to organize a period when you are 'incommunicado'. Switch off that mobile. An answering machine or colleague (possibly on a reciprocal basis) can deal with the phone. Get it known and respected that you are not available for discussion, or whatever, at that time. Obviously, details depend on your individual circumstances; but the principle is that this is an important activity which has to take precedence if you are to do your job properly.

For many people, starting is difficult, both right at the beginning and at each writing session. This is an argument for putting your available time into substantial-sized blocks. One tactic is to finish a session in mid-paragraph so that you know exactly where to pick things up next time. Outlines and structures, as discussed earlier in the chapter, are helpful, but don't feel that you must go through them in a linear manner. In particular, with the scientific journal format, early parts such as the title and abstract, and the final version of the introduction, are best left until you see what the rest of the report is going to look like.

## Revising the draft

Here again there are individual differences in preferred approach. It is often recommended (e.g. Parry, 1996, p. 116) that in producing the first draft you should concern yourself primarily with content, and leave style of writing as a task that you concentrate on when revising.

The aim is to communicate. Go for clear, simple and lively English. There are several useful general guides to writing style, of which the best known is probably Fowler's *Modern English Usage* (Burchfield, 1996), which covers both 'English' English and 'American' English. More specific texts include Day (1983). Barzun and Graff (1977), although oriented towards research in the humanities, has much that is generally valuable on writing. Box 15.5 suggests some guidelines for revising text.

## Box 15.5

### Guidelines for revising the first draft

Whether you can work on the paper as a whole, or only on sections of it, at one time obviously depends on its length.

1   Read the text through.

2   Read the text again and ask yourself:

*   What am I trying to say?
*   Who is the text for?

3   Read the text again and ask yourself:

*   What changes will make the text clearer and easier to follow?

4   To make these changes, you may need:

*   to make *global* or big changes (e.g. rewriting sections); or
*   to make minor *textual* changes.

You need to decide whether you are going to focus first on global changes, or first on text changes.

5   *Global* changes you might like to consider in turn are:

*   reordering parts of the text;
*   rewriting sections;
*   adding examples;
*   changing the examples for better ones;
*   deleting parts that seem confusing.

6   *Text* changes you might like to consider in turn are:

*   using simpler wording;
*   using shorter sentences;
*   using shorter paragraphs;
*   using active rather than passive tenses;
*   substituting positive constructions for negatives;
*   writing sequences in order;
*   spacing numbered sequences or lists down the page (as here).

7   Read the revised text through to see if you want to make any further global changes.

8   Finally, repeat this whole procedure some time (say twenty-four hours) after making your original revisions, and do it without looking back at the original text.

(From Hartley, 1989, p. 90.)

Hartley (1985) used a multiple-method study in evaluating the effectiveness of this procedure, comparing 'before' and 'after' versions of an existing three-page document, and showed that the revised version was easier to read, that the rate of extracting information from it was increased and that judges were more likely to prefer the revised version.

Computers can assist in revising drafts. Word processors usually incorporate a spelling checker, and there is also 'thesaurus' software useful for suggesting alternatives to words that you may tend to over-use. Various 'writer's aids' programs are available which provide facilities such as checking on punctuation as well as on spelling errors, repeated words, split infinitives, long sentences, sexist language, readability indices, etc. However, don't let the 'style police' iron out all individuality in your writing; stylistic conventions should work in the service of communication rather than of total conformity.

## The final typescript

This should be a polished jewel. Spelling, punctuation and typing should be perfect. There should be a simple and consistent system of headings and subheadings, and of spacings between sections. If the report is intended for publication in some form, the publishers will have requirements or preferences about format as well as style. Double spacing and wide margins are required. References often cause problems, including inconsistency in format, parts missing, references mentioned in the text but not present in the reference list (and vice versa), and inconsistencies between the name(s) or dates in the text and those in the list. Tables and figures for work sent for publication go at the end of the text with their position indicated in the text.

Assuming that you are using a word processor, it is at this stage that your expertise in its use and attention to detail will be tested. If you can't reach a high standard, give the job to someone who can. Computer packages are available for graphics, but again require facility in their use, and you may have to use the services of a professional graphic illustrator.

There is no substitute for painstaking proof-reading, preferably by someone else. This is not simply because this is a very boring job, but mainly because your familiarity with the text is likely to impede your effectiveness at the task.

Parry (1996, pp. 105–22) provides a more detailed account angled towards the scientific journal paper, taking the process beyond this stage to the independent review system and possible outcomes.

## Further Reading

Barzun, J. and Graff, H. F. (1977) *The Modern Researcher*. New York: Harcourt Brace Jovanovich. Focuses on the humanities but contains much of value for reporting social research (esp. chapters 11–13).

Becker, H. S. (1986) *Writing for Social Scientists: How to Start and Finish Your Thesis, Book or Article*. Chicago: University of Chicago Press. Excellent on the practicalities. From an experienced writer, researcher and editor.

Burchfield, R. W., ed. (1996) *The New Fowler's Modern English Usage*, 3rd edn. Oxford: Clarendon. Revision of Fowler's classic text. Balanced nondogmatic guide to usage covering both British and American English. Have at your side to cut through confusion (infer or imply? when you *can* split infinitives, etc.). Protects against the regimenting barbarism of word processor grammar checkers.

Day, R. A. (1983) *How to Write and Publish a Scientific Paper*, 2nd edn. Philadelphia: ISI Press. Clear and detailed account on traditional scientific reporting.

Hart, C. (1998) *Doing a Literature Review: Releasing the Social Science Imagination*. Thousand Oaks, Calif., and London: Sage. Detailed coverage including first degree, postgraduate and PhD expectations.

Parry, G. (1996) Writing a Research Report. In G. Parry and F. N. Watts, eds, *Behavioural and Mental Health Research: A Handbook of Skills and Methods*, 2nd edn. Hove: Erlbaum (UK) Taylor & Francis. Clear introduction dealing with issues up to and including how to get a paper published.

Wolcott, H. (1990) *Writing Up Qualitative Research*. Newbury Park, Calif. Sage. Excellent discussion, including writing for different audiences. Not afraid to be controversial.

# Afterword

In the initial plan for this book, the idea was to conclude with a rousing plea for a move towards a society in which enquiry was king (or queen): a society where systematic enquiry provides an engine for the development and improvement of human enterprises such as education and social and health services, and was able to do much the same thing for the important and neglected 'people' aspects of industry and commerce. However, wider reading, reflecting on my own experience and that of others, and the writing itself, left me somewhat less sanguine (= 'ardent, confident and inclined to hopefulness') about such a manifesto.

Things are undoubtedly more complex. Lindblom and Cohen (1979) make a powerful case for 'professional social inquiry' being

> only one among several analytical methods, because other forms of information and analysis – ordinary knowledge and causal analysis foremost among them – are often sufficient or better than [professional social enquiry] for social problem solving. (p. 10)

Donald Schon (1987) makes the same kind of point when considering what is involved in 'educating the reflective practitioner':

> In the terrain of professional practice, applied science and research-based technique occupy a critically important though limited territory, bounded on several sides by artistry. (p. 13)

For him, 'artistry' is 'an exercise of intelligence, a kind of knowing', central to the practice of the high-quality professional person, and recognizable through studying their performance.

Carol Weiss (1986), in discussing what she terms the 'limited partnership' between research and policy-making, concludes:

Researchers need to be aware that the work that they do, no matter how applied in intent and how practical in orientation, is not likely to have major influence on the policy decision at which it is purportedly directed . . . Adherence to all the traditional strictures – acceptance of decision-makers' constraints, focus on manipulative variables, timeliness, jargon-free communication and the like – seems only to increase the application of research results marginally . . . When competing with other powerful factors, such as officials' concern with political or bureaucratic advantage, one limited study (and all studies are limited in some way) is likely to have limited impact. (p. 232)

These sombre warnings argue for a much greater degree of humility among proponents of systematic enquiry. However, advantage can be gained from this initially depressing realization. What is called for is a rapprochement between artistry and research-based technique in professional practice; between ordinary knowledge and professional social enquiry in social problem-solving. And, above, all a realistic appreciation of limits to likely impact.

So, forewarned, you should be better equipped for the challenging and highly enjoyable task of carrying out real world research.

# Appendix A
## Writing a Project Proposal

*These suggestions are targeted at relatively small-scale research or enquiry, such as that carried out as a project on a taught post-graduate course or for a research degree. They may also be of value in connection with small grant applications to funding organizations.*

Research is an activity which is essentially in the public domain. Carrying it out is rarely a totally solo exercise. All research seeks to make links to what other researchers have done previously. It usually involves access to and the use of public resources. Much research, particularly in the arts and social sciences, is in some sense based on other people and their responses and productions. On completion, there is an onus on the researcher to make her findings available through some form of publication (= 'making public').

It is, therefore, appropriate that any proposed research should be laid out for inspection and comment by others, and, in many cases, that it should be approved by others. Any student certainly requires his proposal to be formally approved. Those seeking funding require the approval of the funding agency to which they apply, or they will not receive support. In these cases, there will almost always be some required format to the proposal. It is an obvious part of the professional approach advocated here that any specific rubric should be strictly adhered to. If a maximum of 2,000 words is required for the first of May, you do not send in 3,000 on the eighth.

The concern here is for general issues appropriate to all small-scale research proposals. A useful analogy has been made by several writers between researchers and architects (e.g. Hakim, 1987; Leedy, 1989). Planning is the main link. The architect plans buildings; the researcher draws up plans to investigate issues and solve problems. In each case these plans must say something about structure, about how the task is conceptualized and about the methods to be used in implementing the plans.

For both the researcher and the architect, it is insufficient simply to present the concept of the problem and its suggested mode of solution (tower block or ranch house; survey or experiment). Factors such as the resources needed to carry out the work; the qualifications and experience of those involved; previous work that has already been carried out by the applicant and others; computer facilities; obtaining of any necessary permissions and clearances – all these and many other matters are important.

*The research proposal is your opportunity to persuade the 'client' that you know what you are talking about; that you have thought through the issues involved and are going to deliver; that it is worth their taking the risk and giving you licence to get on with it.*

There is a temptation to think of writing the research proposal as merely an irksome formality, a hurdle that has to be jumped before you can get on with the real work of research. Viewed in this light, it is, literally, a waste of time. It is not unlikely that you will produce a skimped and unconvincing proposal which, quite rightly, gets vetoed. It is much more helpful to see it as an important and integral part of the research process. The work that you do at this stage may not produce the definitive proposal which gives an accurate account of what you are going to do in the research, and what will come out of it. Little research has that degree of certitude. But if you can persuade experienced judges that what you are proposing looks interesting and feasible within the constraints of resources and time that you have available, you should take heart. Remember that you are the one who has most to lose if you get into a situation where the research is a failure, and that you want the best insurance policy that you can get. Viewed in that light, it is well worth investing in a good research proposal.

## How to Recognize a Good Proposal

### A good proposal is direct and straightforward

It tells what you are proposing to do, and why you are proposing to do it. The former is concerned with aims, which should be clear and explicit. For the latter, you will have to show why it is interesting and timely, which will involve a demonstration of your awareness of the empirical and theoretical context.

Good research demands clarity of thought and expression in the doing and the reporting. The proposal provides good evidence on your clarity of thought and expression. Make it pro rather than con.

## A good proposal communicates well

The basic purpose is to communicate your intentions. Anything that gets in the way of this should be cut out. Complex mega-sentences illustrating the complexity and subtlety of your thought processes should be avoided. Fine writing with arcane vocabulary (such as 'arcane') does not help. Unless it is specifically asked for, you do not seek to impress by gargantuan book lists illustrating what you have read, or hope to read. The few key works central to your proposal are more appropriate.

As with any research-related writing, the question of audience is important. Appropriate assumptions may vary for different kinds of proposals, but it is often helpful to regard the reader not as an expert in the exact sub-field of your research, but more as a cross between an intelligent layperson and a generalist in the discipline.

## A good proposal is well organized

The structure of your proposal should be simple and self-evident. It helps to have a consistent system for indicating and, if you need to, lettering or numbering, headings and sub-headings. The expected style is usually standard paragraphing and continuous prose. Don't produce a minutely sectionalized, note-form proposal.

Remember that research demands organization above virtually everything else. A poorly organized proposal does little for your cause.

## The Content of a Research Proposal

If you have to work to a standard format on a proposal form or grant application, this obviously determines how you set things out. However, there is substantial overlap between many of these, and it is likely that you will have to provide the following.

### Abstract or summary

This should be brief, clear and informative, giving a flavour of what is intended and why. This will be the first thing read, so you want to give a good impression. Don't exceed any word limit which is specified.

## Background and purpose

This is a major section where you impress by your commitment and professionalism. It will include a short review of relevant work done by others. It is crucial that you unearth and include any very recent work. Its presence will be reassuring to a specialist reviewer and its absence potentially damning. You want to show that there is a gap to be filled, or a next step to be taken, or a concern arising – and that you have a good idea how this should be addressed.

Relevance is very important. Don't show off by displaying ideas or knowledge which do not contribute directly. It helps to get a sympathetic critic to read your draft. If you have been preparing this for some time, you will be so close to it that you find it difficult to put yourself into the position of someone reading it for the first time. Complex constructions may need unpacking; the implicit made explicit.

Your aim is to lead the reader inexorably towards the conclusion you have reached: that this is the work that must be done, now, with these aims, and in this way.

## The plan of work

Here you go into some detail about the methods and procedures to be used. The detail which is necessary or possible will vary according to the nature of the enquiry. A traditional experiment will require close specification of the design to be used, how variables are to be operationalized, and details of chosen tests or measures (justifying the specific choice if alternatives are possible). If more flexible strategies are used, you still have to demonstrate that you know what is involved (see below).

It is often helpful, and reassuring to the reader, if you have carried out some previous work to prepare the ground for the study. This may have been part of an earlier study or project which inspired you to develop it further. Or you might have carried out specific pilot work, perhaps to demonstrate the feasibility of what you are now proposing. This can get you out of a common 'Catch-22' situation. If you are, say, simply repeating a procedure that others have used, this does not constitute novel research; if you go for a novel procedure, how do you know that it is going to work?

You need to be clear where the research will take place and who will be involved. Will you be doing all the work or is it in some sense a group exercise? If the latter, how is your contribution to be demarcated from the larger enterprise? If it is at all feasible, the scale of the enterprise should be stated (e.g. size of any samples). Any necessary permissions for access, co-operation or involvement will have to be negotiated prior to presenting the proposal and statements about this made here (possibly with documentation, such as confirmatory letters, as well).

The plan will also need to specify how data will be analysed. You should, once again, convince the reader that you have thought through the issues. Above all, you have to guard against the impression that you are going to gather the data and then think about analysis afterwards; or that you will simply subject the data to an unspecified barrage of computer-generated analyses. You should indicate the nature and extent of any computer support needed, and how the need will be met.

## Financial aspects

Any proposal which involves financial implications should spell these out and indicate who is going to pay. For a student, this may involve equipment, computer time, photocopying, printing, telephone, etc. A member of staff or a practitioner or professional doing work for her own organization may also have to include a sum to cover for the time she is involved, and for any additional staff time (whether secretarial, technical or research assistance). Bids for external funding would include all these headings and substantial amounts for overheads. Different institutions and different funding bodies each have their own interpretations of what is admissible, and you obviously have to play the game according to their rules.

There is a general tendency to underestimate the financial implications of any research, particularly when times are hard and money scarce. The best advice is to be as realistic as you can. Research is, by definition, problematic and unforeseen circumstances inevitably tend to increase costs. Cutting corners and skimping financially is a false economy. It may slightly increase your chances of getting approval (though not necessarily; experienced assessors might regard it as an indication of a lack of professionalism), but it will almost certainly decrease your chances of delivering satisfactorily on time. If you find that you do not have the time or resources to complete the project as envisaged, the situation can be sometimes rescued by 'trading down' to a different design (see Hakim, 1987, pp. 120–3).

## Ethical implications

For many forms of research, certainly for much research involving humans, proposals will require ethical vetting. This will seek to ensure that it falls within an appropriate 'code of practice' (see chapter 3, p. 65). It will usually be sensible to seek clearance at an early stage of the preparation of the proposal, when its main features have been settled. The formal proposal would then simply certify that approval had been granted.

There may also be legal implications of certain kinds of research. One which potentially affects much research arises from data protection legislation. This is designed to protect individuals from having personal data stored on computer and other files without their knowledge, agreement and access. If any such data are stored in your research, you need to seek advice on your responsibilities.

## The Problem of Pre-specifying Flexible Design Studies

In the flexible design studies discussed in chapter 6, it is not feasible to pre-specify many of the details of the research project. The design, and the theoretical and conceptual framework, are typically viewed as *emerging* during the project.

Proposals for this type of research must convince that the researcher has both the need for, and the right to, this kind of flexibility. The proposal must justify why the research questions are best dealt with in this way. It must also convince, through its argument and referencing, that you are competent to carry out this style of research and capable of using the proposed methods. Marshall and Rossman (1999) provide helpful suggestions for the development and description of this kind of proposal.

## Shortcomings of Unsuccessful Proposals

There are, of course, an almost unlimited number of ways in which to present an unsatisfactory research proposal which would justifiably be unsuccessful. Leedy (1989, ch. 6) examines the matter thoroughly. He cites a range of analyses of American grant applications which, although they relate to applications for external funding, have considerable relevance to all research proposals. Four major factors come out as shortcomings of poor applications:

*   the problem being of insufficient importance, or unlikely to produce any new or useful information;
*   the proposed tests, methods or procedures being unsuited to the stated objective;
*   the description of the research being nebulous, diffuse or lacking in clarity, so that it could not be adequately evaluated;

---

## Box A.1

## Ten ways to get your proposal turned down

**1** Don't follow the directions or guidelines given for your kind of proposal. Omit information that is asked for. Ignore word limits.

**2** Ensure that the title has little relationship to the stated objectives, and that neither title nor objectives link to the proposed methods or techniques.

**3** Produce woolly, ill-defined objectives.

**4** Have the statement of the central problem or research focus vague, or obscure it by other discussion.

**5** Leave the design and methodology implicit; let them guess.

**6** Have some mundane task, routine consultancy or poorly conceptualized data trawl masquerade as a research project.

**7** Be unrealistic in what can be achieved with the time and resources you have available.

**8** Be either very brief, or, preferably, long-winded and repetitive in your proposal. Rely on weight rather than quality.

**9** Make it clear what the findings of your research are going to be, and demonstrate how your ideological stance makes this inevitable.

**10** Don't worry about a theoretical or conceptual framework for your research. You want to do a down-to-earth study so you can forget all that fancy stuff.

---

- the investigator not having adequate training, or experience, or both, for the research.

Box A.1 gives a list of things you might like to think about when appraising your own research proposal. It is not exhaustive.

### Further Reading

Brooks, N. (1996) Writing a grant application. In G. Parry and F. N. Watts, eds, *Behavioral and Mental Health Research: A Handbook of Skills and Methods*, 2nd edn. Hove: Erlbaum (UK) Taylor & Francis. Angled towards clinical research, but the advice is helpful in connection with making any grant application in social research.

Krathwohl, D. R. (1988) *How to Prepare a Research Project: Guidelines for Funding and Dissertations in the Social and Behavioral Sciences*, 3rd edn. Syracuse, NY: Syracuse University Press. Detailed and authoritative account. Keyed to the American context, but many of the issues are of general validity.

Leedy, P. D. (1989) *Practical Research: Planning and Design*, 4th edn. New York: Macmillan. Chapter 6 is devoted to 'Writing the Research Proposal'. Based on a review of relevant literature on successful and unsuccessful proposals.

Punch, K. F. (2000) *Developing Effective Research Proposals*. London and Thousand Oaks, Calif.: Sage. Detailed and well-structured set of guidelines. Covers both qualitative and quantitative projects.

# Appendix B
## The Roles of Practitioner–Researchers, Researchers and Consultants in Real World Research

This appendix discusses the relative roles of practitioner–researchers, researchers and consultants in real world research, and provides some practical advice on carrying out these roles.

### The Practitioner–Researcher

A practitioner–researcher is someone who holds down a job in some particular area and is, at the same time, involved in carrying out systematic enquiry which is of relevance to the job. In education, this might be the teacher carrying out a study of a way of helping an *individual child* with a learning difficulty; or a project on delivering some aspect of curriculum to a *school class*; or (possibly working with colleagues from the same or other schools) a systematic enquiry into a proposed local authority initiative to improve communication between first and secondary *schools*. Corresponding foci of enquiry, from *individual* through *group* to *organization*, are not difficult to envisage for practitioners in other professions. In all these cases, the carrying out of the enquiry is likely to be in addition to the individual's normal full-time responsibilities. Another version of the practitioner–researcher is the true hybrid: someone whose job is officially part-practitioner, part-researcher. This might be a short-term arrangement to enable the enquiry to take place, or a continuing joint appointment. Or there could be less formal arrangements, with some remission of normal responsibilities.

Increasingly, postgraduate and post-experience study is moving away from the notion that the practitioner–student determines the focus of her studies, and in particular that of any project or thesis work, solely on the basis of her own individual interests. The move is towards study relevant to the professional setting, in part at least determined by the agenda and concerns of that setting. Reduction in individual freedom is balanced by an increasing likelihood of implementation, and of additional resources and time for the practitioner–researcher. As Zeisel (1984) puts it, 'research seen as problem- and situation-specific becomes a tool to achieve someone's purposes rather than an end in itself' (p. 226).

Practitioner–researchers might be thought to be at a considerable disadvantage *vis-à-vis* outside professional researchers, but they have complementing advantages. Box B.1 lists some of them. Anyone carrying out a sequence of studies in a particular setting can build up a specialized expertise about that type of setting which may well be unrivalled.

---

## Box B.1

### Practitioner–researchers compared with 'outside' researchers

*Disadvantages of the practitioner–researcher role*

**1**   *Time*   Probably the main disadvantage. Trying to do a systematic enquiry on top of normal commitments is very difficult.

**2**   *Lack of expertise*   This obviously depends on the individual. There is a need for some background in designing, carrying out and analysing studies. A major problem can be 'not knowing what it is that you don't know'.

**3**   *Lack of confidence*   Lack of experience in carrying out studies leads to lack of confidence.

**4**   *'Insider' problems*   The insider may have preconceptions about issues and/or solutions. There can also be hierarchy difficulties (both ways, i.e. with high-status and low-status practitioner–researchers); and possibly the 'prophet in own country' phenomenon (i.e. outside advice may be more highly valued).

*Advantages of the practitioner–researcher role*

**1**   *'Insider' opportunities*   You will have a pre-existing knowledge and experience base about the situation and the people involved.

**2**   *'Practitioner' opportunities*   There is likely to be a substantial reduction of implementation problems.

**3**   *'Practitioner–researcher' synergy*   Practitioner insights and role help in the design, carrying out and analysis of useful and appropriate studies.

---

Most professional workers in the 'human services' professions, whether in the public or the private sector, are busy people. There appears to be an increasing acceptance that investigation, enquiry, evaluation and innovation are all part of the professional role, in concepts such as 'extended profession-ality' and the 'reflective professional' (Schon, 1983, 1987), but the time and energy to carry them out on top of one's normal load are often lacking. However, Allen-Meares and Lane (1990) have argued, in the context of social work practice, that there is a potential synergy between research and practice, such that their integration is of benefit to both. The traditional solution of creating a division of labour in professional work between practitioners and researchers has its own problems when the intention is to influence practice. Nor does it help in developing the extended professional.

What other solutions are possible? Logically, one could increase the amount of time available for these activities by reducing the weight of other commit-ments. If the extended professional is a better professional, then the time should be found for this extension to take place. Alternatively, the time com-mitment needed to carry out worthwhile studies could be decreased, that is, we look for an *economical* approach to enquiry, such that it is feasible at the same time as managing a substantial practitioner workload. Or again, the practitioner–researcher could be given support, perhaps in terms of research assistance or at a consultancy level. Ex-practitioners have their uses. The for-mer nurse or salesman will retain considerable knowledge and experience and should have high credibility.

These suggestions are not mutually exclusive. The other disadvantages, lack of expertise and confidence, and those arising from the fact that the person is working inside their own organization, could all be mitigated by access to a research consultant. An experienced consultant could, in a short span of time, suggest what is feasible in a given situation, giving the practitioner–researcher confidence as to its feasibility and appropriateness. Similarly it is, paradoxically, often easy for an outsider to spell out the generality of the likely problems to arise from insider status.

Winter (1989, pp. 34–7) presents an insightful analysis of the problems of the practitioner–researcher. He asks how a small-scale investigation by a prac-titioner can lead to genuinely new insights:

> Experienced practitioners approach their work with a vast and complex array of concepts, theoretical models, provisional explanations, typical scenarios, antici-pation of likely outcomes, etc. . . . A 'research' process must demonstrably offer something over and above this pre-existing level of understanding. (p. 34)

This leads to a need to establish a clear *difference* of procedure between the research and the procedures of professional practice itself, to guard against the 'we knew that already' or 'we do that every day of our professional lives.' He also considers that the methods used must be *accessible*, in the sense that they must be readily available to anyone who seeks to adopt them, and *rigorous* – that is, that they are 'systematically grounded in justifiable and coherent principles' (p. 36). Winter considers that practitioner action research cannot simply use the research methods of conventional social science, and advocates a reflexive, dialectical approach (see also Winter, 1987).

However, it is possible to accept Winter's analysis of the problems without necessarily adopting his solutions. The need for a differentiated, rigorous and systematic approach to real life issues as faced by any enquirer is fully accepted and is probably the major theme within this book. Accessibility is an interesting problem. It was argued in chapter 1 (p. 8) that the methods of systematic real world enquiry are not a private garden to which only the social science graduate has access. Some time and effort will certainly be needed by practitioners without this background if they are to enter, but again this is a process facilitated by the sympathetic and experienced adviser or consultant.

## Advice to practitioner–researchers

Part of your time will be devoted to carrying out research. This book is intended as a general resource in aid of this task. There are some features specific to the joint nature of your role.

*Negotiate a time allowance to carry out the enquiry*   If this dual practitioner–researcher role has been agreed, your firm, institution or whatever presumably sees the advantages of an 'insider' carrying out the enquiry. Make it clear that to capitalize on these advantages, you need adequate time to carry out the enquiry properly. In particular, don't forget the time needed to write up the report(s) and disseminate the findings and their implications. If the dual role is a long-term arrangement, it is better to have an agreed proportion of your time allocated to the research work on a continuing basis rather than to negotiate separately for each enquiry.

*Work in a team whenever possible*   Working on an enquiry, particularly if it involves evaluation or has change implications, can be very stressful and it helps for this to be a collective endeavour. There are practical advantages in assessing reliability of observational and other data, and more generally in sharing perceptions about issues, developing conceptual structures, analytical frameworks, etc.

*Seek support*   There is much 'legwork' and drudgery in carrying out even a small-scale enquiry. It is likely to be more cost-effective for your organization to provide clerical and similar support to help with surveys, code question-naires, transcribe tapes etc., rather than have you do it all yourself.

*Seek advice*   Unless you have a strong and up-to-date research methodology background, and considerable experience in carrying out real world enquiries, it is again likely to be cost-effective for your organization to buy in consultancy support. This need not be extensive. Working through this book will not substitute completely for such advice, but should substantially reduce the consultancy time requirement as you will have an appreciation of what it is you need to know, and will be able to return to the book for details about specific methods and techniques of analysis.

There is an increasing number of research consultancy firms, and individuals offering consultancy services. Another tactic is to contact a local university. Their departments in relevant areas are increasingly involved in short-term consultancy work of this kind.

A possibility, which may be helpful in career terms, is to register for a research degree or other postgraduate award and carry out the enquiry as a part of it, receiving supervisory support to do this. Formal training in research methods is increasingly an important part of such programmes. Credit accumulation and transfer schemes, now running in many higher education institutions, permit the kind of prior experience and learning acquired as a part of professional work to count as substantial credit towards qualifications.

Incidentally, university teachers are a particular breed of practitioner–researcher. The good news is that their research could and should have a close link with their teaching role. The bad news is that, in many countries, there is an increasing expectation that you produce the research goods in terms of outputs such as papers in refereed journals at the same time that the demands of the teaching and administration part of your professional life increase with higher student numbers and a decreasing unit of resource. The advice given above to other practitioner–researchers to negotiate a time allowance, work in a team, seek support and seek advice, applies with equal force.

## The Researcher

Persons with research or enquiry expertise can take on a variety of roles in real world research. The main distinction that applies to such roles is that between your actually carrying out the enquiry (with or without colleagues or other support) and your advising other persons who then carry it out for themselves. We will consider the latter separately, under the heading of the 'consultancy role'.

An underlying assumption in this book is that if you are going to carry out an enquiry, it is, in virtually all cases, because someone has asked you to do so. The basic notion is of a client, sponsor or boss who wishes you to do this. This includes the situation where you made the first move – perhaps persuaded your head of unit, or the manager of the firm down the road, that it would be a good thing if . . . and they took the suggestion on board. It also covers the situation on a course in 'Methods of Enquiry' or the like, where it is the course tutor who has asked you to carry out the study, in part as a training for carrying out subsequent real world enquiries. As a researcher rather than a practitioner–researcher, you are most likely to be external to the setting or organization forming the focus of the enquiry, if only because relatively few 'human service' organizations have so far appreciated the wisdom of having a researcher per se on the payroll.

The assumption that the study is carried out for this kind of instrumental purpose does not preclude the possibility that it might make some contribution to understanding in general terms what goes on in the intensive care unit, or the selection process for sales trainees, or whatever. But such a contribution is a spin-off from a well-designed, executed and analysed study rooted in previous work and/or conducted within a particular theoretical framework. The main concern of the study is practical: it seeks to provide answers relevant to that specific context. Does the study help to solve the problem or throw light on the issue presented?

Real world research has tended to be viewed as a methodologically flawed version of 'proper' research. In terms of the traditional model, this is perfectly true – much 'real world' research is messy: uncontrolled variables abound, predictor and criterion measures interact, alternative hypotheses cannot be ruled out, standard statistical measures cannot be applied without massive violation of assumptions (Boehm, 1980, p. 498).

This book has tried to indicate how you might go about things in this difficult situation. The real world investigator's responsibilities often extend further than is expected in traditional models of research. It may not be your responsibility actually to implement the results in the sense of overseeing a change in practice or whatever; but what might somewhat clumsily be termed their 'implementability' has got to be very much in the mind of the enquirer, both in conducting the enquiry and in the form in which the results are presented. Utopian solutions involving impossible staff ratios or physical resources that are way outside budget are of no great help. Recall the teacher who said, when one-to-one teaching sessions were advocated to solve her problems in teaching slow learners to read, 'What do I do when the other twenty-nine are swinging from the lamp-bulbs?' If one-to-one sessions really do provide a solution, then the task of the investigator is widened – either come up with some solution for the other twenty-nine, or give convincing arguments to 'management' for the necessary resources.

## Advice to researchers

*Know the environment of the study*   If you are an outsider, you will need to find out a substantial amount about the client's needs and expectations, and to be aware of the setting and context in which the study will take place. An awareness and recognition of these matters will enhance your credibility and be likely to obtain more interest from participants in the study. You will need to be able to show the link between 'internal' issues and the research questions.

*Be prepared to 'sell' the idea of the research*   Persuasion is one of the many skills you need to carry out this kind of applied work. There seems to be an idea about that it is morally wrong to seek to 'sell' your research project to the client and other likely participants. I don't see this – always provided, of course, that you are acting in good faith, and that you are selling rather than over-selling. Even when the commission to carry out a study comes directly from the client, you are likely to have to persuade them that, for example, while they saw the problem as X, your view is that it is really about Y; or that while they wanted a sample survey, the question would be better addressed by a case study (or vice versa). It is important to try to give your best estimate of the likely costs and benefits, both of the project itself and of any changes that seem likely to arise if its findings were implemented. In an organization, persuasion may well be needed at several levels in the hierarchy, with the message appropriately tailored to the audience.

*Be prepared to 'sell' the findings of the research*   The same case for 'selling' can be made in connection with outcomes from the research. For the client, the findings and their usefulness are the most important part of the process. Persuasion is particularly important when, as is often the case, implementation of some new approach or way of working is indicated. You need understanding of the change process and the likely barriers that will be erected (see chapter 7, p. 219).

*Remember that you are likely to be judged on your communication and interaction skills*   There will be little interest in your knowledge of the literature or of research methodology. Much more important is how you 'present' when interacting with the client and participants, initially during the project and when disseminating the findings.

Hakel et al. (1982) provide a useful analysis of the communication skills required by the applied researcher, summarized in box B.2. They focus on organizational studies but the points that they make have general relevance. Suggestions are provided for role-play (behaviour modelling) exercises designed to develop these skills.

## Box B.2

## Communication skills needed by the real world researcher

1   *Explaining the rationale for a project* (showing the client and others what is in it for them):

- describe objectives in non-technical terms and advantages of conducting the project with suggested methodology;
- ask for and listen to reactions;
- explain how findings will benefit client and organization, and contrast this with consequences or implications of not being involved.

2   *Listening and reacting* (showing understanding and generating confidence in the researcher):

- convince client of your personal interest in the project;
- ask client how their personal or organizational effectiveness might be influenced by the project – listen openly;
- ask client to elaborate on points where you disagree and discuss your own views;
- thank client for views and promise they will be considered before proceeding;
- (if appropriate) set follow-up date to redefine project or get agreement.

3   *Defending or presenting an idea, opinion or project* (showing professional competence and ability to contribute to management/organizational objectives):

- express your opinion and explain why you hold it (versus alternatives);
- explain relationship between what you propose and their objectives;
- ask for and listen to reaction;
- ask for elaboration on points where you disagree;
- discuss and compare your opinion and theirs in reference to the best criteria you can identify for measuring their objectives.

4   *Redirecting or redefining their expressed interest or objectives* (ensuring that research results will be useful and making sure that the research answers the questions they *should* be asking):

- express your understanding of their interests and objectives and suggest a more fundamental perspective, together with your reasons for offering it;

- explain the relationship between your more fundamental perspective and their need;
- ask for and discuss their reactions to your recommendation;
- (if necessary) outline how their interest or objectives will be met by following a more fundamental recommendation.

5   *Getting agreement and commitment* (making sure that they understand what must be done to provide support and follow-up):

- review with client/management the rationale of the project;
- indicate and discuss specific responsibilities, tasks, milestones and deadlines;
- ask for and discuss reactions;
- agree to summarize the schedule and actions in writing, and submit these for record;
- set specific follow-up dates to review progress at each milestone.

(Adapted and abridged from Hakel et al., 1982, pp. 105–8.)

## The Research Consultant (Project Adviser) Role

Organizations make use of many kinds of consultants, such as legal experts, financial advisers and advertising agents. There are also consultants who provide expertise based to a greater or less extent on the theories, findings and methods of the social sciences, such as communications, job training, management, marketing, organizational development (OD), personnel selection and public relations consultants. Consultancy as a role is not limited to formal organizations.

Research consultancy as envisaged here amounts to a personal advisory service to the individual or group charged with mounting some form of enquiry. Indeed, because of these other connotations of the term 'consultant', it may be wiser to refer to the role as 'research adviser' (or even, because of the antipathy to 'research' in some contexts, as 'project adviser'). The aim is to provide advice, information and support so that internal practitioner–researchers can overcome their relative lack of expertise and experience in designing, running, analysing and reporting on the enquiry.

Within this general framework, several variants are possible – mainly reflecting the extent to which the project remains internal; or is a partnership between consultant and internal researchers; or becomes the consultant's project with the internal researchers carrying out most of it. There are advantages and disadvantages of each, although in the latter two the role is not so much consultant as researcher: they provide one way of minimizing the disadvantage of being an outsider by involving internal colleagues. In action research and other approaches focusing on change, the distinction between researcher and consultant becomes blurred. In any case, it is important to establish at a very early stage which role you are expected to play.

The following discussion assumes that you are simply advising rather than taking over the project. A common approach is for the consultant to have a substantial voice in the design, choice of research strategy and methods to be used, but after that simply a watching brief, offering further advice if problems crop up, and when important milestones are achieved.

## The 'giving away' of skills

Your task as consultant is in part to 'give away' skills and experience. This is increasingly seen as a necessary task for social scientists if what these disciplines have to offer, both in terms of theories and findings, and methodologically, is to make an impact on society. However, dangers of misuse and misapplication have to be guarded against.

Work of this kind is open to the criticism that the skills are necessarily esoteric and should be available only to the select few who have completed a full academic and professional training in a relevant discipline. The answer to this is in part through such attempts to give away skills being fully evaluated to determine their success, or otherwise, empirically (e.g. Robson et al., 1988).

In relation to enquiry and the skills needed to carry this out effectively, the pragmatic point is that much of what goes on in the practice of the 'human' professions at individual, group or organization level is not currently subject to systematic enquiry and evaluation. Pressures in that direction may lead to researchers being asked to carry out such studies, which is to be welcomed. However, the trend in many services seems to be to seek to do this 'in-house'. There are clear advantages to this trend, both in extending the professionalism of the practitioners concerned, and in increasing the likelihood of findings being implemented. But the work may be of poor quality. This is where the consultant comes in: not only to provide advice on specifics, but to reinforce the notion that the only worthwhile studies are rigorous, systematic and unbiased.

## Advice to the research consultant (project adviser)

*Seek an early clarification of your role*  Is the role purely advisory? Is it one-off advice in setting up the project, or is there a continuing involvement (e.g. to comment on instruments used or developed; to give advice on development of fieldwork and possible modification of design; to make suggestions about analysis, need for further data, form and content of report, dissemination strategy and tactics)?

*Assess the capability of the practitioner–researcher(s)*   Have they sufficient knowledge/experience/skills to carry out the intended project? Can you assist them so that they can cope? Or can the project be reformulated so they can handle it? Are they sufficiently committed to the ideals of enquiry to produce a full and unbiased study (or would they just do a 'cosmetic' job)? *If you are not happy with these answers, withdraw*; and let them, and the organization, know why – tactfully.

*Seek answers to these questions:*
*   Where does the project come from? (Who wants it done? Why?)
*   What is the problem/issue?
*   What do they see as the research questions?
*   What resources are available (mainly time availability of practitioner/researcher(s))?
*   What is the time-scale of the project?
*   What methodology (strategy, research methods), if any, is proposed?
*   What problems do they envisage? (Opposition? Suspicion?)
*   How will the study be reported?
*   How will the findings be used?
*   What is the position on confidentiality/anonymity?

The extent to which you get answers on these issues gives an indication of their research sophistication, and of the extent to which things have been thought through. This helps you to assess the feasibility of their task within the constraints of time and resources, and to give realistic advice.

## Further Reading

Fuller, R. and Petch, A. (1995) *Practitioner Research: The Reflexive Social Worker.* Buckingham: Open University Press. Focuses on the kind of research feasible for busy practitioners and the linking of research skills to the insights of practice.

Middlewood, D., Coleman, M. and Lumby, J., eds (1999) *Practitioner Research in Education: Making a Difference.* London: Paul Chapman. Wide-ranging set of articles on the effect of practitioner research on individuals, teams and the institution.

# Glossary

*Note:* The glossary entries seek to help you understand the way in which some key terms are to be understood in the context of this book. They are not formal definitions of the terms.

Many terms explained in the text are not included in this glossary. They can be found using the index (p. 587). If there are two or more page entries for a term, the number in **bold** indicates the main page on which it is discussed.

**action research**   Research which is orientated towards bringing about change, often involving respondents in the process of investigation. Researchers are actively involved with the situation or phenomenon being studied.

**agency**   A social force which has an effect on how things are organized. For some, individuals are seen as the main agents. Others would focus on groups, social classes, or organizations.

**case study**   A research strategy focusing on the study of single cases. The case can be an individual person, an institution, a situation, etc. As used in this text, case study design studies the case in its context, typically using multiple methods of data collection. Qualitative data are almost always collected; quantitative data collection can also be used.

**causal relationships**   A relationship between A and B is causal if A causes B to occur. In realism this indicates the operation of a mechanism. The positivist view is that causal relationships are simply the constant conjunction of A and B.

**cause**   The reason why something happens. The central goal of science is commonly viewed as seeking to establish such reasons (usually expressed in terms of developing theories and/or laws). The successionist view of causation is central to positivist science. Realism adopts a generative view of causation.

**closed systems**   Systems from which all external influences have been excluded. Approximated to by laboratories. Real world research takes place in open systems.

**coding**   The process of collecting observations or responses into groups which are like one another, and assigning a symbol (known as a *code*) as a name for the group.

**constant conjunction**   When one thing regularly follows another. It is the successionist view of causation. This empirical regularity is, in the positivist view, all that is meant by causation.

**constructivism**   *See* social constructivism.

**content analysis**   A method of studying the content of documents or other research material. It typically involves categorizing information and then comparing the frequency of occurrence of different categories.

**contingency table**   A table of numbers in which the relationship between two variables is shown by giving frequencies of occurrence for each of the table cells.

**control**   A procedure employed in experimental designs with the purpose of ensuring that extraneous factors or variables do not affect assessment of the effect of the independent variable(s) on the dependent variable(s).

**correlation**   A measure of relationships between variables describing the direction and degree of association between them. The statistic assessing this is known as a correlation coefficient. A correlation matrix is a table containing the values of the correlation coefficients for the variables involved.

**credibility**   Refers to the ability to demonstrate that the research was designed in a manner which accurately identified and described the phenomenon to be investigated. It calls for a detailed specification of the methods used and the justification for their use.

**critical realism**   Version of realism particularly associated with the work of Roy Bhaskar. It is critical of society and holds that social research has an emancipatory purpose.

**data**   The plural of datum, which refers to a record of an observation. Data can be numerical (and hence quantitative) or consist of words or images (hence qualitative), which may, or may not, be subsequently quantified.

**demand characteristics**   The understandings developed by participants about the researcher's expectations. Different demand characteristics can lead to different outcomes of an experiment.

**dependent variable**   The variable in experimental research where one looks for possible effects of the independent variable manipulated by the experimenter.

**discourse**   Refers to systems of knowledge and their associated practices. More narrowly, it is used in discourse analysis to refer to particular systems of language, with a characteristic terminology and underlying knowledge base, such as in medicine.

**elaboration**   An approach to the exploration of causal relationships between variables through the examination of contingency tables. By introducing third variables to bivariate tabulations, arguments about causal direction and spuriousness are tested.

**embeddedness**   Realist view that human action can be understood only in terms of its location within different layers of social reality.

**empiricism**   A school of thought claiming that experience via the senses is the source of all knowledge. It is characteristic of positivism generally. However, empiricism is also the basis for phenomenology which relies on the observation of evidence.

**ethics**   Principles and systems relating to what is right and wrong. Standards and codes of conduct.

**ethnography**   An approach to the description and understanding of the life and customs of people living in various cultures. Originally focused on primitive and exotic cultures, but now commonly used more generally. A full ethnography calls for participation in the culture for a period of months or even years. Ethnographic approaches may, however, be employed in smaller-scale studies.

**ethnomethodology**   Method of identification of the assumptions through which we make sense of the social world. Involves the analysis of rules of conduct and shared cultural assumptions.

**experiment**   A research strategy characterized by the researcher actively manipulating or changing aspects of what is studied. So-called 'true experiments' involve the researcher allocating or assigning participants to different experimental conditions on a random basis. 'Quasi-experiments' are experiments where such random allocation is not feasible.

**experimenter effects**   Effects on the outcomes of experiments due to some aspect of the experimenter (e.g. their expectations).

**fixed design research**   A research strategy where the research design is fixed (i.e. highly pre-specified) prior to the main phase of data collection. Almost always involves the collection of quantitative data and the use of statistical analysis. The experiment is a prime example of fixed design research.

**flexible design research**   A research strategy where the research design develops (emerges, unfolds) during the process of data collection and analysis. Almost always involves the collection of qualitative data, but can also involve collection of quantitative data.

**generalizability**   The characteristic of research findings that allow them to be applied to other situations and other populations.

**generative view (of causation)**   Holds that there is a real connection between things that are causally linked. In seeking an explanation, we are not only concerned with external observable causes, but also with the possibility of there being some internal feature, liability, or power (commonly referred to by realists as a mechanism). Cause describes the potential for change; whether or not the change actually takes place (i.e. the mechanism operates) depends on the conditions and circumstances.

**grounded theory**   An approach which emphasizes the systematic discovery of theory from data, so that theories remain grounded in observations of the social world, rather than being generated in the abstract.

**Hawthorne effect**   The possibility that the mere fact of being observed in a research project can influence the behaviour of those being observed.

**hermeneutics**   The interpretation of texts. Developed from the tradition of biblical scholarship, hermeneutic strategies are now employed in the analysis of all textual materials. Non-verbal things (e.g. clothing, architecture and group interactions) can be viewed as kinds of texts, and treated hermeneutically.

**heterogeneity**   Where different constituent elements differ considerably from each other, or are of different kinds.

**holistic**   In case study, refers to a study focusing on a single case.

**homogeneity**   Having the different constituent elements similar to one another.

**humanistic**   A term with many, widely differing, meanings. Here used to refer to disciplines and approaches where a scientific approach is considered inappropriate.

**hybrid approach**   Approach which brings together in one study characteristics typical of different traditions of doing research.

**hypothesis**   Used in this text in the restricted sense of a predicted or expected answer to a research question. Used more generally as an idea that can serve as a premise or supposition to organise certain facts and thereby guide observations.

**hypothetico-deductive approach**   The view that science proceeds by deriving hypotheses from theories, which are then tested for truth or falsity by observation and experimentation. It is the opposite of the inductive approach, which proposes that theories can be derived from observations.

**independent variable**   A term used in experimental design to refer to the variable which is directly manipulated by the experimenter.

**inductive approach**   The process of making conclusions from the specific and concrete to the general and abstract.

**inferential statistics**   Statistical tests which allow conclusions from sample data to be generalized to the population on a probabilistic basis.

**internal validity**   The extent to which a study establishes that a factor or variable has actually caused the effect that is found (and in particular that it has not been caused by other factors).

**interpretive/ist approaches**   Emphasize the meaningful nature of people's participation in social and cultural life. The focus is on an analysis of the meanings people confer upon their own and others' actions.

**materialist**   Approach which maintains that 'matter' is the only substance.

**mechanism**   Key term within the realist approach to explanation. Effects are considered to take place through the operation (or 'firing') of mechanisms. It is their action which produces results. They are underlying, i.e. typically not observable.

**methodology**   The theoretical, political and philosophical backgrounds to social research and their implications for research practice, and for the use of particular research methods.

**model**   A representation of a system or some other aspect of research interest. It may be expressed in symbols, equations and numbers, or in pictorial images (e.g. boxes and links between them), or in words. Models are mainly used to help explain and understand the phenomena of interest.

**modus operandi**   Way of working.

**multiple correlation**   A form of correlation between a dependent variable and a group of independent variables.

**multivariate analysis**   Analysis of the relationships between three or more variables (as opposed to bivariate analysis involving two variables, or univariate analysis involving one).

**natural science**   The science of 'nature' typified by disciplines such as physics and chemistry. Distinguished here from social science.

**naturalism**   The view that the methods and approach of natural science can and should be used in social science.

**naturalistic**   Term used by ethnographers and others to indicate that they are collecting naturally occurring data. It sounds confusingly similar to naturalism.

**objectivity**   In simple terms, refers to a lack of bias or prejudice. Objectivity is associated with claims to authority, universality and detachment. Typically linked with an empiricist use which assumes that facts and values can or should be separated from each other. Subjectivists contest these claims.

**open systems**   Opposite of closed systems.

**paradigm wars**   Debates between proponents of different research paradigms (e.g. between 'qualitative' and 'quantitative' researchers).

**paradigms**   The overall conception and way of working shared by workers within a particular discipline or research area.

**phenomenology**   A theoretical perspective advocating the study of direct experience taken at face value. It sees behaviour as determined by the phenomena of experience, rather than by external, objective and physically described reality.

**plagiarism**   Passing off the work of someone else as your own.

**policy research**   Research seeking to inform or influence policy. One form of applied, real world research. Distinguished from academic or 'pure' research.

**population**   The universe of elements from which the sample elements are drawn. It can be a literal population (i.e. of people) but is also used more generally (e.g. could be the population of all hospitals in a given region).

**positivism**   A school of thought seeing reality as the sum of sense impressions, equating social sciences with natural sciences, employing a deductive logic and quantitative research methods. An extremely influential intellectual trend from the mid-nineteenth century, forming, until recently, the generally accepted view of science. Although some social scientists still take this position, it is widely discredited by methodologists and philosophers of science.

**postmodernism**   A movement in intellectual circles of the late twentieth century which rejects the view of social science as a search for over-arching explanations of human nature or the social and cultural world. It is characterized by an eclecticism of styles, combining forms from different eras and geographic locations. There is an irreverence for past achievements, which postmodernists wish to 'deconstruct', destroy or ignore.

**pragmatism**   An approach which makes practical consequences the test of truth. It seeks solutions demanded by the problems presented by a particular situation.

**pre-experiments**   Studies which follow a general experimental style, but where the weakness of the design does not allow an adequate interpretation of the findings to be made.

**primary data**   Data collected from original sources and not already published, secondary sources, such as directories or databases.

**probabilistic basis**   When something is known or asserted to a certain degree of probability (i.e. not with certainty).

**probability**   The likelihood that a particular relationship or event will occur. Expressed by a number between 0 (it will not occur) and 1 (it is certain to occur).

**qualitative data**   Non-numerical data (typically but not necessarily in the form of words).

**quantitative data**   Data in the form of numbers.

**random allocation**   A procedure which ensures that there is an equal probability of assignment of participants to the different groups in an experiment
(e.g. by using the toss of a coin to decide whether each participant is allocated to an experimental or to a control group).

**randomized controlled trial (RCT)**   An experimental design which involves
random allocation of participants, either to an experimental group which
receives some form of 'treatment' or intervention, or to a control group
which receives no such special treatment or intervention.

**reactivity**   Changes produced by the process of measurement itself (e.g. by
the presence of an observer).

**realism**   The view that a reality exists independently of our thoughts or
beliefs. Research is seen as referring to this reality rather than constructing
it. Comes in several versions, including critical realism.

**reductionism**   The view that theories at one level of explanation can be
derived from those at a lower level (e.g. that social science theories can be
derived from psychological ones, which can in turn be derived from biological science theories, etc.).

**reflexivity**   The process of researchers reflecting upon their actions and values
during research (e.g. in producing data and writing accounts), and the
effects that they may have.

**regression analysis**   A method used to study the relationship between variables, especially the extent to which a dependent variable is a function of
one or more independent variables. The values of one variable can then be
used to predict the values of another.

**relativism**   A stance which rejects the notion of any absolute standards
for judging truth. Radical versions contend that all explanations of the
world, from science to magic, have equal status. Cultural relativism
asserts that different cultures define phenomena in different ways, hence
the perspective of one culture cannot be used to understand that of
another.

**reliability**   The extent to which a measuring device, or a whole research
project, would produce the same results if used on different occasions with
the same object of study. There are well-established procedures for assessing reliability in fixed design research. The issues are more difficult to deal
with in flexible design research, where some researchers would regard the
concept as inappropriate.

**replication**   Repeating a piece of research in order to establish the reliability
of its findings. Reporting of fixed design research should be in sufficient
detail for replication to be feasible. Anything approaching an exact replication is rarely feasible in flexible design research.

**sample**   The units chosen to be included in a study. The term suggests that
it is drawn from a wider population Sampling can involve attempts to rep-

resent a population statistically, in which case random selection methods should be used.

**scientific**  Relating to science. This, very broadly speaking, refers to knowledge obtained by the collection of evidence or data, critically assessed, systematized and brought under general principles.

**scientistic**  An approach which assumes that, without considering the nature of the subject matter, following the procedures and conventions of (usually natural) science is the way to proceed.

**secondary analysis**  Analysis of data already collected in some other context than the present study.

**social constructivism (or constructionism)**  The view that reality is socially constructed, i.e. that the phenomena of the social and cultural world and their meanings are created in human social interaction.

**social sciences**  The study of people and their ways using a rigorous, systematic approach. Those disciplines that have adopted a scientific model for understanding human beings and their forms of social organization. The social sciences include sociology, political science, anthropology, economics, and parts of psychology, law and geography. A wide range of applied areas and fields relating to people (e.g. business and management studies, education, health-related studies) make use of social science research approaches.

**stakeholder**  Refers to everyone in an organization or other focus of a research study who has some interest (stake) in the research and its outcomes. Includes participants or clients, workers, management, etc. Particularly relevant in evaluation research and other approaches such as action research where there is a focus on change and hence there are likely to be direct effects on such stakeholders.

**statistical inference**  The generalization of findings from a sample to the broader population using a statistical test.

**statistical significance**  Refers to the probability that a particular result of a statistical test could be due to chance factors alone.

**subjectivism**  *See* objectivism.

**successionist view (of causation)**  Causal inferences are made solely on the basis of observational data. By setting up a sequence of observations under carefully controlled conditions, it is possible to differentiate causal links from spurious associations (e.g. as in the true experiment). A 'constant conjunction' between treatment (cause) and outcome (effect) under such conditions, constitutes the evidence for a causal relationship.

**theory**  A proposed explanation for phenomena, or sets of occurrences, or of relationships. A statement describing how some part of the world works. To be a scientific theory, it has to be testable.

**triangulation**   A research approach employing more than one perspective, theory, participant, method or analysis. The notion is that this helps in getting a better 'fix' on the object of study.

**true experiment**   An experimental design in which the allocation of participants to different (e.g. experimental and control) groups is on a random basis. Contrast with a quasi-experiment where some other means of allocation is used.

**trustworthiness**   General, relatively neutral, term referring to the extent to which one can have trust or confidence in a study and its findings.

**validity**   The degree to which what is observed or measured is the same as what was purported to be observed or measured. At its most simple, this refers to the truth status of research reports. However, a great variety of techniques for establishing the validity of measuring devices and research designs has been established, both for quantitative and for qualitative research. More broadly, the status of research as truth is the subject of considerable philosophical controversy, lying at the heart of the debate about postmodernism.

**value-free (value-neutral)**   The notion that values (e.g. of the researcher) do not play a part in research and its outcomes.

**variables**   A measure which can take on different values. The term is widely used in fixed design research.

# References and Author Index

The references incorporate an author index. The numbers in **bold** at the end of each entry indicate where the publication is referred to in this book.

Adair, J. G., Dushenko, T. W. and Lindsay, R. C. L. (1985) Ethical regulations and their impact on research practice. *American Psychologist*, 40, 59–72. **69**

Adams, K. L. and Ware, N. C. (1989) Sexism and the English language: the linguistic implications of being a woman. In J. Freeman, ed., *Women: A Feminist Perspective*. Mountain View, Calif.: Mayfield. **503**

Adelman, C. (1989) The practical ethic takes priority over methodology. In W. Carr, ed., *Quality in Teaching: Arguments for a Reflective Profession*. London: Falmer. **216**

Adler, M. and Ziglio, E. (1996) *Gazing into the Oracle: The Delphi Method and its Application to Social Policy and Public Health*. London: Jessica Kingsley. **288**

Adler, P. A. and Adler, P. (1987) *Membership Roles in Field Research*. Newbury Park, Calif.: Sage. **344**

Adorno, T. W., Frenkel-Brunswick, E., Levinson, D. J. and Sanford, R. N. (1950) *The Authoritarian Personality*. New York: Harper & Brothers. **99, 306**

Agnew, N. M. and Pyke, S. W. (1982) *The Science Game: An Introduction to Research in the Behavioral Sciences*, 3rd edn. Englewood Cliffs, NJ: Prentice-Hall. **310**

Ahern K. J. (1999) Ten tips for reflexive bracketing. *Qualitative Health Research*, 9, 407–11. **172, 173**

Aiken, S., West, S. G., Schwalm, D. E., Carroll, J. L. and Hsiung, S. (1998) Comparison of a randomized and two quasi-experimental designs in a single outcome evaluation: efficacy of a university-level remedial writing program. *Evaluation Review*, 22, 207–44. **145**

Ajzen, I. and Fishbein, M. (1980) *Understanding Attitudes and Predicting Social Behavior*. Englewood Cliffs, NJ: Prentice-Hall. **435**

Aldridge, M. and Wood, J. (1998) *Interviewing Children: A Guide for Child Care and Forensic Practitioners*. Chichester: Wiley. **272, 291**

Alexa, M. and Zuell, C. (2000) Text analysis software: commonalities, differences and limitations. *Quality and Quantity*, 34, 299–321. **464**

Allen-Meares, P. and Lane, B. A. (1990) Social work practice: integrating qualitative and quantitative data collection techniques. *Social Work*, 35, 452–6. **536**

Altheide, D. L. and Johnson, J. M. (1994) Criteria for assessing interpretive validity in qualitative research. In N. K. Denzin and Y. S. Lincoln, eds, *Handbook of Qualitative Research*. Newbury Park, Calif.: Sage. **168**

American Educational Research Association (1992) *Ethical Standards of AERA*. <http://www.aera.net/about/policy/ethics.htm>. Accessed 28 Nov. 2000. **65**

American Psychological Association (1992) *Ethical Principles of Psychologists and Code of Conduct*. <http://www.apa.org/ethics/code.html>. Accessed 28 Nov. 2000. **65**

American Psychological Association (1994) *Publication Manual of the American Psychological Association*. Washington, DC: American Psychological Association. **504**

American Psychological Association (2001) *Finding Information about Psychological Tests*. <http:www.apa.org/science/findingtests.pdf>. Accessed 22 June 2001. **307**

American Sociological Association (1997) *American Sociological Association Code of Ethics*. <http://www.asanet.org/members/ecoderev.html>. Accessed 7 Nov. 2000. **65**

Anastas, J. W. (1998) Reaffirming the real: a philosophy of science for social work. European Evaluation Society Annual Conference. Rome, 29–31 Oct. **30**

Anastas, J. W. and MacDonald, M. L. (1994) *Research Design for Social Work and the Human Services*. New York: Lexington. **4, 5, 167**

Anastasi, A. (1988) *Psychological Testing*, 6th edn. New York: Macmillan. **297**

Anderson, R. A., Baron, R. S. and Logan, N. H. (1991) Distraction, control and dental stress. *Journal of Applied Social Psychology*, 21, 156–71. **11**

Archer, M., Bhaskar, R., Collier, A., Lawson, T. and Norrie, A. (1998) *Critical Realism: Essential Readings*. London and New York: Routledge. **44**

Argyris, C., Putnam, R. and MacLain-Smith, D. (1985) *Action Science*. San Francisco: Jossey-Bass. **216**

Argyris, C. and Schon, D. A. (1974) *Theory in Practice*. San Francisco: Jossey-Bass. **62**

Aronson, E. and Carlsmith, J. M. (1986) Experimentation in Social Psychology. In G. Lindzey and E. Aronson, eds, *Handbook of Social Psychology*, 2nd edn. Reading, Mass.: Addison-Wesley. **111**

Asch, S. E. (1956) Studies of independence and conformity, I: a minority of one against a unanimous majority. *Psychological Monographs*, 70/9, no. 416. **111**

Asmussen, K. J. and Cresswell, J. W. (1995) Campus response to a student gunman. *Journal of Higher Education*, 66, 575–91 (reprinted as Appendix F in Cresswell, 1998). **474**

Atkinson, E. (2000) In defence of ideas, or why 'what works' is not enough. *British Journal of Sociology of Education*, 21, 317–30. **61**

Atkinson, P. and Delamont, S. (1985) Bread and dreams or bread and circuses: a critique of 'case study' research in education. In M. Shipman, ed., *Educational Research, Principles, Policies and Practices*. London: Falmer. **216**

Atkinson, P. and Hammersley, M. (1994) Ethography and participant observation. In N. K. Denzin and Y. S. Lincoln, eds, *Handbook of Qualitative Research*. Thousand Oaks, Calif.: Sage. **186, 188, 190**

Atweh, B., Kemmis, S. and Weeks, P., eds (1998) *Action Research in Practice: Partnerships for Social Justice in Education*. London and New York: Routledge. **216**

Auge, W. K. and Auge, S. M. (1999) Sports and substance abuse: naturalistic observation of athletic drug-use patterns and behavior in professional caliber bodybuilders. *Substance Use and Abuse*, 34, 217–49. **310**

Backman, K. and Hentinen, M. (1999) Model for the self-care of home-dwelling elderly. *Journal of Advanced Nursing*, 30, 564–72. **85**

Bagley, C. and Pritchard, C. (1998) The reduction of problem behaviours and school exclusion in at-risk youth: an experimental study of school social work with cost-benefit analysis. *Child and Family Social Work*, 3, 219–26. **214**

Bakeman, R. and Gottman, J. M. (1997) *Observing Interaction: An Introduction to Sequential Analysis*, 2nd edn. Cambridge: Cambridge University Press. **312, 325, 338, 340, 342, 345**

Baker, T. L. (1988) *Doing Social Research*. New York: McGraw-Hill. **261, 323, 360**

Baldwin, S., ed. (1998) *Needs Assessment and Community Care: Clinical Practice and Policy Making*. Oxford: Butterworth-Heinemann. **213**

Ballenger, B. (1998) *The Curious Researcher*, 2nd edn. Boston: Allyn & Bacon. **76**

Banai, R. (1995) Critical realism, and urban and regional studies. *Environment and Planning B: Planning and Design*, 22, 563–80. **30**

Bannister, D. and Mair, J. M. M. (1968) *The Evaluation of Personal Constructs*. New York: Academic. **367**

Banyard, P. and Hunt, N. (2000) Reporting research: something missing? *The Psychologist*, 13, 68–71. **70**

Barber, A. E. and Roehling, M. V. (1993) Job postings and the decision to interview: a verbal protocol analysis. *Journal of Applied Psychology*, 78, 845–56. **367**

Barber, T. X. (1976) *Pitfalls in Human Research: Ten Pivotal Points*. Oxford: Pergamon. **112**

Barley, N. (1989) *Not a Hazardous Sport*. London: Penguin. **319**

Barlow, D. H., Hayes, S. C. and Nelson, R. O. (1984) *The Scientist Practitioner: Research and Accountability in Clinical and Educational Settings*. Oxford: Pergamon. **146, 153, 326, 347**

Barlow, J. and Harrison, K. (1996) Focusing on empowerment: facilitating self-help in young people with arthritis through a disability organisation. *Disability and Society*, 11, 539–51. **287**

Barnard, N. (1999) *Foods that Fight Pain*. London: Bantam. **35**

Barnett, V. and Lewis, T. (1984) *Outliers in Statistical Data*, 2nd edn. Chichester: Wiley. **410**

Baron, L. and Straus, M. A. (1989) *Four Theories of Rape in American Society*. New Haven, Conn.: Yale University Press. **99**

Barrett, F. J. and Cooperrider, D. L. (1990) Generative metaphor intervention: a new approach for working with systems divided by conflict and caught in defensive perceptions. *Journal of Applied Behavioral Science*, 26, 219–39. **85, 179**

Barton, E. M., Baltes, M. M. and Orzech, M. J. (1980) Etiology of dependence in older nursing home residents during morning care: the role of staff behaviors. *Journal of Personality and Social Psychology*, 38, 423–31. **333, 334**

Barzun, J. and Graff, H. F. (1977) *The Modern Researcher*. New York: Harcourt Brace Jovanovich. **350, 520, 522**

Bassey, M. (1998) Action research for improving educational practice. In R. Halsall, ed., *Teacher Research and School Improvement: Opening Doors from the Inside*. Buckingham: Open University Press. **217, 218**

Batson, C. D., Schoenrade, P. and Ventis, W. L. (1993) *Religion and the Individual*. Oxford: Oxford University Press. **306**

Beaumont, J. G. and French, C. C. (1987) A clinical field study of eight automated psychometric procedures: the Leicester/DHSS project. *International Journal of Man–Machine Studies*, 26, 661–82. **304**

Beck, A. T. and Steer, R. A. (1987) *The Beck Depression Inventory*. San Antonio: The Psychological Corporation/Harcourt Brace Jovanovich. **305**

Becker, H. S. (1986) *Writing for Social Scientists: How to Start and Finish Your Thesis, Book or Article*. Chicago: University of Chicago Press. **523**

Becker, H. S. (1998) *Tricks of the Trade: How to Think about Your Research while You're Doing It*. Chicago: University of Chicago Press. **76**

Bellack, M. S., Hersen, M. et al., eds (1998) *Behavioral Assessment: A Practical Handbook*, 4th edn. Boston: Allyn & Bacon. **307**

Bensman, J. and Vidich, A. (1960) Social theory in field research. *American Journal of Sociology*, 65, 577–84. **489**

Bentz, V. M. and Shapiro, J. J. (1998) *Mindful Inquiry in Social Research*. Thousand Oaks, Calif.: Sage. **20, 26, 50, 89, 93, 98, 196, 216, 498**

Berelson, B. (1952) *Content Analysis in Communications Research*. New York: Free Press. **355**

Berg, D. N. (1988) Anxiety in research relationships. In D. N. Berg and K. K. Smith, eds, *The Self in Social Inquiry*. Newbury Park, Calif.: Sage. **377**

Berger, P. L. and Luckman, T. (1967) *The Social Construction of Reality*. Harmondsworth: Penguin. **196**

Bersoff, D. N. (1999) *Ethical Conflicts in Psychology*, 2nd edn. Washington DC: American Psychological Association. **65**

Bhaskar, R. (1978) *A Realist Theory of Science*, 2nd edn. Brighton: Harvester. **29**

Bhaskar, R. (1979) *The Possibility of Naturalism: A Philosophical Critique of the Contemporary Human Sciences*. Brighton: Harvester. **31, 35**

Bhaskar, R. (1982) Emergence, explanation and emancipation. In P. Secord, ed., *Explaining Social Behavior: Consciousness, Behavior and Social Structure*. Beverly Hills, Calif.: Sage. **29**

Bhaskar, R. (1986) *Scientific Realism and Human Emancipation*. London: Verso. **21, 30, 41**

Bhaskar, R. (1989) *Reclaiming Reality*. London: Verso. **41, 490**

Bhaskar, R., ed. (1990) *Harré and His Critics*. Oxford: Blackwell. **29**

Bickman, L., ed. (1980) *Applied Social Psychology Annual*, vol. 1. Newbury Park and London: Sage. **11**

Birckmayer, J. D. and Weiss, C. H. (2000) Theory-based evaluation: what do we learn? *Evaluation Review*, 24, 407–31. **205**

Blackmore, C. and Ison, R. (1998) Boundaries for thinking and action. In A. Thomas, J. Chataway and M. Wuyts, eds, *Finding Out Fast: Investigative Skills for Policy and Development*. London: Sage. **63**

Blackwell (1995) *Idealist*. Oxford: Blackwell Science. **53**

Blaikie, N. W. H. (1991) A critique of the use of triangulation in social research. *Quality and Quantity*, 25, 115–36. **371**

Blaikie, N. (1993) *Approaches to Social Enquiry*. Cambridge: Polity. **22, 32, 44**

Bloor, M. (1997) Techniques of validation in qualitative research: a critical commentary. In G. Miller and R. Dingwall, eds, *Context and Method in Qualitative Research*. London: Sage. **168, 175**

Blumer, H. (1954) What is wrong with social theory? *American Sociological Review*, 19, 3–10. **489**

Blumer, H. (1969) *Symbolic Interactionism: Perspectives and Method*. Englewood Cliffs, NJ: Prentice-Hall. **197**

Boehm, V. R. (1980) 'Research in the Real World' – a conceptual model. *Personnel Psychology*, 33, 495–503. **539**

Bogardus, E. (1926) The group interview. *Journal of Applied Sociology*, 10, 372–82. **284**

Bogdan, R. C. and Biklen, S. K. (1992) *Qualitative Research for Education: An Introduction to Theory and Methods*, 2nd edn. Boston: Allyn & Bacon. **186**

Bogdewic, S. P. (1999) Participant observation. In B. F. Crabtree and W. L. Miller, eds, *Doing Qualitative Research*. Thousand Oaks, Calif.: Sage. **344**

Borg, W. R. and Gall, M. D. (1989) *Educational research*. White Plains, NY: Longman. **161**

Botterill, T. D. and Crompton, J. L. (1996) Two case studies exploring the nature of the tourist's experience. *Journal of Leisure Research*, 28, 57–82. **366**

Bourgue, L. B. and Back, K. W. (1982) Time sampling as a field technique. In R. G. Burgess, ed., *Field Research: A Sourcebook and Field Manual*. London: Allen & Unwin. **258, 259**

Box, G. E. P. and Jenkins, G. M. (1976) *Time-Series Analysis: Forecasting and Control*. San Francisco: Holden-Day. **448**

Brace, N., Kemp, R. and Snelgar, R. (2000) *SPSS for Psychologists: A Guide to Data Analysis Using SPSS for Windows*. Basingstoke: Macmillan. **392**

Bradburn, N. and Sudman, S. (1979) *Improving Interview Method and Questionnaire Design*. San Francisco: Jossey-Bass. **282**

Bradbury, F. C. S. (1933) *Causal Factors in Tuberculosis*. London: National Association for the Prevention of Tuberculosis. **35**

Bradford, R. (1990) The importance of psychosocial factors in understanding child distress during routine X-ray procedures. *Journal of Child Psychology and Psychiatry*, 31, 973–82. **371**

Brand, M. (1998) Commentary on Carlson et al. (1997). *Evidence-based Nursing*, 1, 14. **84**

Brannen, J., ed. (1992) *Mixing Methods: Qualitative and Quantitative Research*. Aldershot: Avebury. **373**

Breakwell, G. (1986) *Coping with Threatened Identities*. London: Methuen. **62**

Breitenbecher, K. H. and Gidycz, C. A. (1998) An empirical evaluation of a program designed to reduce the risk of multiple sexual victimization. *Journal of Interpersonal Violence*, 13, 472–88. **204**

Brewer, J. and Hunter, A. (1989) *Multimethod Research: A Synthesis of Styles*. Newbury Park, Calif.: Sage. **43, 82, 371**

Brez, S. M. and Taylor, M. (1997) Assessing literacy for patient teaching: perspectives of adults with low literacy skills. *Journal of Advanced Nursing*, 25, 1040–7. **85, 179**

British Association of Social Workers (1996) *The Code of Ethics for Social Work*. Birmingham: British Association of Social Workers. **65**

British Psychological Society (1992) The Late Sir Cyril Burt: Statement. *The Psychologist*, 15, 147. **506**

British Psychological Society (2000) *Code of Conduct, Ethical Principles and Guidelines*. Leicester: British Psychological Society. <http://www.bps.org.uk>. Accessed 7 Nov. 2000. **65**

British Sociological Association (1989a) *BSA Guidelines on Anti-Sexist Language*. London: British Sociological Association (mimeo). **503**

British Sociological Association (1989b) *Anti-Racist Language: Guidance for Good Practice*. London: British Sociological Association (mimeo). **503**

British Sociological Association (n.d.) Statement of ethical practice. *Sociological Research Online*. <http://www.socresonline.org.uk/info/ethguide.html>. Accessed 7 Nov. 2000. **65**

Broad, W. and Wade, N. (1985) *Betrayers of the Truth: Fraud and Deceit in Science*. Oxford: Oxford University Press. **506**

Bromley, D. B. (1986) *The Case-study Method in Psychology and Related Disciplines*. Chichester: Wiley. **177, 179, 180**

Bronson, D. E., Pelz, D. C. and Trzinski, E. (1988) *Computerizing Your Agency's Information System*. Newbury Park, Calif.: Sage. **362**

Brooks, N. (1996) Writing a grant application. In G. Parry and F. N. Watts, eds, *Behavioral and Mental Health Research: A Handbook of Skills and Methods*, 2nd edn. Hove: Erlbaum (UK) Taylor & Francis. **532**

Brown, B. (1995) *Closed Circuit Television in Town Centres: Three Case Studies*. Crime Prevention and Detection Series Paper 73. London: Home Office. **37**

Brown, J. B. (1999) The use of focus groups in clinical research. In B. F. Crabtree and W. L. Miller, eds, *Doing Qualitative Research*, 2nd edn. Thousand Oaks, Calif.: Sage. **286, 287**

Brown, J., Lent, B. and Sas, G. (1993) Identifying and treating wife abuse. *Journal of Family Practice*, 36, 185–91. **287**

Bryman, A. (1988a) *Quality and Quantity in Social Research*. London: Unwin Hyman. **6, 43, 46**

Bryman, A. (1989) *Research Methods and Organisation Studies*. London: Unwin Hyman. **230, 259, 267, 332, 360, 374**

Bryman, A. (1992) Quantitative and qualitative research: further reflections on their integration. In J. Brannen, ed., *Mixing Methods: Quantitative and Qualitative Research*. Aldershot: Avebury. **373**

Bryman, A., ed. (1988b) *Doing Research in Organisations*. London: Routledge. **377**

Bryman, A. and Cramer, D. (1997) *Quantitative Data Analysis for Social Scientists*. London: Routledge. **432, 434**

Bryman, A. and Cramer, D. (1997) *Quantitative Data Analysis with SPSS for Windows: A Guide for Social Scientists*. London: Routledge. **392, 447, 453**

Buchanan, D. A. and Boddy, D. (1982) Advanced technology and the quality of working life: the effects of word processing on video typists. *Journal of Occupational Psychology*, 55, 1–11. **377**

Buchanan, D., Boddy, D. and McCalman, J. (1988) Getting in, getting on, getting out and getting back. In A. Bryman, ed., *Doing Research in Organisations*. London: Routledge. **376, 378**

Burchfield, R. W., ed. (1996) *The New Fowler's Modern English Usage*, 3rd edn. Oxford: Clarendon. **520, 523**

Burgess, R. G. (1981) Keeping a research diary. *Cambridge Journal of Education*, 11, 75–83. **259**

Burgess, R. G. (1983) *Experiencing Comprehensive Education: A Study of Comprehensive Education*. London: Methuen. **321**

Burgess, R. G., ed. (1984) *The Research Process in Educational Settings: Ten Case Studies*. London: Falmer. **377**

Burke, T. B. (1997) Assessing homosexual stress. *Journal of Homosexuality*, 33, 83–99. **366**

Burr, V. (1998) Overview: realism, relativism, social constructionism and discourse. In I. Parker, ed., *Social Constructionism, Discourse and Realism*. London: Sage. **27**

Burton, D. (2000) Using literature to support research. In D. Burton, ed., *Research Training for Social Scientists*. London: Sage. **15**

Butler, B. E. and Petrulis, J. (1999) Some further observations concerning Sir Cyril Burt. *British Journal of Psychology*, 90, 155–60. **506**

Butt, T. (1995) What's wrong with laddering? *Changes*, 13, 81–7. **367**

Byrne, B. M. (1989) *A Primer of LISREL: Basic Applications and Programming for Confirmatory Factor Analytic Models*. New York: Springer Verlag. **434, 435**

Byrne, B. M. (1994) *Structural Equation Modeling with EQS and EQS/Windows*. Thousand Oaks, Calif.: Sage. **434, 435, 453**

Byrne, D. (1998) *Complexity Theory and the Social Sciences: An Introduction*. London: Routledge. **26, 31, 35, 44**

Byrne, D. S., Harrison, S. P., Keithley, J. and McCarthy, P. (1986) *Housing and Health: The Relationship between Housing Conditions and the Health of Council Tenants*. Aldershot: Gower. **35**

Cacioppo, J. T., von Hippel, W. and Ernst, J. M. (1997) Mapping cognitive structures and processes through verbal content: the thought-listing technique. *Journal of Consulting and Clinical Psychology*, 65, 928–40. **368**

Campbell, D. T. (1969) Reforms as experiments. *American Psychologist*, 24, 409–29. **119**

Campbell, D. T. (1988) *Methodology and Epistemology for Social Science: Selected Papers*. Chicago: University of Chicago Press. **104, 116**

Campbell, D. T. and Stanley, J. C. (1963) Experimental and quasi-experimental designs for research on teaching. In N. L. Gage, ed., *Handbook of Research on Teaching*. Chicago: Rand McNally. Also published separately as *Experimental and Quasi-experimental Designs for Research on Teaching*. Chicago: Rand McNally, 1966. **103, 104, 107, 133**

Campbell, J. T., Daft, R. L. and Hulin, C. L. (1982) *What to Study: Generating and Developing Research Questions*. Newbury Park, Calif.: Sage. **55, 56, 61**

Cancian, F. M. (1993) Conflicts between activist research and academic success: participatory research and alternative strategies. *American Sociologist*, 24, 92–106. **216**

Caputo, R. K. (1988) *Management and Information Systems in Human Services*. New York: Haworth. **362**

Carlisle, C. (1998) Commentary on Brez, S. M. and Taylor, M. (1997). *Evidence-Based Nursing*, 1, 29. **85**

Carlsson, R., Lindberg, G. and Westin, L. (1997) Influence of coronary nursing management follow up on lifestyle after acute myocardial infarction. *Heart*, 77, 256–9. **84, 123**

Carney, T. F. (1973) *Content Analysis*. Winnipeg: University of Manitoba Press. **353**

Carr, W. and Kemmis, S. (1986) *Becoming Critical*. London: Falmer. **180**

Cash, K., Anansuchatkul, B. and Busaya-wong, W. (1999) Understanding the psychosocial aspects of HIV/AIDS prevention for northern Thai single adolescent migratory women workers. *Applied Psychology: An International Review*, 48, 125–37. **287**

Cattell, R. B. (1965) *The Scientific Analysis of Personality*. Harmondsworth: Penguin. **305**

Catterall, M. and Maclaran, P. (1998) Using computer software for the analysis of qualitative market research data. *Journal of the Market Research Society*, 40, 207–22. **462**

Chalmers, A. F. (1982) *What Is This Thing Called Science?*, 2nd edn. Milton Keynes: Open University Press. **19**

Chalmers, I., Enkin, M. and Keirse, M. J. N. C., eds (1989) *Effective Care in Pregnancy and Childbirth*. Oxford: Oxford University Press. **118**

Chamberlain, K. (2000) Methodolatry and qualitative health research. *Journal of Health Psychology*, 5, 285–96. **164**

Chapple, C. and Nofziger, S. (2000) Bingo! hints of deviance in the accounts of socia-bility and profit of bingo players. *Deviant Behavior*, 21, 489–517. **487**

Chenitz, W. C. and Swanson, J. M. (1986) *From Practice to Grounded Theory: Qualitative Research in Nursing*. Menlo Park, Calif.: Addison-Wesley. **496**

Cherryholmes, C. C. (1992) Notes on pragmatism and scientific realism. *Educational Researcher*, 21, 13–17. **43**

Chesney, M. (2001) Dilemmas of self in the method. *Qualitative Health Research*, 11, 127–35. **167**

Child, D. (1990) *The Essentials of Factor Analysis*, 2nd edn. London: Cassell. **434**

Clark-Carter, D. (1997) *Doing Quantitative Psychological Research: From Design to Report*. Hove: Psychology Press. **162, 437**

Clarke, L. (1996) Covert participant observation in a secure forensic unit. *Nursing Times*, 92, 37–40. **316**

Clarke, S. (1999) Justifying deception in social science research. *Journal of Applied Philosophy*, 16, 151–66. **67**

Cliff, D. R., Sparks, G. and Gibbs, G. R. (n.d.) *Looking for Work in Kirklees: A Study of the Experience of Unemployment in Kirklees MBC*. Huddersfield: The Polytechnic in collaboration with the Policy and Performance Review Unit, Kirklees MBC. **280**

Clifford, C., Day, A., Cox, J. and Werrett, J. (1999) A cross-cultural analysis of the use of the Edinburgh Post Natal Depression Scale (EPDS) in health visiting practice. *Journal of Advanced Nursing*, 30, 655–64. **84**

Cochrane, A. L. (1979) 1931–1971: a critical review, with particular reference to the medical profession. In *Medicines for the year 2000*, 1–11. London: Office of Health Economics. **118**

Cochrane Controlled Trials Register (1999) In *The Cochrane Library, Issue 3*. Oxford: Update Software. **118**

Coffey, A. and Atkinson, P. (1996) *Making Sense of Qualitative Data: Complementary Research Strategies*. Thousand Oaks, Calif.: Sage. **498**

Cohen, J. (1988) *Statistical Power Analysis for the Behavioral Sciences*, 2nd edn. New York: Academic. **437**

Cohen, J. (1992) A power primer. *Psychological Bulletin*, 112, 155–9. **161**

Cohen, M. B. and Garrett, K. J. (1999) Breaking the rules: a group work perspective on focus group research. *British Journal of Social Work*, 29, 359–72. **288**

Collier, A. (1994) *Critical Realism: An Introduction to Roy Bhaskar's Philosophy*. London: Verso. **41**

Collier, A. (1998) Language, practice and realism. In I. Parker (ed), *Social Constructionism, Discourse and Realism*. London: Sage. **27**

Colliver, J. A. (1996) Science in the postmodern era: post-positivism and research in medical education. *Teaching and Learning in Medicine*, 8, 10–18. **30**

Colman, A. M., ed. (1994) *Psychological Research Methods and Statistics*. London: Longman. **162**

Cook, T. D., Appleton, H., Conner, R., Schaffer, A., Tamkin, G. and Weber, S. J. (1975) *'Sesame Street' Revisited: A Case Study in Evaluation Research*. New York: Russell Sage Foundation. **448**

Cook, T. D. and Campbell, D. T. (1979) *Quasi-Experimentation: Design and Analysis Issues for Field Settings*. Chicago: Rand McNally. **104, 106, 119, 131, 134, 135, 139, 162, 179**

Cooper, H. (1998) *Synthesizing Research*. London: Sage. **52**

Corson, D. (1991) Bhaskar's critical realism and educational knowledge. *British Journal of Sociology of Education*, 12, 223–41. **30**

Corson, D. (1997) Critical realism: an emancipatory philosophy for applied linguistics. *Applied Linguistics*, 18, 166–88. **30**

Cousins, J. B. and Earl, L. M., eds (1995) *Participatory Evaluation in Education: Studies in Evaluation Use and Organisational Learning*. London: Falmer. **7, 217**

Coxon, T. (1988) 'Something sensational': the sexual diary as a tool for mapping detailed sexual behavior. *Sociological Review*, 36, 353–67. **258**

Crabtree, B. F. and Miller W. L. (1992) Primary Care Research: a multi-method typology and qualitative road map. In B. F. Crabtree and W. L. Miller, eds, *Doing Qualitative Research*. Thousand Oaks, Calif.: Sage. **457**

Craig, G., Corden, A. and Thornton, P. (2000) Safety in social research. *Social Research Update*, issue 29. Also available on <http://www.soc.surrey.ac.uk/sru/SRU29.html>. **68**

Crain, R. L. and Mahard, R. E. (1983) The effect of research methodology on desegregation-achievement studies: a meta-analysis. *American Journal of Sociology*, 88, 839–54. **369**

Cressey, D. R. (1953) *Other People's Money: A Study in the Social Psychology of Embezzlement*. New York: Free Press. **490**

Cresswell, J. W. (1998) *Qualitative Inquiry And Research Design: Choosing among Five Traditions*. Thousand Oaks, Calif.: Sage. **165, 166, 195, 199, 462, 497, 498**

Croll, P. (1986) *Systematic Classroom Observation*. London: Falmer. **331**

Crotty, M. (1998) *The Foundations of Social Research: Meaning and Perspective in the Research Process*. London: Sage. **172**

Currie, D. (1988) Re-thinking what we do and how we do it: a study of reproductive decisions. *Review of Sociology and Anthropology*, 25, 231–53. **191**

Czaja, R. and Blair, J. (1996) *Designing Surveys: A Guide to Decisions and Procedures*. Thousand Oaks, Calif.: Pine Forge. **4, 162, 237, 241, 242, 267**

Dancey, C. P. and Reidy, J. R. (1999) *Statistics without Maths for Psychology: Using SPSS for Windows*. London: Prentice-Hall. **427, 437**

Dane, F. C. (1990) *Research Methods*. Pacific Grove, Calif.: Brooks/Cole. **303**

Datta, L. (1994) The paradigm wars. In C. S. Reichardt and S. F. Rallis, eds, *The Qualitative–Quantitative Debate: New*

*Perspectives*. San Francisco: Jossey-Bass. **43**

Davidson, J. O'C. and Layder, D. (1994) *Methods, Sex and Madness*. London: Routledge. **24, 93, 186, 198**

Davies, B. (1998) Psychology's subject: a commentary on the relativism/realism debate. In I. Parker, ed., *Social Constructionism, Discourse and Realism*. London: Sage. **27**

Davis, F. (1960) Interview guide for problems of the handicapped in everyday social situations. Unpublished. Cited in Lofland and Lofland, 1995, pp. 84–5. **281**

Davis, M. Z. (1973) *Living with Multiple Sclerosis: A Social Psychological Analysis*. Springfield, Ill: Charles C. Thomas. **191**

Dawes, R. M. and Smith, T. L. (1985) Attitude and opinion measurement. In G. Lindzey and E. Aronson, eds, *The Handbook of Social Psychology*, 3rd edn. New York: Random House. **298**

Day, R. A. (1983) *How to Write and Publish a Scientific Paper*, 2nd edn. Philadelphia: ISI Press. **520, 523**

Deem, R. (1996) Border territories: a journey through sociology, education and women's studies. *British Journal of Sociology of Education*, 17, 5–19. **377**

Delamont, S. (1992) *Field Work in Educational Settings: Methods, Pitfalls and Perspectives*. London: Falmer. **200**

Delanty, G. (1997) *Social Science: Beyond Constructivism and Realism*. Buckingham: Open University Press. **44**

Delbecq, A. L. (1986) *Group Techniques for Program Planning: A Guide to Nominal Group and Delphi Processes*. Middleton, Wisc.: Green Briar. **57**

Dent, C. W., Sussman, S. Y. and Stacy, A. W. (1997) The impact of a written parental consent policy on estimates from a school-based drug use survey. *Evaluation Review*, 21, 698–712. **382**

Denzin, N. K. (1988) *The Research Act: A Theoretical Introduction to Sociological Methods*, 3rd edn. Englewood Cliffs, NJ: Prentice-Hall. **174, 371, 496**

Denzin, N. K. (1989) *Interpretive Interactionism*. Newbury Park, Calif., and London: Sage. **195**

DeProspero, A. and Cohen, S. (1979) Inconsistent visual analysis of intrasubject data. *Journal of Applied Behavior Analysis*, 12, 573–9. **450**

DeRubeis, R. J., Gelfand, L. A., Tang, T. Z. and Simons, A. D. (1999) Medications versus cognitive behavior therapy for severely depressed outpatients: meta-analysis of four randomized comparisons. *American Journal of Psychiatry*, 156, 1007–13. **368**

de Vaus, D. A. (1991) *Surveys in Social Research*, 3rd edn. London: UCL Press/Allen & Unwin. **245, 246, 268**

DeVries, R. G. (1985) *Regulating Birth: Midwives, Medicine and the Law*. Philadelphia: Temple University Press. **49**

Diaper, G. (1990) A comparative study of paired-reading techniques using parents as tutors to second year junior school children. *Child Language, Teaching and Training*, 6, 13–24. **84, 123**

Dillman, D. (2000) *Mail and Internet Surveys: The Tailored Design Method*, 2nd edn. Chichester: Wiley. **268**

Dilorio, J. A. and Nusbaumer, M. R. (1993) Securing our sanity: anger management among abortion escorts. *Journal of Contemporary Ethnography*, 21, 411–38. **49**

Draper, L. (2001) Being evaluated: a practitioner's view. *Children and Society*, 15, 46–52. **202**

Draucker, C. B. (1999) The critique of Heideggerian hermeneutical nursing research. *Journal of Advanced Nursing*, 30, 360–73. **198**

Drisko, J. W. (1998) Utilization-focussed evaluation of two intensive family preservation programs. *Families in Society: The Journal of Contemporary Human Services*, 79, 62–74. **496**

Drisko, J. W. (2000) Qualitative data analysis: It's not just anything goes! Charleston, SC: Society for Social Work and Research Annual Conference, 30 Jan. **458**

Easton, K. L., McComish, J. F. and Greenberg, R. (2000) Avoiding common pitfalls in qualitative data collection and transcription. *Qualitative Health Research*, 10, 703–7. **176**

Ebaugh, H. R. F. (1988) *Becoming an EX: The Process of Role Exit*. Chicago: University of Chicago Press. **49**

Eichler, M. (1980) *The Double Standard: A Feminist Critique of Feminist Social Science*. London: Croom Helm. **73**

Eichler, M. (1988) *Nonsexist Research Methods: A Practical Guide*. London: Unwin Hyman. **75, 76, 376**

Elliott, C. D. (1983) *The British Ability Scales*. Slough: National Foundation for Educational Research. **306**

Elliott, J. (1991) *Action Research for Educational Change*. Milton Keynes: Open University Press. **216**

Elster, J. (1989) *Nuts and Bolts for the Social Sciences*. Cambridge: Cambridge University Press. **33, 44**

Elsworth, G. R. (1994) Arguing challenges to validity in field research: a realist perspective. *Knowledge: Creation, Diffusion, Utilisation*, 15/3, 321–43. **171**

Ely, M. with Anzul, M., Friedman, T., Gardner, D. and Steinmetz, M. A. (1991) *Doing Qualitative Research: Circles within Circles*. London: Falmer. **278**

Emerson, R. M., Fretz, R. I. and Shaw, L. L. (1995) *Writing Ethnographic Fieldnotes*. Chicago: University of Chicago Press. **344, 511**

Endacott, R., Clifford, C. M. and Tripp, J. H. (1999) Can the needs of a crtically ill child be identified using scenarios? Experiences of a modified Delphi study. *Journal of Advanced Nursing*, 30, 665–76. **57**

Engelman. K. K., Altus, D. E. and Mathews, R. M. (1999) Increasing engagement in daily activities by older adults with dementia. *Journal of Applied Behavior Analysis*, 32, 107–10. **84, 147, 153**

Enkin, M., Keirse, M. J. N. C. and Chalmers, I., eds (1989) *A Guide to Effective Care in Pregnancy and Child-birth*. Oxford: Oxford University Press. **118**

Erickson, F. (1986) Qualitative methods in research on teaching. In M. C. Wittrock, ed., *Handbook of Research in Teaching*. New York: Macmillan. **508**

Ericsson, K. A. and Simon, H. A. (1993) *Protocol Analysis: Verbal Reports as Data*. Cambridge, Mass.: MIT Press. **375**

Esbensen, F.-A., Deschenes, E. P., Vogel, R. E., West, J. Arbott, K. and Harris, L. (1996) Active parental consent in school-based research: an examination of ethical and methodological issues. *Evaluation Review*, 20, 737–53. **70**

Evason, E. and Whittington, D. (1997) Patients' perceptions of quality in a Northern Ireland hospital group: a focus group study. *International Journal of Health Care Quality Assurance*, 10, 7–19. **287**

Everitt, A. and Hardiker, P. (1996) *Evaluating for Good Practice*. London: Macmillan. **28**

Eysenck, H. J. and Crown, S. (1949) An experimental study in opinion–attitude methodology. *International Journal of Opinion and Attitude Research*, 3, 47–86. **298**

Eysenck, H. J. and Eysenck, S. B. G. (1964) *The Eysenck Personality Inventory*. London: Hodder & Stoughton. **305**

Eysenck, H. J. and Eysenck, S. B. G. (1975) *Manual of the Eysenck Personality Inventory*. San Diego, Calif.: Edits. **305**

Fan, D. P. (1997) Possibilities in computer content analysis of text: introduction to symposium. *Social Sciences Computer Review*, 15, 349–50. **358**

Fantasia, R. (1988) *Cultures of Solidarity: Consciousness, Action and Contemporary American Workers*. Berkeley, Calif.: University of California Press. **49**

Festinger, L. Riecken, H. W. and Schachter, S. (1956) *When Prophecy Fails*. New York: Harper & Row. **316**

Fetterman, D. M. (1989) *Ethnography Step by Step*. Newbury Park, Calif.: Sage. **313, 352, 459**

Fetterman, D. M., Kaftarian, S. J. and

Wandersman, A., eds (1996) *Empowerment Evaluation: Knowledge and Tools for Self-assessment and Accountability*. Thousand Oaks, Calif.: Sage. **217**

Feyerabend, P. K. (1978) *Against Method: Outline of an Anarchistic Theory of Knowledge*. London: Verso. **22**

Fibel, B. and Hale, W. D. (1978) The Generalized Expectancy for Success Scale: a new measure. *Journal of Consulting and Clinical Psychology*, 4, 924–31. **296**

Field, A. (2000) *Discovering Statistics Using SPSS for Windows: Advanced Techniques for the Beginner*. London: Sage. **432, 444, 445**

Fielding, N. G. and Fielding, J. L., eds (1986) *Linking Data*. Newbury Park, Calif.: Sage. **489**

Fielding, N. G. and Fielding, J. L. (2000) Resistance and Adaptation to Criminal Identity: Using Secondary Analysis to Evaluate Classic Studies of Crime and Deviance. *Sociology*, 34, 671–89. **360**

Fielding, N. G. and Lee, R. M. (1998) *Computer Analysis and Qualitative Research*. London: Sage. **462**

Fine, M. (1992) Passions, politics, and power: feminist research possibilities. In M. Fine, ed., *Disruptive Voices*. Ann Arbor: University of Michigan Press. **198**

Fisher, R. A. (1935) *The Design of Experiments*. Edinburgh: Oliver & Boyd. **104**

Fitzpatrick, J. M., While, A. E. and Roberts, J. D. (1996) Operationalisation of an observation instrument to explore nurse performance. *International Journal of Nursing Studies*, 33, 349–60. **333**

Flanders, N. (1970) *Analyzing Teaching Behavior*. New York: Wiley. **329, 330**

Fletcher, G. J. O. (1996) Realism versus relativism in psychology. *American Journal of Psychology*, 109, 3, 409–29. **25, 26, 30**

Fliess, J. L. (1981) *Statistical Methods for Rates and Proportions*. New York: Wiley. **342**

Fontana, A. and Frey, J. H. (1994) Interviewing: the art of science. In N. K. Denzin and Y. S. Lincoln, eds, *Handbook of Qualitative Research*. Thousand Oaks, Calif.: Sage. **283**

Fontana, A. and Frey, J. H. (2000) The interview: from structured questions to negotiated text. In N. K. Denzin and Y. S. Lincoln, eds, *Handbook of Qualitative Research*, 2nd edn. Thousand Oaks, Calif.: Sage. **291**

Fortier, A-M. (1998) Gender, ethnicity and fieldwork: a case study. In C. Seale, ed., *Researching Society and Culture*. London: Sage. **85, 186**

Foster, J. (1995) Informal social control and community crime prevention. *British Journal of Criminology*, 35, 563–83. **86, 186**

Foster, J. J. (2001) *Data Analysis Using SPSS for Windows New Edition: Versions 8–10*. London: Sage. **392, 453**

Foster, P. (1996) Observational research. In R. Sapsford and V. Jupp, eds, *Data Collection and Analysis*. London: Sage. **344**

Foster, R. L. (1997) Addressing epistemologic and practical issues in multimethod research: a procedure for conceptual triangulation. *Advanced Nursing Science*, 20/2, 1–12. **371**

Fournier, V. (1997) Graduates' construction systems and career development. *Human Relations*, 50, 363–91. **366**

Fowler, L. P. (1997) Clinical reasoning strategies used during care planning. *Clinical Nursing Research*, 6, 349–61. **367**

Foxen, T. and McBrien, J. (1981) *The EDY Course for Mental Handicap Practitioners*. Manchester: Manchester University Press. **364**

Frankfort-Nachmias, C. and Nachmias, D. (1992) *Research Methods in the Social Sciences*, 4th edn. London: Edward Arnold. **159**

Franklin, R. D., Allison, D. B. and Gorman, B. S., eds (1996) *Design and Analysis of Single-case Research*. Mahwah, NJ: Lawrence Erlbaum Associates. **142, 147, 162**

French, C. (1990) Computer-assisted Assessment. In J. R. Beech and L. Harding, eds, *Testing People*. Windsor: NFER–Nelson. **304**

Fullan, M. (1982) *The Meaning of Educational Change*. New York: Columbia University Press. **219, 220**

Fullan, M. (1991) *The New Meaning of Educational Change*, 2nd edn. London: Cassell. **219**

Fuller, R. and Petch, A. (1995) *Practitioner Research: The Reflexive Social Worker*. Buckingham: Open University Press. **217, 544**

Gahan, C. and Hannibal, M. (1998) *Doing Qualitative Research Using QSR NUD\*IST*. London: Sage. **464, 466, 472**

Gay, L. R. (1992) *Educational Research*, 4th edn. New York: Merrill. **251**

Geertz, C. (1973) *The Interpretation of Cultures*. New York: Basic. **186**

Gergen, K. J. (1985) The social constructionist movement in modern psychology. *American Psychologist*, 40, 266–75. **26**

Gergen, M., Chrisler, J. C. and LoCicero, A. (1999) Innovative methods: resources for research, publishing, and teaching. *Psychology of Women Quarterly*, 23, 431–56. **370**

Gibbs, G. (2001) *Qualitative Data Analysis: Explorations with NVivo*. Buckingham: Open University Press. **464, 498**

Gibbs, G. (n.d.) *Consumer Behaviour and Green Attitudes*. Questionnaire. Huddersfield: The Polytechnic (mimeo). **247**

Gibson, J. M. E. (1998) Using the Delphi technique to identify the content and context of nurses' continuing professional development needs. *Journal of Clinical Nursing*, 7, 451–9. **57**

Giddens, A. (1986) Action, subjectivity, and the constitution of meaning. *Social Research*, 53, 529–45. **197**

Gigerenzer, G. (1993) The super-ego, the ego, and the id in statistical reasoning. In G. Keren and C. Lewis, eds, *A Handbook for Data Analysis in the Behavioral Sciences*. Hillsdale, NJ: Erlbaum. **401**

Gilloran A. J., McGlew, T., McKee, K., Robertson, A. and Wight, D. (1993) Measuring the quality of care in psychogeriatric wards. *Journal of Advanced Nursing*, 18, 269–75. **331**

Gittelson, J., Shankar, A. V., West, K. P., Ram, R. M. and Gnywali, T. (1997) Estimating reactivity in direct observation studies of health behaviors. *Human Organization*, 56, 182–9. **311**

Glaser, B. (1978) *Theoretical Sensitivity: Advances in the Methodology of Grounded Theory*. Mill Valley, Calif.: Sociology Press. **191**

Glaser, B. (1992) *Basics of Grounded Theory Analysis: Emergence versus Forcing*. Mill Valley, Calif.: Sociology Press. **191, 193, 265, 494, 498**

Glaser, B. and Strauss, A. (1965) *Awareness of Dying*. Chicago: Aldine. **191, 496**

Glaser, B. and Strauss, A. (1967) *The Discovery of Grounded Theory*. Chicago: Aldine. **191, 492, 494**

Glaser, B. and Strauss, A. (1968) *Time for Dying*. Chicago: Aldine. **191, 496**

Glass, G. V., Willson, V. L. and Gottman, J. M. (1975) *The Design and Analysis of Time-series Experiments*. Boulder, Col.: Colorado Associated University Press. **448**

Goffman, E. (1969) *The Presentation of Self in Everyday Life*. Harmondsworth: Penguin. **196**

Gold, R. L. (1958) Roles in sociological field observations. *Social Forces*, 36, 217–23. Repr. in G. J. McCall and J. L. Simmons, eds (1969), *Issues in Participant Observation: A Text and Reader*. Reading, Mass.: Addison-Wesley. **319**

Gordon, B. M. (1995) Knowledge construction, competing critical theories, and education. In J. Banks and C. A. McGee-Banks, eds, *Handbook of Research on Multicultural Education*. London: Macmillan. **29**

Gorman, B. S. and Allison, D. B. (1996) Statistical alternatives for single-case designs. In R. D. Franklin, D. B. Allison and B. S. Gorman, eds, *Design and Analysis of Single-case Research*. Mahwah, NJ: Lawrence Erlbaum Associates. **450**

Gottman, J. M. and Bakeman, R. (1998) Systematic observational techniques or building life as an observational researcher. In Gilbert et al., eds, *Handbook of Social Psychology*, 4th edn. Oxford: Oxford University Press. **345**

Gottschalk, L., Kluckhohn, C. and Angell, R. (1945) *The Use of Personal Documents in History, Anthropology and Sociology*. New York: Social Science Research Council. **350**

Grady, K. E. and Wallston, B. S. (1988) *Research in Health Care Settings*. Newbury Park, Calif.: Sage. **50, 82, 382**

Gray, C. D. and Kinnear, P. R. (1998) *SPSS for Macintosh Made Simple*. Hove: Psychology Press. **392**

Green, A. (1995) Verbal protocol analysis. *The Psychologist: Bulletin of the British Psychological Society*, 8, 126–9. **367**

Greenhouse, S. W. and Geisser, S. (1959) On methods in the analysis of profile data. *Psychometrika*, 24, 95–112. **448**

Gregg, V. H. and Jones, D. (1990) Ethics committees. *The Psychologist: Bulletin of the British Psychological Society*, 3, 162–5. **69**

Grinyer, A. (1999) Anticipating the problems of contract social research. *Social Research Update*, issue 27. Department of Sociology, University of Surrey. Also available at <http://www.surrey.ac.uk/sru/SRU27.html>. **379**

Grusky, O. (1963) Managerial succession and organisational effectiveness. *American Journal of Sociology*, 69, 21–31. **360**

Guba, E. G., ed. (1990) *The Paradigm Dialog*. Newbury Park, Calif.: Sage. **43**

Guba, E. G. and Lincoln, Y. S. (1989) *Fourth Generation Evaluation*. Newbury Park, Calif.: Sage. **168**

Guba, E. G. and Lincoln, Y. S. (1994) Competing paradigms in qualitative research. In N. K. Denzin and Y. S. Lincoln, eds, *Handbook of Qualitative Research*. Thousand Oaks, Calif.: Sage. **27, 28**

Gullan, E., Glendon, A. I., Matthews, G., Davies, D. R. and Debney, L. M. (1990) The stress of driving: a diary study. *Work and Stress*, 4, 7–16. **259**

Guttman, L. (1944) A basis for scaling qualitative data. *American Sociological Review*, 9, 139–50. **298**

Hacking, I. (1983) *Representing and Intervening: Introductory Topics in the Philosophy of Natural Science*. Cambridge: Cambridge University Press. **33**

Hagen, R. L. (1997) In praise of the null hypothesis statistical test. *American Psychologist*, 52, 15–24. **402**

Haig, B. D. (1996) Statistical methods in education and psychology: a critical perspective. *Australian Journal of Education*, 40, 190–209. **401**

Hakel, M. D., Sorcher, M., Beek, M. and Moses, J. L. (1982) *Making it Happen: Designing Research with Implementation in Mind*. Newbury Park, Calif.: Sage. **540, 542**

Hakim, C. (1982) *Secondary Analysis in Social Research: A Guide to Data Sources and Methods with Examples*. London: Allen & Unwin. **360, 373**

Hakim, C. (1987) *Research Design: Strategies and Choices in the Design of Social Research*. London: Allen & Unwin. **10, 80, 93, 181, 232, 268, 360, 362, 384, 526, 530**

Hall, D. and Hall, I. (1996) *Practical Social Research: Project Work in the Community*. London: Macmillan. **11, 15, 37, 48, 76, 379**

Hamel, J. (1993) *Case Study Methods*. Newbury Park, Calif.: Sage. **177**

Hammersley, M. (1985) From Ethnography to Theory. *Sociology*, 19, 244–59. **186**

Hammersley, M. (1989) *The Dilemma of Qualitative Method: Herbert Blumer and the Chicago Tradition*. London: Routledge. **188, 320**

Hammersley, M. (1992) *What's Wrong with Ethnography?* London: Routledge. **62, 188, 189, 490**

Hammersley, M. (1995) *The Politics of Social Research*. London: Sage. **72, 73**

Hammersley, M. (2000) The Relevance of Qualitative Research. *Oxford Review of Education*, 26, 393–405. **5**

Hammersley, M. and Atkinson, P. (1995) *Ethnography: Principles in Practice*, 2nd edn. London: Routledge. **200, 488, 489, 498**

Hammersley, M. and Scarth, J. (1993) Beware of wise men bearing gifts: a case study in the misuse of educational research. *British Educational Research Journal*, 19, 489–98. **73**

Handen, B. L., McAuliffe, S., Janosky, J., Feldman, H. and Breaux, A. M. (1998) A playroom observation procedure to assess children with mental retardation and ADHD. *Journal of Abnormal Child Psychology*, 26, 269–77. **311**

Haney, C., Banks, C. and Zimbardo, P. (1973) Interpersonal dynamics in a simulated prison. *International Journal of Criminological Penology*, 1, 69–97. **364**

Hanson, D. J. (1980) Relationship between methods and judges in attitude behavior research. *Psychology*, 17, 11–13. **231**

Harding, S. (1986) *The Science Question in Feminism*. Milton Keynes: Open University Press. **29**

Harding, S., ed. (1987) *Feminism and Methodology*. Milton Keynes: Open University Press. **73**

Harding, S. and Hintikha, M. B. (1983) *Discovering Reality: Feminist Perspectives on Epistemology, Metaphysics, Methodology and Philosophy of Science*. Dordrecht: Reidel. **73**

Hargreaves, D. H. (1997) In defence of research for evidence-based teaching. *British Educational Research Journal*, 23, 405–19. **61**

Harlen, W. and Elliott, J. (1982) A checklist for planning or reviewing and evaluation. In R. McCormick, ed., *Calling Education to Account*. London: Heinemann. **212**

Harlow, L. L., Mulaik, S. A. and Steiger, J. H., eds (1997) *What If There Were No Significance Tests?* Mahwah, NJ: Lawrence Erlbaum Associates. **402**

Harré, R. (1981) The positive-empiricist approach and its alternative. In P. Reason and J. Rowan, eds, *Human Enquiry: A Sourcebook of New Paradigm Research*. Chichester: Wiley. **29**

Harré, R. (1986) *Varieties of Realism: A Rationale for the Natural Sciences*. Oxford: Blackwell. **29**

Harré, R. and Secord, P. F. (1972) *The Explanation of Social Behaviour*. Oxford: Blackwell. **364**

Harrison, R. S., Boyle, S. W. and Farley, O. W. (1999) Evaluating the outcomes of family-based intervention for troubled children: a pretest-posttest study. *Research on Social Work Practice*, 9, 640–55. **84, 135**

Hart, C. (1998) *Doing a Literature Review: Releasing the Social Science Imagination*. Thousand Oaks, Calif., and London: Sage. **523**

Hartley, J. (1985) *Designing Instructional Text*, 2nd edn. London: Kogan Page. **519, 522**

Hartley, J. (1989) Tools for evaluating text. In J. Hartley and A. Branthwaite, eds, *The Applied Psychologist*. Milton Keynes: Open University Press. **521**

Hartley, J. and Branthwaite, A. (1989) The psychologist as wordsmith: a questionnaire study of the writing strategies of productive British psychologists. *Higher Education*, 18, 423–52. **519**

Hartley, J. and Chesworth, K. (2000) Qualitative and quantitative methods in research on essay writing. *Journal of Further and Higher Education*, 24, 15–24. **371**

Hathaway, S. R. and McKinley, J. C. (1967) *The Minnesota Multiphasic Personality Inventory*. Minneapolis: NCS Interpretive Scoring System, University of Minnesota. **305**

Hayes, N., ed. (1997) *Doing Qualitative Analysis in Psychology*. Hove: Psychology Press. **498**

Health Committee (1992) *Second Report, Session 1991–2: Maternity Services*. London: HMSO. **118**

Hearnshaw, L. S. (1979) *Cyril Burt: Psychologist*. London: Hodder & Stoughton. **506**

Heatherton, T. and Polivy, J. (1991) Development and validation of a scale for measuring state self-esteem. *Journal of*

*Personality and Social Psychology*, 60, 895–910. **305**

Heim, A. W. (1970) *Group Test of General Intelligence AH4*. Slough: National Foundation for Educational Research. **306**

Heller, F., ed. (1986) *The Use and Abuse of Social Science*. Newbury Park, Calif.: Sage. **14, 219**

Henry, G. T. (1990) *Practical Sampling*. Newbury Park, Calif.: Sage. **162**

Henwood, K. L. (1993) Women and later life: the discursive construction of identities within family relationships. *Journal of Ageing Studies*, 7, 303–19. **191**

Henwood, K. L. (1997) Adult mother–daughter relationships: two phases in the analysis of a qualitative project. *Feminism and Psychology*, 7, 255–63. **370**

Herrera, C. D. (1999) Two arguments for 'covert methods' in social research. *British Journal of Sociology*, 50, 331–43. **67**

Hersen, M. and Barlow, D. H. (1976) *Single Case Experimental Designs: Strategies for Studying Behavior Change*. Oxford: Pergamon. **449**

Hodgson, R. and Rollnick, S. (1989) More fun, less stress: how to survive in research. In G. Parry and F. N. Watts, eds, *Behavioural and Mental Health Research: A Handbook of Skills and Methods*. Hove: Lawrence Erlbaum. **384**

Hofer, M., Sassenberg, K. and Pikowsy, B. (1999) Discourse asymmetries in adolescent daughters' disputes with mothers. *International Journal of Behavioural Development*, 23, 1001–22. **333**

Hoinville, G., Jowell, R. and Associates (1985) *Survey Research Practice*, 2nd edn. London: Gower. **268, 274**

Hollway, W. (1989) *Subjectivity and Method in Psychology: Gender, Meaning and Science*. Newbury Park, Calif., and London: Sage. **73, 376**

Holstein, J. A. and Gubrium, J. F. (1994) Phenomenology, ethnomethodology, and interpretive practice. In N. K. Denzin and Y. S. Lincoln, eds, *The Handbook of Qualitative Research*. Thousand Oaks, Calif.: Sage. **195, 196**

Holsti, O. R. (1969) *Content Analysis for the Social Sciences and Humanities*. Reading, Mass.: Addison-Wesley. **354**

Homan, R. (1991) *The Ethics of Social Research*. London: Longman. **76**

Hops, H., Davis, B. and Longoria, N. (1995) Methodological issues in direct observation: illustrations with the living in familial environments (LIFE) coding system. *Journal of Clinical Child Psychology*, 24, 193–203. **339**

Horn, R. (1996) Negotiating research access to organisations. *The Psychologist*, 9, 551–4. **378**

House, E. R. (1991) Realism in research. *Educational Researcher*, 20, 2–9. **30, 32, 106**

House, E. R., Mathison, S. and McTaggart, R. (1989) Validity and teacher inference. *Educational Researcher*, 18, 11–15, 26. **106**

Hovland, C. I. and Sherif, M. (1952) Judgmental phenomena and scales of attitude measurement: item displacement in Thurstone scales. *Journal of Abnormal and Social Psychology*, 47, 822–32. **298**

Howard, K. and Sharp, J. A. (1996) *The Management of a Student Research Project*, 2nd edn. Aldershot: Gower. **383**

Howe, K. R. (1988) Against the quantitative–qualitative incompatibility thesis: or dogmas die hard. *Educational Researcher*, 19, 10–16. **43**

Howkins, E. J. and Ewens, A. (1999) How students experience professional socialisation. *International Journal of Nursing Studies*, 36, 41–9. **366**

Huff, D. (1973) *How to Lie with Statistics*. London: Penguin. **412**

Hughes, J. A. and Sharrock, W. W. (1997) *The Philosophy of Social Research*, 3rd edn. London: Longman. **24**

Huisman, M. (2000) Imputation of missing item responses: some simple techniques. *Quality and Quantity*, 34, 331–51. **396**

Hume, D. (1888) *A Treatise of Human Nature*. Oxford: Oxford University Press. (First publ. 1738, London: John Noon). **21**

Husserl, E. (1977) *Cartesian Meditations: An Introduction to Phenomenology*, trans. D. Cairns. The Hague: Martinus Nijhoff. **195**

Hyland, M. E., Bott, J., Singh, S. and Kenyon, C. A. P. (1994) Domains, constructs and the development of the breathing problems questionnaire. *Quality of Life Research*, 3, 245–56. **287**

Impara, J. C. and Plake, B. S., eds (1998) *The Thirteenth Mental Measurements Yearbook*. Lincoln, Nebr.: Buros Institute of Mental Measurement. **303**

Irwin, J. (1985) *The Jail: Managing the Underclass in American Society*. Berkeley, Calif.: University of California Press. **49**

Iwaniec, D. and Pinkerton, J., eds (1998) *Making Research Work: Promoting Child Care Policy and Practice*. Chichester: Wiley. **220**

Jenkins, C. D., Zyzanski, S. J. and Rosenman, R. H. (1979) *Jenkins Activity Survey Form C: Manual*. San Antonio: Psychological Corporation/Harcourt Brace Jovanovich. **306**

Jenkins, D. (1984) Chocolate cream soldiers: sponsorship, ethnography and sectarianism. In R. Burgess, ed., *The Research Process in Educational Settings: Ten Case Studies*. London: Falmer. **74, 514**

Johnson, A. (1996) 'It's good to talk': the focus group and the sociological imagination. *Sociological Review*, 44, 3, 517–38. **284**

Johnson, A. E. (1998) Problems associated with randomized controlled trials in breast cancer. *Journal of Evaluation in Clinical Practice*, 4, 119–28. **116**

Johnson, G. I. and Briggs, P. (1994) Question-asking and verbal protocol techniques In C. Cassell and G. Symon, eds, *Qualitative Methods in Organizational Research: A Practical Guide*. London: Sage. **367, 375**

Johnson, K., Bryant, D. D., Collins, D. A., Noe, T. D., Strader, T. N. and Berbaum, M. (1998) Preventing and reducing alcohol and other drug use among high-risk youths by increasing family resilience. *Social Work*, 43, 297–308. **204**

Johnson, P. (1998) Analytic induction. In G. Symon and C. Cassell, eds, *Qualitative Methods and Analysis in Organizational Research: A Practical Guide*. London: Sage. **321**

Johnson, S. (1997) Continuity and change: a study of how women cope with the transition to professional programmes of higher education. PhD thesis. University of Huddersfield. **62**

Johnson, S. and Robson, C. (1999) Threatened identities: the experiences of women in transition to programmes of professional higher education. *Journal of Community and Applied Social Psychology*, 9, 273–88. **62**

Jones, J. A. (1995) An illustration of the danger of nonresponse for survey research. Paper presented at the annual meeting of the American Educational Research Association, San Francisco, April. **251**

Jones, R. A. (1985) *Research Methods in the Social and Behavioral Sciences*. Sunderland, Mass.: Sinauer. **215, 319**

Joynson, R. B. (1989) *The Burt Affair*. London: Routledge. **506**

Judd, C. M., Smith, E. R. and Kidder, L. H. (1991) *Research Methods in Social Relations*, 6th edn. New York: Holt, Rinehart & Winston. **135, 213**

Kaneko, M. (1999) A methodological inquiry into the evaluation of smoking cessation programmes. *Health Education Research*, 14, 433–41. **30**

Kaplan, A. (1964) *The Conduct of Inquiry: Methodology for Behavioral Science*. San Francisco: Chandler. **15, 204**

Karp, D. A. (1993) Taking anti-depressant medications: resistance, trial commitment, conversion and disenchantment. *Qualitative Sociology*, 16, 337–59. **487**

Kazdin, A. (1982) *Single-case Research Designs: Methods for Clinical and Applied Settings*. Oxford: Oxford University Press. **153, 450**

Kazi, M. A. F. (2000) Evaluation of social work practice in England. *Journal of*

*Social Work Research and Evaluation*, 1, 101–9. **30**

Kazi, M. A. F. and Ward, A. (2001) Service-wide integration of single-subject designs and qualitative methods: a realist evaluation. Paper presented at the Society for Social Work and Research Conference, Atlanta, Jan. **30**

Kelly, G. A. (1970) A brief introduction to personal construct theory. In D. Bannister, ed., *Perspectives in Personal Construct Theory*. London: Academic. **366**

Kemmis, S. and McTaggart, R. (1981) *The Action Research Planner*. Geelong, Victoria: Deakin University Press. **70**

Kemmis, S. and Wilkinson, M. (1998) Participatory action research and the study of practice. In B. Atweh, S. Kemmis and P. Weeks, eds, *Action Research in Practice: Partnerships for Social Justice in Education*. London and New York: Routledge. **7, 217**

Kern, J. M. (1991) An evaluation of a novel role play methodology: the standardized idiographic approach. *Behaviour Therapy*, 22, 13–29. **365**

Kidd, P. S. and Parshall, M. B. (2000) Getting the focus and the group: enhancing analytical rigor in focus group research. *Qualitative Health Research*, 10, 293–308. **288**

Kidder, L. H. (1981) Qualitative research and quasi-experimental frameworks. In M. B. Brewer and B. E. Collins, eds, *Scientific Enquiry and the Social Sciences*. San Francisco: Jossey-Bass. **490, 491**

Kimmel, A. J. (1988) *Ethics and Values in Applied Social Research*. Newbury Park, Calif.: Sage. **69**

King, C. and Kennedy, P. (1999) Coping effectiveness training for people with spinal cord injury: preliminary results of a controlled trial. *British Journal of Clinical Psychology*, 38, 5–14. **85, 135**

King, N. (1994) The qualitative research interview. In C. Cassell and G. Symon, eds, *Qualitative Methods in Organizational Research*. London: Sage. **271**

Kirby, S. and McKenna, K. (1989) *Experience, Research, Social Change: Methods from the Margins*. Toronto: Garamond. **49, 317**

Kirk, J. and Miller, M. L. (1986) *Reliability and Validity in Qualitative Research*. Beverly Hills, Calif.: Sage. **169**

Kirk, R. E. (1995) *Experimental Design: Procedures for the Behavioral Sciences*, 3rd edn. Belmont, Calif.: Brooks/Cole. **123, 162**

Kitzinger, C. (2000) Doing feminist conversation analysis. *Feminism and Psychology*, 10, 163–93. **370**

Kitzinger, J. (1994) Focus groups: methods or madness? In M. Boulton, ed., *Challenge and Innovation: Methodological Advances in Social Research on HIV/AIDS*. London: Taylor & Francis. **287**

Klee, R. (1997) *Introduction to the Philosophy of Science: Cutting Nature at its Seams*. Oxford: Oxford University Press. **21**

Kline, P. (1990) Selecting the best test. In J. R. Beech and L. Harding, eds, *Testing People*. Windsor, Berks: NFER–Nelson. **304**

Kline, P. (2000) *Handbook of Psychological Testing*, 2nd edn. London: Routledge. **307**

Koch, S. (1959) *Psychology: The Study of a Science*, 6 vols. New York: McGraw-Hill. **21**

Kopinak, J. K. (1999) The use of triangulation in a study of refugee well-being. *Quality and Quantity*, 33, 169–83. **86, 370**

Koyré, A. (1968) *Metaphysics and Measurement*. London: Chapman & Hall. **31**

Kraemer, H. C. (1981) Coping strategies in psychiatric clinical research. *Journal of Counselling and Clinical Psychology*, 49, 309–19. **162**

Krantz, J. (1990) Commentary on the Barratt and Cooperrider article. *Journal of Applied Behavioral Science*, 26, 241–3. **85**

Krathwohl, D. R. (1988) *How to Prepare a Research Project: Guidelines for Funding and Dissertations in the Social and Behavioral Sciences*, 3rd edn. Syracuse, NY: Syracuse University Press. **533**

Kratochwill, T. R., ed. (1978) *Single Subject Research*. New York: Academic. **144**

Krippendorff, K. (1980) *Content Analysis: An Introduction to its methodology*. Newbury Park, Calif.: Sage. **350, 351, 374**

Krueger, R. A. and Casey, M. A. (1998) *Focus Groups: A Practical Guide for Applied Research*, 3rd edn. Thousand Oaks, Calif.: Sage. **291**

Kvale, S. (1996) *InterViews: An Introduction to Qualitative Research Interviewing*. Thousand Oaks, Calif.: Sage. **170, 290, 291**

Labonte, R., Feather, J. and Hills, M. (1999) A story/dialogue method for health promotion knowledge development and evaluation. *Health Education Research*, 14, 39–50. **369**

Lam, W. S. E. (2000) L2 literacy and the design of the self: a case study of a teenager writing on the internet. *TESOL Quarterly*, 34, 457–82. **474**

Lamal, P. A. (1991) Psychology as commonsense: the case of findings concerning work motivation and satisfaction. *Psychological Science*, 2, 129–30. **9**

Lane, R. (1996) Positivism, scientific realism and political science: recent developments in the philosophy of science. *Journal of Theoretical Politics*, 8, 361–82. **30**

Langdridge, D., Sheeran, P. and Connolly, K. J. Small is beautiful: the theory of reasoned action and additional variables. *British Journal of Social Psychology*, submitted for publication. **435**

Layder, D. (1993) *New Strategies in Social Research*. Cambridge: Polity. **186**

LeCompte, M. D. and Goetz, J. P. (1982) Problems of reliability and validity in ethnographic research. *Review of Educational Research*, 52, 31–60. **107**

Lee, T. W. (1999) *Using Qualitative Methods in Organizational Research*. Thousand Oaks, Calif.: Sage. **200**

Leedy, P. D. (1989) *Practical Research: Planning and Design*, 4th edn. New York: Macmillan. **526, 533**

Lemon, N. (1973) *Attitudes and their Measurement*. London: Batsford. **293**

Lensing, S. Y., Gillaspy, S. R., Simpson, P. M. and Jones, S. M. (2000) Encouraging physicians to respond to surveys through the use of fax technology. *Evaluation and the Health Professions*, 23, 348–59. **251**

Leon, A. M., Dziegielewski, S. F. and Tubiak, C. (1999) A program evaluation of a juvenile halfway house: considerations for strengthening program components. *Evaluation and Program Planning*, 22, 141–53. **204**

Lerner, M. J. (1980) *The Belief in a Just World: A Fundamental Delusion*. New York: Plenum. **99**

Letherby, G. and Zdrodowski, D. (1995) 'Dear researcher': the use of correspondence as a method within feminist qualitative research. *Gender and Society*, 9, 56–93. **369**

Lewin, K. (1946) Action research and minority problems. *Journal of Social Issues*, 2, 34–6. **216**

Lewin, K. (1951) Problems of research in social psychology. In D. Cartwright, ed., *Field Theory in Social Science*. New York: Harper & Brothers. **61**

Lewis, P. (2000) Realism, causality and the problem of social structure. *Journal for the Theory of Social Behaviour*, 30, 249–68. **32**

Likert, R. (1932) A technique for the measurement of attitudes. *Archives of Psychology*, no. 140. **293**

Lincoln, Y. S. and Guba, E. G. (1985) *Naturalistic Inquiry*. Newbury Park, Calif.: Sage. **27, 170, 172, 176, 315, 490, 511**

Lindblom, C. E. and Cohen, D. K. (1979) *Usable Knowledge: Social Science and Social Problem-solving*. New Haven, Conn.: Yale University Press. **232, 524**

Linsell, S. and Robson, C. (1987) *Study of One Year's Intake at Huddersfield Polytechnic: Their Qualifications and Progress.* Huddersfield: The Polytechnic (mimeo). **395**

Lipsey, M. K. (1990) *Design Sensitivity.* Newbury Park, Calif.: Sage. **162**

Little, C. V. (1999) The meaning of learning in critical care nursing: a hermeneutic study. *Journal of Advanced Nursing,* 30, 697–703. **198**

Locke, E. A. (1986) *Generalizing from Laboratory to Field Settings.* Lexington, Mass.: Lexington. **114**

Locke, E. A. and Latham, G. P. (1991) The fallacies of commonsense 'truths'. a reply to Lamal. *Psychological Science,* 2, 131–2. **9**

Loewenthal, M. (1996) *An Introduction to Psychological Tests and Scales.* London: UCL Press. **294, 305, 306, 307, 433, 434**

Lofland, J. (1971) *Analysing Social Settings.* Belmont, Calif.: Wadsworth. **319, 511**

Lofland, J. and Lofland, L. H. (1984) *Analyzing Social Settings: A Guide to Qualitative Observation and Analysis,* 2nd edn. Belmont, Calif.: Wadsworth. **379**

Lofland, J. and Lofland, L. H. (1995) *Analyzing Social Settings: A Guide to Qualitative Observation and Analysis,* 3rd edn. Belmont, Calif.: Wadsworth. **49, 200, 278, 281, 323, 344, 379**

Long, J. S. (1983) *Confirmatory Factor Analysis.* Newbury Park, Calif., and London: Sage. **433**

Lovie, A. D. (1986) Getting new statistics into today's crowded syllabuses. In A. D. Lovie, ed., *New Developments in Statistics for Psychology and the Social Sciences,* vol. 1. London: Methuen. **410**

Lovie, A. D. and Lovie, P. (1991) Graphical methods for exploring data. In P. Lovie and A. D. Lovie, eds, *New Developments in Statistics for Psychology and the Social Sciences,* vol. 2. London: Routledge. **399**

Lovie, P. (1986) Identifying outliers. In A. D. Lovie, ed., *New Developments in Statistics for Psychology and the Social Sciences,* vol. 1. London: Methuen. **410**

Lumsdaine, E. and Lumsdaine, M. (1995) *Creative Problem Solving: Thinking Skills for a Changing World.* New York: McGraw-Hill. **57**

Luttrell, W. (2000) 'Good Enough' Methods for Ethnographic Research. *Harvard Educational Review,* 70, 499–523. **377**

Lynch, M. (1985) *Art and Artifact in Laboratory Science: A Study of Shop Work and Shop Talk in a Research Laboratory.* London: Routledge & Kegan Paul. **4**

Lynch, P. (1995) Adolescent smoking: an alternative perspective using personal construct theory. *Health Education Research,* 10, 95–106. **366**

Lynd, R. S. and Lynd, H. M. (1929) *Middlestown: A Study in Modern American Culture.* New York: Harcourt Brace Jovanovich. **513**

McColl, M., Hart, G. and Chung, D. (1996) Client Follow-up at the Adelaide Sexually Transmitted Disease Clinic. *Australian and New Zealand Journal of Public Health,* 20, 161–4. **331**

McCracken, G. (1988) *The Long Interview.* Newbury Park, Calif.: Sage. **281**

McCulloch, A. (2000) Evaluations of a community regeneration project: case studies of Cruddas Park Development Trust, Newcastle upon Tyne. *Journal of Social Policy,* 29, 397–419. **215**

MacDonald, G. (1996) Evaluating the effectiveness of social interventions. In A. Oakley and H. Roberts, eds, *Evaluating Social Interventions: A Report of Two Workshops Funded by the Economic and Social Research Council.* Ilford: Barnardo's. **4**

MacDougall, C. and Fudge, E. (2001) Planning and recruiting the sample for focus groups and in-depth interviews. *Qualitative Health Research,* 11, 117–26. **286**

Mackintosh, N. J. (1995) *Cyril Burt: Fraud or Framed?* Oxford: Oxford University Press. **506**

MacMillan, K. and McLachlan, S. (1999) Theory-building with NUD*IST: using computer assisted qualitative analysis in a media case study. *Sociological Research Online*, 4, 135–51. **474**

McWhirter, J. M., Collins, M. Bryant, I., Wetton, N. M. and Bishop, J. N. (2000) Evaluating 'Safe in the Sun': a curriculum programme for primary schools. *Health Education Research*, 15, 203–17. **204**

Madill, A., Jordan, A. and Shirley, C. (2000) Objectivity and reliability in qualitative analysis: realist, contextualist and radical constructionist epistemologies. *British Journal of Psychology*, 91, 1–20. **496**

Madriz, E. I. (1998) Using focus groups with lower socioeconomic status Latina women. *Qualitative Inquiry*, 4, 114–28. **287**

Mahoney, M. J., Moura, N. M. and Wade, T. C. (1973) The relative efficiency of self-reward, self-punishment and self-monitoring techniques for weight loss. *Journal of Consulting and Clinical Psychology*, 40, 404–7. **347**

Mäki, U. (1988) How to combine rhetoric and reality in the methodology of economics. *Economics and Philosophy*, 4, 89–109. **30**

Manicas, P. T. (1987) *A History and Philosophy of the Social Sciences*. Oxford: Blackwell. **29**

Manicas, P. T. and Secord, P. F. (1983) Implications for psychology of the new philosophy of science. *American Psychologist*, 38, 399–413. **30, 34, 40**

Manis, J. G. and Meltzer, B. N., eds (1967) *Symbolic Interactionism: A Reader in Social Psychology*. Boston: Allyn & Bacon. **314**

Manstead, A. S. R. and Semin, G. R. (1988) Methodology in social psychology: turning ideas into action. In M. Hewstone, W. Stoebe, J-P. Codol and G. M. Stephenson, eds, *Introduction to Social Psychology*. Oxford: Blackwell. **80**

Marsh, C. (1982) *The Survey Method: The Contribution of Surveys to Sociological Explanation*. London: Allen & Unwin. **96, 228, 231, 268, 427, 451**

Marsh, C. (1988) *Exploring Data: An Introduction to Data Analysis for Social Scientists*. Cambridge: Polity. **406, 407, 410, 412, 413, 425, 452, 453**

Marshall, C. and Rossman, G. B. (1999) *Designing Qualitative Research*, 3rd edn. Thousand Oaks, Calif.: Sage. **58, 94, 109, 531**

Marshall, H. (1994) Discourse analysis in an occupational context. In C. Cassell and G. Symon, eds, *Qualitative Methods in Organizational Research*. London: Sage. **366**

Martin, J. (1981) A garbage can model of the psychological research process. *American Behavioral Scientist*, 25, 131–51. **81, 377**

Martin, P. and Bateson, P. (1986) *Measuring Behaviour: An Introductory Guide*. Cambridge: Cambridge University Press. **340, 345**

Martusewicz, R. A. and Reynolds, W. M., eds (1994) *Inside Out: Contemporary Critical Perspectives in Education*. New York: St Martin's. **28**

Mason, J. (1996) *Qualitative Researching*. London: Sage. **171, 176, 189, 200**

Mason, S. (1997) Social work research: is there a feminist method? *Affilia: Journal of Women and Social Work*, 12, 10–32. **369**

Maxwell, J. A. (1992) Understanding and validity in qualitative research. *Harvard Educational Review*, 62, 279–300. **104, 106, 171, 176**

Maxwell, J. A. (1996) *Qualitative Research Design: An Interactive Approach*. Thousand Oaks, Calif.: Sage. **50, 63, 81, 94, 106, 176**

Maxwell, S. E. and Delaney, H. D. (1999) *Designing Experiments and Analyzing Data: A Model Comparison Perspective*. Mahwah, NJ: Lawrence Erlbaum Associates. **33, 123, 162, 453**

May, T. (1997) *Social Research: Issues, Methods and Process*, 2nd edn. Milton Keynes: Open University Press. **29**

Maynard, M. and Purvis, J., eds (1994) *Researching Women's Lives from a Feminist Perspective*. London: Taylor & Francis. **73, 376**

Meadows, L. M. and Dodendorf, D. M. (1999) Data management and interpretation using computers to assist. In B. F. Crabtree and W. L. Miller, eds, *Doing Qualitative Research*, 2nd edn. Thousand Oaks, Calif.: Sage. **464**

Medawar, P. B. (1979) *Advice to a Young Scientist*. New York: Harper & Row. **55**

Meddis, R. (1984) *Statistics Using Ranks: A Unified Approach*. Oxford: Blackwell. **415, 441**

Meehl, P. E. (1978) Theoretical risks and tabular asterisks: Sir Karl, Sir Ronald, and the slow progress of soft psychology. *Journal of Consulting and Clinical Psychology*, 46, 806–35. **401**

Meehl, P. E. (1990) Why summaries of research on psychological theories are often uninterpretable. *Psychological Reports*, 66, 195–244. **401**

Mehta, K. (1997) Respect redefined: focus group insights from Singapore. *International Journal of Aging and Human Development*, 44, 205–19. **287**

Menard, S. (1991) *Longitudinal Research*. Newbury Park, Calif.: Sage. **161**

Merriam, S. (1988) *Case Study Research in Education: A Qualitative Approach*. San Francisco: Jossey-Bass. **179**

Mertens, D. M. (1998) *Research Methods in Education and Psychology: Integrating Diversity with Quantitative and Qualitative Approaches*. Thousand Oaks, Calif.: Sage. **15, 51, 94, 157, 158, 161, 198, 251, 255, 494, 507**

Mertens, D. M., Farley, J., Madison, A. and Singleton, P. (1994) Diverse voices in evaluation practice: feminists, minorities, and persons with disabilities. *Evaluation Practice*, 15, 123–9. **28**

Merton, R. K., Fiske, M. and Kendall, P. L. (1956) *The Focused Interview*. Glencoe, Ill.: Free Press. **283, 388**

Merttens, R. (1998) What is to be done? (With apologies to Lenin!). In I. Parker,

ed, *Social Constructionism, Discourse and Realism*. London: Sage. **27**

Middlewood, D., Coleman, M. and Lumby, J., eds (1999) *Practitioner Research in Education: Making a Difference*. London: Paul Chapman. **544**

Miles, M. B. (1979) Qualitative data as an attractive nuisance: the problem of analysis. *Administrative Science Quarterly*, 24, 590–601. **455**

Miles, M. B. and Huberman, A. M. (1984) *Qualitative Data Analysis: A Sourcebook of New Methods*. Newbury Park, Calif.: Sage. **109**

Miles, M. B. and Huberman, A. M. (1994) *Qualitative Data Analysis: An Expanded Sourcebook*, 2nd edn. Thousand Oaks, Calif.: Sage. **63, 64, 176, 179, 200, 459, 467, 472, 473, 475, 477, 480, 481, 483, 484, 488, 498, 507, 508**

Miller, W. L. and Crabtree, B. J. (1999) Depth interviewing. In B. F. Crabtree and W. L. Miller, eds, *Doing Qualitative Research*, 2nd edn. Thousand Oaks, Calif.: Sage. **270**

Milne, E., Corti, B., English, D. R., Cross, D., Costa, C. and Johnston, R. (1999) The use of observational methods for monitoring sun-protection activities in schools. *Health Education Research*, 14, 167–75. **310**

Milroy, L. (1980) *Language and Social Networks*. Oxford: Blackwell. **365**

Milton, J. and Wiseman, R. (1999) A meta-analysis of mass-media tests of extrasensory perception. *British Journal of Psychology*, 90, 235–40. **368**

Mintzberg, H. (1973) *The Nature of Managerial Work*. New York: Harper & Row. **332**

Mishler, E. G. (1991) *Research Interviewing: Context and Narrative*. Cambridge, Mass.: Harvard University Press. **231, 268, 291**

Monnickendam, M. and Markus, E. J. (1996) Effects of a practice-centred cognitive-oriented computer course on computer attitudes: implications for course content. *Social Work and Social Sciences Review*, 6, 175–85. **85, 135**

Morrison, D. E. and Henkel, R. E., eds (1970) *The Significance Test Controversy*. Chicago: Aldine. **401**

Morrow, S. L. and Smith, M. L. (1995) Constructions of survival and coping by women who have survived childhood sexual abuse. *Journal of Counselling Psychology*, 42, 24–33. Repr. in Cresswell (1998). **86, 496**

Morse, J. M. (1994) Designing funded qualitative research. In N. K. Denzin and Y. S. Lincoln, eds, *The Handbook of Qualitative Research*. Thousand Oaks, Calif.: Sage. **199**

Morse, J. M. (1999) Myth #93: reliability and validity are not relevant to qualitative inquiry. *Qualitative Health Research*, 9, 717–18. **170**

Morse, J. M. (2000) Determining sample size. *Qualitative Health Research*, 10, 3–5. **199**

Moustakas, C. (1994) *Phenomenological Research Methods*. Thousand Oaks, Calif.: Sage. **196, 498**

Muijs, D. and Reynolds, D. (2000) School effectiveness and teacher effectiveness in mathematics: some preliminary findings from the evaluation of the mathematics enhancement programme (primary). *School Effectiveness and School Improvement*, 11, 273–303. **333**

Murphy, E., Dingwall, R., Greatbatch, D., Parker, S. and Watson, P. (1998) Qualitative research methods in health technology assessment: a review of the literature. *Health Technology Assessment*, 2/16. **95**

Mutch, A. (1999) Critical realism, managers and information. *British Journal of Management*, 10, 323–33. **30**

Myers, I. B. and McCaulley, M. H. (1985) *A Guide to the Development and Use of the Myers–Briggs Type Indicator*. Palo Alto, Calif.: Consulting Psychologists Press. **305**

Nash, R. (1999) Realism in the sociology of education: 'explaining' social differences in attainment. *British Journal of Sociology of Education*, 20, 107–25. **30**

Nason, J. and Golding, D. (1998) Approaching observation. In G. Symon and C. Cassell, eds, *Qualitative Methods and Analysis in Organizational Research: A Practical Guide*. **344**

Nee, C. and Taylor, M. (2000) Examining burglars' target selection: interview, or ethnomethodology? *Psychology, Crime and Law*, 6, 45–59. **371**

Neilsen, J., ed. (1990) *Feminist Research Methods*. New York: Westview. **73**

Neuman, W. L. (1994) *Social Research Methods: Qualitative and Quantitative Approaches*, 2nd edn. Boston: Allyn & Bacon. **47**

Newcomb, M. D., Rabow, J., Monto, M. and Hernandez, A. C. R. (1991) Informal drunk driving intervention: psychosocial correlates among young adult women and men. *Journal of Applied Psychology*, 21, 1988–2006. **85**

Newman, D. L. and Brown, R. D. (1996) *Applied Ethics for Program Evaluation*. Thousand Oaks, Calif.: Sage. **76**

Nieswiadomy, R. M. (1993) *Foundations of Nursing Research*, 2nd edn. Norwalk, Conn.: Appleton & Large. **195**

Norris, N. (1990) *Understanding Educational Evaluation*. London: Kogan Page. **216**

Northcott, J. and Brown, G. (1998) Butterflies in the rain forest? Ethnography and the business English student. *Edinburgh Working Papers in Applied Linguistics*, 9, 63–72. **260**

Northmore, D. (1996) *Lifting the Lid: A Guide to Investigative Research*. London and New York: Cassell. **8**

Norwich, B. (1999) Pupils' reasons for learning and behaving and for not learning and behaving in English and maths lessons in a secondary school. *British Journal of Educational Psychology*, 69, 547–69. **85**

Novak, J. D. and Gowin, D. B. (1984) *Learning How to Learn*. Cambridge: Cambridge University Press. **63**

Oakes, M. W. (1986) *Statistical Inference: A Commentary for the Social and Behavioural Sciences*. New York and Chichester: Wiley. **401**

Oakley, A. (1981) Interviewing women: a contradiction in terms. In H. Roberts, ed., *Doing Feminist Research*. London: Routledge & Kegan Paul. **369**

Oakley, A. (1996) Who's afraid of the randomised controlled trial? The challenge of evaluating the potential of social interventions. In *What Works? Effective Social Interventions in Child Welfare*. Report of a conference organized by Barnardo's and the Social Science Research Unit, 11 March 1994. Ilford: Barnardo's. **4**

Oakley, A. (1998) Gender, methodology and people's ways of knowing: some problems with feminism and the paradigm debate in social science. *Sociology*, 32, 707–31. **369**

Oakley, A. (2000) *Experiments in Knowing: Gender and Method in the Social Sciences*. Cambridge: Polity. **95, 99, 117, 120, 203**

Oakley, A. and Fullerton, D. (1996) The lamp-post of research: support or illumination? In A. Oakley and H. Roberts, eds, *Evaluating Social Interventions*. Ilford: Barnardo's. **205**

Oliver, M. (1992) Changing the social relations of research production? *Disability, Handicap and Society*, 7/2, 101–14. **29**

Oliver, N. (1990) Work rewards, work values and organisational commitment in an employee-owned firm: evidence from the UK. *Human Relations*, 43, 513–26. **267**

Onyskiw, J. E., Harrison, M. J., Spady, D. and McConnan, L. (1999) Formative evaluation of a collaborative community-based child abuse prevention project. *Child Abuse and Neglect*, 23, 1069–81. **86, 179**

Oppenheim, A. N. (1992) *Questionnaire Design, Interviewing and Attitude Measurement*. London: Pinter; New York: Basic. **245, 308**

Orna, E. with Stevens, G. (1995) *Managing Information for Research*. Buckingham: Open University Press. **53**

Orne, M. T. (1962) On the social psychology of the psychological experiment with particular reference to demand characteristics and their implications. *American Psychologist*, 17, 776–83. **112**

Ortmann, A. and Hertwig, R. (1997) Is deception acceptable? *American Psychologist*, 52, 746–7. **69**

Osgood, C. E., Suci, C. J. and Tannenbaum, P. H. (1957) *The Measurement of Meaning*. Urbana, Ill.: University of Illinois Press. **299, 302**

Oskamp, S. and Schultz, P. W. (1998) *Applied Social Psychology*, 2nd edn. Upper Saddle River, NJ: Prentice-Hall. **15**

Outhwaite, W. (1987) *New Philosophies of Social Science: Realism, Hermeneutics and Critical Theory*. London: Macmillan. **19, 20, 40**

Padgett, D. K. (1998) *Qualitative Methods in Social Work Research: Challenges and Rewards*. Thousand Oaks, Calif.: Sage. **172, 174, 200, 507**

Page, S. (2000) Community research: the lost art of unobtrusive methods. *Journal of Applied Social Psychology*, 30, 2126–36. **348**

Park, P., ed. (1993) *Voices of Change: Participatory Research in the United States and Canada*. Westport, Conn.: Bergin & Garvey. **216**

Parker, I., ed. (1998) *Social Constructionism, Discourse and Realism*. London: Sage. **27**

Parker, I. (1999) Against relativism in psychology, on balance. *History of the Human Sciences*, 12, 61–78. **27**

Parry, G. (1996) Writing a research report. In G. Parry and F. N. Watts, eds, *Behavioural and Mental Health Research: A Handbook of Skills and Methods*, 2nd edn. Hove: Erlbaum (UK) Taylor & Francis. **520, 522, 523**

Patomäki, H. and Wight, C. (2000) After postpositivism? The promises of critical realism. *International Studies Quarterly*, 44, 213–37. **30**

Patton, M. Q. (1981) *Creative Evaluation*. Newbury Park, Calif.: Sage. **206**

Patton, M. Q. (1982) *Practical Evaluation*. Newbury Park, Calif.: Sage. **205, 517**

Pawson, R. and Tilley, N. (1997) *Realistic Evaluation*. London: Sage. **29, 31, 36, 119, 120, 122, 205, 221**

Pearson, J. C. (1985) *Gender and Communication*. Dubuque, Iowa: Wm C. Brown. **503**

Pelosi, M. K., Sandifer, T. M. and Letkowski, J. J. (1998) *Doing Statistics with EXCEL 97*. Chichester: Wiley. **392**

Pervin, K. and Turner, A. (1998) A study of bullying of teachers by pupils in an inner London school. *Pastoral Care*, 30, 4–10. **86, 179**

Peto, R. (1987) Why do we need systematic overviews of randomized trials? *Statistics in Medicine*, 6, 233–40. **117**

Petrosino, A. J., Boruch, R. F., Rounding, C., McDonald, S. and Chalmers, I. (2000) The Campbell Collaboration Social, Psychological, Educational and Criminological Trials Register (C2-SPECTR) to facilitate the preparation and maintenance of systematic reviews of social and educational interventions. *Evaluation and Research in Education*, 14, 602–19. **119**

Pettigrew, T. F. (1996) *How to Think Like a Social Scientist*. New York: HarperCollins. **44**

Piaget, J. (1929) *The Child's Conception of the World*. New York: Harcourt Brace. **282**

Piaget, J. (1930) *The Child's Conception of Physical Causality*. London: Routledge & Kegan Paul. **282**

Pidgeon, N. and Henwood, K. (1996) Grounded theory: practical implementation. In J. T. E.. Richardson, ed., *Handbook of Qualitative Research Methods for Psychology and the Social Sciences*. Leicester: BPS Books. **493, 498**

Platt, J. R. (1964) Strong inference. *Science*, 146, 347–53. **104**

Porperino, F. and Robinson, D. (1995) An evaluation of the reasoning and rehabilitation program with Canadian federal offenders. In R. Ross and R. Ross, eds, *Thinking Straight*. Ottawa: Air Training Publications. **119**

Porter, S. (1993) Critical realist ethnography: the case of racism and professionalism in a medical setting. *Sociology*, 27, 591–609. **487, 490**

Porter, S. and Ryan, S. (1996) Breaking the boundaries between nursing and sociology: a critical realist ethnography of the theory–practice gap. *Journal of Advanced Nursing*, 24, 413–20. **30**

Posovac, E. J. and Carey, R. G. (1997) *Program Evaluation: Methods and Case Studies*, 5th edn. Upper Saddle River, NJ: Prentice-Hall. **221**

Potter, J. and Wetherell, M. (1987) *Discourse and Social Psychology: Beyond Attitudes and Behavior*. Newbury Park, Calif.: Sage. **365, 375**

Powney, J. and Watts, M. (1987) *Interviewing in Educational Research*. London: Routledge & Kegan Paul. **271, 278, 282**

Pratt, A. C. (1995) Putting critical realism to work: the practical implications for geographical research. *Progress in Human Geography*, 19, 61–74. **30**

Presser, S. and Blair, J. (1994) Survey pretesting: do different methods produce different results? *Sociological Methodology*, 24, 73–104. **241**

Prilleltensky, I. (1994) *The Morals and Politics of Psychology: Psychological Discourse and the Status Quo*. **76**

Punch, K. F. (1998) *Introduction to Social Research: Quantitative and Qualitative Approaches*. London: Sage. **59, 65, 495**

Punch, K. F. (2000) *Developing Effective Research Proposals*. London and Thousand Oaks, Calif.: Sage. **533**

Punch, M. (1986) *The Politics and Ethics of Fieldwork: Muddy Boots and Grubby Hands*. Beverly Hills: Sage. **378, 508**

Quinn, M. M., Kavale, K. A., Mathur, S. R., Rutherford, R. B. and Forness, S. R. (1999) A meta-analysis of social skill interventions for students with emotional or behavioral disorders. *Journal of Emotional and Behavioral Disorders*, 7, 54–64. **368**

Quintana, S. M. and Maxwell, S. E. (1999) Implications of recent developments in structural equation modeling for counseling psychology. *The Counseling Psychologist*, 27, 485–527. **434**

Ragin, C. C. (1987) *The Comparative Method: Moving Beyond Qualitative and Quantitative Strategies*. Berkeley, Calif.: University of California Press. **177**

Rathje, W. and Murphy, C. (1992) *Rubbish! The Archaeology of Garbage*. New York: HarperCollins. **347**

Rawlinson, J. G. (1981) *Creative Thinking and Brainstorming*. Aldershot: Gower. **57**

Reason, P. and Rowan, J. (1981) *Human Inquiry: A Sourcebook of New Paradigm Research*. Chichester: Wiley. **196, 374**

Reed, M. I. (1997) In praise of duality and dualism: rethinking agency and structure in organizational analysis. *Organization Studies*, 18, 21–42. **30**

Rees, C. E., Bath, P. A. and Lloyd-Williams, M. (1998) The information concerns of spouses of women with breast cancer: patients' and spouses' perspectives. *Journal of Advanced Nursing*, 28, 1249–58. **287**

Reichardt, C. S. (1979) The statistical analysis of data from nonequivalent group designs. In T. D. Cook and D. T. Campbell, eds, *Quasi-Experimentation: Design and Analysis Issues for Field Settings*. Chicago: Rand McNally. **448, 449**

Reichardt, C. S. and Rallis, S. F., eds (1994) *The Qualitative–Quantitative Debate: New Perspectives*. San Francisco: Jossey-Bass. **27, 43**

Reinharz, S. (1992) *Feminist Methods in Social Research*. Oxford: Oxford University Press. **73, 198, 216, 369, 370, 376**

Rennie, D. L. (1998) Grounded theory methodology: the pressing need for a coherent logic of justification. *Theory and Psychology*, 8, 101–19. **191**

Reviere, R., Berkowitz, S., Carter, C. C. and Ferguson, C. G., eds (1996) *Needs Assessment: A Creative and Practical Guide for Social Scientists*. Washington DC: Taylor & Francis. **213**

Reynolds, P. D. (1979) *Ethical Dilemmas and Social Science Research*. San Francisco: Jossey-Bass. **65**

Richards, L. (1999) Data alive! The thinking behind NVivo. *Qualitative Health Research*, 9, 412–28. **464**

Richards, S. and Postle, K. (1998) Surviving in the field: an exploration of the challenges of participant observation in social work settings. *Issues in Social Work Education*, 18, 7–41. **314**

Richards, T. and Richards, L. (1994) Using computers in qualitative analysis. In N. Denzin and Y. Lincoln, eds, *Handbook of Qualitative Research*. Thousand Oaks, Calif.: Sage. **497**

Richardson, J. T. E. (1990) Variants of chi-square for 2 × 2 contingency tables. *British Journal of Mathematical and Statistical Psychology*, 43, 309–26. **419**

Rigby, A. S. (1999) Editorial. Getting past the statistical referee: moving away from P-values and toward interval estimation. *Health Education Research*, 14, 713–15. **402**

Roberts, H. (1981) *Doing Feminist Research*. London: Routledge. **73, 369**

Robinson, N. (1999) The use of focus group methodology – with selected examples from sexual health research. *Journal of Advanced Nursing*, 29, 905–13. **285**

Robson, C. (1985) Small N: Case Studies? In S. Hegarty and P. Evans, eds, *Research and Evaluation Methods in Special Education*. Windsor: NFER–Nelson. **146**

Robson, C. (1993) *Real World Research: A Resource for Social Scientists and Practitioner–Researchers*. Oxford: Blackwell. **170**

Robson, C. (1994) *Experiment, Design and Statistics in Psychology*, 3rd edn. London: Penguin. **162, 392**

Robson, C. (2000) *Small-scale Evaluation: Principles and Practice*. London: Sage. **207, 214, 221**

Robson, C., Sebba, J., Mittler, P. and Davies, G. (1988) *Inservice Training and*

*Special Educational Needs: Running Short School-focused Courses.* Manchester: Manchester University Press. **212, 364, 543**

Roethlisberger, F. I. and Dickson, W. T. (1939) *Management and the Worker.* Cambridge, Mass.: Harvard University Press. **113**

Rogers, C. R. (1945) The non-directive method as a technique for social research. *American Journal of Sociology,* 50, 279–83. **282**

Rogers, C. R. (1961) *On Becoming a Person.* London: Constable. **67**

Roll-Hansen, N. (1998) Studying natural science without nature? Reflections on the realism of so-called laboratory studies. *Studies in the History and Philosophy of the Biological and Biomedical Sciences,* 29, 165–87. **4**

Rose, J. (1998) Measuring quality: the relationship between diaries and direct observation of staff. *British Journal of Developmental Disabilities,* 44, 30–7. **312**

Rosenberg, M. (1968) *The Logic of Survey Analysis.* New York: Basic. **429**

Rosenthal, R. (1976) *Experimenter Effects in Behavioral Research,* rev. edn. New York: Irvington. **343**

Rosenthal, R. and Rosnow, R. L. (1975) *The Volunteer Subject.* New York: Wiley. **112**

Rosenthal, R. and Rubin, D. B. (1980) Summarising 345 studies of interpersonal expectancy effects. In R. Rosenthal, ed., *New Directions for Methodology of Social and Behavioral Science,* no. 5. San Francisco: Jossey-Bass. **112, 343, 368**

Rosnow, R. L. and Rosenthal, R. (1996) Computing contrasts, effect sizes, and counternulls on other people's published data: general procedures for research consumers. *Psychological Methods,* 1, 331–40. **437**

Rosnow, R. L. and Rosenthal, R. (1997) *People Studying People: Artifacts and Ethics in Behavioral Research.* W. H. Freeman. **49, 98**

Ross, H. L. (1973) Law, science and accidents: the British Road Safety Act of 1967. *Journal of Legal Issues,* 2, 1–75. **206**

Ross, H. L., Campbell, D. T. and Glass, G. V. (1970) Determining the social effects of a legal reform. *American Behavioral Scientist,* 13, 492–509. **144**

Rossi, P. H. (1980) The presidential address: the challenge and opportunities of applied social research. *American Sociological Review,* 45, 889–904. **10**

Rowntree Trust (n.d.) *Research and Development Programme.* York: Joseph Rowntree Memorial Trust. **514**

Ruspini, E. (2000) Longitudinal research in the social sciences. *Social Research Update,* issue 28. Department of Sociology, University of Surrey. Available at <http://www.surrey.ac.uk/sru/SRU28.html>. **161**

Rust, J. and Golombok, S. (1999) *Modern Psychometrics: The Science of Psychological Assessment,* 2nd edn. London: Routledge. 1999. **304, 308**

Ryan, T. P. (1997) *Modern Regression Methods.* Chichester: Wiley. **432**

Sackett, G. P., ed. (1978) *Observing Behavior,* vol. 2: *Data Collection and Analysis Types.* Baltimore: University Park Press. **325, 345**

Sadler, D. R. (1981) Intuitive data processing as a potential source of bias in educational evaluation. *Educational Evaluation and Policy Analysis,* 3, 25–31. **460**

Salmon, P. (1994) Research: a Kellyan perspective. *Changes,* 12, 199–205. **366**

Sapsford, R. (1999) *Survey Research.* London: Sage. **245, 268**

Sapsford, R. and Jupp, V. (1996) Validating evidence. In R. Sapsford and V. Jupp, eds, *Data Collection and Analysis.* London: Sage. **162**

Sarantakos, S. (1998) *Social Research,* 2nd edn. London: Macmillan. **23, 197, 217**

Sawynok, J. (1995) Pharmacological rationale for the clinical use of caffeine. *Drugs,* 49, 37–50. **35**

Sayer, A. (2000) *Realism and Social Science.* London: Sage. **29, 41, 44**

Schensul, J. J. and Schensul, S. L. (1992) Collaborative research: methods of inquiry for social change. In M. D. LeCompte, W. L. Millroy and J. Preissle, eds, *The Handbook of Qualitative Research in Education.* New York: Academic. **7**

Scheurich, J. J. (1997) *Research Method in the Postmodern.* London: Falmer. **11, 15**

Schon, D. A. (1983) *The Reflective Practitioner.* London: Temple Smith. **536**

Schon, D. A. (1987) *Educating the Reflective Practitioner.* San Francisco: Jossey-Bass. **524, 536**

Schratz, M. and Walker, R. (1995) *Research as Social Change: New Opportunities for Qualitative Research.* London: Routledge. **221**

Schwab, D. P. (1985) Reviewing empirically based manuscripts: perspectives on progress. In L. L. Cummings and P. J. Frost, eds, *Publishing in the Organisational Sciences.* Homewood, Ill.: Irwin. **267**

Schwandt, T. A. (1994) Constructivist, interpretivist approaches to human inquiry. In N. K. Denzin and Y. S. Lincoln, eds, *Handbook of Qualitative Research.* Thousand Oaks, Calif.: Sage. **27**

Scott, D. (2000) *Realism and Educational Research: New Perspectives and Possibilities.* London and New York: Routledge/Falmer. **30**

Scriven, M. (1976) Maximizing the power of causal investigation: the modus operandi method. In G. V. Glass, ed., *Evaluation Studies Review Annual,* vol. 1. Newbury Park, Calif.: Sage. **9**

Scriven, M. (1991) *Evaluation Thesaurus,* 4th edn. Newbury Park, Calif.: Sage. **61**

Seale, C., ed. (2000) *Researching Society and Culture.* London: Sage. **462**

Selener, D. (1997) *Participatory Action Research and Social Change,* 2nd edn. Cornell Participatory Action Research Network. Ithaca, NY: Cornell University. **216, 221**

Shames, M. L. (1990) On data, methods and theory: an epistemological evaluation of psychology. *Canadian Psychology,* 31, 229–37. **30**

Shearn, J., Beyer, S. and Felce, D. (2000) The cost-effectiveness of supported employment for people with severe intellectual disabilities and high support needs: a pilot study. *Journal of Applied Research in Intellectual Disabilities,* 13, 29–37. **214**

Shipman, M. D. (1988) *The Limitations of Social Research,* 3rd edn. London: Longman. **109**

Sidman, M. (1960) *The Tactics of Scientific Research.* New York: Basic. **122, 146, 449**

Siegel, H. (1987) *Relativism Refuted: A Critique of Contemporary Methodological Relativism.* Boston: Reidel. **26**

Siegel, S. and Castellan, N. J. (1988) *Nonparametric Statistics for the Behavioral Sciences,* 2nd edn. New York: McGraw-Hill. **415, 454**

Silverman, D. (1985) *Qualitative Methodology and Sociology.* Aldershot: Gower. **376**

Silverman, D. (1993) *Interpreting Qualitative Data: Methods for Analysing Talk, Text and Interaction.* London: Sage. **489**

Silverman, D. (2000) *Doing Qualitative Research: A Practical Handbook.* Thousand Oaks, Calif., and London: Sage. **200, 474, 498, 510**

Sim, J. (1998) Collecting and analysing qualitative data: issues raised by the focus group. *Journal of Advanced Nursing,* 28, 345–52. **177, 287, 289**

Simpson, T. A. (2000) Streets, sidewalks, stores, and stories: narrative and uses of urban space. *Journal of Contemporary Ethnography,* 29, 682–716. **487**

Singh, N. N., Curtis, W. J., Wechsler, H. A., Ellis, C. R. and Cohen, R. (1997) Family friendliness of community-based services for children and adolescents with emotional and behavioural disorders and their families: an observational study. *Journal of Emotional and Behavioural Disorders*, 5, 82–92. **333**

Skinner, B. F. (1938) *The Behavior of Organisms: An Experimental Analysis*. New York: Appleton. **146**

Skinner, B. F. (1963) The flight from the laboratory. In M. Marx, ed., *Theories in Contemporary Psychology*. New York: Macmillan. **111**

Skinner, B. F. (1974) *About Behaviourism*. London: Cape. **146**

Sloan, G. (1999) Good characteristics of a clinical supervisor: a community mental health nurse perspective. *Journal of Advanced Nursing*, 30, 713–22. **287**

Smith, D. (1987) *The Everyday World as Problematic*. Toronto: University of Toronto Press. **73**

Smith, G. D. and Egger, M. (1998) Meta-analysis: unresolved issues and future developments. *British Medical Journal*, 316, 221–5. **368**

Smith, H. W. (1975) *Strategies of Social Research: The Methodological Imagination*. London: Prentice-Hall. **327, 455**

Smith, J. A. (1995) Qualitative methods, identity and transition to motherhood. *The Psychologist: Bulletin of the British Psychological Society*, 8, 122–5. **474**

Smith, J. A. (1997) Developing theory from case studies: self-reconstruction and the transition to motherhood. In N. Hayes, ed., *Doing Qualitative Analysis in Psychology*. Hove: Psychology Press. **474**

Smith, J. K. and Heshusios, L. (1986) Closing down the conversation: the end of the quantitative–qualitative debate among educational researchers. *Educational Researcher*, 15, 4–12. **43**

Smith, M. J. (1998) *Social Science in Question*. London: Sage/Milton Keynes: Open University Press. **20, 44**

Solomon, L. S., Tomaskovic-Devey, D. and Risman, B. J. (1989) The gender gap and nuclear power: attitudes in a politicized environment. *Sex Roles*, 21, 401–14. **159**

Sonnentag, S. (1998) Expertise in professional software design: a process study. *Journal of Applied Psychology*, 83, 703–15. **367**

Spence, I. and Lewandowsky, S. (1990) Graphical perception. In J. Fox and J. S. Long, eds, *Modern Methods of Data Analysis*. Newbury Park, Calif., and London: Sage. **403**

Spradley, J. P. (1980) *Participant Observation*. New York: Holt, Rinehart & Winston. **46, 320**

Stainback, S. and Stainback, W. (1988) *Understanding and Conducting Qualitative Research*. Dubuque, Iowa: Kendall/Hunt. **507**

Stake, R. E. (1995) *The Art of Case Study Research*. Thousand Oaks, Calif.: Sage. **179, 200**

Stanfield, J. H. (1993) Epistemological considerations. In J. H. Stanfield and R. M. Dennis, eds, *Race and Ethnicity in Research Methods*. Newbury Park, Calif.: Sage. **157**

Stanley, L. and Temple, B. (1996) Doing the business: using qualitative software packages in the analysis of qualitative datasets. In R. G. Burgess, ed., *Using Computers in Qualitative Research*. Greenwich, Conn.: JAI. **463**

Stanley, L. and Wise, S. (1983) *Breaking Out: Feminist Consciousness and Feminist Research*. London: Routledge & Kegan Paul. **73**

Stebbins, R. A. (1987) Fitting in: the researcher as learner and participant. *Quality and Quantity*, 21, 103–8. **379**

Steinmetz, G. (1998) Critical realism and historical sociology: a review article. *Comparative Studies in Society and History*, 40, 170–86. **25, 30**

Stenhouse, L. (1982) The conduct, analysis and reporting of case study in educational research and evaluation. In R. McCormick, ed., *Calling Education to Account.* London: Heinemann. **311**

Stephenson, W. (1980) Newton's fifth rule and Q-methodology: applications to educational psychology. *American Psychologist*, 35, 882–9. **303**

Stevens, C. D. (1998) Realism and Kelly's pragmatic constructivism. *Journal of Constructivist Psychology*, 11, 283–308. **366**

Stevens, J. (1997) *Applied Multivariate Statistics for the Social Sciences*, 3rd edn. New York: HarperCollins. **433**

Stewart, D. and Mickunas, A. (1990) *Exploring Phenomenology: A Guide to the Field and its Literature*, 2nd edn. Athens, Ohio: Ohio University Press. **195**

Stewart, D. W. and Shamdasani, P. N. (1990) *Focus Groups: Theory and Practice.* Newbury Park, Calif.: Sage. **285**

Still, A. W. (1982) On the number of subjects used in animal behaviour experiments. *Animal Behaviour*, 30, 873–80. **162**

Stockman, N. (1983) *Antipositivist Theories of the Sciences.* Dordrecht: Reidel. **21**

Stratton, G. and Mota, J. (2000) Girls' physical activity during primary school playtime: a validation study using systematic observation and heart rate telemetry. *Journal of Human Movement Studies*, 38, 109–21. **331**

Strauss, A. (1987) *Qualitative Analysis for Social Scientists.* Cambridge: Cambridge University Press. **63, 109, 498**

Strauss, A. and Corbin, J. (1998) *Basics of Qualitative Research: Techniques and Procedures for Developing Grounded Theory*, 2nd edn. Thousand Oaks, Calif.: Sage. **191, 192, 193, 194, 200, 265, 493, 494, 495, 497, 511**

Strauss, A. and Corbin, J., eds (1997) *Grounded Theory in Practice.* Thousand Oaks, Calif.: Sage. **191, 265**

Stringer, E. (1996) *Action Research: A Handbook for Practitioners.* Thousand Oaks, Calif.: Sage. **216**

Suchman, E. A. (1967) *Evaluative Research: Principles in Public Service and Action Programs.* New York: Russell Sage. **206**

Suhonen, R., Valimaki, M. and Katajisto, J. (2000) Developing and testing an instrument for the measurement of individual care. *Journal of Advanced Nursing*, 32, 1253–63. **304**

Sutton, A. J., Jones, D. R., Abrams, K. R., Sheldon, T. A. and Song, F. (1999) Systematic reviews and meta-analysis: a structured review of the methodological literature. *Journal of Health Services Research and Policy*, 4, 49–55. **368**

Sutton, R. I. and Schurman, S. J. (1988) On studying emotionally hot topics: lessons from an investigation of organisational death. In D. N. Berg and K. K. Smith, eds, *The Self in Social Inquiry.* Newbury Park, Calif.: Sage. **377**

Tabachnik, B. G. and Fidell, L. S. (1996) *Using Multivariate Statistics*, 3rd edn. New York: HarperCollins. **433, 434, 454**

Taplin, P. S. and Reid, J. B. (1973) Effects of instructional set and experimenter influence on observer reliability. *Child Development*, 44, 547–54. **343**

Tashakkori, A. and Teddlie, T. (1998) *Mixed Methodology: Combining Qualitative and Quantitative Approaches.* Thousand Oaks, Calif.: Sage. **6, 43, 374**

Taylor, K. M. and Sheppard, J. A. (1996) Probing suspicion among participants in deception research. *American Psychologist*, 51, 886–7. **69**

Tesch, R. (1990) *Qualitative Research: Analysis Types and Software Tools.* London: Falmer. **27, 457, 499**

Thomas, A. Chataway, J. and Wuyts, M., eds (1998) *Finding Out Fast: Investigative Skills for Policy and Development.* London: Sage. **76**

Thomas, G. (1997) What's the use of theory? *Harvard Educational Review*, 67, 75–104. **61**

Thomas, M. D., Blacksmith, J. and Reno, J. (2000) Utilizing insider–outsider research teams in qualitative research. *Qualitative Health Research*, 10, 819–28. **382**

Thomas, R. (1996) Statistical sources and databases. In R. Sapsford and V. Jupp, eds, *Data Collection and Analysis*. London: Sage. **51**

Thornberry, O. T. and Massey, J. T. (1988) Trends in United States telephone coverage across time and subgroups. In R. M. Groves, P. P. Biemer, L. E. Lyberg, J. T. Massey, W. L. Nichols and J. Waksberg, eds, *Telephone Survey Methodology*. New York: Wiley. **241**

Thurstone, L. L. and Chave, E. J. (1929) *The Measurement of Attitude*. Chicago: University of Chicago Press. **295**

Thyer, B. A. and Geller, E. S. (1987) The buckle up dashboard sticker: an effective environmental intervention for safety belt promotion. *Environment and Behavior*, 19, 484–94. **150**

Tinbergen, N. (1963) On aims and methods of ethology. *Zeitschrift für Tierpsychologie*, 20, 410–33. **325**

Tolson, D., Smith, M. and Knight, P. (1999) An investigation of the components of best nursing practice in the care of acutely ill hospitalized older patients with coincidental dementia: a multi-method design. *Journal of Advanced Nursing*, 30, 1127–36. **86, 370**

Tonkiss, F. (1998) The history of the social survey. In C. Seale, ed., *Researching Society and Culture*. London: Sage. **227**

Tourangeau, R. and Rasinski, K. A. (1988) Cognitive processes underlying context effects in attitude measurement. *Psychological Bulletin*, 103, 299–314. **241**

Trigg, R. (1989) *Reality at Risk: A Defense of Realism in Philosophy and the Sciences*. New York: Harvester Wheatsheaf. **24**

Trist, E. L. (1976) Engaging with large-scale systems. In A. W. Clark, ed., *Experimenting with Organizational Life: The Action Research Approach*. London: Plenum. **10**

Trochim, W. M. K. (1984) *Research Design for Program Evaluation: The Regression–Discontinuity Approach*. Newbury Park, Calif.: Sage. **145**

Tsang, E. W. K. and Kwan, K.-M. (1999) Replication and theory development in organizational science: a critical realist perspective. *Academy of Management Review*, 24, 759–80. **42**

Tudor, R. (1992) *Search Widely, Choose Wisely: A Case Study Exploring Structural and Behavioural Factors in Idea Generation and Evaluation Following Brainstorming on a Strategic Problem*. Manchester: Manchester Business School. **57**

Tufte, E. R. (1983) *The Visual Display of Quantitative Information*. Cheshire, Conn.: Graphics. **407**

Tukey, J. W. (1977) *Exploratory Data Analysis*. Reading, Mass.: Addison Wesley. **399**

Turner, J. (1992) The promise of positivism. In S. Seidman and D. G. Wagner, eds, *Postmodernism and Social Theory*. Oxford: Blackwell. **21**

Turner, C. F. and Martin, E., eds (1986) *Surveying Subjective Phenomena*, 2 vols. New York: Russell Sage. **268**

Valois, P. and Godin, G. (1991) The importance of selecting appropriate adjective pairs for measuring attitudes based on the semantic differential method. *Quality and Quantity*, 25, 57–68. **302**

Valsiner, J., ed. (1986) *The Individual Subject and Scientific Psychology*. New York: Plenum. **179**

Van de Geer, J. P. (1993) *Multivariate Analysis of Categorical Data: Applications*. Newbury Park, Calif.: Sage. **400**

van Dijk, T. A., ed. (1985) *Handbook of Discourse Analysis*, 4 vols. London: Academic. **365**

Vaughan, R. J. and Buss, T. F. (1998) *Communicating Social Science Research to Policymakers*. Thousand Oaks, Calif.: Sage. **221**

Veitch, J. A. and Newsham, G. R. (2000) Exercised control, lighting choices, and energy use: an office simulation experiment. *Journal of Environmental Psychology*, 20, 219–37. **365**

Velleman, P. F. and Hoaglin, D. C. (1981) *Applications, Basics and Computing of Exploratory Data Analysis*. Boston: Duxbury. **399**

von Post, I. and Eriksson, K. (1999) A hermeneutic textual analysis of suffering and caring in the peri-operative context. *Journal of Advanced Nursing*, 30, 983–9. **198**

Waddington, D. (1994) Participant observation. In C. Cassell and G. Symon, eds, *Qualitative Methods in Organizational Research: A Practical Guide*. London: Sage. **314**

Wainwright, S. P. (1997) A New Paradigm for Nursing: The Potential of Realism. *Journal of Advanced Nursing*, 26, 1262–71. **30**

Walker, R. (1985) *Doing Research: A Handbook for Teachers*. London: Methuen. **50, 224, 274, 326, 362**

Walker, R. and Adelman, C. (1975) *A Guide to Classroom Observation*. London: Methuen. **352**

Wallace, R. A. and Wolf, A. (1986) *Contemporary Sociological Theory*. Englewood Cliffs, NJ: Prentice-Hall. **197**

Walsh-Daneshmandi, A. and MacLachlan, M. (2000) Environmental risk to the self: factor analysis and developmental subscales for the Environmental Appraisal Inventory (EAI) with an adult sample. *Journal of Environmental Psychology*, 20, 141–9. **304**

Walston, J. T. and Lissitz, R. W. (2000) Computer-mediated focus groups. *Evaluation Review*, 24, 457–83. **288**

Warner, M. M. (1993) Objectivity and emancipation in learning disabilities: holism from the perspective of critical realism. *Journal of Learning Disabilities*, 26, 311–25. **30**

Watkins, M. and Redfern, S. J. (1997) Evaluation of a new night nursing service for elderly people suffering from dementia. *Journal of Clinical Nursing*, 6, 485–94. **204**

Watson, R. J. D. and Richardson, P. H. (1999) Assessing the literature on outcome studies in group psychotherapy: the sensitivity and precision of Medline and PsychINFO bibliographic database searching. *British Journal of Medical Psychology*, 72, 127–34. **51**

Webb, E. J., Campbell, D. T., Schwartz, R. D., Sechrest, L. and Grove, J. B. (1981) *Nonreactive Measures in the Social Sciences*, 2nd edn. Boston: Houghton Mifflin. **347**

Webb, E. J., Campbell, D. T., Schwartz, R. D. and Sechrest, L. (2000) *Unobtrusive Measures*, rev. edn. (First publ. 1965.) Thousand Oaks, Calif.: Sage. **347, 348, 374**

Weber, R. P. (1985) *Basic Content Analysis*. Newbury Park, Calif., and London: Sage. **358**

Wechsler, D. (1955) *The Wechsler Adult Intelligence Scale*. New York: Psychological Corporation. **306**

Weick, K. E. (1968) Systematic observational methods. In G. Lindzey and E. Aronson, eds, *The Handbook of Social Psychology*, vol. 2, 2nd edn. Reading, Mass.: Addison-Wesley. **327**

Weick, K. E. (1985) Systematic observational methods. In G. Lindzey and E. Aronson, eds, *The Handbook of Social Psychology*, 3rd edn. New York: Random House. **11**

Weiss, C. H. (1986) Research and policymaking: a limited partnership. In F. Heller, ed., *The Use and Abuse of Social Science*. Newbury Park, Calif.: Sage. **524**

Weiss, C. H. (1997) *Evaluation: Methods for Studying Programs and Policies*, 2nd edn. Upper Saddle River, NJ: Prentice-Hall. **221**

Weiss, C. H. and Bucuvalas, M. J. (1980) *Social Science Research and Decision-making*. New York: Columbia University Press. **11**

Weiss, R. (1994) *Learning from Strangers: the Art and Method of Qualitative Interview Studies.* New York: Free Press. **291**

Weitzman, E. A. and Miles, M. B. (1995) *Computer Programs for Qualitative Data Analysis: A Software Sourcebook.* Thousand Oaks, Calif.: Sage. **462, 463, 499**

Wells, G. L. and Luus, C. A. E. (1990) Police line-ups as experiments: social methodology as a framework for properly conducted line-ups. *Personality and Social Psychology Bulletin,* 16, 106–17. **112**

Wenger, N. S., Korenman, S. G., Berk, R. and Liu, H. H. (1999) Reporting unethical research behavior. *Evaluation Review,* 23, 553–70. **54**

Whyte, W. F. (1951) Observational field work methods. In G. Jahoda, ed., *Research Methods in Social Relations,* vol. 2. New York: Dryden. **319**

Whyte, W. F. (1984) *Learning from the Field: a Guide from Experience.* Newbury Park, Calif., and London: Sage. **181, 282, 317, 344**

Wilkinson, M. B. (1996) *Action Research for People and Organizational Change.* Brisbane: Queensland University of Technology. **216**

Wilkinson, S. (1998) Focus groups in feminist research: power, interaction, and the co-construction of meaning. *Women's Studies International Forum,* 21, 111–25. **370**

Wilkinson, S. and Unger, R. K. (1999) Focus groups: a feminist method. *Psychology of Women Quarterly,* 23, 221–46. **370**

Williams, S. J. (1999) Is anybody there? Critical realism, chronic illness and the disability debate. *Sociology of Health and Illness,* 21, 797–819. **30**

Wilson, G. D. and Patterson, J. R. (1968) A new measure of conservatism (C). *British Journal of Social and Clinical Psychology,* 7, 164–9. **306**

Winchester, M. (1999) Interviews and questionnaires as mixed methods in population geography: the case of lone fathers in Newcastle, Australia. *Professional Geographer,* 51, 60–7. **86, 370**

Winter, R. (1987) *Action-Research and the Nature of Social Enquiry.* Aldershot: Gower. **537**

Winter, R. (1989) *Learning from Experience: Principles and Practice in Action-Research.* London: Falmer. **536**

Witkin, B. R. and Altschuld, J. W. (1995) *Planning and Conducting Needs Assessments: A Practical Guide.* Thousand Oaks, Calif.: Sage. **213**

Wolcott, H. F. (1974) The elementary school principal: notes from a field study. In G. Spindler, ed., *Education and Cultural Process: Toward an Anthropology of Education.* London: Holt, Rinehart & Winston. (Repr. in Wolcott, 1994, 115–48, and as Appendix E in Cresswell, 1998.) **487**

Wolcott, H. F. (1990) *Writing Up Qualitative Research.* Newbury Park, Calif.: Sage. **508, 523**

Wolcott, H. F. (1994) *Transforming Qualitative Data: Description, Analysis and Interpretation.* Thousand Oaks, Calif.: Sage. **168, 487, 488, 492**

Wright, P. C. and Monk, A. (1991) A cost effective evaluation method for use by designers. *International Journal of Man– Machine Studies,* 35, 891–912. **367**

Wuest, J. (2000) Negotiating with helping systems: an example of grounded theory evolving though emergent fit. *Qualitative Health Research,* 10, 51–70. **496**

Wulfhorst, J. D. (2000) Collective identity and hazardous waste management. *Rural Sociology,* 65, 275–94. **474**

Yates, B. T. (1996) *Analyzing Costs, Procedures, Processes, and Outcomes in Human Services.* Thousand Oaks, Calif.: Sage. **214**

Yates, B. T. (1998) Formative evaluation of costs, cost-effectiveness, and cost-benefit: toward cost → procedure → process → outcome analysis. In L. Bickman and D.

J. Rog, eds, *Handbook of Applied Social Research Methods*. Thousand Oaks, Calif.: Sage. **214**

Yates, F. A. (1966) *The Art of Memory*. London: Penguin. **324**

Yeung, H. W. C. (1997) Critical realism and realist research in human geography: a method or a philosophy in search of a method? *Progress in Human Geography*, 21, 51–74. **30**

Yin, R. K. (1981) The case study as a serious research strategy. *Knowledge: Creation, Diffusion, Utilisation*, 3, 97–114. **178**

Yin, R. K. (1989) *Case Study Research: Design and Methods*, rev. edn. Newbury Park, Calif.: Sage. **369, 512**

Yin, R. K. (1993) *Applications of Case Study Research: Design and Methods* Newbury Park, Calif.: Sage.

Yin, R. K. (1994) *Case Study Research: Design and Methods*, 2nd edn. Thousand Oaks, Calif.: Sage. **90, 177, 178, 181, 182, 183, 185, 200, 499**

Young, J. and Matthews, R., eds (1992) *Rethinking Criminology: The Realist Debate*. London: Sage. **30**

Youngman, M. B. (1979) *Analysing Social and Educational Research Data*. London: McGraw-Hill. **396**

Zeisel, J. (1984) *Inquiry by Design: Tools for Environment–Behavior Research*. Cambridge: Cambridge University Press. **232, 276, 283, 318, 535**

Zhu, S. H. (1999) A method to obtain a randomized control group where it seems impossible: a case study in program evaluation. *Evaluation Review*, 23, 363–77. **114**

Zigmond, A. S. and Snaith, R. P. (1983) The Hospital Anxiety and Depression Scale. *Acta Psychiatrica Scandinavica*, 67, 361–70. **305**

Zimmerman, D. H. and Wieder, D. L. (1977) The diary: diary-interview method. *Urban Life*, 5, 479–98. **259**

Zuckerman, M. and Lubin, B. (1963) *The multiple affect adjective check list*. San Diego, Calif.: Edits. **305**

# Subject Index

r